Boom, Crisis, and Adjustment

The Macroeconomic
Experience of
Developing
Countries

The World Bank Comparative Macroeconomic Studies series includes country studies that were used in the preparation of this synthesis volume. Studies now published or forthcoming from the World Bank cover Brazil, Colombia, Costa Rica, Côte d'Ivoire, India, Indonesia, Sri Lanka, Thailand, and Turkey. For information on these books and related studies, contact the Office of the Publisher, The World Bank, 1818 H Street, N.W., Washington, D.C. 20433, U.S.A.

Boom, Crisis, and Adjustment

The Macroeconomic

Experience of

Developing

Countries

I. M. D. LITTLE

RICHARD N. COOPER

W. MAX CORDEN

SARATH RAJAPATIRANA

Published for the World Bank

OXFORD UNIVERSITY PRESS

Oxford University Press

OXFORD NEW YORK TORONTO
DELHI BOMBAY CALCUTTA MADRAS KARACHI
KUALA LUMPUR SINGAPORE HONG KONG TOKYO
NAIROBI DAR ES SALAAM CAPE TOWN
MELBOURNE AUCKLAND
and associated companies in
BERLIN IBADAN

© 1993 The International Bank for Reconstruction
and Development / THE WORLD BANK
1818 H Street, N.W.
Washington, D.C. 20433, U.S.A.

Published by Oxford University Press, Inc.
200 Madison Avenue, New York, N.Y. 10016

Oxford is a registered trademark of Oxford University Press

Manufactured in the United States of America
First printing December 1993

The findings, interpretations, and conclusions expressed in
this study are entirely those of the authors and should not be
attributed in any manner to the World Bank, to its affiliated
organizations, or to members of its Board of Executive Directors
or the countries they represent.

Library of Congress Cataloging-in Publication Data

Boom, crisis, and adjustment : the macroeconomic experience of
developing countries / Ian M.D. Little ... [et al.].
   p. cm.
Includes bibliographical references and index.
ISBN 0-19-520891-9
1. Structural adjustment (Economic policy)—Developing countries—
Case studies. 2. Economic stabilization—Developing countries—
Case studies. 3. Developing countries—Economic policy—Case
studies. I. Little, Ian M. D.
HC59.7.B576 1994
339.5'09172'4—dc20   93-27208
                                                             CIP

Contents

Preface

This volume is one outcome of a research project initiated and financed by the World Bank in 1986, entitled, "Macroeconomic Policies, Crisis, and Growth in the Long Run." The aim of the project was to look in depth at the macroeconomic experiences of many developing countries in Africa, Asia, and Latin America, to compare their reactions to the crises they faced in the seventies and eighties, and to consider, among other things, the implications for long-run growth. The emphasis was comparative and reflected a search for policy issues. In the end, the project explored the macroeconomic histories of eighteen countries from the late sixties to the end of the eighties. Studies of the experiences of seventeen countries were commissioned. This volume has drawn not only on these studies but on many other books and articles and on World Bank and International Monetary Fund data sources. We refer to these in the text and in footnotes.

The project, directed by Sarath Rajapatirana of the World Bank staff and an author of this book, faced as its greatest challenge the problem of presenting primary data as consistently as possible. A research project like this does not just take figures from one source blindly but compares different sources and takes note of the statistical situation in different countries. Thus, it is really an education in caution, in not making judgments based on small changes in figures, and in not being misled by neat tables and regressions—let alone by sophisticated techniques resting on the basis of very shaky primary data. In general we have used World Bank and International Monetary Fund figures for our comparative work and our main tables, but these do not always tell precisely the same story as data used by our country authors, or other sources, coming from national sources. If we had another five years we could reconcile all these figures, and we could also determine more precisely which figures rest on very shaky primary sources and which have firmer bases. Here it can only be noted that for some countries the statistical base is quite tenuous. Nigeria is a clear example, and not the only one. The reader should bear this in mind all the time.

We are indebted to many people, starting with the authors listed in appendix I, and the many other authors to whom we refer. Anne Krueger, former vice president for economics at the World Bank, and Deepak Lal, then research adviser, both played major roles in the initiation of the project. This is also true of the following advisers for the project, who made important contributions to the development of the country studies at several conferences: Mario Blejer, Guillermo Calvo, Domingo Cavallo, Vittorio Corbo, Dennis de Tray, Juergen Donges, Bo Karlstrom, Allan Meltzer, and Laurence Whitehead. We also wish to acknowledge the great help of Jariya Charoenwattana, Jennifer Gordon, V. Hugo Juan-Ramon, Miguel Kiguel, Margaret Kienzle, Michael Lewin, Flora Paoli, Pedro Videla, Cherian Samuel, and Debbie Wetzel. Anita Bhatia's role as the project's coordinator, followed by Charles Dade, was invaluable.

This book is a joint effort of all four authors, but the primary authorship was divided up as follows: Ian Little drafted chapters 3, 4, 5, and 11, Max Corden drafted chapters 6, 7, and 8, Richard Cooper drafted chapters 2, 10, and 12, and Sarath Rajapatirana drafted chapter 9. Chapter 13 was jointly drafted. Although the World Bank sponsored this project, it is in no way responsible for its contents. The views expressed should not be regarded as the views of the Bank nor should statistics that are cited be regarded as Bank-endorsed.

Chapter 1

Introduction

Until the 1970s, research on developing countries was mainly concerned with longer-run structural issues. With the harsh economic shocks of the early 1980s and the ensuing debt crises in countries throughout the world, attention turned increasingly to macroeconomic policy and its relation to growth. Growth rates declined in many developing countries in the 1980s because of these macroeconomic problems and—some have argued—because of the adjustment policies that were subsequently followed. This book is a product of that mounting interest in the macroeconomic policies of developing countries.

There is now a large body of literature on this subject, particularly on the implications of accumulated debt and on the impact of the "orthodox" economic policies that have been followed. This literature has dealt primarily with a small number of Latin American countries—notably Argentina, Brazil, and Chile—and one of its principal objectives has been to compare attempts at stabilizing inflation, both the successes and the failures. To that extent, it has been somewhat unbalanced. In an effort to remedy the situation, this book brings a considerably broader perspective to this area of research. It covers eighteen developing countries in four continents, and inflation is but one of the many issues discussed.

Our central purpose here is to review the macroeconomic experiences of these eighteen countries over the years 1974 to 1989. Three distinct periods emerge within this time frame: (a) 1974–79, which covers the time from the first oil shock to the second, when the ease of borrowing on the world capital market led to spending booms in many countries; (b) 1980–83, which was the period of crisis; and (c) 1983–89, the subsequent period of adjustment and, in many cases, growth recovery. At times, we go back further, as far as 1965, to get the proper perspective, and at other times, for countries where there have been important changes, we carry the story forward as far as 1992. We are particularly interested in policy reactions to external shocks and in stabilization or destabilization policies, along with their implications for growth over the longer term. Our aim has been not only to compare the experiences and reactions of these countries, but also to understand why they have differed.

To determine why some countries suffered bigger shocks than others, and why some reacted differently to similar shocks, we investigated whether the shocks were external or internal in origin; what roles fiscal, monetary, exchange rate, and trade policies played; what degree of inflation occurred and why; and what effects macroeconomic policies had on growth. This exercise has yielded some vital lessons for future policies.

Much of this book may be regarded as story telling informed by theory. Its conclusions were arrived at by thoroughly pragmatic or eclectic procedures. Given the limited availability and quality of the data, we were unable to estimate a completely specific dynamic model to deal with the episodes and problems that are the subject of this book.

We have taken note of a large body of cross-country econometric research concerning the impact of macroeconomic policies or outcomes (inflation, real exchange instability, investment, for example) on growth, the relationship between exchange rates and the trade balance or exports, and so on. Usually such research is based on data drawn from many more countries than the eighteen studied here. We have also engaged in cross-country econometric research ourselves (reported mainly in chapters 5 and 11), often with uncertain results. The problem with such work is that many of the numerous factors that may affect the dependent variable are themselves both interrelated and difficult to measure. The so-called independent variables are seldom really independent. Even though multicountry regression analysis often produces equivocal results, it is a natural complement to the kind of country-intensive work reported here.

Intensive studies of many country experiences and of many particular episodes of the kind presented in this volume are particularly valuable because they can generate ideas and suggest cause-and-effect relationships between both economic and political variables that were previously unrecognized or underemphasized. This in turn may not only influence theorizing and model-building but also have a more immediate and beneficial impact on policy formation. Any such contribution may, of course, extend to countries other than those studied. Past macroeconomic theory has been inspired by the experiences of very few countries—primarily Great Britain and the United States and a few developing countries in Latin America. We hope to widen the group of countries whose experiences influence generalizations, theorizing, and hypothesis testing in the field of macroeconomics.[1]

Table 1-1 gives some information about our group of countries. In terms of gross domestic products and populations, the group provides a large representative sample of the total developing world. It includes the five largest developing economies other than China, namely, Brazil, India, the Republic of Korea, Mexico, and Indonesia. Five others—Turkey, Argentina, Thailand, Colombia, and Pakistan—can also be described as large, for in 1989 their gross national products (GNPs) measured US$35 billion or more.[2] We chose only countries that were

Table 1.1 Basic Data on Eighteen Countries, 1965–90

Country	GDP, 1990 (millions US$)	Population mid-1989 (millions)	GNP per capita 1990 (US$)	GNP per capita Average annual growth rate, 1965–90 (%)	Average annual inflation rate, 1980–90 (%)	External debt as % of GNP, 1990	Debts rescheduled 1982–88
Argentina	93,260	32.3	2,370	-0.3	395.2	61.7	*
Brazil	414,060	150.4	2,680	3.3	284.3	22.8	*
Cameroon	11,130	11.7	960	3.0	5.6	56.8	
Chile	27,790	13.2	1,940	0.4	20.5	73.6	*
Colombia	41,120	32.3	1,260	2.3	24.8	44.3	
Costa Rica	5,700	2.8	1,900	1.4	23.5	69.2	*
Côte d'Ivoire	7,610	11.9	750	0.5	2.3	203.9	*
India	254,540	849.5	350	1.9	7.9	25.0	
Indonesia	107,290	178.2	570	4.5	8.4	66.4	
Kenya	7,540	24.2	370	1.9	9.2	81.2	
Korea, Rep.	236,400	42.8	5,400	7.1	5.1	14.4	
Mexico	237,750	86.2	2,490	2.8	70.3	42.1	*
Morocco	25,220	25.1	950	2.3	7.2	97.1	*
Nigeria	34,760	115.5	290	0.1	17.7	117.9	*
Pakistan	35,500	112.4	380	2.5	6.7	52.1	
Sri Lanka	7,250	17.0	470	2.9	11.1	73.2	
Thailand	80,170	55.8	1,420	4.4	3.4	32.6	
Turkey	96,500	56.1	1,630	2.6	43.2	46.3	

Note: The "technical notes" in *World Development Report 1992* explain the meaning and methods of calculation of the figures in the first five columns. The average annual inflation rate (column 5) is measured by the growth rate of the GDP implicit deflator, while other figures of inflation rates in this book refer to the growth rate of the cost-of-living index—but the two measures normally tell very similar stories. External debt in column 6 refers to the total external debt stock, long- and short-term. For column 7, note that Cameroon's debt was rescheduled in 1989.

Source: *World Development Report 1992* (for the first five columns). Column 6 is from the World Bank's *World Debt Tables 1991–92*, Volume 2. Column 7 comes from the International Monetary Fund and chapter 4 of this volume.

market economies at the time—that is, we excluded the ones that used to be described as "centrally planned." The group actually includes all the large developing market economies other than Egypt, Iran, the Philippines, and Venezuela. It also includes Nigeria, which is by far the largest economy in sub-Saharan Africa, but steep depreciation of its currency reduced the value of its GDP to slightly less than $35 billion in 1990. In addition, we looked at some relatively small economies: Chile, Morocco, Cameroon, Côte d'Ivoire, Kenya, Sri Lanka, and Costa Rica. Chile has had some remarkable economic experiences that have been much analyzed, but the literature on the macroeconomics of the other smaller economies is sparse. In 1990 the dollar value of the GDP of all the countries combined was about 60 percent of the dollar value of the gross domestic products of all developing market economies combined.

As table 1-1 shows, the countries are certainly diverse—so the diversity of experiences we report should hardly be surprising. At one end of the spectrum, five countries have a population in excess of 100 million each, while at the other end, seven have a population of 25 million or less. Six of the group count as low-income countries and twelve as middle-income countries, but the low-income countries include all those with a large population, apart from Brazil: namely, India, Indonesia, Nigeria, and Pakistan. Countries with high per capita growth rates over the period 1965–90 (3 percent or more) are Korea, Indonesia, Thailand, Brazil, and Cameroon (in that order). In contrast, Argentina, Nigeria, and Chile had near-zero average growth over that period. The top performers between 1980 and 1990 were Korea, Thailand, Indonesia, India, and Pakistan, while Côte d'Ivoire, Nigeria, Argentina, Mexico, and Cameroon were at the bottom, with negative per capita growth rates (see table 5-2). The great dispersion in per capita growth rates and the outstanding performance of Korea are certainly striking.

The countries are also diverse in other respects. Three (Indonesia, Nigeria, Mexico) are big oil exporters, and their stories have been much affected by this fact, whereas all the rest—except Colombia and Cameroon (both also oil exporters) and Argentina (close to self-sufficient)—are oil importers. Four have experienced high inflation in recent years, with annual average inflation rates of 40 percent or more in 1980–90; at the other end, nine averaged inflation rates of 10 percent or less. Eight of the countries had to reschedule their international debt in the period 1983–88 and were described by the International Monetary Fund as "countries with recent debt-servicing difficulties." This troubled group—consisting of Argentina, Brazil, Chile, Costa Rica, Côte d'Ivoire, Mexico, Morocco, and Nigeria—receives much attention in this book, as it has in both popular and academic discussion. Some of the other ten countries had quite high debt ratios but, as will be shown, their economic performance on the whole turned out to be much more favorable.

In general, the theory underlying this book is quite standard and also eclectic, with no particular commitment to Keynesianism, monetarism, or rational expectations. We certainly do not find support for extreme versions of any of these schools of thought. The theory of macroeconomic policy for developing countries would require a completely separate book, although it would certainly benefit from the kind of material presented in this volume. Here, we draw on bits of theory wherever necessary and expound it briefly where appropriate, or sometimes we take it as known when it is straightforward textbook theory.

The textbook theory of internal and external balance—especially its "dependent economy" version—provides the most useful framework for the discussion of adjustment problems in chapters 4 and 5. It shows that usually the current account of the balance of payments can only be improved through a reduction in domestic expenditure (absorption)—combined with policies that "switch" demand away from tradables toward nontradables, and supply from nontradables to tradables, if an unnecessary fall in total output is to be avoided. Without such "switching," the reduction in domestic demand required to improve the current account would result in excess supply and unemployment in the nontradable sectors of the economy.[3]

Chapter 2 reviews world economic developments over the study period, providing background for the stories that follow. Chapters 3, 4, and 5 then move ahead with a detailed historical account of the macroeconomic experiences and policies of the eighteen countries, with a heavy emphasis on comparisons. Above all, it is essential to "get the story straight" before attempting to arrive at any general conclusions. Although there is some similarity in the external shocks, more striking is the diversity of policy reactions and of the various domestic factors with which external shocks interacted.

Chapter 3 deals with the period after the first oil shock and before the crises of the early 1980s; the story here is one of funds flowing readily from the world capital market and many countries borrowing heavily. As a consequence, their economies boomed, but the foundations were also laid for the later debt crisis. Chapter 4 tells of the crisis of the early 1980s—actually many different crises, and many different policy reactions. Chapter 5 covers the adjustment period between 1983 and 1989, sometimes going into 1990, a period in which some countries launched major structural adjustment programs involving trade and other liberalization measures, and the growth rates recovered in some cases. At the same time, many struggled to cope with the debt problem they inherited from the earlier two periods, and two (Argentina and Brazil) went through episodes of very high (and briefly even hyper-) inflation. Drastic shifts in resource transfers took place at this time owing to higher interest payments and reduced current account deficits—in some cases inward transfers were reduced, and in others they shifted outward. We compare this and the previous period and try to relate the extent of the shifts in resource transfers to various economic outcomes.

In chapters 6 to 10, we deal with critical issues that span the entire study period, sometimes going back to well before 1973: inflation and inflation stabilization, exchange rate policy, fiscal and monetary policies, trade restrictions, and liberalization. Chapter 6 looks at thirteen countries in which inflation rates have generally been low or moderate. Almost all had inflation "bubbles" in the two periods 1973–75 and 1980–82. A distinction is made between adjustment inflation, spiral inflation, and inflation resulting from the monetization of fiscal deficits. Adjustment inflation is essentially temporary and results from relative price adjustments necessitated by various shocks, for example, an improvement or deterioration in the terms of trade; spiral inflation refers to the continuous process wherein wage increases follow a devaluation and set in motion further devaluation, and so on; and the last category refers to cases in which inflation results from an inadequate fiscal policy. Of course, continued monetization is also necessary to sustain spiral inflation. Chapter 7 recounts the high-inflation experiences and the stabilization policies—sometimes successful, sometimes not—of five countries, including Argentina, Brazil, and Mexico, the three largest debtors of the 1980s. It also describes the high inflation and stabilization episode of Indonesia during 1961–70. Chapter 8 takes up the complex exchange rate policies and changes in exchange rate regimes of all the countries over the whole period. Of particular interest is the effect of various regimes on inflation.

In chapter 9 we survey the changes in trade regimes over the study period, noting the importance of variations in quantitative import restrictions as policy responses to balance of payments problems. We also draw attention to the important episodes of trade liberalization and explore the relationship between trade policy and exchange rate policy. In chapter 10 we turn to fiscal policy, and what is largely an adjunct of fiscal policy, monetary policy. We point out that fiscal policy in developing countries, in contrast to that in developing countries, has rarely helped to stabilize output and sometimes has been a significant destabilizing factor. Furthermore, we show that state-owned enterprises, and occasionally provincial governments, have had a large hand in their countries' fiscal problems, and that many states have relied on seigniorage as a source of revenues, sometimes for the government's budget and sometimes off the budget. Some policy conclusions are presented in these five chapters, although they are drawn together in chapter 13.

Chapter 11 is concerned with the effects of macroeconomic policy on long-run growth. The many factors that affect long-run growth—some of which have their roots in history and sociocultural as well as political conditions—operate mainly, if not wholly, through material investment and its productivity, or through changes in the quality of the labor force. Our work was not concerned with the determinants of the latter, or with research and development. The chapter is thus limited to investigating the effects of macroeconomic policy on the ratio of gross investment (as normally defined to exclude investment in human beings) to GNP and the efficiency of investment. Instability appears to be one element accounting for the huge differences from country to country in the relationship of investment to growth: it affects the quality of investment, as well as the level of investment in relation to GNP. Of the doubtless many other influences on the quality of investment, the manner in which public investment choices are made receives particular attention.

Chapter 12 asks *why* governments pursued particular policies; why they reacted in different ways to often similar shocks; why some were more ready to monetize budget deficits and generate inflation, and to allow it to continue, than others; why some reacted quickly and some slowly to crises. The subject here is political economy, and the questions examined are of the kind economists tend to bypass, or at least fail to treat systematically.

At the time of writing, there is a growing awareness of the importance of this subject. It has become clear to us that these questions deserve a book of their own, and chapter 12 only makes a start. We distinguish between the influence of *conviction* on policymakers' decisions—conviction shaped by historical experience, by ideology, by their training—and the influence of the ability to *control*—that is, to achieve the policies they wish to achieve. Success in this area of endeavor depends, among other things, on the strength of the government, the power of pressure groups, and institutional arrangements.

Chapter 13 draws together the conclusions of the various chapters and summarizes the implications for policy that seem to emerge. It asks what lessons can be learned from this particular historical experience of boom, crisis, and adjustment in eighteen developing countries.

The Rate of Devaluation: Two Definitions

There are many references to devaluations, real or nominal, in this book. The *rate* of devaluation can be expressed in two ways. Suppose that the exchange rate of the Indonesian rupiah is changed from 702 per dollar to 970 per dollar. Hence, the dollar value of the rupiah has fallen from 0.00142 to 0.00103. An index would show a decline, and the proportionate fall is 27.5 percent. The first method defines this as the rate of devaluation. The advantage of this method is that it conforms with the idea that "devaluation" represents a fall in value. Note, however, that the rupiah value of a dollar has risen from 702 to 970, which represents an increase of 38.2 percent. The second method defines this increase as the rate of devaluation: "the" exchange rate is then the number of rupiahs per dollar. The advantage of the second method is that it indicates the extent of the domestic price effects of the devaluation, and thus the incentives for the switching of production and demand that are created by the devaluation. In this book we use the *second* method.

Chapter 2

A Brief Survey of the World Economy

This chapter reviews trends in the world economy over the period 1965–90 that had an effect on stabilization and development in our eighteen countries—and indeed in all developing countries. Two that stand out are the continued rapid growth of world trade during the period, especially exports of manufactured goods from developing countries, and the emergence in the early 1970s, as in the 1920s, of a world money and capital market to which many developing countries had ready access. Also important are the move from fixed to floating exchange rates, started in March 1973; two sharp increases (1974 and 1979–80) and one sharp fall (1986) in oil prices; dramatic movements in the prices of several other primary products, notably coffee and copper; a mild economic recession and two deep ones (1975 and 1982); a large appreciation of the U.S. dollar against other leading currencies, followed by an equally large fall (1985–86); and a debt crisis for many developing countries in the mid-1980s when voluntary external lending virtually ceased.

Broadly speaking, the 1960s and early 1970s brought outstanding economic growth and, until 1973, relative price stability. This pattern broke in the mid-1970s with a commodity price boom, the first oil shock, and the deepest recession since the 1930s. Consolidation in the late 1970s was interrupted by a second oil shock, associated with a revolution in Iran. That episode, along with stringent efforts in several large industrial countries to control inflation, led to a second serious recession in 1981–82. The combination of heavy borrowing through earlier difficulties, high interest rates, and recession produced the debt crisis of 1982–83. After a setback in the late 1970s and early 1980s, growth in the industrialized countries resumed. For developing countries, however, the 1980s were years of adjustment, relative stagnation, and, for some, accelerating inflation (see table 2-1).

The chapter opens with a review of the institutional developments over the study period, that is, those connected with formal management of the world economy. The dominant trends in international trade and finance and the major events of the period are discussed next. The concluding section provides a brief comment

Table 2.1   Growth and Inflation, 1965–90

(percent a year)

	1965–73	1973–80	1980–90
GDP growth			
Industrial countries	4.4	2.5	3.1
Developing countries	6.2	5.1	3.2
Per capita	3.7	3.0	1.2
Inflation			
Industrial countries			
GDP deflator	5.4	9.3	4.5
Exports (U.S. dollars)	5.6	12.0	2.6
Developing countries			
GDP deflator	9.7	24.9	61.8
Nonoil exports (U.S. dollars)	4.5	12.5	0.2

Source: Calculated from IMF *International Financial Statistics* (1990), and World Bank, *World Development Report,*1992.

on the intellectual or philosophical climate of the day, which influenced both national and international economic decisionmaking.

Institutional Developments

After the Second World War and the chastening experiences of the 1930s, nations became intent on building a basic framework for economic relations among nations. The monetary elements of this framework were largely embodied in the Bretton Woods Agreement, which laid down basic principles and established the International Monetary Fund (IMF) and the International Bank for Reconstruction and Development (later called the World Bank). In their current account transactions, countries were to make their currencies convertible at fixed exchange rates (except for a 2 percent margin of fluctuation). The fixed rates could be adjusted, with international agreement, to correct a "fundamental disequilibrium" in international payments, and controls could be imposed on capital movements. Countries were to be free, within this framework, to pursue diverse economic and social objectives, and in particular to pursue policies to achieve full employment. The IMF was to oversee the rules and to lend funds to tide countries over temporary imbalances in payments or to ease their adjustment from disequilibrium to a position of payments equilibrium. The World Bank was to intermediate between the private capital markets of the world and capital-short countries, since it was assumed, after the experience of the 1930s, that private lenders would be loath to lend abroad any time soon.

No country was obliged to agree to the Bretton Woods arrangements, but over the years most chose to do so. The exceptions were the Communist countries, for whom currency convertibility was fundamentally inconsistent with central planning; and Switzerland, which remained cooperatively outside the arrangements until the early 1990s, when it decided to join.

The principles governing trade among nations are embodied in the General Agreement on Tariffs and Trade (GATT). The foremost of these is the rule of non-discrimination among trading partners. The GATT also provided for the settlement of disputes, including in extremis controlled retaliation against offending practices, and committed members to a gradual liberalization of trade from the highly restrictive regime prevailing in 1947. Initially, only a few countries adhered to the GATT, but by 1990 about 100 of the 150 members of the IMF and World Bank had joined in.

There were no analogous formal arrangements governing foreign investment. Trade in primary products was in principle covered by the GATT, but some felt from the beginning that an effort should be made to temper wide swings in the prices of primary products. In the 1950s, countries made various attempts at reaching international commodity agreements, but only the ones for tin (founded in 1956) and rubber (dating from 1979) endured with much content, and tin collapsed in 1986.

The Bretton Woods system of fixed but adjustable exchange rates was eventually undermined by two structural flaws. First, the system was directly or indirectly (through the U.S. dollar) based on gold; yet at a fixed nominal price, monetary gold supplies could not grow rapidly enough to support the unexpectedly rapid economic growth that took place in the 1950s and 1960s. The deficiency was filled by the U.S. dollar; but as the ratio of foreign-held dollars to U.S. gold grew over time, the gold convertibility of the dollar became increasingly doubtful, giving rise to the possibility of a run on the U.S. gold stock—and, more seriously, to a breakdown of what seemed to be a well-functioning set of international financial arrangements. To deal with this possible problem, countries in 1967 agreed to the creation of special drawing rights (SDRs) at the IMF. That is to say, a "paper gold" would be created from time to time to satisfy the need of a growing world economy for additional owned reserves that, unlike the dollar, were not some country's national currency. Two allocations of SDRs took place, in 1970–72 and in 1979–81, both for relatively modest amounts. This solution came too late to deal with the problem adequately, a run on U.S. gold did occur, and in August 1971 U.S. President Richard Nixon suspended indefinitely the gold convertibility of the U.S. dollar.[1]

Second, the Bretton Woods system relied on changes in fixed exchange rates to correct a fundamental disequilibrium. By the time authorities recognized that a disequilibrium was "fundamental," everyone else had come to see it as well. People could speculate on the possibility of a step change in the exchange rate, and if they correctly guessed when a change would occur they could profit at the expense of the authorities, selling a currency before depreciation and buying it afterward.

Effective controls on capital movements turned out to be crucial to making the system work. Through leads and lags in payments, it was possible to speculate even through trade transactions; in any case, some important countries did not accept the desirability of having controls on capital movements (nor were they required by the rules, only permitted), and did not have them. As world capital markets revived, currency speculation became easy and extensive. In 1972–73 large movements of funds from dollars into European currencies induced a number of countries to abandon fixed exchange rates. In March 1973 floating exchange rates among major currencies became general. Developing countries then had to decide whether to float their currencies as well, and if not, where to peg their currency. Their responses are discussed at length in chapter 8. In 1978 the IMF's Articles of Agreement were formally amended to abandon both the commitment to gold and the commitment to fixed exchange rates.

The experience of the early 1970s suggested that policymakers needed to do more continuous monitoring of world economic developments. In 1974 the IMF established an "interim committee" of twenty (later twenty-two) finance ministers to meet twice annually with that objective in mind; 1975 saw the first of what subsequently became annual economic summit meetings among five (later seven) heads of government of the major industrialized democracies.

Not satisfied with general floating, eight European countries in 1979 created the European monetary system (EMS), which, like the Bretton Woods system, required a declaration of "central" exchange rates but made the margins of variation around these central rates wider. Under the EMS, changes in central rates were frequent during the initial period, 1979–87, and efforts were made to coordinate the monetary policies of members. The EMS currencies, which came psychologically to center on the German mark, floated against the U.S. dollar, the Japanese yen, the British pound (until Britain joined the EMS in 1990), and other currencies. At first, the U.S. dollar gradually appreciated against the EMS currencies, by about 75 percent between 1980 and the end of 1984, but by 1986 it had fallen back to the 1980 rate. This sharp movement among major exchange rates had a significant influence on foreign trade flows, on commodity prices as conventionally measured (usually in dollars), and on the real value of dollar-denominated external debt, much of which had been acquired by the early 1980s.

By the mid-1960s most of the industrialized countries had eliminated their exchange controls on foreign trade.[2] A round of multilateral trade negotiations, known as the Kennedy Round, concluded in 1967 with the industrialized countries reducing tariffs on manufactured goods by about one-third, over a period of eight years. Even before the conclusion of the Kennedy Round, developing countries, through the UN Conference on Trade and Development (UNCTAD) and other forums, pressed hard to have the GATT requirement for nondiscrimination dropped. In its stead they wanted unreciprocated tariff reductions that would not be extended to developed countries. Gradually this idea came to be accepted, and by the mid-1970s the European Community, Japan, the United States, and other developed countries had extended duty-free treatment to many manufactured goods and processed foodstuffs coming from developing countries, under the generalized system of preferences (GSP). This erosion of a fundamental GATT principle came at a price, however. First, the European Community and the United States stiffened considerably their "safeguards" against import disruption. Second, textiles were excluded from GSP treatment and, moreover, the special arrangements governing trade in cotton textiles were extended in 1974 to cover woolen and man-made textiles under the Multifiber Arrangement, designed to restrain the rate of growth of exports of textiles and (mainly) apparel from developing countries.

At the Tokyo Round of multilateral trade negotiations from 1973 to 1979, participants again agreed to reduce tariffs on manufactured goods by about one-third over a period of eight years and to tighten the rules of GATT somewhat and extend its reach. Thus between 1968 and 1987 there was a steady reduction in tariffs and other barriers to imports into the major industrialized countries. This liberalization enabled developing countries to expand their nonagricultural exports, as many of them did. Import liberalization in developing countries, in contrast, was much more spotty and limited, until the mid-1980s; some countries even increased their restrictions on imports, as discussed in chapter 9, partly in response to the economic shocks they were experiencing.

The Uruguay Round of multilateral trade negotiations was launched in 1986 with the explicit objective of extending the reach of GATT into international trade in services and some aspects of foreign investment. By the end of 1992 this round was still in session because of disagreements over trade in agricultural products, which had not been resolved in previous rounds either, and over the protection of patents and trademarks. The European Community and Japan especially lined up against the liberalization of agricultural imports, while Brazil, India, and a number of other developing countries, joined on a few issues by Canada, resisted strong protection for patents and trademarks.

International agreements were in place at various times during the study period to limit fluctuations in commodity prices, notably on tin, coffee, sugar, cocoa, and natural rubber. By the late 1980s only the rubber agreement, which was structured differently from the others, was still functioning satisfactorily.[3] Another important agreement was the extension in the late 1970s of national control over the management of marine resources out to 200 nautical miles from the coast; this development represented a large-scale national appropriation of territory.[4]

Structural Changes in the World Economy

The institutional developments in the quarter century from 1965 to 1990 were accompanied by important changes in the growth and composition of world trade, the geographical pattern of trade, and the world money and capital market.

World exports, aided by trade liberalization, grew at the compound annual rate of 12.7 percent a year in dollar terms. They grew more rapidly than total world output, as they had done during the period 1950–65. Total exports from developing countries grew nearly as rapidly, because of a particularly strong increase in their exports of manufactured goods. Whereas in 1965 only 26 percent of total exports from developing countries were manufactured goods, including semiprocessed nonferrous metals, by 1990 the share of manufactures had more than doubled to 53 percent. This change was due not only to the rise in relative importance of exporters such as the Republic of Korea and Hong Kong, but also to the growth of manufactured exports from the countries of Latin America, where manufactures as a share of exports had risen from only 7 percent in 1965 to 32 percent in 1990. Brazil, once a classic exporter of primary products (92 percent of exports in 1965), recorded 53 percent of its exports as manufactured goods by 1990. Between 1969 and 1989 manufactured goods from developing countries grew from 5 to 13 percent of OECD imports of manufactures. Sub-Saharan African countries, however, still export mainly primary products, as do the major oil-exporting developing countries.

These changes in export composition have important implications for interpreting movements in the terms of trade. It is no longer appropriate, if it ever was, to associate movements in the prices of primary products in relation to manufactured goods with the terms of trade of developing countries. As noted, many developing countries have become substantial exporters of manufactured goods and, similarly, many are significant importers of primary products, especially petroleum and staple foods such as grains, but also in some cases cotton and other industrial materials.

The most noteworthy feature of the geographic pattern of trade is how *little* it changed in its main features over the quarter century. Developing countries as a group accounted for 27 percent of world exports in both 1965 and in 1988, for instance (table 2-2). Surprisingly, the nonoil exporters of this group gained slightly at the expense of oil exporters, although the latter increased their share temporarily during the periods of large oil price increases. The large changes were among nonoil exporters. In particular, the export share of several east and southeast Asian countries rose markedly over this period as a whole, reflecting also a rapid growth of output and income in those countries. In contrast, the export share of the developing countries of African and the Western Hemisphere declined significantly, by two and three percentage points, respectively. By 1990 Korea alone was exporting more than all of Africa. (The year 1990 saw a slowdown into recession in Britain and the United States, so imports of raw materials were unusually depressed; oil prices, however, were temporarily higher after Iraq's invasion of Kuwait in August.)

Similarly, the share of industrial countries in world exports was virtually unchanged, until the late 1990s, remaining at about 73 percent, and within this group the share of industrial Europe rose only slightly, despite the removal of barriers to intra-European trade during the early part of the period. Japan's share rose sharply, however, from 5 to 10 percent, while that of the United States declined from 16 to 12 percent.[5]

Table 2.2   Share of World Exports, Selected Years
(percent)

	1965	1978	1990
United States	15.9	11.8	11.8
Japan	4.9	7.9	8.6
Industrial Europe	44.7	44.5	47.9
Developing countries	27.3	30.4	26.3
Oil exporters	6.2	12.6	5.7
Nonoil exporters	21.2	17.8	20.6
Four Asian tigers[a]	1.6	3.8	8.8
Africa	4.7	3.8	2.3
Western Hemisphere	6.8	4.8	3.0

a. Korea, Taiwan (China), Hong Kong, and Singapore.
Note: Excludes the former U.S.S.R. and several smaller Communist countries.
Source: IMF, *International Financial Statistics* (1989, 1991).

A third significant development in the world economy was the re-emergence of an effective world money and capital market. The Euro-dollar market started in London in the late 1950s and grew rapidly during the 1960s, but remained a market mainly for banks and other prime borrowers in developed countries. By the late 1960s, however, a number of developing countries had tentatively entered the market, maturities had lengthened, and there were new instruments for credit. By the end of the decade, Euro-currency credits to developing countries were roughly half a billion dollars a year. The international bond market also revived. The Euro-currency market was given a fillip by the first oil shock, since London-based banks found themselves flooded with funds from the newly rich oil-exporting countries. Bank lending to developing countries grew rapidly, reaching $44 billion in 1981, before receding sharply following the 1982 debt crisis. The money and bond markets continued to grow, but the heavily debt-ridden developing countries no longer had ready access to them. Other developing countries, however, continued to borrow in these markets.

Official development assistance, another feature of the post–World War II period, continued to grow in nominal terms throughout our period, although less rapidly than private capital flows until the debt crisis. In real terms these flows were two-thirds higher by 1988 than they had been in 1965. Table 2-3 sets out bilateral development assistance and other capital flows to developing countries. Members of the Organization of Petroleum Exporting Countries (OPEC) offered extensive development assistance when their earnings and surpluses were exceptionally high; this assistance peaked at $9.6 billion in 1980 but by 1988 had declined to $2.4 billion. Net new lending, including structural adjustment loans, by the World Bank and its affiliate, the International Development Association, grew from $2.5 billion a year in the early 1970s to a peak of $25 billion in 1986. The dominant movement was in private capital, which rose fivefold from 1973 to 1981, only to

Table 2.3 Total Net Resource Flows to Developing Countries

Year	Billions of current U.S. dollars[a]				Billions of U.S. dollars at 1989 prices and exchange rates			
	Development assistance	Other official	Private	Total[b]	Development assistance	Other official	Private	Total[b]
1970	8.2	1.0	7.0	20.0	33.2	4.0	28.3	80.9
1971	9.1	1.2	6.9	21.9	34.1	4.5	25.9	82.1
1972	9.8	1.4	9.6	24.2	32.7	4.7	32.0	80.7
1973	12.7	2.3	15.0	33.9	36.3	6.6	42.9	96.9
1974	16.5	2.6	12.2	37.5	43.1	6.8	31.8	97.9
1975	21.0	3.3	23.8	56.6	47.0	7.4	53.3	126.8
1976	20.3	3.3	22.2	56.6	44.3	7.2	48.4	123.4
1977	21.0	3.3	28.8	67.0	41.9	6.6	57.4	133.6
1978	34.0	5.4	46.8	106.0	57.6	9.2	79.4	179.7
1979	31.7	5.7	53.9	104.1	48.5	8.7	82.5	159.3
1980	37.5	8.0	66.0	128.4	52.4	11.2	92.3	179.5
1981	37.2	9.2	74.3	139.1	54.6	13.5	109.0	204.0
1982	33.8	10.3	58.2	116.0	51.2	15.6	88.1	175.6
1983	33.9	8.5	47.8	94.8	51.7	13.0	72.8	144.4
1984	34.8	12.7	31.7	85.4	54.5	19.9	49.6	133.7
1985	37.0	11.6	30.5	83.1	57.4	18.0	47.3	128.8
1986	43.9	11.9	26.7	81.8	54.0	14.6	32.9	100.6
1987	48.2	13.3	33.7	92.6	51.1	14.1	35.7	98.2
1988	51.4	14.1	43.8	107.2	50.7	13.9	43.2	105.8
1989	52.9	12.6	48.3	123.3	52.9	12.6	48.3	123.3
1990	62.6	16.2	60.8	144.2	55.9	14.5	54.3	128.9

a. A billion is 1,000 million. b. Includes voluntary grants.
Source: OECD, Development Assistance Committee.

fall to one-third that level in 1986. In real terms, private capital movements were lower in 1986 and 1987 than they had been in 1973.

Finally, and not least, the International Monetary Fund (IMF) provided substantial emergency credit to developing countries immediately following the two major oil price increases and world recessions. As noted previously, the IMF was created to police certain rules of international financial behavior and to provide *temporary* support to countries experiencing temporary *balance of payments* difficulties or undertaking an adjustment program to restore payments equilibrium. The rules regarding fixed exchange rates were formally altered with an amendment to the Bretton Woods Articles of Agreement in 1978, but those concerning convertibility on current account were not altered.

Paradoxically, the role of the IMF increased significantly *after* the so-called collapse of the Bretton Woods system in 1971–73. Its lending rose sharply in 1974–76, partly out of its ordinary resources, but it also acquired extraordinary loans from the large industrial (G-10) countries and from some OPEC members, and it created an "oil facility" to help finance oil-importing countries while they were adjusting to the higher oil prices. The number of new IMF loans dropped in 1977–79, but then rose sharply again in the early 1980s, with net new credits peaking at $11.3 billion in 1983 and total outstanding credit reaching $38.6 billion in 1985.

The IMF played two other roles as well. First, it offered member countries policy advice on how to adjust to their payments positions. On large loans, the IMF stipulated policy conditions for disbursement of the loan, but it was available for advice under other circumstances as well. Second, governments and banks came to regard IMF endorsement of a country's adjustment policies as a "seal of approval" on debt rescheduling and new lending, both with respect to official debt and bank debt, as discussed further below. IMF approval assured lenders that a viable program had been undertaken.[6]

Major Economic Events

Several dramatic economic events also occurred during the period. To start, the fixed exchange rate feature of the Bretton Woods system broke down in the early 1970s. That was followed by two sharp increases in the price of crude oil, the most important commodity in world trade and a necessary input to all modern economies.

As noted, the decade of the 1960s had brought developed and developing countries alike outstanding economic growth, probably unprecedented in history, at moderate rates of inflation. In the late 1960s the postwar current account surplus of the United States virtually disappeared, but the deterioration was blunted by a strong inflow of capital, due mainly to tight money. When monetary conditions eased in the small recession of 1970–71, capital flows reversed and the overall U.S. payments deficit swung from a surplus of $2.7 billion in 1969 to a deficit of

$11 billion in 1970 and to $30 billion in 1971. These were enormous sums in their time and flooded the rest of the world with dollars, a flood that was augmented through pyramiding in the London-based Euro-dollar market (on which more below), such that the dollar foreign exchange reserves of other countries rose by substantially more than the U.S. deficit.

Under fixed exchange rates, increases in foreign exchange reserves increase domestic money supplies. A few countries, notably the Federal Republic of Germany, were able to sterilize much of the inflow, but money supplies in most countries increased by substantially more than the rise in foreign exchange reserves. This trend suggested that concern for the balance of payments was the principal source of monetary discipline for these countries; when that was relaxed, restraint on domestic monetary expansion was also relaxed. In any case, starting with Canada (in 1970), followed by the United Kingdom (in 1972), one country after another attempted to insulate domestic monetary conditions from external influences by floating its currency. Generalized floating began in March 1973.

That year also produced the highest rate of growth in the industrialized countries (5.7 percent) and in the world that had been seen since the Korean War boom year of 1950 (see figure 2-1). As a consequence of strong fundamental demand, and of changes in agricultural policies in the former Soviet Union (leading to large imports of grain), world commodity prices more than doubled between early 1972 and early 1974, before receding in the 1974–75 recession. For our eighteen countries, the prices of sugar, copper, and phosphates were especially important. (Coffee and cocoa prices, however, were to rise much more in 1975–77, following a severe frost in Brazil; we discuss this event at greater length in chapter 3.) Some of the price increase was undoubtedly speculative in origin, reflecting among other things concern with rising inflation.[7] In October of this boom year came the Yom Kippur War between Israel and Egypt, followed by the Arab embargo on oil sales to the United States and the Netherlands, and the decision in December by OPEC ministers to raise crude oil prices more than threefold, from $3.70 to $11.65 a barrel.

This price increase, effective January 1, 1974, was probably the largest one-quarter economic shock the world economy has ever experienced. More than 10 percent of world payments for trade were redirected in a single quarter. It created an acute dilemma for policymakers in all countries. A sharp increase in oil prices not only pushes up the general price level (= inflation), but in the short run also leads to a reduction in output because of the large change in the distribution of income between oil consumers and oil producers. Since demand for oil is inelastic in the short run, the need for households and firms to spend more for oil products implies they have less available for other purchases, so output declines and unemployment rises. Macroeconomic management is thrown into confusion as countries try to fight both inflation and unemployment at the same time, but with different emphases, and thus find themselves faced with secondary balance of payments problems. Governments of oil-importing countries also had to decide whether to adjust fully to the higher oil prices, even though they might prove to be

Figure 2.1 Price and Output Gap Developments in the Seven Largest OECD Economies, 1970–92

Percent

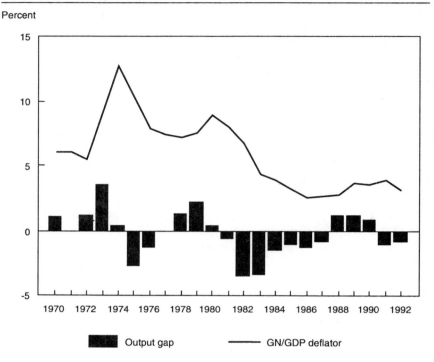

Note: Based on 1987 GDP weights and exchange rates. The output gap is defined as the difference between actual and potential output in relation to potential output. A positive value means that the economy is operating above its potential and a negative value that there is slack in the economy. GNP/GDP deflator is calculated as percentage change from the previous year.
Source: OECD *Economic Outlook* 49 (July 1991).

temporary (as some eminent economists predicted), or whether to borrow to cover their increased import bills.

The United States and Germany, followed with a lag by Japan, put greater weight on fighting inflation; most other countries, developed and less developed alike, chose to proceed on course and borrow as necessary to cover increased expenditures on oil. Funds were amply available, since oil-exporting countries found themselves with revenues far in excess of what they could spend in the short run, and placed their surplus funds in the Euro-currency market, to be re-lent by banks to oil-importing countries.

In 1974–75 a combination of oil price increases and contractionary policies in several major countries produced the sharpest decline in world economic activity since the Second World War. It was the first OECD-wide recession, in the technical sense of a decline in real gross national product for more than two quarters.[8] The recession, of course, increased the borrowing requirements of those countries that attempted to maintain their economic growth; by the same token, the heavy borrowing to support continued spending mitigated the depth of the recession.

Over time the oil-exporting countries increased their expenditures to match their now higher incomes, and their large current account surplus of $67 billion in 1974 became a small deficit of $2 billion by 1978. Oil prices continued to rise slowly in nominal terms but declined slightly in real terms from their 1974 level (see figure 2-2). OECD growth was back to 4.2 percent, modestly lower than during the 1960s, but respectable. The year 1978 suggested a return to normalcy.

But an Islamic revolution occurred in Iran in early 1979. Iranian oil production dropped sharply and world oil prices began a steep rise that was to persist for over two years, from $12.70 a barrel for Saudi light in 1978 to $33.50 a barrel in 1982. Oil-exporter current account surpluses rose to $103 billion in 1980, and again oil-importing countries were faced with rising price levels (since fuels are an important input to modern economies) combined with declining demand for nonfuel production. The macroeconomic policy dilemma was posed again, as it had been in 1974. More countries elected to fight inflation after the second oil shock, but a number continued to borrow heavily, joined on this occasion also by a number of oil-exporting countries—notably Mexico and Nigeria—whose spending plans ran ahead even of their much higher current revenue. So once

Figure 2.2   World Oil Prices—Nominal and Real, 1970–88

U.S. dollars per barrel

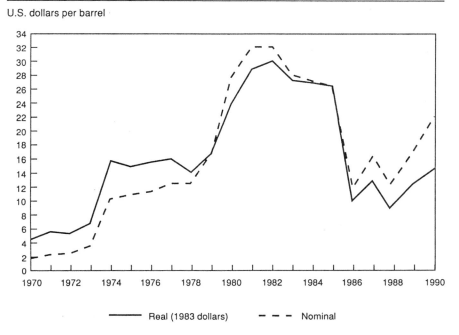

——— Real (1983 dollars)   − − − Nominal

Source: IMF *International Financial Statistics* (various issues).

again external debt took a sharp increase. As a result of the fight against inflation short-term interest rates rose much more in 1980–81 than they had in 1974 (three-month Eurodollar deposit rates averaged 16.9 percent during 1981, up from 8.8 percent in 1978), and a higher portion of bank loans carried floating interest rates, so debtors faced higher interest payments as well as higher oil prices (see chart 2.3).

As in 1974, a combination of the suddenly higher oil prices and the contractionary policies in leading industrial countries (Britain, Germany, Japan, and the United States) induced a second world recession in 1981–82, more severe (in relation to potential output) than the 1975 recession. Again, the recession depressed primary product prices and required many countries to borrow more than they otherwise would. And again, the fact of heavy borrowing itself mitigated the severity of the world recession.

The combination of high accumulated debt, recession, and high interest rates (see figure 2-3) produced a debt crisis. Previously debtors could rely on a decline in interest rates in recessions to compensate in part for their decline in exports.

Figure 2.3 Interest Rates and Nonoil Developing Country Terms of Trade, 1965–90

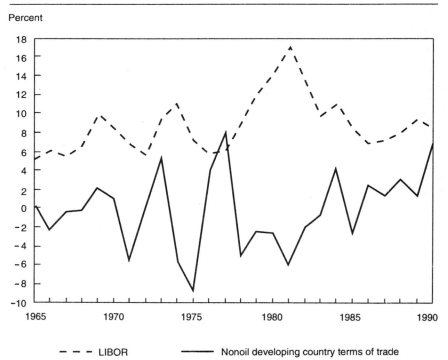

Percent

----- LIBOR   ——— Nonoil developing country terms of trade

Source: IMF *International Financial Statistics* (various issues).

After 1982, debtors were not only unable to borrow more, but they could not even roll over their current debts as they matured. Ironically, the debt crisis became a global issue when in August 1982 Mexico, an oil *exporter*, announced that it could not continue to service its debts. That produced a general hesitation by the major banks of the world to continue to lend to governments in developing countries. Several countries—Turkey, Poland, Costa Rica—had run into debt limits earlier, but with the Mexican crisis, the problem became generalized. Although some voluntary lending continued, especially to Asian countries whose capacity for servicing debt did not seem so severely constrained, the rate of new voluntary lending declined sharply from 1982 on. Net new bank lending to developing countries reached a peak of $44 billion in 1981, having risen sharply from $24 billion in 1979 and 1980; by 1984 it was down to $8 billion, and by 1987 it had fallen to $4 billion.[9] Since the willingness of banks to lend to any borrower depends on the perception that the borrower has access to other lenders, once some banks withdrew, others followed apace, thereby precipitating delays in payment.

Borrowing is based on expectations about the future. It is easy, but beside the point, to criticize past decisions once we learn what the "future" actually brought. It is therefore useful to recall the climate of expectations around 1980, when so much borrowing took place. Inflation in the leading countries was expected to continue at a high rate, without deleterious effects on growth. Oil prices, which rose throughout 1979 and 1980, were expected to continue to rise, albeit at a much lower rate. Concretely, in 1980 the World Bank projected that unit values of exports of manufactured goods from the industrialized countries would increase on average 8.4 percent a year for the coming decade, whereas in the event they increased only 4.6 percent a year. As a result, a ten-year fixed-interest loan made in 1980 ended up carrying a much higher real interest rate than was expected at the time.

More relevant for many developing countries (although not for all, as noted above) was the price of primary products. A composite index (excluding oil) was projected in 1980 to increase on average 9.4 percent a year over the coming decade, for a *real* increase (in terms of manufactured goods) of 0.9 percent a year. This index *declined* 0.5 percent a year, for a real decline of 4.9 percent a year— more than five percentage points less than expected. About the same time, it was thought that oil prices would increase 3 percent a year in real terms for the indefinite future, whereas in actuality they declined sharply from the levels of 1980. Oil-exporting countries borrowed against this expectation, and banks willingly lent to them. Some countries (most notably Brazil) launched large oil-saving investments against the same expectation, again finding willing lenders.

Similarly, the U.S. recession of 1982 was at first not foreseen, and then its magnitude was greatly underestimated.[10] Furthermore, interest rates failed to decline as rapidly as they had in earlier recessions, offsetting for debtors some of the impact of the decline in demand for their exports.

The sharp reduction of new lending after 1982 gave rise to a net outward transfer of resources—defined as interest payments less net new borrowing—from many developing countries to their creditors. Of course, the debtor countries still had the assets that they had purchased with the loans, except where the borrowing had been used for current consumption, for example, in paying for higher oil bills or for current government expenditures or transfers. In some cases, it turned out, the assets purchased were abroad, in private hands, since the public borrowing was indirectly used to finance the outflow of private capital, sometimes called capital flight. The magnitudes were exceptionally large in Argentina, Mexico, and Venezuela, none of which maintained controls on private capital outflow in the early 1980s. The income on these privately held assets was not generally available for servicing the public debts.

In other cases, the loans had been used for large investments where the economic returns were dubious, especially in the 1980s, when growth had fallen off and oil prices had dropped from their 1981 highs. In still other cases, the borrowing had been used for successful investments, which added to national product more than was required to service the debts. The last category was not typical for many debtors.

When a debtor within a country becomes unduly burdened, some kind of debt relief is usually provided—often under court-supervised bankruptcy proceedings. The international community groped toward an international equivalent for sovereign debt during the course of the 1980s. For debt to official creditors (arising from official export credits or development loans), procedures had already been worked out in the so-called Paris Club, a committee of creditors relevant to any particular debtor country, chaired by the French Ministry of Finance. With a satisfactory program, endorsed by the IMF, official claims were rescheduled, in effect stretching the original maturities of the debts. Such rescheduling increased sharply during the 1980s, from one or two a year during the 1970s to a local peak of twenty-one in 1985 and twenty-four in 1989. Nine of the eighteen countries covered in this study experienced debt rescheduling between 1980 and 1988.[11] Early rescheduling involved extensions of maturity, often with a grace period, at unchanged interest rates. Following the 1988 Toronto economic summit, official creditors became considerably more generous and began to offer wider coverage and lower interest rates on some rescheduling.

A procedure called the London Club, which was analogous to that of the Paris Club, was developed by private bank creditors. In this case, a committee of leading creditor banks worked out a program of rescheduling, rollovers, and new lending in response to a satisfactory economic program, endorsed by the IMF, in the debtor country. Meetings of the London Club jumped from seven in 1982 to twenty-two in 1983, but then gradually dropped back to seven again by 1989. By then much of the commercial bank debt had been rescheduled, and the total had declined considerably.

Gradually, the conditions of debt relief became somewhat easier—with longer extensions, longer grace periods, lower interest rates, and eventually swaps of bank debt for equity or for bonds that involved substantial reduction in principal. Between official and commercial bank creditors together, $29 billion in principal and interest were rescheduled in 1985; the amount rose to a peak of $33 billion in 1987, but then dropped to $19 billion in 1989.

Following the 1982 recession, the United States had a long period of steady growth, until 1990. Japan also enjoyed a period of steady growth, but the countries of Europe, other than Britain, remained anemic until late in the 1980s, with the result that over the decade the industrial countries as a group grew nearly two percentage points less than they had during the 1960s.[12] Combined with a heavy debt burden, this lower growth had a number of repercussions in developing countries, whose growth during the 1980s was more than two percentage points lower than it had been in the 1960s. Lower growth in income and consumption in the industrialized countries means not only a slower growth in demand for products from developing countries, but also puts some downward pressure on the prices of primary products, thus worsening the terms of trade of those countries that export primary products.

The 1982 recession and subsequent slow growth also reduced the world demand for oil. In 1980 and 1981 a number of analysts projected that world oil prices would continue to rise and would reach $45 or $50 a barrel by the mid-1980s. Some of the many energy-conserving investments made around the world were predicated on continued increases in oil prices, as was the heavy borrowing by such oil producers as Mexico and Nigeria. The demand for oil weakened, however, and through 1985 oil prices dropped gradually from their 1981 peaks. In command over goods and services, they dropped even further. Declining oil demand led OPEC for the first time to assign production quotas to its members in 1982, thus meeting the formal condition for a cartel. Because assigned quotas tended to exceed demand, prices were maintained as high as they were only by substantial reductions in production by Saudi Arabia, OPEC's largest producer—from more than ten million barrels a day in late 1980 to less than three million barrels a day in 1985. At this point, Saudi Arabia, having warned on several occasions that it would not be the sole swing producer in OPEC, changed its pricing and production strategy, and oil prices quickly fell below $10 a barrel in early 1986. This sharp drop was a bonanza to oil-importing countries, such as Brazil and Korea, but it was a major financial setback to oil-exporting countries such as Mexico and Nigeria. The lesson was apparently learned by OPEC members; restrictions were reimposed on production, and prices rose in late 1986, but they remained about $10 a barrel lower than they had been in early 1985 ($18 as against $28). In real terms, after 1986 they were below the level of 1974, but not as low as they were in 1973, before the first major oil price increase (see figure 2-2).

The broad story is revealed in table 2-4, which shows the emergence of large OPEC payment surpluses in 1974–76 and again in 1979–81, with corresponding deficits in the industrialized countries and the nonoil developing countries. With the sharp drop in the price of oil in 1986, that pattern was reversed, and a partial recovery began in 1987.

Current account deficits of the nonoil developing countries show how borrowing evolved in these countries, since the current account, when properly measured, is equal to the change in net claims on foreigners. Gross borrowing was often higher than the current account deficit because funds were needed to cover the outflows by private citizens and to permit increases in foreign exchange reserves. According to the current account deficits, borrowing increased sharply in 1974 and again in 1979, peaked in 1981, and then took a large drop after the 1982–83 debt crisis. By 1987 the nonoil developing countries had a current account surplus of nearly $12 billion—a *swing* of $111 billion from 1981, indicating the great compression of imports experienced by many developing countries.

Note that the sums of the rows in table 2-4 do not equal zero, nor on the whole do they even come close to it, as they should.[13] After 1977, recorded payments for goods, services, and transfers greatly exceeded recorded receipts for these items.

Table 2.4   Current Account Positions, 1968–90
(billions of dollars)

| Year | Industrial countries | Developing countries | | Total[a] |
		Oil-Exporting	Other	
1968	4.5	1.3	−6.1	−1.2
1969	5.5	0.9	−5.4	0.0
1970	6.9	−1.0	−10.0	−4.1
1971	10.2	1.2	−12.2	−0.7
1972	8.0	3.5	−4.9	6.6
1973	13.6	6.6	−5.4	14.9
1974	−21.4	67.4	−30.5	15.4
1975	9.7	32.6	−39.8	2.5
1976	−10.5	37.9	−27.3	0.1
1977	−15.5	22.2	−23.0	−16.4
1978	14.7	−2.4	−32.6	−20.3
1979	−23.6	59.9	−48.6	−12.3
1980	−59.4	103.5	−76.1	−32.0
1981	−17.6	46.6	−99.3	−70.2
1982	−20.9	−9.3	−74.5	−104.7
1983	−21.7	−20.5	−38.1	−80.4
1984	−56.7	−5.9	−22.2	−84.7
1985	−48.9	4.0	−25.3	−70.2
1986	−16.3	−23.0	−12.1	−51.4
1987	−39.5	−4.2	11.6	−32.1
1988	−50.5	−13.0	5.4	−58.0
1989	−84.4	6.1	−17.7	−96.0
1990	−104.9	−4.2	−17.1	−100.5

a. Excludes the former U.S.S.R., several small centrally planned economies, and China before 1982.
Source: IMF, *International Financial Statistics*, various issues, and *Supplement on the Balance of Payments* (1984).

So OPEC surpluses were less than they appear, or deficits by the other countries were less than they appear. These large discrepancies can be traced to three likely sources: (1) imports into developing countries were overinvoiced, to conceal the export of private capital; (2) purchases of foreign services by governments, especially OPEC governments during the large construction booms in those countries, were underrecorded by countries that exported the services, because of inadequate data-gathering procedures, and (3) interest and dividend payments to private owners of capital, mainly in developing countries, are recorded by the countries in which the assets are located, but not by the countries in which the owners of the financial assets reside. The point is that a number of indebted countries were probably far less indebted than the official figures suggest, but, as a practical matter, the foreign assets owned by their residents were inaccessible to the governments of the indebted countries. Thus, debt problems became mainly *governmental* debt problems.

By the late 1980s the world economy again seemed to have returned to some normalcy—a number of developing countries were working their way out from under their external debt, and growth was returning to Europe, in part because restraints on intra-European trade were scheduled to be removed by the end of 1992. World attention became preoccupied with developments in Eastern Europe and the former U.S.S.R. However fascinating and important those developments were for the countries in question, and for the structure of international security, the only direct implication they had for developing countries was that they created a competing demand for the limited supply of official funds available from the rich countries. They also carried an intellectual message, as explained in the next section.

The Intellectual Climate

Economic policy, like other policy, is strongly influenced not only by events but also by the intellectual milieu of each era. The postwar international economic framework was strongly influenced by the Great Depression and by the ideas that came out of that experience, particularly the notion that governments could stabilize, and had an obligation to stabilize, aggregate demand so as to avoid high and rising unemployment. These ideas sparked the so-called Keynesian revolution in economic thought. They sought also to avoid beggar-thy-neighbor actions by countries in search of higher domestic demand and employment—hence the emphasis on trade liberalization and current account convertibility, a reaction in part to the exploitative bilateral currency arrangements of Nazi Germany in the 1930s.

Two strands of thought have greatly influenced policy in developing countries. The first originated with political leaders in the colonial world and their intellectual guides and supporters; the second originated within the professional world of economics.

Following decolonization and the dismantling of the great European empires, many intellectuals in the newly independent countries reacted negatively to European firms and to European ways. Many felt the same about American firms and American ways because of the close association between the United States and Europe after the war, and because the United States was the leading and most outspoken capitalist country. Instead, they found the U.S.S.R. intellectually appealing, in part because of its anti-imperial stance, and in part because central planning appeared to have been successful in stimulating the growth of the Soviet economy during the 1950s, while attaining a measure of equity. These dispositions were reinforced by the economic development literature of Western economists, who emphasized setting national targets for growth and investment and using government authority to achieve those targets through such instruments as control over credit and over the allocation of foreign exchange, and even through direct commands and government ownership of enterprises. The government was expected not only to provide a framework of physical and social infrastructure, such as commercial law and modern education, but also to serve as entrepreneur, investor, and manager of economic activity.

The hopes for rapid development were so high that many leaders in developing countries were disappointed with their economic performance in the 1960s—ironically, since on average that performance was outstanding by historical standards and is unlikely to be achieved in future periods. They chose to blame this poor performance on the international economic system, arguing that they had played no role in setting its rules (although many Latin American countries were represented at Bretton Woods) and that it was biased against the economic development of poor countries. Collectively, they assaulted the nondiscrimination provisions of the GATT, arguing for tariff and other trade discrimination in favor of developing countries.[14]

These opinion leaders also wanted to carry the dirigisme of many of their domestic economies into the international arena, through such devices as international commodity agreements designed to raise average prices and international endorsement of producer cartels; government-compelled transfers of technology to developing countries; government control over the employment, investment, and export behavior of multinational corporations; international sanction for freedom to expropriate foreign-owned property with appropriate compensation, to be determined solely by the host country; and augmented transfers of resources to developing countries, on concessional terms but with minimal conditions on use, through a variety of channels.

These positions were set forth in several declarations and resolutions, starting with a ministerial level meeting of the Group of 77 (of developing countries in the United Nations) in Algiers in 1967 and culminating with passage by the UN General Assembly in 1974 of the Charter of Rights and Duties of States, by a divisive majority vote. The key sticking points for the United States and several other industrialized countries were the provisions concerning producer cartels, expropriation of foreign-owned property, and management of the international financial system (especially the IMF). The general drift of many provisions, however, implied a degree of governmental involvement in economic matters that the industrialized countries (most openly, Britain, Germany, and the United States) found uncongenial and ultimately unacceptable. The provisions did, however, reflect a point of view widely accepted around the world in the mid-1970s, especially a distrust of private enterprise, and these attitudes underlay the booms in public investment in developing countries discussed in the next chapter.[15]

Economists, meanwhile, had begun to doubt the wisdom of the "Keynesian" emphasis on maintaining high employment through the manipulation of monetary and, especially, fiscal policy. The naive but widely espoused versions ignored the possibility of accelerating inflation under "Keynesian" economic management, something Keynes himself had recognized and acknowledged as a problem thirty years earlier. As inflation accelerated during the 1970s, attention turned increasingly to the "monetarist" approach to macroeconomic management, with its focus on some measure of the money supply and its relation to the price level. Monetarism came into vogue in the late 1970s. Like the Keynesian perspective, monetarism had its naive variants, especially when attempts were made to make it quantitatively operational, and these versions were discredited during the 1980s when postulated relationships between particular definitions of money supply and price level broke down in many countries.

Other notions that were gaining currency among academic economists and that found their way into macroeconomic policymaking in some countries were so-called rational expectations and the new classical economics. The latter emphasized the high degree of perfection of markets, not only for commodities and securities, but also for manufactured goods and labor. The former made the important observation that, in making their decisions, economic agents (households and firms) are likely to take into account all the information that is available to them, and to anticipate the future consequences of their actions and those of others, rather than merely extrapolate past behavior. Unfortunately, when academic economists translate this common-sense observation into their economic models, it is introduced as perfect foresight except for truly random fluctuations.

Perfect foresight is an analytically powerful and convenient assumption, but one that is extraordinarily naive when applied to actual economic decisionmaking. Nonetheless, the power of these intellectual currents was such that during the late 1970s and 1980s the two sets of ideas led some policymakers in Britain, Chile, Argentina, and the United States to believe that inflation could be reduced relatively painlessly if only the government showed sufficient resolution with respect to monetary control, and, in the case of Chile and Argentina, demonstrated that resolution by fixing the exchange rate. The latter two experiments are discussed at length in chapter 7.

In the industrialized countries, there was also a general philosophical reaction to big—and growing—government with the emergence of neoconservatism and neoliberalism, two schools of thought that were not far apart on matters of economic and social policy, as both contended that the efficacy of government action was questionable, even if well-intentioned. In addition, neoconservatives questioned how well-intentioned many such interventions were, pointing rather to the self-interest of politicians in their pandering to the public on issues of general concern while privately recognizing that proposed solutions could not solve the stated problems, and to the self-interest of bureaucrats in greater government intervention so as to enhance their own social status, decisionmaking power, and remuneration.

These philosophical currents, reinforced by the public's disenchantment with inflation and the government's apparent inability to bring it under control, led to the election of a more conservative group of leaders in several major countries: Margaret Thatcher in Britain (1979), Joe Clark in Canada (1980), Ronald Reagan in the United States (1980), and Helmut Kohl in Germany (1981). (In 1981, however, France's Fifth Republic elected its first socialist president, François Mittérrand; it was not a good period for incumbents.)

The strong political attack on big government as being both incompetent and oppressive was reinforced by the clear failure, by the 1980s, of central planning in the U.S.S.R. and in other Communist countries. China in 1978 inaugurated major reforms to decentralize economic decisionmaking both in agriculture (where it was highly successful) and in industry (where success was more modest). Hungary and Poland moved more tentatively in a similar direction. And in 1985 the U.S.S.R. began a program of *glasnost* (openness of expression) as a necessary prelude to *perestroika* (restructuring of the economy). By the end of the decade, Poland, Czechoslovakia, Hungary, and Mongolia had formally abandoned communism as a political system and central planning as the principal mechanism for allocating resources, in favor of open markets; East Germany had been unified with West Germany under the latter's principles of economic organization; and Bulgaria and Romania had taken steps to dismantle their systems of central planning. In 1991 the U.S.S.R. fragmented into its constituent republics, each of which was struggling with economic and political reform, but none seemed likely to return to a system of central control over the allocation of resources.

Indeed, the desire for less government control, more private enterprise, more autonomy for government-owned enterprises, and more reliance on competition (including import competition) as a regulator of resource allocation was worldwide, extended to many developing countries by the late 1980s and no doubt helps explain their growing interest in trade liberalization. By the end of our period, these philosophical currents had drastically changed the environment both for national economic policymaking and for international negotiation on economic matters.

Chapter 3

The Period of Cheap and Easy Credit, 1973–1979

Two notable features of the period from 1973 to 1979 were the new supply of international credit at low interest rates and the dramatic rise in oil prices in 1974. These were large exogenous changes that produced important policy reactions in most of the eighteen countries under study here. As this chapter points out, the change in credit conditions had a more lasting effect than the change in oil prices.

The new credit conditions were favorable for almost all these countries.[1] Meanwhile, the oil price increase had differential effects. For the oil exporters Indonesia and Nigeria, it was favorable. For countries that were roughly self-sufficient in oil, such as Colombia and Argentina, the shock was not too serious. For yet others, the shock was offset by increases in other commodity prices, as in Sri Lanka and Côte d'Ivoire in 1974 and Morocco in 1974 and 1975. Since a change in the terms of trade has rather similar effects however produced, we shall consider it to be the relevant magnitude.

Table 3-1 gives estimates of the size of the 1974 and 1975 terms-of-trade shock in relation to the gross domestic product (GDP) and exports of the previous year. The countries are arranged in three groups, in descending order of the size of the terms-of-trade shock in relation to GDP (combining 1974 and 1975). The first group consists of the seriously affected, with a total effect exceeding 3 percent of GDP. For the five countries in the second group, the terms-of-trade effect was very small in relation to GDP, but large in relation to exports, except in Colombia. The three countries in the third group gained—Nigeria and Indonesia enormously, and Morocco significantly.[2]

All the countries achieved positive growth in 1974, although barely so in the case of India and Chile. Their poor performance had little to do with the oil price rise, however. In most countries the growth was rather slower than in 1973.

The year 1975 was again similar for most, the growth rate falling further in eleven cases, and recovering in the others. The exception was Chile, which

Table 3.1   Terms-of-Trade Shocks, 1974 and 1975

(percent)

Country	Total effect on GDP_{t-1}		Total effect on $Exports_{t-1}$		Change in debt (PPG)/ GNP, 1973–75[a]	GDP growth rate			
	1974	1975	1974	1975		1973	1974	1975	1976
Chile	−12.4	−5.1	−48.2	−27.8	+32.0	−5.5	0.8	−13.2	3.6
Cameroon	−3.8	−3.7	−20.3	−16.7	+0.6	5.5	10.7	−0.8	4.3
Côte d'Ivoire	−0.9	−6.4	−2.6	−16.1	+1.4	4.3	6.2	10.2	5.8
Kenya	−4.1	−3.0	−13.4	−8.0	+2.5	5.8	3.6	1.3	2.2
Costa Rica	−5.1	−1.0	−22.6	−4.0	+7.2	7.8	5.4	2.0	5.4
Pakistan	−3.1	−2.8	−21.4	−22.0	−18.9	7.1	3.4	4.1	5.3
Korea, Rep.	−4.0	+0.9	−16.6	+4.0	+0.8	15.2	8.9	7.7	13.5
Sri Lanka	−3.1	−0.6	−21.9	−3.8	−1.1	9.5	3.8	6.5	3.5
Thailand	−0.8	−3.0	−5.3	−16.6	+0.7	9.8	4.3	4.8	9.4
Brazil	−2.6	−0.5	−33.3	−7.0	+3.0	14.4	9.0	5.2	9.8
Mexico	−0.9	−0.6	−22.5	−15.8	+1.5	8.2	6.1	5.7	4.2
Turkey	−1.1	−0.3	−18.1	−5.2	−5.1	4.2	8.6	8.9	8.8
Argentina	−0.9	−0.3	−19.5	−7.7	+8.1	3.8	5.5	−0.5	−0.2
India	−0.9	+0.0	−25.0	+1.0	0.0	3.4	1.2	9.2	1.7
Colombia	+0.9	−1.1	+7.6	−9.5	−1.6	6.7	5.7	2.1	4.8
Morocco	+3.0	+1.3	+20.8	+5.9	+2.5	3.5	5.4	6.7	11.0
Indonesia	+17.0	−3.0	+90.9	−11.1	−5.6	8.7	7.7	5.0	6.9
Nigeria	+23.1	−2.6	+136.7	−9.8	−3.5	7.6	11.2	−3.2	9.2

a. Percentage points.
Note: The effect on the terms of trade must be regarded as giving an order of magnitude only: there are considerable divergences in several cases between World Bank data and those given in the country studies. (But only in the case of Kenya were World Bank data clearly wrong.)
Source: All World Bank data, except for Kenya, for which the data are from Bevan, Collier, and Gunning (unpublished). The debt figures are for public and public guaranteed debt only and are from *World Debt Tables 1980–81*.

experienced a catastrophic fall of 12 percent in real GDP, partly because of a fall in copper prices. Except in Chile, there were no very serious recessions. GDP fell in Nigeria, mainly because of a reduction in the quantity of oil produced, but real income, of course, rose with the rise in oil prices.

In 1976 growth improved for most of the countries. This was the first year of the coffee boom, and among the noncoffee exporters that had sustained a serious shock in 1974, Korea, Pakistan, Thailand, and Turkey experienced a rapid rise in GDP. This rapid recovery is striking. The decline in growth following the 1974 shock was clearly over.

All the countries that suffered a negative shock increased their borrowing, as was to be expected; but the increases in 1974 and 1975 were not excessive. Almost as many countries reduced the ratio of public and publicly guaranteed debt (PPG) to GNP as increased it (see table 3-1). Only Chile experienced a very large rise, and this was due mainly to a fall in GNP rather than a large rise in borrowing.

The varying effects of the 1974 shock and the subsequent growth of GDP cannot be understood without examining policy reactions in our countries. First, we consider what would have been optimal or rational reactions to the oil price rise, given the knowledge available at the time. For five of our countries, the coffee boom of 1976–78 was soon to overshadow the oil price rise, and therefore optimal reactions to this favorable shock are also considered. Next, we describe the actual policy reactions to the 1974 shock and the reactions of the coffee exporters to their windfall. Complicating circumstances make the evaluation difficult, even with hindsight, although the new ease of borrowing was clearly more influential than changes in the terms of trade, as indicated by the investment booms in almost all our countries.We argue that the great increases in borrowing were devoted mainly to investment.

Optimal Policy Reactions to Exogenous Changes

Policy reactions to the cheapening and increased ease of foreign borrowing and to the change in the terms of trade resulting from the oil price rise would have depended on whether authorities expected the changes to be temporary or permanent, or, at least, long-lasting. In particular, a country's decision about whether to borrow and how much—that is, about the extent to which it should run a current account deficit—would have depended on a number of factors that might push in opposite directions. Another important consideration would have been whether its terms of trade had worsened (as in most cases) or improved.

Consider, first, whether the greater ease and cheapness of borrowing was expected to be permanent. Although commercial banks had already begun to increase their lending to developing countries before 1973, it was the oil price rise that caused real rates of interest to fall drastically and commercial bank loans to rise rapidly, beginning in 1974. The leading oil exporters could not absorb the huge increase in their earnings, and the large countries of the Organization for Economic Cooperation and Development, fearful of inflation, were unwilling to pursue expansionary policies. It was a buyers' market for "petro-dollars." Surely this state of affairs should not have been expected to last, even if the increase in the real price of oil was believed to be permanent. The surpluses of the oil exporters would undoubtedly be reduced as they learned to spend, and the industrialized countries would become less wary of deficits. Long-term real interest rates might have been expected to rise from the zero or negative levels of 1974 and 1975 to 3–4 percent, which seems to be a long-term norm.

It was rational for a country to take advantage of a temporary period of low real interest rates by borrowing and investing more than it otherwise would in that period, although the extent of the advantage would have been severely limited by the difficulty of raising the level of investment efficiently for a short period.

Loans are contracted at nominal rates. The expected rate of inflation had become very uncertain, and so also had real interest rates. After 1976 debt was therefore increasingly contracted at variable rates. Since borrowers could not be sure that the real interest rate on medium- or long-term loans of this type might not turn out to be high, borrowing should have become a less attractive proposition. Yet many countries began to borrow heavily for investment in 1974 and 1975, and these investment booms continued long after low interest rates were ensured.

As for the oil price rise itself, there were good reasons to suppose that the rise would be permanent, or long-lasting, at any rate. Undoubtedly, the consensus was that the price rise had come to stay, although there were, of course, some dissenters. It is rational for a country (or a person) to adapt immediately to a new circumstance that is expected to be permanent. A permanent fall in real income should in principle be followed by a rapid reduction of consumption. Borrowing to maintain consumption would require a bigger adjustment later. A fall in investment should also occur unless the change in circumstances increased the real yield of investment or reduced the cost of foreign borrowing. In fact, the real yield of investment in oil substitutes and measures that would economize in the use of oil went up, while that in energy-using industries and activities went down. Brazil, for one, embarked on an extensive oil-substituting investment program. Although this turned out to be a poor investment and was probably ill-considered at the time, in principle, at least, a shift in the pattern of investment, both toward tradables (exports and import-competing industries), to reduce the current account deficit, and toward oil-saving activities seemed rational.

Another important factor to consider is the difficulty of making rapid adjustments in response to a current account deterioration. Such a deterioration could not be rectified overnight without a loss of domestic output. Temporary borrowing is therefore justified until the relative price changes made in order to restore external balance have the desired effect, for it permits the level of output to be maintained during this period. Some expansionary fiscal or monetary measures might be necessary to maintain demand during the transition, since both real incomes and real cash balances would have fallen in the face of the rise in import prices.

Another way of looking at the problem is to ask how a rise in borrowing (or use of reserves) could be avoided. In the short run, this could be achieved only by reducing the quantity of imports, generally by means of deflationary measures that would also reduce the demand for, and hence the output of, nontradables. It is true that a devaluation or import controls could switch the pattern of demand away from imports toward nontradables, hence maintaining demand for the latter. Neither of these measures may produce much "switching" in the short run. Indeed, they may reduce domestic output further because of the higher domestic cost of imported inputs brought about by devaluation or by their physical shortage resulting from controls. Thus a rapid reduction of demand, sufficient to improve the current account and so avoid borrowing or the use of reserves, even if accompanied by devaluation or tighter import controls, could have a considerable deflationary effect.[3]

The upshot is that some rise in borrowing, as indeed occurred, was certainly rational for a short period, say two to three years, in the case of all of the countries that suffered the terms-of-trade shock of 1974. Thereafter, one should expect some adjustment, which would imply devoting a higher proportion of GDP to exports or import savings, with a fall in either consumption or investment (in relation to GDP). This switching would require a movement of relative prices in favor of tradable goods, in other words, a real devaluation.

The foregoing assumes that countries were borrowing an optimal amount when the terms-of-trade shock hit them. In reality, prior to 1974 borrowing on international markets was constrained. Thus some higher level of borrowing, to reduce any fall in investment or raise its level, would be justified by the increased ease and cheapness of borrowing; and this consideration might justifiably postpone the adjustment to worsened terms of trade beyond the two- to three-year period suggested. This would depend on the existence of sound investments that had previously been frustrated by the inability to borrow or by high interest rates on marginal borrowing. Remember, too, that however high the returns to investment, there is a prudential limit to borrowing abroad (see chapter 4).

The oil price rise of 1973–74 came on top of a general rise in world prices. The reaction of countries was in some cases influenced by the fear of "importing" inflation. It is questionable, however, whether fighting such a price rise—either by controls or by deflationary action on the domestic front—was a good idea. A jump in world prices such as that of the early 1970s would tend to result in a once-and-for-all desirable adjustment of and rise in domestic prices.[4] This is referred to as "adjustment inflation" in chapter 6.

Countries that benefit by an improvement in the terms of trade (expected to be permanent) could expect some rise in both consumption and investment. As long as real foreign interest rates were very low, they would favor domestic investment. They would have difficulty achieving a rapid rise in domestic investment, however, without embarking on ill-chosen and very low-yielding projects. Furthermore, the price of nontraded capital goods, primarily construction, may be forced up, also limiting the rise in efficient investment. If the gain from the change in the terms of trade were large, then a period of investment in foreign assets would be optimal while the country organized itself to sustain a somewhat higher level of domestic investment with adequate social returns.

In the case of our countries, it is important to remember not only the oil shock but also the coffee boom of 1976–78. For five of them—Cameroon, Colombia, Côte d'Ivoire, Costa Rica, and Kenya—this boom dwarfed the oil shock that preceded it. Yet the boom could not be expected to last and did not therefore cancel any need to adapt to the oil price rise that was expected to be permanent. This applies in particular to Costa Rica, Côte d'Ivoire, and Kenya, since the other two did not suffer as a result of the oil price rise.

A temporary windfall should be devoted almost entirely to savings, to be matched by domestic or foreign investment. As we have already emphasized, good domestic investments take time to prepare, and the increased expenditure may be delayed for several years. The best strategy is to buy foreign assets that can later be sold when more profitable domestic investment expenditures are made. In this respect, the optimal reaction to a temporary windfall does not differ from a sudden improvement in the terms of trade that is expected to last.

Unlike oil production, coffee production is usually in the hands of small producers. The government may or may not permit the windfall to accrue to them. If it does, they too will normally want to save most of the windfall, but acquiring foreign assets is difficult for them, even if it is legal. Adequately attractive domestic financial assets may also be unavailable. What would be optimal for a country and its citizens may thus be prevented by financial controls or by the underdeveloped state of domestic financial markets. It may even be difficult to "invest" in durable goods. As a result, the windfall recipients may be driven to consume more than they otherwise would or to make low-yielding direct investments in house or farm improvements.

Reactions to exogenous events may also be affected by the initial state of the economy, whether it is in good shape or is besieged with problems. Inflation was among the most important of such problems, notably in Argentina, Brazil, and Chile, but to a lesser extent in most other countries (see chapters 6 and 7). Reactions may in addition be affected by exogenous events that are peculiar to the country in question, such as droughts in India. We now turn to actual policy reactions in the eighteen countries.

The Policy Responses of the Countries Adversely Affected by the 1974 Terms-of-Trade Shock

Three consequences of the terms-of-trade shock were of concern to policymakers in the eighteen countries: the deterioration in the balance of payments, an acceleration of inflation, and a fall in demand for domestic output. We consider first the ten major losers from this point of view, beginning with the four that chose to deflate: Chile, Sri Lanka, Kenya, and Thailand.

Chile's current balance in 1974 was virtually unchanged despite a deterioration in the terms of trade, since the volume of copper and other exports had risen sharply. At the end of 1974, however, the copper price fell from $1.50 per pound to $0.50 per pound. Since the Pinochet regime believed that the anticipated large current account deficit could not be financed, it initiated a massive fiscal and monetary contraction. There was an across-the-board reduction in public sector spending of 15 percent, together with tax increases. The fiscal deficit of 5.5 percent of GDP in 1974 became a surplus of 1.2 percent in 1975, an amazingly large turnaround in a short time. The public sector wage bill and investment were drastically cut. GDP fell by about 12 percent, and real income by much more as a result of the deteriorating terms of trade. The external deficit was thereby contained. While the dollar value of exports fell by 26 percent, that of imports fell by 20 percent, despite the rise in import prices. The result was a further rise in the current account deficit, from about $300 to $500 million. Of the ten countries, Chile was the only one to experience a recession, that is, an absolute fall in GDP. The others did no worse than suffer a fall in the rate of growth of GDP.

Were the savage deflationary policies undertaken solely because of the belief that the projected deficit could not be financed? There were other disturbances in Chile. In 1974 the *quarterly* rate of inflation was nearly 50 percent, but the authorities devalued faster than the rate of inflation until the second quarter of 1975 and thus did not appear to be unduly concerned about inflation. It was only in April 1975, when quarterly inflation reached 70 percent, that the authorities began to tackle inflation explicitly; the quarterly rate was quickly halved. Chile's efforts to control inflation are considered at length in chapter 7. Another factor that was at least concordant with the public expenditure cuts was a determination to reduce the role of the public sector.

Sri Lanka was another country whose government did not believe it could finance the deficit that would arise if no action was taken. It tightened already tight exchange restrictions and also took deflationary fiscal action, mainly by reducing food subsidies. Aid flows and borrowing rose from about 1 percent to nearly 4 percent of GDP, and it seems that the deflationary measures taken were probably necessary. They were not so severe as to cause a recession. Devaluation was not contemplated.

Like Chile and Sri Lanka, Kenya suffered a large terms-of-trade shock. It was already fighting a balance of payments problem arising from an earlier public investment boom. It borrowed further from the IMF and the World Bank, and also from some commercial sources. As in Sri Lanka, there was also some tightening of restrictive import and credit controls. Government investment was reduced, and other investment also fell, no doubt as a result of the credit squeeze. Government consumption rose, however, supported by foreign borrowing. Kenya was one of the few countries in which investment fell as a result of the terms of trade shock. GDP growth was very low in 1974 and 1975 (and fell on a per capita basis). There was a devaluation of 14 percent in 1975. The balance of payments was turned around by the coffee boom in 1976, and strong growth was resumed.

Thailand experienced a fairly severe terms-of-trade shock in 1974 and was one of the few countries to take immediate deflationary action. The growth of public expenditure was moderated, while tax revenue proved to be buoyant. The consolidated public sector balance changed from a deficit of 3.5 percent of GDP in 1973 to a surplus of 0.5 percent in 1974 (Warr and Nidhiprabha, forthcoming). The Bank of Thailand also adopted a mild deflationary policy. This appears to have been done more because of the inflation bubble that had begun in 1973 and reached 24 percent in 1974 than because an excessive current account deficit was feared. As it turned out, the current account deficit was actually well below its long-run average. Output suffered insofar as the rate of growth was only about 4.5 percent in 1974 and 1975, well below the average of more than 7 percent for the 1970s. Expansionary policies were resumed in 1975 when the inflation rate came back to 5 percent. There was no adjustment to the changed terms of trade, and deficits continued into the 1980s at higher levels than in the previous decade.

Our analysis of optimal policy might suggest that these four countries should not have taken deflationary action. It is not clear that political conditions or the ideological bent of economic policies would have permitted further borrowing in the case of Chile or Sri Lanka, and Chile's reactions were also much influenced (in the year of 1975) by the extremely high inflation inherited from the Allende period. The fairly mild deflationary action in Kenya and Thailand might perhaps have been avoided with somewhat greater recourse to foreign borrowing in 1974 and 1975.

Brazil and five other countries suffered losses because of the shocks while avoiding deflation. Along with Brazil, the others—Costa Rica, Côte d'Ivoire, Cameroon, Pakistan, and Korea—apparently expected a fall in demand because of the oil price shock. A less positive interpretation would be that these countries showed no concern for the balance of payments deterioration because they rightly believed that they could easily borrow. They also showed little concern for the jump in inflation, probably believing, in most cases correctly, that it was a worldwide phenomenon that would reverse itself (see chapter 6).

Brazil's reaction was to tighten import controls somewhat and exercise some mild fiscal and monetary restraint in 1974, which was in any case justified by the fact that the economy was already probably overheated before the oil price rise. This policy of restraint was temporary, however. Before the end of the year, the government initiated a large new program of long-gestation import-substituting investment in the energy field. It made no other adjustment to the adverse terms-of-trade shock. Indeed, the oil price increase was not fully passed on to consumers or producers. The exchange rate policy (consisting of frequent small devaluations intended to achieve purchase power parity) was unchanged. High levels of borrowing continued throughout the 1970s, and inflation increased.

In Costa Rica, there was a huge rise in the current account deficit and a burst of inflation. Although Costa Rica was accustomed to price stability, the authorities nevertheless permitted domestic credit to expand rapidly in order to avoid any reduction in aggregate real expenditure. On top of this, they initiated a public investment boom in 1975. The coffee boom of 1976 permitted this exuberant neglect of adjustment to continue for a while.

Côte d'Ivoire started a large public investment program in 1974. The terms-of-trade shock in that year was negligible, since improved cocoa and timber prices had offset the oil price increase. Although the terms-of-trade shock in 1975 was severe and the current account deficit rose to about 10 percent, the public investment plans were not modified. In 1976 they were supported by the beginning of the coffee boom, when borrowing was reduced, only to rise to very high levels in 1978 and after, as the terms of trade worsened again. There was, of course, no change in the nominal exchange rate, since Côte d'Ivoire is a member of the Franc zone.

Cameroon's exports were, in 1974, very similar to those of Côte d'Ivoire. Not surprisingly, its terms of trade over 1974 and 1975 were also similar. Unlike Côte d'Ivoire, Cameroon took no expansionary action in 1974, and its GDP fell marginally in 1975, in contrast to a strong rise in Côte d'Ivoire. Thereafter, GDP grew rapidly in both countries. Oil was discovered in Cameroon in 1973, and the investment booms of 1976 and later years was partly due to Cameroon's investment in oil production.

Pakistan had just started an ambitious program of public sector investment (in 1973) when the oil shock hit. The effects of this shock were compounded by a fertilizer price rise, serious floods, and the international textile recession. The current account deficit went from 1 percent to 10 percent of GDP, but this jump was easily financed by borrowing on favorable terms, mainly from the members of the Organization of Petroleum Exporting Countries. Although inflation rose to 23 percent, this did not alarm the authorities and produced virtually no policy reaction. The government made some unsuccessful attempts to reduce current expenditure but planned no cuts in capital expenditures and made no change in the nominal exchange rate. In short, Pakistan borrowed its way through the unfavorable exogenous shock.

Korea was among the countries concerned with the loss of output that would stem from the terms-of-trade shock. Like Pakistan, Korea felt some repercussions from the world textile recession of 1974. The terms-of-trade shock was quite large, and the current account gap widened in 1974 to more than 10 percent of GNP. It was easily financed, however, mainly by the use of reserves and by borrowing from the IMF. The public sector deficit was allowed to increase, and the won was devalued by 21 percent in December 1974. The growth rate fell to about 8 percent in 1974 and 1975—almost a recession by Korean standards. By 1977 the current account deficit had been eliminated. Inflation rose moderately but became a matter of concern only later. The required adjustment was thus achieved with little or no loss of output.

The exogenous shocks also had some adverse effects on Argentina, Colombia, Mexico, Turkey, and India. Although these countries felt only a small terms-of-trade shock in relation to GDP, it was large in relation to exports, except in Colombia. Since there was no shock in Colombia, no policy reaction was needed. Easy borrowing allowed Argentina, Mexico, and Turkey to ignore the balance of payments deterioration. They had all initiated public sector investment booms in 1973 or earlier, and these booms were allowed to continue.

India is a special case because its policy response was extensive, although it responded more to inflation than to the balance of payments deterioration. The inflation in turn was due far more to bad harvests than to the rise in import prices. The years 1971–72 and 1972–73 had brought drought and a decline in cereal production. Moreover, in the recovery year 1973–74 both cereal output and general agricultural production were still below trend.[5] Largely for this reason, but also because of expansionary fiscal and monetary developments, inflation accelerated. It rose from about 6 percent in 1971–72 to 10 percent, 20 percent, and 25 percent in the following three years. (Anything above 10 percent is regarded as critical in India.) Of course, the rise in import prices contributed to inflation in 1973–74 and 1974–75, but it did not play as large a role as in many countries, since import and export prices are small components of the costs of production and living in India. The fiscal laxity of the early 1970s, which was reversed only in 1973–74, was a contributory cause. This in turn can be at least partly explained by exogenous events—the brief war with Pakistan in 1971, the influx of nearly 10 million Hindu refugees from Bangladesh in that year, and the relief requirements, including food subsidies, arising from the drought in 1972–73.

The policy response began quietly in 1973–74. Government expenditures were reduced (by 2.3 percent of GDP) and monetary policy was also tightened in mid-1973. Nonetheless, inflation continued, and severe budgetary measures were taken in March and July 1974, when the emphasis was on reducing disposable incomes via taxation and incomes policy, though public investment was again reduced. Inflation actually went into reverse in the fall of 1974.

The quite modest deficits were easily financed by the use of reserves and borrowing from the IMF. They would, of course, have been larger without the deflationary measures described. The current account turnaround was dramatic, with a surplus of nearly 2 percent of GNP by 1976–77. A large part of the explanation is that inflation fell below the world rate for several years, with a consequent depreciation of the real exchange rate and a boom in exports. Large stocks of foreign exchange and cereals were accumulated. It could be (and was) argued that India overadjusted.

Three Gainers from the 1974 Terms-of-Trade Shock:
Indonesia, Nigeria, Morocco

Two of the three countries that experienced a positive terms-of-trade shock were the oil exporters Indonesia and Nigeria. The shock was greater for Nigeria. By 1973 oil production was about 17 percent of GDP in Nigeria and 12 percent in Indonesia. Oil made up 85 percent and 50 percent of their total exports, respectively.

Nigeria also experienced a large rise in the quantity produced from 1970-74 on. This was an exogenous event, but it was not strictly a shock for it was expected. For the period 1974–78, Gelb (1988) estimates the windfall (counting both quantity and prices as windfall) at about 23 percent of nonmining GDP in the case of Nigeria and 16 percent in the case of Indonesia.[6] In both countries, the domestic windfall accrued in the first instance entirely to the government. Therefore the domestic consequences depended on what the government did with its new revenues. If, for instance, it used it all to buy foreign assets, there would have been no domestic consequences at all.

In 1974 both countries had a large turnaround in the current account, about 5 percent of GNP in Indonesia and 16 percent in Nigeria. From 1975 through 1978, both reverted to current account deficits, owing to massive increases in investment as a proportion of (a rapidly rising) GNP. Between the first half of the 1970s and the second half, the average investment share in Nigeria rose from 17 percent of GNP to 25 percent, and in Indonesia from 20 percent to 25 percent.[7]

In both countries the shares of consumption fell. This drop was even more pronounced in the case of private consumption.[8] The main reason for this reaction was probably that the government had wanted a higher level of investment but could not previously achieve it without unpopular measures. The government was able to keep all or most of the windfall for investment or public consumption without imposing an actual burden on the people. Moreover, it might have been quite difficult to transfer most of the windfall to the private sector without disturbing reductions in taxation, and in Nigeria a total elimination of nonoil taxes would not have been enough to transfer the whole of the windfall. The choice between investing at home or abroad went heavily in favor of domestic, mainly public, investment. In both countries this had the expected effect of bringing about a real appreciation, that is, a rise in the price of nontradables in relation to nonoil tradables.

In the early 1980s, Nigeria's GDP fell heavily while Indonesia continued to progress and avoided any debt rescheduling (chapter 4). Their different performances in the 1980s can be traced back to differences in the treatment of their 1974 windfalls, particularly Indonesia's better choice of new investments. In contrast to Nigeria, it devoted a much higher proportion of public development and capital expenditure to agriculture and rural development. This move would have helped to offset the depressing effect on agriculture of the real exchange rate appreciation. Furthermore, in November 1978 Indonesia devalued the rupiah from 415 per U.S. dollar to 625. This was done not for any balance of payments reason, but mainly to reverse the real appreciation and hence stimulate agricultural and other traditional outputs and exports. The different treatment of agriculture had important consequences. Nigerian exports, other than oil, virtually vanished, while Indonesian nonoil exports rose from 25 percent of the total in 1975 to 43 percent in 1979.

The third country to benefit from the terms of trade in 1974 was Morocco, whose gain from the quintupling of phosphate prices far outweighed the loss from the oil price increase. Even before the phosphate boom, it had stepped up public investment, in 1973, and although it had done so largely for internal political reasons, the increasing ease of borrowing that was already evident in 1973 may have had some influence. In 1976 the price of phosphate fell 50 percent, but the government kept to its investment plans. The current account, which had been in surplus in 1974, deteriorated to a deficit of 17 percent in 1977. Investment rose from 17 percent in 1973 to 35 percent in 1977, while consumption approximately maintained its share of GNP. False expectations and an inability to retreat quickly when expectations proved to be false led Morocco into deep trouble.

The Coffee Boom

Unlike the oil price shock, the coffee boom of 1976–78 should certainly have been perceived as temporary. The boom had a large impact on five countries in our study: Cameroon, Colombia, Costa Rica, Côte d'Ivoire, and Kenya.[9] Although Brazil is also a major coffee producer, and frost in Brazil was the cause of the boom, it is excluded from this survey because Brazilian exports are not dominated by coffee.

The average price of coffee in 1977 was three times the 1975 average. Table 3-2 compares the terms of trade for these countries between the period 1973–75, which catches the oil price shock, and 1975–77, which catches the coffee shock. For all five countries, the coffee boom was more powerful than the oil price shock, so all had better terms of trade in 1977 than 1973. Then the coffee boom died away in the late 1970s, leaving Cameroon, Costa Rica, and Kenya with worse terms of trade than before the oil price shock. Colombia had not suffered an oil shock, and its terms of trade in 1979 were much better than in 1973. Côte d'Ivoire, less dependent on oil imports than Costa Rica or Kenya, also enjoyed better terms of trade in 1979 than in 1973.

The countries differ greatly in the extent to which the windfall accrued to the producers or to the government. In Costa Rica and Kenya, the whole price rise accrued to producers. Colombia had an export tax, and also a coffee fund, to help stabilize the price producers received. About 75 percent of the rise from 1975 to 1977 was passed on to producers (but the amount withheld was not ranked as government revenue). The West African countries used governmental commodity stabilization funds not only to stabilize the receipts of farmers but also to tax them heavily. In Cameroon, producer prices rose about 60 percent when world prices rose 200 percent. Producers in Côte d'Ivoire received about half the world price, less when it was high and more when it was low.

Despite these differences, government revenues in four of the five countries roughly doubled from 1975 to 1978. In Costa Rica and Kenya, the rise was only an indirect consequence of the boom, but no less rapid. Only in Côte d'Ivoire did revenues rise much higher—close to 170 percent—owing to the surplus of the

Table 3.2   Terms-of-Trade Index for Five Coffee Exporters, Selected Years

Country	1973	1975	1977	1979
Cameroon	100	69	131	91
Colombia	100	100	196	144
Costa Rica	100	76	109	87
Côte d'Ivoire	100	85	152	123
Kenya	100	81	124	92

Source: World Bank data except for Kenya, in which case see Bevan, and others (unpublished).

stabilization fund. It did not take long for government expenditures to catch up with, and overtake, revenue. Only Colombia ran a budget surplus over the period of 1976 through 1978. Côte d'Ivoire, with its huge rise in public revenue, achieved a small public sector surplus in 1976 and 1977, but this turned into huge deficits in 1978 and later years.

Government reactions differed in the two West African countries. Côte d'Ivoire had already started increasing public investment in 1974. The coffee (and cocoa) boom supported this policy and may have magnified it. When coffee and cocoa prices started to fall in 1978, public investment probably stopped rising as a proportion of GNP, but remained very high for several years. Borrowing exceeded 15 percent of GNP. Cameroon experienced a more modest investment boom, which was related to the exploitation of its newly found oil reserves. Fiscal policy was much more conservative, and 1978 saw a surplus, although oil revenues were as yet a trickle.

Of the two Latin American coffee exporters, Colombia had somewhat the same experience as Cameroon, and Costa Rica's was like that of Côte d'Ivoire. Although the proceeds of the coffee price rise accrued mostly to the private sector in Colombia, the boom was moderated by appropriate fiscal and monetary policy. Both the budget and the current accounts were in surplus through the period 1976–78. Colombia was the only coffee boom country in which domestic investment as a proportion of GNP did not rise (or fall), although reserves rose by about $2 billion. By contrast, Costa Rica was already experiencing a surge in government-led investment when coffee prices rose and helped support the surge. Despite higher revenues from coffee, the budget deficit increased, and the current account deficit, although reduced in 1976 and 1977, remained very high (about 8 percent of GNP). As coffee prices fell, the deficits became enormous, as in Côte d'Ivoire. In both countries, the adverse effects of the oil price shock reasserted themselves when the coffee high died away.

Kenya also experienced an investment boom starting in 1976. This is the only case in which the investment boom was clearly a consequence of the coffee boom. The windfall accrued initially to the producers. Bevan and others (unpublished) reckon that 60 percent of the rise in income was saved, a clear indication that the peasant producers understood the price rise would not last. The investment boom was more private than public. While public investment also rose, the increase in public consumption was greater and proved hard to compress when coffee prices retreated.

Were government and private reactions to the coffee boom rational or optimal? Certainly, a rise in savings was a rational reaction. The Kenyan experience might suggest that more of the windfall would have been saved had more remained in private hands or been passed on through reduced tax rates. Another interesting question is how much of the savings should have been devoted to domestic investment and how much to the acquisition of foreign assets. It would seem best to have devoted a large proportion to foreign assets, including reserves. A sudden burst of real domestic investment that may last for only a very few years is most unlikely to be efficient, unless there is a shelf of already planned and appraised projects, which is seldom or never the case. Furthermore, investments always have a considerable local component (particularly in construction) that cannot usually be expanded quickly. Any attempt to do so will withdraw resources from traded goods sectors through higher prices of nontradeables. Considerable price and resource movements in response to a temporary situation are to be avoided. Except for Colombia, the coffee boom countries did not organize or permit any build-up of foreign assets. Perhaps they were influenced by a view prevalent twenty years earlier—namely, that reserves are a waste of development potential.

The Investment Booms in Sixteen Countries, 1974–81

We have argued that raising the proportion of GNP devoted to investment would have been a rational reaction to both the easier credit conditions and the coffee boom. The same may not be true for the supposedly permanent deterioration of the terms of trade arising from the rise in oil prices. Higher oil prices would tend to raise profitability and hence investment in energy production and energy saving, but reduce investment in those industries that are heavy users of energy. In such situations the terms-of-trade deterioration should be countered by a real depreciation that raises profitability and investment in tradeable goods production but reduces it in nontradeables. Thus the outcome is ambiguous.

In fact, in every one of the countries except Brazil and India a big investment boom began between 1973 and 1978. In Brazil there was a boom from 1970 to 1975, but the level of investment in relation to GNP was the same in 1979 as in 1973. In India there was a slowly rising trend of investment from 1968 to 1985, but no surges.

In nearly all of the other countries the investment boom was predominantly public. The only clear exceptions were Chile and Kenya, and possibly Cameroon.[10] Changes in the level of public investment would have been made as a matter of policy, while the level of private investment would have been determined by profit expectations, possibly tempered by credit or other controls. In some of our countries, public investment was partly offset by a fall in private investment; this was true of Colombia, Mexico's first boom, Pakistan, and Thailand. In most cases private investment also rose, though less than public investment. Table 3-3 indicates the dates and sizes of the booms. Most started about the time of the oil price shock or a little later. In Colombia, Kenya, Mexico (second boom), and Sri Lanka, the boom began in 1977 or 1978.

The Oil and Phosphate Gainers

As already mentioned, the rising price of oil sparked an investment boom in both Indonesia and Nigeria. Since the windfall accrued to their governments, the

Table 3.3   Investment Booms

Country	Period	Investment as a percentage of GDP					
		Public		Private		Total	
Argentina	1973–77	8.4	13.4	13.3	10.7	21.7	24.1
Cameroon	1974–79	4.5	4.6	11.1	17.4	15.6	22.0
Chile (F)	1976–81	5.1	4.2	7.7	16.8	12.8	21.0
Colombia (F)	1978–83	5.5	9.1	9.9	8.1	15.4	17.2
Costa Rica (F)	1975–79	7.0	8.9	15.0	16.4	22.0	25.3
Côte d'Ivoire	1974–78	11.3	21.0	8.1	8.7	19.4	29.7
Indonesia	1974–81	8.0	13.2	8.6	16.7	16.6	29.9
Kenya (F)	1977–80	9.0	10.7	9.1	13.0	18.1	23.7
Korea, Rep.	1976–79	5.5	7.5	18.8	25.8	24.3	33.3
Mexico (1)	1971–75	4.7	8.9	13.3	12.5	18.0	21.4
Mexico (2)	1977–81	7.7	11.7	11.9	14.0	19.6	25.7
Morocco	1973–77	4.7	20.7	12.2	13.5	16.9	34.2
Nigeria	1974–76	4.8	17.3	11.9	14.1	16.8	31.4
Pakistan	1973–77	7.1	15.3	7.1	5.9	14.2	21.2
Thailand (F)	1974–81	3.7	9.2	19.7	16.5	23.4	25.7
Sri Lanka	1977–82	6.5	16.7	7.3	15.2	13.8	31.9
Turkey	1973–77	8.5	12.5	9.6	10.1	18.1	22.5

Note: F indicates gross fixed capital formation.
Source: Country studies for this volume (except for Korea). The figures for total investment differ from those derived from the World Bank data base (which are expressed as a percentage of GNP, not GDP) given in the appendix tables at the end of this chapter. But there is no serious conflict. The figures for Korea are from Servén and Solimano (1993).

economic consequences depended on the regime's preferences and its ability to impose them.

Nigeria's military government was inexperienced in formulating economic policy and thus left this task to the bureaucracy, which it protected from the politicians. In consequence of the rise in military expenditure during the civil war, the military already had more than enough resources. Political pressures on the bureaucracy were thus weak, and it could pursue its own objectives. These included Africanization and industrialization in the capital-intensive import-substituting manner that was then still in line with development thinking in most developing countries, whether radical or nationalist. This philosophy and the great haste with which investment expenditure was undertaken resulted in enormous waste.

In Indonesia, the windfall and the investment boom were of more modest proportions. Some of the oil windfall was devoted to what might be considered a noninflationary form of investing abroad—namely, paying off the debts of Indonesia's state oil firm Pertamina (see chapters 10 and 12 for accounts of the Pertamina affair). The Pertamina scandal weakened the influence of the advisers and officials who were most keen on capital-intensive industrial investments while it strengthened the position of the economic team popularly known as the "Berkeley Mafia" (they had received their economic training at the University of California, Berkeley). Above all, it sent out an early warning about the dangers of short-term borrowing. Thus, public investment in Indonesia rose less and more slowly than in Nigeria, and was more devoted to agriculture and rural development. Although Indonesia was also an autocracy, its governmental decisions were influenced by a greater variety of interests than decisions in Nigeria. Those who have studied both countries are quite clear that Indonesia's investment was much more productive than that of Nigeria.[11]

In contrast, the investment boom in Morocco was not a consequence of improved terms of trade. Rather, it had been initiated in the Five-Year Plan for 1973–77, before the phosphate boom of 1974 (and before it could have been anticipated). The plan owed much to the king's difficulties. The army had become murderously untrustworthy, and the king sought new allies within the middle class (managers, directors, bureaucrats), which therefore needed to be strengthened.

At the time, Morocco accounted for one-third of the world's phosphate exports (and had nearly three-quarters of the world's known reserves). No cartel could be formed, but for a while Morocco was a successful price leader. When the price quintupled, the government seized on the false expectation that the high price could be sustained, especially in view of the similar expectation for oil prices. The already expansionary Five-Year Plan was therefore revised upward. Although the reasons for the boom were originally exogenous (from an economic point of view), it was greatly magnified as a response to a favorable external shock (the excess of the windfall gain from phosphate over the windfall oil loss) that was expected to persist.

According to Claassen (unpublished), the chosen investments focused too much on irrigation that benefited larger landowners and their export crops for the European market. Although it could hardly have been anticipated in 1973, the prospects for such exports grew dim when Portugal, Spain, and Greece joined the European Economic Community. There was also a large capital-intensive investment in phosphate derivatives, which may or may not have been very productive.

The Coffee Gainers

The investment surge among the coffee gainers was not a result of the coffee windfall, except in Kenya. As noted earlier, Colombia succeeded in stabilizing the windfall and experienced no rise in investment during the coffee boom. Its later public investment program was planned to counter the deflationary effects of the subsequent fall in coffee prices.

Costa Rica seemed to have difficulty containing the income demands of different sections of the population and thus experienced some breakdown of the distributional equilibrium that had prevailed earlier.[12] The increase in public investment and central government expenditures preceded the coffee boom but was soon supported by it. Costa Rica's rather minor public investment boom therefore seems to have been a mixed case of an economically exogenous increase in response to political pressures and an increase induced by the coffee boom, which could not be resisted because of political economy pressures.

In Côte d'Ivoire, it was perceived that the economy could no longer rely on the source of the outstanding growth of the 1960s, agricultural development. Furthermore, there were large and growing inequalities between the North and the South, the latter having been the main beneficiary of growth. These factors evidently convinced President Houphouët-Boigny of the need for a vigorous government impetus, and he initiated the Programme du Nord at the end of 1974. This was the first time that Côte d'Ivoire had experimented with massive public investment expenditures. More than $415 million was to be spent on one sugar-growing and processing project (SODESUCRE). The program was accelerated as revenues rose with the cocoa and coffee boom, but the new strategy of growth (to be led by public sector investment) had been decided before coffee and cocoa prices rose.

Cameroon's investment surge began in 1974, largely in response to the need to exploit its new oil discoveries. Because of the coffee boom, this could be accomplished without excessive current account deficits and foreign borrowing. According to table 3-3, the boom was mainly private, but in Cameroon's case parastatal investment is counted as private.

Kenya's brief investment boom from 1976 to 1978 occurred mainly in the private sector and was clearly a result of the rise in incomes. Although the windfall accrued directly to producers, government revenue also rose substantially (because of general taxation, also because of some relaxation of import restrictions, which brought a rise in tariff revenues). A large part of the growing public revenue was spent on consumption, although public investment also rose. The greatest increase in investment in this period occurred in the private sector. The way in which government macroeconomic policy affected private savings and the efficiency of this private investment are particularly interesting.[13]

Owing to exchange controls, private savings could not be invested abroad. Import quotas were in force but were relaxed, so that there was a surge in imports of durable consumption goods, partly, no doubt, because it could be anticipated that quotas would soon become less relaxed again, and capital gains would be made. Such imports count as consumption, of course, although they were really a form of personal investment in this case. Furthermore, the policy of financial repression with low controlled interest rates implied that the acquisition of financial assets was an unattractive form of savings. Real investment, especially in construction, therefore received an unwarranted impetus. The upshot was that the private sector received strong incentives to acquire real assets immediately. With freer markets, the use of the windfall would have been spread over a longer period, and the resulting investment would presumably have been more efficient.

The Eight Losers

Consider now the situation in the eight countries that were adversely affected by the 1974 terms-of-trade shock and that did not benefit from the coffee boom. In five of these, investment started picking up either well before the terms of trade shock (in Argentina, Turkey, and Pakistan, and in Mexico during the first boom) or was more or less contemporaneous with it (in Thailand). Note that in every case the boom began for essentially political reasons and was not interrupted by the adverse terms-of-trade shock, which was quite large in relation to exports. The ease of borrowing permitted this.

Mexico had two booms in the 1970s. The first (from 1971 to 1975) had entirely internal—political, institutional, and personal—origins and dates back at least to the student revolt of 1968. It led to increasing concern about the inequality of income distribution, and this inspired leftist elements within the governing political party, helping them to gain influence. During the first year of Echeverria's presidency (1971), the Treasury maintained its traditionally powerful role, but Echeverria soon became convinced that policy in 1971 had been too restrictive, and departments were ordered to double the spending levels of the 1971 budget. He personally initiated the investment boom and was responsible for the erosion of the conservative countervailing powers of the Treasury. This erosion was completed by the succession to that office of the next president, Lopez Portillo. The boom and rising public deficits were sustained by foreign borrowing (and a rise in the inflation tax) until 1976, when there was a devaluation and moderate correction of the deficit.

Huge new oil deposits had been discovered and by 1977 oil exports amounted to $1 billion. This was still only a trickle compared with the flood that was to come. The flood could be anticipated, however, and the availability of foreign finance seemed to be unlimited. Therefore, although the public deficit was very high by historical standards (3.3 percent of GDP), the second public investment boom (1977–81) was initiated. The second boom had its origins both in the political and institutional changes associated with the first boom (which had after all not ended in disaster), and in favorable exogenous events, both internal and external.

In Argentina, the public investment boom began with the Peronist government of 1973–75. Initial conditions were favorable, with high reserves and a current account surplus in 1973 resulting from high prices for wheat and meat. It was evidently part of a rather typical program designed to restrain inflation by price and wage agreements within the framework of a "social pact" and to promote real growth through increased investment and fiscal deficits. The new investments were understandably concentrated in the energy and defense sectors. The investment boom continued under the military government that succeeded in 1975, despite a large current account deficit in that year. It continued through the Martinez de Hoz period, until early 1981. The major investments were undertaken by public enterprises, many of which were under military control. Their expenditures were beyond the control, and probably even the knowledge, of the Finance Ministry.

They were the main reason for the public sector deficits that undermined the Martinez de Hoz attempt to conquer inflation in Argentina (see chapter 7).

In Turkey, a party with an explicit social democratic ideology (the Republican People's Party) took the lead in the 1973 elections, obtaining a plurality of seats rather than a majority. The growing strength and aspirations of distributional coalitions implied, at least in the eyes of the government, that these could be contained and satisfied only by rapid growth. Also in 1973, there was a surge in remittances from Turkish workers, mostly in Germany, and this peaked in 1974. The public sector expansion was planned before the oil price shock of 1974, which, together with the Cyprus war, put the current account back into deficit. The new opportunities of borrowing permitted the public sector-induced boom to continue for a while. The political economy explanation of the boom is very similar to that given for Costa Rica.

Several factors lay behind the public investment boom in Pakistan, which was embarked on in 1974 at virtually the same time as the oil shock. Although the shock was quite severe, it was largely offset by a rise in remittances from Pakistani workers in the Middle East. Furthermore, instant cheap loans were available from Islamic oil-producing countries. Thus, despite increases in the price of oil and fertilizer, external circumstances permitted the boom.

In Thailand, the rise in total investment from 1974 to 1981 was quite small, but it was not matched by any rise in savings and therefore added to the current account deficits. The increase in public investment, mainly for power and irrigation, was large but was partly offset by a fall in private investment.

In Chile, Korea, and Sri Lanka, the investment boom began well after the terms of trade shock, which affected all three severely. Chile and Sri Lanka were among the few countries that took deflationary action in 1974. Chile's subsequent investment boom was in effect a recovery from a deep recession. The ratio of investment to GDP did not rise above the normal levels for the years before the disturbances of the Allende socialist government in 1970–73. Nevertheless, it was remarkable in several respects. It was wholly private and arose out of a major liberalization of domestic capital markets that produced a huge increase in financial transactions and a rampant stock market boom. (The financial boom and subsequent crisis are discussed further in chapter 10.) The confidence in the future engendered by the liberal reforms of the Pinochet regime is evident from the surge of domestic borrowing, often at very high real interest rates. The boom lasted into the 1980s and was accompanied in its later stages by massive foreign borrowing. The story of the collapse is recounted in chapter 4.

Sri Lanka suffered greatly from the changes in international prices in 1973 and 1974. In response, its increasingly autocratic United Front government imposed extreme austerity, associated with yet further import repression. There was some relief in 1976 and 1977 as tea prices rose (a blip in Sri Lanka's almost ever-declining terms of trade), but this was too late for the United Front. The United National party under J. R. Jayawardana won an overwhelming victory in the 1977 elections. This was the first time any single party had obtained a majority.

In addition, external circumstances (in the form of rising tea prices) and the austerity of the previous government had helped Sri Lanka accumulate substantial reserves, totaling as much as ten months of imports. The new government immediately embarked on extensive economic liberalization somewhat akin to that in Chile under Pinochet and that in Turkey in 1980. Aid donors responded enthusiastically and underwrote the changes by large increases in aid. There was, perhaps, some tension between the (relatively) free-market liberalization policy and the government's effort to spearhead growth by a massive increase in public investment. The program was to some extent populist (the huge Mahaweli power and irrigation project, and the housing program, for example, were expected to benefit large numbers of people). It was also probably felt that this was the only way to absorb quickly the large amounts of aid that were on offer. The notable feature of Sri Lanka's investment splurge is that it was associated with a major change in economic policy and with foreign support. It resembles Turkey in 1980–81 in these respects.[14]

Korea's investment boom of the mid-1970s originated in a decision made in 1972 to transform the structure of the national economy in the direction of heavy and chemicals industries (HCI). One factor influencing this decision seems to have been President Park's perception, based on a (mis)reading of the so-called Nixon Doctrine, that Korea needed to become more self-reliant in manpower and in firepower for the sake of its national defense and therefore needed to build up its steel, shipbuilding, machinery, and associated industries. Another factor was the perception that Korea's wages were moving out of the "cheap labor" category and that the country would gradually have to yield its strong labor-intensive export products to those with cheaper labor. With an eye on the model of Japan, some of its officials believed that a strong public initiative was required to shift the structure of production toward the more capital-intensive products that Korea could plausibly hope to export profitably, after a settling-in period.

To this end, Korea in 1973 launched an ambitious investment plan that was overwhelmingly private but with government direction, encouragement, and credit and tax advantages. It was derailed almost immediately by the first oil shock but was put back on track in 1976 after a relatively rapid adjustment to that shock (aided by strong export performance, including income from overseas construction, and energy conservation measures). By 1978 the economy was clearly overheated, and in March 1979 a major stabilization program was introduced to combat inflation and the loss of export competitiveness as domestic prices rose in the presence of a fixed exchange rate (unchanged against the dollar from December 1974 to January 1980). The stabilization program was largely planned before the second oil shock, although President Park's decision to scale back the HCI program (some of its inefficiencies had become manifest by this time) may have been influenced by the early effects of the oil shock. The Korean ratio of investment to GNP rose from 25 percent in 1973 to a peak of 36 percent in 1979 before being scaled back to 31 percent in 1981.

The Causes of the Investment Booms

In only three cases—in Indonesia, Kenya, and Nigeria, can the investment booms in our countries be traced to a favorable external exogenous shock. The second boom in Mexico was partly caused by the internal exogenous shock of new oil discoveries. In four other cases (Cameroon, Costa Rica, Côte d'Ivoire, and Morocco), a rise in commodity prices supported, and in at least one case magnified, a public investment boom that was already under way.

In Colombia, and perhaps Pakistan, the boom was motivated by an *unfavorable* change in economic circumstances that was expected to depress domestic output. In short, it was instituted for standard Keynesian reasons—a countervailing policy permitted by substantial reserves or ease of borrowing.

Internal political reasons seem to have played a large role in the booms of Argentina, Costa Rica, Côte d'Ivoire, Mexico, Morocco, and Turkey. Apparently these countries felt that increased government investment, and no doubt the induced rise in output, would relieve internal tensions. In Turkey and Sri Lanka, a change of government was associated with a radical change in economic philosophy.

The Korean boom, although mainly private, began as a result of the structuralist theory that the economy required a big shove by the government to move to the more capital- and skill-intensive phase of development that was becoming appropriate. Chile was exceptional in that its boom was wholly private and started from a very low level.

The only common element in all the countries was the greater ease and cheapness of foreign borrowing. Even those in which the boom was caused by a favorable shock did not take long to start borrowing.

The Uses of Borrowing

In view of the debt crisis that ensued, the next important question to ask is, What uses were made of the borrowed funds? In principle, if a country borrows to increase investment there should be no debt problem. This statement, however, carries two important provisos. The first is that the investments have a real economic return that is at least equal to the real rate of interest. Since the borrowing is presumably in foreign currency, the required equal rate of return must also be expressed in foreign currency. This does not mean that investments should not go into nontraded good sectors. They, too, may have important indirect earnings or savings of foreign exchange. Indeed, the value of every input and output of any investment project in the final analysis depends on its estimated direct and indirect use, savings, or earnings of foreign exchange, and the required methods of estimating that value are prescribed in one of the standard systems of cost-benefit analysis.[15] The second proviso is that repayments should not be scheduled so as

Table 3.4   Investment, Consumption, and Net Borrowing
(percentage of GDP)

Country	National investment 1970–73	74–79	Consumption 1970–73	74–79	Net borrowing 1970–73	74–79	Growth of real consumption per head
Argentina	20.3	24.5	79.5	74.3	1.1	−1.5	0.6
Brazil	20.5	23.2	80.5	80.2	1.6	3.8	9.4
Cameroon	18.5	20.9	91.4	89.7	3.2	2.5	3.3
Chile	13.5	16.9	90.0	86.9	3.0	4.6	9.4
Colombia	19.0	18.6	84.3	80.6	2.8	−0.5	3.3
Costa Rica	20.7	22.5	86.6	87.2	6.1	9.1	6.7
Côte d'Ivoire	22.0	27.0	79.1	79.2	4.6	7.4	3.4
India	17.8	21.1	83.3	79.6	0.7	−0.4	1.0
Indonesia	18.4	23.3	81.5	73.7	2.1	0.0	4.5
Kenya	24.8	23.5	81.5	84.0	4.3	6.3	1.7
Korea, Rep.	23.2	29.8	83.3	76.5	4.8	4.6	10.3
Mexico	19.8	21.9	85.5	83.0	1.6	2.3	3.4
Morocco	17.1	26.6	86.1	88.1	0.2	9.0	2.3
Nigeria	16.0	22.4	86.2	76.4	0.9	−2.0	−2.2
Pakistan	14.6	17.0	91.0	93.8	3.7	5.6	2.4
Sri Lanka	17.0	17.8	86.4	87.8	1.9	1.8	7.3
Thailand	23.9	26.1	77.9	78.0	0.9	3.6	3.4
Turkey	19.1	22.1	83.9	85.6	−1.5	3.6	6.5

Note: Last column is average annual rate of growth of real consumption per head (including public consumption), 1970–79.
Source: See the tables in the appendix to this chapter.

to run ahead of the benefits. Usually, however, creditors can be prevailed upon to reschedule payments if the ultimate soundness of the loan is not in doubt.

Table 3-4 shows the average ratios of consumption and investment (public and private combined) to GNP for 1970–73 and 1974–79. National investment is here defined to exclude the usually small part that was foreign financed in the form of direct and portfolio investment and thus includes only investment financed out of domestic savings and out of foreign borrowing or the use of reserves. Columns 5 and 6 show the ratio of "net borrowing" abroad to GNP, that is, the current account deficit less inflows of direct and portfolio investment.[16]

To what extent were the magnified foreign deficits and "net borrowing" of the period 1973–79 associated with a rise in investment (rather than consumption)?[17] The story of the investment booms suggests a close relationship.

Every country except Colombia and Kenya raised its investment ratio. Of these sixteen, nine also raised the level of net borrowing. Six countries managed to raise investment significantly while reducing "net borrowing." These were the two oil exporters, Indonesia and Nigeria, and also Argentina, Cameroon (which began to benefit from oil only in 1979), India, and Korea. Ten countries in all borrowed a higher proportion of GNP. All of these except Kenya increased the investment ratio, and most raised the investment ratio more than they raised the borrowing ratio. Thus, Kenya is the only clear case of a country that borrowed primarily to support consumption. Indeed, consumption fell as a proportion of GNP in the majority of countries, and only in Kenya and Pakistan did it rise by more than 2 percent of GNP.

This does not, of course, imply that real consumption fell. According to the figures in column 7 of table 3-4, the annual rate of growth of real consumption per head (including public consumption) from 1970–79 was high in several countries, most notably Brazil, Chile, Costa Rica, Korea, Sri Lanka, and Turkey. These figures are suspect, however. Total current price consumption is deflated by the cost-of-living index, which is not appropriate for much public consumption, and is also known to be biased downward in several countries.

By and large, from the viewpoint of 1980, and on the basis of only macroeconomic information, there was little reason to worry about the debt. The debt problem could have been serious only if (1) the raised levels of investment yielded little or nothing, or little or nothing that could be transformed into foreign exchange, or (2) if the increased public debt was incurred to finance the private acquisition of foreign assets rather than current account deficits.

Summing Up the Period 1973–79

Most of the oil-importing countries managed a reasonably high growth rate from 1974 to 1979, despite the oil price shock (table 3-5, columns 1 and 2). Argentina and Chile were the exceptions. In most cases, however, the rate was lower than in the years 1970–73, which are generally regarded as a golden age. Even so, seven countries managed to achieve a higher growth rate—Cameroon, Chile, India, Morocco, Pakistan, Sri Lanka, and Thailand.

Although most countries raised the ratio of investment to GNP, the returns can have contributed little to growth in the period. Much of the new investment was in long-gestation capital-intensive projects, which, even if well chosen, would have had little impact by 1979. Moreover, there is evidence, albeit mostly anecdotal, that some, and possibly a good deal, of the investment can now be judged, with the benefit of hindsight, to have been ill-chosen (see chapter 11). The investment booms and associated foreign borrowing would have contributed to growth in another way. The increased demand for domestic labor ensured that any slack in the economy was taken up. Thus, the fairly high growth rates of the 1974–79 period were probably a Keynesian phenomenon in the main, and it is unlikely that this kind of growth could have lasted much longer.

Column 9 of table 3-5 indicates a deterioration in the terms of trade for all the countries except two oil exporters (Indonesia and Nigeria) and two coffee exporters (Côte d'Ivoire and Colombia). The deterioration was severe (greater than 20

Table 3.5   Some Key Indicators, 1970–79

(percent)

Country	GNP growth 1970–73	1974–79	Debt/GNP 1973	1979	Debt int/GNP 1973	1979	CA def/GNP 1973	1979	Terms of trade 1973/79
Chile	1.7	2.8	31.1	37.3	0.6	2.9	2.7	5.9	51
Cameroon	2.7	8.6	14.8	33.0	0.6	1.3	1.0	2.3	91
Côte d'Ivoire	6.4	5.8	26.8	47.0	1.2	3.2	9.6	16.9	123
Kenya	9.7	5.6	30.3	38.5	1.2	2.1	5.3	8.3	92
Costa Rica	7.4	5.2	27.0	43.7	1.6	3.0	7.5	14.4	87
Pakistan	4.7	4.8	64.4	40.7	1.3	1.1	1.3	4.2	63
Korea, Rep.	9.1	9.6	29.2	24.5	1.9	1.8	2.3	6.5	88
Sri Lanka	3.1	5.2	17.0	30.3	0.5	0.83	1.2	6.8	90
Thailand	7.0	7.3	8.4	14.5	0.5	1.2	0.4	7.7	76
Brazil	11.9	6.1	16.5	26.4	1.0	2.4	2.8	4.8	64
Mexico	8.5	5.8	15.7	25.1	0.9	2.4	2.5	4.0	61
Turkey	6.3	5.3	14.4	17.0	0.4	1.1	−3.2	2.1	82
Argentina	3.6	2.4	8.9	10.0	1.07	1.07	−1.8	1.0	64
India	2.4	3.4	13.2	12.2	0.3	0.3	0.5	0.3	73
Colombia	7.2	5.3	23.0	13.9	1.0	0.9	0.5	−1.6	144
Morocco	3.9	5.6	16.9	48.2	0.7	2.9	−1.6	9.8	94
Indonesia	8.5	6.6	38.7	31.3	0.7	2.0	2.8	−1.9	250
Nigeria	9.8	3.9	6.3	5.1	0.2	0.3	0.0	−2.2	330

Note: Debt and interest are long- and medium-term only. Short-term debt figures are available for most countries only from 1977. Debt figures are for end of year.

Source: World Bank, except for Kenya's terms of trade which are taken from Bevan and others, (unpublished).

percent) for seven: Chile, Pakistan, Thailand, Brazil, Mexico, Argentina, and India.

Table 3-5 also shows that all the countries with worsened terms of trade, except India, increased the size of their current account deficits (or turned a surplus into a deficit, in the case of Turkey, Argentina, and Morocco). The current account deficit became very large (greater than 5 percent of GNP) in Chile, Côte d'Ivoire, Kenya, Costa Rica, Korea, Sri Lanka, Thailand, and Morocco.

The definition of a sustainable current account deficit is discussed in chapter 4. It is, of course, related to the optimum level of borrowing. To anticipate, we can say that a deficit of more than 2-3 percent of GNP is unsustainable in the long run. The higher or more burdensome the existing debt, the more urgent it becomes to adjust, in the sense of changing policies so as to reduce the current deficit.

The burden of debt, as judged by interest in relation to GNP, was still nowhere extremely high in 1979, and had reached 3 percent only in Côte d'Ivoire and Costa Rica. Some countries with high current account deficit ratios also had high debt ratios—notably Chile, Côte d'Ivoire, Kenya, Costa Rica, and Morocco. Here the need to adjust was becoming urgent.

As explained in chapter 1, most of our eighteen countries would have required both "switching" and "absorption" policies to correct an unsustainable balance of payment deficit. The classic switching policy is a change in the nominal exchange rate, but for various reasons, good and bad, many governments were reluctant to make this change. Import and export taxes could also have been changed, but, being developing countries, most preferred to try to switch demand away from imported goods and toward import substitutes through controls, and to switch production toward exports through some form of subsidy.

There was little use in switching policies in the period 1974–79, in comparison with what was to come later. The high inflation countries—Argentina, Brazil, Chile, and Colombia—resorted to frequent nominal devaluations (until Argentina and Chile experimented with fixing the rate). This was also true of Turkey after 1975. The purpose of these devaluations, however, was to prevent relative domestic and world prices from getting too far out of line rather than to effect a change. There was no policy change as a result of the oil price shock.

Early in 1974 Costa Rica unified its exchange rates, devaluing the official rate by 29 percent. It is not clear how far this was a response to the deteriorating balance of payments, or how large the effective change was. In December 1974, Korea devalued by 20 percent, in response to the terms-of-trade shock and the large rise in the current account deficit. Kenya also devalued, by a more modest 16 percent in 1975. In 1976 Mexico ran into a balance of payments crisis and devalued by a massive 60 percent; the previous boom and associated inflation had clearly resulted in a large overvaluation of the peso. At the end of 1977, Sri Lanka also effected a large devaluation of 87 percent against the dollar; this was part of a major change of economic policy under a new government, which in addition removed most import and exchange controls as well as export incentive schemes. The primary purpose was to permit a more open economy (in this respect the devaluation rather resembles that of India in 1966). The most interesting devaluation (of 51 percent) was that of Indonesia in 1978. This came out of the blue: there was no pressing balance of payments problem; the objective, which was achieved, was to improve the viability of the nonoil tradable sectors, which were suffering from appreciation of the real exchange rate. These changes in exchange rates, their motivation, and their effects, are discussed in chapter 8.

Some countries used controls on and off to help switch production and expenditures. For instance, Brazil, India, Kenya, and Sri Lanka tightened import controls somewhat in 1974. Some of the coffee-boom countries relaxed and tightened import controls as the value of exports waxed and waned (see chapter 9). Export subsidies were also used, for example, in Sri Lanka.

As for our countries' absorption policies—fiscal and monetary—the terms-of-trade shock of 1974 was naturally deflationary, both because domestic incomes were squeezed and because the associated imported inflation caused the real money supply to shrink. Some of the suffering countries took no action, allowing already expansionary policies to continue. Others initially took mild deflationary fiscal and monetary action but quickly opted for borrowing and expansion. Only in Chile was the reaction so severe as to cause a major recession. In most of the countries, GDP grew more slowly in 1974 and 1975, but then 1973 had been an exceptional year.

Fiscal policy was the main instrument, and, within fiscal policy, expenditure (including subsidies). Few countries significantly increased their tax rates—Chile, India, and Korea were exceptions. Some countries used monetary or credit policy, however. Open market operations were nowhere significant, so that the monetary base could not be influenced independently of fiscal and payments balances. Credit controls were possible, however, and were used in several countries, notably in India. In some other countries, credit was more or less out of control as parastatal organizations were authorized to borrow directly from the central bank. In yet others, central bank losses were also important. (For more details on the uses of fiscal and monetary policy see chapter 10.)

No country, excepting India, made a sustained attempt to adjust to the worsened terms of trade. A few countries initially took some action to ameliorate the deterioration in their external payments situation, but this sooner or later gave way to expansionary policies supported by borrowing. Although in some cases the combination of high debt and very large current account deficits was threatening, on the whole the debt situation was not regarded as a serious problem at the time, largely because countries were borrowing mainly to increase the ratio of investment to GNP.

Appendix

The appendix tables to this chapter contain columns for investment (Inv), divided into direct and portfolio investment (DFI + P) and national investment (NI); consumption (Con); the current account (CA); remittances (R); and error.

The relationship between these concepts may be explained by the following identities.

In the absence of "remittances" (public and private unrequited transfers, in the jargon of the IMF's *International Financial Statistics*),

$$(3.1) \qquad \text{GDP} = \text{Consumption (C)} + \text{Investment (I)} + \text{Exports} - \text{Imports.}$$

Adding in net factor income (F), we have

$$(3.2) \qquad \text{GNP} = \text{C} + \text{I} + \text{CA (current account).}$$

Remittances (R) contribute to the current account but not to GNP. Given their existence, we therefore have

(3.3)   GNP = C + I + CA - R.

Some investment consists of direct foreign investment (DFI) and portfolio investment (P). This investment (DFI + P) belongs to foreigners. We therefore write

(3.4)   GNP = C + NI + (DFI + P) + CA - R

where NI stands for national investment. (DFI + P) goes to finance a balance of payments deficit without corresponding borrowing or the use of reserves. In the following country tables, these right-hand side magnitudes are expressed as percentages of GNP. They should, in principle, add to 100. In practice they do not, and the tables therefore include an error term, which is positive when the other terms exceed 100. In table 3-4, we used the concept "net borrowing" (B), which is -CA - DFI - P. In this table NI + CON - B = 100 + R + error. All magnitudes are expressed as percentages of GNP; therefore the error is CON + INV + CA - R - 100.

Table 3A.1   Argentina

Year	Inv	DI+PI	NI	CON	CA	R	Error
1970	21.8	0.4	21.4	79.3	−0.7	−0.0	0.4
1971	21.0	0.5	20.5	79.0	−1.6	−0.0	−1.6
1972	21.1	0.1	21.0	79.4	−0.9	−0.0	−0.4
1973	18.2	−0.2	18.4	80.1	1.8	0.0	0.1
1974	19.5	−0.1	19.6	80.3	0.2	0.0	0.0
1975	26.1	−0.1	26.2	75.2	−3.4	0.0	−2.1
1976	27.2	−0.1	27.3	69.7	1.7	0.0	−1.4
1977	27.5	0.3	27.2	70.6	2.7	0.1	0.8
1978	24.7	0.7	24.0	72.5	4.4	0.2	1.4
1979	22.9	0.4	22.5	77.8	−1.0	0.1	−0.4
1980	22.4	0.7	21.7	81.0	−8.5	0.0	−5.1
1981	19.3	1.6	17.7	84.2	−8.4	−0.0	−4.9
1982	17.3	1.1	16.2	88.5	−4.5	0.1	1.2
1983	18.8	1.4	17.4	85.0	−4.1	0.0	−0.3
1984	12.2	0.9	11.3	91.1	−3.4	0.0	−0.1
1985	9.3	0.5	8.8	92.3	−1.6	0.0	−0.0
1986	9.4	0.0	9.4	94.2	−3.8	0.0	−0.3
1987	17.4	−0.8	18.2	88.2	−5.5	−0.0	0.1
1988	17.3	0.3	17.0	84.5	−1.8	0.0	0.0
1989	13.2	—	—	88.7	−2.4	0.0	−0.5

— Not available.
Source: World Bank Date and IMF, *International Financial Statistics* (various years).

Table 3A.2   Brazil

Year	Inv	DI+PI	NI	CON	CA	R	Error
1970	20.7	1.0	19.7	80.6	−2.0	0.1	−0.8
1971	21.3	1.1	20.2	81.4	−3.4	0.0	−0.7
1972	21.4	1.0	20.4	81.2	−2.9	0.0	−0.3
1973	23.5	1.7	21.8	78.7	−2.7	0.0	−0.5
1974	25.6	1.2	24.4	81.2	−7.3	0.0	−0.5
1975	27.2	1.0	26.5	78.2	−5.7	0.0	−0.3
1976	23.5	0.9	22.6	80.5	−4.4	0.0	−0.4
1977	22.4	1.0	21.4	79.9	−3.0	0.0	−0.7
1978	23.5	1.1	22.4	80.1	−3.6	0.0	−0.0
1979	23.4	1.5	21.9	81.5	−4.8	0.0	0.1
1980	24.1	0.8	23.3	81.6	−5.6	0.1	−0.0
1981	24.0	0.9	23.1	80.7	−4.7	0.1	−0.1
1982	22.1	1.0	21.1	83.9	−6.1	−0.0	−0.1
1983	17.5	0.6	16.9	86.0	−3.6	0.1	−0.2
1984	16.2	0.6	15.6	83.8	0.0	0.1	−0.1
1985	17.9	0.5	17.4	82.3	−0.1	0.1	0.0
1986	20.1	−0.1	20.2	82.0	−2.1	0.0	0.0
1987	22.9	0.2	22.7	77.6	−0.5	0.0	0.0
1988	22.6	—	—	76.1	1.3	0.0	0.0
1989	23.3	—	—	78.0	0.2	0.0	1.5

— Not available.
Source: World Bank data and IMF, *International Financial Statistics* (various years).

Table 3A.3   Cameroon

Year	Inv	DI+PI	NI	CON	CA	R	Error
1970	16.7	1.5	15.2	86.0	−2.7	0.9	−0.9
1971	17.9	0.2	17.7	94.2	−3.9	0.8	7.4
1972	19.8	0.2	19.6	95.1	−7.0	0.5	7.4
1973	21.6	−0.0	21.6	90.4	−1.0	−0.4	11.4
1974	18.6	1.5	17.1	87.4	−0.8	0.1	5.1
1975	21.7	1.0	20.7	90.0	−6.0	0.9	4.8
1976	19.0	0.3	18.7	94.3	−3.2	1.3	8.8
1977	23.5	0.1	23.4	87.2	−3.0	1.0	6.7
1978	24.2	0.8	23.4	87.1	−4.5	0.0	6.8
1979	23.4	1.2	22.2	92.3	−2.3	0.0	13.4
1980	20.7	2.0	18.7	92.6	−5.8	0.0	7.5
1981	27.1	2.0	25.1	85.4	−5.8	0.1	6.6
1982	25.0	1.6	23.4	82.0	−4.8	−0.2	2.4
1983	26.1	3.0	23.1	76.0	−0.7	−0.0	1.4
1984	22.3	0.2	22.0	71.9	2.7	−0.1	−3.0
1985	26.6	3.8	22.8	68.5	4.3	−0.4	−0.2
1986	24.4	0.0	24.4	80.9	−6.0	−0.6	−0.1
1987	21.1	0.0	21.1	87.6	−10.2	−1.0	−0.5
1988	18.3	—	—	87.6	−7.5	−1.2	−0.4
1989	13.0	—	—	90.4	−1.9	−0.6	2.1

— Not available.
Source: World Bank data and IMF, *International Financial Statistics* (various years).

Table 3A.4   Chile

Year	Inv	DI+PI	NI	CON	CA	R	Error
1970	16.9	−1.1	18.0	85.0	−1.1	0.1	0.7
1971	14.7	−0.7	15.4	87.6	−2.0	0.1	0.2
1972	12.3	−0.1	12.47	92.4	−4.0	0.1	0.6
1973	8.0	−0.1	8.1	95.0	−2.7	0.1	0.2
1974	21.5	−5.2	26.7	79.4	−2.7	0.1	−1.9
1975	13.6	0.6	13.0	92.5	−7.1	0.2	−1.2
1976	13.2	−0.1	13.3	85.7	1.6	0.5	−0.0
1977	14.7	0.1	14.6	89.2	−4.2	0.7	−1.0
1978	18.2	1.2	17.0	87.5	−7.2	0.6	−2.1
1979	18.3	1.4	16.9	87.2	−5.9	0.5	−0.9
1980	21.6	0.6	21.0	85.7	−7.4	0.0	−0.1
1981	23.7	1.2	22.5	91.4	−15.1	0.0	−0.0
1982	12.2	1.7	10.5	97.7	−10.2	−0.1	−0.2
1983	10.7	0.7	10.0	95.2	−6.2	−0.0	−0.3
1984	15.1	0.4	14.7	96.8	−12.2	−0.0	−0.3
1985	15.4	0.8	14.6	93.9	−9.9	−0.2	−0.4
1986	16.5	2.1	14.4	91.9	−8.0	−0.4	0.8
1987	18.4	5.3	13.1	86.1	−4.7	−0.7	0.5
1988	18.4	5.0	13.0	82.3	−0.8	−0.7	0.6
1989	22.1	—	—	82.7	−3.3	−0.3	1.8

— Not available.

Source: World Bank data and IMF, *International Financial Statistics* (various years).

Table 3A.5   Colombia

Year	Inv	DI+PI	NI	CON	CA	R	Error
1970	20.8	0.5	20.3	83.7	−4.2	0.5	−0.2
1971	19.9	0.5	19.4	86.6	−5.9	0.4	0.2
1972	18.5	0.2	12.4	84.3	−2.3	0.4	0.1
1973	18.7	0.6	18.1	82.5	−0.5	0.3	0.4
1974	21.8	0.3	21.5	80.9	−2.9	0.4	−0.6
1975	17.3	0.2	17.1	82.9	−1.3	0.4	−1.5
1976	17.9	0.1	17.8	81.0	1.1	0.3	−0.3
1977	19.0	0.2	18.8	78.4	1.9	0.2	−0.9
1978	18.4	0.3	18.1	79.6	1.1	0.3	−1.2
1979	18.3	0.3	18.0	80.6	1.6	0.4	0.1
1980	19.1	0.2	18.9	80.6	−0.6	0.5	−1.4
1981	20.7	0.6	20.1	83.4	−5.5	0.7	−2.1
1982	20.8	0.9	19.9	85.1	−8.0	0.4	−2.5
1983	20.3	1.4	18.9	84.6	−8.0	0.4	−3.5
1984	19.5	1.5	18.0	83.8	−3.8	0.8	−1.3
1985	19.6	3.0	16.6	82.0	−5.4	1.4	−5.2
1986	18.7	2.0	16.7	77.9	1.1	2.3	−4.6
1987	21.1	1.0	20.1	81.4	1.0	2.9	0.6
1988	23.4	0.5	22.9	81.2	−0.6	2.7	1.3
1989	21.0	—	—	81.5	−0.5	2.8	−0.8

— Not available.
Source: World Bank data and IMF, *International Financial Statistics* (various years).

Table 3A.6   Costa Rica

Year	Inv	DI+PI	NI	CON	CA	R	Error
1970	20.8	2.7	18.1	87.4	−7.6	0.6	0.0
1971	24.7	2.1	22.6	87.3	−10.8	0.7	0.5
1972	22.7	2.8	19.9	87.1	−8.3	0.5	1.0
1973	24.7	2.5	22.2	84.5	−7.5	0.5	1.2
1974	27.4	2.9	24.5	90.3	−16.4	0.6	0.7
1975	22.3	3.6	18.7	89.6	−11.5	0.5	−0.1
1976	24.4	2.7	21.7	84.8	−8.6	0.6	0.0
1977	24.9	−2.2	22.7	83.2	−7.5	0.5	0.1
1978	24.2	2.0	22.2	86.9	−10.6	0.5	−0.0
1979	26.3	1.1	25.2	88.2	−14.4	0.3	−0.2
1980	27.9	3.7	24.2	88.0	−14.4	0.3	1.2
1981	32.7	2.7	30.0	85.5	−17.6	1.2	−0.6
1982	29.6	1.1	28.5	86.7	−12.3	1.6	2.4
1983	27.0	1.9	25.1	85.6	−9.9	2.5	0.2
1984	24.8	1.6	23.2	84.1	−4.5	4.2	0.2
1985	27.4	1.4	26.0	82.2	−3.5	6.0	0.1
1986	26.9	1.3	25.6	78.7	−1.9	3.7	0.9
1987	29.0	1.8	27.2	82.4	−6.1	5.3	0.0
1988	25.7	1.6	24.1	84.3	−4.2	6.0	−0.2
1989	26.0	—	—	84.7	−8.6	3.3	−1.2

— Not available.

Source: World Bank data and IMF, *International Financial Statistics* (various years).

Table 3A.7   Côte d'Ivoire

Year	Inv	DI+PI	NI	CON	CA	R	Error
1970	23.8	2.4	21.4	74.9	−2.7	−1.5	−2.5
1971	23.4	0.9	22.5	79.7	−3.9	−1.8	1.0
1972	22.4	1.1	21.3	80.2	−7.0	−1.6	−2.8
1973	25.4	2.5	22.9	81.5	−1.0	−3.0	8.9
1974	23.9	0.8	23.1	76.8	−0.8	−3.3	3.2
1975	24.4	1.9	22.5	84.2	−10.6	−4.0	2.0
1976	25.4	1.0	24.4	79.1	−5.9	−6.1	4.7
1977	29.9	0.1	29.8	72.6	−3.1	−5.2	4.6
1978	32.9	1.1	31.8	78.8	−11.7	−5.9	5.9
1979	31.2	0.9	30.3	83.8	−16.9	−7.0	5.9
1980	29.8	1.0	28.8	82.3	−18.4	−7.1	0.8
1981	27.6	0.4	27.2	86.5	−17.8	−6.1	2.4
1982	24.9	0.7	24.2	85.4	−14.4	−5.1	1.0
1983	22.3	0.6	21.7	87.7	−14.8	−4.7	−0.1
1984	11.8	0.0	11.8	83.6	−1.2	−4.3	−1.5
1985	13.9	0.4	13.5	82.2	1.1	−4.0	1.2
1986	12.0	0.8	11.2	83.3	−3.4	−4.1	−4.1
1987	12.6	—	—	89.8	−10.2	−4.3	−3.5
1988	15.7	—	—	86.5	−12.0	−4.2	−5.6
1989	11.3	—	—	95.6	−14.5	−3.8	−3.8

— Not available.
Source: World Bank data and IMF, *International Financial Statistics* (various years).

Table 3A.8   India

Year	Inv	DI+PI	NI	CON	CA	R	Error
1970	17.2	0.0	17.2	84.0	−0.7	0.5	−0.0
1971	18.6	0.0	18.6	82.8	−0.6	0.8	−0.0
1972	17.2	0.0	17.2	83.7	−0.5	0.3	0.1
1973	18.3	0.0	18.3	82.5	−0.5	0.3	−0.0
1974	19.8	0.0	19.8	81.5	−0.9	0.4	0.0
1975	20.9	0.0	20.9	79.7	0.3	0.9	0.0
1976	21.0	0.0	21.0	78.4	1.7	1.1	0.0
1977	19.8	0.0	19.8	79.8	1.8	1.3	0.1
1978	22.3	0.0	22.3	78.9	0.1	1.3	0.0
1979	22.8	0.0	22.8	79.2	−0.3	1.7	−0.0
1980	22.8	0.0	22.8	80.3	−1.3	2.0	−0.2
1981	25.7	0.0	25.7	77.5	−1.7	1.6	−0.1
1982	23.6	0.0	23.6	79.6	−1.4	1.6	0.2
1983	22.4	0.0	22.4	80.5	−1.3	1.5	−0.1
1984	22.6	0.0	22.6	80.6	−1.6	1.6	−0.2
1985	25.6	0.0	25.6	78.3	−2.7	1.3	−0.1
1986	24.5	0.0	24.5	79.1	−2.5	1.2	−0.1
1987	23.1	0.0	23.1	80.5	−2.4	1.2	−0.0
1988	24.7	0.0	24.7	79.8	−3.1	1.3	0.1
1989	23.9	0.0	23.9	80.3	−2.8	1.2	0.0

Source: World Bank data and IMF, *International Financial Statistics* (various years).

Table 3A.9   Indonesia

Year	Inv	DI+PI	NI	CON	CA	R	Error
1970	15.8	0.9	14.9	85.8	−3.2	0.7	−2.3
1971	18.4	1.4	17.0	83.1	−3.8	0.5	−2.8
1972	22.1	1.8	20.3	78.3	−2.9	0.4	−2.9
1973	21.2	0.1	21.2	78.9	−2.8	0.3	−3.0
1974	20.1	−0.2	19.9	74.2	2.3	0.2	−3.6
1975	24.3	1.5	22.8	76.1	−3.5	0.1	−3.2
1976	24.4	0.9	23.5	74.6	−2.3	0.0	−3.3
1977	23.8	0.5	23.3	73.0	−0.1	0.1	−3.4
1978	24.4	1.3	23.1	75.1	−2.7	0.0	−3.2
1979	27.8	0.5	27.3	69.4	1.9	0.1	−1.0
1980	25.4	0.3	25.1	65.5	4.0	0.3	−5.4
1981	30.6	0.2	30.4	68.6	−0.6	0.3	−1.7
1982	28.9	0.6	28.3	75.7	−5.9	0.1	−1.4
1983	30.0	0.8	28.2	74.2	−7.7	0.1	−3.6
1984	27.5	0.3	27.2	73.7	−2.2	0.2	−1.2
1985	29.2	0.3	28.9	73.2	−2.3	0.1	0.0
1986	29.4	0.7	28.7	75.8	−5.1	0.3	−0.2
1987	32.9	0.5	32.5	70.5	−2.9	0.4	0.1
1988	33.1	0.5	32.6	69.4	−1.7	0.3	0.5
1989	36.5	—	—	66.0	−1.2	1.0	1.0

— Not available.
Source: World Bank data and IMF, *International Financial Statistics* (various years).

Table 3A.10   Kenya

Year	Inv	DI+PI	NI	CON	CA	R	Error
1970	25.3	0.9	24.4	79.3	−3.2	1.7	−0.3
1971	24.7	0.3	24.4	85.2	−6.5	3.4	−0.0
1972	23.0	−0.1	23.1	82.2	−3.3	1.9	−0.0
1973	27.2	−0.1	27.3	79.4	−5.3	1.3	0.0
1974	26.8	−0.0	26.8	84.9	−10.8	1.1	−0.2
1975	18.9	0.4	18.5	90.0	−7.0	1.6	0.3
1976	21.2	1.1	20.1	83.0	−3.8	0.4	−0.0
1977	24.7	1.3	23.4	76.2	0.6	1.5	−0.0
1978	31.1	0.6	30.5	83.7	−13.0	1.8	0.0
1979	23.1	1.3	21.8	86.7	−8.3	1.5	0.0
1980	30.2	1.2	29.0	84.5	−12.6	2.1	0.0
1981	28.6	0.1	28.5	83.0	−8.4	3.3	−0.1
1982	22.7	0.1	22.6	85.3	−4.8	2.2	1.0
1983	21.5	0.2	21.3	82.3	−0.8	3.2	−0.2
1984	21.5	0.1	21.4	83.4	−2.1	3.0	−0.2
1985	26.5	0.2	26.3	78.4	−1.9	3.3	−0.3
1986	22.6	0.4	22.2	80.9	−0.5	3.0	0.0
1987	25.4	0.5	24.9	83.9	−6.5	2.8	0.0
1988	26.5	0.1	26.4	83.5	−5.6	4.3	−0.0
1989	26.6	—	—	83.9	−7.3	4.8	−1.6

— Not available.
Source: World Bank data and IMF, *International Financial Statistics* (various years).

Table 3A.11   Republic of Korea

Year	Inv	DI+PI	NI	CON	CA	R	Error
1970	24.6	0.7	23.9	84.5	−7.0	2.0	0.1
1971	25.1	0.4	24.7	85.3	−8.6	1.7	0.1
1972	20.9	0.6	20.3	84.2	−3.5	1.6	−0.0
1973	24.7	0.7	24.0	79.0	−2.3	1.4	−0.0
1974	31.8	0.6	31.2	80.1	−10.8	1.2	−0.1
1975	27.5	0.3	27.2	82.8	−9.1	1.1	0.1
1976	25.7	0.5	25.2	76.9	−1.1	1.2	0.3
1977	27.7	0.4	27.3	73.6	0.0	0.6	0.7
1978	31.9	0.2	31.7	72.5	−2.2	1.0	1.2
1979	36.0	0.0	36.0	72.9	−6.5	0.7	1.7
1980	32.8	0.1	32.7	78.4	−8.8	0.7	1.7
1981	30.7	0.2	30.5	78.8	−6.9	0.7	1.9
1982	29.8	−0.1	29.9	77.2	−3.7	0.7	2.6
1983	29.7	0.2	29.5	74.2	−2.0	0.7	1.2
1984	30.9	0.5	30.4	72.6	−1.6	0.6	1.3
1985	30.3	1.3	29.0	71.9	−1.0	0.6	0.6
1986	29.7	0.6	29.1	67.2	4.5	1.0	0.4
1987	29.9	0.2	29.7	64.1	7.7	0.9	0.8
1988	30.2	0.1	30.1	62.5	8.4	0.9	0.2
1989	34.8	—	—	63.2	2.4	0.1	0.3

— Not available.
Source: World Bank data and IMF, *International Financial Statistics* (various years).

Table 3A.12   Mexico

Year	Inv	DI+PI	NI	CON	CA	R	Error
1970	22.1	0.8	21.3	84.5	−2.9	0.1	3.6
1971	19.7	0.8	18.9	86.2	−2.1	0.1	3.7
1972	19.8	0.8	19.0	86.0	−2.0	0.1	3.7
1973	20.8	0.9	19.9	85.4	−2.5	0.1	3.6
1974	22.6	0.8	21.8	84.3	−3.9	0.2	2.8
1975	23.1	0.8	22.3	84.0	−4.4	0.2	2.5
1976	21.9	1.2	20.7	84.7	−3.7	0.2	2.7
1977	22.5	2.3	20.2	82.4	−2.2	0.2	2.5
1978	23.2	1.5	21.7	82.3	−3.0	0.2	2.3
1979	25.6	0.7	24.9	80.5	−4.0	0.2	1.9
1980	28.0	1.2	26.8	77.3	−5.7	0.2	−0.6
1981	28.4	1.7	26.7	78.0	−6.7	0.1	−0.4
1982	24.3	1.6	22.7	76.4	−3.9	0.2	−3.4
1983	22.1	−0.1	22.2	74.0	3.9	0.2	−0.2
1984	21.0	−0.2	21.2	76.5	2.5	0.2	−0.2
1985	23.0	−0.3	23.3	76.8	0.6	0.6	−0.2
1986	19.4	0.3	19.1	81.6	−1.4	0.4	−0.8
1987	20.3	1.1	19.2	77.9	3.0	0.5	0.7
1988	21.7	1.4	20.3	81.2	−1.5	0.3	1.1
1989	18.6	—	—	87.9	−2.0	0.4	4.1

— Not available.
Source: World Bank data and IMF, *International Financial Statistics* (various years).

Table 3A.13   Morocco

Year	Inv	DI+PI	NI	CON	CA	R	Error
1970	18.7	0.5	18.2	86.4	−3.2	1.9	0.0
1971	18.2	0.5	17.7	85.8	−1.4	2.5	0.1
1972	15.5	0.3	15.2	86.5	1.0	2.8	0.2
1973	17.1	−0.0	17.1	85.5	1.6	4.0	0.2
1974	20.8	−0.3	21.1	80.7	3.0	4.3	0.2
1975	25.4	−0.0	25.4	86.5	−5.8	5.8	0.3
1976	28.5	0.4	28.1	92.6	−15.0	5.5	0.6
1977	34.8	0.5	34.3	87.7	−16.9	5.2	0.4
1978	26.1	0.4	25.7	90.4	−10.2	5.9	0.4
1979	25.2	0.3	24.9	90.9	−9.8	6.0	0.3
1980	25.0	0.5	24.5	89.1	−7.8	6.1	0.2
1981	27.4	0.4	27.0	92.9	−12.6	7.5	0.2
1982	29.5	0.5	29.0	90.1	−12.7	6.8	0.1
1983	25.1	0.4	24.7	88.8	−6.7	7.4	−0.2
1984	26.5	0.4	26.1	89.4	−8.1	7.7	0.1
1985	28.8	0.2	28.6	87.1	−7.3	8.9	−0.3
1986	25.5	0.0	25.5	85.4	−1.3	9.6	0.0
1987	23.6	0.3	23.3	85.3	1.0	9.8	0.1
1988	24.9	0.4	24.5	80.6	2.2	7.7	0.0
1989	25.1	—	—	84.6	−3.7	7.5	−1.5

— Not available.
Source: World Bank data and IMF, *International Financial Statistics* (various years).

Table 3A.14 Nigeria

Year	Inv	DI+PI	NI	CON	CA	R	Error
1970	13.4	1.5	11.5	90.3	−3.0	0.5	0.2
1971	17.5	1.9	15.5	89.2	−3.0	0.0	3.7
1972	19.7	1.8	17.9	85.5	−2.2	−0.1	3.1
1973	20.7	2.0	18.8	81.1	−0.0	−0.3	2.1
1974	15.1	0.8	14.3	71.8	16.3	−0.3	3.5
1975	22.2	1.0	21.2	79.0	0.1	−0.3	1.6
1976	27.7	0.7	27.0	74.6	−0.8	−0.3	1.8
1977	27.3	0.8	26.6	75.8	−2.0	−0.3	1.4
1978	25.3	0.4	25.0	80.5	−6.8	−0.4	−0.6
1979	20.6	0.4	20.2	76.4	2.4	−0.5	−0.1
1980	21.2	−0.7	22.0	73.1	5.7	−0.6	0.6
1981	21.9	0.6	21.4	84.1	−7.3	−0.6	−0.7
1982	15.6	0.5	15.1	92.1	−9.4	−0.5	−1.2
1983	11.6	0.4	11.2	93.4	−5.6	−0.4	−0.2
1984	6.1	0.2	5.9	93.7	0.1	−0.4	0.3
1985	7.7	0.6	7.3	91.3	3.3	−0.3	2.6
1986	9.9	0.3	9.9	94.6	0.9	−0.2	5.5
1987	12.1	0.3	12.5	88.1	−0.3	−0.1	0.0
1988	13.2	3.1	10.5	91.0	−0.7	−0.0	3.5
1989	13.5	—	—	85.0	3.8	0.3	2.0

— Not available.
Source: World Bank data and IMF, *International Financial Statistics* (various years).

Table 3A.15   Pakistan

Year	Inv	DI+PI	NI	CON	CA	R	Error
1970	15.8	0.2	15.6	91.0	−6.7	1.2	−1.1
1971	15.7	0.0	15.7	91.5	−4.6	1.7	0.9
1972	14.1	0.3	13.7	90.6	−2.6	1.9	0.2
1973	13.1	−0.1	13.2	91.1	−1.3	3.0	−0.1
1974	13.5	0.0	13.5	94.4	−5.7	2.3	−0.1
1975	16.4	0.2	16.2	95.9	−9.5	3.0	−0.2
1976	17.4	0.1	17.3	93.1	−6.3	3.6	0.6
1977	19.5	0.1	19.4	91.5	−6.1	4.9	−0.0
1978	18.0	0.2	17.8	92.3	−2.8	7.6	−0.1
1979	18.1	0.3	17.8	95.3	−4.2	9.2	−0.0
1980	18.7	0.3	18.4	94.3	−3.7	9.2	0.1
1981	18.9	0.4	18.5	91.6	−2.7	9.0	−1.2
1982	19.5	0.2	19.3	92.6	−3.7	9.3	−0.9
1983	19.1	0.1	19.0	92.9	−0.6	12.1	−0.7
1984	18.5	0.2	18.3	93.6	−2.1	10.9	−0.9
1985	18.6	0.9	17.7	95.3	−3.9	10.1	−0.1
1986	19.1	0.6	18.5	90.9	−2.3	10.6	−2.9
1987	19.5	0.8	18.7	88.0	−1.0	9.0	−2.5
1988	18.4	0.8	17.6	89.5	−2.9	7.4	−2.4
1989	18.0	—	—	90.7	−3.3	6.8	−1.4

— Not available.
Source: World Bank data and IMF, *International Financial Statistics* (various years).

Table 3A.16   Sri Lanka

Year	Inv	DI+PI	NI	CON	CA	R	Error
1970	19.3	0.0	19.3	85.6	−2.6	0.6	1.7
1971	17.3	0.0	17.3	86.1	−1.6	0.7	1.1
1972	17.5	0.0	17.5	85.3	−1.3	0.6	0.9
1973	13.9	0.0	13.9	88.4	−0.9	0.6	0.8
1974	15.8	0.0	15.8	92.5	−3.8	1.5	3.0
1975	15.7	0.3	15.4	92.6	−2.9	2.7	2.7
1976	16.4	0.0	16.4	86.9	−0.2	2.4	0.7
1977	14.5	0.0	14.5	82.5	3.5	2.7	−2.2
1978	20.2	0.1	20.1	85.2	−2.4	2.9	0.1
1979	25.9	1.4	24.5	86.6	−6.8	5.7	0.0
1980	34.0	1.1	32.9	89.4	−16.4	6.9	0.1
1981	28.4	0.1	28.3	90.3	−10.3	8.4	−0.0
1982	30.4	0.3	30.1	90.2	−11.4	8.8	0.4
1983	29.0	0.7	28.3	88.8	−9.1	8.7	0.0
1984	26.6	0.6	26.0	81.8	0.0	8.2	0.2
1985	23.9	0.4	23.5	90.2	−7.0	7.4	−0.3
1986	23.8	0.5	23.5	90.1	−6.5	7.4	−0.0
1987	23.4	0.9	22.6	89.3	−4.9	7.4	0.4
1988	22.8	0.4	22.2	90.3	−5.7	7.5	−0.1
1989	21.9	—	—	90.1	−6.0	6.8	−0.8

— Not available.
Source: World Bank data and IMF, *International Financial Statistics* (various years).

Table 3A.17   Thailand

Year	Inv	DI+PI	NI	CON	CA	R	Error
1970	25.5	0.8	24.7	78.7	−3.5	0.7	0.0
1971	24.2	0.6	23.6	78.7	−2.4	0.6	−0.1
1972	21.8	1.0	20.8	79.6	−0.6	0.7	−0.1
1973	27.1	0.8	26.3	74.7	−0.4	1.3	0.1
1974	26.7	1.5	25.2	75.7	−0.6	1.8	0.0
1975	26.7	0.2	26.5	77.9	−4.2	0.5	−0.1
1976	24.0	0.5	23.5	78.7	−2.6	0.3	−0.2
1977	27.0	0.5	26.5	78.8	−5.6	0.2	−0.0
1978	28.4	0.5	27.9	76.6	−4.8	0.2	−0.0
1979	27.5	0.9	26.6	80.4	−7.7	0.2	−0.0
1980	26.6	0.9	25.7	80.5	−6.5	0.7	−0.1
1981	26.7	1.0	25.7	81.3	−7.5	0.5	−0.0
1982	23.5	0.7	22.8	79.9	−2.9	0.5	0.0
1983	26.1	1.2	24.9	81.9	−7.3	0.7	0.0
1984	25.2	1.4	23.8	80.4	−5.2	0.4	−0.0
1985	24.5	2.9	21.6	80.2	−4.2	0.5	0.0
1986	22.5	0.6	21.9	77.4	0.6	0.6	−0.1
1987	26.3	1.1	25.2	75.3	−0.8	0.5	0.3
1988	29.3	2.8	26.5	73.9	−2.8	0.4	−0.0
1989	31.5	—	—	72.2	−3.7	0.4	0.2

— Not available.
Source: World Bank data and IMF, *International Financial Statistics* (various years).

Table 3A.18   Turkey

Year	Inv	DI+PI	NI	CON	CA	R	Error
1970	19.9	0.5	19.4	83.1	−0.3	2.6	0.1
1971	17.9	0.4	17.5	86.3	0.3	4.6	−0.1
1972	21.1	0.3	20.8	82.6	1.3	4.9	0.1
1973	19.1	0.4	18.7	83.7	3.2	6.0	0.0
1974	21.7	0.2	21.5	85.3	−1.9	5.1	0.0
1975	23.3	0.3	23.0	85.4	−4.6	4.0	0.1
1976	25.3	0.0	25.3	82.3	−4.9	2.7	0.0
1977	25.4	0.1	25.3	83.5	−6.6	2.3	0.0
1978	18.9	0.1	18.8	85.6	−2.4	2.1	0.0
1979	18.9	0.1	18.8	85.8	−2.1	2.6	0.0
1980	22.3	0.0	22.3	87.7	−6.1	3.9	0.0
1981	22.5	0.2	22.3	85.5	−3.4	4.5	0.1
1982	21.2	0.1	21.1	85.1	−1.8	4.4	0.0
1983	20.2	0.1	20.1	87.2	−3.9	3.5	0.0
1984	20.1	0.2	19.9	87.2	−2.9	4.4	0.0
1985	21.5	0.2	21.3	84.3	−2.0	3.9	−0.1
1986	25.2	0.2	25.0	80.8	−2.6	3.4	0.0
1987	26.1	0.1	26.0	78.7	−1.2	3.6	−0.0
1988	24.6	0.5	24.1	76.3	2.3	3.1	0.1
1989	22.9	—	—	80.5	1.2	4.6	0.0

— Not available.
Source: World Bank data and IMF, *International Financial Statistics* (various years).

Chapter 4

Heading for Crisis: 1979–1982

The period from 1979 to 1982 began with the second oil shock and ended with Mexico's debt moratorium. That moratorium marked a critical change in the availability of international credit that affected most, but not all, of our eighteen countries. During these four years, and for some time after, most of these countries found their terms of trade deteriorating, and most of them increased their debt, some to extremely high levels. The ensuing crises brought home the dangers of heavy foreign borrowing.

The Situation in 1979

As pointed out in chapter 3, our countries made little adjustment to the oil price rise of 1973–4. All the net oil importers except India increased their current account deficits in the 1970s, and most increased their debt. Furthermore, most countries were significantly less well placed to meet an external shock in 1979 than they were in 1973 (see table 3-5). Table 4-1 shows how the situation worsened from 1979 to 1982. (Note that the debt and interest figures in table 4-1 include short-term debt, which is excluded from table 3-5 because short-term debt figures are not available for 1973.)

In 1979, several of the countries were running unsustainable current account deficits.[1] A current account deficit becomes unsustainable when the ratio of a country's deficit to its gross national product (GNP) exceeds the rate of growth of GNP multiplied by the debt/GNP ratio—in other words, when the debt/GNP ratio rises (this ignores inward equity investment, which was nowhere of quantitative importance in the eighteen countries).

An unsustainable deficit is not necessarily undesirable. There is no reason to eschew an increase in the debt ratio if it is well below some critical level. Indeed, it is sound policy to let the ratio rise as long as the increased borrowing is used to

Table 4.1   Debt and Current Account Ratios, 1979 and 1982

(percentage)

Country	Debt/ GNP		Debt interest/ GNP		Current account/ GNP		Total debt service/ exports		Debt/ exports	
	1979	1982	1979	1982	1979	1982	1979	1982	1979	1982
Argentina	15	84	1.9	6.9	1.0	4.5	23	50	211	447
Brazil	31	36	2.1	4.5	4.7	6.1	63	81	336	395
Cameroon	37	37	1.2	2.6	2.2	4.8	10	19	122	133
Chile	45	77	2.8	10.6	5.9	10.2	39	71	190	336
Colombia	21	27	0.9	2.8	-1.6	8.0	13	30	68	204
Costa Rica	53	167	2.9	5.4	14.4	12.3	34	21	182	317
Côte d'Ivoire	58	111	2.8	10.0	16.9	14.4	25	46	173	277
India	15	13	0.3	0.6	0.3	1.4	10	14	151	191
Indonesia	35	29	2.0	2.1	-1.9	5.9	20	18	85	124
Kenya	46	57	2.1	4.1	8.3	4.8	17	33	164	217
Korea	36	52	1.8	5.8	6.5	3.7	14	22	114	132
Mexico	31	52	2.4	6.8	4.0	3.9	68	57	252	312
Morocco	53	84	2.9	5.3	9.8	12.7	38	43	347	327
Nigeria	8	14	0.3	1.4	-2.2	9.4	2	16	32	100
Pakistan	43	38	1.1	1.4	4.2	3.7	20	16	324	215
Sri Lanka	34	55	1.6	2.5	6.8	11.4	9	15	96	160
Thailand	23	35	2.4	3.1	7.7	2.9	15	21	74	130
Turkey	22	38	1.1	3.2	2.1	1.8	41	30	513	196

Note: Countries in italics are those whose debt was rescheduled in the period 1985–88. A current account deficit is shown as positive. Debt includes public and private, long- and short-term.

Source: The figures for 1982 are from *World Debt Tables* (1990–91); those for 1979 are from *World Debt Tables* (1980–81) and national account data base. Current Account/GNP figures are from the appendix to chapter 3.

finance investments with a real social return greater than the marginal real rate of interest paid on the increased borrowing.

There is no objectively definable upper limit to the debt/GNP ratio. It should be limited either by the inability to find promising enough investments or by risk. There are several distinguishable risks. A change in circumstances may reduce the yield on the chosen investments or even turn them into liabilities. Interest rates on outstanding debt may be higher than expected because of a change in world capital markets. Also, GNP growth may be less than expected, so servicing the debt may become difficult. For one reason or another, whether as a result of bad luck or bad management, the country may become uncreditworthy and the expected capital inflow may dry up. The necessary adjustment might create severe internal problems and loss of output.

Suppose, for the sake of illustration, that a country should take action to stabilize the debt/GNP ratio when it reaches 40 percent. If it is considered imprudent to expect GNP to grow at a rate of more than 5 percent, then the current account deficit should not exceed 2 percent of GNP (.05 x .4 x 100).

Foreign lenders tend to look more at the levels of debt in relation to exports. They do this because amortization and interest on foreign debt are reckoned in dollars, and a country may have difficulty finding the dollars if there is a fall in export receipts (or surge in imports), even though the payments are modest in relation to GNP. Figures for total debt service (amortization and interest) and for total debt in relation to exports (table 4-1) show that countries with low ratios of exports to GNP may have high ratios of debt to exports and of total debt service to exports, even though the debt in relation to GNP is modest. This was the situation in Brazil and Turkey in 1979. For a given debt/export ratio, the lower the interest rate and the longer the maturity of the debt, the lower the total ratio of debt service to exports. The given debt/export ratio is then less risky. Bearing this in mind, suppose further that a country should be taking steps to limit the debt/export ratio when it reaches 2. By analogous argument to that of the preceding paragraph, the current account deficit should not exceed 10 percent of exports if the expected growth rate of the dollar value of exports is 5 percent a year. In recent years (1973–79), Morocco and Turkey experienced a growth rate of the dollar value of exports of less than 5 percent a year; but their debt/export ratio was very high in 1979 (347 percent and 513 percent, respectively), and that of their current account to exports exceeded 10 percent.

Consider, too, what might happen when the growth rate of export value is less than the rate of interest paid on foreign borrowing. To see the significance of this, partition the current account deficit into its interest component and the noninterest component, termed the primary current account deficit. Now suppose the primary deficit is, and remains, zero. The debt will then grow at r percent per year where r is the rate of interest. If r exceeds the rate of growth of export value, the debt/export ratio will grow indefinitely. A sufficient primary surplus is then needed to prevent this outcome.[2] By 1979, many of our countries must have been paying a higher interest rate on new commitments than the growth rate of export value that could be reasonably expected. Almost all were running primary deficits.

Chile, Costa Rica, Côte d'Ivoire, Kenya, Morocco, and Pakistan had, by 1979, reached a debt/GNP ratio in excess of 40 percent. All had large current account deficits in relation to GNP, ranging from 4.2 percent (Pakistan) to 16.9 percent (Côte d'Ivoire). Except for Pakistan, because of its relatively low deficit and its ability to borrow at low interest rates from other Islamic countries, these countries were running dangerously unsustainable current account deficits.

The 1979–81 Shocks

The first step in discussing the shocks of 1979–81 is to distinguish them from unfavorable exogenous events. If an event is expected, it can hardly be described as a shock. In 1979 there was a dramatic increase in oil prices, triggered by the fall of the Shah of Iran. The average price rose from $14.7 per barrel in 1978 to $31.3 in 1979. It rose somewhat further in 1980 and 1981, to $34.1, before falling slowly until the collapse of 1986.[3] These price movements were certainly shocking.

There were other commodity price movements, the most important for our countries being the fall in the price of coffee (though copper was also important for Chile, and phosphates for Morocco). Since coffee is subject to sudden periodic booms (when Brazil freezes, coffee boils) followed by longer declines, the fall in coffee prices after 1978 can hardly be described as a shock, although it contributed substantially to the worsening terms of trade for the coffee exporters. In table 4-2 we have simply calculated the total terms-of-trade effect that allows for all commodity price changes, whether or not these could properly be described as shocks.[4]

A third unfavorable event was the rise in interest rates. Nominal rates began to rise in 1977, when the London interbank offered rate (LIBOR) three-month dollar rate averaged 6 percent. They then rose almost continuously through 1981, when the same rate averaged 16.5 percent; but it had already reached 15 percent in the last quarter of 1979. Thus, the heavy new borrowing in the period under review was made at interest rates that were known to be high, and it would be misleading to include the whole of the rise in interest payments as an adverse shock. In table 4-2 we therefore show how much interest payments would have risen in each of the recorded years if no fresh debt had been incurred. This does not show the increase in interest payments, but only that part due to changes that were not in the country's power to control.[5]

Yet another unfavorable change resulted from the lower growth experienced by the countries of the Organization for Economic Cooperation and Development (OECD). From 1976 through 1979, the GDP of OECD countries grew an average 3.8 percent per year. In contrast, from 1980 through 1983, it was only 1.2 percent, with a slight fall in 1982. This decline had some effect on the volume of exports from developing countries. The volume of imports into OECD countries fell in the years 1980–82 by about 0.5 percent a year. We have not quantified this effect.[6]

It is worth noting, however, that for ten of the eighteen countries the volume of exports to the developed world was higher in 1982 than in 1979, despite the recession. The losers were Argentina (-17 percent), Colombia (-13 percent), Costa Rica (-5 percent), Côte d'Ivoire (-7 percent), India (-9 percent), Indonesia (-9 percent), Kenya (-24 percent), and Nigeria (-43 percent). The rise in the price of oil, together with the recession, naturally reduced the world demand for oil, but Nigeria's huge loss had other reasons, as is suggested by the relatively small fall in Indonesia's exports.[7]

Several highlights can be seen in table 4-2:

- The interest rate shock was small, particularly in relation to the terms-of-trade effect.
- Nigeria and Indonesia gained greatly. Mexico also gained from the terms-of-trade effect, but this was offset by the rise in interest rates. Note,

Table 4.2   Terms of Trade and Interest Rate Effects
(percentage of GDP and merchandise exports)

Country	Year	Terms-of-trade effect		Interest rate effect		Total effect	
		GDP_{t-1}	$Exports_{t-1}$	GDP_{t-1}	$Exports_{t-1}$	GDP_{t-1}	$Exports_{t-1}$
Côte d'Ivoire	1979	−0.66	−2.25	−0.26	−0.88	−0.92	−3.13
	1980	−5.28	−19.20	−1.75	−6.35	−7.03	−25.55
	1981	−4.38	−14.72	−0.97	−3.25	−5.35	−17.97
						−13.30	−46.65
Sri Lanka	1979	−2.42	−7.83	−0.40	−1.28	−2.82	−9.11
	1980	−3.81	−13.03	−0.04	−0.13	−3.85	−13.16
	1981	−2.63	−9.94	−0.10	−0.36	−2.73	−10.30
						−9.40	−32.57
Chile	1980	−1.82	−9.72	−2.03	−10.83	−3.85	−20.55
	1981	−2.21	−13.05	−0.82	−4.82	−3.03	−17.87
	1982	−1.01	−8.41	−1.30	−10.90	−2.31	−19.31
						−9.19	−57.73
Korea, Republic of	1979	−0.68	−2.69	−0.13	−0.50	−0.81	−3.19
	1980	−3.17	−13.60	−2.21	−9.47	−5.38	−23.07
	1981	0.93	1.54	−1.05	−3.78	−0.12	−2.24
						−6.31	−28.50
Thailand	1979	−0.90	−5.30	−0.18	−1.04	−1.08	−6.34
	1980	−1.88	−9.70	0.13	0.69	−1.75	−9.01
	1981	−2.78	−13.76	−0.45	−2.23	−3.23	−15.99
						−6.06	−31.34
Cameroon	1979	−3.03	−17.61	−0.03	−0.17	−3.06	−17.78
	1980	−0.89	−4.65	−1.15	−5.47	−2.04	−10.12
	1981	−0.27	−1.43	−0.24	−1.31	−0.51	−2.74
						−5.61	−30.64
Brazil	1979	−0.79	−12.53	−0.61	−9.73	−1.40	−22.26
	1980	−1.41	−21.39	−0.99	−15.02	−2.40	−36.41
	1981	−0.81	−9.77	−0.58	−6.97	−1.39	−16.74
						−5.19	−75.41
Kenya	1980	−1.04	−5.83	−1.38	−7.69	−2.42	−13.52
	1981	−1.44	−8.19	−0.24	−1.35	−1.68	−9.54
	1982	−0.42	−2.50	0.17	1.02	−0.25	−1.48
						−4.35	−24.54

Country	Year	Terms-of-trade effect		Interest rate effect		Total effect	
		GDP_{t-1}	$Exports_{t-1}$	GDP_{t-1}	$Exports_{t-1}$	GDP_{t-1}	$Exports_{t-1}$
Colombia	1979	−0.55	−4.23	−0.12	−0.90	−0.67	−5.13
	1980	−1.63	−13.75	−1.39	−11.83	−3.02	−25.58
	1981	−0.92	−7.79	0.36	3.03	−0.56	−4.76
						−4.25	−35.47
Costa Rica	1979	−0.44	−1.80	−0.31	−1.25	−0.75	−3.05
	1980	−2.23	−9.65	−0.56	−2.43	−2.79	−12.08
	1981	−1.67	−8.07	1.47	7.09	−0.20	−0.98
						−3.74	−16.11
Morocco	1979	−0.12	−1.07	−0.34	−3.03	−0.46	−4.10
	1980	−0.72	−6.12	−1.37	−11.67	−2.09	−17.79
	1981	−0.57	−4.33	0.04	0.32	−0.53	−4.01
						−3.08	−25.90
Turkey	1979	−0.11	−2.48	0.39	9.09	0.28	6.61
	1980	−0.63	−19.69	0.09	2.84	−0.54	−16.85
	1981	−0.59	−11.95	−1.01	−20.36	−1.60	−32.31
						−1.86	−42.55
Argentina	1980	−0.44	−6.16	−0.99	−13.94	−1.43	−20.10
	1981	−0.12	−2.32	−0.27	−4.77	−0.39	−7.09
	1982	−0.46	−7.47	0.42	6.89	0.04	−0.58
						−1.78	−27.77
Pakistan	1979	−0.82	−9.94	−0.09	−1.04	−0.91	10.98
	1980	−0.35	−3.31	−0.50	−4.76	−0.85	−8.07
	1981	−0.25	−2.29	0.23	2.12	−0.02	−0.17
						−1.78	−19.22
India	1979	−0.29	−5.59	−0.04	−0.84	−0.33	−6.43
	1980	−0.39	−7.04	−0.07	−1.25	−0.46	−8.29
	1981	0.26	5.31	−0.03	−0.62	0.23	4.69
						−0.56	−10.03
Mexico	1979	0.18	3.32	−0.58	−10.64	−0.40	−7.32
	1980	1.34	21.32	−1.08	−17.21	0.26	4.11
	1981	0.65	8.13	−0.77	−9.64	−0.12	−1.51
						−0.26	−4.72

(The table continues on the following page)

Table 4.2   (continued)

Country	Year	Terms-of-trade effect		Interest rate effect		Total effect	
		GDP_{t-1}	$Exports_{t-1}$	GDP_{t-1}	$Exports_{t-1}$	GDP_{t-1}	$Exports_{t-1}$
Indonesia	1979	4.75	22.60	−0.55	−2.63	4.20	19.97
	1980	5.63	19.81	−0.50	−1.74	5.13	18.07
	1981	1.55	5.51	−0.17	−0.61	1.38	4.90
						10.71	42.94
Nigeria	1979	4.57	28.81	−0.28	−1.77	4.29	27.04
	1980	8.25	37.86	−0.69	−3.16	7.56	34.70
	1981	1.50	5.99	0.08	0. 32	1.58	6.31
						13.43	68.05

Note: The countries are arranged in order of highest to lowest total adverse shock as percentage of GDP.
Merchandise exports are f.o.b.
Source: World Bank data.

however, that Mexico's gain from the terms of trade is understated because the recent rise in oil exports resulted in oil being underweighted in the terms-of-trade index. For similar reasons, Cameroon's loss is overstated.

- The big losers with regard to GDP were Chile, Côte d'Ivoire, Korea, Sri Lanka, and Thailand.
- With regard to exports, Brazil was also a big loser over the three years. Every losing country, except India and Pakistan, suffered considerably in relation to exports in at least one year (total effect as a percentage of exports was 10 percent or more).
- The terms-of-trade shock in 1979–80 was very similar to that of 1974–75, but, because of the world recession, the terms of trade in 1981 continued to worsen for most countries, which is why we have included 1981 in the table. The terms-of-trade shock was less in the latter period for most countries, as might be expected from the fact that the percentage increase in the price of oil was less and some countries had reduced their dependence on oil.

As in chapter 3, we again ask what might have been reasonable expectations in 1979 and 1980 concerning commodity prices and interest rates. In short, was the shock expected to be permanent or temporary?

The World Bank projected—as is now well-known—that the high oil price would not only be permanent but would go on rising at about 3 percent a year in real terms.[8] In dollar terms, the price fell in 1986 to half the average level of 1979. No doubt, expectations varied greatly. Certainly, a good deal of misinvestment resulted. In any event, it is safe to assume that none of the oil-importing countries thought their predicament would soon be relieved by a fall in the price of oil, nor did the oil exporters expect their good fortune to fade away.

Next in importance for several of the countries are coffee prices. After hitting a peak in 1977, they took a sharp fall in 1978, recovered slightly in 1979, dropped once more (in dollar terms) in 1980 and 1981, and then began a slow recovery. Copper prices went up from 1978 to 1980, then went into a sustained fall through 1986 that took them back to the dollar price levels of the late 1970s. Similarly, phosphate prices rose from 1978–81 and then fell back to the levels of the late 1970s. Although the expectations for these volatile commodities are not fully known, countries should have recognized that coffee prices were bound to fall from the exceptional levels of 1978.

As noted in chapter 2, most of the commercial loans that were incurred carried a floating interest rate. So it is possible that they expected some reversal of the rise in rates, which lasted until the third quarter of 1981. Previous experience would have suggested that nominal and real short-term interest rates were likely to fall in a recession.

By and large, the conclusion has to be that the countries could hardly have been expecting any significant reversal of the adverse changes that took place in 1979–81. In fact, the terms-of-trade changes in 1982 and 1983 were somewhat unfavorable for many of our countries, but they were small in comparison with the 1979–81 period.

Chile, Costa Rica, Côte d'Ivoire, Kenya, and Morocco—with a high debt in relation to GNP and a large current account deficit that was rapidly adding to that debt—were already crying out for adjustment in 1979. Korea, Sri Lanka, and Thailand also had huge current account deficits, but their debt was still moderate. All eight, except Costa Rica and Morocco, are to be found in the top half of table 4-2—that is, they suffered relatively large shocks.

Two countries with special problems were Argentina and Brazil. The debt/export ratio was high in both countries, as was inflation: 160 percent in Argentina and 53 percent in Brazil.

Of the eight countries for which the 1979–81 shock was either favorable or fairly small, Indonesia and Nigeria had gained greatly from the 1979 oil price rise and were running current account surpluses. They continued to gain in 1980 and 1981. Mexico had a large current account deficit, but the debt level was still moderate, and the volume of oil production and export was rapidly growing. Cameroon was similar. Pakistan was not so well placed, but its debt was on favorable terms. Colombia and India had modest debt levels; Colombia actually had a current account surplus.

To what extent did our countries' external positions improve or worsen from 1979 to 1982, and to what extent was this change related to the seriousness of their positions in 1979? Broadly, thirteen countries were in a worse position, including most of the countries that were badly placed in 1979 as well as those that were relatively well placed. It was a period in which a potentially modest debt crisis turned into a serious one for many countries. After reviewing the policy reactions, we shall see that neither their initial positions in 1979 nor the depth of the shocks of 1979–82 would have foretold which countries were to suffer recessions and a "debt crisis" (and would have to reschedule their debt or run into arrears, or both). Macroeconomic management was more important than good or bad luck.

The Policy Reaction

As mentioned earlier, Chile, Costa Rica, Côte d'Ivoire, Kenya, Korea, Morocco, Sri Lanka, and Thailand were unfavorably placed in 1979 to meet the impending shock.

Eight Badly Placed Countries

It is instructive to examine the eight cases individually.

CHILE. The events in Chile beginning in 1979 led up to a disastrous recession in 1982 and 1983 and were perhaps the most complex (and fascinating to economists) of those in any of our countries.[9] Here we give only a highly compressed account of the policy reactions. In 1979, Chile was already in the early stages of an investment (and consumption) boom that was unique among our countries in that it was private and was, in its later stages, based on private borrowing abroad. Earlier, from 1978 to 1980, copper prices had risen by 50 percent and masked the oil price rise, as in 1974. The boom continued until the end of 1981.

Initially, the authorities seemed to direct their attention almost exclusively toward reducing inflation (see chapter 7). The public sector deficit had been eliminated, and in 1979 the tablita (a schedule of preannounced devaluations) was ended. The exchange rate was pegged to the dollar, and it was expected that inflation would soon be reduced to world levels. It was in fact reduced, but not very quickly, to about 7 percent a year by the end of 1981. The increases in the current account deficit and foreign borrowing were not regarded as problems. If private institutions overborrowed and went bankrupt, that was a matter of concern only to themselves and their foreign creditors. Provided that the public sector was not in deficit, the money supply could also be left to look after itself.

A great deal went wrong, however. Partly because of the combination of a fixed nominal exchange rate (the peso was pegged to the dollar, which appreciated after 1979) and wage indexation, but also because of a great inflow of foreign funds, the real exchange rate became greatly overvalued. Although GDP continued to rise until the end of 1981, the traded goods sectors experienced increasing difficulty and unemployment mounted. The financial and banking sectors were oligopolistic and largely unsupervised. Many bad loans were made at high interest rates.

In 1981 it became obvious to many that the government's policies were unsustainable, and expectations of devaluation increased. The current account deficit worsened (it reached 15 percent of GNP in that year) as a result of speculative imports of durable goods and higher real interest rates. The collapse came early in 1982. Foreign creditors lost confidence and severely reduced the inflow of funds. This, together with the falling copper price (which fell by a third from 1980 to 1982, back to the level of 1978) and rapidly rising interest payments forced a drastic fall in domestic expenditure. Investment more than halved. At first, the authorities were determined to maintain the fixed exchange rate, and they relied on automatic deflation resulting from the balance of payments deficit to deal with the external problem. In August 1982, after an inadequate 19 percent devaluation in June, they floated the rate. This was a radical departure from previous policies. By the end of 1982, Chile's currency had depreciated by 86 percent in relation to the earlier fixed rate.

COSTA RICA AND COTE D'IVOIRE. These countries have much in common besides their littoral location. Both had an enormous current account deficit in 1979, more or less matched by public sector deficits stemming from public investment and current expenditure booms that continued after the collapse of the coffee boom. Both seem to have undergone a serious loss of fiscal control. The parastatals in both countries, and in Costa Rica's case the central bank, incurred large deficits. The booms had also produced an appreciation of the real exchange rate. A deep recession hit both in 1982 or 1983.

Costa Rica desperately resisted a devaluation, although the colon was probably already overvalued in 1979. In 1982 it became absurdly overvalued when the rate of inflation jumped to 90 percent. The fixed rate had effectively collapsed by 1980 with the development of parallel markets, but the official rate was not devalued until December 1981, and even then not to a realistic level. Fiscal action was delayed until the second half of 1982. During this period, public authorities managed to continue borrowing heavily, despite a moratorium on interest payments to commercial banks that was declared in mid-1981 and lasted two years. Multiple and chaotic experiments took place with the exchange rate regime, to suppress symptoms rather than attack the cause, before the exchange rate was again unified in November 1983.

Côte d'Ivoire did not experience the high inflation of Costa Rica. Its currency was pegged to the French franc, which was depreciating against the dollar, and was probably much less overvalued than Costa Rica's; but devaluation was, in any case, out of the question because Côte d'Ivoire was a member of the franc zone (the implications of this are further discussed in chapters 8 and 10).

Côte d'Ivoire moved to deal with fiscal policy more quickly than Costa Rica did. Public investment was reduced in 1979 and 1980, and controlled interest rates were raised, but serious action was delayed until 1981. The International Monetary Fund (IMF) and the World Bank were approached in November 1980, and funds were obtained from both in 1981. Public investment was drastically cut, and by 1983 was down by 30–40 percent in real terms. Subsidies were reduced and credit tightened. In Costa Rica also, taxes were raised in 1981 and public investment reduced.[10] Despite this action, the deficits were only slightly reduced in 1982, the fiscal measures being offset by rapidly rising interest payments. In both countries, the outcome was severe recession, magnified in the case of Côte d'Ivoire by the drought of 1983.

To sum up, both countries were ill-prepared to meet the terms-of-trade and interest rate shocks, which were especially large for Côte d'Ivoire. Both delayed action, and control of public finances was inadequate. In Costa Rica the refusal to devalue, and the consequently chaotic exchange rate regime, contributed to the problems. Neither country was able to prevent a huge rise in the external debt.

KENYA. The story of Kenya, another coffee exporter, was similar to that of Costa Rica and Côte d'Ivoire, except that it was less dramatic. Government investment and consumption rose as a consequence of rising revenues from the coffee boom, but fiscal discipline was lost, and expenditure rose much faster than revenue. External debt was high, and the current deficit serious in 1979, though neither was as high or as serious as in the case of Costa Rica or Côte d'Ivoire. The terms-of-trade and interest rate shock was much less severe than for Côte d'Ivoire, but similar to that for Costa Rica.

As elsewhere, the authorities were slow to react and foreign and domestic borrowing rose, the former mainly from the IMF and World Bank. Import controls were also tightened. There was some fiscal retrenchment, mainly cuts in public investment in 1981–82, and controlled interest rates were raised. The public deficit was halved between 1980–81 and 1982–83. The government resisted an IMF recommendation to devalue in 1979 but subsequently decided to devalue by 16 percent in 1981 and 24 percent in 1982.

Kenya experienced no actual recession in the period 1980–83, but the growth rate was low, well below the annual population growth rate of about 4 percent.

KOREA. Korea's current account deficit in 1979 was 6.5 percent of GNP and the debt ratio was 36 percent. This threatening situation was primarily the result of a major investment boom in heavy industry promoted by President Park. Since Korea imports all its oil, the terms-of-trade shock was severe.

Some scaling back of the heavy industry program had already started before the oil price rise, since there was some concern that the economy was becoming overheated while exports were losing their competitiveness (the won had been pegged to the dollar since 1974). The 1979 budget was contractionary, and the won was devalued by 36 percent in January 1980. Thus, the Korean authorities acted far more rapidly than those in our other countries.

The situation grew complicated in 1980, however, when the rice crop failed miserably and total agricultural output dropped by about 15 percent. As a result, GNP fell by more than 5 percent—the only recession in Korea since the 1950–53 war. With the help of large loans from the IMF, the authorities moved to counter the recession by expansionary budgetary action in 1980 and 1981. This action was quickly reversed with the strong recovery of output in the period 1981–83. After the devaluation, the exchange rate regime was shifted to a managed float and the won depreciated against the dollar (but not the yen) throughout this period. Like many other countries, Korea experienced an inflationary bubble in 1979–81 (especially in 1980 with the harvest failure), but the exchange rate was manipulated to keep the real exchange rate roughly constant.

With the rapid recovery of output and cautious monetary and fiscal policy in 1982 and 1983, inflation subsided while the dynamism of Korea's exports asserted itself. The current account was almost in balance by 1983. Korea never lost its creditworthiness in the crisis years primarily because the high growth rate of exports kept the debt/export ratio low, even though the debt continued to grow during this period.

MOROCCO. The public investment boom of the mid-1970s, which continued even when phosphate prices were falling, left Morocco with a very high debt, despite some mild retrenchment in 1978, and an unsustainable current account deficit in 1979.

Phosphate prices then began rising in 1979 (and peaked in 1981). Because the increase almost compensated for the oil price rise, Morocco suffered only a small terms-of-trade shock. Undeterred, and apparently mesmerized by phosphate prices, Morocco embarked on a new but short-lived public investment boom. This was brought to an end in 1982 by *force-majeur*. The huge deficits from 1976 through 1981 had been mainly financed by loans from Saudi Arabia and by commercial borrowing. Saudi Arabia now cut its loans, and net loans from commercial banks turned negative. In 1983 Morocco appealed to the IMF and World Bank. Major reforms were initiated (see chapter 5).

In 1973 Morocco had adopted a managed flexible exchange rate after depegging from the French franc. The nominal exchange rate (against a basket of nine currencies) was kept almost constant until 1984, with a small appreciation of the real exchange rate. Import controls were also used to influence the trade balance. Morocco made no attempt to adjust until forced to do so. In 1979–83 real GNP rose by about 2.7 percent a year, despite a recession in 1981 caused by drought.[11]

SRI LANKA. As mentioned in chapter 3, Sri Lanka's new government initiated a phenomenal public sector investment boom in 1977 that brought total investment from about 15 percent of GNP to 34 percent in 1980. Macroeconomic conditions were favorable in 1977. The previous government's contractionary measures, together with a tea boom and increases in remittances and tourism, had produced a current account surplus (the first in a decade or more) despite a large budget deficit (9 percent of GDP). The reserves had risen to an all-time high of eleven months of imports. The mainly concessional debt, at 29 percent of GDP, was not serious. Even more important, aid donors were enthusiastic.

The large terms-of-trade shock beginning in 1978 and continuing to 1983 was caused by falling tea prices, as well as the oil price rise. Between 1978 and 1982 the purchasing power of exports almost halved. The current account balance moved from a surplus of 5 percent of GDP in 1977 to a deficit of 7 percent of GDP in 1979. The authorities did not change their policies in response to the terms-of-trade shock in 1979, for the large deficit was more than covered by concessionary loans. Throughout 1980 the reserves fell and at year-end were equal to only two months of imports. The fiscal deficit reached a phenomenal 26 percent of GNP, and the current account deficit 16 percent.

Some stabilization measures were taken at the end of 1980, two years after the terms-of-trade deterioration became apparent. The budget speech of 1980 noted that the large inflows of foreign aid had undermined financial discipline in several areas of government activity. There was an overall cut-back of capital expenditures, although the "lead" investments—the huge Mahaweli irrigation and power project and the housing program—were by and large protected. The budget deficit was somewhat reduced, but remained very high, about 20 percent through 1983. Interest rates were also raised, and the growth rate of money (M1) reduced. The current account deficit came down to about 10 percent of GNP over the three years 1981–83. From 1979 through 1983, the nominal exchange rate (flexible since 1977) was allowed to depreciate, but the real exchange rate rose.

THAILAND. As in several other cases, the terms-of-trade shock in Thailand came toward the end of a public investment boom. From 1978 through 1981 the growth rate of GDP was very high, averaging nearly 7 percent. Meanwhile, the terms-of-trade deteriorated sharply and continued to do so until 1982. As a result, the current account deficit rose to about 6 percent of GNP in the years 1979–83.

At the same time, several policy adjustments did take place. There was some tempering of the public investment boom after 1981. Thailand has a tradition of conservative monetary policy, and the Bank of Thailand enjoys a measure of independence. Thus, as inflation rose from 8 percent in 1978 to 20 percent in 1980, monetary policy was tightened, so that by 1983 inflation was down to 4 percent, an impressive achievement for it was brought about without a recession—just a decline in the growth rate in 1982 to 4 percent, with a recovery in 1983. The average growth rate for the whole of 1979–83 was more than 5 percent. Thailand is clearly a very flexible economy.

Reserves, which had been equal to about six months of imports at the beginning of the terms-of-trade shock, fell to a low of two months during 1982. There was a minor, and reluctant, devaluation in 1981, putting an end to the long-standing fixed exchange rate regime. Given the deterioration in the terms of trade, more depreciation might have been appropriate. The total (including short-term) debt continued to grow—from 25 percent of GNP in 1980 to 35 percent in 1983. The sustained high growth rate of GNP kept the debt/GNP ratio from rising to intolerable levels in the face of the large current account deficit.

Thailand seems to react in an appropriate manner to changes in the main economic indicators—the reserves, the foreign balance, and inflation—that is, by using monetary, fiscal, and exchange rate policies. It reacts gently, however, which is indeed conservative behavior. By 1983 the overall position was not much different from 1979. There was no crisis. The current account deficit remained quite high, but there was no loss of creditworthiness.

Two Special Cases

Argentina and Brazil are high-inflation countries. Both experimented with using the exchange rate to control inflation. For these reasons, their stories are more fully told in chapter 7. Here we deal briefly with the problems of the 1979–83 period and the preceding events.

ARGENTINA. The regime of Martinez de Hoz as finance minister under General Videla from 1976 to 1981 was marked by efforts to reduce inflation from the very high annual level of 440 percent in 1976, combined with some liberalization of trade and financial markets, and fiscal reform. The fiscal deficit and inflation were reduced in 1977 and 1978. Nonetheless, both remained high, and in December 1978 the government instituted preannounced exchange rate changes (a "tablita") in an effort to reduce inflationary expectations. This did help to bring inflation down to a rate of about 100 percent by the end of 1979 and during 1980. Still, inflation did not fall fast enough to prevent a real appreciation of the peso, accompanied at first by an inflow of capital, which lasted as long as the tablita was believed (international financial transactions had been liberalized).

In 1980, the mild success in reducing the government deficit since 1976 was reversed. This together with the increasing overvaluation of the peso undermined the credibility of the policy, and the capital inflow turned to massive capital flight. During 1980 there was also a major domestic financial crisis, resulting from high real interest rates, low profitability, and bad loans. The Martinez de Hoz policies were in tatters, and the new president, General Viola, made it clear that they would not be continued. Martinez de Hoz left office in March 1981. During 1981 and 1982, there was no coherent policy and economic chaos was magnified by the Malvinas (Falklands) war. Capital flight continued, and the government deficit, inflation, and the foreign debt all rose out of control.

BRAZIL. As mentioned in chapter 3, Brazil made no attempt to adjust to the first oil shock. The expansionary policies continued in the period 1976–78. Through a flexible exchange rate policy, the government was able to keep the real exchange rates reasonably constant. The current account deficit averaged about 4 percent of GNP during this period. The foreign debt doubled, but Brazil was in part borrowing to increase reserves, which rose by about $6 billion in the three years 1976–78, so that the net debt rose much less—by about 30 percent. At the end of 1979, interest on the debt as a proportion of GNP was still modest, but since Brazil, like India, exports little of its output, interest payments were becoming high as a proportion of exports.

In March 1979 a new government under General Figueiredo took office. It was already apparent that the balance of payments was deteriorating, and that inflation was accelerating. Initially, with the well-known economist Mario Simonsen as planning minister, it planned a reduction of the government deficit and some reform of the price mechanism. Delfim Neto then took over as manager of economic policy in August and led Brazil into a full-fledged crisis.[12] He restored policies oriented to accelerated economic growth, despite the deteriorating international situation. Subsidies were increased (including that on petroleum), and interest rates reduced with an anti-inflationary intent. Subsidies rose to more than 3 percent of GDP. Some attempt was made to deal with the current account deficit, which was 4.8 percent of GNP in 1979. Export subsidies were increased, and import deposits required. At the end of the year there was a 30 percent devaluation. Inflation rose to more than 100 percent a year, and the real effects of the December 1979 devaluation were wiped out in a few months. At the end of 1980, the authorities introduced some measures of retrenchment. There was some monetary restriction and increased reliance on bond financing, with the result that interest rates rose. Nevertheless, the inflation-adjusted deficit of the public sector remained high at around 7 percent of GDP in 1981 and 1982.[13] The current account deficit averaged about 5.5 percent over the same period, although there was a sharp recession in 1981 and stagnation in 1982. The public sector deficit was reduced only after it became difficult to borrow abroad following the Mexican moratorium of 1982.

The policies of 1979 and 1980 clearly overheated the economy, which was already producing to capacity, and were certain to worsen the already deteriorating external position, despite superficial measures to limit the trade deficit. The Brazilian mystique of high growth proved to be its own worst enemy. Faced with the need for a relatively minor adjustment, Brazil—rather like Morocco and Sri Lanka—reacted with anti-adjustment.

Eight Well-Placed Countries

The eight well-placed countries divide easily into those that were favored by the oil shock and those that were not. The latter four consist of Colombia, India, Pakistan, and Turkey. None of these countries suffered a serious external shock and they are not to be found in the top half of table 4-2.

COLOMBIA. In contrast to other coffee exporters, Colombia had managed to sterilize the monetary effects of the coffee boom at least in part and had built up reserves, recognizing that the coffee price boom would last only about three years. The authorities initiated a public investment boom in 1979 to counter any recession that the fall in coffee prices might cause. The economy was well placed to take this Keynesian action. The debt was low, the current account was in surplus, the consolidated public sector was in balance, and reserves were high. Thus until the balance of payments crisis in 1984, the government continued stimulating the domestic economy by fiscal and monetary expansion, with ever-increasing public sector and current account deficits financed by a fall in reserves as well as heavy foreign borrowing. A recession was avoided, but the average rate of growth in the years 1980 through 1983 fell to little more than 2 percent a year.

From the point of view of maintaining demand for domestic output in the face of the fall in coffee prices and generally reduced world demand, this stimulation of demand appeared appropriate, at least as a short-run policy. Even so, there was a conflict between internal and external balance. This might have been resolved with a greater rate of nominal depreciation, leading to real depreciation. Although Colombia had for long practiced a crawling peg exchange rate regime, the real exchange rate had appreciated during the coffee boom and was allowed to appreciate further in 1980–83 with a view to restraining inflation, which was running at more than 20 percent a year.

INDIA. India shows some similarity to Colombia. Through cautious fiscal policies it built up large reserves of foreign exchange (and cereals) during the second half of the 1970s. The current account was in surplus in 1978. The foreign debt was trifling, and inflation was zero. Unlike Colombia, India suffered a serious shock in 1979. The terms-of-trade shock in relation to GDP was modest, but there was a severe drought and foodgrain production fell 18 percent. Exports were also sluggish, partly because the real exchange rate appreciated with the burst of inflation in 1979–80, and oil production was disrupted by political and industrial disturbances in Assam.

In sharp contrast to 1974, the government decided not to take deflationary action (the shocks must have helped reduce the demand for nonagricultural goods and services in any case) but to allow some rise in public sector borrowing and to finance the external deficit by the use of reserves and borrowing. Although GDP fell by more than 5 percent in 1979, it recovered sharply in 1980–81 and grew further in 1981–82. The government took some restrictive fiscal action in that year, and inflation subsided. It also obtained a large loan from the IMF.

As in Colombia, the real exchange rate was allowed to appreciate, and the current account scarcely improved, running at about 1.5 percent of GNP from 1981 through 1984. Unlike Colombia, however, India had no balance of payments crisis in 1984. Although both countries had similar public sector deficits from 1981 to 1983, India's current account deficit and foreign borrowing were much smaller. Private domestic savings financed a much larger proportion of the public borrowing requirement.

PAKISTAN. Pakistan's terms-of-trade shock in 1979 and the following years was minor and was largely offset by rising remittances from Pakistani workers in the Middle East. Nevertheless, fiscal and monetary policies were quite tight, and the public sector deficit was reduced. Even so, GNP grew rapidly in 1979–80 (by more than 8 percent). Although the current account deficit was little changed (at about 4–5 percent), reserves were low, and an IMF loan was negotiated. As in the case of the later IMF loan to India, this seems to have been obtained mainly for precautionary reasons. In January 1982, the dollar peg was abandoned in favor of a managed float. The real exchange rate, which had appreciated significantly since 1979, was thereafter allowed to depreciate. The current account deficit averaged about 3 percent of GNP over the period 1980–81 to 1983–84, and the debt/GNP ratio remained constant. The growth rate of GNP remained high, averaging more than 6 percent. Pakistan reacted quickly and appropriately and never let matters get out of hand.

TURKEY. Turkey had its debt crisis in 1977, ahead of the rest of the developing world. It had borrowed massively to finance the public spending boom, as well as the higher costs of oil imports. In addition, the income from remittances declined. The current account deficit rose to 6.9 percent of GNP in 1977. Most of the debt was short-term. With the debt/export ratio reaching unsustainable levels (particularly because Turkey's export/GDP ratio was exceptionally low), there was a crisis of confidence, and private capital inflow suddenly dried up. As a result of import restrictions and a decline in investment, the current account improved. Even so, inflation rose to 57 percent in 1978 and reached 110 percent in 1980, when there was a big devaluation. The question of the extent to which the current account improvement was connected with the increase in inflation in this and other episodes is discussed in chapter 7.

By 1979 the debt situation had become viable because of a massive rescheduling in 1978 (short-term debt was reduced from about half the total in 1978 to less than a quarter in 1979). The terms of trade did deteriorate in 1979 and 1980 as a result of the oil price rise, but this hardly seems to have been noticed amid the political and civil turmoil and the economic consequences of the "bust" of 1977. The current account deficit rose to 6.1 percent of GNP in 1980, but with IMF support this was easily financed.

The Demirel government, elected in November 1979, initiated major reforms in January 1980. They encompassed all areas of macroeconomic policy, the trade regime and the exchange rate, fiscal policy, and interest rates. They should be seen more as a delayed response to the events of 1977 and the turmoil of the next two years than as anything to do with the oil price shock. They also constituted a complete change of economic philosophy from the highly dirigiste inward-looking regime that had prevailed since the 1950s toward an open economy that would rely much more on the incentives of the price mechanism. This change was well supported by the IMF and bilateral donors. Among our countries, only Chile in 1974 and after, and Sri Lanka in 1977, reoriented policies as dramatically as Turkey did.

In January 1980, the exchange rate was devalued by 100 percent, and thereafter frequent adjustments resulted in further real depreciation. Export subsidies were increased, and imports were increasingly liberalized in 1981–83. The export response was dramatic despite the recession in OECD countries. The dollar value of exports doubled in 1980–82 and led the way out of the recession of 1979 and 1980. Over the next three years, GDP rose by more than 4 percent a year. Current account deficits were reduced to manageable levels. Budget deficits remained rather high—more than 5 percent of GDP, but in 1982 inflation fell from 110 percent to 31 percent. Problems remained, but Turkey had finally recovered from the 1977 crisis, taking the terms-of-trade deterioration in its stride.

The other four well-placed countries were the oil exporters: Cameroon, Indonesia, Mexico, and Nigeria. The favorable terms-of-trade shock in 1979 for Indonesia and Nigeria was huge. For Mexico it was small, and for Cameroon apparently negative, but oil output and exports were rising fast in both countries. Thus, in Mexico mining accounted for about 4 percent of GNP in 1979, rising to 10 percent in 1982, by which time oil accounted for about 75 percent of exports. (In Indonesia in 1982, comparable figures were 19 percent and 67 percent.) In Cameroon, oil production rose from about 3 percent of GDP in 1979 to 27 percent in 1982, and oil exports from 9 percent of the total to 48 percent.[14]

CAMEROON. The terms-of-trade shock for Cameroon was concentrated in 1979, which marked the end of the coffee and cocoa boom. Oil exports began in 1977 but were still only 10 percent of total exports in 1979. There were some deflationary changes in 1979 as the central budget changed from balance to a 3 percent surplus (of GDP), and domestic credit expansion was reduced. Despite this reduction and the fall in export prices, GDP apparently rose by 5 percent, and inflation fell from 12 percent to 7 percent.

After 1979, rising oil exports overcompensated any balance of payments effect of the terms-of-trade deterioration. By 1982 oil exports were about 50 percent of the total. The current account nevertheless deteriorated in 1980 and 1981 before improving and becoming a surplus in 1984. Cameroon's current account and budgetary figures are highly unreliable, however, especially since oil receipts are an official secret. Except for 1982, when there was a setback (but no recession) as a result of drought, GDP grew rapidly. The debt/GNP ratio remained roughly constant.

The notable feature of Cameroon's policy is that the authorities did not borrow on top of the rise in export and government revenues, as happened in Nigeria, Mexico, and to a lesser extent Indonesia. Indeed, they sequestered oil revenues abroad, in part by prepaying external debt, and thereby largely avoided Dutch disease effects.[15] Apparently, they had learned from the disastrous results of the oil boom in Nigeria.

INDONESIA. The rupiah was devalued by 51 percent in November 1978 (chapter 3), primarily to give a boost to the production and exports of the nonoil tradable sectors, agriculture and manufacturing. This objective was met in 1979 with a leap in both the volume and value of nonoil exports. However, the oil price rise of 1979 boosted inflation. Indonesia spent the oil revenues, and the monetary effects could not be sterilized. The effects of the devaluation on the real exchange rate (PPP measure) were eroded by 1981, although the price of tradables in relation to nontradables still favored tradables as compared with 1978. The current account changed from a deficit of 2.7 percent in 1978 to a surplus of 4.0 percent in 1980, and the reserves rose. The investment boom, which had begun in 1975, continued, and investment/GNP remained on a high plateau of about 30 percent in 1981–83; GDP rose very fast until 1982, when there was a slight recession caused by bad weather. In contrast, the balance of payments began to deteriorate in 1981 and continued to do so through 1983. The volume of oil exports fell in 1982 as a result of a reduction in the quotas of the Organization of Petroleum Exporting Countries (OPEC), and the fall in oil prices started in the same year; other export prices also weakened. The dollar value of exports fell by about 9 percent, while that of imports rose by 41 percent from 1980 to 1982. The current account deficit reached 5.9 percent from the surplus of 4 percent in 1980.

The authorities reacted quite strongly. They devalued the rupiah by 38 percent in March 1983, cut public investment, and put many other reforms into effect. They took this action even though the debt/GNP ratio had actually fallen from 1979 to 1982. Note, too, that the debt-service ratio was only 18 percent in 1982 because of the relatively high export/GNP ratio and the favorable composition of the debt. Indonesia never rescheduled and remained creditworthy. The contrast with Mexico and Nigeria is interesting, and we return to this later.

MEXICO. After pausing for breath in 1976, Mexico initiated a second major public investment and expenditure boom in 1977. This was floated on the tide of rapidly rising oil revenues, and the terms-of-trade "shock" of 1979 was favorable. As happened in most other countries where revenue was booming, the rise in expenditure greatly exceeded the rise in revenue. The situation was still under control in 1980, but there was no attempt to slow the momentum of the rise in public expenditures. Inflation reached 30 percent and, as the exchange rate was fixed to the dollar, the real exchange rate appreciated. During 1981 the public deficit became enormous—about 14 percent of GDP[16]—although GDP rose by about 8 percent (as it had been doing since 1978). The current account deficit was 6.7 percent of GNP. Interest rates had risen, and the oil price had peaked, but public expenditure continued to rise in 1982, when the crunch came. Meanwhile, a massive capital flight had begun in 1981 in anticipation of a devaluation, which continued through February 1982, when the peso was devalued by 68 percent (over the whole of 1982 the nominal devaluation was 268 percent). The public deficit, however, was not reduced; it was financed by inflation, which rose to nearly 100 percent. The balance of payments and financial crisis lasted throughout 1982.

The story of this crisis year, the belated efforts to deal with the crisis, and the events of the later 1980s belong to chapter 5. Here we note only that the debt rose beyond 50 percent of GNP, while GDP began to fall, despite the rise in public expenditure. In 1982 it fell by 0.5 percent and in 1983 by 5.3 percent.

Mexico's crisis came a little earlier than in most other countries and precipitated problems in some of them when Mexico's moratorium on debt repayment began to undermine confidence in international lending. The crisis was entirely self-inflicted. The ship could be seen to be heading for the rocks, but the captain did not shorten sail, let alone change course.

NIGERIA. In 1978, Nigeria was still near the summit of the great investment boom of the 1970s, but a fall in the quantity and price of oil exports in that year resulted in both a fall in GDP and a large current account deficit. The oil price rise came to the rescue in 1979 and 1980, when GDP rose and the current account moved to a large surplus (5.2 percent of GNP in 1980).

There was also a return to democracy and civilian government in 1979, which lasted through 1983—a dark period in Nigeria's economic history, eclipsed only by the civil war of the 1960s. Competitive distributional demands ensured that public expenditure continued to mushroom and that there was a shift of emphasis from investment to consumption, although a few huge projects were retained, notably the steel works and the new capital at Abuja. The public sector and the current account were in massive deficit in 1981 and 1982. The naira was clearly overvalued, and capital flight became important. Despite this, the current expenditure estimates in the 1982 budget were almost doubled.

The three years 1981–83 were marked by fiscal irresponsibility and the absence of any coherent policy. The states were allowed to borrow abroad from 1980 and both they and the federal government did so until this easy way out began to be closed by foreign creditors in 1982. Even so, several states defaulted on domestic payments in 1981, and many projects were halted as a result. Some federal action was forced in April 1982 by the shortage of foreign exchange. Devaluation was not considered, but there was some reduction in public expenditure and imports were cut by licensing, an increase in duties, and an import deposit scheme. This was insufficient, and both trade and interest arrears were incurred. In January 1983, import licensing became even more restrictive, inflation rose to more than 20 percent in that year, and GNP slumped by 5 percent (it had already fallen by 7 percent in 1981 with no change in 1982). From 1981 to 1983, investment collapsed from 22 percent to 12 percent of GNP while consumption rose from 84 percent to 93 percent. The government fell to a military coup in January 1984. The foreign debt had risen from 8 percent of GNP at the end of 1979 to 21 percent. Although this was still low by world standards, Nigeria had lost all credibility. The economy was depressed, and suffering from import starvation. Inflation was high, and the exchange rate by now grossly overvalued. The policies of the new military government are discussed in chapter 5.

Indonesia Compared with Mexico and Nigeria

Some key features of the three economies for the period 1979–83 are given in table 4-3. To begin with, oil as a proportion of GNP was much smaller in Mexico than in Indonesia. Thus, mining in Mexico was only 4.3 percent of GNP in 1979, rising to 12 percent in 1983. In Indonesia, the production of oil and liquid natural gas was 25 percent of GNP in 1979, falling to 18 percent in 1983. These figures are not exactly comparable, of course, but they show the orders of magnitude. Mexico's total exports were only 12 percent of GDP in 1979, whereas Indonesia's were 30 percent. Mexico's oil exports were 45 percent of the total in 1979, rising to 71 percent in 1983. Comparable figures for Indonesia were 57 percent and 64 percent, respectively. Thus, there was not a big difference in the importance of oil for the balance of payments in the period we are considering. Both countries ran into large and similar current account deficits, Mexico in 1981 and Indonesia in 1983, on the order of 7–8 percent of GNP. Neither country used exchange controls.

Why then did Mexico experience a shipwreck in 1982, while Indonesia sailed through the troubled waters? There are two main reasons: one is that Mexico had been imprudent in the constitution of its debt, and the other is that the authorities seemed to have lost control. At the end of 1981, Mexico's debt/GNP ratio was not much higher than that of Indonesia, 33 percent against 25 percent. But the ratio of debt service to exports in 1981 was *very* different, 52 percent against 14 percent, owing to the high proportion of Mexico's short-term debt (which required more amortization) and its low export ratio. In 1981 the Mexican economy was obviously in a serious disequilibrium, but the authorities did nothing either to reduce the public sector deficit or to ameliorate the increasing overvaluation of the peso as inflation accelerated. There was massive capital flight well before the devaluation in February 1982, and even then fiscal action was still delayed. In contrast, the Indonesian authorities did not lose credibility. In the light of their far better debt-service position and higher reserves, the situation was much less threatening in Indonesia in 1982 than in Mexico in 1981, but Indonesia devalued and also took fiscal action in March 1983. There was no significant capital flight.

It is also interesting to compare Indonesia and Nigeria.[17] Both countries incurred current account deficits of about 8 percent of GNP, Nigeria in 1982 and Indonesia in 1983. There, apart from the importance of oil, the resemblance ends. From 1980 to 1983 the volume of Nigeria's crude oil exports was cut in half, while that of Indonesia remained unchanged. The oil ministry in Nigeria had played a losing game against the market: first, it overpriced and lost sales; and later, in 1980, it reneged on contracts when the spot market price rose above the contract price, with the result that buyers reneged when the spot price fell in 1981. Because of these strategies, and also because nonoil exports rose in Indonesia and fell in Nigeria, the dollar value of Nigeria's exports fell by 60 percent from 1980 to 1983 and those of Indonesia by only 14 percent.

Indonesia thus ran into a large deficit mainly because of a rise in imports. Nigeria incurred a similar deficit *despite* a large fall in imports. Nigeria's huge loss of export income necessitated a reduction in imports that was damaging to production in the nonoil sectors of the economy. It also lost creditworthiness. Indonesia, with a relatively small fall in export value, retained creditworthiness and had no need to curtail imports. Except in 1982, GDP continued to grow, while the Nigerian

Table 4.3   Three Major Oil Exporters, 1979 and 1983
(percentage, billions of dollars)

Item	Year	Indonesia		Mexico		Nigeria	
Oil production/GNP	1979	25		4		27	
	1983	18		12		15	
Oil exports/total exports	1979	57		45		93	
	1983	64		71		96	
Current account deficits/							
GNP	1979	−1.9		4.0		−2.4	
	1983	7.7		−3.9		5.6	
Maximum current	1981			6.7			
account deficits/GNP	1982					9.4	
	1983	7.7					
Debt/GNP	1981	25		33		13	
	1983	39		66		21	
Debt service/exports	1981	14		5		29	
	1983	20		52		24	
		Exports	*Imports*	*Exports*	*Imports*	*Exports*	*Imports*
Trade data							
(balance of payments	1979	15.2	9.2	9.3	12.1	16.8	11.9
basis, f.o.b., billions	1980	21.8	12.6	15.5	18.9	25.9	14.8
of dollars)	1981	23.3	16.5	20.1	23.9	18.1	18.9
	1982	19.7	17.9	21.2	14.4	12.2	14.9
	1983	18.7	17.7	22.3	8.6	10.3	11.4

Source: *International Financial Statistics* and *World Debt Tables* (1989–90). Data for production taken from country studies and World Bank data.

economy was deeply depressed. Indonesia devalued in January 1983 and reversed the real appreciation of the currency that both countries had been experiencing since 1980. In Nigeria, the real appreciation continued until 1985, and import starvation worsened.

In contrast with Nigeria, Mexico's crisis was not due to a fall in exports, but to a jump in imports. As already explained, a similar surge in imports did not produce a crisis in Indonesia. Both Mexico and Nigeria had overvalued currencies in 1981 and 1982, and both suffered from capital flight. Both countries were in recession in 1982 and 1983 with a severe compression of imports.

The Nature of the Crisis and Its Causes

What distinguishes the countries that were in deep trouble by the end of 1982? In table 4-4 the countries are arranged in three groups. The first includes the eight debt-crisis countries whose debt was to be rescheduled. Some, including Costa Rica, Mexico, and Nigeria, had already declared a moratorium or were in arrears on commercial debt, but for the others the debt crisis was still in the future. Before discussing the determinants of "deep trouble," we therefore need to say more about its meaning.

Debt and the Current Account

"Deep trouble" means a lack of creditworthiness (or adequate reserves) combined with a severe current account deficit. This combination forces a large and rapid deflation (to improve the trade balance) or a default on the debt service, or both. The required improvements in the trade balance usually cannot be brought about without causing a recession. In such a situation, a country will normally request debt rescheduling in order to avoid default and to reduce the magnitude of the required improvement in the trade account.

As can be seen in table 4-1, the current account deficit in 1982 was enormous for Chile, Costa Rica, Côte d'Ivoire, and Morocco (in excess of 10 percent); and very large for Brazil (6.0 percent) and Nigeria (7.9 percent). Only Argentina and Mexico had relatively modest deficits (less than 5 percent). Whether such deficits can be financed depends, of course, on the existing debt situation. The debt/export ratio was extremely threatening for Argentina, Brazil, Chile, Côte d'Ivoire, Mexico, and Morocco. Although Costa Rica's debt to GNP was the highest of all, and the debt/export ratio also high, the debt-service ratio was only moderately high: but Costa Rica had already defaulted and rescheduled, and was obviously not creditworthy. Nigeria's debt and debt service were low, but it was nevertheless in arrears, and fiscal mismanagement rendered it uncreditworthy.

For the second group of three "intermediate" countries in table 4-4—Colombia, Kenya, and Sri Lanka—their current account and debt statistics suggest trouble, but they managed to avoid a debt crisis and recession. Colombia needs some explanation, for the current account deficit in 1982 was very high (8 percent), and the debt/export ratio quite high—although the debt/GNP and interest/GNP ratios were modest. About half of the debt was to official creditors, including the World Bank. Reserves were very high in 1980 (more than twelve months of imports). They were run down but remained high (eight months) even at the end of 1982. Colombia was determined to service the debt, and lenders, including the commercial banks, were prepared to continue lending on a scale that permitted this.

Kenya's deficit, though still high, had been much reduced since 1979. The debt ratios were quite high, but Kenya's policies seemed reasonably orthodox and flexible. Some adjustment was in train, and the exchange rate was used. The IMF

Table 4.4   Disequilibrium Factors

Country	Bad start	Big bad shock	Inaction	Lack of fiscal control	Real ex-change rate appreciation	Recession 1980–82
Troubled						
Argentina	N	N	Y	Y	N[a]	Y
Brazil	N	Y	Y	Y	N[a]	Y
Chile	Y	Y	Y	N	Y	Y
Costa Rica	Y	N	Y	Y	N[a]	Y
Côte d'Ivoire	Y	Y	Y	Y	N	Y
Mexico	N	N	Y	Y	Y	Y
Morocco	Y	N	Y	N	N[b]	Y
Nigeria	N	N	Y	Y	Y	Y
Intermediate						
Colombia	N	N	Y	Y	N	N
Kenya	Y	Y	Y	Y	N	N
Sri Lanka	Y	Y	N	N	Y	N
Untroubled						
Cameroon	N	Y[c]	N	N	N	N
India	N	N	N	N	Y	Y
Indonesia	N	N	N	N	Y	Y
Korea	Y	Y	N	N	N	Y
Pakistan	N	N	N	N	N	N
Thailand	Y	Y	N	N	Y	N
Turkey	N	N	N	N	N	Y

Note: Whether or not a country could be characterized by the title of the column heading is indicated by a Y or N in the appropriate cell. Bad start—current account deficit/GDP > 5.6% in 1979 (see Table 4.1) Big shock—total negative effect/GDP > –4.3% in 1979 (see Table 4.2). Inaction—see text. Lack of fiscal control—see text. Recession—actual fall in annual GDP. Real exchange rate appreciation—percentage appreciation of the real exchange rate from 1979(1) to 1982(2) > 15%.
a. These countries all had periods of rapid real appreciation. In Argentina, there was a huge apprecia-tion from 1978(1) to 1981(1), followed by a fall back to the levels of 1978. In Brazil the real exchange rate fell from 1978(1) to 1980(1), but then rose by 45% to 1982(3). In Costa Rica, the real exchange rate appreciated from 1978(1) to 1980(4), before falling back to 1978 levels.
b. The lack of real appreciation in the period 1979–82 does not imply that the currency was not over-valued during that period. In the case of Morocco our author argues that the dirham was overvalued relative to 1970, taken to be an equilibrium year for the exchange rate.
c. In Cameroon the terms-of-trade shock was offset by a rising volume of oil exports.
Source: World Bank data.

helped with standbys, and Kenya did not default or demand rescheduling. It took pride in meeting its commitments, a high proportion of which were to official lenders.

In the case of Sri Lanka, the current account deficit was enormous. Although the debt/GNP ratio was also high, the terms were favorable and debt service quite low. Above all, aid donors and the World Bank were happy with the liberal reforms and were prepared to give much support.

The remaining seven "untroubled" countries require little comment. In 1982, their current account deficits were very modest, except for Cameroon and Indonesia, where the debt figures were not alarming. They remained creditworthy.

Inaction and Fiscal Control

Whether or not the countries identified as "troubled," "intermediate," or "untroubled" in table 4-4 could be characterized as having suffered a "bad start," "big bad shock," "inaction," "lack of fiscal control," "currency overvaluation," or "recession" is indicated by a Yes (Y) or No (N) in the table. The criteria for this assessment are given in the note to table 4-4.

The categories "inaction" and "lack of fiscal control" need some discussion, since it is a matter of judgment whether a country has these loosely defined characteristics, and we could be accused of taking a peep into the future before deciding. "Inaction" means a failure to try to reduce absorption by fiscal or monetary action. We believe our ascriptions are well supported by the country studies on which this volume is based, although it should be noted that "inaction" may include obviously inadequate or very delayed action. Kenya is a borderline case. It was already experiencing a serious problem in 1979, but fiscal action was delayed until 1981–82. Nonetheless, the public deficit was halved from 1980–81 to 1982–83. Chile is a special case in that inaction refers to the failure to devalue, for Chile was running a public sector surplus.

Of course, if no action was required, there is no point in recording inaction. In fact, all the countries for which table 4-4 records No (N) for inaction did take some deflationary fiscal or monetary action in the period, except possibly Indonesia.

Lack of fiscal control means that the Finance Ministry was unable to control public expenditure, usually because parastatal institutions or state governments were able to borrow, either from the central bank or abroad, without the sanction or even knowledge of the Finance Ministry. It could also be because political conditions made the Finance Ministry too weak to curb other central government ministries. This lack of control is ascribed only if our country studies refer to it explicitly. A No (N) does not mean, however, that fiscal discipline was as good as may be desirable.

It is clear from table 4-4 that fiscal and monetary inaction, often accompanied by lack of fiscal control, is by far the best discriminant of whether a country was in deep trouble by the end of 1982. Indeed, table 4-4 strongly suggests that the initial conditions have little significant independent explanatory value.

Real Exchange Rate Appreciation

The *y* sign in table 4-4 indicates a real effective exchange appreciation in excess of 15 percent between the first quarter of 1979 and the second quarter of 1982. Appreciation does not necessarily imply that the currency was overvalued, but the country studies suggest that this was the case. At first glance, it might seem that there was no relation between overvaluation and the debt crisis in the countries that experienced the appreciation, but the footnotes to table 4-4 indicate that Argentina, Brazil, and Costa Rica, had large real appreciations during part of the period. The Moroccan country study for this volume (Claassen unpublished) also suggests that the dirham was overvalued in the period 1979–82.

This evidence for overvaluation in turn suggests a relationship with the debt crisis, as might be expected. When the exchange rate becomes incredible, and the authorities delay devaluation, large capital outflows are probable. Capital flight may be moderated by high real interest rates, but they would have to be extremely high, and disturbing for the internal financial system and for domestic investment, if a maxidevaluation is widely expected. Exchange controls may be used but are unlikely to prevent major outflows where the incentive to evade them is strong. In the early 1980s, huge flows of capital poured out of Argentina, Mexico, and Nigeria, and, to a lesser extent, from Brazil and Chile. Indonesia—which has no exchange controls—recognized the need to devalue in time, and avoided the problem. Exchange controls and capital flight are further discussed in chapter 8.

Since the debt crisis and recession are closely associated, as table 4-4 shows, an association of overvaluation and recession follows. Korea and Turkey are exceptions; they experienced a recession but no real currency appreciation. The recession in Korea was caused wholly or mainly by drought, while Turkey's recession of 1980 was a hangover from the troubles of the late 1970s, soon to be replaced by recovery.

There are only three cases of probable overvaluation without recession: India, Sri Lanka, and Thailand. In India, the exchange rate was irrelevant for imports because of extensive controls, while exports were far too small in relation to GDP for their sluggish behavior to have caused a recession in this period. In Sri Lanka, the overvaluation was caused by the high capital inflow that supported the boom; the investment boom caused a real appreciation, without the latter causing a recession. To a lesser extent, the same applied to Thailand, where the real appreciation was, in any case, quite modest.

Recessions, 1980–83

All the countries in the first group of table 4-4 experienced a recession in the period 1980–83, as well as serious trouble on the external front. The reasons for the recession varied, and included natural disaster, falling export earnings and private investment, and cuts in public expenditures to combat inflation or improve the balance of payments. The withdrawal of foreign credit was the immediate cause in only a minority of cases.

In Argentina, the recession originated with the overvaluation of the currency resulting from the predetermined exchange rate scale—that is, the tablita. This was followed by the collapse of the tablita and capital flight, which led to very high interest rates, bank failures, and general uncertainty. Both public and private investment collapsed. In Brazil in 1981, monetary restrictions and increased reliance on bond financing in the face of inflation also resulted in very high interest rates and a fall in investment. In Chile, overvaluation of the currency, falling copper prices, rapidly rising interest payments, and bank failures combined to cause a collapse of investment, which more than halved from 1981 to 1983. As in 1975, Chile had the biggest recession of all in 1982, with a 15 percent fall in GDP. Costa Rica had its own debt crisis in 1981. As elsewhere in Latin America, investment fell sharply in 1981 and 1982. The currency had become highly overvalued. A delayed large devaluation in 1981 added to the inflation that had made it necessary. This produced a severe monetary squeeze, in addition to which the government raised taxes to try to reduce the yawning budgetary deficit. A rise in net borrowing especially from official sources coincided. In Côte d'Ivoire, the authorities undertook deflationary action in 1981, including large cuts in public investment, in the face of a huge current account deficit (18 percent of GNP). Net borrowing peaked in 1982 when the recession began. It was exacerbated in 1983 by a fall in agricultural production due to drought. In Mexico, the fall in borrowing in 1982 was combined with capital flight. The consequential and necessary massive correction of the current account deficit in 1982 and 1983 could not be achieved without deflation and extremely severe cuts in imports. Between 1981 and 1983 the current account moved from a deficit of 6.7 percent of GNP to a surplus of 3.9 percent. Investment fell by about 45 percent, and the volume of imports by about 60 percent; GDP fell by about 5 percent. In Nigeria, the recession of 1981 through 1983 was accompanied by a large rise in net borrowing and inward transfer of resources. The fall in oil exports (quantity and price) and the widening of the deficit prompted a severe compression of imports, by means of controls. This, together with a burst of inflation and the consequential monetary squeeze, and the uncertainty caused by chaotic internal conditions, resulted in a collapse of investment (from 22 percent of GNP to 12 percent). Morocco's recession in 1981 was mainly due to drought. Investment continued to rise, and the recession was short-lived as agricultural output recovered in 1982. In both these respects, Morocco differs from the other reschedulers. It did have a crisis in 1983, however, as a result of the withdrawal of credit. There was a large fall in inward transfers, which nonetheless remained positive, and investment fell. The recession was slight and short-lived.

Only a few recessions occurred in the nonrescheduling countries in the period 1980–83. Turkey's GDP fell in 1980; this was the tail end of a recession caused by the debt crisis of 1977. Korea, too, had a recession in 1980, but it was entirely due to agricultural failure. Indonesia's slight recession in 1982 was mainly due to bad weather.

Clearly, few of the recessions of the early 1980s can be attributed to a drying up of foreign credit. It was the immediate cause only in Mexico and Morocco (in 1983), and perhaps in Costa Rica and Turkey with their own prior debt crises. The recessions among the other reschedulers were, except for Morocco in 1981, a byproduct of trying belatedly to cope with high and rising current account deficits, and with inflation in some of the Latin American countries. Chapter 5 examines further the contribution of the fall in foreign credit and high debt service to the slow recovery from recession.

The recessions experienced by all eight reschedulers, except for Morocco, extended over several years, whereas the few recessions among the others were one-year affairs. The pre-recession annual level of output was exceeded only after three years in Côte d'Ivoire, four years in Costa Rica and Mexico, five years in Brazil, and six years in Chile. In Argentina and Mexico, the output level of 1988 was still below that of 1980. Except in Morocco, all these recessions were far deeper than anything experienced in the developed countries since 1945. From peak to trough, they ranged from about 4.5 percent in the case of Côte d'Ivoire to about 14 percent in Chile. Five of these deep recessions were in Latin America.

These varying recession episodes raise important issues, some of which are taken up again later in this book (chapters 5, 7, and 11), while some require more research to resolve. Most have in common a fall in real aggregate demand caused either by external events or by government intervention to correct an unviable balance of payments, or both. This fall in demand typically results in a Keynesian recession.

In no country are prices and wages completely flexible downward, so there is no mystery about such a recession. The degree of downward flexibility is likely to vary, however, but to be less in more urbanized or industrialized countries. In 1981 in Latin America, the proportion of the GDP arising in agriculture ranged from 7 percent in Chile to 23 percent in Costa Rica. In Nigeria, the proportion was 23 percent and in Côte d'Ivoire, 27 percent. Our country studies show that during the 1980s real wages fell substantially in most Latin American countries, including Argentina, Brazil, and, above all, Mexico. This does not mean, however, that nominal wages were instantaneously flexible downward when there was a decline in nominal demand. The declines in real wages were accompanied by inflation. Inflation in a depressed real economy led to a fall in real wages.

In addition, in some countries, notably Mexico and Nigeria later, recessions induced by external shocks had a "supply-side" element. Imports had to be reduced drastically, this being done quickly with quantitative import restrictions, and the reduced availability of imported inputs then led to reduced domestic production. This is "import starvation." Import restrictions, like a devaluation, might be expected to switch demand away from imports toward domestically produced goods, and so to moderate a recession, but this effect is likely to take some time. In the short run, the import starvation effect is usually stronger.

Nominal devaluation should also switch expenditure toward home-produced goods, at least provided that it leads to real devaluation for a reasonable length of time (see chapter 8). This switching effect would certainly not be instantaneous. If there is a sharp fall in demand, some recession is inevitable.

Recessions may not only be induced directly or indirectly by external shocks or by a correction of previous overexpansionary policies; they may also (notably in India) result from droughts—which is a domestic supply-side effect—or from inflation stabilization policies (chapter 7). A usual byproduct of such policies is a real appreciation, which makes the production of tradables uncompetitive.

The experiences of Chile and Mexico are instructive in this regard. The Chilean recession was far greater. Chile's GDP fell 14 percent in 1982, compared with Mexico's decline of 4.2 percent in 1983. Both countries suffered severe terms-of-trade declines, but Chile more so, and the reduction in inward resource transfer between 1980 and 1983 was about the same (although much greater for Chile in comparison with the boom year 1981). Since Chile had wage indexation and was also more urbanized, its economy was in all likelihood more rigid. Both devalued in 1982, although Chile was a little slower to do so, and its policymakers have been criticized on that ground. Chile's growth rate rapidly recovered after the recession, however, while Mexico's stayed low. Furthermore, Mexico continued to struggle with high inflation, while Chile settled at a moderate inflation rate (about 20 percent). The depth of the Chilean slump may have had some longer-term benefit in moderating inflation in later years.

Chapter 5

A Slow Recovery for Most: 1983–89

A dominant feature of the 1980s was the reduction in resource transfers to developing countries after 1982. The reason for this change was not that international capital had become more expensive. In real terms (adjusted by the U.S. gross domestic product [GDP] deflator), the LIBOR (London interbank offered rate) remained in the range of 6.5–7.0 percent from 1981 to 1984 and then fell to 4 percent in 1987. Transfers declined primarily because some countries, including those that had absorbed much capital in 1978–82, lost their creditworthiness.

Almost all of our eighteen countries relied less on an inflow of resources from abroad (hereinafter referred to simply as transfers) after 1982 than before. The transfers are measured by the current account deficit less interest paid abroad plus remittances. Remittances are here defined as the sum of public and private unrequited transfers as given in international financial statistics. They consist mainly of remittances from nationals working abroad and grants from official donor agencies. Appendix tables 5A-1 to 5A-18 give the figures country by country and year by year.

In the case of some highly indebted countries, interest reached more than 10 percent of the GNP. Interest payments have been erratic, however, especially in countries that failed to pay and whose debt was rescheduled.[1] Table 5-1 therefore shows the average resource flows for the sexennia 1977–82 and 1983–88; it also shows the current account, interest, and remittance components of the 1983–88 transfers separately, and the maximum fall in transfers from one year to the next. The countries are arranged in order of size of reduction in inward transfers (column 3).

The presence of the Republic of Korea in the top half of table 5-1 is sufficient warning that it must be interpreted with care. The change in transfers is not always an exogenous event outside the country's control. Korea did not lose creditworthiness, but considered it desirable to reduce the foreign debt. Its large current account deficits around 1980 were rapidly reduced and became large surpluses after 1986.[2]

Table 5.1 Resource Transfers, Current Account Deficit, and Outward Interest Payments

(percentage of GNP)

Country[a]	Average inward resource transfer, 1977–82 (1)[b]	Average inward resource transfer, 1983–88 (2)[c]	Reduction in inward resource transfer (3)[d]	Average current account deficit, 1983–88 (4)	Average interest paid, 1983–88 (5)	Average remittance income, 1983–88 (6)	Maximum annual change in transfers (7)	Year of maximum change in transfers (8)
Côte d'Ivoire	2.7	−7.5	−10.2	6.5	9.7	−4.3	−14.6	1984
Costa Rica	9.8	0.8	−9.0	5.0	8.8	4.6	−15.8	1983
Chile	4.0	−4.1	−8.1	6.8	10.6	−0.3	−9.9	1982
Mexico	1.0	−7.0	−8.0	−1.2	6.2	0.4	−8.0	1983
Morocco	14.5	7.1	−7.4	3.4	4.8	8.5	−5.6	1983
Korea, Rep.	2.0	−5.4	−7.4	−2.6	3.6	0.8	−4.2	1986
Kenya	7.2	2.2	−5.0	2.9	4.0	3.3	−4.6	1982
Brazil	1.8	−2.9	−4.6	0.8	3.7	0.1	−3.2	1984
Turkey	5.2	1.7	−3.5	1.7	3.6	3.7	−4.9	1988
Nigeria	1.4	−2.1	−3.5	0.6	2.4	−0.2	−5.5	1984
Thailand	3.8	0.9	−2.9	3.3	2.9	0.5	−4.3	1982
Cameroon	2.8	−0.1	−2.9	2.7	2.3	−0.6	−3.9	1984
Argentina	−1.0	−2.9	−1.9	3.4	6.3	0.0	−4.5	1982
Sri Lanka	11.3	11.2	−0.2	5.6	2.2	7.8	−9.4	1984
Pakistan	10.9	10.8	−0.1	2.3	1.5	10.0	−3.2	1987
Colombia	0.4	1.1	0.7	2.6	3.3	1.8	−5.3	1986
India	1.7	2.7	1.0	2.3	1.0	1.4	−0.5	1982
Indonesia	−1.1	0.4	1.4	3.7	3.6	0.2	−6.0	1984

a. The countries in italics rescheduled their debts during the period.
b. Minus sign indicates outward transfer.
c. Column 4 − 5 + 6.
d. Column 2 − 1. Negative sign represents reductions in inward transfer or shift to outward transfer.
Source: Appendix 5-A.

For most of the other ten countries whose transfers fell by 3.5 percent or more, the change was more or less forced. They could not continue to finance current account deficits on the previous scale. They had to reduce both amortization and interest payments or somehow effect an improvement in the trade balance, or both. All except Korea, Kenya, and Turkey went into arrears or rescheduled the debt, or both. All except Kenya reduced their current account deficits, despite large increases in their interest costs (not shown in the table 5-1). It should be emphasized, however, that current account deficits continued, and somehow had to be financed (even if only by payment arrears), for every country except Korea and Mexico (column 4). Mexico achieved a current account surplus despite interest payments of 6.2 percent of GNP, but at a high cost in recession and slow growth.

The shock was enormous (it exceeded 7 percent of GNP) for the first six countries in table 5-1. From 1983 to 1988 interest reached more than 10 percent of GNP for Chile, while Mexico and Côte d'Ivoire transferred 7 percent or more of GNP abroad. Resource transfers deteriorated for all our countries except Colombia,

India, and Indonesia, although they remained positive, as was also the case for Costa Rica, Morocco, Kenya, Turkey, Thailand, Sri Lanka, and Pakistan (column 2). In six of these seven (Thailand being the exception), it was aid remittances that sustained the positive inflow (column 6).

The decline in lending to developing countries was the main feature of the 1980s. Changes in the terms of trade, which had been so important in the preceding decade, became less important, at least until 1986. From 1982 to 1986 there were no important changes in the terms of trade, except for a tea boom in 1984 that affected Sri Lanka. Then in 1986 oil prices collapsed, creating serious problems for the oil exporters. Both for this reason, and because there was a minor coffee boom in the same year, Côte d'Ivoire, Costa Rica, Kenya, Korea, and Thailand experienced a considerable improvement in their terms of trade. After 1986 the coffee countries again lost out. Côte d'Ivoire was the hardest hit, since the cocoa price also collapsed. Chile, in contrast, gained because copper reached an all-time high (in dollar terms) in 1988. We return below to the problems of the oil and coffee exporters after 1986.

Conditions in the Early 1980s

One obvious question to raise is to what extent growth was influenced by conditions prevailing in 1982: by the level of indebtedness and the state of the current account of the balance of payments, and by whether the economy was in recession or not. Inflation is another possible determinant.

Debt and the Current Account

Debt service and the current account of our countries at the end of 1982 was given in table 4-1 of the previous chapter. Of the eight countries that we deemed to be in trouble in 1979 because of the debt and their current account deficits, three (Kenya, Korea, and Thailand) had reduced their current account deficits by 1982. Sri Lanka's current account deficit was worse, but this was no immediate problem, for it remained a donors' darling.

The other four—Chile, Costa Rica, Côte d'Ivoire, and Morocco—had either increased their current account deficit or failed to reduce it. All four had deficits in excess of 10 percent of GNP in 1982, with debt to GNP ratios of 77 percent or more. They either had demanded or were soon to demand rescheduling. This was also the case for the two nonoil exporters that were in difficulty in 1979, Argentina and Brazil. Inflation was the primary problem for Argentina, while Brazil was struggling with both inflation and a very high ratio of total debt service to exports. Both countries had increased current account deficits and debt ratios, Argentina to 84 percent of GNP. Two of the eight countries that were favorably placed in 1979—the oil exporters, Mexico and Nigeria—had joined the ranks of the distressed, as described in chapter 4. This accounts for the eight reschedulers (see the countries in italics in table 5-1).

Recessions in the 1980–83 Period

As explained in chapter 4, these eight countries experienced an actual fall in GDP in 1981 or 1982, or in both years. Only in Mexico itself could the recession be traced to the credit rationing that was consequent on the shock of Mexico's moratorium in 1982. In Costa Rica, Morocco, Brazil, Nigeria, and Argentina, the recessions began in 1981. Three of these countries (Costa Rica, Morocco, and Nigeria) actually experienced a rise in inward transfers in that year. This may happen when a fall in export prices or a failure of domestic supply (Morocco) causes both a worsening of the current account and a fall in domestic demand. In Chile, the very severe recession began before the Mexican crisis (see chapters 4 and 7). In Côte d'Ivoire, GDP did not fall on an annual basis until 1983, but the recession began in 1982. Whether or not a country is in recession will influence its later growth.

The Influence of Some Initial Conditions on Growth in the 1980s

To investigate whether growth in the later 1980s was dependent on macroeconomic conditions in 1982, we estimated simple regressions of the growth of GNP per capita from 1982 to 1989 on the current account, on debt (measured alternatively as the ratio of total debt to GNP and total debt service to exports) and on inflation in the year 1982. All coefficients had the expected sign—that is, growth was negatively associated with the current account deficit, debt, and inflation. However, none was significant even at the 10 percent level. The coefficient of a dummy variable for recession in the period 1980–83 was also insignificant. The lack of any significant simple correlation between the initial conditions and subsequent growth may seem surprising, although it does not, of course, imply that they would remain insignificant if other variables were included (or if the sample of countries had been larger).

It is not surprising that recession is insignificant, because its effects can go either way. On the one hand, a low level of activity leaves room for recovery; on the other hand, it is the result of difficulties that may be hard to overcome. The insignificance of debt, however, will probably surprise most readers. The reasons for the insignificant correlation become obvious from figure 5-1. Costa Rica had a huge debt but grew somewhat faster than the mean rate. Korea was quite highly indebted, but grew famously. Nigeria had negligible debt, but its GNP declined more than that of any other country except Côte d'Ivoire. Exclude these three, and debt would certainly be significant. The fact that debt was statistically an insignificant variable in our sample certainly does not imply that it was irrelevant! As shown later in this chapter, regressions in our sample countries are often heavily

Figure 5.1 Growth Rate of GNP, 1982–89 and Debt/GNP, 1982

Growth rate of GNP per capita 1982 –89

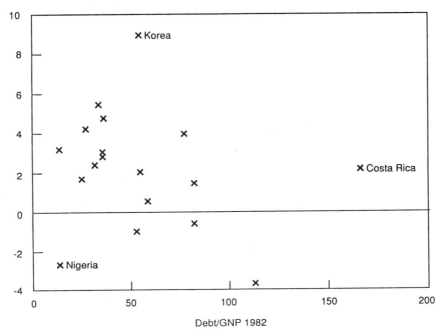

Debt/GNP 1982

Source: Table 4.1 and 5.2.

influenced by outliers; but if one shoots the outliers, one destroys the theoretical basis of significance tests.

It is, in any case, obvious that events occurring during the period 1983–88 may dominate the story and render initial conditions relatively unimportant. Money is not always made by backing the horse that carries the lowest weight in a handicap race. Furthermore, the initial condition variables themselves influence other variables for the period 1983–88, and the inclusion of these latter variables may render the former statistically insignificant.

The Record of the 1980s

In evaluating the record of the 1980s, it is particularly important to examine our countries' experience with rescheduling, investment, and growth in this period.

Table 5.2   The Record of the 1980s

Country	(1)	(2)	(3)	(4)	(5)	(6)	(7)
	Current account deficit[a]/GNP		Change in investment[b]	Mean investment 1983-88	Change in resource transfer[b]	Inward resource transfer[c] 1983-88	Growth rate of GNP per head[d] 1982-89 percent per year
	1982	1988					
Reschedulers							
Argentina	4.5	1.8	−9.9	12.5	−1.9	−2.9	-0.6
Brazil	6.0	−1.3	−3.4	19.3	−4.6	−2.9	2.3
Chile	10.2	0.8	−2.4	15.7	−8.1	−4.1	4.0
Costa Rica	12.3	4.2	−0.5	27.1	−9.0	0.8	2.1
Côte d'Ivoire	14.4	12.8	−14.4	15.0	−10.2	−7.5	−3.6
Mexico	3.9	1.5	−4.2	21.1	−8.0	−7.0	−1.0
Morocco	12.7	−2.2	−2.2	25.7	−7.4	7.1	1.4
Nigeria	7.9	0.7	−11.6	10.4	−3.5	−2.1	−2.7
Mean (unweighted)	9.0	2.3	−6.1	17.1	−6.6	−2.3	0.2
Remainder							
Cameroon	4.8	7.1	−2.9	21.1	−2.9	−0.1	−1.1
Colombia	8.0	0.6	+0.8	20.2	+0.7	1.1	1.7
India	1.4	3.2	+1.1	23.9	+1.0	2.7	3.3
Indonesia	5.9	1.7	−1.4	25.4	+1.4	0.4	4.1
Kenya	5.0	5.6	−2.5	24.5	−5.0	2.2	0.7
Korea	3.7	−8.4	−1.4	30.1	−7.4	−5.4	8.9
Pakistan	3.7	3.1	+0.1	18.9	−0.1	10.8	2.8
Sri Lanka	11.4	5.8	−0.6	25.0	−0.2	11.1	2.0
Thailand	2.9	2.8	−1.2	25.4	−2.9	0.9	5.5
Turkey	1.8	−2.3	+1.4	23.0	−3.5	1.7	3.1
Mean (unweighted)	4.9	1.9	−0.7	23.6	−1.9	2.5	3.1

a. Minus sign indicates surplus.
b. A comparision of the mean values for 1983-88 compared with the mean value for 1977-82. Column 5 is from table 5.1, column 3.
c. Column 6 is from table 5.1, column 2. Minus sign indicates outward resource transfers.
d. Fitted expotential rate.
Source: Appendix A to this chapter.

Rescheduling, Investment, and Growth

The eight reschedulers were the countries that ran into deep trouble in the period 1981–83. All were also in recession in that period. If growth is measured from a state of recession, there may be an upward bias. Therefore, to determine whether the troubles of the early 1980s affected the long-run growth performance of countries, it is better to compare the level of real GNP in the years 1986–88 with the years 1976–78 (using a three-year average to even out peculiarities in any individual year). We do this in chapter 11, where we deal specifically with longer-run issues. Here, we look at the recovery of the afflicted, or lack of it, and at the experience of the better-placed countries over the 1980s.

Table 5-2 gives some relevant information. The first set of countries contains the reschedulers, and the second set the rest. The last column gives the rate of growth of GNP per capita in the period 1982–89. The striking features here are the significant differences in the mean growth rates, changes in resource flows, and changes in investment. Although (or because) the reschedulers were all in recession in the period 1981–83, their subsequent growth in per capita GNP was much worse than that of the others, none of which was in recession in that period (except for a slight recession in Indonesia in 1982). Argentina, Côte d'Ivoire, Mexico, and Nigeria experienced negative growth. Brazil and Costa Rica recovered moderately well, while Chile's GNP rose very rapidly after 1985. As already mentioned, Morocco suffered only a brief agricultural setback. In contrast, half of the others grew rapidly (3 percent or more in per capita GNP). Even Kenya, which experienced a large turnaround in transfers, managed to achieve positive growth.

There is no suggestion that rescheduling is important in explaining the countries' relative performance. It should be regarded more as a consequence of other factors that drove countries to seek relief from the burden of servicing their debt. It is no accident that six of the eight reschedulers experienced a negative change of resource flows in excess of 4 percent, against two of the others (Kenya and Korea). Eight out of this latter group of ten continued to enjoy an inflow of resources in 1983–88, and only Korea experienced considerable outflow. In contrast, all the reschedulers except Costa Rica and Morocco suffered an outflow, which reached more than 4 percent of GNP for Chile, Côte d'Ivoire, and Mexico.

Despite this strong association between rescheduling and both the change in resource flows and growth in the period 1982–89, there is no significant correlation between the latter two ($r = .16$).[3] Figure 5-2 illustrates this apparent paradox. A glance is enough to show that there is little correlation, but the reschedulers (marked with crosses—X) are clearly a class apart from the others (marked with naughts—0). They tend to exhibit slow growth and a high fall in transfers, whereas the opposite is the case for the others. Regressing growth on the change in transfers and a dummy variable for rescheduling showed the latter to be significant.

Rescheduling is also strongly associated with changes in investment. Thus the mean fall in investment/GNP for the reschedulers was about six percentage points, and for the others less than one percentage point. One would expect a close positive relationship between a fall in inward transfers and a fall in investment (both associated with rescheduling). On general grounds, it is to be expected that when the current account has to be improved it will be investment that suffers most. There is indeed some positive relationship ($r = .38$), but it is weak and barely significant, as shown in figure 5-3. Excluding Argentina, Côte d'Ivoire, and Nigeria, there would be only an extremely weak positive relationship.

Investment levels and growth are significantly correlated ($r = .67$), but the correlation depends yet again on a few outliers—Argentina, Côte d'Ivoire, Korea, and Nigeria (see figure 5-4). There is a stronger correlation between changes in

Figure 5.2 Growth Rate of GNP per Capita, 1982–89 and Fall in Inward Transfers

Growth rate of GNP per capita, 1982–89

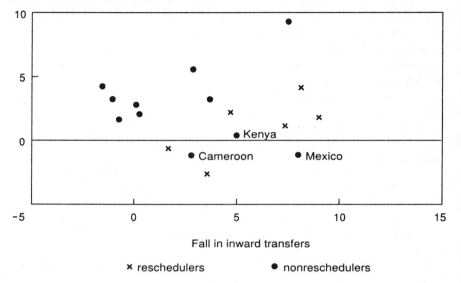

Fall in inward transfers

× reschedulers   ● nonreschedulers

Source: Table 5.2.

Figure 5.3 Changes in Investment and Resource Flows

Fall in investment

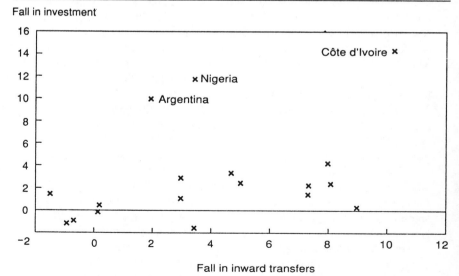

Fall in inward transfers

Source: Table 5.2.

investment (from 1977–82 to 1983–88) and growth ($r = .70$) than between the investment ratio in the second period and growth. Even this result, however, depends heavily on a few outliers (see figure 5-5). This suggests that low or negative growth and a fall in investment were both caused by other factors, rather than that low or negative growth resulted from a low level of investment. Thus there are alternative stories. The first and most conventional is that a turnaround in resource transfers results in investment cuts, and that a reduced level of investments results in lower growth. The correlations described do not support this first story very well because of the weak correlation between the reduction in inward transfers and fall in investment. Furthermore, although the falls in investment are significantly correlated with the level of investment in the second period ($r = .72$), they "explain" only about half of the variance of the level of investment in that period. It is the latter that should in theory explain growth, even if only after several years.

The second story is that the turnaround in transfers is related both to rescheduling, which is an effort to reduce its severity, and to a struggle to improve the trading account. This latter can usually be achieved in the short and medium run only by a fall in imports, which is mainly a consequence (but also in part a cause) of a low level of activity. Falls in private investment are caused in part by the low level of activity and expected growth, and in part by import cuts. Public investment cuts are part of the deflationary policies required to improve the current account.[4] Although reduced investment after a few years can be expected to become a cause of lower growth, this effect may not be of much significance in a six-year period,

Figure 5.4 Growth Rate of GNP per Capita, 1982–89 and Investment/GNP, 1983–88

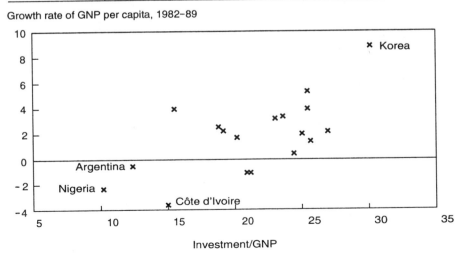

Growth rate of GNP per capita, 1982–89

Investment/GNP

Source: Table 5.2.

Figure 5.5. Growth Rate of GNP 1982-89 and Fall in Investment
(Percentage points)

Growth rate of GNP per capita, 1982-89

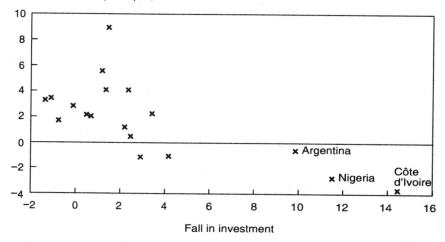

Fall in investment

Source: Table 5.2.

especially when there is reason to believe that the marginal investments of the earlier period were of very low productivity.

The second story is better supported. That is to say, rescheduling is an indicator of the difficulty that countries had in balancing their external accounts, even at a reduced or low level of activity. Rescheduling is closely associated with recession and low growth, and with changes in both resource flows and investment (Korea is the main exception). Surprisingly, as already pointed out, there is no significant correlation between growth and changes in transfers. This suggests the following interpretation. The changes in transfers resulted in reduced growth only when the country found itself in severe balance of payments difficulties, as indicated by rescheduling, which was the only means of moderating the need to improve the trade balance. The balance of trade could not be improved without a reduced level of activity; lower public investment was an instrument, while lower private investment would also result from a lower expectation of growth, and in some cases also from a rise in interest rates and an increase in the stringency of import controls. As noted in chapter 4, Kenya is the prime example of a country that did not reschedule, although it faced quite severe balance of payments problems. It suffered a steep fall in investment, mainly public.

What is the essential difference between the stories we have told? The second story still has it that a fall in inward transfers will cause a fall in investment, but with the proviso that it will do so severely only if the struggle to improve the current account requires deflation in general, and cuts in public investment and a tightening of import controls in particular.[5] This implies that a rapid growth of exports may relieve the situation. The weak correlation between falls in inward transfers and falls in investment, and the insignificant correlation between falls in inward transfers and growth, may be explained by differences in export performance. This hypothesis is supported by multiple regression analysis of the variables so far discussed, with the addition of some terms of trade and export variables (see appendix 5B).

Influence of the Terms of Trade and Export Performance

The above analysis amounts to saying that growth after the crisis of 1982–83 depended to a considerable extent on the need to switch output to the task of restoring the balance of payments and on the difficulties experienced in bringing about such a switch. This need through the period 1982–88 in turn depended not only on the extent of the disequilibrium at the beginning but also on the course of the terms of trade. We referred to the terms of trade above but did not bring out the relationship to growth.

Figures for the terms of trade for 1982 and 1985 through 1989 are given in table 5-3, together with the value in 1988 compared with 1982, and 1989

Table 5.3   Terms of Trade, Selected Years

(1980 = 100)

Country	1982	1985	1986	1987	1988	1989	1988/82 (%)	1989/85 (%)
Argentina	90	90	85	82	87	90	97	97
Brazil	90	89	109	97	116	120	129	130
Cameroon	95	92	65	66	64	67	67	70
Chile	80	80	72	79	94	98	118	118
Colombia	96	98	100	70	68	59	71	69
Costa Rica	93	95	104	85	98	93	105	103
Côte d'Ivoire	87	96	105	87	92	80	96	96
India	107	114	119	119	119	120	111	104
Indonesia	101	94	70	69	70	68	69	74
Kenya	90	91	111	81	92	86	102	101
Korea, Rep.	104	106	112	104	109	112	105	103
Mexico	104	98	66	74	66	72	63	67
Morocco	91	89	104	100	102	81	112	115
Nigeria	101	90	45	54	40	46	40	44
Pakistan	94	88	95	99	107	98	114	122
Sri Lanka	92	99	97	96	102	96	111	103
Thailand	78	74	84	81	82	80	105	111
Turkey	91	91	109	110	115	105	122	126

Source: World Bank data.

compared with 1985. We have already suggested that the terms of trade figures may be even more unreliable than most of those we use, although when 1982 is compared with 1988, they at least show the direction of change where a large change is indicated. The correlation between the growth of GNP per capita and the indicated change in the terms of trade is .43, which is significant.

The main influence was the fall in the real price of oil, in the first half of 1986. The only important losers were the oil producers—Cameroon, Colombia, Indonesia, Mexico, and Nigeria (table 5-3). Brazil, Chile, and Turkey were large gainers. The fall in the oil price in 1986 exacerbated the problems of the oil producers. Cameroon, Mexico, and Nigeria fell into recession in 1986 or 1987, while Colombia and Indonesia escaped.

It should be noted that in the discussion and analysis of exports throughout this chapter we consider only exports to the developed world as measured by imports into developed countries. Experts consider these figures much more reliable than exports as recorded by the developing countries. The latter are more subject to errors because of over- and underinvoicing and inadequate recording and classification. There are also more gaps in the statistics and greater delays in obtaining them. The disadvantages are that exports to socialist countries and to other developing countries are ignored. In a few cases the rate of growth of the value of exports to the developed world may be significantly different from that of total exports. Nevertheless, in our judgment the figures we use are the best available measures of export success and failure.

THE OIL EXPORTERS. Although the main shock of the 1980s for many countries was the fall in inward transfers, the steep fall in oil prices in 1986 was of greater importance for oil exporters. Oil revenues dropped sharply in 1985–89, except in Colombia, where increasing quantities produced and exported more than offset the price fall. Table 5-4 records indices of the dollar value of fuel and other exports, imports, and changes in real GDP for these countries. The appendix tables to this chapter that give current account deficits and resource transfers are also relevant.

Cameroon's oil exports were cut in half in 1986 and did not recover. Nonoil exports were sluggish, with coffee and cocoa prices also falling after 1986. The current account moved from a large surplus in 1985 to a series of large deficits. With the fall in export income, GDP fell by 17 percent from 1986 to 1989.

Colombia is a coffee country as well as a fuel exporter. In 1986 there was a coffee boom, after which the collapse in coffee prices was compensated by a large rise in the quantity of fuel exports (coal as well as oil). From 1985 to 1989 the value of fuel exports more than trebled, despite the fall in price. Manufactured exports also grew strongly. The total dollar value of exports rose by 56 percent. Not surprisingly, GDP grew satisfactorily, despite a large outward transfer of resources.

In 1986 Indonesia suffered a 23 percent fall in the dollar value of exports, but the resultant widening of the current account deficit could be financed with only a small fall in imports. In September it announced a 45 percent devaluation and

Table 5.4   Trade Performance of the Oil Exporters, 1985–90
(percentages of 1985 merchandise exports in dollars)

Country	1985	1986	1987	1988	1989	1990
Cameroon						
Merchandise exports	100	73	77	68	72	
Fuel	66	32	38	29	34	
Nonfuel	34	41	39	39	38	
Manufactures	2	2	2	2	2	
Merchandise imports	46	63	73	63	49	
Growth rate of GDP	7.7	8.0	−6.5	−7.7	−3.4	−2.5
Colombia						
Merchandise exports	100	151	144	142	156	
Fuel	13	21	40	34	47	
Nonfuel	87	130	104	108	109	
Manufactures	11	14	16	22	51	
Merchandise imports	114	106	117	140	147	
Growth rate of GDP	3.3	6.1	5.4	4.1	3.4	3.9
Indonesia						
Merchandise exports	100	77	87	95	109	
Fuel	75	49	50	47	51	
Nonfuel	25	28	37	48	58	
Manufactures	6	9	15	20	27	
Merchandise imports	75	71	74	80	112	
Growth rate of GDP	2.7	5.8	4.9	5.8	7.3	7.2
Mexico						
Merchandise exports	100	84	101	110	127	
Fuel	51	25	29	23	26	
Nonfuel	49	59	72	87	101	
Manufactures	34	40	52	66	75	
Merchandise imports	50	43	46	71	88	
Growth rate of GDP	2.8	−3.9	1.9	1.5	3.2	4.0
Nigeria						
Merchandise exports	100	61	60	57	78	
Fuel	97	58	57	52	74	
Nonfuel	3	3	3	5	4	
Manufactures	0	1	1	1	1	
Merchandise imports	72	58	50	50	54	
Growth rate of GDP	10.2	−0.6	−1.8	9.9	6.0	5.7

Note: The value of merchandise exports is estimated as the value of each country's merchandise imports into developed countries. We have not recorded the terms of trade in this table because of divergences between different World Bank sources, and also between Bank sources and country sources.
Source: World Bank data. (The change in GDP is taken from appendix table AII.1.)

began liberalizing imports as well as promoting exports, with the result that nonoil exports grew sharply. The value of manufactured exports more than quadrupled from 1985 to 1989, and the total dollar value of exports rose past the level of 1985, although there was no recovery in the value of oil exports.

Mexico also experienced a large fall in exports in 1986 (16 percent) after also suffering a major earthquake in December 1985. With inflation rising to more than 100 percent in 1986 and a huge public sector deficit, Mexico could not avoid deflationary measures and a sharp recession, despite significant supportive action from the IMF and the World Bank. Nevertheless, it continued reforming the trade regime. There was a slow recovery in 1987–89, accompanied by a doubling of the value of nonoil exports from 1985 to 1989. Although the value of total exports rose by 50 percent from 1986 to 1989, imports were severely restricted, especially in 1986 and 1987, when the outward transfer of resources averaged 7 percent of GNP. Mexico's recovery was handicapped by heavy interest payments on the debt and by capital flight.

Nigeria's merchandise dollar exports (virtually all oil) fell by 39 percent in 1986, and merchandise imports by 19 percent. How the resultant current account deficit was financed is unclear (with huge errors and omissions figure). There are severe statistical problems with Nigeria's national accounts, but it appears that GDP fell in 1986 and 1987, but then recovered in 1988 and 1989 with the arrival of better weather and an increase in oil exports. Nigeria undertook major reforms of its exchange rate regime from 1986 to 1989, which are discussed at length in chapter 8.

Thus all these countries except Colombia suffered a serious loss of export income from oil. The importance of nonoil exports is clear. In Indonesia and Mexico, the value of nonoil exports doubled in 1985–89, and this more than offset the fall in oil revenues. Manufactures accounted for a large part of the rise. Colombia's export success came both from new oil finds and from a sensational rise in manufactured exports. In contrast, in Cameroon and Nigeria the loss of oil export revenue was not offset by a significant rise in the value of nonoil exports. Largely as a result, the dollar value of imports in 1989 was about the same in Cameroon as in 1985, and the real value would have been significantly lower. In Nigeria the dollar value of imports was 25 percent lower in 1989 than in 1985.

Thus it is not surprising that Colombia and Indonesia grew satisfactorily from 1985 to 1989, and that Cameroon and Nigeria experienced recessions. Mexico's poor performance, as compared with that of Indonesia, needs further explanation, since both countries doubled the value of nonoil exports. The main reason is not far to seek. Mexico, still suffering severely from its indebtedness and capital flight, was transferring a high proportion of GNP abroad. Despite export success, this could be achieved only by a much more severe compression of imports than in Indonesia, as compared with the early 1980s. For example, the dollar value of imports in 1987 was 51 percent of 1981, while the value of Indonesian imports was 74 percent of 1981.

THE COFFEE AND COCOA EXPORTERS. The coffee boom of 1986 and the ensuing bust in 1987 created little disturbance compared with the coffee boom of the 1970s. The boom was much smaller (prices rose by 28 percent in 1986, against a rise of 216 percent in 1975–77), although the subsequent fall in 1987 was severe (37 percent against 32 percent in 1978). Furthermore, coffee was a much lower proportion of exports in Kenya, Colombia, and Costa Rica than it had been in 1977.

We have already considered Cameroon and Colombia as oil exporters. Costa Rica more than compensated for the fall in coffee export income after 1986 by a rapid rise in exports of manufactures to developed countries. The dollar value of these exports rose 128 percent from 1986 to 1989, and the total value of exports rose by 37 percent. Imports rose even more rapidly, however, and the current account deficit reached more than 7 percent of GDP in 1989.

Côte d'Ivoire, like Cameroon, experienced a deep recession in the period 1987–89. As in the case of both Cameroon and Kenya, there was no significant rise in other exports to offset the fall in export revenue from cocoa and coffee after 1986. The value of exports to developed countries fell by 25 percent from 1986 to 1989. Côte d'Ivoire has both a huge external debt (and is in arrears of interest) and a current account deficit approaching 10 percent of GNP. Without export growth, it is hard to envisage a revival of growth.

In Kenya, the fall in coffee revenues after 1986 was not offset by growth in other exports. Although the export value of manufactures rose by 60 percent, this increase started from a very low level. Note, too, that the value of exports to developed countries fell by 12 percent from 1986 to 1989. At the same time, the value of imports rose 34 percent and the current account deficit averaged more than 6 percent of GNP from 1987 to 1989. Although GDP rose by about 5.5 percent a year, this was at the expense of an unsustainable current account deficit.

The Mechanism of Growth in the 1980s

The simple cross-country correlations considered in this chapter suggest that growth in the 1980s depended greatly on the need to improve the current account, and on the extent to which the countries studied were able to meet this challenge without having to create or permit a reduced level of economic activity. This implies that foreign trade variables may play an important role in the explanation of growth. The terms of trade in the 1980s certainly affected the magnitude of the task faced by the countries. The main changes were the fall in the price of oil in 1986, and in cocoa and coffee prices in 1987. As expected, subsequent growth in 1986–89 was related to nontraditional export performance, as well as the continued ability to borrow.

We therefore carried out multiple regression analysis of the growth of GNP per capita in 1982–89 on the "independent" variables already discussed, together with some trade variables. This is reported in appendix 5B, the concluding sentences of which are as follows:

However, the so-called independent variables are too endogenous and interrelated for such regression analysis to indicate the causal mechanisms involved. Although the inclusion of all the variables discussed thus adds but little to our understanding of the period, we nevertheless believe that the regression provides support for the view that export performance was an important cause of growth in this period.

The relationship between export performance and growth does not arise merely because exports are part of GDP. Except for a handful of countries, the value of exports was not a very high proportion of GDP even in 1988 (see table 5-5, column 8), and in most cases the *value added* from exports as a proportion of GDP was probably quite low. In the main, it appears that rapid export growth relieves a country in balance of payments difficulties from having to compress imports by import restrictions or deflationary action. It permits a more liberal trade regime with all the benefits associated with the exploitation of comparative advantage (the relationship here is a virtuous circle—liberal trading policies both encourage and are encouraged by rapid export growth). It also makes a country more creditworthy, while relief from a dominating concern with debt and the balance of payments permits authorities to pursue economic reforms outside the field of trade and payments.

The Policies of the 1980s

The next important question to consider is how growth in the 1980s was affected by country policies.

Exchange Rates and Exports

Columns 1 and 2 of table 5-5 give the growth rates of dollar value and volume of exports in 1982–88. In ten of our countries the growth rate of dollar value exceeded 9 percent, with Korea, Pakistan, Thailand, and Turkey experiencing growth rates of more than 15 percent. The performance in terms of volume was similar, except that Chile's high value growth was largely due to a boom in copper prices, while the slow growth in volume in the case of Cameroon, Indonesia, and Nigeria became negative in value owing to a deterioration in their terms of trade. Table 5-5 also includes the growth rate of the value of manufactures to developed countries in the periods 1982–88 and 1986–89. World trade in manufactures in 1982–88 grew by 13 percent a year, while that of manufactures from all developing countries exported to developed countries grew by 18 percent a year. Thus developing countries were relatively successful. Within our group, Indonesia, Turkey, Thailand, Costa Rica, Chile, Mexico, and Korea were the stars (in that order).

Table 5.5   Growth of Exports, 1982–88

| Country | Growth rate of exports (% p.a.), 1982–88[a] | | Real exchange rate[b] | | | Growth rate of $ value of manufactured exports[c] | | Exports/ GDP % | Manu-factured exports/ total exports % |
	$ Value	Volume[d]	1985/82	1988/85	1988/82	1982–8	1986–89	1988	1988
Argentina	5.6	3.9	86	85	74	9.0	24.2	10	25
Brazil	10.2	9.0	78	103	80	16.8	15.9	10	48
Cameroon	−2.3	1.1	110	120	132	9.6	10.2	16	13
Chile	9.7	3.4	64	74	47	24.1	40.8	37	15
Colombia	9.3	11.5	79	65	51	15.7	20.2	16	25
Costa Rica	10.5	8.1	111	75	83	25.3	27.6	36	40
Côte d'Ivoire	1.6	0.5	92	128	118	17.3	19.2	33	12
India	8.3	5.7	99	72	71	14.3	22.2	7	73
Indonesia	−2.6	1.8	76	54	42	31.4	36.8	25	29
Kenya	4.8	6.2	100	73	72	17.4	16.0	19	17
Korea, Rep.	20.7	18.2	90	93	81	21.1	20.0	41	93
Mexico	4.4	7.8	105	80	84	21.3	21.0	16	55
Morocco	9.4	6.7	82	91	75	19.1	24.0	25	50
Nigeria	−12.0	0.4	146	18	26	18.3	27.0	25	2
Pakistan	15.6	14.8	91	102	65	18.0	15.2	14	69
Sri Lanka	10.1	8.6	104	78	81	19.9	19.8	26	43
Thailand	15.9	12.5	90	81	73	26.6	37.6	34	52
Turkey	18.0	14.9	93	79	74	28.2	36.0	24	64
Means	7.6	7.5	95	80	74	19.6	24.1	23	40
World	8.3					13.0	13.8		
Developing countries	4.2					18.2	20.2		

a. Growth rates are point-to-point compound annual rates.
b. Ratio of the later year to the earlier year.
c. Exports are the dollar value of the recorded f.o.b. value of imports of industrialized countries taken from United Nations sources, except that the last two columns use World Bank estimates.
d. For export volumes the value figures are deflated by World Bank export prices indices for each country.
Source: World Bank and IMF data.

A feature of the 1980s was the more flexible use of nominal exchange rates. Most countries for most of the time managed the exchange rate to make and keep exports more competitive. They succeeded in bringing about a depreciation in the real exchange rate, which is a measure of competitiveness. Different measures of the real exchange rates are explained in chapter 8. Real exchange rate indices as measured by the IMF are given in table 8-1. Table 5-5 records changes from 1982 to 1985, 1985 to 1988, and 1982 to 1988. All countries except Cameroon and Côte d'Ivoire, whose currencies were pegged to the French franc, experienced an important real devaluation over the six-year period. In eleven of the sixteen countries, this occurred mainly or wholly in the second half of the period. Thus in Costa Rica, Mexico, Nigeria, and Sri Lanka, the real exchange rates actually appreciated from 1982 to 1985, whereas in India and Kenya there was virtually no change.

The nominal exchange rate regimes through which these changes were effected are examined at length, country by country, in chapter 8. The central question in this chapter is the extent to which export growth, to which we have attached such importance, was a consequence of the real depreciations and therefore an indirect result of the change in exchange rate policies. This issue is also taken up again in chapter 8. An obvious first step suggested by economic theory in the context of a single country is to correlate the change in real exchange rates with the growth of the volume of exports across the spectrum of our countries.[6] The correlation coefficient turns out to be virtually zero. At first glance, this might seem surprising, but some reflection suggests that cross-country correlation is an inappropriate method of investigating the relation between export growth and the change in real exchange rates. The following points may be made:

- At the most general level, it is clear that countries may differ greatly in how far they need to realign the real exchange rate to achieve any given rate of export growth. Obviously, countries differ both in the initial degree of uncompetitiveness and in the composition of exports. Some exports have a greater elasticity of supply than others. Nontraditional exports, especially manufactures, are likely to be in more elastic supply.
- More particularly, where oil was a high proportion of exports in 1982, the growth of export volume from 1982 to 1988 was bound to be slow, whatever happened to the real exchange rates. Exports for members of the Organization of Petroleum Exporting Countries were limited by quota. Coffee exports were also governed by quota arrangements.
- The supply of exports may be seriously affected by nonprice factors. These include drought, frost, and disease, in the case of agricultural products, and discoveries or the depletion of resources in the case of minerals.
- As already pointed out, the depreciation of the real exchange rates came at different times in the period, and could be expected, other things being equal, to have a greater effect the earlier it came.
- The exchange rate is not the only element in trade policies that affects the profitability of exports. Changes in taxes and subsidies have been important in some countries (but are not reflected in table 5-5). Import liberalization and the credibility of a government's commitment to the maintenance of a trade regime that is favorable to exports are also important.

In the medium term, the exchange rate can be expected to have the greatest effect on exports of manufactures and of agricultural products other than tree crops. Since agriculture in the developed world is heavily protected, the great opportunities lie with manufactures. In our countries, the big real devaluations

Figure 5.6 Growth of Manufactured Exports ($ value), 1986–89 and Change in Real Exchange Rates, (RER), 1988–85

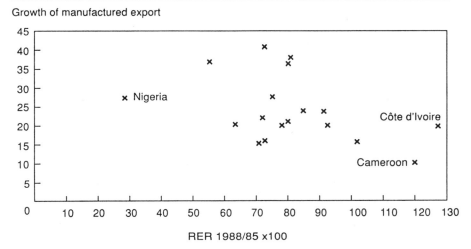

Source: Table 5.5.

came in the second half of the study period. Table 5-5 gives the growth rate of manufactured exports in 1986–89, as well as the change in the real exchange rates in 1985–88. There is a significant correlation between these two ($r = .40$), as shown in figure 5-6.

Developing countries were very successful in penetrating the markets of the developed countries in this period. The dollar value of world exports of manufactures grew by 13.8 percent a year, while that of all developing countries grew by 20.2 percent, and that of our set of countries by 24.1 percent. Only one of our set of countries—Cameroon—failed to beat the world average. The export success of particular countries is discussed further in chapter 8.

A government's commitment to open trading policies is of great importance for the growth of exports. The requirement of credibility has been rightly stressed in recent economic analyses (see, for example, Calvo 1986). If industrialists are not convinced that a favorable climate for exports exists, which includes the freedom to import, then they will not make the appropriate investments. The real exchange rate does not adequately measure this aspect of export performance.

In addition to flexible exchange rates, a major and apparently sustained shift in the first half of the 1980s to export orientation, combined with import liberalization, took place only in Morocco (1984) and Turkey (1980). Many of our other countries made some move to liberalize imports and reduce protection, but these efforts were not very substantial or comprehensive, as in the case of India, or were simply a continuation of a long-standing trend toward reduced protection, as in

Korea and Thailand. More substantial reforms came in the second half of the 1980s (see chapter 9 for the details of the trade liberalization).

In Morocco there was a considerable liberalization of imports in 1984, combined with a devaluation of 20 percent. The growth of the volume of exports rose from 5.6 percent a year in 1982–85 to 8.3 percent in 1985–88, despite a fall in phosphate exports in the latter period. After Korea and Thailand, Turkey had the most striking export performance of any country in the 1980s, although the figures may be somewhat exaggerated as a result of overinvoicing.

> With an early emphasis on export promotion, a clear signal was given to producers that output recovery would be induced by export expansion. The maxi-devaluation of January 1980 was followed by frequent mini-devaluations through May 1981. From May 1981 onwards (to the end of 1983) the exchange rate was adjusted daily against a currency basket. Besides devaluations, export incentives included tax rebates, credit subsidies, an exchange retention scheme, and duty free imports for the production of exportables. (Celásun and Rodrik 1989, p. 668)

Liberalization of imports followed later. Apart from these incentives, exports were favored by widespread initial excess capacity and the Iraq-Iran war. It should also be noted that these trade regime measures were part of a broader program of reform that reduced controls and increased the role of the price mechanism. In the 1970s Turkey had been a classic case of a highly controlled economy dominated by import substitution. The rather massive reorientation of incentives (as well as luck) may well have been needed because the industrial structure inherited from the 1970s was not in line with comparative advantage.[7]

After 1985, especially in the last years of the decade, and in 1990, all the countries in our group that had not already embarked on major reforms of the trade regime began to reduce protection and adopt more liberal trading policies, especially by reducing import controls (see chapter 9). As the industrialized countries became more protectionist, the developing countries began to abandon their long-cherished faith in protection and import substitution. Mexico's liberalization, begun in 1986, was probably the most comprehensive, and it has been sustained, despite inflation and a temporary freezing of the exchange rate from December 1987 to December 1988. Mexico's determination was signaled by its decision to join the General Agreement on Tariffs and Trade (GATT) and its proposal for a free trade area with the United States. Indonesia has also continued the liberalization process since 1986. Nigeria began a dramatic change in its exchange rate and trading regimes in 1986, as described in chapter 8. We saw earlier that these countries rapidly expanded nonoil exports, although this was from an extremely low level in the case of Nigeria. In other cases the reforms have either been modest (as in Pakistan, and India until 1991), or of questionable credibility because of inflation (as in Argentina and Brazil). In yet other cases where there seems to be a determined reform (for example, in Costa Rica, which like Mexico has joined the GATT), it is too soon to make any appraisal of the effects.

Fiscal and Monetary Policies

Whereas export success and related policies played an important role in the growth of per capita GNP in our countries in the period 1982–89, the effect of fiscal and monetary policies on growth is less clear. They certainly helped reduce current account deficits, as was essential when borrowing became more difficult. (Fiscal and monetary policy is discussed at length in chapter 10.) Central government deficits were reduced in about half our countries between 1982 and 1987, despite the large rise in interest payments for all but a few. Primary deficits, which may be a better measure of the fiscal impact of the government, were reduced in all but six countries, and the reduction was very large in the cases of Colombia, Korea, Morocco, and Thailand. By 1987, half of the countries were running primary surpluses. Thus the later 1980s were years of general budgetary restraint. Nevertheless, fiscal deficits remained the major problem for many of the countries in 1989. Note that India did not practice fiscal restraint in the late 1980s, just as it was the odd country out in the second half of the 1970s in adjusting, or overadjusting, to the first oil shock. Political developments began to erode India's fiscal conservatism in the 1970s, as reflected in rising government deficits in the 1980s, which reached more than 10 percent of GDP by 1989–90, with a primary borrowing requirement of over 7 percent of GDP.

The Heightened Importance of Official Lending

Appendix tables 5A-1 to 5A-18 give the sources of borrowing in 1980–88. In the period 1980–82, most of our countries borrowed predominantly from private sources. The exceptions were Cameroon, Costa Rica, India, Kenya, Morocco, Pakistan, and Turkey, which relied heavily on bilateral official lending. Multilateral official lending (by the World Bank and the IMF) was also important in Côte d'Ivoire, India, Pakistan, and Turkey.

In 1983–88 net private lending was greatly reduced, but it remained significant for most countries. In the cases of India, Thailand, and Turkey its relative importance actually increased, but it became negligible or negative for Cameroon, Costa Rica, Kenya, Nigeria, Pakistan, and Sri Lanka. Among these, only Costa Rica and Nigeria rescheduled the debt in the period 1983–88 (and Cameroon in 1989). In Korea, however, private borrowing remained very important through 1985, but then in 1986–88 the government repaid more than US$10 billion. Private lending continued to be very important for the big Latin American debtors: Argentina, Brazil, Chile, and Mexico. This, however, was reluctant, concerted lending undertaken in the course of restructuring the debt and in an effort to ensure continued payment of interest. Côte d'Ivoire and Morocco were two other re-schedulers that continued to receive loans (though not from the commercial banks).

The relative decline in private lending to all countries except India, Thailand, and Turkey was matched by a relative increase in public lending. This section, however, focuses primarily on the IMF and the World Bank. In the period 1983–88 as a whole, net borrowing from the IMF was negligible or negative for most countries. This was because they either had no monetary relations with the IMF (as in the case of Colombia and Nigeria) or were repaying loans incurred in the late 1970s or early 1980s. In contrast, IMF loans were quantitatively very important for Argentina and Mexico, and moderately so for Brazil, Chile, and Morocco. The weight of IMF loans in this period, however, is measured not only by the size of the loans. More important in some cases is the fact that countries facing a balance of payments crisis were required to accept an IMF stabilization program in order to qualify for rescheduling or for new lending by commercial banks.[8] This has also been a condition for new lending by bilateral donors and for World Bank lending. Thus World Bank structural adjustment loans (SALs) have been associated with IMF loans in Argentina, Brazil, Cameroon, Chile, Costa Rica, Côte d'Ivoire, Kenya, Mexico, Morocco, Pakistan, Thailand, and Turkey.[9]

The World Bank initiated SALs in 1980. They grew to a disbursement plateau of about $3 billion in 1986 and subsequent years, or about 25 percent of all World Bank (and IMF) lending. As a result of this policy of making loans that could be disbursed quickly to support economic reforms, and of the decline in commercial lending, the World Bank in the second half of the 1980s acquired an important presence in several of our countries where it had been a minor lender earlier, such as Argentina, Morocco, Nigeria, and Pakistan. In certain years it also played a leading role in Brazil, Chile, and Mexico. For a few other countries—for example, Colombia, India, Indonesia, Kenya, and Turkey—it was an important lender throughout the 1980s, often in conjunction with a bilateral donors' consortium. All our countries except India and Sri Lanka received SALs, although several only in the second half of the 1980s (Argentina, Chile, Colombia, Indonesia, and Cameroon).

There is no doubt that the World Bank and the IMF played a large role in the policy reforms discussed above. Although the jury is still out as to the success and sustainability of the more recent reforms, the World Bank was also closely associated with the earlier reforms in Morocco and Turkey, which have been very successful. However, it is beyond the scope of this project to assess the success of IMF and World Bank policies, which in any case involve many more countries than those in our sample.[10]

Economic Circumstances at the End of the Decade

Table 5-6 presents some figures that are crucial to an assessment of the problems that our countries faced at the end of the 1980s. Two debt indicators are given. The interest paid as a percentage of exports of goods and services is some indication of the immediate burden caused by the debt, but it is a poor indicator of long-run problems, if only because eight of the countries were in interest payment arrears. Therefore, total debt as a percentage of GNP is also given.

Column 1 shows that investment had fallen to very low levels in Argentina, Côte d'Ivoire, and Nigeria. It was also rather low in Cameroon, Colombia, Mexico, and Pakistan. Elsewhere, it was high enough to sustain a high rate of growth, provided public investments were well chosen and provided a distorted price mechanism did not result in private investments of low social productivity.

Table 5.6   Key Magnitudes for 1989
(percent)

Country	Gross investment/ GNP (1)	Inflation (CPI) 1989 (2)	Interest/ exports of goods and services (3)	Debt/ GNP (4)	CA balance/ GNP (5)	GDP growth rate (6)
Argentina	9.8	3,079	18[a]	119	−2.4	−4.1
Brazil	21.4	1,287	15[a]	26	+0.2	3.3
Cameroon	18.6	0	8[a]	45	−1.9	−3.4
Chile	22.4	17	17	77	−3.3	10.9
Colombia	20.8	26	19	45	−0.5	3.4
Costa Rica	26.9	17	9	95	−8.5	5.6
Côte d'Ivoire	11.2	7	16[a]	187	−14.5	−1.0
India	23.9	6	14	25	−2.8	6.2
Indonesia	35.9	6	15	61	−1.2	7.3
Kenya	26.8	10	14[a]	72	−7.3	4.6
Korea, Rep.	34.7	6	4	16	+2.4	6.1
Mexico	18.1	20	25	47	−2.0	3.2
Morocco	23.5	3	19[a]	101	−3.7	2.3
Nigeria	11.4	41	17[a]	119	−3.8	6.0
Pakistan	18.0	8	10[a]	46	−3.4	4.8
Sri Lanka	21.9	12	7	73	−6.0	2.1
Thailand	31.5	5	6	34	−3.6	12.2
Turkey	22.9	70	14	54	+1.2	1.6

a. Denotes interest payments in arrears.
Source: Columns 1 and 2 are from *Trends in Developing Economies 1990*. Columns 3 and 4 are from *World Debt Tables 1991–90*, and column 6 is from table 5.7.

Column 2 shows that inflation was a dire problem only in Argentina, Brazil, and Turkey, although it was still uncomfortably high in Chile, Colombia, Mexico, and Sri Lanka. In several other countries, the high public sector deficits to which we refer below threatened a rise in inflation.

The immediate burden of debt reported in table 5-6 is measured by interest actually paid as a proportion of exports (column 3). It exceeded 15 percent for Chile, Colombia, and Mexico, countries that continued to meet their obligations; but eight other countries were in arrears, and in this sense had a debt problem.

Half of the countries had a debt/GNP ratio in excess of 60 percent. Among these the current account deficit for 1990 implied that the debt/GNP ratio was still rising in the cases of Costa Rica, Côte d'Ivoire, and Kenya, even given a rise in GNP of 5 percent a year.

By 1990, all of our countries except Cameroon, Côte d'Ivoire, and Mexico were using exchange rate flexibility to encourage exports, and many were also using export subsidies and other incentives. All had made some progress in eliminating import quotas and in rationalizing and reducing tariffs (trade interventions are discussed in chapter 9), but most were still having difficulty achieving a viable fiscal balance. Fiscal figures are not included in table 5-6 because they are unreliable and it may be misleading to compare them between countries. The coverage of published figures varies, and only in a few countries are figures for public enterprises consolidated. Yet for many, their losses have been the heart of the problem. Even when reliable figures are given for the consolidated nonfinancial public sector, it may turn out that the central bank has been incurring large losses (see chapter 10).

The deficit figures that are available for 1989, even if they do not tell the whole story, are clearly large enough in several cases to suggest that they constituted the central problem facing the government, and that they were seriously endangering the country's prospects. Overall budget deficits in 1989 exceeded 7 percent of GDP in Argentina, Cameroon, Côte d'Ivoire, India, Kenya, Pakistan, and Sri Lanka.[11]

Such deficits can be financed only by rapidly increasing debt, or to some degree by inflation. The danger of excessive foreign borrowing has become all too apparent. High domestic borrowing increases interest rates, which drives out private investment and magnifies interest payments on the rising public debt. This story is examined in some detail in chapter 10.

The relatively good growth of GNP in India, Kenya, Pakistan, and Sri Lanka in the period 1982–89 was thus supported by deficits that could hardly be sustained for much longer. India was a newcomer to the list of countries with lax fiscal discipline. Although the 1990 figures for India as given in table 5-6 were not obviously alarming, it had been clear for several years that India's traditional fiscal conservatism was breaking down, and that a crisis was impending.[12]

A Postscript on the Early 1990s

Our survey of the 1980s (obviously) ends with 1989 or 1990, but history does not stand still. We note here some of the more important developments from 1990 to 1992 in our countries. Of course, there are always ups and downs in the main variables—fiscal and current account deficits, inflation rates, growth rates, and so on. The main questions are whether there have been any large shifts in variables and policies.

The most important changes have taken place in Argentina, Brazil, and India. All three engaged in, or committed themselves to, major trade liberalization programs.

In Argentina, the Menem administration took over in the midst of the hyperinflation of 1989. It struggled right through 1990 and early 1991 with the inflation problem, and finally—when Domingo Cavallo took over as minister of the economy in March 1991—embarked on a radical reform program that, by mid-1992, had virtually put an end to serious inflation (down to less than 20 percent a year). Fiscal equilibrium was, more or less, restored, and the value of the currency was firmly fixed to the dollar (see chapter 7).

In Brazil, President Fernando Collor de Melo, the first directly elected president in more than twenty years, took over in 1990 and introduced radical liberalization measures. Hyperinflation was indeed ended, but several plans designed to reduce inflation to reasonable levels did not succeed, and by mid-1992 inflation in Brazil was again at very high levels (about 20 percent a month). In 1992 Brazil had by far the highest inflation rate of any of our countries.

India at last faced its problem of growing public deficits in June 1991. During the May/June election Mr. Rajiv Gandhi was assassinated. The succeeding prime minister, Mr. Narasimha Rao, immediately appointed Dr. Manmohan Singh, a distinguished economist, as finance minister. This was a sign of the seriousness of the situation (India was on the verge of default), for Dr. Singh had never been a politician and was not a member of the Lok Sabha (Parliament). Known as a cautious man, he acted with unprecedented boldness and speed. Within a month, the rupee was devalued twice, interest rates raised, and trade policy reforms announced. Steps were also taken to reduce the public sector deficit, mainly by cutting subsidies. The immediate financial crisis was resolved by loans from the Bank of England and Bank of Japan, and then from the IMF and World Bank.

Many of the extensive controls over private sector investment and production have been scrapped and the conditions governing direct foreign investment have been made more welcoming. Announcements of impending reform add up to a major liberalization, embracing trade, financial, and industrial policies, including the role of the public sector. There are serious political hurdles to overcome, but if the package goes through, India will become a very different economy from that of the entire postindependence period to date.

In all the other countries, the tendencies evident in 1989 continued into the 1990s. Many continued or embarked upon liberalization and structural adjustment measures. Notably, Colombia reduced trade barriers substantially in 1990 and

1991. Mexico continued with extensive reforms—including privatization and trade liberalization—designed to increase the efficiency and flexibility of the economy. Its success in reducing inflation to less than 20 percent in 1991 is discussed in chapter 7. It made a far-reaching agreement in 1991 with its creditors under the aegis of the Brady plan, which significantly reduced the burden of the debt and prompted a reversal of earlier capital flight. By 1992 there was every sign that Mexico's recovery was under way. An outstanding event was the transition to democracy in Chile in 1990. Wisely, the new government chose to continue the successful orthodox macro- and microeconomic policies of its predecessor.

Aside from Korea, the high-growth countries of the period were Thailand and Indonesia. From 1987, and continuing into 1992, Thailand had the biggest boom in its history. The growth rate in 1990 was 10 percent and in 1991 it was 8 percent. This was fed by massive private capital inflow, much of it going into the booming export sector. The fiscal situation remained sound, although inflation rose above the low level usual for Thailand, reaching nearly 6 percent in 1990. As was to be expected, monetary policy was tightened in 1991. Indonesia's story was similar— it was marked by a capital inflow, an export boom, rather high inflation (9 percent in 1991), and a 7 percent growth rate.

Cameroon and Côte d'Ivoire were the two countries in crisis, both with negative growth rates, because they had been slow to adjust to the shocks of the 1980s. The interesting question, taken up in chapter 8, is to what extent this situation was connected with the rigid exchange rate regime to which membership of the franc zone committed them. Both were in arrears to domestic and foreign creditors, both were dependent on loans from the IMF and the World Bank, and both were subject to adjustment programs. In Côte d'Ivoire, impressive public expenditure reductions were achieved in 1990, lowering the noninterest (primary) deficit from 7.6 percent to 2 percent of GDP. A new, technocratic government embarked on structural reforms in 1991.[13]

Appendix 5A

The following tables show the resource transfers for each country for each year between 1970 and 1988, and also the net debt flows and their components. An inward resource transfer is positive and an outward transfer is indicated by a negative sign. A current account surplus is represented by a negative sign. Interest payments refer to actual payments made, not payments that were due. The item "remittances" refers to public and private "unrequited transfers," a main element of which is often remittances from workers overseas.

The resource transfer concept used here differs from the "resource balance" concept in some World Bank publications, notably *Trends in Developing Economies 1990* (World Bank 1990c), in that interest paid, rather than total net payments for factor services, is subtracted from the current account deficit.

Table 5A.1   Argentina

	Resource transfers (percentage of GNP)						
	1970	*1971*	*1972*	*1973*	*1974*	*1975*	*1976*
A. Current account deficit	0.72	1.55	0.86	−1.81	−0.22	3.33	−1.71
B. Interest payments	1.54	1.37	1.42	1.17	0.95	1.87	1.24
C. Remittances	0.00	0.00	0.00	0.00	0.00	0.00	0.00
D. Inward resource transfer (A − B + C)	−0.82	0.18	−0.56	−2.98	−1.17	1.46	−2.95

	1977	*1978*	*1979*	*1980*	*1981*	*1982*	*Average 1977–82*
A. Current account deficit	−2.70	−4.33	1.01	8.51	8.43	4.52	2.57
B. Interest payments	1.32	1.76	1.87	4.15	6.15	6.88	3.69
C. Remittances	0.10	0.20	0.10	0.00	0.00	0.10	0.08
D. Inward resource transfer (A − B + C)	−3.92	−5.89	−0.76	4.36	2.28	−2.26	−1.03

	1983	*1984*	*1985*	*1986*	*1987*	*1988*	*Average 1983–88*
A. Current account deficit	4.10	3.45	1.57	3.84	5.52	1.86	3.39
B. Interest payments	9.15	6.04	8.38	5.78	5.30	3.25	6.32
C. Remittances	0.00	0.00	0.00	0.00	0.00	0.00	0.00
D. Inward resource transfer (A − B + C)	−5.05	−2.59	−6.81	−1.94	0.22	−1.39	−2.93

	Net debt flows (millions of dollars)								
	1980	*1981*	*1982*	*1983*	*1984*	*1985*	*1986*	*1987*	*1988*
Long-term private	2,797	6,326	5,665	1,134	15	2,350	345	900	−29
Long-term official	21	−4	68	301	−38	141	−5	39	226
World Bank	37	74	26	30	20	76	274	662	299
IMF	0	0	0	1,367	0	1,000	159	622	23
Total	2,855	6,396	5,759	2,832	−3	3,567	773	2,223	519

Note: The current account deficits shown may differ from those shown in annex table AII.3.
Source: For resource transfers, World Bank data; for net debt flows, *World Debt Tables*, various issues.

Table 5A.2   Brazil

	Resource transfers (percentage of GNP)						
	1970	*1971*	*1972*	*1973*	*1974*	*1975*	*1976*
A. Current account deficit	1.98	3.33	2.89	2.73	7.20	5.67	4.29
B. Interest payments	0.53	0.60	0.73	0.94	1.40	2.41	1.12
C. Remittances	0.10	0.00	0.00	0.00	0.00	0.00	0.00
D. Inward resource transfer (A − B + C)	1.55	2.73	2.16	1.79	5.80	3.26	3.17

							Average
	1977	*1978*	*1979*	*1980*	*1981*	*1982*	*1977–82*
A. Current account deficit	2.90	3.51	4.66	5.52	4.64	6.00	4.54
B. Interest payments	1.15	1.56	2.11	3.39	4.09	4.49	2.80
C. Remittances	0.00	0.00	0.00	0.10	0.10	0.00	0.03
D. Inward resource transfer (A − B + C)	1.75	1.95	2.55	2.23	0.65	1.51	1.77

							Average
	1983	*1984*	*1985*	*1986*	*1987*	*1988*	*1983–88*
A. Current account deficit	3.51	−0.02	0.11	1.97	0.45	−1.13	0.78
B. Interest payments	4.83	4.54	4.16	2.88	2.39	3.54	3.72
C. Remittances	0.10	0.10	0.10	0.00	0.00	0.00	0.05
D. Inward resource transfer (A − B + C)	−1.22	−4.46	−3.95	−0.91	−1.94	−4.84	−2.89

	Net debt flows (millions of dollars)								
	1980	*1981*	*1982*	*1983*	*1984*	*1985*	*1986*	*1987*	*1988*
Long-term private	3,944	7,760	6,896	3,103	3,988	−377	−893	−862	2,046
Long-term official	413	704	640	457	353	484	−18	−141	−19
World Bank	242	250	405	931	965	356	1,004	40	40
IMF	0	0	551	2,167	1,788	−65	−616	−1,149	−438
Total	4,599	8,714	8,492	6,657	7,094	398	−523	−2,112	1,629

Note: The current account deficits shown may differ from those shown in annex table AII.3.
Source: For resource transfers, World Bank data; for net debt flows, *World Debt Tables*, various issues.

Table 5A.3   Cameroon

	Resource transfers (percentage of GNP)						
	1970	*1971*	*1972*	*1973*	*1974*	*1975*	*1976*
A. Current account deficit	2.59	3.90	7.00	0.97	0.75	6.00	3.20
B. Interest payments	0.43	0.49	0.49	0.63	0.58	0.62	0.68
C. Remittances	0.90	0.80	0.50	−0.40	0.10	0.90	1.30
D. Inward resource transfer (A − B + C)	3.06	4.21	7.01	−0.06	0.27	6.28	3.82

							Average
	1977	*1978*	*1979*	*1980*	*1981*	*1982*	*1977–82*
A. Current account deficit	3.00	4.50	2.17	5.79	5.85	4.84	4.36
B. Interest payments	0.92	1.09	1.22	2.18	2.21	2.58	1.70
C. Remittances	1.00	0.00	0.00	0.00	0.10	−0.20	0.15
D. Inward resource transfer (A − B + C)	3.08	3.41	0.95	3.61	3.74	2.06	2.81

						Average
	1983	*1984*	*1985*	*1986*	*1987*	*1988*	*1983–88*
A. Current account deficit	0.75	−2.69	−4.24	5.82	9.61	7.01	2.71
B. Interest payments	2.38	2.70	2.15	2.22	2.00	2.13	2.26
C. Remittances	0.00	−0.10	−0.40	−0.60	−1.00	−1.20	−0.55
D. Inward resource transfer (A − B + C)	−1.63	−5.49	−6.79	3.00	6.61	3.68	−0.10

	Net debt flows (millions of dollars)								
	1980	*1981*	*1982*	*1983*	*1984*	*1985*	*1986*	*1987*	*1988*
Long-term private	279	97	56	233	93	−252	−68	−51	40
Long-term official	176	189	65	61	74	60	103	91	239
World Bank	3	42	46	48	43	34	49	52	14
IMF	−5	−10	−3	−1	−3	−6	−8	−9	85
Total	493	318	164	341	207	−164	76	83	378

Note: The current account deficits shown may differ from those shown in annex table AII.3.
Source: For resource transfers, World Bank data; for net debt flows, *World Debt Tables*, various issues.

Table 5A.4   Chile

	Resource transfers (percentage of GNP)						
	1970	*1971*	*1972*	*1973*	*1974*	*1975*	*1976*
A. Current account deficit	1.11	2.00	4.00	2.70	2.64	7.20	−1.50
B. Interest payments	1.27	1.06	0.42	0.63	1.03	2.70	2.58
C. Remittances	0.10	0.10	0.10	0.10	0.10	0.20	0.50
D. Inward resource transfer (A − B + C)	−0.06	1.04	3.68	2.17	1.71	4.60	−3.58

							Average
	1977	*1978*	*1979*	*1980*	*1981*	*1982*	*1977–82*
A. Current account deficit	4.20	7.20	5.90	7.37	15.13	10.21	8.34
B. Interest payments	1.98	2.49	2.81	4.46	5.67	10.57	4.66
C. Remittances	0.70	0.60	0.50	0.00	0.00	−0.10	0.28
D. Inward resource transfer (A − B + C)	2.92	5.31	3.59	2.91	9.46	−0.46	3.96

							Average
	1983	*1984*	*1985*	*1986*	*1987*	*1988*	*1983–88*
A. Current account deficit	6.16	12.20	9.34	7.61	4.65	0.83	6.80
B. Interest payments	9.43	13.45	13.65	11.23	9.55	6.26	10.60
C. Remittances	0.00	0.00	−0.20	−0.40	−0.70	−0.70	−0.33
D. Inward resource transfer (A − B + C)	−3.27	−1.25	−4.51	−4.02	−5.60	−6.13	−4.13

	Net debt flows (millions of dollars)								
	1980	*1981*	*1982*	*1983*	*1984*	*1985*	*1986*	*1987*	*1988*
Long-term private	2,237	3,462	1,499	945	928	686	391	180	336
Long-term official	−153	−80	−90	92	261	224	79	148	303
World Bank	5	18	19	12	18	211	340	269	324
IMF	−52	−64	−40	613	221	199	114	−73	−67
Total	2,037	3,336	1,388	1,662	1,428	1,320	924	524	896

Note: The current account deficits shown may differ from those shown in annex table AII.3.
Source: For resource transfers, World Bank data; for net debt flows, *World Debt Tables*, various issues.

Table 5A.5   Colombia

	Resource transfers (percentage of GNP)						
	1970	*1971*	*1972*	*1973*	*1974*	*1975*	*1976*
A. Current account deficit	4.07	5.80	2.20	0.53	2.85	1.31	−1.06
B. Interest payments	0.82	0.86	0.93	1.00	1.08	1.04	1.02
C. Remittances	0.50	0.40	0.40	0.30	0.40	0.40	0.30
D. Inward resource transfer (A − B + C)	3.75	5.34	1.67	-0.17	2.17	0.67	−1.78

							Average
	1977	*1978*	*1979*	*1980*	*1981*	*1982*	*1977–82*
A. Current account deficit	−1.93	−1.11	−1.57	0.62	5.42	7.96	1.56
B. Interest payments	0.79	0.84	0.90	2.07	2.06	2.85	1.58
C. Remittances	0.20	0.30	0.40	0.50	0.70	0.40	0.42
D. Inward resource transfer (A − B + C)	−2.52	−1.65	−2.07	−0.95	4.06	5.51	0.40

							Average
	1983	*1984*	*1985*	*1986*	*1987*	*1988*	*1983–88*
A. Current account deficit	7.92	3.76	5.33	−1.10	−0.99	0.60	2.59
B. Interest payments	2.59	2.51	3.62	3.40	3.74	3.76	3.27
C. Remittances	0.40	0.80	1.40	2.30	2.90	2.70	1.75
D. Inward resource transfer (A − B + C)	5.73	2.05	3.11	−2.20	−1.83	−0.46	1.07

	Net debt flows (millions of dollars)								
	1980	*1981*	*1982*	*1983*	*1984*	*1985*	*1986*	*1987*	*1988*
Long-term private	531	1,125	856	535	741	393	967	−333	290
Long-term official	124	102	215	346	309	514	392	168	250
World Bank	153	174	184	168	308	424	276	64	85
IMF	0	0	0	0	0	0	0	0	0
Total	808	1,401	1,255	1,049	1,358	1,331	1,635	−101	625

Note: The current account deficits shown may differ from those shown in annex table AII.3.
Source: For resource transfers, World Bank data; for net debt flows, *World Debt Tables*, various issues.

Table 5A.6   Costa Rica

	Resource transfers (percentage of GNP)						
	1970	*1971*	*1972*	*1973*	*1974*	*1975*	*1976*
A. Current account deficit	7.51	10.80	8.30	7.50	16.40	11.50	8.60
B. Interest payments	1.42	1.39	1.45	1.57	1.86	1.89	1.70
C. Remittances	0.60	0.70	0.50	0.50	0.60	0.50	0.60
D. Inward resource transfer (A − B + C)	6.69	10.11	7.35	6.43	15.14	10.11	7.50

	1977	*1978*	*1979*	*1980*	*1981*	*1982*	*Average 1977–82*
A. Current account deficit	7.5	10.60	14.40	14.43	17.57	12.25	12.79
B. Interest payments	1.69	2.41	2.87	3.87	6.06	5.42	3.72
C. Remittances	0.50	0.50	0.30	0.30	1.20	1.60	0.73
D. Inward resource transfer (A − B + C)	6.31	8.69	11.83	10.86	12.71	8.43	9.80

	1983	*1984*	*1985*	*1986*	*1987*	*1988*	*Average 1983–88*
A. Current account deficit	9.55	4.45	3.46	1.92	6.10	4.20	4.95
B. Interest payments	19.44	7.69	9.85	6.27	4.37	4.97	8.77
C. Remittances	2.50	4.20	6.00	3.70	5.30	6.00	4.62
D. Inward resource transfer (A − B + C)	−7.39	0.96	−0.39	−0.65	7.03	5.23	0.80

	Net debt flows (millions of dollars)								
	1980	*1981*	*1982*	*1983*	*1984*	*1985*	*1986*	*1987*	*1988*
Long-term private	198	49	17	96	−27	42	−11	−14	0
Long-term official	150	126	98	191	110	67	−28	43	9
World Bank	22	13	8	6	18	63	26	−18	−32
IMF	8	51	−4	106	−25	13	−36	−62	−54
Total	378	239	119	399	76	185	−49	−51	−77

Note: The current account deficits shown may differ from those shown in annex table AII.3.
Source: For resource transfers, World Bank data; for net debt flows, *World Debt Tables*, various issues.

Table 5A.7   Côte d'Ivoire

	Resource transfers (percentage of GNP)						
	1970	*1971*	*1972*	*1973*	*1974*	*1975*	*1976*
A. Current account deficit	2.80	7.20	5.60	9.60	2.20	10.60	5.90
B. Interest payments	0.83	1.02	1.03	1.15	1.40	1.52	1.52
C. Remittances	−1.50	−1.80	−1.60	−3.00	−3.30	−4.00	−6.10
D. Inward resource transfer (A − B + C)	0.47	4.38	2.97	5.45	−2.50	5.08	−1.72

							Average
	1977	*1978*	*1979*	*1980*	*1981*	*1982*	*1977–82*
A. Current account deficit	3.10	11.70	16.90	18.36	17.83	14.39	13.71
B. Interest payments	1.87	2.42	2.82	4.77	7.81	10.09	4.96
C. Remittances	−5.20	−5.90	−7.00	−7.10	−6.10	−5.10	−6.07
D. Inward resource transfer (A − B + C)	−3.97	3.38	7.08	6.49	3.92	−0.80	2.68

							Average
	1983	*1984*	*1985*	*1986*	*1987*	*1988*	*1983–88*
A. Current account deficit	14.82	1.20	−1.08	3.43	7.70	12.80	6.49
B. Interest payments	10.39	11.79	12.28	10.67	6.95	6.10	9.70
C. Remittances	−4.70	−4.30	−4.00	−4.10	−4.30	−4.20	−4.27
D. Inward resource transfer (A − B + C)	−0.27	−14.89	−17.36	−11.34	−3.55	2.50	−7.49

	Net debt flows (millions of dollars)								
	1980	*1981*	*1982*	*1983*	*1984*	*1985*	*1986*	*1987*	*1988*
Long-term private	925	675	1,130	198	660	624	320	247	439
Long-term official	91	36	161	141	114	72	71	183	230
World Bank	79	34	200	178	186	26	61	290	−17
IMF	38	377	127	166	9	−45	−79	−148	−64
Total	1,133	1,122	1,618	683	969	677	373	572	588

Note: The current account deficits shown may differ from those shown in annex table AII.3.
Source: For resource transfers, World Bank data; for net debt flows, *World Debt Tables*, various issues.

Table 5A.8   India

	Resource transfers (percentage of GNP)						
	1970	*1971*	*1972*	*1973*	*1974*	*1975*	*1976*
A. Current account deficit	0.77	0.60	0.50	0.50	0.90	–0.30	–1.71
B. Interest payments	0.36	0.38	0.39	0.34	0.31	0.31	0.31
C. Remittances	0.50	0.80	0.30	0.30	0.40	0.90	1.10
D. Inward resource transfer (A – B + C)	0.91	1.02	0.41	0.46	0.99	0.29	–0.92

							Average
	1977	*1978*	*1979*	*1980*	*1981*	*1982*	*1977–82*
A. Current account deficit	–1.71	–0.10	0.03	1.30	1.70	1.40	0.48
B. Interest payments	0.29	0.32	0.30	0.36	0.41	0.57	0.37
C. Remittances	1.30	1.30	1.70	2.00	1.60	1.60	1.58
D. Inward resource transfer (A – B + C)	–0.70	0.88	1.70	2.94	2.89	2.43	1.68

							Average
	1983	*1984*	*1985*	*1986*	*1987*	*1988*	*1983–88*
A. Current account deficit	1.30	1.508	2.60	2.49	2.45	3.20	2.26
B. Interest payments	0.71	0.89	0.89	0.99	1.03	1.19	0.95
C. Remittances	1.50	1.60	1.30	1.20	1.20	1.30	1.35
D. Inward resource transfer (A – B + C)	2.09	2.21	3.01	2.70	2.62	3.31	2.66

	Net debt flows (millions of dollars)								
	1980	*1981*	*1982*	*1983*	*1984*	*1985*	*1986*	*1987*	*1988*
Long-term private	490	511	645	572	1,564	1,170	1,913	1,350	1,473
Long-term official	194	–3	21	110	148	158	299	809	541
World Bank	740	1,121	1,299	1,225	986	1,218	1,062	1,713	2,087
IMF	1,014	652	1,968	1,306	67	–264	–648	–1,082	–1,210
Total	2,438	2,281	3,933	3,213	2,765	2,282	2,626	2,790	2,891

Note: The current account deficits shown may differ from those shown in annex table AII.3.
Source: For resource transfers, World Bank data; for net debt flows, *World Debt Tables*, various issues.

Table 5A.9   Indonesia

	Resource transfers (percentage of GNP)						
	1970	*1971*	*1972*	*1973*	*1974*	*1975*	*1976*
A. Current account deficit	3.18	3.76	2.92	2.82	-2.26	3.54	2.33
B. Interest payments	0.47	0.59	0.75	0.70	0.70	1.03	1.26
C. Remittances	0.70	0.50	0.40	0.30	0.20	0.10	0.00
D. Inward resource transfer (A – B + C)	3.41	3.67	2.57	2.42	-2.76	2.61	1.07

							Average
	1977	*1978*	*1979*	*1980*	*1981*	*1982*	*1977–82*
A. Current account deficit	0.11	2.65	-1.86	-4.00	0.63	5.91	1.57
B. Interest payments	1.28	1.35	1.99	1.94	1.91	2.14	1.77
C. Remittances	0.10	0.00	0.10	0.30	0.30	0.10	0.15
D. Inward resource transfer (A – B + C)	-1.07	1.30	-3.75	-5.64	-0.98	3.87	-1.05

							Average
	1983	*1984*	*1985*	*1986*	*1987*	*1988*	*1983–88*
A. Current account deficit	7.83	2.25	2.33	5.17	2.95	1.70	3.71
B. Interest payments	2.46	2.94	2.98	3.78	4.70	4.54	3.57
C. Remittances	0.10	0.20	0.10	0.30	0.40	0.30	0.23
D. Inward resource transfer (A – B + C)	5.47	-0.49	-0.55	1.69	-1.35	-2.54	0.37

	Net debt flows (millions of dollars)								
	1980	*1981*	*1982*	*1983*	*1984*	*1985*	*1986*	*1987*	*1988*
Long-term private	806	1,070	1,342	2,681	1,312	222	759	-78	-968
Long-term official	466	650	866	701	560	421	481	1,536	1,576
World Bank	341	336	501	458	722	644	591	1,012	1,214
IMF	0	0	0	454	-4	-386	0	606	-56
Total	1,613	2,056	2,709	4,294	2,590	901	1,831	3,076	1,766

Note: The current account deficits shown may differ from those shown in annex table AII.3.
Source: For resource transfers, World Bank data; for net debt flows, *World Debt Tables*, various issues.

Table 5A.10   Kenya

	Resource transfers (percentage of GNP)						
	1970	*1971*	*1972*	*1973*	*1974*	*1975*	*1976*
A. Current account deficit	3.18	6.48	3.33	5.29	10.80	7.14	3.80
B. Interest payments	1.13	1.03	0.96	1.23	1.44	1.48	1.52
C. Remittances	1.70	3.40	1.90	1.30	1.10	1.60	0.40
D. Inward resource transfer (A – B + C)	3.75	8.85	4.27	5.36	10.46	7.26	2.68

	1977	*1978*	*1979*	*1980*	*1981*	*1982*	*Average 1977–82*
A. Current account deficit	–0.60	13.07	8.30	12.60	8.40	4.95	7.79
B. Interest payments	1.46	1.76	2.07	3.37	3.69	3.69	2.67
C. Remittances	1.50	1.80	1.50	2.10	3.30	2.20	2.07
D. Inward resource transfer (A – B + C)	–0.56	13.11	7.73	11.33	8.01	3.46	7.19

	1983	*1984*	*1985*	*1986*	*1987*	*1988*	*Average 1983–88*
A. Current account deficit	0.84	2.15	1.93	0.55	6.50	5.60	2.93
B. Interest payments	3.50	3.68	6.78	3.38	3.58	2.88	3.97
C. Remittances	3.20	3.00	3.30	3.00	2.80	4.30	3.27
D. Inward resource transfer (A – B + C)	0.54	1.47	–1.55	0.17	5.72	7.02	2.23

	Net debt flows (millions of dollars)								
	1980	*1981*	*1982*	*1983*	*1984*	*1985*	*1986*	*1987*	*1988*
Long-term private	191	–21	–37	13	–168	–11	129	50	90
Long-term official	106	175	113	117	258	65	93	97	35
World Bank	105	63	156	102	143	76	66	60	81
IMF	85	27	147	92	–17	46	–116	–122	75
Total	487	244	379	324	216	176	172	85	281

Note: The current account deficits shown may differ from those shown in annex table AII.3.
Source: For resource transfers, World Bank data; for net debt flows, *World Debt Tables*, various issues.

Table 5A.11   Republic of Korea

	Resource transfers (percentage of GNP)						
	1970	*1971*	*1972*	*1973*	*1974*	*1975*	*1976*
A. Current account deficit	6.97	8.64	3.41	2.22	10.80	9.08	1.09
B. Interest payments	0.85	1.03	1.50	1.89	1.28	1.59	1.48
C. Remittances	2.00	1.70	1.60	1.40	1.20	1.10	1.20
D. Inward resource transfer (A − B + C)	8.12	9.31	3.51	1.73	10.72	8.59	0.81

	1977	*1978*	*1979*	*1980*	*1981*	*1982*	*Average 1977–82*
A. Current account deficit	−0.03	2.19	6.54	8.79	6.95	3.71	4.69
B. Interest payments	1.41	1.60	1.77	4.70	5.68	5.66	3.47
C. Remittances	0.60	1.00	0.70	0.70	0.70	0.70	0.73
D. Inward resource transfer (A − B + C)	−0.84	1.59	5.47	4.79	1.97	−1.25	1.95

	1983	*1984*	*1985*	*1986*	*1987*	*1988*	*Average 1983–88*
A. Current account deficit	2.02	1.78	0.99	−4.49	−7.67	−8.38	−2.63
B. Interest payments	4.54	4.50	4.54	3.62	2.38	1.73	3.55
C. Remittances	0.70	0.60	0.60	1.00	0.90	0.90	0.78
D. Inward resource transfer (A − B + C)	−1.82	−2.12	−2.95	−7.11	−9.15	−9.21	−5.40

	Net debt flows (millions of dollars)								
	1980	*1981*	*1982*	*1983*	*1984*	*1985*	*1986*	*1987*	*1988*
Long-term private	1,776	2,784	1,397	2,369	2,915	2,540	−1,173	−7,846	−1,514
Long-term official	463	773	466	619	167	25	−281	−609	−2,542
World Bank	187	264	560	409	393	110	−103	−279	1,812
IMF	582	631	78	161	314	−229	−125	−1,174	−497
Total	3,008	4,452	2,501	3,558	3,789	2,446	−1,682	−9,908	−2,741

Note: The current account deficits shown may differ from those shown in annex table AII.3.
Source: For resource transfers, World Bank data; for net debt flows, *World Debt Tables*, various issues.

Table 5A.12   Mexico

	Resource transfers (percentage of GNP)						
	1970	*1971*	*1972*	*1973*	*1974*	*1975*	*1976*
A. Current account deficit	2.90	2.06	1.96	2.48	3.88	4.44	3.72
B. Interest payments	0.77	0.77	0.75	0.90	1.09	1.21	1.49
C. Remittances	0.10	0.10	0.10	0.10	0.20	0.20	0.20
D. Inward resource transfer (A − B + C)	2.23	1.39	1.31	1.68	2.99	3.43	2.43

							Average
	1977	*1978*	*1979*	*1980*	*1981*	*1982*	*1977–82*
A. Current account deficit	2.21	3.01	3.96	5.70	6.66	3.85	4.23
B. Interest payments	1.89	2.15	2.44	3.21	4.05	6.81	3.42
C. Remittances	0.20	0.20	0.20	0.20	0.10	0.20	0.18
D. Inward resource transfer (A − B + C)	0.52	1.06	1.72	2.69	2.71	−2.76	0.99

							Average
	1983	*1984*	*1985*	*1986*	*1987*	*1988*	*1983–88*
A. Current account deficit	−3.86	−2.53	−0.64	1.37	−2.98	1.50	−1.19
B. Interest payments	7.12	6.74	5.71	6.64	6.05	5.03	6.22
C. Remittances	0.20	0.20	0.60	0.40	0.50	0.30	0.37
D. Inward resource transfer (A − B + C)	−10.78	−9.07	−5.75	−4.87	−8.53	−3.23	−7.04

	Net debt flows (millions of dollars)								
	1980	*1981*	*1982*	*1983*	*1984*	*1985*	*1986*	*1987*	*1988*
Long-term private	6,026	11,565	6,349	2,635	789	−832	−978	2,754	−1,374
Long-term official	462	580	1,345	−453	406	302	918	488	298
World Bank	333	354	275	177	430	505	592	418	680
IMF	−134	−70	222	1,072	1,234	300	723	419	−93
Total	6,687	12,429	8,191	3,431	2,859	275	1,255	4,079	−489

Note: The current account deficits shown may differ from those shown in annex table AII.3.
Source: For resource transfers, World Bank data; for net debt flows, *World Debt Tables*, various issues.

Table 5A.13   Morocco

Resource transfers (percentage of GNP)							
	1970	*1971*	*1972*	*1973*	*1974*	*1975*	*1976*
A. Current account deficit	3.17	1.37	−0.95	−1.57	−2.96	5.94	15.26
B. Interest payments	0.64	0.69	0.71	0.71	0.60	0.64	0.84
C. Remittances	1.90	2.50	2.80	4.00	4.30	5.80	5.50
D. Inward resource transfer (A − B + C)	4.43	3.18	1.14	1.72	0.74	11.10	19.92

	1977	*1978*	*1979*	*1980*	*1981*	*1982*	*Average 1977–82*
A. Current account deficit	17.08	10.35	9.83	7.79	12.67	12.72	11.74
B. Interest payments	1.57	2.27	2.90	3.97	5.37	4.94	3.50
C. Remittances	5.20	5.90	6.00	6.10	7.50	6.80	6.25
D. Inward resource transfer (A − B + C)	20.71	13.98	12.93	9.92	14.80	14.58	14.49

	1983	*1984*	*1985*	*1986*	*1987*	*1988*	*Average 1983–88*
A. Current account deficit	6.70	8.13	7.36	1.30	−0.97	−2.23	3.38
B. Interest payments	5.10	5.34	4.90	4.52	4.30	4.57	4.79
C. Remittances	7.40	7.70	8.90	9.60	9.80	7.70	8.52
D. Inward resource transfer (A − B + C)	9.00	10.49	11.36	6.38	4.53	0.90	7.11

Net debt flows (millions of dollars)									
	1980	*1981*	*1982*	*1983*	*1984*	*1985*	*1986*	*1987*	*1988*
Long-term private	460	146	643	-40	376	245	166	177	102
Long-term official	671	1,008	681	320	397	230	249	212	148
World Bank	36	63	97	124	205	220	254	240	226
IMF	190	163	441	94	125	54	−313	137	−105
Total	1,357	1,380	1,862	498	1,103	749	356	766	371

Note: The current account deficits shown may differ from those shown in annex table AII.3.
Source: For resource transfers, World Bank data; for net debt flows, *World Debt Tables*, various issues.

Table 5A.14   Nigeria

Resource transfers
(percentage of GNP)

	1970	1971	1972	1973	1974	1975	1976
A. Current account deficit	2.79	2.73	2.00	0.04	−14.64	−0.11	−0.72
B. Interest payments	0.21	0.20	0.18	0.20	0.12	0.11	0.09
C. Remittances	0.50	0.00	−0.10	−0.30	−0.30	−0.30	−0.30
D. Inward resource transfer (A − B + C)	3.08	2.53	1.72	−0.46	−15.06	−0.52	−1.11

	1977	1978	1979	1980	1981	1982	*Average 1977–82*
A. Current account deficit	1.81	6.15	−2.20	−5.13	6.65	7.89	2.53
B. Interest payments	0.09	0.11	0.33	0.91	1.23	1.36	0.67
C. Remittances	−0.30	−0.40	−0.50	−0.60	−0.60	−0.50	−0.48
D. Inward resource transfer (A − B + C)	1.42	5.64	−3.03	−6.64	4.82	6.03	1.38

	1983	1984	1985	1986	1987	1988	*Average 1983–88*
A. Current account deficit	4.90	−0.12	−2.97	0.80	0.30	0.70	0.60
B. Interest payments	1.60	2.12	1.96	1.37	2.53	5.08	2.44
C. Remittances	−0.40	0.40	−0.30	−0.20	−0.10	0.00	−0.23
D. Inward resource transfer (A − B + C)	2.90	−2.64	−5.23	−0.77	−2.33	−4.38	−2.07

Net debt flows
(millions of dollars)

	1980	1981	1982	1983	1984	1985	1986	1987	1988
Long-term private	1,413	2,320	2,633	1,146	−500	−1,071	−485	366	52
Long-term official	15	94	113	528	39	−360	144	72	101
World Bank	39	45	111	150	224	229	446	261	49
IMF	0	0	0	0	0	0	0	0	0
Total	1,467	2,459	2,857	1,824	−237	−1,202	105	699	202

Note: The current account deficits shown may differ from those shown in annex table AII.3.
Source: For resource transfers, World Bank data; for net debt flows, *World Debt Tables*, various issues.

Table 5A.15   Pakistan

	Resource transfers (percentage of GNP)						
	1970	*1971*	*1972*	*1973*	*1974*	*1975*	*1976*
A. Current account deficit	6.66	4.56	2.60	1.30	5.70	9.50	6.30
B. Interest payments	0.77	0.56	1.21	1.31	0.97	0.91	0.99
C. Remittances	1.20	1.70	1.90	3.00	2.30	3.00	3.60
D. Inward resource transfer (A − B + C)	7.09	5.70	3.29	2.99	7.03	11.59	8.91

	1977	*1978*	*1979*	*1980*	*1981*	*1982*	*Average 1977–82*
A. Current account deficit	6.10	2.80	4.20	3.70	2.70	3.70	3.87
B. Interest payments	0.96	1.04	1.10	1.43	1.04	1.25	1.14
C. Remittances	4.90	7.60	9.20	9.20	9.00	9.30	8.20
D. Inward resource transfer (A − B + C)	10.04	9.36	12.30	11.47	10.66	11.75	10.93

	1983	*1984*	*1985*	*1986*	*1987*	*1988*	*Average 1983–88*
A. Current account deficit	−0.60	2.20	4.20	2.50	1.00	3.10	2.27
B. Interest payments	1.40	1.30	1.31	1.59	1.68	1.72	1.50
C. Remittances	12.10	10.90	10.10	10.60	9.00	7.40	10.02
D. Inward resource transfer (A − B + C)	10.10	11.80	12.99	11.51	8.32	8.78	10.79

	Net debt flows (millions of dollars)								
	1980	*1981*	*1982*	*1983*	*1984*	*1985*	*1986*	*1987*	*1988*
Long-term private	168	−21	448	−86	163	−189	42	140	−146
Long-term official	480	364	448	213	300	334	244	111	593
World Bank	60	67	173	109	128	134	203	283	375
IMF	169	414	409	272	−72	−185	−368	−429	−312
Total	877	824	1,478	508	519	94	121	105	510

Note: The current account deficits shown may differ from those shown in annex table AII.3.
Source: For resource transfers, World Bank data; for net debt flows, *World Debt Tables*, various issues.

Table 5A.16   Sri Lanka

	Resource transfers (percentage of GNP)						
	1970	*1971*	*1972*	*1973*	*1974*	*1975*	*1976*
A. Current account deficit	3.00	1.80	1.70	1.20	4.90	3.80	0.18
B. Interest payments	0.54	0.48	0.54	0.54	0.47	0.55	0.65
C. Remittances	0.60	0.70	0.60	0.60	1.50	2.70	2.40
D. Inward resource transfer (A − B + C)	3.06	2.02	1.76	1.26	5.93	5.95	1.93

							Average
	1977	*1978*	*1979*	*1980*	*1981*	*1982*	*1977–82*
A. Current account deficit	−5.30	2.49	6.82	16.44	10.32	11.40	7.03
B. Interest payments	0.76	1.47	1.60	1.72	1.97	1.99	1.59
C. Remittances	2.70	2.90	5.70	6.90	8.40	8.80	5.90
D. Inward resource transfer (A − B + C)	−3.36	3.92	10.92	21.62	16.75	18.21	11.34

							Average
	1983	*1984*	*1985*	*1986*	*1987*	*1988*	*1983–88*
A. Current account deficit	9.07	−0.01	7.03	6.54	4.90	5.84	5.56
B. Interest payments	2.27	2.13	2.22	2.12	2.35	2.18	2.21
C. Remittances	8.70	8.20	7.40	7.40	7.40	7.50	7.77
D. Inward resource transfer (A − B + C)	15.50	6.06	12.21	11.82	9.95	11.16	11.12

	Net debt flows (millions of dollars)								
	1980	*1981*	*1982*	*1983*	*1984*	*1985*	*1986*	*1987*	*1988*
Long-term private	86	182	222	59	81	43	9	−63	−92
Long-term official	117	137	118	169	170	223	249	168	231
World Bank	18	26	56	71	90	74	82	82	57
IMF	29	144	−6	−13	−12	−53	−84	−116	97
Total	250	489	390	286	329	287	256	71	293

Note: The current account deficits shown may differ from those shown in annex table AII.3.
Source: For resource transfers, World Bank data; for net debt flows, *World Debt Tables*, various issues.

Table 5A.17   Thailand

			Resource transfers (percentage of GNP)				
	1970	*1971*	*1972*	*1973*	*1974*	*1975*	*1976*
A. Current account deficit	3.52	2.37	0.63	0.43	0.63	4.20	2.60
B. Interest payments	0.46	0.54	0.50	0.51	0.62	0.70	0.63
C. Remittances	0.70	0.60	0.70	1.30	1.80	0.50	0.30
D. Inward resource transfer (A – B + C)	3.76	2.43	0.83	1.22	1.81	4.00	2.27

							Average
	1977	*1978*	*1979*	*1980*	*1981*	*1982*	*1977–82*
A. Current account deficit	5.57	4.84	7.71	6.49	7.49	2.86	5.83
B. Interest payments	1.28	1.98	2.44	2.50	3.35	2.98	2.42
C. Remittances	0.20	0.20	0.20	0.70	0.50	0.50	0.38
D. Inward resource transfer (A – B + C)	4.49	3.06	5.47	4.69	4.64	0.38	3.79

							Average
	1983	*1984*	*1985*	*1986*	*1987*	*1988*	*1983–88*
A. Current account deficit	7.32	5.18	4.19	–0.61	0.77	2.80	3.28
B. Interest payments	2.79	2.81	3.51	3.08	2.70	2.45	2.89
C. Remittances	0.70	0.40	0.50	0.60	0.50	0.40	0.52
D. Inward resource transfer (A – B + C)	5.23	2.77	1.18	–3.09	–1.43	0.75	0.91

				Net debt flows (millions of dollars)				
	1980	*1981*	*1982*	*1983*	*1984*	*1985*	*1986*	*1987*	*1988*
Long-term private	1,255	949	668	417	849	939	–451	–13	624
Long-term official	423	360	303	441	397	371	243	63	95
World Bank	124	284	354	398	261	209	77	–24	–493
IMF	23	547	33	242	–74	101	–172	–247	–260
Total	1,825	2,140	1,358	1,498	1,433	1,620	–303	–221	–34

Note: The current account deficits shown may differ from those shown in annex table AII.3.
Source: For resource transfers, World Bank data; for net debt flows, *World Debt Tables*, various issues.

Table 5A.18   Turkey

	Resource transfers (percentage of GNP)						
	1970	1971	1972	1973	1974	1975	1976
A. Current account deficit	0.35	−0.35	−1.30	−3.18	1.92	4.60	4.94
B. Interest payments	0.35	0.44	0.40	0.40	0.34	0.33	0.41
C. Remittances	2.60	4.60	4.90	6.00	5.10	4.00	2.70
D. Inward resource transfer (A − B + C)	2.60	3.81	3.20	2.42	6.68	8.27	7.23

							Average
	1977	1978	1979	1980	1981	1982	1977–82
A. Current account deficit	6.59	2.43	2.07	6.11	3.41	1.81	3.74
B. Interest payments	1.45	1.69	1.07	1.44	2.47	2.90	1.84
C. Remittances	2.30	2.10	2.60	3.90	4.50	4.40	3.30
D. Inward resource transfer (A − B + C)	7.44	2.84	3.60	8.57	5.44	3.31	5.20

							Average
	1983	1984	1985	1986	1987	1988	1983–88
A. Current account deficit	3.82	2.92	2.00	2.70	1.20	−2.30	1.72
B. Interest payments	3.30	3.42	3.49	3.47	3.61	4.52	3.63
C. Remittances	3.50	4.40	3.90	3.40	3.60	3.10	3.65
D. Inward resource transfer (A − B + C)	4.02	3.90	2.41	2.63	1.19	−3.72	1.74

	Net debt flows (millions of dollars)								
	1980	1981	1982	1983	1984	1985	1986	1987	1988
Long-term private	641	−11	150	139	303	−15	1,092	1,207	1,446
Long-term official	973	754	345	−43	534	−38	249	46	80
World Bank	267	390	414	371	499	477	397	467	356
IMF	485	365	202	190	−43	−251	−376	−451	−431
Total	2,366	1,498	1,111	657	1,293	173	1,362	1,269	1,451

Note: The current account deficits shown may differ from those shown in annex table AII.3.
Source: For resource transfers, World Bank data; for net debt flows, *World Debt Tables*, various issues.

Appendix 5B

We did multiple regression analysis of the growth of per capita GNP for 1982–89 on the "independent" variables discussed in the text, together with some trade variables. We also included the growth rate of GNP from 1974 to 1981. This was intended to pick up continuing background influences on growth not specified in the other "independent" variables. The list of variables, with their acronyms and sources, is as follows:

Dependent Variable
G = Exponential annual growth rate of GNP per capita, 1982–89 (table 5.2, column 7).

Independent Variables
$CADEF$ = The current account deficit as a percentage of GNP, 1982 (table 5.2, column 1).
INV = The mean of total investment as a percentage of GNP, 1983–88 (table 5.2, col. 4).
ΔINV = INV minus the similar mean, 1977–82 (table 5.2, col. 3).
ΔT = The mean of inward transfers as a percentage of GNP, 1983–88 less the similar mean, 1977–82 (table 5.2, column 5).
$CHTOT$ = Terms of trade 1988/1982 (table 5.3).
$GVALEX$ = Exponential growth rate of the dollar value of exports (table 5.5, column 1) (estimated as the dollar value of imports into developed countries).
$GVOLEX$ = Exponential growth rate of the "volume" of exports estimated (table 5.5, column 2) as $VALEX$ divided by the Bank's export price index.
$G7481$ = The growth rate of GNP, 1974–81.

Apart from the above we also tried a dummy for rescheduling. This was never significant, because of its high correlation with INV, ΔINV, and ΔT. The change in average inflation between 1977–82 and 1983–88 was also tried but was never significant, although the coefficient had the expected negative sign. The $CADEF$ was

Table 5B.1   Correlation Matrix

	G8289	INV 8388	ΔINV	ΔTrs	CADEF	CHTOT 88/82	GVOLX	GVALEX	G7481
INV 8388	.67	1							
ΔINV	.70	.72	1						
ΔTrs	.16	.01	.38	1					
CADEF	-.23	-.18	-.12	-.04	1				
CHTOT	.43	.29	.33	-.18	.28	1			
GVOLEX	.69	.53	.61	.07	-.46	.44	1		
GVALEX	.72	.53	.60	-.07	-.12	.75	.88	1	
G 7481	.43	.49	.42	.10	-.12	-.10	.13	.12	1

included because it was the least insignificant variable when growth was regressed on this and other initial conditions.

We saw earlier that some surprising results emerged from estimating simple correlations because they were dominated by a few extreme outliers—Korea, Nigeria, and sometimes also Cameroon, Costa Rica, and Côte d'Ivoire. Multiple regression analysis also suffers from a high degree of multicollinearity. That is, some pairs of "independent" variables are themselves highly correlated. This is shown in the correlation matrix. In particular, both the volume and value of exports are strongly correlated with the investment variables, while growth in the earlier period 1974–81 is also quite strongly correlated with investment in 1983–88.

A brief account follows of some actual equations estimated. First we used all the "independent" variables except *VALEX*, since it made little sense to include all three trade variables. None were significant. Δ*INV*, *CADEF*, and Δ*T* were then successively eliminated in order of insignificance. *GVOLEX* alone became significant at this stage. Successive elimination of *CHTOT* and *G7481* left the equation (*t* values in parentheses):

$$(5B\text{-}1) \quad G = -5.3 + .24\,INV + .26\,GVOLEX$$
$$\phantom{(5B\text{-}1) \quad G = } (2.2) \qquad (2.4)$$

$$\begin{aligned} R^2 &= 0.60 \\ F &= 11.40 \\ DW &= 2.60 \end{aligned}$$

When *GVALEX* was used instead of *CHTOT* and *GVOLEX*, it alone was found to be significant even when all other variables were included. Successive elimination of insignificant variables resulted in

$$(5B\text{-}2) \quad G = -1.5 + .54\,G7481 + .26\,GVALEX$$
$$\phantom{(5B\text{-}2) \quad G = } (2.3) \qquad\quad (4.4)$$

$$\begin{aligned} R^2 &= 0.64 \\ F &= 13.60 \\ DW &= 2.40 \end{aligned}$$

Notice that *G7481* is strongly correlated with INV ($r = .49$), and hardly correlated with *GVALEX* ($r = .12$), while INV is strongly correlated with *GVALEX* ($r = .53$). This explains why G7481 enters equation (5-2) rather than INV. Substituting the latter for the former produces the equation

$$(5B\text{-}3) \quad G = -4.4 + .22\,INV + .19\,GVALEX$$
$$\phantom{(5B\text{-}3) \quad G = } (2.1) \qquad (2.8)$$

$$\begin{aligned} R^2 &= 0.63 \\ F &= 13.00 \\ DW &= 2.50 \end{aligned}$$

What, if anything, do we learn from this? Initial conditions, and indicators of short- and medium-term economic turmoil (*CADEF*, ΔINV, and ΔT) have little or no explanatory value when the investment ratio and measures of export success are included among the "independent" variables. Earlier growth is as good an explanatory variable as investment, but is less robust (it dropped out of the first set of equations described) and has less theoretical appeal than the investment ratio. The investment ratio alone explains statistically 45 percent of the variance of growth, and the growth of the value of exports explains 52 percent. Together, they explain 63 percent; however, the so-called independent variables are too endogenous and interrelated for such regression analysis to indicate the causal mechanisms involved. Although the inclusion of all the variables discussed adds but little to our understanding of the period, we nevertheless believe that the regressions provide support for the view that export performance was an important cause of growth in this period.

Chapter 6

Inflation in the Eighteen Countries

In this chapter and the next, we look at inflation in our eighteen countries. We are particularly interested in the connection between exogenous shocks and inflation and in the outcome of stabilization attempts. Chapter 7 describes in greater detail the experiences of two chronically high-inflation countries—Argentina and Brazil—and also the episodes of high inflation in Chile, Mexico, Turkey, and Indonesia.

Historical Overview

For most of our countries, as for most members of the Organization for Economic Cooperation and Development (OECD), 1973 was a watershed year from the point of view of inflation. Hence, the chapter opens with an overview of the situation on the eve of the disturbances of 1973–75.

Inflation before 1973

In the early 1970s, developing countries in general were thought to be high-inflation countries, but this image is contradicted by the average CPI figures for 1970–72 (column 2 of table 6-1), if we assume high to mean in excess of 50 percent, or even 20 percent. Argentina, Brazil, and Chile were in the main responsible for this image, but they were clearly not representative. Even the two Central American countries in our group—Mexico (5 percent) and Costa Rica (4 percent)—were low-inflation countries up to 1972. Brazil's average inflation rate of 20 percent over these three years was actually rather low compared with earlier years.

Clearly, Argentina (36 percent) and Chile (42 percent) stand out. By the standards of those years, any inflation rate from 10 to 20 percent would be regarded as

Table 6.1   Inflation Rates and Bubbles, 1960–89

(annual average CPI inflation rate)

Country	1960–69	1970–72	First bubble 1973–75	1976–79	Second bubble 1980–82	1983–89	End of period 1988–89
Argentina	22.9	35.6	313.4[b]	238.7	123.3	755.3	3,079.8[m]
Brazil	45.9	19.7	28.2[c]	44.3	95.4	415.7	1,287.0[m]
Cameroon	2.0[a]	6.0	17.2[e]	10.9	14.9[h]	7.4	4.3
Chile	25.1	42.4	413.7	94.3	27.4[f]	21.3	15.9
Colombia	11.2	9.8	22.7	23.9	26.2	22.3	27.0
Costa Rica	2.0	4.1	20.9	5.7	53.3[g]	17.9	18.7
Côte d'Ivoire	3.4[a]	2.7	17.4[e]	17.3	10.3	4.0	4.1
India	6.0	4.9	22.8[d]	2.4	12.2[i]	8.4	7.8
Indonesia	100.6	7.7	35.8[d]	13.8	17.1[j]	8.1	7.2
Kenya	1.8	3.9	18.5[c]	12.8	15.4	8.9	9.1
Korea, Rep.	12.0	13.7	24.8[c]	14.6	25.0[i]	3.8	6.4
Mexico	2.7	5.2	17.0	20.1	80.3[h]	82.5	20.0[m]
Morocco	2.5	3.1	17.6[e]	9.8	10.8	6.2	2.8
Nigeria	3.5	11.1	29.1[b]	17.9	20.8[l]	27.5	52.5
Pakistan	3.7	5.1	23.5	7.9	11.9[i]	6.2	8.3
Sri Lanka	2.2	5.0	11.0[d]	6.4	22.1[i]	10.5	12.8
Thailand	2.2	1.7	19.9[d]	7.4	16.2[i]	2.9	4.6
Turkey	3.5	11.5	16.8	37.1	110.2[k]	48.1	69.3

a. 1961–69.   b. 1975–76.   c. 1974–75.   d. 1973–74.   e. 1974.   f. 1980–81.   g. 1981–83.
h. 1982–83.   i. 1980–81.   j. 1979–80.   k. 1980.   l. 1981.   m. 1989.
Source: World Bank data.

moderately high—well above the OECD average rate of 5 percent. Five countries fell into this "moderately high" category—Brazil (20 percent), Korea (14 percent), Turkey (12 percent), Nigeria (11 percent), and Colombia (10 percent). The remaining eleven countries averaged less than 8 percent inflation during those three years, Thailand being the lowest, at 2 percent. Thailand has had remarkably low inflation over long periods.

The first column of table 6-1 shows the average inflation rates during the 1960s (for annual figures, see table AII.2 in annex II at the end of the book). Indonesia stands out here. Under the Soekarno regime, it experienced very high inflation in 1962–66, which topped 600 percent in 1966. This was followed by a successful stabilization that brought the inflation rate down to 10 percent by 1969 (see chapter 7). The Korean average inflation rate during the 1960s was only moderately high (12 percent), but during the Korean War it hit 500 percent in 1951 and 108 percent in 1952. By 1953 it was down to 30 percent. Thus, Korea, like Indonesia, experienced an episode of very high inflation foilowed by successful stabilization.

In the case of the three "traditional" high-inflation countries—Brazil, Argentina, and Chile—the averages for the 1960s actually hide great variations. The Brazilian average inflation rate was 46 percent, but it reached 92 percent in 1964 and then gave way to a period of remarkably successful stabilization that brought the inflation rate down to 23 percent by 1969. The Argentinian average inflation rate was 23 percent, but in 1959 it moved up to 114 percent and there were actually two stabilization episodes during the period. The same pattern occurred in Chile, where the average was 25 percent and the peak 45 percent, with two stabilization episodes during the period.

The Colombian average inflation rate during the 1960s was only 11 percent, but the rate was very variable and reached 32 percent in 1963 (owing to an exceptional, and temporary, increase in the fiscal deficit in 1962). The Indian inflation rate averaged 6 percent but was also variable, averaging 12 percent during the four years 1964–67. Indian inflation during that period was increased by drought and, to a lesser extent, by the 1966 devaluation. For the remaining ten countries, including Mexico and Costa Rica in Latin America, inflation rates in the 1960s were similar to or a little higher than those prevailing in the developed countries—usually averaging 3 percent or even less. This low inflation was accompanied by fixed exchange rates.

Inflation Experience 1973–89

The three traditional high-inflation countries were certainly special cases during the period 1973–89. Brazil's inflation rate rose to a new plateau (averaging 44 percent) as a result of the first oil shock, moved to an even higher plateau (95 percent average) as a result of the second oil and real interest rate shock, and jumped to 189 percent as a result of the third shock of the debt crisis. This was followed from 1986 by several stabilization plans that failed and by hyperinflation in 1989. Argentina also had a variable high-inflation experience that culminated in hyperinflation in 1989. Chile was different. It began the period with extreme inflation resulting from the policies of the socialist Allende regime, but the drastic stabilization policies of the Pinochet regime after 1976 brought the rate down to 10 percent by 1982. Since then inflation has gone up again, but never into the really high ranges.

From around 1972 to 1973, two countries—Mexico and Turkey—gradually became transformed into high-inflation countries, as also discussed in chapter 7. This leaves thirteen low- or moderate-inflation countries.

All thirteen of these countries, except Colombia and Korea, had fixed exchange rates during the world inflation of 1972–73 and the first oil shock. Given the fixed rates, it was inevitable that world inflation would be transmitted to the domestic price level of tradable goods, and that some of the impact would be transmitted to wages and nontradables. Several other factors played an important role as well.

In developed countries government spending had been increasing faster than real output, and there was a spirit of expansionism—a kind of euphoria about what was possible. This spirit also came to be transmitted to many developing countries, where it led to increases in domestic spending that, sometimes with a lag, had inflationary effects through increasing demand for domestically produced goods. In addition, it increased the demand for imports and thereby contributed to a later balance of payments crisis and, in several cases, to devaluation.

Changes in the terms of trade brought further effects. As observed in chapter 3, the terms of trade improved in three of the thirteen countries (Indonesia, Nigeria, and Morocco), showed no significant change in one (Colombia), and in 1974 deteriorated in the nine that were oil importers. Four of these countries (Costa Rica, Kenya, Côte d'Ivoire, and Cameroon), as well as Colombia, benefited from the short-lived coffee boom of 1976–78. That left five Asian countries (India, Pakistan, Sri Lanka, Korea, Thailand) with a deterioration in the terms of trade uncompensated by any improvement until oil prices fell in the 1980s.

In all thirteen countries, whether their terms of trade improved or worsened, the rate of inflation increased sharply in 1973 or 1974, or both (table 6-1, column 3). In most cases, this was an "inflationary bubble," for the rate of inflation declined again in 1975 or 1976, though not always to the pre-1973 level.

As a result of the shocks described in chapter 4, sometime in the period 1980–83 (mostly in 1980–81), almost all the countries experienced another inflationary bubble—very marked in some cases, modest in others. This can also be seen from table 6-1. After that, inflation rates went down, except in Colombia, Nigeria, Brazil, Argentina, Mexico, and Turkey. Costa Rica had an exceptional bubble. Developments in Colombia, Costa Rica, and Nigeria since 1980 are discussed in some detail later in the chapter.

The pattern over the whole period becomes clearer when the inflation position at the end of the period (1988–89 average) is compared with the initial 1970–72 position (table 6-1). In 1989 Argentina and Brazil were both in the hyperinflation range in comparison with the 36 percent and 20 percent, respectively, experienced earlier. Chile and Turkey changed places in a drastic turnabout: from 42 percent to 16 percent for Chile, and from 12 percent to 69 percent for Turkey. Mexico in 1989 had only 20 percent inflation, a steep descent from the preceding 100 percent levels, bringing it closer to its 5 percent inflation of 1970–72. Nigeria joined the high-inflation category, going from 11 percent to 53 percent. The only other country with more than 20 percent inflation was Colombia (27 percent). Costa Rica (19 percent) and Sri Lanka (13 percent) went up somewhat. Korea became a low-inflation country (from 14 percent to 6 percent). Finally, eight countries that had inflation rates below 10 percent before were still at that level at the end of the period, although several had gone through "bubble" episodes.

Thus, by the end of the period only six had 20 percent or more inflation, and among the entire group, Argentina and Brazil were very unusual. To repeat a point made earlier, these figures prove false the common impression that developing countries in general tend to be very inflationary. They also show tremendous variety among the countries. Obviously, there is much to explain.[1]

Adjustment Inflation, Spiral Inflation, and Monetization: A Framework of Analysis

Inflation can take three forms, a classification that provides a useful framework for sorting out the varying reactions to shocks in our eighteen countries, as long as it is remembered that all three kinds may come together. The first kind, "adjustment inflation," is temporary and thus leads to inflationary "bubbles." It represents a process of getting to a new equilibrium. The second is "spiral inflation," which may be more prolonged and is essentially a disequilibrium process. The third is "seigniorage inflation," which results from monetization of fiscal deficits.

Adjustment Inflation

For the oil-importing countries—that is, countries that suffered a terms-of-trade deterioration in 1974 and again in later years—the direct effect of the oil price rise was that the price to domestic consumers and to industrial users of oil went up, and they then passed on the increased costs to consumers. This is a relative price adjustment and in itself would not bring about continuous inflation; but such an adjustment usually does not happen all at once, so it does lead to a rise in the rate of inflation for one or two years—and hence to an "inflationary bubble." This direct transmission effect was related not only to the oil price rise but also to the world inflation in tradable goods in general. The oil price rises of 1973–74 were preceded by a general commodity boom that raised import prices for many countries.

Furthermore, an oil price rise will worsen the balance of payments and hence lead to a decline in reserves, and it may then induce a devaluation of the exchange rate. Realistically, this assumes that the effects of the decline in reserves on the domestic money supply are sterilized, so that domestic demand is maintained and an automatic mechanism for improving the balance of payments is not allowed to operate. The devaluation then leads to a further rise in domestic prices. This effect is also a price adjustment and will add to the inflation bubble. In fact, only a few countries out of the thirteen discussed in this chapter did devalue as a result of the first oil shock (Korea, Kenya, Costa Rica), but there were more devaluations in the 1980–82 period (see table 8-2).

These two effects—the direct price effect and the exchange rate effect—produce the domestic relative price adjustment necessitated by the oil price rise. This adjustment involves a gradual or possibly quite sudden rise in the average domestic price level.

Next, consider the effects on inflation of an improvement in the terms of trade through a rise in export prices. Between 1973 and 1979, those of our countries that experienced such an improvement were Indonesia and Nigeria (oil), Morocco (phosphates), and the five coffee exporters (Cameroon, Colombia, Costa Rica, Côte d'Ivoire, Kenya).

When a rise in export income is saved, it can lead to an increase in foreign exchange reserves, reduced foreign borrowing, or capital outflow, public or private. In these cases it will not affect inflation one way or the other. In all of our countries, at least part—and in some cases all—of the gains were spent, either mainly by the government or partly by the government and partly by the private sector. Some of the funds went for imports and some for domestically produced goods. Insofar as such gains are spent on domestic goods and services—including labor—domestic prices and wages will tend to rise. A rise in the relative price of nontradables to tradables is required to restore equilibrium in the market for non-tradables or, more generally domestic goods, when any of the gains from a boom are spent on such goods. Given a fixed nominal exchange rate, this is brought about by a domestic price and wage adjustment. It is the "spending effect" of a boom, and thus gives rise to adjustment inflation in the form of an inflation bubble.

Note that when the terms of trade deteriorate because import prices rise (as in the case of our oil importers), adjustment inflation also takes place. Then, the relative price of domestic goods or nontradables needs to fall, not to rise, as in the case of increased export income. It may seem curious that both a terms-of-trade deterioration and a terms-of-trade improvement would bring about the same kind of inflationary bubble. An external shock, whether unfavorable or favorable, requires a relative price change (at least, provided that it leads to changes in spending on domestic goods), and this relative price change is in practice brought about by an absolute price increase in both cases. When the terms of trade deteriorate in response to rising import prices, the relative price change is brought about by this rise in import prices, supplemented in some cases by devaluation; and when the terms of trade improve in response to rising export prices, the change is brought about by a rise in the prices of domestically produced (essentially nontraded) goods and services.

Adjustment inflation may also take place when the prices of goods and services sold by the public sector rise as a result of an effort to reduce a public sector deficit. Such adjustments in public sector prices—in particular public utility prices—are usually the ingredients of a structural adjustment program and may also be required as a result of a deterioration in the terms of trade that usually increases a budget deficit. This, together with a large devaluation, helps to explain the exceptionally high (110 percent) Turkish inflation in 1980.

Spiral Inflation

The initial domestic price increases brought about by an oil price rise, by increases in the foreign prices of other imports, or by devaluation may generate "spiral inflation." In such instances, higher prices lead to higher wages, hence higher costs, higher prices of nontradables, further wage increases, possibly more devaluation, and so on. The initial price effects in themselves might cause only a bubble, but in certain circumstances they can start off an inflationary process. This is "spiral inflation." Such a process can only continue if the money supply is steadily increased. When a deterioration in the terms of trade initially leads to a reduction in real wages, sometimes nominal wages are increased in the hope of restoring real wages. At the same time, monetary expansion may take place to maintain employment, by raising prices ahead of wages. A wage-price process of this kind may be destabilizing: the rate of inflation may accelerate as monetary expansion becomes less and less successful in raising prices ahead of wages and thus in keeping real wages down and employment up. More often, the process begins but then peters out at the cost of unemployment and temporarily reduced growth because of monetary tightness.

Some inflationary bubbles seem to be greater than can be readily explained by pure adjustment inflation and may contain an element of temporary spiral inflation. Evidence of spiral inflation is clearest in the case of Brazil, but it has probably been a factor in all six Latin American countries.

Seigniorage Inflation

So far, monetary policy has played a rather subsidiary role in our analysis. Yet the growth of the money supply resulting from fiscal deficits is obviously one of the factors that give rise to prolonged inflation. Consequently, whether inflation is moderate (as in Colombia, Costa Rica, and Nigeria) or high (as in the countries discussed in chapter 7), it cannot be fully understood without some information on fiscal conditions.[2]

Fiscal deficits are financed to some extent—and sometimes primarily—by money creation, and such continuous monetization is often the principal cause of inflation. If inflation is to be reduced, fiscal deficits have to be reduced. The ability of a state to finance its deficit through money creation—that is, to obtain real resources through its monopoly of the supply of domestic money—is called seigniorage, and when the need to generate seigniorage is responsible for the growth of the money supply, the country is experiencing "seigniorage inflation."

Seigniorage is a form of revenue for the government. It will not cause inflation if the supply of money merely keeps up with the growth in the demand for money in real terms, because of the growth of real gross domestic product (GDP) and other factors that make money demand rise faster than real GDP, such as increased monetization of the economy resulting from economic development. When the money supply expands beyond such growth in real demand, inflation occurs. Inflation lowers the real value of existing holdings of money, and the increases in the money supply generating seigniorage restore it again. Holders of money are able to restore their real balances by savings that are designed to obtain the additional money supply, and these savings, in effect, finance the government deficit. Thus the government obtains real resources through taxes on money balances, this being the inflation tax, which is a part—often a very large part—of seigniorage. In addition, inflation tends to reduce the real wage as prices rise ahead of nominal wages for various reasons. The redistribution of income within the private sector from wages to profits would probably raise private savings and so reduce absorption.

The process is actually far more complex than this simple description suggests. To begin with, the fiscal deficit itself may also depend on the rate of inflation. This is an important relationship called the Tanzi effect.[3] If tax revenue assessed on 1988 incomes is received in 1989 and meanwhile prices have risen 50 percent, the real value of these revenues will have fallen in comparison with their value in 1988. The higher the rate of inflation and the greater the lags in tax collection, the lower will be tax revenue in real terms for any given set of formal tax rates.

The Tanzi effect interacts with seigniorage inflation in the following way. Government expenditure in real terms may increase and so raise the deficit and the rate of growth of the money supply, and subsequently the rate of inflation. We can assume tax rates to be constant. The higher inflation then reduces tax revenue in real terms owing to the Tanzi effect and so raises the deficit further, which causes further inflation, which increases the deficit, and so on. Provided the Tanzi effect is not too large (a low elasticity of the deficit in response to inflation), the process will be stable: an equilibrium rate of inflation and fiscal deficit for the given increase in real government expenditure will be attained.

Deficits can also be debt-financed, and this solution may not be inflationary, at least immediately. A shift from monetization to debt financing of the deficit would then reduce inflation. Many issues arise here, some of which will be discussed further in chapters 7 and 10. An increase in a deficit that is debt-financed may have a direct demand-expanding effect, and hence may bring about some rise in prices. Although this would not directly cause continuous inflation, it might raise the future deficit through the accumulating interest burden, and eventually this might lead to more inflation. Debt in relation to GDP cannot accumulate indefinitely. Eventually the deficit must be reduced through the generation of a noninterest surplus (a *primary* surplus), or it must be monetized.

Note, too, that expected inflation tends to raise nominal interest rates. For a given real interest rate, the higher the expected inflation, the higher the nominal interest rate. The higher interest rate compensates for the expected decline in the real value of given nominal debt. This increase in the interest rate then raises the nominal fiscal deficit, because of higher interest payments on new debt and on existing debt as it matures and is rolled over. Yet the end result will not be a real increase in the deficit, since at the same time inflation will reduce the real value of existing debt.

One can calculate an inflation-adjusted fiscal deficit, which subtracts from the nominal deficit that part that is explained by the higher interest bill caused by expected inflation. If holders of debt wished to maintain the real value of their financial assets during a period of inflation, they would use the extra nominal interest receipts resulting from expected inflation for the purchase of more nominal debt. If interest rates are controlled, however, or if there is an element of surprise inflation, the compensation will not be complete; some net inflation tax of debt will then remain. Alternatively, if debt is not held entirely voluntarily, holders may be compelled to let the real value erode. In Brazil, Mexico, and some other countries, the deficit adjusted for the effect of inflation on the government's interest payments is called the *operational deficit*, a concept that will be referred to again in chapters 7 and 10. It should be distinguished both from the *primary deficit*, which excludes net interest payments altogether, and from the total nominal deficit of the public sector—the *public sector borrowing requirement*—which covers the whole of the interest bill, including that part caused by expected inflation.

Yet another point to note is that the demand for money itself depends on inflation. The higher that inflation is expected to climb, the lower will be the demand for money as asset holders seek to shift out of money (an asset that is expected to yield a negative rate of return) into other assets, both financial assets and goods, that they expect to yield a positive rate of return, or at least one that is not as low as that on money. The demand for money thus depends on the expected rate of inflation, which is likely to respond to the actual rate of inflation.

Normally, an increase in the actual rate of inflation would gradually raise the expected rate, though the latter will also depend on many other factors, notably indications of the future fiscal policy of the government. Even if the expected rate of inflation rises, the demand for money may not fall much or immediately. It may take time for people to find ways of economizing on money and to find adequate substitutes, and for institutions to develop that can provide such alternatives easily.

Similarly, a decline in inflation, or evidence of a policy change expected to push down inflation, will raise the demand for money, and hence help reduce inflation further. An announcement of a change in fiscal policy that would eventually lead to reduced monetization—even though there is no immediate effect on the rate of growth of the money supply—could immediately reduce the rate of inflation through an increase in the demand for money. Thus, it is possible for a stabilization program to have a very quick effect through its influence on expectations, though finally it will depend on what happens to the actual rate of money growth.

The three kinds of inflation described here are not mutually exclusive or contradictory. They simply reflect different motivations. An increased growth in the money supply for whatever reason is likely, within limits, to generate more seigniorage, and so permit a higher fiscal deficit than otherwise (for given debt finance). The motivation for the increase could come primarily from the need to finance a higher deficit—the result being the seigniorage kind of inflation. Alternatively, it could come from an attempt to forestall the deflationary effects of import price increases, or price increases resulting from wage pressures (accommodating inflation). In such cases, the higher seigniorage is an incidental by-product.

Monetary expansion could also result from the accumulation of foreign exchange reserves when the exchange rate is fixed and there is an export boom or capital inflow, as there was in Colombia during the coffee boom. In such cases, adjustment inflation and temporary monetary expansion go hand in hand.

The seigniorage motivation—and not just the other two kinds—could possibly explain some of the increases in inflation in oil-importing countries after the two oil shocks. The oil price increases typically had adverse effects on budgets: governments were direct users of oil and competing fuels; profits of parastatal enterprises that were oil users fell or losses increased; and tax revenue fell because of lower profits and incomes in the private sector, and because of reduced spending on taxable non-oil imports. The immediate response to this fiscal problem in oil-importing countries was some combination of more foreign borrowing, domestic borrowing from the private sector, and monetization. After the first oil shock, the most common response was to increase foreign borrowing. Insofar as the monetization road was chosen, the oil price rise set off an inflationary process.

Inflation and the Current Account: The Tradeoff Model

A simple model that involves seigniorage inflation sheds considerable light on what happened in several countries in response to the 1982 debt crisis and also on other occasions. It features a "tradeoff" between the current account and inflation. We start with a given operational fiscal deficit. Suppose that initially a large part of it has been financed by foreign borrowing. Next, suppose that a debt crisis arises and that the further supply of funds obtainable on normal commercial terms begins drying up.

The government has several possible options here. It can reduce the fiscal deficit by reducing government spending or raising taxes. It may be able to continue with a current account deficit by financing the budget deficit through emergency borrowing from official or private sources (in the latter case, perhaps, through concerted lending programs of private banks), or by going into arrears. It might shift from foreign financing to domestic borrowing, thus raising domestic interest rates and crowding out private borrowers and so reducing private investment. Finally, it might switch from foreign borrowing to borrowing from the central bank, that is, to monetization.

In practice, all four choices were made in response to the 1981–83 crises, but a major tradeoff was between continued current account deficits financed by foreign borrowing and monetization of fiscal deficits, and hence, directly or indirectly, increased inflation. Some countries chose, or stumbled into, increased inflation as a result of the need to reduce the current account deficit. The large group of low-inflation countries avoided this approach: in the 1980–83 crisis period, some chose to borrow abroad further, and most improved their fiscal positions. Several also made the "inflation choice," an outstanding example being Mexico. Mexico faced a tradeoff between the current account and inflation: the more the current account improved, and hence the less the reliance on debt finance, the higher the inflation rate. This tradeoff could have been avoided by cutting the fiscal deficit sufficiently (which was done eventually), but this was difficult to do quickly.

Another way of putting this matter is that the loss of foreign financing for the budget deficit requires the current account to be improved. Such an improvement calls for a reduction of real expenditures (absorption), which could be brought about either by a reduction of government expenditures or by a tax increase that reduces private expenditures. One form of tax is the inflation tax: it is a way of generating private savings (designed to restore real balances) and hence reducing absorption sufficiently. In addition, as noted above, inflation is likely to reduce real wages, and thereby may also reduce absorption in the short run.

It may seem paradoxical to say that an improvement in the current account is brought about by higher inflation, because one may have a fixed nominal exchange rate in mind. In that case, inflation would bring about continuous real appreciation, which would have an increasingly adverse effect on the current account for any given level of real expenditures. The assumption of the tradeoff model is that the nominal exchange rate is appropriately depreciated to avoid real appreciation. If a country is experiencing higher inflation than its trading partners, it would have to depreciate continuously. In fact, if absorption is reduced through a shift from foreign borrowing to the inflation tax, it is necessary in most circumstances to associate the reduction in absorption with a real devaluation (or other "switching measure") to maintain the demand for domestic goods and services.

The nominal devaluations that did usually take place in response to the crises, and that are indicated when a shift from foreign borrowing either to the inflation tax or to a reduction in the fiscal deficit is made, in addition produced temporary adjustment inflation, and in some cases spiral inflation. In some countries, then, an increase in the rate of growth of the money supply and of seigniorage could be explained by the tradeoff model or alternatively by the desire to avoid the economic contraction that would otherwise result from the devaluation-wage-price spiral. Of course, such monetary expansion weakens the impact of the nominal devaluation on the real exchange rate.

Inflation 1973–78: Bubbles and Adjustment

The inflation experiences of our thirteen low- or moderate-inflation countries between 1973 and 1978 can be summarized according to what happened among the oil importers, among the oil or phosphate exporters, and among the coffee boom countries.

What Happened to Inflation in the Oil Importers?

From 1973 to 1975 inflation increased in all the oil-importing countries. In many cases there was high domestic credit expansion in 1972 and 1973 (as in most developed countries), and this, combined with the sharp deterioration in the terms of trade, led to a severe deterioration in the current account, which in turn led to devaluation in three countries—Korea, Kenya, and Costa Rica. The rise in import prices, combined with an increase in the money growth rate and combined also with devaluation in three cases, explains the inflation bubble.[4]

In the case of Korea, wages also rose rapidly in 1974 and 1975, the result of a tight labor market in the preceding years. That period witnessed a similar explosion of nominal and real wages in the OECD countries, other than the United States. In the case of India, drought and unusual monetary expansion were probably more important than the rise in import prices in explaining the steep rise in the Indian inflation rate.

Table 6-1 shows that in all except Côte d'Ivoire, the inflation rate fell after 1975 or 1976. In general, there were few signs of spiral effects or of significant increases in monetization and, most important, the bubbles did not raise inflationary expectations. The 1974–75 bubble was, in the main, a case of adjustment inflation.

Côte d'Ivoire is an exception among the oil importers because its bubble lasted much longer. It was and is a member of the franc zone, so that inflation was bound to be limited by the fixed exchange rate commitment, but inflation did not decline because of the public investment boom. This boom began in 1974, kept going through 1975 (the year when the terms of trade deteriorated), and from 1976 was supported by income from the coffee boom. Thus, Côte d'Ivoire's inflationary bubble lasted from 1975 to 1980, having been caused by adjustment to a spending boom that was financed both by foreign borrowing and by the proceeds of the coffee boom.

The Oil or Phosphate Exporters: Indonesia, Nigeria, Morocco

Indonesia provides a good example of adjustment inflation. The oil revenue went to the government and was spent, almost wholly, on investment. The result was a big increase in the money supply (40 percent in 1974). In 1974 the current account was in surplus (3 percent of GDP) since it took some time for spending to increase but, as before 1974, it quickly turned into a modest deficit (averaging 2 percent of GDP in 1975–78), so that spending exceeded real income. The net effect was a big increase in demand for nontraded goods, leading inevitably to a substantial real appreciation.

The Indonesian rupiah was fixed to the dollar at a constant rate from 1972 to 1978, so that the real appreciation could result only from domestic inflation. In 1973 the inflation rate jumped to 31 percent and in 1974 to 41 percent, falling back to 19 percent in 1975. Real appreciation continued until the nominal devaluation of 1978: the inflation rate after the initial boom, that is, from 1975–78, averaged 14.5 percent. Because of a "balanced budget rule" (discussed in chapter 12), there was essentially no monetization of a fiscal deficit, and hence also, in the absence of a domestic capital market, limited scope for reducing inflation through reduced monetization when tax revenue increased as a result of the oil boom. The government could, of course, have restrained its increase in spending and instead built up (sterilized) cash reserves at the central bank, or invested abroad, as Cameroon did.

In 1972, on the eve of this favorable shock, the Indonesian inflation rate was only 7 percent, having been brought down from very high rates a few years earlier. The sustained real appreciation and quite prolonged inflationary episode from 1973 were clearly brought about by the spending effects of the oil boom. In 1973, a role was also played by the "rice crisis," a sharp rise in the price of rice owing to a low harvest and a doubling of the world price of rice.

Nigeria's inflation and real exchange rate story is much the same as Indonesia's. The nominal exchange rate was also fixed, and inflation rose to 34 percent in 1975, and averaged 22 percent over 1976–78. In 1974–75, a current account surplus of 17 percent of GDP resulted from the oil price rise, followed by a deficit in the next four years that averaged 2.5 percent. The money supply rose 90 percent in 1974. For Nigeria, as for Indonesia, this episode was thus a period of adjustment inflation. The one crucial difference is that in 1978 Indonesia devalued, restoring its real exchange rate, whereas Nigeria continued to adhere to its fixed nominal rate, and hence continued appreciating in real terms until 1984.

The third country to have a terms-of-trade gain and export boom in 1974 was Morocco. The gains from the rise in phosphate prices far outweighed the losses from the oil price rise. A public spending boom began a year earlier. The country maintained a fixed exchange rate to the French franc. Moroccan inflation also increased, so that there was a real appreciation, but it was modest. The jump to 18 percent inflation in 1974 was no doubt explained by the oil price rise, as well as the spending boom. In the following four years inflation averaged 10 percent, which was not much different from the French inflation rate.

Five Coffee Boom Countries

The policy reactions to the brief coffee boom (1976–78) in five of our countries (see chapter 3) show clear indications of adjustment inflation and in Costa Rica a tendency to reduced monetization.

In the case of Colombia, the story is straightforward. Colombia had not been affected by the oil shock and had not embarked on a public spending boom earlier. Thus, the effects of the coffee boom should be easy to see. Note, too, that in 1973 the Colombian inflation rate had jumped to 21 percent (from an average of 10 percent in 1970–72), the result of an exceptional increase in the money base in 1972–73. The current account and budget went into surplus, and the foreign exchange reserves increased. The money base boomed as a result. Private spending increased, but there was, notably, no public spending boom. Essentially, the effects were sterilized to some extent after the coffee price increase. The inflation rate rose somewhat, peaking at 33 percent in 1977. This was a pure case of moderate adjustment inflation.

The two franc-zone countries had little scope for monetizing their budget deficits and hence also for reducing monetization. In both, notably Côte d'Ivoire, there were signs of adjustment inflation. Cameroon had a fiscal surplus and a modest investment boom related to the exploitation of the newly found oil reserves. Inflation apparently increased somewhat in 1977 and 1978. Côte d'Ivoire had embarked on a massive public spending boom before the rise in coffee and cocoa prices, and this continued and even accelerated as a result. The inflation rate—clearly a case of adjustment inflation—increased, reaching a peak of 27 percent in 1977.

The fruits of the Kenyan coffee boom went directly to the private sector, but in various ways led to higher public revenues. There was a private investment boom and also an increase in public spending, both stimulated by the coffee boom. This, too, was a clear case of adjustment inflation. The inflation rate had peaked at 19 percent in 1975, partly owing to the devaluation that year. In 1976 it fell to 12 percent. As a result of the coffee boom, inflation increased again, to 15 percent in 1977 and 17 percent in 1978, dropping to 8 percent in 1979.

In the case of Costa Rica, the low inflation rate during the coffee boom years 1976–78 is striking. There had been an "oil shock" bubble 1974–75, with an average inflation rate of 25 percent, and by 1976 inflation was down to a more traditional 3.5 percent, aided by some import liberalization and some price controls on basic foods. The benefits of the boom went principally to the private sector. At the same time, there was a large increase in public spending, only partly covered by increased revenues. The budget deficit quadrupled between 1976 and 1980, financed both by domestic banks and by foreign borrowing, and thus laid the foundation for the 1981 debt crisis. This increase in spending, if temporary, could have been expected to lead to adjustment inflation, but if unchecked, ran the risk of becoming spiral inflation.

Ten Low-Inflation Countries, 1979–89: Bubbles and Stabilization

The last two periods we surveyed consist of the crisis years of 1980–82 and the subsequent "stabilization" years 1983–89 (these correspond to the periods covered in chapters 4 and 5, respectively). The eighteen countries can be readily classified into three categories, the ten low-inflation countries, the three moderate-inflation countries (Colombia, Costa Rica, Nigeria), and the five high-inflation countries (discussed in chapter 7).

The low-inflation countries are those in which inflation rates averaged 10 percent or less during 1983–89. Of course, inflation rates were higher during their "bubbles." This group consists of the six Asian countries and also Morocco,

Kenya, Cameroon, and Côte d'Ivoire. A question of particular interest regarding these countries is how they managed to achieve low inflation rates after their bubbles. Technically, it is primarily a matter of the interaction of monetary-fiscal policies with exogenous shocks. Fundamentally, the answer depends on political economy. The broad story for these ten countries is as follows.

As a result of the external shocks described in chapter 4, they had inflationary bubbles in 1980–82, which in each country tended to be somewhat lower than the earlier bubble of 1974–75. The explanation is that, like the OECD countries, they had become more wary of inflation as a result of the first shock, and so applied tighter monetary policies. Any tendencies to spiral inflation were quickly nipped in the bud by those policies. The average inflation rate during the second bubble for all ten countries was 16 percent, compared with 21 percent during the first bubble. Country figures are given in table 6-1. The biggest bubbles were in Korea (25 percent) and Sri Lanka (22 percent); in Korea's case, this was the same as the earlier inflation peak (in 1974–75), and in Sri Lanka's case it was much higher (11 percent in 1974–75).

In all cases this was followed by stabilization, which in some cases, as table 6-1 shows, was quite remarkable. During the seven years 1983–89, the nine countries' average inflation rates were all below 10 percent, and Sri Lanka's was 10.5 percent.[5]

These low rates were not necessarily the result of a fixed exchange rate regime, as might be expected, for by the end of 1983 only four of these ten countries still had fixed exchange rate regimes (Thailand, Morocco, Cameroon, and Côte d'Ivoire). By the end of 1989 this was true of only the last two—both members of the franc zone. Furthermore, all except these two had devalued their currencies, the result being real depreciations at some stage during the period. Hence, one cannot conclude on the basis of the experiences of these eight countries that devaluations or shifts to flexible exchange rate regimes lead to high inflation. The effects of exchange rate regimes on inflation, or vice versa, are discussed further in chapter 8.

In chapter 5, rescheduling was viewed as an indication of severe problems, whether the result of external shocks or domestic policies. Here it should be noted that eight of the ten low-inflation countries did not reschedule in the period 1982–88; this includes the six Asian countries. The only reschedulers among the ten were Morocco and Côte d'Ivoire.[6] This does not mean that most of the ten did not suffer big shocks either in the 1980–82 period or later. As shown in chapters 4 and 5, Sri Lanka, Côte d'Ivoire, Korea, and Thailand were heavy terms-of-trade losers (in relation to GDP) in the 1979–82 period. In addition, Côte d'Ivoire, Kenya, and Morocco were badly in need of adjustment owing to earlier spending booms. The shifts in resource transfer from inward to outward were huge (in relation to GDP) in the case of Côte d'Ivoire, Morocco, Korea, and Kenya (see the first column of table 5-1). Finally, in 1986 Indonesia and Cameroon lost from the oil price fall. Thus out of the ten only India and Pakistan were not faced with major adjustment problems as a result of external shocks or earlier spending booms.

It is therefore significant that in all these countries (with the exception of Sri Lanka), the need for adjustment did not lead to increased inflation. Their governments did not choose the inflation tax road, nor did they allow spiral inflation to develop. The "tradeoff model" outlined earlier did *not* apply to these countries. In fact, inflation in the 1983–89 period was generally lower than in 1976–79 (see table 6-1). For the group as a whole, the average inflation rate fell from 10 percent to 7 percent. Outstanding examples of successful adjustment with low inflation come from Indonesia and Korea.

In Indonesia the second inflation bubble came relatively early, in 1979–80, as a result of both the 1978 devaluation and then the domestic monetary impact of the second oil shock. This was adjustment inflation, averaging 17 percent. Then the inflation rate fell both in 1981 and 1982, but the 1983 devaluation led to a minibubble of 12 percent in 1983–84. For the whole period 1983–89, the average inflation rate was only 8 percent, which should be compared with 14 percent for 1976–79.

At first sight, the modest Indonesian inflation rate after the 1986 oil shock (average of 8 percent inflation 1987–89) seems really impressive when one notes the extent of the reduction in the inward resource transfer combined with the decline in the terms of trade. The excess of imports of goods and services other than debt service over exports other than oil and gas fell from 14.9 percent of GDP in 1984 to 6.7 percent in 1988. This very large shift measures the combined effects of increased principal repayments of long-term debt, higher interest payments, and greatly reduced income from oil and natural gas imports. Inflation increased a little over 1985 and 1986, but basically the resource shift was brought about without increased, or high, inflation. The tradeoff model clearly did not apply in this case.

The crucial policy instruments were the 1983 and 1986 devaluations, and successful efforts to reduce government expenditures and raise revenue from nonoil taxes. Indonesia has a "balanced budget rule," instituted in 1967, which does not allow the government to finance deficits by borrowing from the central bank. The budget is defined as including revenue from foreign loans, so that, if the latter has to be reduced, there is no alternative to fiscal contraction. The tradeoff model is not applicable to Indonesia because the inflation financing road is ruled out. Of course, there can still be adjustment inflation and also monetary expansion through growth of foreign exchange reserves and through credit creation for the private sector.

How did the Indonesian government manage to adhere to its balanced budget rule? And how did it manage to bring about such a great fiscal improvement? The answers to these questions lie at a deeper level.[7] It is even more noteworthy that, apparently, the adjustment was achieved while at the same time the incidence of poverty declined and income distribution became more even.

The reduction in public spending consisted mostly of a postponement of capital-intensive (and hence import-intensive) public investment projects. Current expenditures affecting vulnerable groups were not, on the whole, reduced. This outcome was only possible because the capital investment program had been very large (it fell from 10 percent of GDP in 1984 to 8 percent in 1987). In addition, major tax reforms were introduced at the end of 1983 and a value added tax instituted in 1985. The non-oil sector had been undertaxed and a great deal of tax evasion had taken place. As a result of various reforms introduced from 1983, nonoil tax revenue rose by more than 2 percent of GDP.

By any standards, Indonesia followed sound policies in this period. Its government was stable (in power since 1965), essentially autocratic, and, to a great extent, technocratic. The advisers known as the "Berkeley Mafia" played a key role in economic policy from 1965 on. They had competition, but on the main issues, their views generally prevailed with President Suharto, in whom eventual authority was concentrated. Conservative and cautious attitudes, rooted in the culture, with an emphasis on consensus, and a concern with maintaining political support in the rural areas—where most of the population and most of the poor were—all played a role. In addition, the bad experiences of the years before 1967 had made policymakers conscious of the dangers of losing macroeconomic control.

Another example of successful adjustment comes from Korea. It had embarked on an anti-inflation program in March 1979, involving tighter fiscal policy, increases in reserve requirements for banks (introduced in 1978 in advance of the full program), and sharp increases in interest rates on both loans and deposits. At about the same time, world oil prices began their dramatic two-year increase, followed more tentatively by a rise in the price of other raw materials. Korea then experienced an exceptionally bad harvest in 1980, resulting in the only decline (by 5 percent) in real GDP since the 1950s. Then the world recession of 1982 impeded Korea's export sales.

Despite its anti-inflation program, Korea devalued the won in January 1980 to recover from the real appreciation that had taken place since the previous devaluation in 1974. In mid-1980 the Korean authorities altered their macroeconomic course, introducing an expansionist supplementary budget and cutting bank reserve requirements in half (and halved again in 1981); interest rates were reduced more gradually. Despite this two-year reversal in policy, inflation hit its peak rate of 29 percent in 1980, dropping modestly to 21 percent in 1981 and then dramatically to 7.2 percent in 1982. Inflation remained below 5 percent until 1988.

Korea resumed its anti-inflation policy in earnest in mid-1982, with a stiff budget proposal for 1983 and a modest increase in bank reserve requirements. Partly to reduce expenditures, partly to set an example for the private sector, wage growth ceilings had been imposed on public employees in 1981, and these were gradually lowered to zero in 1984. Wage guidelines were promulgated for the private sector, enforced in part through the denial of bank loans to firms that had exceeded the guidelines without justification.

The Korean case is clearly an example of bubble inflation, but unlike Costa Rica (discussed further below), Korea ended up with a lower rate of inflation after the bubble than before. The inflationary impetus from a currency devaluation, or from a sharp increase in oil prices, will naturally recede over time, provided it does not trigger a wage-price spiral. Through monetary, budget, and wage policy—

accompanied by extensive publicity on the need to restrain inflation and the rationale for the macroeconomic strategy—the Korean authorities managed to reduce inflation despite a temporary interlude of expansionist action.

The anti-inflationary program launched in 1979 was in response to wide public concern over "inflation" (especially urban land prices) and alleged profiteering in 1978, reinforced by a strong but latent desire by economic technocrats to reign in the excessive investment in heavy industry. They took advantage of this public discontent to press their case once again, with greater vigor, on President Park.

General Chun led a political coup in May 1980, thus coming to power with doubtful legitimacy. To justify his regime, he launched a program of "purification," to rid the country of corruption, inflation, and lack of civic-mindedness. After a brief expansionist policy in response to the slowdown of 1980–81, Chun resumed the stabilization program under the strong influence of economic adviser Kim Je Ik, who felt that large firms needed a stable environment and competitive pressure in order to perform well. To that end, he favored a tight budget and tight credit policy (but low interest rates), along with a slightly overvalued currency and trade liberalization, all of which were sought from late 1982.

Public opposition, which was often confused with opposition to the Chun regime, was suppressed early in the 1980s in various ways, including legislation to weaken the power of labor unions. Opposition to the stiff anti-inflation program, mainly from business associations, grew over time, but for a while Chun supported the technocrats, urging them among other things to explain clearly the reasons for the policy to the public and to business groups.

The sharp decline in inflation, however, actually preceded the severe budget and other measures of 1983–84. It resulted from effective control over fiscal and monetary instruments even during the expansionist phase of policy in 1980–81, combined with improvements in the international terms of trade from the terrible level of 1980 and a recovery of domestic production of cereals in 1981.

For the ten low-inflation countries, their achievements cannot be explained simply by low budget deficits. Budget deficits in some of the ten countries have been very high, but they have not been monetized to a significant extent (see table 10-11). There is no correlation between budget deficits in relation to GDP and inflation rates. The obvious explanation is that there are two other ways of financing deficits, namely, borrowing abroad (including concessional borrowing) and borrowing domestically. India stands out as a country that financed a large part of its high budget deficit from domestic savings. All ten countries except Korea borrowed abroad during the period 1983–89. The biggest net foreign borrowers relative to GDP in the 1983–88 period were Côte d'Ivoire, Sri Lanka, Pakistan, and Morocco. (This is indicated by the current account deficits in the fourth column of table 5-1.)

Three Moderate Inflation Countries, 1979–89

Each of the three countries that experienced intermediate inflation has its own story.

Colombia

Colombia is an interesting case. Essentially, it had developed a "core" rate of inflation above that of low-inflation countries, but well below that of high-inflation countries, and, at least since 1967, this rate has been relatively stable. From 1960 to 1972, the average ("core") inflation rate was 11 percent, and in 1973 it jumped to reach an average of 24 percent over 1973–89. The inflation rate was outside the 20–28 percent range in only four of these seventeen years. The inflation rate has been closely related to the money base, with variations explainable in terms of money base variations. Because of the coffee boom in 1976–79, the main cause of money base expansion was the growth in foreign exchange reserves. In other years, and especially after 1981, the base expanded primarily because of the monetization of public sector deficits.

Since 1967 Colombia has followed a crawling peg exchange rate policy. This does not mean that the real exchange rate has remained constant. Adjustments in the nominal exchange rate have been steadily, and usually automatically, made in the light of the excess of domestic over foreign (usually U.S.) inflation rates, and insofar as there have been *real* changes, they have resulted from policy. Thus the real exchange rate was allowed to appreciate during the coffee boom, a point already noted, and there was a sharp real depreciation in 1985 as part of a balance of payments adjustment process. Colombia avoided one of the worst consequences of continuous high or moderate inflation, namely, continuous real appreciation well beyond what is justified by increases in export income or capital inflow.

The variations in Colombian inflation rates and, more generally, Colombian macroeconomic policy leave two impressions.

First, there has not been stability. Mistakes have been made. They have taken the form of excessive fiscal deficits for limited periods, which have led to monetary expansion and, in the 1981–84 period, to excessive foreign borrowing. As described in chapter 4, the end of the coffee boom was followed by a public spending boom designed to maintain domestic demand and avoid a recession that the decline in export income would otherwise have caused. Hence, this boom had a Keynesian motivation. It led to a crisis, and thus to crisis measures, including real devaluation, and eventually fiscal contraction. Since 1986 there has been a resumption of growth, helped by increases in oil, coffee, and other exports.

The second impression is that, despite the mistakes, over a long period macroeconomic management in Colombia has been fundamentally conservative. It has been similar to that in the ten low-inflation countries. Why Colombia has been so different in this respect from the other South American countries has to do with its political economy. The Colombian authorities have never allowed an imbalance to get out of hand. When inflation increases, or when a current account financing problem emerges, appropriate steps are taken quite quickly to rectify matters. The 1983–84 crisis was quite brief, and drastic steps were taken.

The lesson is that even in a well-managed country, mistakes can be made or serious problems can arise, but the art is to move quickly and to an adequate extent to put matters right. Hence, Colombia has had a number of one- or two-year inflation bubbles, and also current account problems, but that is as far as the matter has gone. Moreover, during the coffee boom Colombia ran current account surpluses—surely the appropriate response—and partly sterilized the domestic monetary effects by cutting the public sector deficit and reducing credit to the private sector. It is true that in 1973 core inflation jumped, but this happened all over the world.

Costa Rica

As can be seen from table 6-1, Costa Rica was a low-inflation country up to 1979. There was a bubble in 1973–75, in association with a balance of payments crisis and a devaluation, similar to those of other low-inflation countries. Costa Rica's fixed exchange rate regime collapsed in 1980, the result of the spending and borrowing boom described in chapter 3. Then it experienced a quite exceptional bubble in 1981–83, with the inflation rate rising to 90 percent in 1982. An impressive stabilization from 1983 involved both a big shift from inward to outward resource transfer and also inflation stabilization: by 1984 the inflation rate was down to 12 percent, and from 1984 to 1989, it averaged 16 percent.

It is not difficult to explain an inflationary bubble in 1982; the inward resource transfer fell by 5 percent of GDP (table 5-12), so that we have here an example of the "tradeoff" model: money financing of the public sector deficit partly replaced foreign financing. In addition, the colon depreciated over 300 percent as a result of the breakdown of the fixed rate system, and some of the controls on prices were relaxed. The rate of growth of the money supply rose from 17 percent in 1980 to 47 percent in 1981 and 70 percent in 1982. An important factor was a large central bank deficit (6 percent of GDP in 1982). Hence, 90 percent inflation in 1982 is not too surprising, although it also contained a substantial element of adjustment inflation.

Of particular interest is the subsequent stabilization brought about by the new government that came into power in 1982. The main feature was the remarkable reduction in the deficit of the nonfinancial public sector. It was 14 percent of GDP in 1981 and was virtually eliminated by 1987. The deficit of the central bank (which was additional to the deficit of the nonfinancial public sector) also fell, but was still above 3 percent of GDP in 1987. From an inflation point of view, there are three points to make.

First, both the outward resource transfer was increased *and* inflation was reduced: hence, while the tradeoff model helps to explain the inflationary bubble of 1982–83, it does not explain the subsequent decline in the inflation rate. The public sector deficit (including central bank deficit) was reduced sufficiently both to switch the resource transfer from inward to outward, and to reduce the monetization of deficits. Second, the brevity of the bubble and the earlier history of low inflation meant that the bubble did not start up inflationary expectations and create inertia and credibility problems, which, as we shall see in chapter 7, are considered extremely important in some other countries, notably Argentina and Brazil. The government drew consciously on the low-inflation history of the country, and hence relied on some "money illusion" and regressive expectations of the public.[8] It was thus largely able to prevent adjustment inflation from becoming spiral inflation. The inflation rate responded quickly to the decline in the money growth rate. The latter fell from 40 percent in 1983 to 15 percent in 1984, while the inflation rate fell from 33 percent to 12 percent. Third, in view of the earlier history of low inflation, the government had a strong commitment—for which it had public support—to reduce the rate of inflation. Inflation stayed, at least until 1990, well above its precrisis levels (16 percent average in 1984–89, compared with 8 percent in 1976–79), but Costa Rica's stabilization since 1983 is an achievement.

Nigeria

The problems that Nigeria faced as a result of its spending boom and the inability to adjust to the fall in oil income in 1982–83 were outlined earlier. There was severe import compression brought about by quantitative import restrictions. In every year of the period 1982–84, the dollar value of imports fell by over 20 percent. The exchange rate was kept fixed until 1985. Inflation increased sharply in 1983 and 1984, reaching 40 percent in 1984. This reflected monetary expansion resulting from budget deficits in 1982 and 1983, as well as the supply scarcities, especially of food imports. In 1985 the inflation rate fell to 7 percent owing to an excellent harvest and the improved fiscal position and hence reduced money growth from 1984.

Then came the 1986 fall in the oil price and a huge depreciation. The dollar value of imports fell 50 percent in that year. The drastic shift in exchange rate regime and eventual move to a floating rate are described in chapter 8. Despite these events, the inflation rate stayed low in that year and the following (6 percent and 11 percent). That is a little surprising. Although it has been suggested that the depreciation had little effect on prices as they already reflected the parallel exchange rate, the supply of goods did fall drastically. The supply of money and quasi money hardly increased in that year because of the decline in foreign exchange reserves, and this must have been a major factor explaining the low inflation of 1986–87. In 1986 the structural adjustment program began. All price controls were ended, but they had in any case been ineffective.

In 1988 food prices rose owing to a poor agricultural season. In addition there was monetary expansion in 1987 and 1988, and these two factors together apparently explain the return of high inflation—to 40 percent a year in 1988 and 1989. In 1989, however, monetary policy was tightened again and the general budget deficit was reduced to 3.5 percent of GDP, so that by 1990 the inflation rate was again below 10 percent.

The consumer price index for Nigeria (the national composite CPI) is heavily weighted by rural consumption patterns, which get an 88 percent weight. The food component carries 60 percent weight, which explains both the importance of changes in domestic and imported food supplies in affecting the inflation rate, as well as the flexibility of the index. Owing to the size, diversity, and dispersion of the Nigerian market, there are (as in other countries also) considerable data problems: changes in the index should be interpreted with caution. Nevertheless, some rough conclusions can be drawn.

First of all, since the crisis that began in 1983, the average inflation rate has ratcheted upward: it was 14 percent from 1977 to 1982 (17 percent in 1974–82), and in 1983–89 it averaged 23 percent. Second, in the last period there were two bubbles, namely, 1983–84 and 1988–89. Each bubble can be explained by earlier monetary-fiscal expansion combined with supply shortages, in the first case reduced import supplies and in the second a poor harvest. Third, the flexibility of prices in response to both changing monetary policy and changing food supplies is striking. Finally, even more significant is the relative flexibility of fiscal-monetary policies. Each bubble was ended with the help of tighter monetary policies.

A key question is whether Nigeria's departure from a fixed rate regime in 1985 has been a cause of the increase in inflation. This general issue with regard to all the countries will be taken up again in chapter 8. Here one can note that Nigeria had big inflation bubbles in 1975 (34 percent) and 1984 (40 percent), in spite of the fixed rate regime, and for the whole period 1974–84, when the exchange rate was fixed (as it also was before then), the inflation rate averaged 20 percent. Of course, some rate of inflation above that of trading partners could be justified up to 1981 as bringing about an appropriate real exchange rate adjustment to the boom in oil export income.

As seen in 1990, Nigeria could be described as a country with fairly low inflation that suffered two adverse shocks in the 1980s and thus had two inflation bubbles, both high because of the exceptional flexibility, upward and downward, of food prices.[9]

Conclusion

This chapter has examined thirteen countries with low or moderate inflation. One interesting question concerning the ten low-inflation countries is whether their experience can be explained by the availability of foreign or domestic savings to finance budget deficits. If foreign or domestic financing had been less, would the deficits have been reduced by raising taxes or reducing noninterest government spending, or would the gap have been filled by the inflation tax? Clearly, much depends on the commitment of a country's government to a belief in the desirability of low inflation and the virtues of conservative monetary policy.

The "gap-filling" role of the inflation tax is implied by the tradeoff model whereby the reduced inward resource transfers that result when less foreign financing becomes available lead to more inflation. Similarly, the "unpleasant monetarist arithmetic" of Sargent and Wallace (1981) suggests that a growing need for domestic financing resulting from the build-up of domestic debt must eventually lead to more monetization and hence to higher inflation.[10] At the same time, in many countries the inward resource transfer greatly declined from 1977–82 to 1983–88 (table 5-1), and yet inflation did not increase significantly; added to this is the Indonesian adjustment to the 1986 terms-of-trade shock mentioned earlier. In all these countries, public sector borrowing in relation to GDP was reduced; increased inflation was not chosen as the way out.

The experiences of the ten low-inflation countries yield two lessons.

First, some temporary increases in inflation rates at times of external or domestic shocks appear to be unavoidable. Furthermore, devaluations and also domestic price adjustments resulting from tighter fiscal policies (for example, increases in public utility prices) are bound to raise the rate of inflation at least temporarily. The important policy requirement is that adjustment inflation leads only to inflationary bubbles and does not turn into spiral inflation, and that monetization habits do not develop.

Effects on expectations also need to be borne in mind. If the inflation rate rises owing to external or domestic shocks, governments should make clear that this may be a necessary adjustment, but that a firm commitment to a low-inflation policy will continue. Inflation bubbles should not be construed as the beginning of a prolonged inflationary process. While some temporary easing of monetary policy may be necessary—and is sometimes the unavoidable effect of an export or a capital inflow boom—it has to be understood as a temporary measure. Broadly speaking, inflation in the ten low-inflation countries has not been fueled very much by expectations and, allowing for lags, the monetary authorities have been able to keep it relatively low. Even quite modest increases in inflation (by the standards of other countries) have often been seen as major problems. This has been a healthy attitude that has prevented countries from getting started on the high-inflation road and also has prevented an outburst of inflationary expectations.

The second lesson is that, subject to shocks and lags and allowing for some bubbles, economic policy can ensure relatively low inflation, on average. It is a matter of monetary-fiscal policy. The crucial requirement is the political will—the anti-inflation resolve—of policymakers and their ability to enforce their resolve through budgetary policies that keep fiscal deficits within the limits of what can be financed through borrowing abroad or at home.

With respect to the three moderate-inflation countries, the lesson from Colombia is that it is possible to sustain moderate inflation combined with a crawling peg exchange rate over a long period. As has been noted, the basic approach must still be cautious and conservative, with a readiness to take strong fiscal measures quickly when the situation deteriorates. The situation in Costa Rica did get seriously out of control for a longer period, so that in this case there is an example of a successful stabilization program following upon a crisis comparable to some discussed in the next chapter. Lessons in this case have been drawn above: the rapid and sustained decline in inflation (though not back to earlier low-inflation elements) is explained both by the willingness to take strong fiscal measures and the failure for inflationary expectations to ignite owing to the earlier low-inflation history. As for Nigeria, favorable lessons can hardly be drawn from its adverse experience, although it appears to have a high degree of price flexibility (attributable principally to the flexibility of food prices) and a certain willingness to tighten monetary policy when inflation does increase. The latter suggests that some of the same anti-inflation attitudes that can be found in the ten low-inflation countries do also exist in Nigeria.

Chapter 7

Stories of High Inflation and Stabilization

This chapter provides details of the inflation experiences and various stabilization attempts, successful and unsuccessful, of Brazil, Argentina, Chile, Mexico, Turkey, and Indonesia. Only the first two have been consistently high-inflation countries, and in 1989 they both suffered hyperinflation. Both have gone through numerous stabilization episodes. Chile and Mexico have had episodes of very high inflation followed by stabilization, Chile in the 1970s, and Mexico in the 1980s. Turkey is a borderline case, having experienced inflation comparable to moderate Latin American levels (50–75 percent) in 1988–90. In the Indonesian case, we deal only with the period 1961–71, when there was very high inflation followed by a successful stabilization. This episode is of particular interest both because of its success and because, unlike the Latin American experiences, it is not well known by scholars of inflation in developing countries.

Brazil: High and Variable Inflation 1960–89

For much of the time between 1960 and 1989, Brazil had high and variable inflation (table 7-1, column 1).[1] Only in 1972 and 1973 was the inflation rate below 20 percent. From 1968 to 1985, Brazilians were fairly comfortable with inflation: they had learned to live with it because, by the standards of the times, it was high but, until 1981, not extreme—that is, not above 100 percent a year—and, above all, because adverse effects were reduced by indexation. This willingness to live with inflation was no doubt one reason why inflation continued.

Table 7.1   Inflation Rates in Five High-Inflation Countries, 1960–90

(percent)

Year	Brazil	Argentina	Chile	Mexico	Turkey
1960	29.5	27.3	11.6	4.9	1.3
1961	33.4	13.4	7.7	1.6	0.5
1962	51.8	28.3	14.0	1.2	2.9
1963	70.1	23.9	44.1	0.6	3.1
1964	91.9	22.1	46.0	2.3	1.7
1965	65.7	28.6	28.8	3.6	5.9
1966	41.3	31.9	23.1	4.2	4.4
1967	30.5	29.2	18.8	3.0	6.8
1968	22.0	16.2	26.3	2.3	0.4
1969	22.7	7.6	30.4	3.4	7.9
1970	22.4	13.6	32.5	5.2	6.9
1971	20.1	34.7	20.0	5.3	15.7
1972	16.6	58.5	74.8	5.0	11.7
1973	12.7	61.3	361.5	12.0	15.4
1974	27.6	23.5	504.7	23.8	15.8
1975	29.0	182.9	374.7	15.2	19.2
1976	42.0	444.0	211.8	15.8	17.4
1977	43.7	176.0	91.9	29.0	27.1
1978	38.7	175.5	40.1	17.5	45.3
1979	52.7	159.5	33.4	18.2	58.7
1980	82.8	100.8	35.1	26.4	110.2
1981	105.6	104.5	19.7	27.9	36.6
1982	97.8	164.8	9.9	58.9	30.8
1983	142.1	343.8	27.3	101.8	31.4
1984	197.0	626.7	19.9	65.5	48.4
1985	226.9	672.2	30.7	57.8	45.0
1986	145.2	90.1	19.5	86.2	34.6
1987	229.7	131.3	19.9	131.8	38.9
1988	682.3	343.0	14.7	114.2	75.4
1989	1,287.0	3,079.8	17.0	20.0	63.3
1990	2,397.8	2,314.0	26.0	26.7	60.3

Note: Consumer price index inflation rates.
Source: World Bank data (annex II) and direct country sources.

An Overview

There has been a consistent expansionary bias in Brazilian policies. Brazilian pol-icymakers and opinionmakers have always been heavily committed to stimulating growth with demand expansionary policies and, even more important, they have been inclined to avoid inflation-reducing measures if these might adversely affect growth in the short run. The main exception to this pattern has been the highly successful Bulhoes-Campos stabilization episode of 1965–67. In general, however, the government has been reluctant to incur short-term costs in the form of a recession for the sake of price stabilization. The tendency has been to give up quickly on a stabilization program well before it has fully done its job. The reluctance to persist in the fight against inflation may also be due to the fact that various interested parties, including those in the financial sector, actually gain from inflation and the associated economic instabilities and complexities.

As indicated in earlier chapters, from 1974 to 1983 Brazil was subject to the same external shocks that adversely affected other oil-importing and debtor countries. In Brazil, none of these shocks led to an inflation "bubble," as in the countries discussed in chapter 6. Rather, inflation rates rose to new plateaus (table 7-1, column 1). As a result of the first oil shock, the average inflation rate rose from 20 percent (1970–72) to 44 percent (1976–79), the second oil and real interest rate shock brought it to 95 percent (1980–82), and the third shock (debt crisis and world recession) to 189 percent (1983–85). The year of the failed Cruzado (stabilization) Plan, 1986, inaugurated a period of extreme inflation instability and very high inflation, wholly the result of domestic policies. It is important to remember that world oil prices fell sharply in 1986, which was a very favorable event for Brazil. Fluctuations before 1973 resulted also purely from domestic policies.

Brazilian economic history from 1960, and especially the history of inflation, is complicated by frequent changes in policy and an addiction to complex schemes and programs. Again and again, attempts have been made to bring inflation down, and again and again, they have turned out to be inadequate or the government has failed to persist with them. Up to 1990 the one exception was in the 1964–73 period.

From the point of view of inflation, Brazilian economic history since 1960 can be divided into three periods: the inflation-stabilization-miracle period of 1960–73, the 1974–85 period of the three external shocks, and the period from 1986, which can be called "Cruzado and After." None of these are simple episodes, since all include numerous policy shifts and raise complex issues. One concerns the impact of indexation—of the exchange rate, of wages, and of financial assets. The central policy issue, endlessly debated inside Brazil and outside, is whether orthodox fiscalist or monetarist theories can explain these events and can also provide the correct principles for developing stabilization plans, or whether "structuralist" or "heterodox" explanations and policies are more appropriate or, at least, need to supplement orthodoxy.

First Period, 1960–73: Inflation, Stabilization, Miracle

The late 1950s marked the beginning of the first major inflationary surge, caused by the monetization of an increasing government deficit. The explanation of inflation is perfectly clear here, and it is hard to see how any structuralist can give it any other explanation. In early 1961 Brazil made an attempt at stabilization, with some monetary contraction, but it did not succeed in reducing the rate of inflation. Of course, one should not expect quick results, but to some this provided support for structuralist theories. The populist President Goulart took over in 1962, and his loose monetary and fiscal policies helped accelerate inflation, which by 1964 was up to about 90 percent. In hindsight, this seems a "typical Brazilian" episode: failed stabilization followed by expansionary policies leading to accelerating inflation.

A military coup in 1964 led to a drastic change in policy and, indeed, to the implementation of an orthodox stabilization program known as the Bulhoes-Campos program (1964–67). Firm wage restraint measures were implemented, so that the real wage fell 25 percent over the period. The most important feature was a reduction in the rate of monetary growth brought about both by a fiscal improvement (tax increases and expenditure reductions) and a shift from money to debt financing. The effects were impressive: by 1967 the inflation rate was down to 31 percent and the federal deficit fell from 4 percent of GDP in 1963 to 1 percent in 1966, with a heavy shift to debt financing. The real growth rate of GDP for the three years 1965–67 averaged 4 percent, which was well below the average up to 1962, although it was an improvement on the 3.3 percent average of 1963–64. In 1965 there was a recession in the industrial sector.

The years from 1968 to 1973 are known as the years of the "Brazilian miracle." During this time, the nation's average real growth rate jumped to 11 percent and the inflation rate steadily fell from 22 percent in 1968 to 13 percent in 1973 (which is the lowest it had reached since 1952). As noted in chapter 6, these rates were still high by world standards, but they were certainly an achievement compared with what had gone before.

The "miracle" was undoubtedly the result of many factors. There was a shift to outward-oriented policies that led to a remarkable export boom, private capital inflows increased, and real wage growth was restrained by a particular kind of forward-looking indexation that brought real wage decreases. Nominal wages were indexed to "expected" prices, the latter set by the government on an optimistic basis; that is, it assumed a faster decline in the rate of inflation than actually took place. It was certainly more than helpful that the world economy was booming, and Brazil seized the opportunity. Most important, in 1968 it introduced a crawling peg exchange rate system and thus avoided an appreciation of the real exchange rate, even though inflation remained above world levels. This was a crucial step for allowing an export boom to continue.

During this period Brazil first learned to live with inflation. There were pervasive "price guidelines," so that advocates of "heterodox policies" (which are explained later) can also find some support from these happy years. Notwithstanding these various factors, it seems obvious that macroeconomic stability—as manifested by a slowly declining and moderate rate of inflation, with no drastic shifts in policies—provided a crucial environment for this growth episode. And this was only made possible by the earlier Bulhoes-Campos stabilization.

To sum up the period: a populist expansion, leading to a low point of 2 percent growth in 1963 and to 92 percent inflation in 1964, was followed first by an orthodox stabilization episode, which brought inflation down drastically and raised the growth rate moderately, and then by six miracle years of very high growth and a continued decline in inflation.

Second Period, 1974–85: Three Shocks and Increasing Inflation

The story of this period has already been told in chapters 4 and 5, and its details—reflecting frequent shifts in policies—need not be repeated. Exchange rate policy is discussed later.

From 1974 to 1979, Brazil sought to ride out the first oil shock through borrowing, and the inflation rate ratcheted upward. As described in chapter 4, Delfim Neto became manager of economic policy in August 1979, and his expansionist policies led Brazil into a full-fledged crisis. Inflation in 1981 was in excess of 100 percent, partly because of a big devaluation, followed by the usual response of wages. This led to a switch in policy—a deflationary episode carried out without IMF involvement—but tighter fiscal policies were not sustained, and the internal public debt increased. The period 1983–84 was one of policy orthodoxy, partly with IMF support, and it included a big devaluation, some fiscal contraction that led to some domestic demand contraction, an impressive export boom, and increasing inflation, which reached 197 percent in 1984, the year of the export boom.

In March 1985 a democratic government took over and introduced big real-wage increases and, again, expansionary policies, which pushed real growth to 8 percent in 1985 and 1986, but also drove inflation to 227 percent in 1985, the highest annual rate since 1960 (or earlier). The stage was set for some drastic anti-inflationary measures.

Third Period, 1986–89: Cruzado and After

The year 1986 saw the rise and fall of the Cruzado Plan. This was a "heterodox" stabilization program and had much in common with Argentina's Austral Plan initiated in 1985. The term "heterodox" refers to programs that go beyond "orthodox" measures of fiscal and monetary restraint (which are central to IMF programs) and include fixing of the nominal exchange rate, wage controls or an incomes policy, and, above all, price controls. The logic of heterodox plans will be discussed more fully at the end of this chapter.

Wages were adjusted upward and then frozen, prices and the exchange rate were frozen, indexation of all kinds was eliminated, and complicated arrangements were made for adjusting contracts. Inflation was stopped in its tracks, but there were two major failures: real wages were increased at the outset, so that a demand-led temporary growth boom followed; and the authorities failed to ensure the necessary fiscal contraction, that is, to ensure that the "heterodox" component was associated with the crucial "orthodox" policies. So it all broke down. External conditions were certainly favorable, since, as noted above, Brazil benefited from the 1986 oil price decline.

Two more attempts at stabilization plans of this kind were made, the Bresser Plan of 1987 and the Summer Plan of 1989, but here, too, the orthodox components of fiscal and monetary restraint were inadequate. The result was a great instability in the inflation rate: first, as expectations of a new plan developed, the inflation rate increased; then it dropped sharply as a direct result of the controls; as the economy overheated and failure became apparent, the inflation rate started going up again. By 1989 the government had completely lost its credibility where its financial policies were concerned, and Brazil had begun sliding into hyperinflation. Attempts at firm action were made by newly elected President Collor de Melo in 1990, who ordered fiscal retrenchment, a blocking of the highly liquid Cruzado balances, and a price freeze. His measures succeeded in ending hyperinflation (inflation peaked at 84 percent *a month* in March 1990). GDP fell 4.2 percent in 1990, the worst slump since 1981 (see table A-1). By the end of 1991, with inflation still more than 20 percent a month and a fiscal problem as serious as ever, Brazil continued to face uncertain prospects.

Has Inflation in Brazil Been Caused by Budget Deficits?

Consider now the central question that arises with all high-inflation experiences: Were high budget deficits the fundamental cause of inflation? In the case of Brazil, a distinction must be made between the public sector borrowing requirement (PSBR), which is the total nominal deficit of the various parts of the Brazilian public sector (federal government, states, municipalities, and public enterprises) that needs to be financed every year, and the "operational deficit." The latter is a Brazilian concept that is now being used in other high-inflation countries. It is derived by subtracting from the PSBR the cost of "the monetary correction," which is the indexation of the principal of loans—that is, the additional nominal payment over the original value of a bond—that compensates holders of public debt for inflation. The correction has not always been exact in its compensation (as will be noted again below), but it is near enough. Roughly, then, the operational PSBR is the inflation-adjusted public deficit. Of course, the whole PSBR requires financing, not just the operational deficit, but the part of the PSBR accounted for by the monetary correction is a compensation to the government's creditors for the reduction in the real value of existing debt that would otherwise take place.

To give an idea of orders of magnitude, in the three years 1983–85, the PSBR averaged 24 percent of GDP while the operational deficit averaged 4 percent. As expected, the data show that the total PSBR rises with inflation because of the increase in the monetary correction. That relationship is no surprise. The more interesting question is whether the operational deficit caused inflation—through monetization or other processes—and, especially, whether changes in it can be correlated with changes in the rate of inflation.

A little less than half of the operational deficit for the years from 1983 to 1985 was financed by monetization (1.8 percent of GDP)—that is, by an increase in base money or seigniorage—while the rest (2.2 percent of GDP) was financed by an increase in real public debt.[2] With debt financing, it is clearly possible for the deficit to rise while seigniorage falls, though generally they have moved together. As will be discussed below, an increase in debt could also have inflationary effects, but for the moment, let us focus on the growth of base money as the source of inflation.

Here, the question is whether there is a clear relationship between the growth of the base and the inflation rate. If the demand for money falls, or if the extension of credit exceeds the growth in base money, inflation will be greater than the growth of nominal base money. Between 1983 and 1985, the base (in nominal terms) grew 971 percent and prices increased by 1,100 percent. Hence there was a pretty close correspondence. In later years, as inflation exploded the nominal base grew relatively less. In particular earlier years also, the nominal base grew much more slowly than the inflation rate. Thus, in 1980 the base only grew 57 percent, while the inflation rate was 83 percent or so.

The general tendency in Brazil has been for the value of the base in relation to GDP, as also of M1, to fall (that is, for income velocity to rise) because of a steady decline in the demand for money. Thus, growing seigniorage cannot explain accelerating inflation, especially since 1986, in an arithmetic sense. Over the whole period 1970 to 1985, seigniorage as a share of GDP has been fairly constant at around 2 percent, while the inflation rate has steadily increased. As discussed in chapter 10, a seemingly small monetized deficit of 2 percent can produce high inflation rates if the public has become habituated to high inflation and holds a very low ratio of non-interest-bearing money to income. In Brazil the ratio of reserve money to following-year GDP was just 1.1 percent in 1984. By way of comparison, it was 5.1 percent in the United States and 5.9 percent in Korea at that time.

The central question is: What determines changes in the demand for money? In the Brazilian case, inflationary expectations and a gradual adaptation of the institutions of the society to increasing inflation have clearly reduced the demand for money, especially for narrow non-interest-bearing money, namely, M2. From 1979 to 1988, M2 as a proportion of GDP, fell from 14 percent to 7.5 percent.

This explanation of the decline in the demand for money may not explain changes in particular years, when the income velocity may have risen because of supply-side factors (oil price rise, devaluation, politically determined wage increases) that brought about jumps in the average price level. As described in chapter 6, these factors produced "inflationary bubbles" in most other countries. Brazil is different, according to many Brazilians and others, because of wage indexation and entrenched inflationary expectations. In Brazil real incomes would fall if money supply did not accommodate, and such a recession would fail to bring the rate of inflation down again within a reasonable time. Brazilians have been reluctant to put to the test the possible responsiveness of the rate of inflation to declines in real output. They have preferred to accommodate the supply-side factors with monetary expansion. And the knowledge that this will happen has kept up inflationary expectations.

As for the main question of whether budget deficits explain inflation, the inflationary explosion of 1962–64 was caused by the monetization of fiscal deficits. The subsequent stabilization was successful to a great extent because of reduced deficits and the reduced monetization of given deficits. So here the answer is clear, as it is with regard to the fiscal failures of the Cruzado Plan and later stabilization attempts.

The issue of why the level of inflation rose following supply-side shocks is more complex. In the period 1973 to 1982, supply-side shocks were generally accommodated by monetary expansion for the reasons discussed above, and it could be (and has often been) argued that this, rather than continued operational deficits, explain the accelerating inflation. A strong counterargument can also be put. If the Brazilian authorities had wanted to reduce the operational deficit or avoid its increase, they could have done so while still accommodating the supply shocks by monetary expansion: they could have pursued a mix of a loose monetary and tight fiscal policy. The fact that they did not do so suggests at least the possibility that the budget deficits were a causal factor, the point being that fiscal expansion was not inevitable even if they had wanted to accommodate the shocks by monetary expansion.

Inflationary Effects of the Domestic Debt

An aspect of macroeconomic policy that has been very important in Brazil is the domestic debt. Borrowing domestically by issuing indexed debt has been significant since 1964, and especially so since 1982. In recent years the greater proportion of the operational budget deficit has been financed not by seigniorage as conventionally understood, but by domestic debt. Financing through foreign debt has, of course, practically disappeared. Domestic debt has returned a positive real interest rate to its holders, and the real interest bill has been growing. Some of the domestic debt has been formally indexed against inflation, while some has paid an interest rate that was not formally indexed but took into account short-term inflation. By 1989 most of the debt was very short-term and not formally indexed.

Naturally, the more debt that is issued, the higher the real interest rate has to be to induce the private sector to hold the growing stock of debt, and this has further effects on the budget. It increases the deficit and thus leads either to further issue of debt or, eventually, to monetization. Eventually the growing debt service must lead to increased monetization of the debt, hence to increased inflation later. This is the "unpleasant monetarist arithmetic" of Sargent and Wallace (1981), who conclude that a current shift from monetization to debt finance might reduce inflation now but would increase inflation later, essentially through increasing future budget deficits. Thus, shifting from monetization to debt only postpones the problem. Going further, and getting a bit extreme, it can be argued that such a shift will lead to higher inflationary expectations now, which will reduce the demand for money and so actually increase inflation now. This extreme conclusion may apply to Brazil after 1986.

There is another consideration that seems to be rather special to Brazil. The debt that the Brazilian government issued from 1985 to 1990 was very short-term and thus highly liquid. In fact, for its holders it could be described as interest-bearing money. This fact had two implications.

First, it meant that the debt could readily be turned into dollars or other foreign currency, so that any increase in inflationary expectations would quickly bring about a portfolio shift, thus depreciate the exchange rate, hence increase inflation, and justify the expectations after the event. The accumulation of highly liquid debt was thus conducive to generating an explosive expectations-based inflationary process.

Second, such liquid debt was a much closer substitute for M1 (currency plus checking deposits) than for long-term private assets, equities, and so on. Therefore, a continuously increasing supply of it reduced the demand for M1. The difference between M1 and this other interest-bearing quasi money was that holders of interest-bearing bonds were protected against the inflation tax. The whole of the tax thus had to be applied to the exceedingly narrow base of M1, which by 1988 was only 10 percent of all money (including quasi money) and about 7.5 percent of GDP. And the liquid short-term debt became inflationary because it reduced the demand for non-interest-bearing money.

One way of reducing inflation in the short term would be to make these very liquid bonds less liquid, that is, to demonetize them. This would increase the demand for M1, reduce the ability to move quickly into dollars, and make the bonds closer substitutes for real assets. The demand for the latter would therefore decline and thereby produce a disinflationary (crowding-out) effect, such as is normally associated with the issue of bonds. Of course, the crowding out of domestic investment is also not desirable, nor is a growing interest burden, so the first-best policy would be to reduce or eliminate the operational budget deficit. This step—demonetizing these bonds by blocking them—was actually part of President Collor de Melo's 1990 stabilization program.[3]

The Role of Indexation

Brazil has been the indexed economy par excellence and—at least until 1985—has learned to live with inflation over a long period as a result. In this respect, it is unique. Three main forms of indexation are relevant here—exchange rate, wage, and financial market indexation—and they all have different implications. Perhaps most important has been indexation of the exchange rate.

Exchange Rate Indexation: Crawling Peg since 1968

Before 1968 Brazil had various exchange rate systems—multiple rates, exchange auction system, and floating rates—but in the immediately preceding period it had a nominal rate (fixed to the dollar, with occasional devaluations). Consequently, the real exchange rate appreciated over periods, a sharp depreciation would follow, then real appreciation would begin again, and so on. In other words, the real exchange rate was highly unstable. In 1968 the crawling peg system was introduced: the nominal rate was frequently adjusted by small changes to maintain a version of purchasing power parity, using the U.S. wholesale price index as an index of the foreign price level. This must have been an important factor in encouraging and maintaining the export boom.

This system lasted until December 1979. Over the period 1968–79, the real exchange rate was remarkably stable. After the first oil shock, the real exchange rate should have depreciated to prevent intensification of import restrictions and to improve the current account, so that such stability was not really first-best. It was better, however, than the situation at various times in many developing countries when inflation has led to increasing real appreciation owing to slowness in devaluing the nominal exchange rate. In many developing countries, such continued real appreciation has been the main adverse effect of inflation. The particular example of Nigeria since 1983 was cited in chapter 6.

The real effects of the 1979 devaluation were quickly eroded because in 1980 depreciation was predetermined at only 50 percent when the inflation rate was much higher (83 percent). (This was a short-lived "tablita" episode, unusual for Brazil. The tablita concept, originating in Argentina, is discussed later in the chapter.) After a 39 percent devaluation in February 1983, the real exchange rate stayed constant for the next three years—until the nominal rate was pegged again in 1986 as part of the Cruzado Plan. During 1983–86, then, the real exchange rate was at an exceptionally competitive level and sparked another export boom. With the Cruzado Plan in 1986, real exchange rate stability in Brazil ended. During the various plans, the nominal exchange rate was fixed, but then it depreciated when the plans broke down. Since mid-1989, Brazil has had a managed floating exchange rate system.

Wage Indexation

Brazil has had numerous schemes of wage indexation and wage control, too numerous and complicated to summarize here. Indexation has usually been "backward-looking" (that is, wages have been adjusted on the basis of past inflation rates), the adjustments have been made at quite long intervals (for example, a year or six months), although the length of the intervals has been varied as a way of changing the average level of the real wage. When the rate of inflation is rising, the longer the interval, the more nominal wages lag behind and hence the lower the real wage. Similarly, when the rate of inflation is falling, reducing the lag raises the real wage.

Wage indexation has by and large set lower rather than upper limits to wages, so that there has been plenty of scope for market forces to influence wages. Also, the coverage of indexation has not been complete. Real wages have certainly not been rigid in Brazil. Notably, they fell 25 percent during the Bulhoes-Campos program, and they also fell after 1982, principally as a result of the 1983 real depreciation. They rose sharply in 1985 following the 1984 boom and the arrival of the new democratic government. Indeed, in recent years real wages may have been determined more by market forces than by indexation arrangements. Yet there is little doubt that from 1968 until at least 1982 wage indexation made some difference to the actual levels of real wages, though less than is often suggested.

Given that wage indexation had some effect, it has been the source of "spiral inflation" —wage increases following price rises, with ensuing monetary accommodation, and so on. As noted above, it may at least help to explain why the two oil shocks led not just to inflationary bubbles but to permanent increases in the rate of inflation, and also why authorities were reluctant to apply orthodox contractionary policies at times of high inflation. Indeed, it may account for the "heterodox" belief that orthodox policies would fail to reduce inflation.

Financial Asset Indexation: Monetary Correction

Until 1964 it was illegal in Brazil to correct nominal assets for inflation, and, in addition, its usury laws put a ceiling on the interest rate. Naturally, with a negative real interest rate, the government found it difficult to sell its bonds. Since a goal of the Bulhoes-Campos program was to shift from money financing to debt financing of the budget deficit, it became necessary to make government bonds more attractive. This could have been done by allowing the market to fix interest rates on the basis of inflationary expectations as well as general portfolio preferences. The path chosen in 1964 and ever since was to issue Indexed Treasury Bonds (ORTNs), on which was paid a "monetary correction," to compensate for inflation, and something extra, so as to yield a positive real interest rate. Later, indexed savings deposits were also introduced, even though nonindexed financial assets also remained.

The aim was to divert private funds to the government; the funds were to come from increased savings as well as from crowding out private investment. A very important effect was to attract foreign capital inflows and to discourage capital flight. Here, again, Brazil has differed greatly from some other countries, notably Argentina and Mexico, where failure to depreciate the currency or to increase domestic interest rates sufficiently has led at various times to vast capital flight. Until 1986, capital flight was not really a problem for Brazil, mostly because of the indexation of financial assets (although there were also exchange controls).

The advantage to savers of an indexed bond over a bond having the interest rate determined in the market on the basis of inflationary expectations is that it avoids inflation risk, that is, the risk of expectations turning out wrong. It should then be possible for the Treasury to raise a given amount of funds at lower cost on average, since there is no need to compensate for that particular risk. A qualification here is that the monetary correction in Brazil has not always been sufficient to compensate for inflation. Another adverse aspect has already been mentioned, namely, that the more attractive these bonds are, the less will be the demand for money.

In 1978 Brazil introduced an ORTN that was linked to the dollar—that is, indexed to the exchange rate. This became a very popular asset when in 1980 the monetary correction for the ordinary ORTN was fixed in advance (rather than expost) on the basis of an inflation rate well below the actual 100 percent inflation outturn in 1981. After the 1982 crisis this corrected ORTN became the country's most important domestic financial asset. This situation created a fiscal problem in 1983. When the real exchange rate stays roughly constant, it does not matter much whether an asset is indexed ex post to the domestic price level or to the dollar. It does matter when the real exchange rate changes. These assets produced a serious budgetary problem as a result of the 39 percent devaluation in 1983, which did lead, as already mentioned, to a real devaluation that was sustained for three years. The budgetary cost in cruzeiros of the monetary correction required to maintain the dollar value of the bonds constant rose sharply. The fiscal problem is exactly the same as when a devaluation raises the fiscal cost of interest payments on a government-held debt that is denominated in foreign currency.

Argentina

In many ways, the Argentinian inflation and stabilization story is similar to that of Brazil.[4] It is one marked by inflation, numerous policy changes and stabilization attempts, accelerating inflation in recent years culminating in hyperinflation, and fiscal problems. Nevertheless, there are important differences.

First, the inflation rate of Argentina has been more unstable than that of Brazil, and the shift to sustained high inflation (more than 100 percent a year) began much earlier, namely, in 1975. In no year from then up to 1991 was the annual rate below 100 percent (except briefly under the Austral Plan in 1986). Second, inflation can be traced more clearly to fiscal deficits, and its variations to variations in the deficit as a ratio of GDP. There was a primary (noninterest) deficit in every year from 1961 to 1989. Third, the real exchange rate has been much more variable. Argentina has not been a consistently indexed economy and has not had the long periods of real exchange rate stability that Brazil had after 1968. As a result of this and many other factors, especially the general instability of economic policy, Argentina experienced low growth for the whole period since 1952. Its "miracle" years were in the early part of the century and the 1920s. After 1975, per capita GDP fell almost every year.

The Argentinian story is very complex because of frequent policy changes, the details of which can be confusing. Hence, the importance of fiscal policy as the source of inflation and of its variations should be stressed at the beginning. The argument that inflation and its continuance were largely the result of inertia and adverse external shocks can be made much more convincingly for Brazil than for Argentina.

For Argentina, two econometric exercises should be noted here. Rodriguez (1988, pp. 205–6) correlated the deficit/GDP ratio with the rate of growth of the consumer price index. He found that variations in government deficits from 1965 to 1986 were closely correlated with variations in inflation. Kiguel and Neumeyer (1989) report that seigniorage has been an important source of government revenue in Argentina, exceeding 3 percent of GDP for most of the period.

The Period up to 1974: Inflation Instability

The early period of Argentina's inflation history, from 1950 to 1974, can be summarized briefly. As in the case of Brazil and Chile, inflation was always high when compared with that in almost all other developing countries, though of course it was much lower than in the 1970s and 1980s. It was also quite variable, as table 7-1 shows. There were only two prolonged periods, namely, 1953–56 and 1968–70, when the inflation rate was below 20 percent. The country experienced two significant stabilization episodes of an essentially orthodox nature: one occurred in 1959, under President Frondizi, and it briefly bore fruit in getting the inflation rate down to 13 percent in 1961, after which it increased again; the other, the Krieger-Vasena episode, took place in 1967, and it managed to get the inflation rate below 20 percent for three years. The latter episode included wage and price controls.

The Isabel Peron Episode: Hyperinflation, 1975–76

The hyperinflation at the beginning of 1976 can be regarded as a significant divide in Argentinian inflation history. These were Isabel Peron's last months as president. Inflation reached 54 percent per month (over 1,000 percent a year) and after that, even after a substantial stabilization effort, the annual rate of inflation never got below 100 percent. Thus, from the point of view of inflation, it was clearly a watershed—a leap from chronic moderate inflation to chronic high inflation.

The increase in the annual rate of inflation actually took place in 1975 (from 24 percent the year before to 183 percent) as the result of various populist policies. Of course, 1975 was a disturbed year for many countries. The Argentine terms of trade deteriorated by 21 percent owing to the recession of grain and meat prices from their 1973 highs, but the extent of the disequilibrium clearly had a domestic origin. The fiscal deficit jumped to 14 percent of GDP in 1975. There was a balance of payments crisis, interest rates were controlled, there were price controls across the economy, and black markets developed.

This chaotic episode provided the stimulus for the subsequent "Martinez de Hoz" stabilization attempt to be discussed below. One might wonder why the memory of that year had not inoculated the people of Argentina more against inflation. The growth rate in these two years was about zero. Clearly, 1975–76 did not have the adverse, traumatic effect that the 1923 German hyperinflation had, or that the hyperinflation and chaos of the Allende years (to be referred to later) had in Chile. Presumably the explanation is that the hyperinflation lasted only a few months in 1976. It took the shock of the hyperinflation of 1989 to make Argentinians ready for serious reforms.

From 1976 to 1989, the government made two major stabilization attempts, both raising important issues. The first was the "Martinez de Hoz" episode of 1976–80, which involved, in its latter phase, the use of an exchange rate tablita as an instrument of anti-inflationary policy. The second was the Austral Plan, which was implemented from June 1985 to March 1986 and was a heterodox stabilization program. The intervening period—from 1981 to 1985—was one of failed stabilization programs and large macroeconomic imbalances. These were also the years of the Falklands War and the transition from the military regime to the democratic Alfonsin government. The period after the Austral Plan was chaotic as well, as successive attempts were made to slow up inflation. The economy was essentially breaking down, with net investment negative, and things culminated in hyperinflation in 1989. A new stabilization attempt of an orthodox kind was made by newly elected President Menem's government in 1990. It failed, but was followed in 1991 by a successful stabilization, which has put Argentina on a new path.

Martinez de Hoz and the Tablita, 1976–80

Few episodes in Latin American economic history have been mulled over more than the five Martinez de Hoz years. (Martinez de Hoz had a longer period in office as finance minister than anyone else since 1952.) The complexity of this episode has been a challenge to economists. The central feature was the attempt to reduce inflationary expectations by exchange rate management.[5]

From 1976 to 1978 policies were fairly orthodox, though rather moderate. Owing to some monetary and fiscal restraint, which affected expectations favorably, the inflation rate dropped drastically, though it never fell far below 100 percent, and the real interest rate rose. For a short period price controls were imposed. The consolidated public sector deficit dropped from 12 percent of GDP in 1976 to 6.5 percent in 1978 (roughly equal to the 1971–73 average, certainly a great improvement, but still too high). There was capital inflow and real appreciation. Capital inflow was attracted by the high interest rate (caused by the combination of budget deficit and monetary tightness) and the apparent and unusual "soundness" of economic policy, as well as the ready availability of funds during that period. The exchange rate was frequently adjusted.

In December 1978 a *tablita* was established. This was really a crawling peg exchange rate, with advance announcement of the rate at which the exchange rate would be devalued. The idea was that the exchange rate tablita would be an anchor for inflation, influencing inflationary expectations. The rate of devaluation was programmed to decline much faster than the rate of domestic price, and wage inflation turned out to decline, so that a very large real appreciation resulted over the tablita period. (On the basis of IMF figures, the real effective exchange rate index rose by 83 percent from 1978[4] to 1980[4], though other sources give a smaller rise.) As noted, there had already been real appreciation in 1976–78, owing to the high interest rate and capital inflow. The tablita produced more real appreciation.

One might ask why the rate of domestic inflation did not fall faster, thus avoiding so much real appreciation. No doubt there was some inertia, as many have argued. A plausible view is that the crucial factor was the continued high fiscal deficit, which was 7.5 percent of GDP in 1980. The public took this to mean that inflation would not decline as much as the tablita implied. Eventually, more devaluation than the tablita indicated would be required and there would be a reversal of the real appreciation. Of course, the public was correct.

The fiscal deficit kept up real interest rates because the government financed it by issuing domestic bonds in the newly liberated capital market. At first the high real interest rates attracted capital into Argentina, but as the real appreciation continued and it became obvious that the tablita could not last—and that Martinez de Hoz might not stay in power—there was massive capital outflow. It is important to note that this capital outflow was made possible, or at least made easier, by the capital market liberalization that Martinez de Hoz had introduced. After the event, the financial liberalization has been much criticized.

If a monetary authority wishes to sustain a particular exchange rate, or an exchange rate tablita, and if the market is convinced that it will not succeed and that devaluation can be expected, capital will flee and the monetary authority will be forced to draw on its reserves or borrow abroad. This was the problem of the Bretton Woods adjustable par value system: if the prediction of eventual devaluation is correct, it gives the agents in the market an opportunity to make assured profits at the expense of the central bank.

To sustain the exchange rate for a time, the central bank or government has to borrow abroad while private people export capital and hence lend abroad. This was the outcome at the time in Argentina. Since private savings were quite high, the problem was not a current account deficit: the current account was actually in small surplus during 1976–78. As private citizens shifted their portfolios into foreign financial assets (mostly in 1981 and 1982), the government had to borrow abroad, and it built up a huge debt. In view of the expectations, no reasonable domestic interest rate could have been high enough to prevent this.

The tablita policy was influenced by the fixed exchange rate version of the monetary theory of the balance of payments. Monetary policy in that model sustains the exchange rate commitment, and the money supply itself becomes endogenous, being determined by the demand for money. If the demand for money is less than supply, the balance of payments goes into deficit, so that the reserves decline and the foreign assets of the banking system fall as required. The reserves change so as to ensure that the supply of money becomes equal to the demand. When the demand for money falls because of lack of confidence in the currency— leading to capital outflow—the reserves fall. And when the reserves get too low, the government has to borrow, which is what happened in this case. In addition, if domestic credit is created to finance a fiscal deficit (more credit than is required to meet extra demand for money resulting from given inflation)—as there was— there will be a further decline in reserves.

The exchange rate (or tablita, in the Argentinian case) could have been sustained indefinitely if there had been a willingness to live with the necessary contraction of domestic credit in real terms. In other words, the domestic interest rate would have had to be sufficiently high. If the public had really believed that this would be the policy reaction, the exchange rate regime would not have been expected to break down and there would not actually have been so much capital flight, if any. In practice, credibility could not be established because of the continued high fiscal deficit and because there was simply no basis for believing that Martinez de Hoz could make the regime last even if he wanted to—as no doubt he did.

Breakdown, 1981–85

There was massive capital flight from 1980. The period of breakdown and crisis might be dated from late 1980, when President Viola was appointed to take over the next year but declined to make an exchange rate commitment ("Viola's silence"), so that devaluation came to be expected. There was thus a crucial policy hiatus. Alternately, it could be dated from March 1981, when President Viola embarked on a new economic policy regime under a new finance minister. This period goes up to June 1985, when the Austral Plan was implemented.

The system really collapsed during this 1981–85 period. The situation was so chaotic that there is little point in describing it in detail. There were several big devaluations (ten from 1981 to 1983). The financial system collapsed, the government took over private international debt, there was a flight from money, and inflation soared, reaching 344 percent (annualized) in mid-1983. High inflation led to lags in tax collections (the Tanzi effect, noted in chapter 6), so that a high budget deficit continued—for this reason as well as others. Yet Argentina actually generated a trade surplus. To some extent, the latter part of this period could be regarded as an illustration of the "tradeoff" model expounded in chapter 6: an improvement in the noninterest current account in real terms—forced by the need to service the foreign debt, by the drying up of "new money" from the banks, and by the worse terms of trade—was brought about at the expense of increased inflation.

The Austral Plan and After

The heterodox Austral Plan—which involved wage and price controls, exchange rate management, and orthodox fiscal and monetary policies—was implemented from June 1985 to March 1986. We have already described the Brazilian Cruzado Plan of 1986; it was very much influenced by the Austral Plan, though there were some differences.

The Austral Plan succeeded in stopping hyperinflation. The inflation rate dropped drastically, although at the end it was still fairly high by other countries' standards: the wholesale price increase averaged 49 percent a year from April to June 1986. There was monetary prudence and the demand for money rose. And all this was achieved with little loss in output. The immediate outcome was thus much more favorable than that of the Cruzado Plan, particularly because it was not associated with an expansion of demand caused by a rise in real wages, as was the case in Brazil.

If the immediate Austral Plan outcome could have been sustained, this episode would be judged a success. The next period, from April to September 1986, was one of monetary ease and abandonment of the freeze. Wage indexation returned. There was a wages push. As in the case of Brazil, and in many episodes earlier and later in Argentina, prudent policies were not sustained long enough.

The question then arises whether the Austral Plan had truly succeeded in bringing down inflationary expectations—so that the wage-price freeze could be ended without inflation reigniting—or whether the freeze itself was considered the key policy instrument by the public, in which case its ending would just reignite inflation. In the latter case, there would have been no point in applying a heterodox freeze at all, since price and wage controls cannot be permanent. The key point surely is that fundamental monetary and fiscal policies must be noninflationary, and must be seen to be so, for expectations to adjust. As long as there was some belief that fiscal equilibrium would be reestablished, the demand for money rose, and this helped to keep inflation down. Once this belief was lost, the end of price control would just reignite inflation. In any case, even if higher inflation were not actually expected, loose monetary and fiscal policies would in due course accelerate inflation again even with given expectations.

Tight money was applied from October 1986 to February 1987, and this did lead to a decline in the rate of inflation. At the same time, tight money combined with continued fiscal ease caused the real interest rate to rise, so that the peso became overvalued again. The inflation rate accelerated once more in 1987, and in February 1987 a new price freeze was temporarily imposed. In 1988 the inflation rate was 343 percent a year (7 percent a month), and 1989 was a year of hyperinflation. The fundamental problem was the fiscal deficit. Interest payments on external debt were an element of this problem, but the debt service problem has to be seen in perspective. While government interest payments to foreigners averaged 6 percent of GNP in 1983–88, net outward transfers averaged only 3 percent. Additional funds, provided reluctantly by commercial creditors and international agencies, eased the burden, and in 1988 interest arrears were 2 percent of GNP. Note, in particular, that net outward transfers in 1986–88 averaged only 1 percent of GNP.

By mid-1989, when President Menem took over, the economy was clearly breaking down, and at last society seemed ready for drastic measures. It was, as Menem said, "Argentina's last chance." He proceeded to a drastic austerity program and temporarily ended hyperinflation. With a loss of confidence, it returned at the end of the year. The whole of 1990 was a year of endlessly changing plans and of crises (though structural reforms—including improvements in the fiscal situation, trade liberalization, and privatization—continued to be made). In February 1991 the monthly rate of inflation was 27 percent. In March 1991 the new minister of the economy, Domingo Cavallo, introduced a radical new plan to fix the Austral to the dollar, make it convertible (fully backing it with dollar and gold reserves), and undertake to avoid financing a budget deficit with money creation. The Convertibility Law proscribed money creation other than through increases in net foreign reserves. Hence, it disciplined monetary policy. In addition, further deregulation and reform measures—especially designed to eliminate the fiscal imbalance—were introduced during 1991. As a result, the inflation rate fell dramatically during 1991 and by mid-1992 was about 20 percent a year.

The Argentinian Fiscal Problem

Running right through the Argentinian story has been the fiscal problem.[6] Unless that was dealt with, other measures designed to regulate prices, influence expectations, and so on, notably exchange rate management, could not work other than temporarily. In the short run, expectations about fiscal policy determine expectations about inflation, so that reasonably credible announcements of policies to tighten fiscal policies can immediately reduce the rate of inflation. This happened in March 1990 when President Menem's new orthodox policy program was announced and the monthly inflation rate fell quickly, from about 80 percent to 10 percent. In the medium and longer run, fiscal policy determines the rate of growth of money and hence the inflation rate for any given expectations.

As noted earlier, primary (noninterest) public sector deficits were incurred in every year from 1961 to 1989. Until 1975, deficits were almost wholly financed by monetization. Under the Martinez de Hoz regime of 1976–80, the government shifted to foreign financing, and hence, as mentioned above, the inflation rate fell somewhat. After 1980, domestic debt financing played a role, financing variable proportions of the deficit; but periodic devaluations kept down the real value of the domestic debt (that is, nominal interest rates have lagged behind inflation outcomes), so that by 1985 domestic public debt was only 6 percent of GDP and by the end of 1988, 11 percent. It rose to 17 percent in 1989. Domestic debt has thus been much less important than in Brazil. On the whole, the primary deficits have been financed by monetization, while interest payments have been rolled over through new debt. Commercial banks were required to maintain reserves with the central bank, so that the interest bill was the main element in the central bank's so-called quasi-fiscal deficit, which in some years has been even greater than the total nonfinancial public sector deficit discussed above.

At various times, price controls have reduced the rate of inflation immediately, and sometimes quite drastically, but when they have been removed, inflation has risen again. Hence, beginning with the Austral Plan, the country has experienced short-term inflation cycles explained by the imposition and removal of controls. These cycles have been superimposed on underlying inflationary trends determined by fiscal policy and by inflationary expectations that have steadily reduced the demand for non-interest-bearing money.

Behind the fiscal problem have been the more fundamental problems of Argentine society: the high level of government spending (and its growth between 1972 and 1987 from 29 percent of GDP to 40 percent); the difficulty of raising or collecting noninflation taxes; the difficulty of reducing the deficits of parastatal enterprises by raising their prices to the public and increasing efficiency; and the difficulty of restraining public sector wage demands. Thus, the fiscalist or seigniorage explanation does not fully account for the problem; the deeper explanation has to tell us why management of the public finances has been so much more difficult in Argentina than in all developed countries (with which Argentina should really be compared) or even in many Latin American countries, notably Chile and Mexico in recent years.

The central objective of the reforms undertaken by the Menem government has been to close the fiscal gap through action on both the revenue and the spending side. A value added tax was expanded, the efficiency of tax administration was improved, the size of the federal government's labor force was reduced, and nearly all public enterprises were privatized, or at least there was partial divestiture. The losses of these enterprises had been a burden on the public finances. As a result, the primary (noninterest) balance of the federal government moved into surplus in 1992, changing from a deficit of 10.5 percent of GDP in 1989. At the time this book went to press, the Argentinian situation appeared to have been truly transformed.

Chile

During the twenty years from 1950, Chile was a chronic-inflation country and had one of the highest average inflation rates in Latin America, roughly equal to Brazil's.[7] Over the whole period, the inflation rate averaged 31 percent. It reached a peak of about 84 percent in 1955, and in 1970 it was 34 percent. The essential explanation was a lax fiscal policy. In contrast with Brazil, Chile had a low growth rate. Three stabilization programs were tried out in these years, and they did succeed in bringing very high rates down, notably in 1957 (from 66 percent to 29 percent) and in 1964 (from 46 percent to 29 percent), but they did not cure Chile of chronic inflation.

Chilean Inflation 1970–73

The most dramatic developments took place during the brief socialist regime of the Allende government, from 1970 to 1973 (it was overthrown in October 1973). There was an unprecedented expansion of the public sector: the public sector deficit rose to 30.5 percent of GDP in 1973. It did not help that the terms of trade dropped about 17 percent during that period. At first, the nominal exchange rate was maintained and the reserves were used up, so that temporarily high inflation was avoided. The visible crisis really began in 1972, when there was an inevitable shift from a current account deficit to inflation tax (the tradeoff model again). The peso was devalued 71 percent in 1972, and this stimulated inflationary expectations. As a result, inflation jumped to 75 percent (from 33 percent in 1970), and by the end of 1973 it had soared to 362 percent. GDP fell by 5.5 percent in that year.

Stabilization, 1974–82: Exchange Rate-Based Stabilization from 1979

The remaining inflation story of Chile can be divided into three stages. In the first stage, 1974–78, inflation was reduced drastically, with the big reduction beginning in 1976, and by mid-1979 it was 33 percent. Real wages fell sharply in 1974 and 1975, and there was a big devaluation. During this period, the fiscal deficit was reduced and by 1978 was down to 1 percent of GDP. Essentially, it was a period of orthodox stabilization, which led to a severe recession in 1975, and of various important microeconomic reforms. As already noted in chapter 4, the severity of the recession was policy induced, being the result of a drastic "shock" program designed to reduce inflation. Fiscal and monetary contractions reinforced the effects of the decline in the terms of trade. The second stage, lasting from 1978 to 1982, is the most interesting—indeed, it is one of the most analyzed, debated episodes in the macroeconomic history of any developing country. It can be described as an episode of "exchange rate-based stabilization," similar to the Martinez de Hoz episode in Argentina described above.

This episode started with massive private sector foreign borrowing and hence a current account deficit and private sector debt accumulation, and ended in a serious balance of payments crisis and recession, as outlined in chapter 4. What makes this period so interesting is that exchange rate policy was used as a way of reducing inflationary expectations and hence inflation. In this respect it was successful. By the end of 1982, inflation was down to 10 percent, but there was a real appreciation during that period, with unemployment continuing at a high level, and it ended in crisis. Hence, there has been much debate about the wisdom of the anti-inflation exchange rate policy.

Policymakers understood full well that the fundamental cause of inflation had been the large Allende and immediate post-Allende budget deficits. At the end of 1977 the inflation rate was still high (about 92 percent), even though the budget deficit had been eliminated, so in 1978 the authorities introduced a tablita; that is, they undertook an assured declining rate of devaluation. At the end of 1978, the inflation rate was still about 40 percent and the policymakers (the "Chicago Boys") became impatient and decided that from mid-1979 the exchange rate in relation to the dollar should be fixed. Inflation continued at least for two more years, so that the real exchange rate in relation to the United States appreciated. The real appreciation of the trade-weighted exchange rate was increased by the tie to the U.S. dollar, since, unexpectedly, the U.S. dollar also appreciated in relation to other major currencies over this period. The net effect was a real appreciation of about 30 percent.

This fixed exchange rate policy was much criticized subsequently, because it caused a large real appreciation that contributed to continued high unemployment; sometimes it is blamed for the excessive capital inflow and high interest rates, as well as the capital outflow at the very end of the period. It is more plausible, however, to argue that the large private capital inflow from 1979 to 1981 made real appreciation inevitable: if the exchange rate had been flexible, the peso would have appreciated in relation to the dollar. Most important, it is argued that the system of lagged wage indexation that had been instituted in 1979 was incompatible with a fixed exchange rate regime and a process of disinflation. (The implication of lagged wage indexation will be discussed later in this chapter.) It has to be recognized that the exchange rate policy was successful in its main objective: by 1982 the inflation rate was down to about 10 percent. By contrast, in the same year, after a somewhat similar episode (though starting from much higher inflation in 1978), Argentina's inflation rate was over 100 percent.

Crisis and Stabilization from 1982

As described in chapter 4, Chile suffered external shocks (a rise in oil prices and in world interest rates) at the end of 1979 but foreign borrowing by the private sector staved off the crisis until 1982. Then new foreign lending suddenly dried up, the copper price fell, domestic investment stopped, and there was a financial sector breakdown and a drastic decline in demand that brought about a huge postwar recession: GDP dropped by 14 percent in 1982, the biggest recession during that period of any in the eighteen countries in this study.

In June 1982, the fixed exchange rate was reluctantly abandoned, and Chile entered the third stage. The peso was devalued 19 percent, but this just increased expectations of further devaluation, so that in August the rate was floated. In hindsight, it can be seen that the devaluation should have taken place in 1981, when the current account problem became apparent and the economy showed signs of slowing down. Since 1982 the exchange rate has been frequently adjusted, and there have been several large nominal and real devaluations. As a result, the inflation rate rose again from its end-1982 low of 10 percent to 27 percent in 1983.

From 1983 to 1989 Chile went through another thoroughly orthodox stabilization period: with a reduction in the fiscal deficit (close to zero in 1987), a stable and moderate (but by no means zero) inflation rate, and a very large real devaluation. There were two big devaluations in 1985, and policy during this period focused on adjusting the peso regularly to prevent real appreciation—a big change from the 1979–81 policies. From the point of view of inflation, the main feature to note is that any attempt to get the inflation rate really low seems to have been given up. Clearly, a lesson was learned from the 1981–82 episode: an attempt to reduce a modest inflation rate to a really low level can be very costly in terms of the temporary loss of real output. Over the whole period from 1983 to 1991, inflation averaged 22 percent and was also 22 percent in 1991.

Mexico

Mexico's inflation history falls into four parts: (1) an early period up to 1972 when Mexico was a low-inflation country like most of the countries discussed in the previous chapter and quite unlike Brazil, Argentina, and Chile; (2) an intermediate moderate-inflation period from 1973 to 1981 (average inflation rate 22 percent), when (as already discussed in chapters 3 and 4) the seeds for later problems were sown; (3) a high-inflation period in 1982–87; and (4) the low-inflation "Pacto" stabilization period of 1988–92.[8] Closest attention will be given here to the third, the high-inflation, period and to the recent highly successful stabilization episode.

Stabilizing Development, 1954–72

The first period was one of "stabilizing development," in the sense of high growth, a fixed exchange rate to the dollar, and low inflation. The Mexican exchange rate was devalued in 1954 and then stayed fixed until 1976. This period, at least up to 1972, was one of remarkable price stability: from 1956 to 1972, the inflation rate averaged less than 3 percent. This was, of course, a natural outcome of the Mexican fixed exchange rate commitment. The Mexican economy was part of the Bretton Woods system, which produced that kind of inflation rate in most of the world. From the point of view of inflation, the four South American countries within the group of countries considered in this study are the special cases. Mexico is not remarkable. Mexican per capita growth averaged 3.3 percent. An essential feature was the pursuit of conservative monetary and fiscal policies. A key role in this respect was played by Ortiz Mena, who was finance secretary from 1958 to 1970.

Period of Moderate Inflation: Two Spending Booms, 1973–81

The principal features of the second period (1972–81) are the two public sector spending booms, which led to very large fiscal deficits (already described in chapters 3 and 4), and to the 82 percent devaluation in 1976. To a great extent, the spending booms manifested themselves not in higher inflation—though inflation did increase—but in current account deficits financed by foreign borrowing. Hence, this was a period of debt accumulation, which led to the 1982 crisis.

The increase in the inflation rate in 1973 to 12 percent and 1974 to 24 percent, when the fixed exchange rate still prevailed, can be explained to some extent by the import of inflation from the United States, as in the rest of the world outside the United States. Quite a few members of the Organization for Economic Cooperation and Development were experiencing similar inflationary bubbles. By 1975, the Mexican inflation rate was down to 15 percent. In addition—and much more important—a public spending boom began with the Echeverria administration in 1972, the fiscal deficit effects of which were partly monetized, and this led to a substantial increase in the money supply, so that much of the rise in inflation from 1973 must be attributed to that boom.

The public spending boom led to a crisis and hence a maxidevaluation in 1976—the first devaluation after twenty-two years. As a result, the inflation rate rose to 29 percent in 1977. More noteworthy is the favorable outcome of the stabilization program—that is, of the maxidevaluation and the fiscal tightening. In 1976 the public borrowing requirement was 10 percent of GDP, and by 1977 it was down to 6.7 percent. A substantial *real* devaluation of more than 20 percent resulted. The exchange rate was kept fixed at its new level until the crisis broke in 1982. There was a devaluation in February 1982 and another one in August, the month of massive capital flight and the beginning of the debt crisis. After 1977 the inflation rate fell again, bottoming in 1978 at 17.5 percent, and then it crept up, so that in the precrisis year of 1981 it was back at 28 percent. Note, too, that by 1980 real wages had fallen 8 percent from their peak in 1977.

The development of new oil reserves led to a second, even larger, public spending boom, which in turn generated large fiscal deficits, especially in 1980 and 1981. By 1981 the public sector deficit was about 14 percent of GDP. The crisis year 1982 inaugurated the high-inflation period of 1982–88.

High Inflation and Two Crises, 1982–86

The events of 1982 to 1988 have already been described in chapters 4 and 5. Here we seek only to put the inflation experience—which can hardly be isolated from the various changes in the "real" economy—into an analytical framework. In 1983 the inflation rate suddenly shot past 100 percent (from around 26 percent in 1980 and 28 percent in 1981). It then fell until it reached a low of about 58 percent in early 1985. It rose again to more than 100 percent in 1987, the result of a monetization of the fiscal deficit and of devaluation (both brought about by the third oil shock), and declined somewhat in 1988, until the new, radical, stabilization program was begun. There were big devaluations in 1982 and 1986, both a part of structural adjustment programs.

The increase in the inflation rate in this period over the previous period can be explained in terms of the "tradeoff" model. This Mexican episode is the outstanding example of the model at work. Because of the rise in interest rates on the accumulated foreign debt and the decline in the terms of trade in 1982, the current account deteriorated drastically. The drying up of new commercial loans called for an improvement in the current account. At the same time, the primary fiscal deficit could not be reduced as quickly as necessary. Hence, there had to be a switch from foreign financing to monetization of the fiscal deficit, and this was the main cause of the increase in inflation.

This inflation arrived through two channels. The first was the exchange rate. Credit creation to finance the deficits led (or would have led) to a continuous decline in foreign exchange reserves; continuous or frequent devaluations were required to avoid such a decline. If the exchange rate floated freely (which it did not in the Mexican case), it would have led automatically to continuous depreciations. Second, in the absence of perfect capital mobility, monetization of fiscal deficits leads, even with a fixed exchange rate, to continuous expansion of the money supply, and hence to greater aggregate demand, and thus inflation.

There were two maxidevaluation episodes, in 1982 and 1985–86, leading to real devaluations in each case of about 50 percent (the latter in two stages, one in 1985 and the other in response to the 1986 oil price fall). These created adjustment inflation, which helps to explain the exceptional inflation rates of 1982 and 1986–87. There was also an element of spiral inflation, but until 1987 this was not so crucial. Real wages fell over the whole period, and effective indexation was only intermittent. The remarkable fall in real wages (about 40 percent in the manufacturing sector between 1981 to 1987) is particularly worth noting. There was certainly no indication of real-wage rigidity. Clearly, inflation was the cause of the erosion in real wages. One cannot imagine that a real wage decline to that extent could have been brought about by conceivable nominal wage decreases.

It is important, however, not to overlook the equally remarkable improvement in the primary fiscal balance that took place—a shift from a deficit of 7 percent of GDP in 1982 to a surplus of 7 percent in 1988. This happened in spite of the decline in the oil price in 1986, which had severely adverse effects on revenue. Nevertheless, because of the high real interest bill, the operational deficits continued, except in 1987. The operational deficit was down to almost zero in 1984, but by 1988 was up again, to more than 4 percent, being mostly financed by domestic debt, but also partly monetized.

Real Exchange Rate Targeting, 1987

The high and accelerating inflation rate of 1987 requires special explanation. The primary fiscal *surplus* was already remarkably large in 1987, at 5 percent of GDP, and there was actually an operational surplus of 2 percent of GDP. A factor operating in 1987 explains the high growth of the money supply in spite of the fiscal (operational) surplus.[9]

As already noted, there had been a big devaluation in 1986. The objective of monetary policy in 1987 was to keep the real exchange rate at its new, highly competitive level. Thus 1987 became a year for targeting a real exchange rate. This yielded two benefits: it allowed a boom in manufactured exports to be sustained and encouraged, and it discouraged capital flight—which had been a serious problem since 1982. The net result was that in 1987 the foreign exchange reserves more than doubled over 1986. It even became possible to use some reserves to buy back debt at a discount. This was truly remarkable in view of the sharp deterioration in the terms of trade in 1986. At the same time, the policy was inevitably highly inflationary.

As nominal wages and prices of domestic goods increased, because of previous inflation, inflation inertia set in. The nominal exchange rate was then increased sufficiently to maintain the real exchange rate target. The increase in reserves that resulted from the current account surplus (2.6 percent of GDP) and the return of flight capital increased the monetary base, and so provided the increase in the money supply that supported the inflation. Put another way, the continuous nominal depreciation at an increasing rate was due to the continuous wage inflation (explained by past inflation), and this increased the demand for money, which was then satisfied by increased supply through the increase in the foreign assets of the banking system. Temporarily, the country was in effect on a "wages standard," since the wage increases determined the inflation rate. This episode raises issues about exchange rate policy to be discussed further in this chapter and in chapter 8.

The question is, what did this inflation tax finance when there was no operational fiscal deficit? It financed the accumulation of reserves through the current account surplus.

This was a brief episode, however. The accelerating inflation of 1987 led to the implementation in 1988 of a new, radical stabilization plan, in which real exchange rate targeting was given up. In 1988 there was another outflow of private capital, and the current account again went into deficit. One cause of the deterioration in the current account was a much-needed boom in private investment.

The Pacto Stabilization Program of 1988–90

In December 1987, an economic solidarity pact (the Pacto) was negotiated with labor unions and other interest groups by President de la Madrid. It was renewed several times by President Salinas (who took over at the end of 1988) and was still operative—under the name of Pact for Stability and Economic Growth—in 1992. It involved a comprehensive stabilization program, the central points of which were further fiscal restraint and, initially, a freezing of the nominal exchange rate in relation to the dollar. It was supplemented by a freeze of minimum wages and public sector prices and tariffs, price controls on some private sector goods, and various structural adjustment measures, notably accelerated trade liberalization and public enterprise divestiture.

This program represented a complete reversal of the 1987 policy. In 1987 the real exchange rate had been targeted, so that wage inflation determined the inflation rate and the nominal exchange rate. By contrast, during the Pacto, the nominal exchange rate was targeted and this eventually affected the inflation rate, the aim of other policies being essentially to sustain the exchange rate. The real exchange rate became endogenous and appreciated by 25 percent during 1988. The program had some similarities with the Martinez de Hoz episode in Argentina. A central feature of the Mexican Pacto, successfully implemented, was the thoroughly orthodox policy of fiscal and monetary restraint. The Pacto was less complex than the Cruzado and Austral plans, differing from both in having a strong and consistently maintained orthodox component of fiscal and monetary restraint, and differing particularly from the Cruzado Plan in leading to a significant (about 10 percent) decline in real wages during 1988.

The inflation rate fell drastically during the year. At the beginning of 1988, it had reached a peak of about 180 percent a year. By the last quarter, it was at an annual rate of about 20 percent, and that is, roughly, where it stayed through 1989 and 1990. Both the primary and operational fiscal balances improved and the primary surplus reached more than 7 percent of GDP in 1989. Contrary to expectations, a recession was not created, but the growth rate, at 1 percent to 1.5 percent in 1988 and 1989, was still low, still yielding a decline in per capita GDP. The lower inflation rate naturally reduced the nominal interest rate, so that the nominal interest bill of the public sector fell sharply, and with it the public sector's borrowing requirement (from 16 percent of GDP in 1987 to about 7 percent in 1989), but this was no surprise. The problem, to be discussed, was that the nominal interest rate did not fall more; that is, there was a sharp rise in the real interest rate.

It should be added here that in 1989 the nominal exchange rate ceased being fixed, and a tablita system—that is, a predetermined crawling peg system—was introduced involving an approximately 20 percent nominal devaluation over 1989. The result was that in 1989 and early 1990, the real exchange rate stayed approximately constant at the appreciated level it had reached at the end of 1988. In 1990 and 1991, the rate of crawl was reduced so much that the exchange rate was practically—though not formally—fixed. In 1991 there was a 9 percent real appreciation, associated with a current account deficit that was only possible because of the revival of capital inflow.

From the point of view of inflation stabilization, the Pacto was clearly a success. In particular, it maintained and strengthened the crucial orthodox part of the program, namely, the tight fiscal policy, and was able to avoid a wages push that would have led to a breakdown of the program. There was a problem, however. It arose from the very high real interest rates during the early stages of the Pacto period and their adverse effects on the operational deficit and hence in preventing further fiscal improvement. This was a completely new problem because from 1983 to 1987 the real interest rate on the large domestic peso-denominated debt had been negative, since nominal rates had failed to keep up with inflation. In 1988 and 1989, the interest rate was high because the market did not expect the exchange rate (or the tablita) to last, but expected more depreciation. Hence, there was still a credibility problem affecting not wages and the real exchange rate, but the interest rate. This is a characteristic problem of stabilization programs.[10]

Of course, monetary policy could have been less tight. Lower domestic real interest rates would then have led to massive capital flight, given the exchange rate expectations. This would have been a repeat of the last stage of the Martinez de Hoz episode in Argentina, and also of the Mexican period of high capital flight in 1980–82. Such a policy was sensibly avoided, but this action had a severe, though temporary, fiscal cost. Hence, the benefits of the reduction of the primary deficit were temporarily lost through the increase in the interest bill on domestic debt. In 1988 the interest bill on peso-denominated debt was in excess of 7 percent of GDP. In contrast, the interest bill on foreign currency-denominated debt was 5 percent of GDP in that year. In July 1989 the interest rate on dollar-denominated Mexican debt was about 20 percent. This contained a large amount of country risk. The interest rate on peso-denominated debt was 55 percent, giving (with 20 percent inflation) a real interest rate of 35 percent, and implying an expected depreciation of about 30 percent, which can be compared with the 20 percent annual depreciation implied by the tablita. By the end of 1989 the situation had changed. Successful debt negotiations reduced the annual resource transfer Mexico would have to make by about 2 percent of GDP. There was a restoration of confidence both because of the success of the debt negotiations, which reduced perceived country risk as well as expected depreciation, and because it did seem that the Pacto would last. The interest rate on dollar-denominated debt fell to 15 percent, and the rate on peso debt was down to 36 percent, implying a 16 percent real interest rate, roughly equal to the rate on dollar-denominated debt. Exchange rate expectations were now in accord with the tablita's annual 20 percent depreciation.

To sum up this aspect of the Pacto, it was built around exchange rate stabilization or, at least, a tablita that basically anchored the inflation rate. Appropriate wage restraint was maintained, but, through high interest rates, the credibility problem of 1988 and 1989 fed back into the budget, and hence into the key orthodox aspect of the program.

An Assessment of Mexican Experience: Crucial Role of Exchange Rate Policy

It is interesting to compare the Mexican with the Brazilian experience since 1981. In relation to GNP, the Mexican foreign debt was greater than that of Brazil: 66 percent for Mexico in 1983 and 50 percent for Brazil (though in relation to exports, Brazil's debt ratio was actually higher then). In addition, in 1986 the Brazilian terms of trade improved owing to the decline in the oil price, whereas Mexico's worsened, and by 1988 Brazil's debt ratio had fallen to 31 percent and Mexico's only to 58 percent. The Mexican authorities seem to have a far better control of economic policy, the reasons for which can be found in the whole political and social situation.

They can bring about significant real devaluations that last for some time. They can drastically cut the primary budget deficit in a short period. In Brazil, declines in real wages tend to be short-lived, and in 1985 there was an 8 percent rise in real wages, while Mexican real wages fell from their 1981 peak (42 percent by

1986). The observation by Pazos (1972) that Latin American countries (the four southern ones that he studied) appeared unwilling to apply sustained stabilization policies because of a reluctance to accept inevitable short-term costs, clearly does not apply to Mexico. Mexico, in effect, followed a heterodox stabilization program with a strong orthodox component in 1988–90, but this strategy worked, unlike Brazil's Cruzado Plan.

During the period 1982–90, Mexico's per capita GDP declined at an average annual rate of about 1 percent, so that Mexico's experience can hardly be considered a complete success story, in spite of the remarkable achievements in macroeconomic policy. Much of the short-term macroeconomic success was achieved at the cost of a reduction in investment, both public and private, and this no doubt explains to a considerable extent the low growth rate—and creates problems for the future. There is also another side: in a sense, Mexico invested quite unusually in the future, and substantial fruits could emerge in due course if policies are sustained. It invested in structural policies—trade liberalization, privatization of inefficient public enterprises, a reduction of uneconomic subsidies, administrative improvements—all of which were long needed. In addition, it invested in credibility.

There was a modest growth recovery from 1989 with an average growth rate of 3.5 percent (implying per capita growth of 1.5 percent) in the three years from 1989 to 1991. Per capita growth, however, was still well below that of 1965–80 (over 3 percent).

The Mexican macroeconomic experience over the whole period between 1972 and 1990 exhibits a clear pattern: the attempt to keep inflation in check through exchange rate policy, an attempt that, until 1989, was not successful, but led instead to severe real exchange rate instability. In this respect, the Mexican experience runs counter to that of Brazil until 1986. Mexico has never chosen to "live with inflation," or, except in the unusual year 1987, to allow the nominal exchange rate to follow domestic costs and prices so as to maintain the real rate. In the tradeoff between trying to slow up inflation at the risk of real exchange rate instability and trying to maintain a real exchange rate, it has always (except in 1987) chosen the first. The result is a pattern of real exchange rate instability beginning in 1972, with the most recent real appreciation beginning in 1988.

In the 1980s, Mexico was no longer truly following a fixed exchange rate policy: there were too many devaluations, and in 1990 there was a tablita, but it still hankered after a fixed nominal rate. When credibility cannot be ensured, this can create difficulties in inducing capital outflow or in compelling very high domestic real interest rates to prevent such outflow. When such an outflow cannot be prevented, the instability just referred to inevitably sets in. Insofar as the attempt to keep the exchange rate fixed encourages tight monetary and fiscal policies and is believed to do so—and thus contributes to the credibility of stabilization policies—it is helpful in keeping inflation down. With regard to expectations and to a commitment to low inflation as an objective, Mexico may still be benefiting from the memory of its long history of exchange rate and price level stability.

Turkey

As described in chapter 4, Turkey had a debt crisis in mid-1977, several years ahead of other countries, and this was the point at which Turkey went from being a low, or moderately low, inflation country to a moderately high one.[11] From an inflation point of view, Turkey only becomes interesting from mid-1977 onward.

The Early Period, 1960–77

From 1960 to mid-1977, the inflation rate was generally below 20 percent and Turkish experience was rather similar to that of many countries described in the previous chapter. In the 1960s, inflation averaged only 5 percent and the exchange rate was fixed. There was a 66 percent devaluation in 1970. A spending boom began in 1971, encouraged by a boom in workers' remittances and thus a surplus in the current account. After 1974, as described in chapter 3, Turkey suffered an adverse shock as a result of the oil price rise and a decline in workers' remittances, so that the current account went into deficit. While inflation rose somewhat from 1971, it was still only 17 percent in 1976. The disequilibrium that emerged from 1974 to 1977 manifested itself in a current account deficit, not in greatly increased inflation.

The exchange rate was fixed to the dollar, and from 1970 to 1977 there were only some minor devaluations. Presumably, the (more or less) fixed exchange rate policy—made possible by the availability of foreign finance—played a leading role in keeping the inflation rate down until 1977. At the same time, this fixed exchange rate policy contributed to the 1977 crisis, as the real exchange rate appreciated, and workers' remittances fell in the expectation of devaluation.

Crisis and Adjustment, 1977–80

The two-and-a-half years from mid-1977 to 1979 were, in the words of Celásun and Rodrik (1989), years of "crisis without adjustment." They present (pp. 656–64) a clear statement of the tradeoff model. Their argument is that inflation occurred because Turkey failed to adjust in response to the decline in foreign funding: "Turkish governments of 1978–79 handed over to inflation the disagreeable job of cutting real expenditures." The current account deficit reached 5.4 percent of GNP in 1976 and a peak of 6.9 percent of GNP in 1977, and as a result of the Turkish debt crisis it fell to 2.6 percent in 1978 and 2.1 percent in 1979. At the same time, the inflation rate started rising sharply in August 1977. It was 17 percent in 1976, 45 percent in 1978, and 59 percent in 1979. Thus, an improvement in the current account went with a marked increase in inflation.

The external problem was transmitted into domestic inflation essentially through shortages of imported commodities that raised domestic prices, and through reduced leakages of domestic credit creation into the balance of payments. As a result, the money base expanded, even though domestic credit creation did not increase. Real wages fell sharply (24 percent in the two years 1978 and 1979) owing to the lag in adjustment of nominal wages to unexpected inflation, and this reduced private consumption.

A key element in the current account improvement was a sharp decline in private investment. Compare 1976, the precrisis year, with 1979, the preadjustment year when the inflation rate had risen to 60 percent. The current account improvement was brought about by a combination of lower private investment and higher private savings—in spite of a worse fiscal balance. Owing to the Tanzi effect, the fiscal deficit rose from 3.5 percent of GNP in 1976 to nearly 7 percent in 1979. Private investment fell from 13 percent to 9 percent. In addition, private savings rose from 11 percent to 13.5 percent. The net result was that the current account deficit fell from 5.4 percent to 2 percent of GNP. It is doubtful that the reduction of private investment was caused primarily by inflation, although there may have been some effect of that kind. The reduced availability of imported goods, brought about by controls, must have been a major factor. Essentially, the failure to adjust fiscally can be said both to have caused inflation (and hence generated bigger private savings) and to have reduced investment.

Although it might be argued that 1978 and 1979 provide an example of the tradeoff model—increased inflation resulting from an improvement in the current account—the peak inflation rate of 110 percent reached in 1980 must be explained somewhat differently. In part, it was due to the monetary expansion of the previous year, but in the main it was an inflationary bubble caused by adjustment inflation. As described in chapter 4, a radical structural adjustment program was introduced in January 1980. The lira was devalued, from 35.35 per dollar to 70.70. In addition, prices charged by state economic enterprises (SEEs) were sharply increased, many by more than 100 percent (for example, electricity by 153 percent), and agricultural support prices rose as subsidies were reduced. The price of wheat rose 100 percent. Thus the inflation bubble of 1980 is not hard to explain.

Money supply (M2) grew 67 percent during that year, much less than the rate of inflation, so that there was a severe decline in real money balances, which produced a temporary recession. The recession helps to explain why the inflation rate was down to 37 percent in 1981. Turkey received substantial official loans from 1980 as a result of its structural adjustment program and the concern of European countries, especially, with Turkey's strategic position. This meant that there was a continued inward resource transfer in spite of the debt crisis, and hence it was easier to get the inflation rate down again. Severe wage restraint imposed by the military government also helped the inflation stabilization process. (Real wages fell 25 percent in 1980.) By 1982, the inflation rate was down to 31 percent. From the end of 1983 it started rising again.

High Growth and High Inflation, 1981–90

Although Turkey experienced impressive growth during the entire period of 1981–90, especially in exports, inflation was high, especially in 1988 and 1989. From 1981 to 1987 the inflation rate (consumer price index, CPI) averaged 38 percent and during 1988–90 it averaged 66 percent.

With the January 1980 devaluation, the exchange rate was given up as a nominal anchor. The policy from 1980 until 1988 was to depreciate the nominal exchange rate sufficiently to maintain the real rate and also to bring about further substantial real depreciation. The dominant objective was to maintain the high export growth rate, regarded correctly as the primary engine of growth during this period. As noted, 1988 and 1989 were years of very high inflation, and this led to a change in exchange rate policy in 1989, the real rate being allowed to appreciate about 30 percent.

The Turkish inflation of this period was a straightforward case of fiscal deficits being partly financed by monetization. Before 1977, fiscal deficits were primarily foreign financed, and as a result Turkey began to incur current account deficits and accumulate debt. Since then it has shifted toward the monetization of deficits, as well as toward domestic debt financing. Current account deficits have continued, but have been relatively lower.

The political difficulty of reducing fiscal deficits and the use of budgetary policies to generate support before elections were the causes of Turkey's continued inflation.[12] In addition, there was a steady decline in the demand for base money. Until recently there were few signs of price and wage inertia, and the inflation was obviously not wage led. Of course, a continuation of the high inflation rates of the 1988–90 period is likely to change this. Empirical work also suggests that large short-term variations in the inflation rate can be explained to a considerable extent by variations in the size of fiscal deficits.

The demand for base money has fallen, and this has increased the inflation rate for given seigniorage. In 1988 the average stock of base money stood at 6.6 percent of GNP, compared with 11.2 percent in 1982. The inflation rate rose from 31 percent in 1983 to 75 percent in 1988, but the ratio of seigniorage to GNP was only up from 3 percent to 4.4 percent. This decline in the demand for money can be explained by three factors. First, the liberalization of exchange controls in December 1983 and later made it easy to hold foreign currency, so that there has been considerable currency substitution. Second, domestic financial liberalization allowed interest rates to rise and led to a shift from non-interest-bearing money or money requiring relatively low reserve requirements into interest bearing assets. Third, the demand for money must have fallen as a result of inflationary expectations gradually catching up with actual inflation, especially in 1988 and 1989.[13]

Finally, the system of wage determination in Turkey during this period can be summarized as compulsory arbitration leading, in effect, to two-year overlapping contracts with partial—very partial—lagged indexation. The inflation from 1978 to 1980 reduced real wages by 43 percent, and they fell further after that, especially due to the inflation rates since 1988. By 1991 it was probable that real wages were so low that further falls were hardly possible. Reducing inflation would no doubt raise real wages.[14]

Indonesia: Inflation and Stabilization, 1961–70

Indonesia's story begins with the crisis that developed in the period 1961–70.[15]

Origins of the Crisis

In 1961, while in the last stage of the Soekarno regime, Indonesia embarked on a monetary expansion fed by budget deficits. In response, inflation jumped from 20 percent in 1960 to 95 percent in 1961. It steadily increased after that, exploding in 1965 with an annual rate of 306 percent and going even higher (topping 1,000 percent) in the peak second quarter of 1966. Seigniorage peaked at about 8 percent of GDP in 1965. The rise in the inflation rate was boosted by a rise in the velocity of money, vastly so in the two peak inflation years.

Table 7-2 shows the relevant data. It should be borne in mind that there are many data problems, so that not much emphasis should be given to precise figures. For example, the cited inflation rates are based on the Jakarta cost of living index, which in an overwhelmingly rural country can only be indicative of the rate of national inflation; GDP figures must also be regarded as having large margins of error.

According to table 7-2, the big increase in the budget deficit occurred in 1961 (from 2 percent to 5 percent of GDP), following a rise in expenditure. After that, public expenditure in relation to GDP actually fell as it was unable to keep up with inflation. The continued fiscal deficit, and its increase in 1965, was brought about by a drastic reduction in revenue, from 13 percent of GDP in 1960 and 1961 to only 4 percent during 1964–66. This was not caused primarily, if at all, by lags in tax collections (the Tanzi effect), but by two distinct factors that were connected with, but not wholly explained by, inflation: first, the breakdown of public administration including the tax collection system and the increase in smuggling that led to evasion of trade taxes; and second, the decline in export and tariff revenue, owing to reduced trade.

The Indonesian budget was overwhelmingly dependent on taxes on trade, especially export taxes, direct and indirect (through a multiple exchange rate system), and this is where the problem lay. Exports fell because of reduced output, owing to general economic dislocation; real appreciation, as exchange rate adjustments became inadequate to compensate for the accelerating inflation; increased domestic absorption of exportables; and declining terms of trade. To some extent, the decline in revenue was caused by inflation—in particular, by the real appreciation that it brought about—but also there was a common cause for both inflation and the decline in revenue, namely, general economic dislocation and mismanagement.

Table 7.2   Indonesian Data, 1960–70

(percent)

	1	2	3	4	5	6	7	8a	8b	8c
					Govt	*Govt*	*Budget*	Current account		
	CPI	*Money*	*GDP*	*Vel.*	*rev.*	*exp.*	*deficit*	*$m*	*$m*	*of GDP*
1960	20	37	2	8	13	15	2	-58		
1961	95	42	6	12	13	19	5	-466		
1962	156	99	2	16	5.5	9	4	-212		
1963	129	95	-2	18	5	10	5	-201		
1964	135	156	3.5	17	4	10	5.5	-205		
1965	594	281	1.1	31	4	11	7	-222	84	-4.5
1966	636	763	2	27	4	9	5	-108	130	-2
1967	112	132	2	25	7	10	3	-254	115	-4
1968	85	126	11	24	7	9	2	-225	-24	-3
1969	10	58	7	17	8	12	3	-336	-74	-3
1970	6.5	34	6.5	14	11	14	3.5	-310	-271	-3

Note: Figures have been deliberately rounded off to avoid a misleading impression of precision given by decimal places, when there are such large margins of error. Column 1 = growth rate per year of Jakarta, cost-of-living index; 2 = growth rate of M1; 3 = growth rate of real GDP; 4 = ratio of nominal value of GDP, using CPI, to average M1; 5–7 = revenue, expenditure, and deficit figures as percentage of GDP (from 1969, figures refer to a fiscal year that starts in April; figures for 1960–64 come from Sundrum 1973, p. 74, and later figures from Woo and others forthcoming); 8a = current account balance in U.S. dollars from *International Financial Statistics*; 8b = current account balance as revised by Rosendale (1978); 8c = current account balance (from *International Financial Statistics*) as a percentage of GDP.

Source: Columns 1-3 from *International Financial Statistics*, Column 4 calculations from *International Financial Statistics*, Column 5-7 from Sundrum 1973, p. 74, and later figures from Woo and others (forthcoming).

Regime Change and Stabilization, 1966–70

A dramatic political crisis in October 1965 led to the fall of Soekarno and the emergence of the Suharto regime, which twenty-five years later was still in power. The regime transition was actually gradual, but politically it was completed in March 1966. A change in the economic policy regime was beyond doubt. Soekarno had militantly proclaimed his hostility to Western economics and to orthodox macroeconomic principles. Hence, there was no doubt at all that "unorthodox" economic policies were responsible for the economic crisis. Now a group of U.S.-educated economists (the "Berkeley Mafia") became the economic policymakers. A comprehensive stabilization and rehabilitation program was launched in October 1966 and implementation began in 1967.

Debt rescheduling of principal and interest payments, and foreign concessional credits, were negotiated. This was undoubtedly an important feature of the stabilization. In the last years of the previous regime all foreign loans had dried up. Some part of the budget deficit could now be financed by foreign borrowing rather than by monetization. The current account swung from surplus to deficit from 1968, and by 1970 the deficit was about 3 percent of GDP.[16]

The import licensing system was abolished, most price controls were ended, the system of trade taxes and multiple exchange rates was gradually simplified, and private foreign investment was encouraged. The program was drawn up with the advice of an IMF mission.[17]

There was a large switch in the pattern of government expenditure, away from wasteful projects and activities of various kinds toward desperately needed infrastructure improvements. The budget deficit fell sharply—not because of a decline in overall expenditure but because revenue recovered. This revenue recovery is explained, above all, by the recovery of exports, as well as the general improvement in the economy.

The growth rate of money fell from more than 700 percent in 1966 to 130 percent in 1967. A fall in the fiscal deficit from 5 percent of GDP to 2–3 percent, supplemented by some shift to foreign financing, presumably generated the large decline in the growth rate of money. The inflation rate in 1967 (106 percent) was about the same as the money growth rate. Hence in 1967 there was apparently no change in the demand for real balances, so that the inflation and money growth rates were about the same. It must be reiterated that these figures should be regarded as very approximate indeed, in view of the data problems.

There was no evidence of any slump in 1967, in spite of the drastic fall in the growth rate of money. It is clear that prices and wages were flexible, and problems of inertia did not arise. Hence, from the point of view of effects on output and employment, it hardly mattered whether the recovery program was credible, other than in one respect: the agreement of foreign creditors to rescheduling of existing debt repayments and to new concessional loans made possible the increased flow of essential imports that was clearly crucial to the restoration of output. The credibility of the program was certainly relevant for the creditors. In addition, as we shall see, credibility did matter for effects on the demand for money.

During the period 1962–66 it is likely that average per capita growth was negative. In 1968 there was a considerable recovery leading to an 11 percent real growth rate, the result of many factors associated with the stabilization, including the increased availability of vital imports financed by foreign credits. As table 7-2 shows, growth continued to be high in the following years, though the 1968 growth rate was exceptional. The high growth rate in 1968 naturally raised the demand for money and hence made it possible for the money growth rate to continue at the relatively high level of 126 percent.

The big change in the inflation rate took place in 1969. The growth rate of money dropped to 58 percent, but inflation actually fell to 10 percent. By 1970—after three years of the program—inflation stabilization was complete with an inflation rate of 6.5 percent. This was a remarkable result.

Some Issues: Velocity, Exchange Rate, Sources of Success

It is particularly interesting to see what happened to the income velocity of money, since its short-term changes are likely to reflect changes in inflationary expectations. Income velocity did not fall significantly until 1969, after which it continued falling steadily, hence making it possible for the inflation rate to decline faster than the growth rate of money. In this way, the economy was remonetized. Sometimes the need for remonetization in an inflation stabilization program is seen as a problem, but here, as also in other historical cases, such as the stabilization following the German hyperinflation, it happened through the gradual reduction in the rate of growth of money. A rise in nominal interest rates on demand deposits, designed to produce positive real rates, was part of the stabilization program, and must have played some role in raising the demand for money and hence lowering income velocity. The recovery in the demand for money was such that by 1972 income velocity (at about 10) was roughly back to where it had been in the late 1950s.

The lag of two years in the decline of velocity suggests that it did take time for price expectations to adjust. In spite of the clear and drastic change in the political and economic regime, credibility was not established immediately. It is not difficult to imagine the skepticism of many Indonesians about new policies that were so different from what had gone before.

Under the 1966 stabilization program, the authorities simplified the complex exchange rate system and announced a big devaluation. Unification of this system was completed in 1970, when exchange controls were also abolished. From 1966 until 1971, the nominal exchange rate was regularly adjusted so as to approximately maintain the real exchange rate. In August 1971, when the stabilization was complete, the rupiah was firmly fixed to the dollar and stayed fixed at the new rate until October 1978. The nominal exchange rate was fixed only when the stabilization was completed. This particular stabilization program was thus *not* one based on the exchange rate, wherein a commitment to a fixed nominal rate is made so as to constrain policies or signal a new low inflation regime.

In addition, the stabilization program was not based on targeting or on making a commitment to a particular rate of growth of money even though the need to cut the growth rate of money was clearly seen as a central objective. As noted above, after a sharp initial fall in 1967, the money growth rate only declined gradually. It was not even a fiscal-policy-based stabilization, since the decline in the budget deficit in relation to GDP was not large, partly because of a shift from money financing to foreign credits. In absolute real terms the decline in the deficit was even less because of the high real growth rate of GDP from 1968.

In a sense, the stabilization was "program-based." Improvements in the pattern of expenditure, policies to restore exports and tax revenue, adjustment of the exchange rate and simplification of the exchange rate system—all played their part. Today it would be described as a structural adjustment program in which the reduction in the money growth rate was a crucial element, required for the decline of the inflation rate. The program achieved credibility with foreign creditors and with holders of money because of its coherence, the nature of the principal policy-makers, and its early achievements.

The stabilization effort was obviously successful for a number of reasons, a primary one being that prices and wages were flexible (explained mainly by the low industrialization and unionization of the Indonesian economy), so that a sharp decline in the growth rate of money did not cause a recession. Second, the economy had been in such a bad way for several years, with almost certainly a negative growth rate per capita on average, that there was full support for a drastic policy change and scope for improvements that quickly produced a growth recovery. The high growth rate it produced also helped boost the demand for money. Third, the consistency and soundness of the policies depended on the high quality of the economist policymakers and the willingness of a firmly entrenched president to delegate macroeconomic policymaking to them. Finally, the willingness of foreign creditors to reschedule and to provide new concessional loans was crucial. Few other countries have produced these four conditions, especially the first and the fourth.

The Sources of Inflation in Six Countries: Summary

Can any general conclusions be drawn about the sources of high inflation, or sharp increases in inflation rates, in the six countries discussed in this chapter? In particular, can these stories be interpreted in terms of the classification suggested in the previous chapter (adjustment inflation, spiral inflation, seigniorage inflation—that is, the monetization of fiscal deficits)?

Certainly, the stories are dominated by fiscalist themes. To a great extent, inflation in all these cases can be explained by monetization of fiscal deficits.

First, in some cases, high inflation began or accelerated as the result of brief periods of populist fiscal expansions and thus clearly had domestic origins. There are many examples: the Goulart expansion in Brazil in 1962–64; the 1985–86 expansion in Brazil, initiated by the outgoing military regime and pursued further by the new democratic government; the Isabel Peron episode in Argentina, which led to hyperinflation in 1975–76; the socialist Allende inflationary explosion in Chile in 1972–73; and finally the Indonesian Soekarno episode of 1961–65.

Second, there are cases of *prolonged* periods of inflation readily explained by prolonged monetization of fiscal deficits, in turn explainable in political terms. The clearest case is that of Argentina, probably for all the years since 1950, and certainly from 1971. For the whole period from 1971 to 1986, the inflation tax averaged 7.6 percent of GDP. Much of Brazilian inflation history can also be explained in these terms, though spiral inflation has also played an important role there. Turkish inflation since 1981 is clearly due to fiscalist factors.

Third, many episodes are best described by the tradeoff model: an adverse external shock leads to the monetization of a deficit, so that increased inflation is caused by the reduction in foreign financing or by a decline in the terms of trade. The clearest examples come from Mexico in 1982 and in 1986–87. Other examples come from Brazil in 1981–84, Argentina in 1983–84, and Turkey in 1978–79. In some cases the deficits originated in public spending booms (described in chapter 3) that initially led to foreign borrowing, the shift to inflation-financing coming at the end of the booms. The principal examples are Mexico in 1980–82 and Turkey in 1977–79.

Elements of spiral inflation—resulting from an adverse external shock that usually led initially to real devaluation—can be found in Argentina and Mexico. Brazil—with its three shocks, each raising the inflation rate to a new plateau—is the most important example, wage indexation clearly playing an important role in the process. Among the six countries discussed in this chapter, there are just a few examples of adjustment inflation, involving devaluation and leading to an inflationary bubble: Mexico in 1976 and Turkey in 1980. Finally, it might be asked where "inflation inertia" comes in. This cannot explain how inflation begins or accelerates but only why it is difficult to stop.

Stabilization Experiences of Six Countries: Summary

Among the many stabilization episodes described in this chapter, there are two clear-cut success stories, namely, the Brazilian Bulhoes-Campos program of 1964–67, and the experience of Indonesia in 1966–70. In both cases not only was the inflation rate reduced in a short period—vastly so in the Indonesian case—but stabilization was followed by a period of high growth. Both were essentially orthodox episodes, but the Brazilian stabilization included severe wage restraint. The Indonesian stabilization was greatly helped by foreign financing.

Two other stabilization episodes can be described as qualified successes. The Chilean stabilization in 1974–82 certainly brought the inflation rate down from its very high (500 percent or so) level, but it was associated with, or led to, low growth as well as other problems (real appreciation, excessive private borrowing). Nevertheless, it did lay the groundwork for the growth recovery from 1983. The Mexican Pacto stabilization of 1988–92 has also been an outstanding success, and an endorsement for a program consisting of a combination of orthodox policies with nominal exchange rate targeting, wage restraint, and some price controls. By 1991 it had brought the inflation rate down from 100 percent to 20 percent without a decline in the growth rate. A judgment made in 1992 has to be qualified, however, because the growth rate is still low (estimated at 3.6 percent a year for 1991), and time is required to see whether low inflation will last.

Finally, there are the many failures of Brazil and Argentina. In one of the Argentinian episodes—the Martinez de Hoz episode of 1976–80—the basic failure was, as usual, in fiscal policy (although, given this, the use of the exchange rate as nominal anchor might be criticized). The episode following the introduction of the heterodox Austral Plan could be described as a qualified success initially, but it was soon followed by further monetary expansion and wage increases. The Brazilian Cruzado Plan failed completely because of the initial wage increases and the fiscal failure. The battle against inflation continues in Brazil, but in 1992 the Menem government's stabilization of 1991–92 was showing clear signs of success.

Four Stabilization Issues

There are four much-debated issues concerning inflation stabilization programs. We review them here in the light of the six country experiences just discussed.[18]

Can Stabilization Be Achieved without Fiscal Retrenchment?

It may be possible in some high-inflation countries to reduce inflation without having to reduce government spending or raise tax rates and without increasing foreign or domestic borrowing in real terms. This is certainly an attractive "soft option." Possibly a given amount of seigniorage in relation to GNP can be obtained with both a high rate of inflation and a low rate, and the problem is to shift from the high to the low one by reducing inflationary expectations sufficiently and by ending indexation. With lower inflationary expectations the demand for money would rise, making the same seigniorage compatible with lower inflation. This is an example of the "Laffer curve" argument—namely, that a given inflation tax revenue can be obtained with both a high rate of inflation tax and a low rate, and that a reduction of the inflation tax rate may actually cause inflation tax revenue to rise (see chapter 10). In the present case, the argument is that a reduction in the inflation tax rate might actually cause revenue from seigniorage to rise, or not fall, owing to the rise in the demand for money. Furthermore, because of the Tanzi effect working in reverse, as inflation falls, ordinary tax revenue would rise in real terms, so that the deficit would naturally decline.

Although it would be unfair to suggest that the architects and advocates of the heterodox Cruzado Plan believed that high Brazilian inflation could be brought down without any fiscal measures at all, there was certainly a tendency to downplay the fiscal problem, and to rely primarily on the ability of the plan to end inflation inertia and finally raise the demand for money sufficiently. This may have appeared reasonable because the money-financed fiscal deficit was not very large (averaging only about 2 percent of GDP since 1974).

There are two objections to this approach.

First, it is really an empirical matter whether the country is in a situation where a reduction in the inflation rate would eventually raise seigniorage, or at least not lower it. The evidence suggests that it is only true in very high inflation cases. No soft option is available for countries with, say, annual inflation of 100 percent or less. Given the uncertainty, a moderately high inflation country that relies on this in formulating its inflation stabilization program is running the risk of failure—and hence the risk of damaging the credibility of further anti-inflation programs. In the case of Brazil, seigniorage has been low because of the indexation of most financial assets, as discussed earlier. The inflation tax has been much more important in Argentina, so that a large reduction of inflation also required a large fiscal improvement. At the same time, it appears that the very high Argentinian inflation rate of 1984 (in excess of 600 percent compared with 300–400 percent in 1983) led to a decline in the ratio of inflation tax revenue to GDP (from 14 percent to 10 percent), which suggests that in that year, at least, lower inflation would have yielded more seigniorage—even though any effort to bring inflation below 300 percent a year would surely have required a reduced fiscal dependence on the inflation tax.

Second, the crucial requirement of this approach is to reduce inflationary expectations. These will be greatly affected by the fiscal situation, since it was usually the monetization of fiscal deficits that was the original cause of inflation. If the fiscal situation is not improved, inflationary expectations will not fall—or not sufficiently or for a long enough time—in spite of various heterodox measures. This was clearly the situation in the two major Argentinian stabilization attempts from 1976 to 1986 and also the Cruzado Plan.

Thus it may be necessary to tighten fiscal policy to convince economic agents that the program is serious and does not just depend on its heterodox components. Confidence-inspiring measures may require not just a reduction in monetization but also a reduction in the overall fiscal deficit, including the parts financed by domestic and foreign borrowing. If these measures are successful, eventually inflationary expectations will fall, the demand for money will rise, and it will be appropriate—and indeed desirable—to increase the money supply somewhat by monetary policy or by shifting from bond finance to money finance of deficits.

Are Heterodox Measures Necessary or Desirable for Inflation Stabilization?

Orthodox anti-inflation programs are programs that involve or emphasize monetary restraint, and since the principal source of monetary expansion is usually through the monetization of fiscal deficits, whether directly or indirectly, this involves primarily policies of fiscal contraction. Of course, monetization could be reduced by shifting the financing of budget deficits away from monetization toward domestic or foreign borrowing; there are circumstances when this is justified—since optimal borrowing is not necessarily zero—but it may just shift problems, including higher inflation, into the future. For the reasons just discussed, programs that do not satisfy the orthodox requirements are unlikely to be successful or, at least, run a high risk of failure.

The question now is whether there is a supplementary role for other policies, that is, policies that have been described as heterodox since the time of the Austral and Cruzado Plans and the Israeli stabilization program. Here one must distinguish several components of heterodoxy, in particular (a) exchange rate stabilization, or the establishment of a tablita, (b) wage controls or an incomes policy, and (c) price controls. We shall discuss the exchange-rate based stabilization approach later; here we consider (b) and (c).[19]

There is really nothing heterodox or new about the idea of controlling or limiting wage increases, either by government fiat or by an incomes policy based on agreement with trade unions. This was a staple of macroeconomic policies in many European countries, notably Britain, in the 1960s and early 1970s, and was practiced by Korea in the early 1980s. Given a monetary policy commitment to full employment and a view that prices tend to be fixed as markups on costs, inflation can only be reduced by moderating wage increases. If there is not a commitment to full employment, and the rate of growth of the money supply (roughly determining the rate of growth of nominal demand) is reduced anyway, unemployment will result if the rate of growth of wages does not also respond: hence, in the absence of a flexible labor market, measures to reduce wages growth are needed to avoid severe recession.

Eventually, of course, growing unemployment would reduce the rate of growth of wages, but this market process usually works slowly. Thus, inflation stabilization is brought about at a cost of temporarily high unemployment, possibly quite severe. The more organized the labor force, and, in particular, the more wage indexation, formal or informal, is practiced, the bigger the problem. We shall return to the wage indexation issue below.

One can certainly make a convincing case for tough wage restraint policies to be associated with orthodox stabilization measures. This should avoid—or reduce—the temporary increase in unemployment. This is exactly what happened in the case of the successful Brazilian program of 1964–67, and of the Mexican program of 1988–90, the very heart of which was a Pacto with the trade unions. It must also be noted that such policies can create microeconomic distortions in the labor market, and usually controls and incomes policies are only effective for limited periods. Often in practice they only apply to minimum wages, so that there is plenty of room for market forces to work. Eventually, wage increases must be moderated by a reduction in inflationary expectations. Wage restraint measures are usually only possible as transitional measures.

Were wage restraint measures needed in the various stabilization experiences discussed in this chapter?

In Chile in 1976–81 and Brazil for much of the period since 1974, there was indeed a wages problem. Both countries were committed to indexation. In the Chilean episode inflation was reduced but unemployment increased. In Brazil the reluctance to practice orthodox restraint for a sufficiently long period, and hence to bring down inflation, can be explained by the reluctance to allow a recession to last for any length of time. If wages had been more flexible, the recession problem would have been reduced. Wages have been much more flexible in Argentina and the failures of so many stabilization attempts, or the reluctance to continue with them for a sufficient length of time, appears to be much more readily explained by the fiscalist approach than by a concern with the adverse employment effects of orthodox contractionary measures. The same applies to Turkey, though there the experience with fairly high inflation is much briefer. Finally, Indonesia in 1966–70, with its low level of industrialization and urbanization in the period, did not have a wages problem.

Mexico provides the outstanding recent example of how orthodox measures can be combined with effective measures of wage restraint; the net result was a reduction of inflation combined with the maintenance, and then recovery, of growth. Korea in the period 1983–84 also provides an example.

As for the more heterodox element of "heterodoxy," namely, price control, this was practiced comprehensively in the Austral and Cruzado Plans, and in the Mexican Pacto. It was also practiced to a modest extent in the Brazilian 1964–67 program, during the 1968–73 "miracle" period, and intermittently during President Collor's stabilization attempts of 1990–91.

There are two arguments in favor of price controls, the first being strong, the second weak. The strong argument is that sometimes it is only politically possible to obtain wage restraint by fiat or agreement with trade unions if there is some price control. The weak argument is that price controls will quickly reduce inflationary expectations. There is something in it since, presumably, for the period of the controls, price inflation will indeed be determined by the controls, and this will obviously affect expectations as well as actual inflation. Hence, price controls helped explain in large part the rapid declines in inflation at the beginning of the Austral Plan and the Cruzado Plan and the various other plans that followed the latter. Price controls are rarely permanent, though, and expectations will take that into account.

One argument against price controls is that they usually create severe microeconomic distortions through affecting relative prices, and this manifests itself in the form of shortages of goods where controls are effective, or of price slippage, where they are not. In addition, if controls are severe in relation to the decline in the rate of nominal demand growth, there will be overall shortages. The argument against long-term comprehensive price controls is surely overwhelming from an administrative and microeconomic distortions point of view. In practice, the main element in price control programs is usually the control of the prices of goods and services supplied by state enterprises or the government directly, or of certain wage goods that are subsidized, and in that case the controls increase the budget deficit and thus worsen the orthodox component of the stabilization program.

Is There a Role for Wage Indexation?

During the last stage of the Chilean stabilization, from 1979 to 1981, there was lagged indexation.[20] Hence, the rate of decline of nominal wages lagged behind the rate of decline of price inflation, so that the real wage increased. This has often been cited as a cause of the real appreciation and the low growth rate of this period. Actually, the problem was not so much wage indexation as such, but the fact that, inevitably, it was lagged. If indexation had been instantaneous, the inflation stabilization program would not have led to an increase in real wages.

Given lagged indexation, a decline in the rate of inflation raises the real wage and tends to have a recessionary effect, and the longer the lag, the greater the rise in the real wage and probably the greater the recession. Conversely, a rise in the inflation rate lowers the real wage and is likely to have a stimulating effect. An adverse exogenous shock—for example, a deterioration in the terms of trade—usually requires a fall in the real wage. With lagged indexation, this can be brought about by an increase in inflation. The longer the lag, the less inflation has to rise to produce a given decline in the real wage. Wage indexation may be the principal cause of spiral inflation, but the existence of a lag can explain why inflation reaches a new plateau after an adverse exogenous shock, but does not indefinitely accelerate.

It was noted earlier that after each of Brazil's three adverse shocks (1974, 1979, 1982), the inflation rate ratcheted upward to reach a new plateau. Of course, it could not have stayed at the higher levels if there had not been ratification of higher inflation rates through monetary expansion. In other words, the interaction of shocks and indexation increased inflation, and monetary expansion ensured that this did not lead to serious recessions—which would have reduced inflation through market forces.

The question then arises whether a system of wage indexation, which is inevitably lagged, is desirable. When there is uncertainty about monetary policies, an argument in favor of indexation can be made. In the absence of indexation—with wages slow to adjust to changes in prices—an unexpected monetary expansion causing an increase in the inflation rate would reduce real wages more than workers are willing to accept and possibly even the government wishes to bring about. Conversely, an unexpected decrease in monetary growth and hence the inflation rate would bring about a greater rise in the real wage than either party wants. Indexation would then reduce uncertainty.

Suppose that wages were not determined by indexation but rather by forward-looking expectations. If the government is pursuing an inflation stabilization program but cannot establish credibility—so that inflationary expectations do not decline when it embarks on its tight money policies—real wages will then rise as prices respond more quickly than wages. Forward-looking wage determination based on false expectations will lead to a bigger rise in real wages and hence a bigger recession than backward wage indexation if the lags in the latter are less than the lags in the adjustment of expectations. Thus there could be some logic in making wage indexation part of a stabilization program.

The crucial question is thus what the alternative to wage indexation is. One alternative is market-based wage determination, with wages determined by inflationary expectations. One must then compare the adverse effects of lagged indexation with the (possibly greater) adverse effects of market-determined wages when expectations are slow to adjust. The other alternative is to have highly flexible wages that quickly respond to the current market situation and thus do not allow real wages to rise to levels where significant involuntary unemployment is created. Outside the public sector, this may well be the situation in many of the countries discussed here, even in some in Latin America, including Mexico. In that case, the introduction of wage indexation would make real wages more rigid.

Wage indexation based on an unwavering formula is clearly undesirable when there is an adverse exogenous shock that requires real wages to fall if employment is to be maintained. Indexation then leads either to increased unemployment, possibly very large, or (as in the case of Brazil) to higher inflation. In the absence of indexation, higher prices caused by worse terms of trade would naturally lead to declines in real wages, and there would be no spiral effect. If the fall in real wages is not enough initially, unemployment will result, and this would then gradually cause wages to adjust—at least provided the adverse shock was expected to continue.

It follows that any country that institutes wage indexation as part of an inflation stabilization program (as Brazil did in the 1960s) should make provision for the formula to be adjusted when there is such an adverse shock. The real wage should be deliberately reduced by means of nominal wage reduction in relation to price increases. Experience shows that in the absence of such provision, or a willingness to give up indexation at times of shocks, the effects of indexation can be highly adverse. It should also be added that once inflationary expectations have been stabilized at a low or moderate level, it may well be best to leave wage determination as far as possible to decentralized market forces and to avoid the rigidities that indexation imposed by the government or centralized agreement inevitably imposes.

Is Exchange Rate-Based Stabilization Desirable?

We have described the exchange rate-based stabilization episodes of Argentina, Chile, Brazil, and Mexico. Either there was a tablita or a fixed exchange rate.

There is a case for using the exchange rate as a nominal anchor in preference to either having a commitment to a monetary target (a method that has not been used in any of the countries), or pursuing fiscal contraction and reduced monetization of deficits, with a fiscal rather than a monetary target.

The exchange rate is a clear-cut, well-defined anchor, especially when the domestic currency is fixed to a particular foreign currency—the dollar in all the cases discussed here—rather than a basket of currencies. It is supposed to represent a firm commitment by the monetary authorities and, given its credibility and its clarity, it should affect expectations. Nothing seems simpler in a country with 100 percent inflation than to announce that henceforth the exchange rate will depreciate only at an annual rate of 20 percent, and this will then set the domestic inflation rate. This explains why a number of stabilization programs—including the Austral and Cruzado Plans—have included exchange rate targets. There are two problems here.

The first is that wages and the prices of nontradable goods may be slow to adjust. There will then be a severe squeeze on the profitability of the sectors producing tradables, and the real exchange rate will appreciate. This is exactly what happened in the Argentinian and the Chilean episodes of 1979–81. In the Chilean case one reason, at least, was lagged wage indexation. In the Argentinian case the exchange rate policy was insufficiently credible for a number of understandable reasons: previous stabilization efforts had all been short-lived, and the necessary fiscal measures were not being taken. We have discussed this in detail above. As noted earlier, this kind of problem—slowness of expectations to adjust and hence inevitable recession—would also result from a policy of monetary contraction aimed, say, not at maintaining a particular exchange rate or tablita, but more directly, at the rate of price inflation.

The second problem is that an attempt to fix an exchange rate or a tablita is likely to lead to a balance of payments crisis unless monetary (and hence fiscal) policy is appropriate at the same time.

The real appreciation and the squeeze on tradables, which, at least in the short run, seems inevitable, would worsen the current account, and in the absence of capital mobility would lead to a decline in the foreign exchange reserves. If this is to be avoided, domestic absorption must be reduced by some combination of fiscal and monetary contraction.

In the presence of capital mobility, a lack of credibility of the exchange rate target would lead to capital outflow unless the domestic interest rate was raised sufficiently. Hence, there has to be appropriate monetary tightness. If the domestic monetary effects of capital outflow were not sterilized, the reduction of reserves would automatically bring about some monetary contraction, but the reserves might run out—or there might be a balance of payments crisis—before equilibrium has been restored. The problem can be avoided if there is sufficient domestic credit contraction to raise domestic interest rates so as to eliminate the incentive for capital flight. Failure to do this in Argentina and in Mexico in 1982 caused massive capital flight. When a big devaluation is expected, very high domestic interest rates may be required, possibly higher than is possible from a domestic point of view.

At this point, one should note the relevance of fiscal policy. An exchange rate policy cannot substitute for an improvement in fiscal policy. If fiscal deficits are being partly or wholly monetized, continued deficits lead to continued domestic credit creation and thus prevent the necessary contraction in the real money supply. While the foreign assets of the central bank fall, the domestic assets rise. This was what happened in Argentina in 1979–82, as described earlier.

It follows that a successful exchange rate-based stabilization program really requires two associated policies.

First, some kind of incomes policy designed to slow the rate of nominal wage increase, at least temporarily, is needed—except when expectations adjust very quickly because the program has high credibility. This is the so-called heterodox element. Second, domestic monetary policy must fit in with the exchange rate commitment: expectations of devaluation must be offset by increases in domestic interest rates. And this means that there cannot be an independent fiscal policy leading to the monetization of fiscal deficits. This is the orthodox element. As we saw earlier, the Mexican Pacto stabilization program of 1988–90 did indeed have both these associated policies—a wages pact combined with a willingness to raise interest rates as required and a reduction in the fiscal deficit, actually producing an operational surplus.

It is possible to pursue an exchange rate-based stabilization program without an explicit incomes policy, although this could result in severe, albeit temporary, recession. Such a program cannot be pursued when the fiscal problem has not been addressed. In the latter case, the attempt to fix the exchange rate will just lead to a balance of payments crisis.

The position by 1992 was that the need for fiscal discipline in order to bring about and maintain inflation stabilization was widely understood and agreed upon. Brazil had not succeeded, but this was a purely political problem. The role of the exchange rate, however, was a controversial, and less resolved, issue among policymakers. Chile followed a flexible rate policy, having learned lessons from its 1979–82 fixed rate experiment which led to real appreciation and ended in crisis. By contrast, in 1992 both Mexico and Argentina followed tablita or fixed rate policies, the Argentinian fixed rate commitment being stronger. In both countries the key fiscal problem was dealt with—and that was the great achievement—but the real exchange rates were appreciating substantially, appreciations that were only possible because of the revival of capital inflow or repatriation of earlier flight capital. Once the capital inflow abates, devaluations may well be needed.

Chapter 8

Exchange Rate Policy: Devaluations and Regime Changes

A distinction must now be made between the study of devaluations and of changes in exchange rate regimes. Beginning in 1974 there were numerous "one-shot devaluations," and for two or three years after 1984 many real devaluations took place (see table 8-3). Why they occurred, what their effects were, and why some countries did not devalue in the face of certain shocks are three of the questions explored in this chapter. The effects of devaluations are bound to be difficult to unravel because they almost always took place in combination with other policy changes, possibly an adjustment program involving a reduction in aggregate domestic spending, or a liberalization or restructuring of the trade regime. Another question that has to be asked is whether exchange rate adjustment has a necessary role at a time of balance of payments crisis.

During the study period, most countries changed their exchange rate regimes from a "fixed but adjustable" exchange rate system to one in which the rate is pegged in the short term but is adjusted frequently—called a "flexible peg" system here—or even to a system in which the currency floats. In discussing the concept of "exchange rate regime" and the various kinds of regimes in the eighteen countries, we will be particularly concerned with the effect of a more flexible exchange rate on each country's adjustment to shocks and on inflation.

This chapter makes many references to the "real exchange rate." We have already referred to this concept earlier. It can be given a number of meanings, and also presents some measurement problems.

As noted in chapter 1, the nominal exchange rate is defined as the number of rupiahs (home currency) per dollar (foreign currency). An increase is a devaluation and the rate of devaluation is the proportionate increase. A real exchange rate index takes into account both changes in the nominal exchange rate (weighting appropriately the exchange rates with different trading partners, and also allowing for multiple rates), and the rates of inflation in the home country and in its trading partners. If E is Indonesia's nominal effective exchange rate, $P*$ is the rate of inflation of Indonesia's trading partners, P is the rate of inflation in Indonesia, and the real exchange rate is R, then $R = EP*/P$. The figures cited in this chapter, which usually come from the International Monetary Fund, are based on this simple approach, with consumer price indices measuring rates of inflation. Annual indices are reproduced in table 8-1. We have also made some use of quarterly figures which are not reproduced there but which provide the basis for real devaluation calculations in this chapter and elsewhere in this volume.[1] Frequently it is also necessary to consider the relative price of tradables to nontradables. This is likely to move in the same direction as the real exchange rate as reported here, but it is not the same. These issues are discussed in more detail in the appendix to this chapter.

We begin with a historical overview, dealing both with devaluations and with regime changes. The story is inevitably rather complicated, owing to the diversity of exchange rate policies among our countries and over time. Next we consider the effects of devaluations and the implications of regime changes. Last, we discuss the lessons of these experiences for exchange rate policy.

Historical Overview

The exchange rate histories of our countries fall into four periods: the Bretton Woods period, which ended in 1973, and then the three periods covered in chapters 3, 4, and 5, which can be called, respectively, the exchange rate interregnum period (1974–79), the regime transition period (1980–83), and the flexible peg period (from 1983 on). As pointed out in chapter 2, the Bretton Woods "fixed but adjustable" exchange rate system ended for developed countries in 1973, and by the end of that year the currencies of major economies were floating. By contrast, most developing countries—including most in our group—continued fixing their exchange rates. Thus, in the interregnum period from 1974 to 1979 (or later in some cases) many countries in our group struggled to maintain a fixed exchange rate regime of some kind in a world where major currencies floated.

In the crisis or regime transition period of 1980–83, many of these countries made stabilization attempts that included devaluations and at the same time changed their exchange rate regimes. Usually the regime changed to a flexible peg: although the rates did not float after that, there were no longer commitments to particular nominal rates. Nominal rates were adjusted continuously in many cases and large real devaluations were brought about in the period 1984–89.

The four periods are summarized in table 8-2, which shows dates of devaluations and regime changes. Table 8-3 gives rates of nominal devaluation for the second and third periods and rates of real depreciation for the last period.

Table 8.1   Real Effective Exchange Rates, 1978–90
(1980 = 100)

Country	1978	1979	1980	1981	1982	1983	1984	1985	1986	1987	1988	1989	1990
Argentina	55	77	100	91	51	43	50	44	44	41	37	34	50
Brazil	123	113	100	121	128	104	104	100	95	95	103	—	—
Cameroon	103	102	100	92	90	93	95	99	110	123	119	111	114
Chile	85	86	100	118	107	87	85	69	58	54	51	53	52
Colombia	95	98	100	108	115	114	105	91	68	61	59	58	51
Costa Rica	87	91	100	64	73	83	82	81	73	66	60	63	62
Côte d'Ivoire	89	98	100	86	78	75	72	72	85	92	92	95	97
India	90	90	100	104	100	103	102	99	85	76	71	66	60
Indonesia	122	93	100	109	118	95	92	90	69	51	49	50	49
Kenya	104	101	100	97	100	95	102	100	87	79	73	70	63
Korea, Rep.	98	107	100	104	107	103	101	96	81	80	89	101	99
Mexico	84	89	100	114	82	72	84	86	60	56	69	74	76
Morocco	103	103	100	92	90	84	79	74	71	69	67	68	64
Nigeria	91	94	100	111	114	134	185	166	91	29	30	27	25
Pakistan	102	100	100	113	104	100	102	95	83	70	65	64	59
Sri Lanka	81	87	100	106	113	112	125	117	104	93	91	86	88
Thailand	91	92	100	103	106	109	107	95	85	80	77	79	80
Turkey	118	128	100	98	84	81	78	78	65	62	62	66	74

— Not available.

Note: The real exchange rate indices are derived from trade-weighted nominal rate indices (that is, "nominal effective exchange rates"). They are corrected by relative rates of inflation on the basis of consumer price indices.

Source: International Monetary Fund (IMF), Information Notice System.

Table 8.2   Devaluations and Regime Changes in Sixteen Countries

Country	1965–73		1974–79		1980–83		1984–90	
Cameroon		a		a		a		a
Chile			R	(1974)	a	R	(1982)	(1985–86)
Colombia								(1985–86)
Costa Rica		a		(1974)	a	R	(1981)	(1986–87)
Côte d'Ivoire		a			a		a	a
India	(1966)	a		(R)				(1985–88)
Indonesia	(1970)	a		(1978)	a	R	(1983)	(1986) F
Kenya		a		(1974)	a	R	(1982)	(1985–87)
Korea, Rep.			R	(1974)	a	R	(1980)	(1985–86)F
Mexico		a		(1976)	a	R	(1982)	R (1985–86)b
Morocco		a			a		a	R (1984–85)
Nigeria		a			a		a	R (1985–88)F
Pakistan	(1972)	a			a	R	(1982)	(1985–86)
Sri Lanka	(1967)	a	R	(1977)				(1985–87)
Thailand		a			a		a	R (1984)
Turkey	(1970)	a			a	R	(1980)	(1985–87)F

R = Regime change during period; from fixed to flexible, or opposite. F = Floating rate (usually managed) at end of period. Letters: a = Fixed rate regime at end of period, all others have flexible rate, b =Tablita at end of period. Dates of nominal devaluations in the first three periods (if more than 10 percent) and of real devaluations in last period. See the text for details and qualifications.
Source: IMF and research by the authors.

The Bretton Woods Period: Thirteen Fixed Exchange Rate Countries

Up to 1973 the story is quite simple. Thirteen countries had fixed exchange rates for long periods, going back usually to the 1950s. The exceptions were the relatively high inflation countries of South America—Argentina, Brazil, Chile, and Colombia—and surprisingly, the Republic of Korea. Since Argentina and Brazil have already been discussed in detail in chapter 7, they will be excluded from this historical survey. They are, in any case, very special cases.

Eight of the fixed exchange rate countries had completely fixed rates without devaluations since the 1950s. For example, Mexico devalued the peso in 1954 to 12.50 to the dollar, where it stayed until 1976. Thailand's exchange rate was 21 baht to the dollar from 1955 to 1981. The group included Morocco, Cameroon, and Côte d'Ivoire, which fixed to the French franc. Indeed, the latter two were part of the franc zone and did not have their own central bank. Five countries (Turkey, India, Pakistan, Indonesia, Sri Lanka) had fixed rate regimes but each also had a significant devaluation (or two) in the period 1960–73.

Table 8.3   Rates of Devaluation in Fourteen Countries, 1974–89

	Year or period[a]	Change in rate of local currency per dollar	Nominal devaluation (percent)	Real depreciation[b] (percent)
Chile	1974	.36–1.87 pesos	419	
	1982	39–73.4 pesos	88	
	1984(3)–1986(4)			57
Colombia	1985(1)–1987(1)			67
Costa Rica	April 1974	6.650–8.570 colones	29	
	1981	8.570–36.090 colones	321	
	1985(1)–1987(4)			33
India	1985(3)–1987(1)			30
Indonesia	November 1978	415–625 rupiahs	51	
	April 1983	702.5–968 rupiahs	38	
	September 1986	1,125–1,633 rupiahs	45	55[c]
Kenya	1974	7,143–8,260 shillings	16	
	1982	10,286–12,725 shillings	24	
	1985(1)–1987(4)			44
Korea, Rep.	December 1974	397.5–484 won	22	
	1980	484–660 won	36	
	1983–1986			26
Mexico	1976	12.50–19.95 pesos	60	
	1982	26.23–96.48 pesos	268	
	1985(2)–1987(1)			79
Morocco	1984(1)–1985(4)			14
Nigeria	1985(1)–1986(4)			461
Pakistan	1982	9,900–12,840 rupees	30	
	1985(1)–1987(4)			52
Sri Lanka	November 1977	8.530–15.950 rupees	87	
	1985(1)–1987(4)			37
Thailand	July 1981	21–23 baht	9.5	
	1983(4)–1989(1)			42
Turkey	January 1980	35.35–70.70 lira	100	
	1984(4)–1986(2)			28

Note: a. When a single year is given (without quarter or month), the nominal or real devaluation is from the end of the previous year to the end of that year. From 1983 onward, depreciations were frequent; hence only real depreciations, calculated from the quarterly IMF figures, are given. b. The periods chosen from 1983 were periods during which there were substantial real depreciations. c. The real devaluation figure refers to the whole year and the nominal one only to the month.
Source: IMF *International Financial Statistics*, mostly (*Supplement on Exchange Rates*) (1985), for column 2; and IMF real exchange rate figures for column 4.

The Interregnum Period 1974–79: Fixed Exchange Rates and Seven Devaluations

After the first oil shock, most countries maintained their fixed exchange rate regimes, though seven of them devalued. Seven other countries (Nigeria, Morocco, Turkey, Pakistan Thailand, and the two franc zone countries) kept their exchange rates completely fixed, and we shall discuss later why this was so. Chile and Korea actually moved from flexible to fixed rate regimes, while India and Sri Lanka moved in the opposite direction. Colombia and Indonesia have their own stories.

Colombia has had a crawling peg system since 1967. In this respect, it is unique among our eighteen countries. Its crawling peg regime was instituted in reaction to previous periods of real exchange rate instability resulting from attempts to peg the nominal rate, attempts that usually failed and were thus followed by devaluations. Since 1967 the Colombian exchange rate has been regularly adjusted at short intervals primarily on the basis of relative rates of inflation, but also in the light of balance of payments considerations—and not on the basis of a predetermined tablita—so there is much scope for discretion. From 1975 to 1983, the real rate was allowed to appreciate somewhat.

Chile had a similar crawling peg system from 1965 to 1970. The complex events after this until 1982 have already been described in chapter 7. A major regime change took place in 1978, when a tablita was established, and in 1979 the exchange rate was fixed.

Korea's exchange rate, while formally fixed to the dollar, was managed flexibly until 1974. Big devaluations in 1961 and 1964 greatly improved Korean competitiveness and helped its famously successful export drive. After that the nominal rate was depreciated almost every year to keep the real rate relatively constant. The high inflation of 1973, combined with the first oil shock, led to a stabilization program and a 20 percent devaluation in 1974. In order to discourage further inflation, the Korean won was then pegged to the dollar, where it stayed for five years until January 1980.

India and Sri Lanka entered the period 1974–79 with a fixed rate and then changed their regime. In both cases, the change was not a reaction to a crisis.

After its 1966 devaluation, India continued to peg to sterling until 1975. This could hardly continue in a world of floating rates, but India was reluctant to establish a peg to the dollar, since, in view of the general hostility to devaluation in India, it would have been difficult to change the peg later. So India went onto a multicurrency peg that allowed its authorities to "devalue by stealth" and depoliticized exchange rate policy. It is a matter of opinion whether India truly changed regime at that time; some might still argue that it stayed on a fixed rate. The trade-weighted nominal rate actually depreciated about 6 percent in 1975–78, but after that it remained fairly steady right through the second oil shock and world recession, until 1983.

Sri Lanka's regime change in 1977 was a major event because it was associated with drastic trade and capital market liberalization. Sri Lanka suffered heavily from the first oil shock, but the United Front government was determined to avoid devaluation and chose to deal with the problem by severely intensifying import controls. The United National Party returned to power in 1977 and embarked—with the great approval of the IMF and the World Bank—on a liberalization program. The dual exchange rate system was abolished, quotas were turned into tariffs, and exchange restrictions were ended. This was accompanied by an 88 percent devaluation of the par value. From then on, any commitment to a fixed exchange rate was ended.

The Indonesian devaluation of 1978 was unusual. When Indonesia unexpectedly devalued in October 1978 by 51 percent, there was clearly no balance of payments problem, nor was this devaluation associated with significant trade liberalization. The government was primarily concerned with the consequences of the Dutch Disease—the adverse effects of the real appreciation since 1972 on nonoil export industries. The real appreciation had resulted from the combination of a fixed nominal exchange rate and domestic inflation well above world levels, averaging nearly 20 percent from 1972 to 1978. It can be regarded as part of the domestic economy's adjustment to the boom in petroleum and gas income.

Thus in 1978 Indonesian authorities used the devaluation to protect the sectors of the economy producing "nonbooming" tradables, primarily agricultural exports. This move can be considered a case of "exchange rate protection." No doubt policymakers also foresaw a decline in oil exports owing to the growing domestic oil consumption in relation to production. Thus, they anticipated a balance of payments problem, for the sake of which they wished to preserve nonoil export industries.

The Crisis Years 1980–83: Nine Devaluations and Regime Transition

Policy reactions to the shocks described in chapter 4 also differed. All countries encountered shocks of some kind, although India, Pakistan, and Colombia felt the least impact. Some countries (notably Korea and Turkey) experienced crises and the reactions to them earlier than others, and some (notably Sri Lanka) chose to ride out the shocks with borrowing for several years.

Eight undertook significant devaluations (amounting to more than 10 percent) in the 1980–83 period (see table 8-2). These were all motivated by balance of payments problems and associated with stabilization programs of some kind. In Turkey and Korea, especially the former, substantial trade liberalization was initiated shortly afterward. In addition, Thailand (1981) devalued by 9.5 percent, which was a significant move only because it ended a period of twenty-six years of an unchanged exchange rate to the dollar.

All eight devaluers made regime transitions (marked by an R in table 8-2) to a flexible peg or to managed floating. For example, Pakistan shifted to managed floating with a trade-weighted basket. The Costa Rican fixed rate system collapsed in 1980 with a dual-rate system emerging, and the rates were unified again in 1983. Regime changes in Thailand, Nigeria, and Morocco were to take place in the next period.

1984–90: The Era of Flexible Exchange Rates and Real Depreciations

Between 1984 and 1990, all except the two franc-zone countries devalued or depreciated to some extent or other, in both nominal and real terms. In addition, Thailand, Morocco, and Nigeria finally gave up their fixed rate regimes. The average real depreciation from the end of 1983 to the end of 1988 for eleven countries (excluding Mexico, Korea and Nigeria) was remarkably high, at 51 percent.[2]

Eight countries had changed to a flexible peg regime earlier: India, Pakistan, Sri Lanka, Korea, Costa Rica, Chile, Turkey, and Kenya. No longer did they engage in one-shot devaluations. Indeed, a high-inflation country like Turkey had to depreciate its nominal rate continually. During certain years some of these countries depreciated their nominal rates just sufficiently to maintain the real rates roughly constant (this was a "crawling peg"). They all devalued substantially in real terms over this period, mostly from 1985 to 1987, and some later.

These real depreciations did not take place in crisis conditions. Sometimes they were postcrisis adjustments; more often, they forestalled new crises. Under a flexible peg system, exchange rate adjustments take place more quickly and do not necessarily wait for crisis conditions to emerge, as in a fixed but adjustable regime. When real depreciations take place not through a one-shot devaluation in a crisis but over several years and in a context in which the bilateral nominal rates are frequently changing anyway, they tend to be less noticed. In some countries the real devaluations can also be explained by a tendency to avoid appreciating in relation to the dollar, so that they reflected in part at least the depreciation of the dollar in world markets from 1985.

Colombia could be added to this group of countries, except that it faced a crisis situation in 1984, having avoided one earlier. Its government acted boldly and embarked on a big adjustment program in 1985, which included a rapid depreciation of the nominal exchange rate within its long established crawling peg system (which brought about a real depreciation of about 40 percent) during 1985 and 1986. This certainly more than offset the earlier real appreciation.

Thailand devalued by 17 percent in 1984, and ended its formal peg to the dollar. This devaluation had the simple aim of canceling out the real appreciation that had taken place since 1981 because the baht had been moving with the dollar. There was a current account problem but no crisis. The devaluation was made reluctantly (as might be expected from a country that had maintained an unchanged parity to the dollar from 1955 to 1981) and was made possible by the low inflation of 1984, which eased fears of the inflationary consequences of devaluation. In spite of the formal shift to a flexible peg regime in 1984, in fact, Thailand has continued to maintain a fairly stable rate to the dollar. This means that the baht depreciated on a trade-weighted basis after 1984. Like Indonesia, Thailand appeared to have stayed almost on a dollar standard. Hence, an *apparently* almost fixed exchange rate since 1984 has led to improved Thai competitiveness.

Morocco faced a crisis in 1983 and proceeded to a structural adjustment program from 1984, which included trade liberalization. It devalued in relation to the

French franc in 1984–85 and changed the regime to a flexible peg (close to a managed float). From 1985 to 1987 the nominal and real effective rates depreciated about 18 percent. On a trade-weighted basis, there had been real depreciation since 1981 owing to the appreciation of the dollar.

The three oil exporters—Mexico, Indonesia, and Nigeria—all suffered from the third oil shock in 1986, and all faced major crises. All three undertook structural adjustment programs, which included large nominal and real devaluations, as well as trade and capital market liberalization. Mexico's devaluations of 1985 and 1986 (yielding about 50 percent real devaluation) were followed in 1987 by a crawling peg policy designed to keep the real exchange rate constant, and from 1988 on by an inflation stabilization program that included, first, a fixed nominal exchange rate, and second, a tablita (and hence real appreciation). Indonesia devalued 44 percent in relation to the dollar in 1986. Owing to the devaluation of the dollar at that time, the real devaluation during 1986 was even greater. At the end of 1989, Indonesia shifted to a float with a good deal of intervention.

Nigeria is an interesting case. It faced a balance of payments crisis as a result of the oil price decline (and also reduction in the volume of exports) in 1982–83, as did Mexico and Indonesia. Whereas two countries devalued in 1982 or 1983, Nigeria held on to its exchange rate (fixed on a trade-weighted basket) and severely tightened its import restrictions instead. With high inflation in 1983 and 1984, the real exchange rate appreciated further, having already done so in 1981–82, and nonoil exports became quite uncompetitive. Nevertheless, Nigeria was forced to adjust, and did so from 1984 with fiscal tightening. This, combined with severely tightened import controls, radically improved the current account position in 1984 and 1985. The striking feature of this episode is that—like Sri Lanka in 1974–76—Nigeria chose to adjust to a big deterioration in terms of trade by using import restrictions rather than devaluation as the switching device.

From 1985 to August 1986, the naira was steadily depreciated (about 100 percent) and this break with a fixed exchange rate system was the first regime change for Nigeria. In September 1986 a foreign exchange auction conducted by the central bank was introduced, with most of the supply of foreign exchange coming from the government's oil revenues. Import licensing was abolished (except for some import prohibitions). The value of the naira dropped precipitously. In January 1989 the auctions were replaced by a straightforward free-floating exchange rate system conducted by private authorized dealers, and the rates were completely unified. The net result of the auction and free floating was that from September 1986 to June 1989, the naira depreciated another 117 percent.

Summary

From 1980 to 1983, most of the fourteen countries discussed here changed regime from a fixed rate to a flexible peg of some kind (see table 8-2), so this was certainly a major transition period. India (1975) and Sri Lanka (1977) changed earlier, and Thailand (1984), Morocco (1984), and Nigeria (1985) changed later. There were also some reverse movements: Korea (1974–80) temporarily moved to a fixed rate, and Chile (1978–82) temporarily to a tablita and then a fixed rate, while Mexico moved to a fixed rate and then a tablita in 1988.

By 1990, all fourteen countries, with the exception of Mexico, had a flexible peg or floating rate of some kind. Mexico, uniquely, had gone back to a tablita. In addition, the two franc-zone countries, of course, stayed with fixed rate regimes.

There were seven significant devaluations (10 percent or more) in the period 1974–79 and eight in the period 1980–83. Only two of these fifteen—Sri Lanka (1977) and Indonesia (1978)—can be regarded as not having been part of a normal balance of payments adjustment process. The devaluations of 1984–90 are more difficult to sort out because most real depreciations did not result from one-shot nominal devaluations but took place over a period of several years. In some countries, nominal rates were continually depreciating owing to inflation. During this period, the real exchange rates of all the countries depreciated significantly. Between 1985 and 1987 there were ten real devaluations of 30 percent or more.

Effects of Devaluations

Of the sixteen countries just surveyed, only five devalued during the 1974–76 crisis period. All except Mexico were oil importers and their terms of trade deteriorated, although in the case of Chile the principal reason for the deterioration in the terms of trade was the fall in the price of copper resulting from the world recession. Three countries—Mexico, Chile, and Korea—had domestic spending booms in the preceding period, and these had not only appreciated their real exchange rates (vastly in the case of the Chilean "Allende boom") but had also generated current account deficits. Thus, there were both external and domestic shocks.

Why Some Countries Devalued and Some Did Not

Why did the other eleven not devalue? The answer is simple for six of them. Indonesia, Nigeria, and Morocco benefited from export booms and obviously had no reason to devalue. The adverse shock was negligible for Colombia, and from 1976 it was to benefit from the coffee boom. The franc-zone countries could not devalue while staying in the zone. That leaves five "nondevaluations" to explain.

In the face of its big terms-of-trade shock, Sri Lanka tightened import restrictions severely and pursued deflationary policies. It also relied on aid flows. Thailand similarly deflated and borrowed. India's terms-of-trade shock was mild, but, as in some other countries, there had been a spending boom as well and some other problems. The policy response consisted of fiscal and monetary restraint combined with some tightening of import restrictions. Pakistan just borrowed its way through the shock. Finally, Turkey borrowed massively, and at the same time initiated a public investment boom.

All these countries except Turkey were strongly averse to devaluation, even though India "devalued by stealth" in 1975, as noted earlier. Most of the countries that devalued tightened import restrictions at the same time. This was particularly true of Kenya. To the policymakers in all the countries, import restrictions seemed a natural way of dealing with a balance of payments problem and were much preferred to devaluation. Usually devaluation was chosen only if there was a severe balance of payments problem or if the real exchange rate had been appreciating considerably. In all countries the tightening of import restrictions was seen as the principal alternative, as well as supplement, to devaluation.

It seems a reasonable hypothesis that, at least implicitly, the first decision made was whether to adjust (that is, reduce spending) or to borrow abroad. Then, if the decision was to adjust, a choice would be made between devaluation and various degrees of tightening import restrictions. Countries did not borrow to finance continuous current account deficits because of their reluctance to devalue. Current account deficits reflected, rather, a reluctance to adjust. The reluctance to devalue explains, rather, the use of import restrictions.

As already noted, the Sri Lankan devaluation of 1977 was associated with trade liberalization, and not a balance of payments crisis; similarly, the 1978 Indonesian devaluation was designed to offset the real appreciation of 1970–78 and was not provoked by a balance of payments problem. As also noted, in the period 1980–83 nine countries devalued as an obvious response by that time to a combination of external and domestically generated (public spending) shocks. In the case of Turkey, the devaluation was combined with large-scale trade liberalization.

The seven that did not devalue in the period 1980–83 consisted of the franc-zone countries; of Nigeria and Morocco, where the adverse external shocks emerged late, namely, in 1983; and of India, Sri Lanka, and Colombia, which all chose to borrow for some time, and also to make use of official aid flows in the case of the first two. India and Sri Lanka avoided reimposing or tightening import restrictions, but all the others intensified restrictions. The striking case of Nigeria in 1983–84 has already been noted. The real exchange rate appreciated greatly owing to domestic inflation combined with a fixed exchange rate. Up to 1984 it borrowed, and then it combined fiscal tightening with severely tightened import controls. The devaluation came in 1985.

It was often said during the period 1974–82 or so that many countries had "overvalued" exchange rates and that this was their main—or a major—problem. In other words, they should devalue. This idea can be given two interpretations. This distinction is important, and often neglected. It could mean that the country should reduce aggregate demand (usually by fiscal contraction) and combine this with devaluation, and hence improve the current account. In other words, it really implies a criticism of the policy of borrowing. Alternatively, it could mean that the country should reduce or abolish its import restrictions and combine this with devaluation, possibly with no net effect on the current account. Undoubtedly, the second interpretation underlay World Bank and IMF advice in the 1970s. In that case, it implied a concern with the adverse effects of import restrictions. It might, of course, mean both—in which case the devaluation would have to be all the greater, and this is both just what was required and happened in many countries from 1985 on.

Analyzing the Effects of Devaluations: Some Difficulties

It is difficult to observe the effects of a devaluation on its own, for two reasons. First, devaluation is almost always part of a policy package. If a devaluation is followed by a contraction of output, it is highly likely to have resulted from the contraction of demand that accompanied it. The demand contraction is meant to make resources available for export- and import-substituting industries, but the transfer of resources, especially labor, is likely to take place with a lag, so that in the short run aggregate output may well decline. Similarly, when a devaluation is associated with trade liberalization and other reform measures—as it was in Pakistan in 1972, Sri Lanka in 1977, and Turkey in 1980—only the effects of the whole package can be observed.

Second, important devaluation effects will surely take time to work themselves out, but over this time other events intervene. For example, the effects of the 1974–76 devaluations were cut short by the public spending booms of the devaluing countries.

A principal purpose of a devaluation is to increase export volume, and here the response is quick only if there are very special conditions—for example, if the expectation of devaluation has led to hoarding of stocks of goods that might be exported or if there are easy substitution possibilities between goods produced for the home market and for export. An example comes from the Indonesian devaluation of 1978. There was actually a sharp increase in nonoil exports in 1979, but the second oil shock at the end of 1979 inevitably led to monetary expansion, hence increased inflation, and so helped to erode the real effects of the devaluation.

To What Extent Were Real Devaluations Eroded, and Why?

If a nominal devaluation failed to bring about a real devaluation for a reasonable length of time, there would be little point in devaluing. After all, the nominal effects are bound to be adverse, at least in the short run—that is, to be inflationary—so there have to be benefits on the real side. Furthermore, if it is widely expected that a real devaluation will be quickly eroded, even though there is initially some real devaluation, resources are unlikely to be moved into tradable industries. In particular, there is unlikely to be any expansion of exports.

Erosion of a devaluation results when the excess of domestic inflation over the inflation rate of trading partners exceeds further nominal depreciations. If there is a one-shot nominal devaluation and then the exchange rate is fixed, some subsequent erosion is almost inevitable since the domestic rate of inflation is likely to exceed the inflation rate of trading partners. This was the position after 1974. On the other hand, erosion can be avoided by continuous depreciation after the one-shot devaluation—that is, by a flexible peg or managed floating system of some kind, as was practiced by most countries after 1982.

As explained in chapter 6, the devaluation itself usually led to an inflationary bubble, so that the rate of inflation would fall after rising immediately with the devaluation. The important question, however, is whether the subsequent inflation is high, and possibly accelerating, in relation to the rate that prevailed before the devaluation. A one-shot devaluation might be considered a success if the inflationary bubble that it generated were followed by an inflation rate that was lower, or at least no higher, than the one that prevailed before the devaluation. That was the case in the Korean devaluation of 1974, but the real devaluation was still eroded in Korea. A fixed nominal rate and a rate of inflation above the world rate are not compatible with a stable real exchange rate.

The path of inflation subsequent to the devaluation depends both on wage responses—on the possibility of a cost-price spiral because of explicit or implicit indexation—and on fiscal and monetary policies. The latter are crucial. A devaluation that is unaccompanied either by trade liberalization or by some contraction of demand is highly likely to be eroded, possibly quite rapidly. It is the policy package that matters.

In general, the 1974–76 devaluations were partly eroded but were followed by inflation rates that were no higher, and sometimes less, than those that prevailed before the devaluations. Thus, these devaluations might be regarded as successes. One complication is that public spending booms, which led to increased inflation, started a few years after these devaluations. The resultant erosion of the earlier real devaluations should be attributed to new shocks, not to the initial policy packages. This was particularly true of the Sri Lankan 1977 devaluation. Six of the crisis devaluations (1980–83) were not eroded at all, whereas Costa Rica's and Mexico's were. Most of the 1985–87 devaluations, which took place in flexible peg regimes, were not eroded, the one exception being Mexico, which had partial erosion. The switch to flexible pegs generally prevented erosions, but in certain cases this favorable real outcome may have been at the expense of higher inflation. We come back to the effects on inflation later.[3]

The country that has not been typical is the "erosion country" par excellence—Mexico. The real effects of each of the three depreciations of 1976, 1982, and 1986 were significantly eroded in subsequent years, although not completely in the last period, 1986–90. In the two periods after 1976 and after 1986, the essential factor was the attempt to fix the exchange rate; but in the period 1983–86, the problem was simply that the domestic inflation rate was very high, the result of the need to generate a high outward resource transfer. The depreciation of the nominal exchange rate did not keep up with the inflation rate that was generated by the need to finance a budget deficit resulting primarily from the debt crisis. The erosion of the real exchange rate was thus a by-product of the workings of the "trade-off model" discussed in chapter 7.

Did Devaluations Increase Exports?

A substantial devaluation, when combined in a policy package with similarly substantial demand contraction, should, after some time, surely increase exports. A devaluation combined with the liberalization of imports should also do so, especially if imports of goods that are inputs into exports are liberalized. This can be expected even when there is continued high inflation, as in the case of Turkey, provided the nominal exchange rate continues to be depreciated so as to maintain the real exchange rate at its devalued level.

The broad impression that emerged from our study of the eighteen countries is that traditional agricultural and mineral exports do not clearly respond, at least in the short run, to real devaluations, but that the effect is usually very marked in the case of nontraditional exports, especially manufactured ones. (Of course, for some countries, such as India and Korea, manufactured exports should really be described as "traditional.") This effect was particularly noticeable as a result of the large real devaluations that took place over the period 1985 to 1987.

The seven devaluations of 1974–79 yield a mixed story, because so many other things happened at the same time or shortly afterward. The Chilean real devaluation of 1974 was huge; to an extent, it compensated for trade liberalization, as well as earlier real appreciation, and was partly offset by the real appreciation (discussed in chapter 7) from 1975 to 1981. The annual value of manufactured exports rose 150 percent (from a very low base) from 1974–75 to 1977–78. The Kenyan, Mexican, and Costa Rican devaluations had no marked effects on exports (though, no doubt some exports would eventually have fallen if the devaluations had not taken place); the Korean devaluation was followed by some real appreciation, but nevertheless very high export growth also followed. As noted below, the 1978 Indonesian devaluation led to a short boom in the rate of growth of manufactured exports. Finally, the Sri Lankan package of policies in 1977 apparently had a major effect in increasing manufactured exports, particularly apparel and textiles, but there were also other factors (discussed below).

The devaluations of 1980–82 did not have quick effects because the world was in recession. The notable exception was Turkey, referred to below. By contrast, the export booms of the late 1980s in a number of countries were at least helped by the recovery of the economies of the major developed countries, and especially by the boom in U.S. imports. Exports of manufactures from almost all our countries actually grew faster than total imports of manufactures by the developed countries, so there is something left to explain, once allowance for the growing world economy is made.

Over the period 1985 to 1988, twelve countries experienced real devaluations of 25 percent or more. The value of manufactured exports to developed countries from ten of these twelve (all except Kenya and Pakistan) grew by 20 percent or more a year over the subsequent period, 1986–89—an impressive outcome. (The value of total imports of manufactures by developed countries grew by 14 percent a year.[4]) As pointed out in chapter 5, the relationship between the size of the real devaluations and the extent of growth of exports of manufactures was statistically significant.

The real devaluations of Korea and Morocco over the period were under 10 percent, but the value of exports still grew by more than 20 percent a year. Korean export growth is hardly a surprise and was part of a trend. There was a real depreciation in 1986, but appreciation in 1988–89. In the case of Morocco, a significant real depreciation (14 percent) took place earlier, in 1984–85. Furthermore, the substantial trade liberalization combined with the credibility of the exchange rate policy in a low-inflation country help to explain the 24 percent surge in annual growth of manufactured exports from Morocco. By contrast, it seems that Kenya's small, highly protected manufacturing sector was simply too uneconomic to respond greatly to devaluation.

Four countries stand out in the late 1980s as export boom economies—Chile, Indonesia, Thailand, and Turkey—and in these cases exchange rate policy clearly played a key role, even though other conditions, notably trade and other liberalization, were also helpful. A new readiness to welcome foreign investment often is also an important element in the expansion of exports of manufactures. In most of our countries, major devaluations were part of a comprehensive policy package, including trade liberalization and deregulation of various kinds, all of which were, in time, favorable for exports.

Chile's real devaluation over the period 1982–88 (in two steps) was 53 percent. This led not only to a very large growth in exports of manufactures but also to growth in exports of agricultural products—food exports to the United States—which doubled in value between 1985 and 1989.

Indonesia's three devaluations (1978, 1983, 1986) all had clear effects on exports of manufactures, though not to the same extent in the three cases. There was an immediate effect in 1979 (25 percent volume increase, apparently) and continued but more modest rates of growth after that. In the three years after 1983, export volume rose 43 percent. The 1986 devaluation and associated measures had the biggest effect. The volume of exports of manufactures rose 80 percent in 1986–88, and growth continued into 1989 and 1990. The rapid responses in all cases suggest that there was considerable excess capacity.[5]

Turkey had a remarkable export boom after 1980, clearly the result both of substantial real devaluation and of expanded export promotion and liberalization measures. The initial boom took place in spite of world recession, though exports to the Middle East were helped by the oil price rise and special circumstances associated with the Iran-Iraq war. The January 1980 nominal devaluation of 100 percent (combined with high inflation) led to real devaluation by the end of 1980 of about 30 percent. Subsequent frequent depreciations of the nominal exchange rate led to a further real devaluation of 64 percent by the end of 1987. (After stabilizing in 1988, the real rate actually appreciated in 1989 and 1990, the result of attempts to stabilize inflation.) Exports of manufactures were about 30 percent of total exports in 1980 and by 1989 were nearly 80 percent. In value terms, they grew 42 percent a year or so in 1980–85 and continued growing after that.[6]

Thailand also had an extraordinary rise in exports of manufactures, beginning in 1985. The annual rate of growth in 1985–89 was 44 percent. The nominal devaluation of the baht in relation to the dollar in 1984, combined with the later depreciation relative to other currencies as the dollar depreciated, as well as the remarkably low Thai inflation, led to a real devaluation of 44 percent over the period 1984–88. The export boom (mainly in clothing and textiles) was no doubt helped by the large inflow of foreign, mainly Japanese, investment, as well as by the improvement in the trade incentive structure.

An econometric exercise done for Sri Lanka for the years 1965 to 1985 examined the short-run effects on export volume of changes in the real effective exchange rate, taking into account both export taxes and export subsidies, as well as the real exchange rate based on the nominal exchange rate and relative price movements at home and abroad (Athukorala and Jayasuriya forthcoming). The results showed that the three traditional exports (tea, rubber, coconuts) were inelastic in short-run supply response (which is not surprising for tree crops). The results for exports of textiles and garments—which boomed since 1979—were complicated by other factors (availability of quotas for exports to developed countries, and a more receptive approach to foreign investment since 1977), and a clear short-run exchange rate effect could not be found. For the remaining category ("other manufactures"), the real effective exchange rate coefficient was highly significant, and suggests a 1.5 percent lagged response to a given 1 percent change in relative prices.

The vast literature on the effects of devaluations on trade has been concerned primarily with the trade balance rather than the effects on exports and has usually looked for short-term effects. The main problem there is that import restrictions may be varied at the same time that an exchange rate is changed. A devaluation together with trade liberalization may well succeed in increasing exports, and yet there may be no net effect on the trade balance. Furthermore, there may be offsetting changes in domestic expenditure that would affect imports.

The relevant literature has been surveyed by Kamin (1988). An early study by Cooper (1971) examined twenty-four devaluations imposed by developing countries between 1959 and 1966 and compared trade flows from the year before with the year after devaluation. He found that the trade balance improved in fifteen cases. Bhagwat and Onitsuka (1974) also researched devaluations in the 1960s and found evidence of long-term export responses. When Edwards (1989a, pp. 279–81) looked at thirty-nine developing country devaluations over the period 1961–82 (including fifteen from our group of countries), he observed the ratios of the current account to GDP one year after and three years after the devaluation in each case. The results cannot be easily summarized here, but it is worth noting that "while in a number of countries there was a deterioration in the short run, the situation changed through time, and after three years there was a substantial improvement" (p. 279).

Kamin (1988) analyzed 104 devaluation episodes from 1953 to 1983 (including 32 from our group) and compared the devaluing country's performance with the average performance of the entire sample during the period corresponding to the devaluation episode. His elaborate method is also difficult to summarize here. He found a positive short-run effect on exports. In fact the results are quite surprising, with exports rising immediately after devaluation in relation to the control group. "The very fast positive response of exports to devaluation observed in the data appears to contradict the presumption of 'short-term elasticity pessimism' to be found in much of the literature" (p. 17).

Pritchett (1991) has looked at the relationship between the real exchange rate and the trade surplus, using time-series data from 1965–88 for sixty-four nonoil developing countries (including thirteen of the group in the present study). He concludes that there is no consistent, significant relationship between the real exchange rate and the trade surplus. By contrast, multivariate regressions show that a terms-of-trade improvement improves the trade balance and a rise in absorption worsens it.[7]

How Were Growth Rates Affected by Devaluations?
Were Devaluations Contractionary?

Normally, one expects a devaluation to have an expansionary effect by switching demand away from imports and making export industries more competitive. This is the standard "switching" effect. It may also induce domestic industry to use more local instead of imported inputs. The impact on potential import-competing industries is more doubtful; in most of the countries, import restrictions have insulated such industries from foreign competition, so that improved competitiveness would make little difference to them; at the same time, such industries may be adversely affected by the higher domestic cost of imported inputs.

In addition, a devaluation is likely to affect aggregate demand (absorption) directly. If demand is reduced, a net contractionary effect is possible: the reduction in aggregate demand may reduce the demand for home-produced goods more than the switching effect increases it. A standard argument is that the fall in real wages and shift of incomes toward profits or toward the rural sector that usually result from a devaluation are likely to reduce aggregate demand because the marginal propensity to save out of wages tends to be relatively higher.[8] Probably a more important consideration is that a devaluation may increase government revenue from taxes on trade or from oil exports. A devaluation will raise the domestic currency value of taxes on trade and of the profits from exports—notably oil exports—when these go to the government. Provided that government expenditure is not increased as a result, the fiscal position will improve. Hence, aggregate demand will be reduced on that account, and possibly there will be less monetization of deficits.

Such a net contractionary effect of a devaluation is sometimes regarded as undesirable, but in fact it must be welcome, since it reduces the need to contract absorption by other means that are usually politically painful. If the reduction in absorption resulting from devaluation is really so great that it exceeds the contraction required for the policy package, nothing is easier and more politically attractive than to offset its effect by some fiscal relaxation. The real problem arises in the opposite case: when a devaluation has an expansionary effect on aggregate demand, so that deliberate absorption-reducing policies must be greater than otherwise.

The expansionary effect of devaluation can be attributed mainly to the impact on the budget of higher foreign debt-service payments in domestic currency terms. Interest and amortization payments on foreign debt in all the developing countries are denominated in foreign currency, principally dollars, and a devaluation would thus have an adverse effect on the budget on that account.

The balance of these various effects could go either way. In the case of Brazil, taxes on trade are not significant sources of revenue, but the government's foreign debt service has been high, so that a real devaluation would have an adverse fiscal effect. Indonesia presents a good case study of the net fiscal effect of a devaluation when both the positive and the negative effects are significant. A devaluation raises revenue in rupiah (but not in dollars, of course) from oil exports, and thus has a favorable effect on the budget. It also raises the rupiah cost of debt service. The greater is the debt, the higher is the interest rate, and the lower is the oil price, the more likely is it that the net effect of a devaluation will be adverse for the budget. Just focusing on these two elements of the budget—oil revenue and debt service— calculations show that the 1978 and 1982 devaluations must have improved the budgetary position while the 1986 devaluation—by which time the debt was higher and the oil price lower—worsened it (Woo and others forthcoming).

All this is interesting, but in the final analysis the direct expansionary or contractionary effects of devaluation were probably overwhelmed by the effects of other policies that made up the policy packages, as well as by changes in the terms of trade that affected not just government revenue but also private spending. This is certainly what the evidence, inconclusive as it is, seems to suggest.

The policy packages that included a devaluation tended—after a lag—to raise growth rates in relation to the crisis years in which the packages were implemented, but not necessarily in relation to the years before the crisis. No clear conclusions about the short-run effects on aggregate output and growth rates of devaluations on their own, or even of stabilization programs as a whole, can be reached. Indeed, many different stories can be told. It is obvious that many of the factors discussed elsewhere in this book other than devaluations were at work.

One stylized story is as follows. Growth was high at first, owing to a public spending boom. This was demand-led growth. It ended in the period 1980–83 in a balance of payments crisis and a sharp reduction of demand, and hence of growth. The decline in demand resulted both from reduced spending out of export income and lower private and public investment. A devaluation happened quickly, or perhaps a little later, together with a demand-reducing stabilization program. Sometimes this reduced growth further. If it did so, it was not because of the devaluation but because of the deliberate fiscal and monetary contraction. After a time, the economy recovered. Notably, exports—especially nontraditional exports—started growing. The growth rate increased, though not necessarily back to the precrisis level. Often there was further devaluation (as in 1985–87), and then further growth and export expansion.

The postcrisis period, 1984–88, is compared with the precrisis one, 1976–79, in table 8-4. In eight cases the growth rate is lower and the real exchange rate devalued. An extreme example of this is provided by Mexico. The average growth rate dropped from 6 percent to 1 percent, and the average real exchange rate was devalued 19 percent. Surely this cannot be construed as evidence that devaluation lowered the growth rate, in view of all the other factors that we know to have played a part. There is certainly no evidence that if Mexico had not devalued but had intensified import restrictions instead, or had deflated more, without devaluation, that its growth rate would have been higher. In speculating on what the effects of devaluation, or the failure to devalue, might have been, we have, of

Table 8.4   Growth Rates and Real Exchange Rates, 1976–79 and 1984–88

Country	Real exchange rate index 1976–79[a]	Real exchange rate index 1984–88	Real devaluation[b]	Average growth rate[c] 1975–79	Average growth rate[c] 1984–88
Cameroon	103	109	(6)[d]	10.2	1.5
Chile	86	63	37	7.5	5.5
Colombia	97	77	26	5.7	4.5
Costa Rica	89	72	24	6.4	4.5
Côte d'Ivoire	94	83	13	5.6	0.8
India	90	87	3	2.4	5.7
Indonesia	108	70	54	7.4	5.2
Kenya	103	88	17	6.5	5.0
Korea, Rep.	104	89	17	10.7	10.3
Mexico	87	71	23	6.2	1.2
Morocco	103	72	43	5.8	5.3
Nigeria	93	100	7[d,e]	4.2	2.9
Pakistan	101	83	22	5.2	6.5
Sri Lanka	84	106	(21)[d]	5.1	3.5
Thailand	92	89	3	8.6	7.7
Turkey	123	69	78	4.0	6.1

a. Owing to unavailability of IMF figures for the early years for the following countries, the average is only 1978 (1), 1978 (4), and 1979 (4): Morocco, Turkey, India, Indonesia, Pakistan, Côte d'Ivoire, Thailand, Korea. For others it is the average of the fourth quarter of all four years.

b. A decrease in the index is a real devaluation. Because the real devaluation between the two periods is measured as the change in EP*/P, it is calculated here as being the change as a proportion of the lower (devalued) figure.

c. Arithmetic average of annual GDP growth rates.

d. Real appreciation.

e. The Nigerian real exchange rate was highly appreciated 1984–85, and only depreciated drastically from the end of 1986.

Source: IMF figures for columns 1 and 2, and World Bank data for columns 4 and 5.

course, the laboratory experiment of the two franc-zone countries, which have never devalued. Their growth rates were modest in 1984–88 and negative in each of the three years 1989 to 1991.

In the course of the postcrisis period from 1984, many countries continued to devalue their real exchange rate and their growth rate continued to rise. Should this gradual recovery in the growth rate be attributed to the further devaluations?

The answer is that the path of growth rates depended not just on the effects of the devaluation, but on fiscal and monetary policies followed for several years after the devaluations, and on whether external or internal shocks intervened after a while. For example, Sri Lanka's growth rate was quite high over the period 1978–82 (average of 6 percent), but this was not just the result of the devaluation-cum-liberalization of 1977, but also of a foreign-financed public spending boom. Sri Lanka devalued further in 1985 and after, but from 1987 its growth rate slumped owing no doubt to domestic social instability.

Some of the stories from the post-1983 period suggest that devaluations, combined with other policies, led, after a lag, to higher growth rates. It seems reasonable to conclude that the high growth rates of Thailand in 1987–90 were export-led, and that the real devaluation of 1984–87 played some role in this. Indonesia has had an impressive recovery in its growth rate since its 1986 devaluation. India had a growth boom in 1988–90, and its exports also increased in that period. The growth boom was probably not related to the real devaluation of 1986–88, for India's exports are only about 5 percent of GDP. The increase in the Indian growth rate was connected much more with an expansion in domestic demand.

In the case of Chile, the immediate effect of its 1974–75 stabilization program—which included a big devaluation—was a huge slump. This was also true of the 1982–83 stabilization. Again, it included a devaluation, and it produced (or was associated with) a huge slump. In both episodes, growth recovered after the slump and became quite high.

How Much Real Exchange Rate Instability Was There?

It is often argued that real exchange rate instability has adverse effects on growth, because it creates uncertainty (which reduces investment), causes resources to move back and forth between tradables and nontradables and, more generally, generates unnecessary adjustment costs. The implication is that instability is not predictable. If an exchange rate cycle were predictable, private decisionmakers with some degree of foresight would not move resources around unnecessarily, nor would investment be discouraged. Another consideration is that real exchange rate instability may just be a symptom of more general instabilities affecting an economy—either exogenous shocks or instabilities of domestic policies. The real exchange rate may simply respond—possibly optimally—to an unstable environment.

In any case, what can be said about the experience of real exchange rate instability in our eighteen countries? To answer that question, one must first decide how to measure instability. If a country has one or more one-shot devaluations, each followed by relatively stable real exchange rates, does that mean the exchange rate is "unstable"? If instability is measured by the deviations around an average real rate over a period, the resulting instability index may be high. We have made calculations on this basis for the period 1978–88. We have calculated the standard deviation around the mean for the period 1978–88 for all our countries, using the IMF index (from table 8-1). The unstable countries (defined on this rather unsatisfactory basis) turn out to be Nigeria (46), Indonesia (23), Argentina, Chile, Turkey (all 21), and Colombia (19).[9]

Even if one uses as a measure deviations from trend, rather than deviations from a mean, high instability will emerge, essentially because the devaluations have taken place in large discrete steps rather than in small steps in the form of a crawling peg (or managed floating) depreciation process.[10] Yet, exogenous shocks may fully justify the steps, and gradual adjustment of the exchange rate in response to a sharp unexpected decline in the terms of trade may be an inferior policy to a sharp devaluation designed to cope with or indeed prevent a crisis. In an unstable environment the optimal real exchange rate path is also likely to be unstable. The common view that real exchange rate instability is undesirable really rests on the assumption—applying to many countries at various times, and notably to Argentina—that such instability is a response to domestically generated instability, that is, in monetary and fiscal policies. It is thus a symptom of undesirable domestic policies.

One possible approach is to search for real exchange rate cycles. A cycle consists of a period of absolute real appreciation that is followed by a real devaluation, either at one time, or over a period. A country can be said to have had an unstable real exchange rate experience if it has had many or several large cycles. Bearing in mind that the general trend over the period, and even earlier, was for real exchange rates to depreciate, one must then look for episodes of real appreciation.[11]

Of the eighteen countries, Argentina seems to stand out. It has had two vast cycles, in 1972–75 and 1978–82.[12] It is no wonder that economists who have studied Argentina put heavy emphasis on the adverse effects of real exchange rate instability. The other countries with highly unstable experiences are Mexico, Chile, Brazil, and Nigeria. Mexico has had three large cycles over the period 1972–90, with real appreciations in 1972–76, 1977–82, and 1983–86, each followed by a large one-shot devaluation. Chile had two large cycles (in 1972–74 and 1978–85). Brazil is something of a surprise because it is well known for its two periods of real exchange rate stability—1968–73 and 1975–79—in spite of high inflation. Since 1979 it has had three cycles associated with unsuccessful inflation stabilization attempts. Nigeria had one large cycle, culminating in the huge devaluations of 1985–86.[13]

Noticeable cycles can be found in Colombia, Sri Lanka, Indonesia, Turkey, and Costa Rica. Even Thailand might be included here: Thai inflation did increase in 1979–81, and during that period the real exchange rate appreciated. The 1984 depreciation corrected this. Also, Korea had two mild cycles, culminating in the devaluations of 1974 and 1980. Colombia's real exchange rate has certainly been much more stable than that of the other Latin American countries; it owes this stability to its sustained adherence to a crawling peg regime. It did not have any short sharp cycles, but there was a period of gradual real appreciation from 1975 to 1983 (about 25 percent), which was followed by a sharp real depreciation in 1985–86.

Although no country has completely avoided some real appreciation eventually followed by a devaluation, the countries in which such cycles have been modest—the truly stable countries—are India, Pakistan, Morocco, and Kenya.

Exchange Rate Regimes

So far we have made a simple distinction between fixed and flexible rate regimes and have focused on shifts between these broad categories. Of the eighteen countries, thirteen had fixed rate regimes of some kind in 1973. By 1979 this was still true of thirteen (though not precisely the same list of countries), but by 1989, only the two franc-zone countries were left in this category, all others having switched to a flexible rate regime. Distinctions now have to be made within each category.

Various Kinds of Regimes

The two franc-zone countries continue to have an institutional commitment to a fixed exchange rate with the franc. The remaining eleven countries have had no such institutional commitment. They had fixed but potentially adjustable exchange rates over the study period. The rates were fixed in the sense that there was a clear commitment to a rate, but the possibility of adjustment remained. Up to 1974, and sometimes after, such adjustment was made reluctantly, and even here a further distinction can be made. Many countries—for example, Thailand and Mexico—had long periods with no change in the rate in relation to the dollar or sterling—and the commitment was almost as strong as if it were institutionalized, as in the case of the franc-zone countries. Others, such as Sri Lanka and Indonesia, had several devaluations in their recent history, and both India and Pakistan, one major one.

A further distinction can be made between fixing to a single currency—dollar, sterling, or franc—and fixing to a basket of currencies (a multicurrency peg). The breakdown of the Bretton Woods system in 1973 required countries to make important decisions in this regard, as exchange rate relationships among the major currencies altered, sometimes rather unpredictably. The most common development was a switch from sterling to the dollar peg, and later, from the dollar peg to a multicurrency peg. If these are considered regime changes, then there were many regime changes in the period 1973–79.

Fixing to a single currency, such as the franc or the dollar, had clear advantages. First, it made the exchange rate commitment very clear and so sent out a credible signal of commitment to a fixed rate. A multicurrency peg is much less clear. This factor clearly weighed heavily with the Thai authorities when they chose to stick with the dollar for a long period. Second, it enabled them to make use of existing forward markets in the currency to which the country had pegged. There was also an obvious disadvantage. The effective (trade-weighed) rate would vary as a result of changes in the value of the currency to which the country pegged. Thus, the franc-zone countries have been depreciating and appreciating with the franc, notably as a result of the sharp appreciation in the dollar up to 1985 and depreciation thereafter. This disadvantage was clearly the reason that most countries switched to multicountry pegs in the 1973–79 period, and sometimes later.

Distinctions also need to be made among the flexible regimes. The most common type of regime now is what has been called a flexible peg here. The central bank fixes a rate on any day or over some period and maintains it by intervention; but it makes no firm commitment to a particular rate and, indeed, changes its rate frequently.[14]

In countries with inflation rates above those of their trading partners, the rate steadily depreciates in nominal terms—that is, it crawls. Not only is there no commitment to a particular exchange rate; there is also no commitment to a particular rate of crawl or to a particular rigid rule. Hence (when the general tendency is steady nominal depreciation), this can be called a "discretionary crawling peg regime" (Joshi 1990). In practice, the regimes of most of our countries since 1982 could be put under this heading. Sometimes governments state that there are various considerations—notably the balance of payments and relative rates of inflation—that are taken into account. This is the system pioneered in the 1960s by Chile, Colombia, and Brazil. The currency of intervention is usually the dollar, but relationships with other currencies are also considered.

This system is to be contrasted with the tablita regime, discussed in chapter 7 principally with respect to Argentinian and Chilean stabilization experiments and instituted in 1989 by Mexico. In that case a nominal rate of devaluation is announced in advance, implying a firm commitment to the rate of devaluation. This is really more like a fixed rate system.

Four countries—Nigeria, Turkey, Indonesia, and Korea—moved to floating rates (with considerable management through intervention) in the period 1988–90. In considering why they did so, note that a floating rate, even with apparently no intervention, does not mean that the government cannot influence the exchange rate. Management of the rate is inevitable. In fact, the distinction between a flexible peg and a managed float regime can be quite unclear. In both cases, the monetary authorities are likely to take a view about the exchange rate and can bring about changes. The main difference is this: in the case of the flexible peg, the authorities automatically intervene by fixing the rate, so that a change in the rate to take into account market conditions represents a kind of initiative, while in the case of the managed float, the market is likely to determine the daily rate and hence short-term fluctuations in the rate, so that intervention to influence the rate requires some initiative.

In the case of Nigeria and Indonesia, the principal sources of foreign exchange for the market are the governments, which are the recipients of the oil revenues. A government can depreciate the rate, for example, by reducing the supply of foreign exchange to the market and keeping more of it for its reserves. In addition, monetary policy can influence the exchange rate—as in the case of all developed countries with floating rates.

What were the reasons for the moves to floating rates? The Nigerian shift to a free-floating market represented a progression from the exchange auction system and was part of a general policy (encouraged by the IMF) of freeing market forces. It must also have been motivated by the difficulty of estimating an equilibrium rate—even a short-term one—at a time of very large adjustments and uncertainties. Indonesia and Turkey have removed exchange controls (which were hard to enforce anyway) and thus have very high capital mobility. Hence, it becomes difficult to manage the exchange rate in the short run except at the cost of substantial changes in reserves or in monetary policy. Korea's decision to reduce intervention in the foreign exchange market was, among other things, designed to deflect U.S. criticism that its exchange rate was manipulated, hence artificially strengthening Korean competitiveness. Of course, the exchange rates of all our countries have been manipulated in some way. The critics suggested that Korea devalued excessively to protect its export industries, hence engaging in "exchange rate protection." In fact, since 1988 the won has appreciated in real terms. It might be added that one attraction of a floating rate in relation to a flexible peg—an attraction relevant for many countries—is that it depoliticizes the rate: political pressure on the central bank to prevent depreciation of the rate is reduced, and blame for a depreciation or appreciation can be shifted to an impersonal "market."

Does a Fixed Rate Regime Discourage Inflation?

The relationship between the exchange rate regime and inflation can go two ways. On the one hand, a country committed to an exchange rate that is fixed to a low-inflation currency or currency basket might be reluctant to monetize its fiscal deficits and hence might inhibit inflation. The exchange rate is the nominal anchor: it anchors the price level. In the short run, some domestic demand expansion might increase inflation and so bring about real appreciation, but the loss of competitiveness would soon lead countries to reverse or at least moderate their expansionary policies. Clearly, a country with a fixed rate cannot indefinitely have an inflation rate higher than that of its trading partners. Of course, for a limited period there can be real appreciation; this may be part of the adjustment process to a capital inflow or a terms-of-trade improvement as—for example—in the case of Indonesia in 1972–78.

The first reaction to loss of competitiveness, as well as to an adverse terms-of-trade shock, has usually been to tighten import restrictions. This was true of almost every one of our countries. The problem is that import restrictions cannot cope with the consequences of a continual loss of competitiveness of exports;

eventually, the country will be starved of essential imports. As many of our countries learned, the fixed exchange rate commitment is likely to break down if monetary discipline is not maintained, particularly when there are exogenous shocks. The question really is what the strength of the exchange rate commitment is. If it is really strong, monetary expansion (and the fiscal deficits that usually cause it) will be moderated in good time. In that case, the fixed exchange rate is a true anchor.

On the other hand, the relationship between the exchange rate regime and inflation can also go the other way, and indeed is very likely to. Countries have been able to maintain fixed exchange rates because they wanted and achieved low inflation. Asian countries, in particular, have had low inflation not because of their fixed exchange rates, but because their policymakers were heavily committed to low inflation as a fundamental policy objective. This has already been noted, and will be further discussed in chapter 12. They followed conservative monetary policies and hence made it possible to maintain a fixed exchange rate. Furthermore, they felt that a devaluation would be inflationary and for a long time tried to avoid it for that and other reasons.

In the case of India, the balance of payments and competitiveness were clearly not big concerns and, in any case, import restrictions were always used to protect domestic industries irrespective of competitiveness. Until 1975 the inflow of imports was regulated so as to maintain the foreign exchange reserves at desired levels. Other Asian countries were more concerned with their balances of payments, as were Nigeria, Kenya, and Morocco, but also made extensive use of import restrictions. Examples of the use of import restrictions in preference to the exchange rate are Sri Lanka's immediate policy response in 1974–76 to the serious terms-of-trade deterioration resulting from the first oil shock, and Morocco's response in 1981–82 to its problems. In all these cases, inflation was relatively low over long periods, not because of the fixed exchange rate, but because of the belief that low inflation was a desirable end in itself.

The evidence does not clearly support the view that a shift from a fixed to a flexible exchange rate leads to more inflation. Such a shift certainly does not *have* to do so. Furthermore, a commitment to a fixed exchange rate does not always prevent inflation. As usual, different countries reveal different stories. We leave aside again the high-inflation countries of Argentina and Brazil and also the franc-zone countries.

The changes in exchange rate regimes and inflation rates between 1970–72 and 1988–89 are instructive here (see table 8-5). Ten countries changed their regimes from fixed to flexible over this period.

In three cases the regime shift resulted in (or was associated with) a sharp rise in inflation: Costa Rica from 4 percent to 18.5 percent, Nigeria from 11 percent to 40 percent, and Turkey from 12 percent to 73 percent. These cases might suggest that a switch of exchange rate regime from fixed to flexible is likely to lead to more inflation or, alternatively, that higher inflation compelled a switch of exchange rate regime. In 1988–89, however, Nigeria was still going through a

Table 8.5   Inflation Rates in Two Time Periods Related to Regime Switches
(CPI inflation rate averages)

Country	1970–72	1988–89
Countries that switched from fixed to flexible regimes		
Costa Rica	4.1	18.7
Nigeria	11.1	52.5
Turkey	11.7	69.3
India	4.9	7.8
Indonesia	7.7	7.2
Kenya	3.9	9.1
Morocco	3.1	2.8
Pakistan	5.1	8.3
Sri Lanka	5.0	12.8
Thailand	1.7	4.6
Countries that had flexible regimes in both periods		
Chile	42.4	15.9
Colombia	9.8	27.0
Korea, Rep.	13.7	6.4
Fixed or tablita regime in both periods		
Cameroon	6.0	4.3
Côte d'Ivoire	2.7	4.1
Mexico	5.2	67.1

Note: Arithmetic average of annual inflation rates.
Source: World Bank data.

difficult adjustment process (and inflation fell to under 10 percent in 1990), so perhaps only Costa Rica and Turkey are relevant here.

A different conclusion emerges from the experience of the remaining seven countries—five of them in Asia. Exchange rate flexibility clearly did not open the inflationary floodgates for them. Sri Lanka did show a significant increase in inflation, from 5 percent to 13 percent, but the average increase for the remaining six was only from 4.4 to 6.7 percent.

Consider, too, the four countries in which the regimes were broadly the same in the two periods. Two of them—Colombia and Korea—had flexible peg regimes in both periods. The Colombian inflation rate rose from 10 percent to 27 percent, while the Korean inflation actually fell, from 14 percent to 6 percent. Korea, like the other Asian countries, thus managed to have low inflation in 1988–89 in spite of exchange rate flexibility. Chile and Mexico have special stories and therefore cannot be compared over the two time periods. (In 1970–72, Chile went through the inflationary explosion of the Allende regime, while in 1988–89, Mexico began a process of inflation stabilization.)

Furthermore, episodes of high and accelerating inflation occurred in three countries—Turkey, Mexico, and Nigeria—that had commitments to fixed rates at the time. The apparent commitment to a fixed exchange rate did not prevent inflation in these cases. In these episodes the exchange rate was clearly not an effective "nominal anchor."

The outstanding instance here is Turkey in 1977–79. The exchange rate had been fixed since 1970, but, owing to the domestic spending boom described in chapter 3, the inflation rate rose to 27 percent in 1977, 45 percent in 1978, and 59 percent in 1979. Naturally this culminated in a crisis, leading to devaluation and an adjustment program. In the year of devaluation and other adjustments, the inflation rate soared (as described in chapter 7), but this was the usual bubble. The important point is that a fixed exchange rate did not prevent very high and increasing inflation before that. In the period 1973–76, the Mexican inflation rate increased from its previously low level, in spite of the fixed exchange rate since 1954, and after the 1976 devaluation the exchange rate was again fixed, and yet, again, inflation rose, this time to 27 percent, in 1980–81. In the Nigerian episode of 1983 and 1984, inflation rose to 23 percent and 40 percent in spite of the fixed rate.

Increasing Capital Mobility and Exchange Rate Policy

In most of the eighteen countries, international capital mobility has been increasing and is now high. Here we are concerned with short-term mobility, that is, with short-term flows and the incentives for such flows. This has important implications for exchange rate policy. In no cases are the foreign exchange reserves completely immune to the effects of speculation on the exchange rate. The reasons for the general tendency to more mobility and the easing of exchange controls during the 1980s are broadly the same as in the case of the developed countries since 1973 and especially in the 1980s, although this major development took place in the developing countries some years later.

What Determines Mobility and Short-term Capital Movements?

Capital mobility depends on the absence or limited scope of exchange controls, and if there are controls, on a failure to enforce them fully. It also depends on the availability of institutions to engage in short-term capital movements. Outward capital movements on a large scale are sometimes pejoratively termed "capital flight." There have been major episodes of such capital flight, notably in 1981 and 1982 out of Argentina and Mexico, but the absence of capital flight episodes is not necessarily an indication of absence of capital mobility. The incentives for moving funds out may not exist. For this reason, many countries have not experienced episodes of large-scale and prolonged short-term inward or outward capital movements.

The incentive for short-term outward capital movements exists if a nominal depreciation of the domestic currency is expected and this is not adequately offset by an excess of relevant domestic interest rates over foreign interest rates. In addition, various risk factors are relevant: capital will tend to move out because of political risk and general uncertainty about the exchange rate.[15] The aim may be to evade taxation. If a country's real exchange rate has been appreciating and this generates expectations of nominal depreciation—and if this is not offset by a sufficient tightness of domestic credit to generate high domestic interest rates—capital will tend to flow out. Capital is less likely to flee a country like Brazil that has generally avoided prolonged real appreciation, in comparison with a country like Argentina, which at various times seeks to reduce inflation by fixing the nominal exchange rate or having a tablita.

Short-term capital movements out of a country may not only take the form of explicit, recorded capital movements but may also be indirect. Such indirect capital outflows take place through leads and lags—paying for imports ahead of time and lagging receipts of export income or its conversion into domestic currency—and by the overinvoicing of imports and underinvoicing of exports. Furthermore, multinational companies can vary the rate of internal transfers across borders. An important factor in a number of countries—notably Pakistan, Turkey, and Morocco—has been workers' remittances, that is, funds sent home by their citizens working abroad. Variations in the flow of these funds, or their conversion into domestic currency, have been a method of foreign exchange speculation.

Capital mobility obviously depends on exchange controls. Most of the eighteen countries have such controls at least on outward capital flows, and sometimes also on inward flows. The notable exceptions are Indonesia, Mexico, and the two franc-zone countries. It is the existence of such controls that primarily explains the low degree of capital mobility in some countries during the 1970s, a period when it was rapidly increasing among the developed countries. The monetary authorities of the countries have varied in their ability to enforce their controls. For example, Korea's enforcement ability is far higher than that of Nigeria. In the 1980s some countries liberalized capital controls upon realizing that their enforcement ability was diminishing sharply. In particular, they could do little about indirect capital movements. This explains at least in part the absence of controls in Indonesia.

All countries have parallel free markets for foreign exchange, sometimes legal and sometimes not—in the latter case "black" markets. The parallel market premium on foreign exchange over the official exchange rate can be some indication of the degree of capital mobility. A low premium suggests that capital mobility is high—that is, foreign exchange can be obtained in order to export capital out of a country by direct or indirect means without having to pay a premium. The premium also depends on the incentive for capital exports: for example, the more a depreciation of the official rate is expected, the greater the premium.[16]

Other things being equal, anything that tends to increase capital mobility will also tend to reduce the premium. For example, remittances have fed parallel market supplies of foreign exchange and helped to reduce the parallel market premiums. Short-run variations in the premium usually reflect variations in exchange rate expectations, while a long-run downward tendency may reflect either a long-run tendency for the incentive to decline (perhaps owing to a greater tendency to avoid real appreciation), or a decline in the effectiveness or even the removal of exchange controls.

How High Was Capital Mobility in Eighteen Countries?

Capital mobility in all the six Latin American countries was high by the end of the 1980s, indeed very high in Mexico and Argentina, although formal controls remained in all countries other than Mexico.[17]

In the early 1980s, economists devoted a great deal of attention to the problem of capital flight in Latin America. The concern was that international banks were being asked to reschedule debts or to lend to countries whose private citizens were at the same time exporting capital. It could be argued that private citizens were simply diversifying their portfolios, which was considered a legitimate activity for investors elsewhere. Other factors played a role, too: the attempt to escape taxation, the general loss of confidence in governments, and—most important of all—expected devaluations.

Capital flight is difficult to measure and there are conceptual issues. The simplest approach is (broadly) to take the net short-term capital outflow figure in the balance of payments (excluding official and bank flows) plus the "errors and omissions" item.[18] Nevertheless, the various measures presented a fairly clear picture. There was massive flight out of Argentina in 1980 and 1981 and out of Mexico in 1981 and 1982.[19]

The difficulties of Argentina in 1980 and 1981, in the last stage of the Martinez de Hoz episode, leading to huge private capital outflows in those years, have already been described in chapter 7. Capital flight out of Mexico was explained by the attempt to hold the exchange rate through 1981 and much of 1982 as the balance of payments crisis developed. Exchange controls, as evidenced by the large (more than 80 percent) premium in the free market that emerged in 1982, did not prevent the export of capital, estimated at nearly $11 billion for 1981 alone. By the end of 1989 the premium had practically disappeared. This could be explained by a monetary policy that was designed to prevent capital outflow in an environment where mobility was known to be high.

In contrast, capital flight from Brazil was not significant up to 1984 (although there was some in 1980 owing to expected devaluation).[20] Brazil had strict, well-enforced foreign exchange regulations. Furthermore, there was little incentive for capital flight because of the crawling peg exchange rate regime and the indexation of financial assets. In later years, the controls were really placed under pressure, and from 1986 there was certainly evidence of capital flight; but the parallel market premium in 1989 was 170 percent, which certainly suggests that the controls still made a difference. Chile had a brief episode of capital flight in 1982. In 1990 inflows were generally free, responding to interest rate differentials and to exchange rate expectations, but outflows were restricted.[21] Colombia has always had quite strict exchange controls, and their effectiveness to a modest extent has been reflected in parallel exchange markets. In recent years the illegal drug economy has also surely made capital very mobile. Because of the flexibility of exchange rate policy—the crawling peg system combined with the willingness to depreciate the real rate when the balance of payments required it—has discouraged large-scale capital flight.[22]

The countries outside Latin America can be simply classified. In the late 1980s, Indonesia, Côte d'Ivoire, Cameroon, and Turkey were high-mobility countries. Mobility in Thailand, Pakistan, and Nigeria has been increasing and might now also be classified as rather high, especially in Thailand, even though all have controls on capital outflows by residents. Morocco is a borderline case (with a 17 percent premium in 1988). India, Sri Lanka, Korea, and Kenya were low-mobility countries.

Indonesia is the extreme case among the eighteen countries. Exchange controls were abolished in 1970, when the exchange rate system was unified. In view of the geographic characteristics of Indonesia and the integration of its main trading-financial community (the Chinese) in the larger southeast Asian economy, controls would have been difficult to enforce. There is inevitably some speculation on the exchange rate, as was the case before the devaluations of 1983 and 1986, but each time serious problems were avoided by speedy and substantial devaluation.

Côte d'Ivoire and Cameroon have both unrestricted capital mobility within the franc area. Côte d'Ivoire is a country with many foreign workers, and the outflow of workers' remittances accounts for nearly 5 percent of GDP. These outflows vary with the interest differential between the domestic and the comparable French rate.[23]

In Pakistan from 1984 to 1987, recorded remittances (from workers in the Middle East) were on average 7 percent of GDP. A regression by Khan (1992) relating the ratio of remittances to exports to the percentage change in the real effective exchange rate confirms the expectation that remittances rise when there is real depreciation (implying no further expected nominal depreciation or even expected appreciation) and fall when there is real appreciation. In 1985 the Pakistani authorities introduced interest-bearing foreign exchange bearer certificates. These offered a way for Pakistani residents to buy and sell foreign exchange with no questions asked. The market in them operated as a legalized parallel market. The market was fed primarily by foreign exchange from remittances. The premium has varied, but was 13 percent in 1988. Other econometric work by Khan (1992) strengthens the conclusion that capital mobility in Pakistan is high: there is a close link between domestic credit and international reserves.

The situation is somewhat similar in Turkey and Morocco. In both cases workers' remittances have been important (about 3 percent of GDP in Turkey and

7 percent in Morocco), and their variations have also reflected expected exchange rate changes, as well as domestic monetary conditions. By 1990 Turkish residents could make purchases of foreign securities freely, so Turkey had clearly become, like Indonesia, a high-mobility country.

Until 1986 Nigeria applied strict exchange controls on current and capital transactions. Because of the huge data problems, nothing can be said with certainty; but comparisons of Nigerian and partner country trade data suggest that before 1986 capital flight through overinvoicing of imports and underinvoicing of exports was substantial, as might be expected. Given the scope for smuggling across the uncontrolled borders, capital mobility would have been high in spite of the controls. Since 1986 variations in exchange rate expectations have been reflected in the floating official rate, so that the premium has declined sharply.

Of the four low-mobility countries (India, Sri Lanka, Kenya, and Korea), India has always had stringent capital controls, and they have been effective. Abolition has never been seen as a serious option. The basic reason for low mobility, apart from the controls themselves, is that India, with a low trade ratio and low foreign investment, has not been as integrated in the world economy as the other countries. Nevertheless, there was probably some capital flight in the 1980–84 period when, arguably, the rupee was overvalued.[24] The other countries also have had strict exchange controls. In Korea particularly, these have been efficiently enforced and very effective—in spite of the fact that Korea is a great trading nation.

Implications of Capital Mobility for Exchange Rate Policy

The increase in capital mobility, direct and indirect, has two implications for exchange rate policy: it increases speculative capital movements stimulated by exchange rate expectations, and it reduces the efficacy of exchange rate intervention. In the extreme case it abolishes the distinction between exchange rate policy and monetary policy.

High capital mobility means that an expected devaluation will lead to high, possibly massive, capital outflows. The attempt to maintain the exchange rate will deplete the reserves and is liable to create a balance of payments crisis. Once the devaluation has taken place, the funds will come back; operators in the market will have bought foreign currency when it was cheap and sold it when it became dear, hence making a profit at the expense of the central bank. Such experiences in the early 1980s help to explain the large losses that central banks in some Latin American countries incurred. If a significant devaluation is expected, no reasonable rise in domestic interest rates can prevent such movements.

Given that fundamentals will eventually require a devaluation, the remedy is then to devalue quickly and in small steps, as expectations build up. Hence, when capital mobility becomes high, there is a case for moving away from the fixed but adjustable regime to a flexible peg, or even to floating. The objection to floating is that it produces a degree of short-term volatility that is unwelcome, so that some intervention—that is, management—is almost inevitable. This by and large explains why many of our countries moved from fixed-but-adjustable regimes to flexible pegs or to managed floating regimes in the 1980s.

An alternative solution for the "speculation problem" is to move to a regime in which exchange rate changes are so rare that they only take place when there are major changes in "fundamentals." The question, then, is whether a commitment to maintain the rate—and hence pursue the appropriate domestic policies—is clearly perceived by the participants in the foreign exchange market. If it is, then capital movements induced by shifts in expectations might also be rare and the problem discussed here would disappear. But this has its own problems. The exchange rate would then be almost given up as an instrument of policy. Furthermore, once there has been a devaluation or appreciation, it might be difficult to re-establish confidence that further exchange changes would indeed be rare.

With respect to the second implication of capital mobility, few, if any, countries in our group have such high capital mobility that the nominal exchange rate has ceased to be a separate instrument of policy. It is still possible, for example, for a country to choose to depreciate the nominal exchange rate with the aim of also depreciating the real exchange rate, while at the same time pursuing a tight monetary policy designed to reduce inflation. This happened in many countries during the 1980s. Hence, the second problem created by capital mobility is not yet serious for most of the eighteen countries—but it might become so. Possibly Mexico, Argentina, Indonesia, and Turkey are countries in which capital mobility is now so high that the scope for separate exchange rate and monetary policies is now quite limited. An intervention designed to depreciate the currency would inevitably increase the money supply as sterilization would have little effect. The exchange rate could only be depreciated by a policy of monetary expansion or appreciated by monetary contraction. While monetary policy could be targeted on the exchange rate, perhaps with the aim of either stabilizing the nominal rate or the real rate, it could not at the same time be targeted directly on domestic inflation or short-term output, or some combination of the two. Furthermore, fiscal policy would then also be tied down, except insofar as nonbank sources of government finance are developed.

One response would then be to target monetary policy directly on domestic objectives while allowing the exchange rate to float. A second would be to treat the exchange rate as the "nominal anchor" of the system (an idea to which we return below), and so give priority to a nominal exchange rate target. An example of such a policy comes from Mexico. In the period 1988–90, Mexico chose to target the exchange rate (in the form of a tablita rather than a completely fixed rate in 1989–90) and monetary policy then became endogenous. In fact, the exchange rate target represented the anti-inflation target.

A third possibility would be to make the exchange rate target real rather than nominal. Monetary policy would be targeted on the nominal exchange rate, but the nominal exchange rate target would, in turn, be aimed to attain a particular real exchange rate. A nominal anchor for the economy would then be lost completely, leaving the price-level indeterminate. The effects might be highly inflationary, as in the case of Mexico in 1987. The movements of nominal wages, as well as various real factors in the economy, would determine the extent of nominal depreciation required to reach the desired real exchange rate. The real exchange rate target itself would be determined by real objectives, such as improving the competitiveness of export industries or increasing foreign exchange reserves.

Lessons from Cameroon and Côte d'Ivoire

Cameroon and Côte d'Ivoire are members of the franc zone, and the exchange rates of their currencies are, and have always been, firmly fixed to the French franc. These two countries provide laboratory experiments for the main issues discussed in this chapter. Their monetary systems are described in chapter 10.

Franc-zone membership has a number of advantages. First, the countries are able to obtain short-term financing through the system. Second, the firm and credible fixing of rates is helpful for trade with France, and more important, for investment from France. Third, traders can use French forward markets for trade with other countries. Fourth, and no doubt most important, the system guarantees an inflation rate not much higher than that of France over the longer term. It does so both by providing a firm discipline on the monetization of fiscal deficits and through the exchange rate commitment itself, which must limit the inflation of traded goods prices. If one accepts the view that other sources of revenue are usually preferable to the inflation tax (though usually these other sources are politically more difficult), this is an advantage. Finally, through the institutionalization of the fixed exchange rate regime, franc-zone membership gives complete credibility to the low-inflation commitment—at least if we assume relatively low inflation in France, itself now constrained by membership in the European monetary mechanism. The credibility problem discussed in chapter 7 thus does not arise.

The disadvantages are also clear. First, franc-zone membership means that the real exchange rates on a trade-weighted basis tend to move with the French franc. Over the period 1981–89, when the dollar first appreciated and then depreciated in relation to other major currencies, the real exchange rates of these two countries thus moved also. The real depreciation in the 1984–85 period was welcome; the appreciation later has been quite inopportune. It should be noted, however, that the instability of real exchange rates has been far outweighed by the instability of export (coffee, cocoa, and oil) prices.

The second disadvantage is the main one: the fixed exchange rate deprives the government of an instrument of policy at a time of external shock. The countries suffered very adverse terms of trade shocks from 1981 (in Côte d'Ivoire) and in 1986 (in both countries). These shocks inevitably led to more use of import restrictions, and the fixed exchange rate made it difficult later to liberalize trade as part of a structural adjustment program and probably led to more foreign indebtedness than otherwise.

The crises of the two countries were described in chapters 4 and 5. The Côte d'Ivoire crisis was explained by a combination of public spending boom in the

1970s and the severe slump of coffee and cocoa prices from their previous exceptionally high levels. In the 1980s Côte d'Ivoire became a highly indebted country in an almost continuous state of crisis. Cameroon was a great contrast until 1986. It borrowed little and husbanded its oil income to a considerable extent. But the 1986 oil shock pushed it suddenly into crisis. In both cases a fixed exchange rate has not been a guarantee against fiscal deficits, given that foreign borrowing is possible. Indeed, one should not expect it to be.

Côte d'Ivoire was a high-growth country until 1978, when its terms of trade started deteriorating after a sharp rise, but after that its growth rate has fluctuated, generally having been very low, and even negative in some years. Cameroon's growth rate has been high but turned negative in 1987. The African franc-zone countries, of which these two are major members, appeared to do well in relation to other African countries up to 1978 or so, but this is no longer true.[25] One gets no support for their monetary arrangements from looking at growth rates. In 1991 the growth rates of both countries were negative: they were the only countries among our eighteen in which this was so. Neither had succeeded in overcoming its crisis.

The fact that franc-zone countries have pegged to a single currency rather than to a trade-weighted basket seems a minor point. The central issues are clearly two. First, to what extent would a shift to a flexible peg—meaning a breach with the system—have led to more inflation? Second, to what extent would a devaluation, or perhaps frequent depreciations, contribute to solving balance of payments problems without undue unemployment? Would a devaluation have lasting real effects?

As noted, membership in the franc zone is certainly a guarantee that high inflation will be avoided, and the two countries belong to our large moderate-inflation group. Nevertheless, there have been inflationary bubbles, and the Côte d'Ivoire inflation rate during the boom and borrowing period 1975–79 was quite high, averaging 17 percent. Compared with the inflation in the two other major West African countries not in the zone (Ghana and Nigeria), it has certainly been far lower. (Ghana's inflation in 1973–88 averaged 50 percent.) Ghana and Nigeria are warnings of what might happen if the two countries were to leave the zone. A comparison with seven other countries listed in table 8-4, however, leads to the opposite conclusion. In particular, Kenya—which moved to a flexible rate in 1982— has remained a low- or moderate-inflation country. A useful comparison can be made with Morocco, which fixed to the franc until 1974. Morocco also had several inflation bubbles, but it has remained a low-inflation country even though it devalued and moved effectively to a flexible peg in 1984. It has been able to combine the benefits of devaluing the exchange rate—and hence actually making some trade liberalization possible in spite of a serious current account problem—with the maintenance of relatively low inflation. In addition, as already noted, flexible peg countries in Asia have remained moderate-inflation countries.

If the firm exchange rate commitment were breached by Cameroon and Côte d'Ivoire and the possibility of devaluation were allowed, would there be enough commitment to low inflation as an objective in itself for monetary policy to be appropriately restrained? This is the fundamental issue with regard to inflation. There has been such a commitment in Morocco, Kenya, and the Asian countries. Some institutional safeguards might have to be built in. Some hesitation to move away from the franc-zone system is understandable. This is true even though so many developing countries have moved to a discretionary crawling peg, or even to floating of some kind (as in Ghana and Nigeria). It is much more drastic to move away from an institutionalized fixed rate regime of the franc-zone type than to make a switch from a fixed but adjustable regime to a flexible regime, as other countries have done. The institutionalized regime provides a firmer discipline and has much more credibility for the markets than any alternative regime. Once such a regime is abandoned, it is highly unlikely that equivalent credibility could be restored.

The other main issue is whether a nominal devaluation—or frequent nominal depreciations—would bring about sufficiently long-lasting real devaluation and desirable shifts in resource allocation toward exports and would allow import restrictions to be removed and tariffs to be lowered. Devaluations appear to have done so in many and probably most of the fourteen countries discussed in this chapter so far, although, as we have seen, the stories are not uniform. Of course, the central problem is always to reduce absorption, a matter primarily of reducing public spending in real terms. Beyond that, this issue has two sides.

First, can a devaluation succeed in bringing about real wage reductions that could not be brought about otherwise, that is, by explicit reduction in nominal wages? Real wages in the urban sector in Côte d'Ivoire have been exceptionally high by African standards. Although they may have fallen since 1982, they remain high, and this reduces Côte d'Ivoire's competitiveness and ability to build up manufactured exports.[26] Would further real wage reductions brought about by increases in domestic prices of imports be accepted when explicit reductions in nominal wages are not? This is a classic issue. It is highly plausible that a devaluation is more likely to bring about a uniform, or widespread, reduction in real wages than could be brought about by politically practical nominal wage reductions. Furthermore, a replacement of import restrictions and tariffs by an equivalent devaluation does not necessarily require a fall in real wages, while it would ensure a more efficient use of foreign trade.

The other issue is whether there is really scope for increasing nontraditional (primarily manufactured) exports even if incentives were improved. It might be noted here that schemes to subsidize exports directly, and hence to provide incentives for exports that are a substitute for devaluation, have presented administrative and fiscal problems in Côte d'Ivoire. Are nontraditional export supply elasticities much above zero? This cannot be answered here, and there are differences of opinion on this. It has not been put to the test in Côte d'Ivoire and Cameroon, nor in many other African countries. The evidence cited earlier from countries outside Africa, and also Morocco, suggests that in those countries elasticities—allowing for lags—are not low.

To conclude, Cameroon and Côte d'Ivoire have been laboratory experiments of fixed rate regimes and can be compared with other countries in our group. Inflation has indeed been moderate, though not always low, but import restrictions have been much used, this being a major disadvantage of the system. Growth rates have been high in the past—though no higher than in many Asian countries. Cameroon has followed conservative policies—the "Thailand of West Africa" —and only faced a crisis with the 1986 oil shock. Côte d'Ivoire was a notable success story until 1974, but since then the combination of public spending booms and terms-of-trade shocks has turned it into a heavily indebted country with low growth and big problems.

The fact that in 1991 these two were the only countries with negative growth among our eighteen can be given the following interpretation. They suffered severe terms-of-trade shocks at similar times as many other countries (1980–81 and 1986), but they have taken much longer to overcome them and, in fact, by 1991 had not done so. It is surely no coincidence that these are the only two countries that did not devalue. A fixed exchange rate commitment may be favorable for growth when external circumstances are favorable, but when they turn severely adverse, prolonged low growth is inevitable—created by a reduction of aggregate demand and by "import starvation" brought about by tightened restrictions. Other countries also suffered from such adverse effects but, as we have seen, in many cases exports were stimulated by real devaluations. Furthermore, devaluing countries could remove or reduce import restrictions without having to deflate excessively for the sake of the balance of payments.

Lessons for Exchange Rate Policy

There are two principal arguments favoring devaluation when the current account has to be improved. The first is concerned with the labor market, and the second with the tendency to use import restrictions as an alternative.

First, because prices and especially nominal wages usually show some downward rigidity or sluggishness, deflation alone would impose bigger losses in output than would a deflation associated with devaluation. This is the orthodox argument for the exchange rate as a "switching device." It appears to be valid in many of the countries, although these inflexibilities only apply normally in the urban sector of a developing economy, and some countries do appear to have some nominal wage flexibility, especially in a general context of inflation.

At the same time, real wages must be flexible downward if a nominal devaluation is not to be eroded. It must be possible for price increases brought about by devaluation to effect declines in real wages for some time. Of course, eventually, rising productivity should allow real wages to recover again, and in the long run real wages should be higher in countries that manage to adjust smoothly to crises than in those that do not. There are clearly limits to the extent to which real wages can be reduced (or should be reduced), but many countries show evidence of a decline in urban real wages in the course of the 1980s, in association with inflation and devaluations. An important example comes from Mexico: real wages in man-ufacturing appear to have fallen by at least 30 percent from 1982 to 1986 (and the minimum wage more).

Second, the alternative to devaluation—or adequate devaluation—is almost always the use of import restrictions. This is an important observation. The evi-dence indicates that the alternative to devaluation at a time of crisis has *not* been just to contract demand and rely on downward flexibility of wages and prices to bring about the required relative price changes in favor of tradables. The frequent use of import restrictions for balance of payments reasons is clearly evident from the episodes studied here (and further in chapter 9). Furthermore, once import re-strictions have been imposed, it becomes difficult to moderate or remove them un-less the exchange rate can be devalued at the same time. The principal episodes of liberalization have always been associated with devaluation.

Four possible arguments against devaluation or frequent depreciation are usu-ally advanced.

The first argument is that nominal devaluations do not lead to sustained real devaluations, primarily because of wage indexation. If it is believed that such real-wage rigidity does exist in particular cases, the argument for devaluation is surely weakened—although it could still be made if a devaluation involved primarily a replacement of import restrictions or a decline in real asset values leading to lower spending. With regard to actual experience, the evidence, as just noted, indicates a good deal of real wage flexibility downward. Furthermore, in the many cases ex-amined earlier where there has been some erosion of real devaluations, this can be readily explained either by subsequent public spending booms—that is, by fail-ures to sustain the initial policy packages—or by external shocks. It was noted that the real devaluations of the 1980s do seem to have lasted for some time so far (up to 1991).

The second, quite ancient, argument is that elasticities in international trade are low. If this were so, devaluations, whether associated with deflationary poli-cies or with trade liberalization, would fail to increase export volumes significant-ly. Moreover, they would fail to induce the substitution of domestic for imported inputs by domestic producers. With regard to the latter, we do not have any evi-dence of significant effects (but this has not really been studied). Some evidence on export growth (presented above) suggests that in general, though not always, there have been significant effects. These effects seem to be mainly in manufactured exports. Sometimes they have operated quite quickly, and sometimes with lags.

The third argument is that a devaluation can have severely adverse effects on some sections of the community. Notable losers are usually wage earners in the public sector whose real wages fall with higher prices of imports and with higher prices of certain exportables that enter their consumption, and firms and employees in domestic industries that use imported inputs, the costs of which will rise. Con-sumers of their products will also lose insofar as the higher costs are passed on.

These adverse effects are the by-products of relative price changes that are highly desirable, from consumption and resource allocation points of view. They are meant to pull production toward exports and domestic industries that use imports less draw consumption away from tradables or tradable-intensive domestic products. The issue is not usually that the poor will be affected adversely (since the poor are often in the rural sector, and in that case usually gain from devaluation), but that the losers are urban groups that are politically influential, so that devaluation can—and sometimes has—brought about political destabilization (though not in any of our eighteen countries in the period 1974–89).

These considerations suggest that gradual depreciation, possibly as part of a discretionary crawling peg system, may usually be preferable to big devaluations. In fact, many countries have recognized this. The adverse effects would be less at any time, and would be less noticed.

It should be added that, insofar as devaluation is associated with the easing of import restrictions, the redistributive effects would not be of the kind just discussed. Users of imported inputs, including export industries, may actually gain, real wages will not necessarily fall, and the principal losers may be the privileged receivers of the rents from the restrictions.

The fourth argument against devaluation is the "nominal anchor argument" : a fixed nominal exchange rate (or a tablita) can act as a nominal anchor—as a bulwark against inflation (see Aghevli and others 1991; Bruno 1991; and Corden 1991a). It may limit the monetization of fiscal deficits, hence limiting inflation, and it may provide a clear and credible signal to the labor market that should discourage nominal wage increases based on inflationary expectations. The argument gets some support from the theory of rational expectations which throws doubt on the presumption that a nominal policy instrument like the nominal exchange rate can have lasting real effects—that is, on real wages and resource allocation. This approach suggests that nominal policies should be aimed at nominal targets, and surely the obvious target in this case is price stability.

This nominal anchor argument is not to be dismissed, although the evidence presented in this chapter does not really support it. Perhaps the strongest support comes from the Mexican experience with a fixed rate and then a tablita 1988–90, which has not only brought down inflation—as such policies did in Chile in 1978–81—but has also been associated with a recovery in the rate of growth.

Since 1984, many countries have devalued greatly in real terms as part of the flexible peg system. In these cases, more time is needed to see whether inflationary expectations have permanently increased and whether financial discipline has been relaxed because of the change in the exchange rate regime. So far only Turkey, Costa Rica, and possibly Chile, especially Turkey, provide any support for the nominal anchor approach. Only in these cases has the rate of inflation increased significantly while the exchange rate regime has moved from fixed to flexible. It is possible that a fixed exchange rate was a nominal anchor for some of the low-inflation Asian countries (notably Thailand in the 1970s and earlier), but the evidence suggests that a fundamental commitment to low inflation, brought about by conservative monetary policies, has been more important and has indeed survived the changes in exchange rate regime. The issues for the franc-zone countries have already been discussed.

It must also be realized that an unsuccessful nominal anchor can be worse than none at all. When the fiscal deficit fails to decline, an attempt to maintain a fixed nominal exchange rate may simply lead to a balance of payments crisis. In addition, when inflationary expectations fail to fall, the attempt will lead to real appreciation and thus unemployment in tradable sectors.

The exchange rate peg will then be given up in crisis conditions, a sharp devaluation will follow, and the result will be real exchange rate instability, especially if there are several such episodes. Many stories of this kind, mainly from Latin America, have been presented in this and the previous two chapters: perhaps the outstanding examples come from Argentina, Mexico, and (in one episode) Costa Rica.

So far we have discussed whether there should be a strong commitment to a fixed exchange rate. A further issue arises once a decision in favor of some exchange rate flexibility is made. Is it preferable to have a fixed but adjustable system, a discretionary crawling peg, or a float? This is a particularly important question because so many of the fourteen countries discussed mainly in this chapter have indeed made a regime transition from the first to the second.

A strong case for a fixed but rarely adjusted exchange rate can certainly be made. The adjustments, in the form of devaluation, would only take place when there are severely adverse terms-of-trade shocks or genuine domestic real shocks. A once-for-all decision to engage in trade liberalization could be regarded as a domestic real shock. Otherwise, the nominal exchange rate commitment (whether to a single currency or a basket) would be maintained. This would be an attempt to obtain the benefits both of the exchange rate as a nominal anchor and of the real effects of exchange rate adjustments.

The problems have already been referred to and explain why this type of regime has been abandoned by many countries. Large stepwise devaluations are accompanied by considerable distributional and political problems. There are inevitable losers from devaluation. Big losers are usually the industries that use imported inputs and the consumers who buy their products. Private debtors who owe foreign-currency (usually dollar) denominated debt will lose, and may be bankrupted. Hence a financial crisis may result, a matter that is further discussed in chapter 10. Real incomes of consumers of imported goods and services will fall, in the absence of complete and rapid indexation. It follows that "devaluation by stealth" will seem easier. Most important, a fixed-but-adjustable regime is difficult to maintain with high capital mobility because of the speculation problem. The alternative is the discretionary flexible peg regime (or a managed floating rate) which by 1990 all except Mexico and the franc-zone countries had chosen.

Appendix 8A: Meaning and Measurement of the Real Exchange Rate

Here, we look more carefully at the concept of the real exchange rate, and particularly at the IMF method of calculating the real exchange rate indices for developing countries reported in table 8-1 and used throughout this chapter.[27]

The Real Exchange Rate and the Salter Model

We start with the "dependent economy" (or Salter) model with two goods, traded (*T*) and nontraded (*NT*). The terms of trade are given exogenously, so that importables and exportables can be aggregated into one composite commodity, namely, "traded" goods.[28]

The price of *T* in foreign currency is p^*, the nominal exchange rate is *e* (pesos per dollar where the peso is the domestic and the dollar the foreign currency), p_t is the domestic price of *T* and p_n the price of *N*. We can define $R = p_t/p_n$ as the real exchange rate of the home country. This is the "Salter ratio." It is one possible definition. Assuming that $p_t = ep^*$, we then have $R = ep^*/p_n$. A rise in *R* (a real depreciation) means that incentives are set up for "switching," that is, for output of *T* to rise and relative demand for *T* to fall. Hence, the balance of trade will tend to improve. One cannot say that the home economy as a whole has become more "competitive," but one can say that *T* production has become more competitive in relation to *N* production. It is reasonable to suppose that a real exchange rate index should aim to indicate or measure changes in *R*, and hence the incentives for balance of trade improvement at any given level of absorption.

Measurement Problems

The practical problem is to find proxies for measuring $\hat{e}$, $\hat{p}^*$ and $\hat{p}_n$ (where $\hat{\imath} = di/i \cdot 1/dt$).

1. *Weighted average of bilateral exchange rates.* The nominal exchange rate *e* has to be a weighted average of bilateral exchange rates, and there are possibilities of different weights, depending on the choice of year(s) for the weights, and various principles that might be applied. Should only trade be used to determine the weights, or also services and (for example) remittances? Usually "trade-weights" are used. The IMF calls the trade-weighted nominal exchange rate the "nominal effective" exchange rate. Most countries trade significantly with several countries that have exchange rates that fluctuate in relation to each other. In these cases, a trade-weighted exchange rate index is clearly preferable to an index based purely on a bilateral rate, such as the dollar rate. During the years 1982–87, the dollar sharply appreciated in relation to other major currencies and then depreciated, so that it makes a big difference for calculating *R* whether the dollar rate or the effective (trade-weighted) rate is used.[29]

In addition, a country may have multiple exchange rates. Many of the countries in this study have had a dual rate system at some time or other, with a free and an official rate, and sometimes more than two. Depending on the purpose, a weighted average nominal rate must then be calculated, perhaps for trade with each major trading partner. Many different calculations are then possible. In practice, since 1973 the official rates have, in most countries, been the dominant ones for trade (if not capital movements), so this has not usually been an important problem.

2. *How to measure foreign inflation.* The foreign inflation rate $\hat{p}^*$ should indicate the rate of inflation abroad not just of the prices of goods exported to the country concerned, but also of domestic goods competing with the home country's own exports, and of exports to third countries of goods competing with the country. Essentially it should measure only inflation of foreign traded goods prices; it should, as far as possible, exclude nontraded ones. Several different measures are possible.

The CPI usually has a large element of nontraded goods and services, so it is not ideal for the purpose. Foreign prices of N (p_n^*) may rise in relation to the prices of T (p_t^*), perhaps owing to productivity growing faster in T than in N abroad. The use of the CPI measure for foreign inflation will then overstate the relevant foreign inflation rate (which is p_t^*) and so overstate a rise in R, perhaps showing a trend increase that does not truly represent an increase in the home country's Salter ratio. The use of the wholesale price index (WPI) of the foreign country is preferable since the nontraded content in it is less. In practice the CPI and WPI tend to move closely together, so the distinction is usually not important, at least not when large inflation differentials are involved. CPI indices are available for longer periods for more countries. The IMF indices used in this book use the CPI while other calculations often use the WPI.[30]

3. *Choice of index of general price level.* Sometimes an index of domestic nontraded goods and services prices, p_n, can be calculated. This requires decomposing a more general index, such as the CPI or the GDP deflator, and is clearly a desirable method, if data are available. In that case p_t might also be calculated directly, rather than relying on figures for p^* and e separately. Such disaggregated calculations are rarely available for long periods, and certainly not for many countries, though they have been made, for example, for Chile and Indonesia.[31] Usually it is necessary to make use of a general price index, which measures changes in a general price level, p_g, in the home country. This is either the CPI index or the WPI. The IMF uses the CPI, which is the most widely available index for all countries.

Such general price indices are always weighted averages of p_t and p_n, with the weights changing. The inclusion of p_t presents a serious problem when the effects of a devaluation are being analyzed. Suppose there is a rise in e (a nominal devaluation), no change in p^*, and no change in p_n. Hence, R rises in the same proportion as e. If the actual measure that is used is $R' = ep^*/p_g$, the real exchange rate will appear to rise by less. In other words, the rise in R' will be less than the rise in R when there is a devaluation. The greater the weight of p_t in the index, the more p_g rises and hence the greater the divergence between R' and R: the more a real devaluation may appear to be eroded as a result of domestic inflation.

Anything that raises p_n will lower both R and R', and if finally $p_n = p_t$ (complete erosion), then $\hat{R} = \hat{R'} = 0$. It also follows that if a choice can be made between several home country general price indices, the one with the biggest weight for N relative to T should be chosen: this means preferring CPI over WPI.

In view of all the possible ways of calculating a real exchange rate index and all the possible weighting systems, it is not surprising that quite divergent figures for R can be obtained. An example can be given for Chile (Meller 1990), where the following indices for the period 1980–86 have been compared: IMF index, World Bank index, Central Bank of Chile index, relative price index (p_t/p_n). The IMF index uses CPIs for Chile and trading partners, while the Central Bank index uses WPI for trading partners and CPI for Chile (for reasons given above, the latter is the more desirable method); all indices are trade-weighted. The relative price index was also compiled by the Central Bank. What was Chile's real devaluation between 1983 and 1986? The figures yielded by the four indices, respectively, are 57 percent, 48 percent, 42 percent and 49 percent.

The Real Exchange Rate and Trade Liberalization

A distinction should really be made between the prices of imports p_m and the prices of exports p_x, even though in the dependent economy model they are combined into one p_t.

First, consider a change in the terms of trade. Let $p_m{}^*$ be the foreign price of the home country's imports and $p_x{}^*$ the foreign price of the home country's exports. In the Salter formula, p^* is a weighted average of these two. Suppose that the terms of trade deteriorate. If $p_x{}^*$ falls, R will fall, and if $p_m{}^*$ rises, R will rise (for given e and given p_n). During the crisis period 1980–83, a common situation for the countries in this study was that $p_x{}^*$ fell relative to the measured general foreign price index $p_g{}^*$ (based on CPIs or WPIs), which kept on increasing. Thus real depreciation was less than appeared, or real appreciation more. Basically, $p_g{}^*$ was not weighted heavily enough toward $p_x{}^*$. The adverse effect on export industries of the fall in export prices was insufficiently reflected in the real exchange rate indices.

Next, consider a change in the trade regime. This is an important complication. The basic ideas can be explained in terms of a simple case. Imports have a domestic price p_m, and there is a given tariff t. Hence, $p_m = p_m{}^*e(1 + t)$. Let p^* be a weighted average of $p_m{}^*$ and $p_x{}^*$ and t' a weighted average of t and the net zero subsidy on p_x. We then have $R = p^*e(1 + t')/p_n$.

Then there is trade liberalization: t is reduced. At the same time, e is raised. This is the familiar situation where trade liberalization is associated with nominal devaluation. Examples have been given for Pakistan (1972), Sri Lanka (1977), and Morocco (1984–85), among others. The aim is to maintain the relative profitability of tradables as a whole in spite of the reduction of tariffs or the liberalization of the quantitative restrictions regime. At the same time, p^* and p_n may be changing.

One can now construct two kinds of indices. The first is the strict "Salter index" R, where a fall in t' may be offset by a rise in e. While the domestic price ratio p_m/p_x will fall, the ratio p_t/p_n (where p_t is an average of p_m and p_x) may not change at all, or much less. For example, when Pakistan devalued about 100 percent in 1972, its associated trade liberalization meant that the net devaluation— indicative of the change in the Salter ratio—was much less, possibly 40 percent on the import side. In such cases one must really make a distinction between the net devaluation for imports and for exports, since they may be very different. An average is likely to obscure the main effects.[32]

The alternative approach is to define a real devaluation as excluding the effects of trade liberalization or the imposition of trade restrictions. Similarly, it would ignore the effects on domestic prices of changes in export subsidies. This means that the calculation of a real exchange rate takes into account only the changes in the nominal exchange rate and in the two general price indices, that is, p^* and p_g, where p_g is a proxy for p_n. It does *not* take into account a change in t. This kind of real exchange rate $R^{\text{``}}$ is thus defined as $R" = p^*e/p_n$ where $p^*e \neq p_t$. This is indeed the conventional measure, including the IMF measure reported. Normally a large fall in t (trade liberalization) needs to be associated with a rise in e. This approach then yields also a rise in the measured real exchange rate, that is, a rise in $R^{\text{``}}$.

The attraction of this approach is that nominal and real exchange rates (so defined) are likely to move in the same direction, unless there is an offsetting change in p^*/p_n. By contrast, the Salter measure R might yield no change in R, or a rise or fall, depending (for given p^*/p_n) on relative magnitudes of changes in t and e and also on weighting measures used.

Imperfect Substitution

The assumption of the dependent economy model that import-competing goods are perfect substitutes for imports, so that their domestic prices rise to the same extent as the prices of imports (the "law of one price" assumption), is surely not realistic. All evidence indicates imperfect substitutability.

This means that one really needs a model with at least four goods, namely M (imports), IC (import-competing goods), N (nontraded goods), and X (exports). All but M are produced at home and all but X are consumed at home. A rise in e will raise p_{ic} less than it raises p_m. Indeed, initially a devaluation may raise p_{ic} very little. A devaluation will cause production to switch out of N into X (as before) and also into IC, and demand in the opposite direction. As before, demand will shift from M to N. In addition, IC will become more competitive relative to M, and demand will shift away from M toward IC. Output of IC must rise. Measuring R as p^*e/p_n is still appropriate (as is also the use of various types of p_g to proxy p_n), but one can no longer say that p_t (an average of p_m, p_{ic}, and p_x) moves precisely with p^*e.

There is an interesting paradox here. Suppose that a nominal devaluation, leading to an increase in p_m, does not initially bring about any rise in p_{ic}: prices in import-competing industries are slow to rise. Gradually, over the following year or so, p_{ic} does rise, until finally it has risen to much the same extent as p_m. As p_{ic} rises, p_g (measured by the CPI or the WPI) will rise. When R is measured as p^*e/p_g, it will then appear to rise at first, and subsequently, as p_{ic}, and with it p_g, rise, the increase will appear to be eroded. Yet, during this period, when apparently there is real appreciation, the true Salter ratio p_t/p_n is actually rising; when one defines the real exchange rate in terms of this ratio, there is further real depreciation.

Alternative "Competitiveness" Measures

The four-good model leads to an alternative way of defining the real exchange rate. In this approach it is regarded as a measure of competitiveness of *IC* relative to *M*, ignoring *N*. This approach was common before the dependent economy model became fashionable but may still be appropriate for developed countries. This measure does not indicate the incentive for the crucial switching effect between *N* and *X* or *N* and *IC*. One would then define the real exchange rate as p^*e/p_{ic}.

In addition, for a large country that exports manufactures—that is, the major developed countries—one could assume that export prices p_x are not given externally, but are determined by domestic costs, so that a real exchange rate index would be defined as a measure of competitiveness of all tradables, both *IC* and *X*, relative to foreign goods, that is, as p^*e/p_t where p_t is a weighted average of p_{ic} and p_x. A labor cost index for tradables, usually defined as manufactures, might measure p_t; this is one of the common methods used by the IMF when calculating real exchange rate indices for developed countries.[33]

Other Complications

Various other complications, calling for a departure from the simple dependent economy model assumptions, might also be noted here.

First, foreign importers may partly absorb the effects of a devaluation, and similarly export prices in pesos may not rise to the full extent of the devaluation. We then have $p_t = ap^*e$ where a falls when e rises. Hence, an increase in e does not lead to an equal rise in p_t, and thus in R; for this reason, the real exchange rate effects of a devaluation may be overstated by the usual measures, at least in the short run.

A second complication is that domestic production of import-competing goods (*IC*) is often protected by quantitative restrictions rather than tariffs. If these restrictions do not change, domestic prices of *IC* are then isolated from world prices. In fact, quantitative restrictions turn *IC* into *N*. This does not change the analysis. It just means that a real devaluation may lead to resource movements out of *IC* into *X*, rather than from *N* into *IC*.

Finally, one must allow for imported inputs (*IM*) into *IC* and *N*. A real devaluation will raise their relative prices and will induce substitution away from *IM* toward domestically produced inputs. This is a normal switching effect. In addition, p_n and possibly p_{ic} will be raised by the devaluation. There will thus be an understatement of the rise in *R* resulting from a rise in *e*. Ideally, only the value added element in p_n, not the whole of p_n, should be in the denominator of the p_t / p_n ratio. The problem is similar to the one mentioned earlier that arises because a general price index, such as the CPI index, is used to represent p_n; in that case, also, the rise in *R* resulting from a rise in *e* is understated because the denominator consists not of p_n but of a weighted average of p_n and p_t.

Chapter 9

Trade Policies: Tightening and Liberalization

Between 1965 and 1990 all eighteen countries made use of trade restrictions of one kind or another. Indeed, for many years an increase in import restrictions was the normal response to a balance of payments problem. There were also many episodes of liberalization, however, and the tightening and liberalization in response to changes in macroeconomic circumstances became a complex matter. A principal aim of this chapter is to provide a coherent exposition of what actually happened, and why. Inevitably we have to simplify a great deal. After providing a historical overview, we address a number of issues: in particular, how variations in restrictions were related to exchange rate policy and what effects such variations had on current accounts and on fiscal positions. A large literature analyzes the microeconomic effects of trade interventions and also their effects on long-run growth, but these important topics are beyond the scope of the present chapter.

There are two kinds of trade policies. One consists of price-oriented measures: tariffs, export taxes or subsidies, retention schemes, duty exemptions, and import deposits. The other includes quantity-oriented measures: import quotas, import bans, licensing of imports, and export quotas or price measures related to export targets. The measures used by the eighteen countries run the entire gamut, from a total ban on certain imports to minor changes in letters of credit.

The most common and effective method has been the *quantitative restriction of imports* (QRs for short) by means of a system of quotas, which has usually consisted of shifting import items from a free list to a QR list. Conversely, trade policies have been liberalized by increasing the number of items on the free list. At times, quantitative restrictions have been applied to all imports. Some countries have subjected all imports to QRs unless they are included in a "positive list." Others have freely admitted all imports unless included in a "negative list." A switch from a positive list system to a negative list system could represent a substantial liberalization.

The analysis in this chapter is concerned with these tightening and liberalizing trade "episodes." From 1965 to 1990 our countries experienced twenty-six tightening and thirty-three liberalizing episodes (table 9-1), identified on the basis of changes in import quotas, tariffs, export taxes, and subsidies in each. As just noted, import quotas were the most common tool. Tariffs, export subsidies, and taxes played a minor role in these episodes. In most instances, tariffs were imposed mainly for revenue purposes. At times, export taxes were raised with a devaluation so as to siphon off the higher export revenues in domestic currency resulting from a devaluation. Sometimes, export subsidies were used to offset the bias against exports arising from an increase in the items subject to quotas or an accompanying increase in tariffs.

The discussion focuses first on the changes in direction of trade policy, next on the extent of the change (as judged by the changes in QRs, tariffs, and subsidies from their existing levels), and then on the duration of the policy episode. The trade liberalization episodes identified coincide with the turning points established through the use of a "trade liberalization index" (Papageorgiou and others 1991).[1] The duration of each trade policy episode was measured as the period the policy was maintained from the time it was introduced. The episodes have been identified on the basis of detailed information obtained from the project's country studies, from World Bank sources, and from Papageorgiou and others (1991).

Historical Overview

Table 9-1 distinguishes the same four periods used to describe changes in exchange rate policies in chapter 8 (see table 8-2). It can be seen, for example, that Argentina had five episodes over the four periods, three liberalizing episodes and two tightening episodes. Argentina and Brazil, with their characteristically ever-changing policy regimes, had the largest number of episodes. Table 9-2 shows that in the first ("Bretton Woods") period, there were six "tightenings" and nine "liberalizings." As might be expected, the second ("interregnum") and the third ("crisis") periods were mainly characterized by tightening, while the last ("flexible exchange rate") period was mainly one of liberalizing.

The question is whether it is possible to make some reasonable generalizations. To that end, we have not only looked at all episodes in detail, but have also related them to current account developments. In other words, we have tried to determine to what extent changes in current accounts determined changes in trade policies.

To begin with, we found that the first three periods, but not the last, were marked by many trade policy tightenings, always preceded by a deterioration in the current account. Econometric investigations confirm the hypothesis that trade policy tightenings are related to the current account balance (see hypothesis 1 in the appendix to this chapter). The coefficient for the lagged current account bal-

Table 9.1   Trade Policy Episodes by Analytical Periods and Exchange Rate Regimes

Country	Bretton Woods 1965–73		Interregnum 1974–79	Crisis years 1980–83		Flexible exchange rate 1984–90
Argentina	(-) 1967	(+) 1971–73	(-) 1976	(+) 1982 devaluation		(-) 1989
	flexible rate		flexible rate	flexible rate		flexible rate
Brazil	(-) 1967		(+) 1973–74	(-) 1979–80	(+) 1981–84	(+) 1988
	flexible rate		flexible rate	flexible rate		flexible rate
Cameroon			(+) 1973–74 (+) 1976–7			
	CFA, fixed rate		fixed rate	fixed rate		fixed rate
Chile	(-) 1968–70	(+) 1971–73	(-)[a] 1974–79			
	flexible rate		devaluation flexible rate until 1974	devaluation flexible rate		Adopted flexible rate
Colombia	(+) 1967			(+) 1982		(-) 1984–87
	flexible rate crawling peg			crawling peg		1985 crawling peg
Costa Rica			(+) 1974	(+) 1982–84 devaluation/1981		(-) 1986–88 adopted
			devaluation	unified rate/1983		flexible rate
Cote d'Ivoire			(+) 1975–78	(+) 1982		(-) 1986
	CFA fixed rate		fixed rate	fixed rate		fixed rate CFA
India	(-) 1966–68		(+) 1973–74	(-) 1980–85		
	devaluation 1966 fixed rate		fixed rate	fixed rate		
Indonesia	(-) 1966–71					(+) 1983–84 (-)[a] 1986–89
	devaluation fixed rate		devaluation/1978			devaluation/1983 devaluation/1986
Kenya	(+) 1971–75		(-) 1976–78	(+) 1979–84		(-) 1988–89
	fixed rate		devaluation/1974 fixed rate thereafter	devaluation/1982		adopted flexible rate

Table 9.1   (continued)

Country	Bretton Woods 1965–73	Interregnum 1974–79	Crisis Years 1980–83	Flexible Exchange Rate 1984–90
Korea, Rep. of	(-)[a] 1965–67 flexible rate	(-) 1978–79 devaluation/1974 fixed rate thereafter devaluation 1979	(-) 1981 devaluation/1980 fixed rate	adopted flexible rate
Mexico	fixed rate	(-) 1977–79 devaluation/1976 fixed rate thereafter	(+) 1980–82 devaluation/1982	(-)[a] 1985–90 devaluation/1985 devaluation/1986 fixed rate/1988
Morocco	fixed rate	(+) 1978–80 fixed rate	devaluation/1982	(-)[a] 1984
Nigeria	(+) 1967–70 fixed rate	(-) 1973–74 fixed rate	(+) 1983–84 fixed rate	(-)[a] 1986–88 devalued and adopted flexible rates
Pakistan	(+) 1965–71 fixed rate (-) 1972–73 devaluation/1972	(+) 1979–80	fixed rate	(-) 1986–88 flexible rate
Sri Lanka	(-) 1968–70 fixed rate (depreciated dual rate)	(+) 1973–75 fixed rate (-)[a] 1977 devaluation		adopted flexible rate
Thailand	fixed rate	fixed rate	devaluation/1981 (small)	(+) 1983–84 (-) 1986–88 devaluation/1984 flexible rate
Turkey	(-) 1970 devaluation fixed rate		(-)[a] 1979–80 devaluation/1980 fixed rate (-) 1983–85	(-) 1989 adopted flexible rate
Totals	15 episodes +6 -9	16 episodes +9 -7	13 episodes +8 -5	15 episodes +3 -12

Note: Negative sign indicates liberalizing episodes.

a. Indicates regime change.

Source: Papageorgiou, Michaely, and Choksi (1991) and World Bank data.

Table 9.2   Trade Policy Episodes, Trade Regime Changes and the Exchange Rate, 1965–90

	1965–73	*1974–79*	*1980–83*	*1984–90*	*1965–90*
Trade policy tightening	6	9	8	3	26
Exchange rate devalued or flexible during episode	3	1	7	2	13
Exchange rate fixed during episode	3	8	1	1	13
Trade policy liberalization	9	7	5	12	33
Exchange rate devalued or flexible during episode	9	4	5	11	29
Exchange rate fixed during episode	0	3	0	1	4
No changes in trade policy	6	4	10	5	22
Trade regime changes	1	2	1	4	8
	Korea 1965–67	Chile 1974–79 Sri Lanka 1977	Turkey 1980	Morocco 1984 Indonesia 1986–89 Mexico 1985–90 Nigeria 1986–88	

Source: Country Studies; Papageorgiou, Michaely, and Choksi (1991); and World Bank sources.

ance is highly significant for trade tightenings, as seen in equation 9-2. The coefficient increases when the current account of the previous year is taken as the independent variable, as in equation 9-3. Of course, this finding is hardly surprising. The natural, even obvious, tendency is to tighten quantitative import restrictions, usually by shifting items from a free to a restricted list, when a current account problem develops. The variation of trade policy was in most cases an important instrument of balance of payments policy, sometimes the only one. Although trade tightenings were usually preceded by current account deteriorations, it was not inevitable, however, that a current account problem would lead to trade tightening. Thus, Korea and Thailand suffered from both oil shocks but did not tighten restrictions as a result. Indeed, in 1978 Korea started liberalizing again. Clearly, a country could live with a deteriorating current account for some time if it was able to borrow, and this is what happened in many cases in the second and third periods. Table 9-2 shows that in the third ("crisis") period, ten countries did not tighten trade restrictions. This included several countries adversely affected by the oil and interest rate shocks: Korea and Thailand, already mentioned; Chile, which encountered a severe crisis but did not fundamentally alter the liberalized regime adopted during the second period; and Pakistan and Sri Lanka, which financed their trade deficits with workers' remittances and big foreign aid flows.

Second, we found some asymmetry in response. Improvements in the current account were less likely to lead to liberalizing episodes than deterioration was likely to lead to tightenings. Notably, Indonesia did not liberalize after the first and second oil shocks. Nevertheless, the modest liberalizations by Kenya, Mexico, and Nigeria in the second period can be explained by the favorable effects of the coffee boom and the first oil shock.

Third, the relationship between the balance of payments situation and the change in trade policy altered—indeed, quite drastically—in the fourth period. Only one significant trade tightening in that period—Brazil's—could be readily explained by the balance of payments. In eight other cases, deterioration of the current account led to a package of crisis policies that included trade liberalization. We shall call this "the new liberalization." Hence, the earlier relationship was reversed. While the coefficient for the current account balance is highly significant in the equation that relates trade policy episodes to the current account balance in the first three periods, the structure of this relationship changes in the 1984–89 period. (See equations 9-3a and 9-3b in the appendix to this chapter. There is a significant difference between the intercepts for equation 9-3c, which uses a dummy variable to distinguish between the 1965–83 and 1984–89 periods.)

In 1986 the three major oil exporters—Indonesia, Mexico, and Nigeria—all suffered severe adverse shocks, and all three turned to radical stabilization and structural adjustment programs, recommended by the IMF and World Bank (one of the Bank's loan conditions was trade liberalization). In seven other cases, current account deficits were followed by some trade liberalization, significantly in Côte d'Ivoire, Colombia, Kenya, and Morocco. Thailand and Turkey, both quite open economies by the beginning of this period owing to earlier liberalizations, liberalized from a more favorable balance of payments situation than the others.

Fourth, external shocks played only a limited role in shaping the various episodes. The first period brought no significant external shocks (other than the commodity boom at the end). Trade tightenings resulted from current account problems that, in turn, resulted from domestic policy shocks. Except in Korea, liberalization came through either improvements in the current account or through attempts to rectify severe distortions caused by earlier trade tightenings. In the second and third periods, the external shocks did play a significant role, but they did not always have the expected effects. As already noted, favorable current account effects did not always lead to liberalization, while unfavorable effects did not always lead to trade tightening. In the fourth period, the principal external shock was the adverse 1986 shock for the oil exporters, and we have already referred to the responses in that case.

The thirty-three liberalization episodes can be classified in various ways. Of the nine episodes in the first period, only three—those of Brazil, Indonesia, and Korea—had significant effects. The Brazilian episode was probably a leading cause of the 1968–73 "miracle" described in chapter 7, and followed the Bulhoes-Campos stabilization. The Indonesian episode was part of the Suharto stabilization and reform program also described in chapter 7. We come to the Korean case below. In later periods, it is also possible to distinguish significant episodes from more minor ones.

An important subgroup of liberalization episodes can be described as *regime changes*. There were eight of these (see tables 9-1 and 9-2). These cases consisted not only of substantial—sometimes drastic—trade liberalization, but also of a sustained effort not to use trade tightening policies to counter a balance of payments problem.

In Korea, the regime change took place in 1965–67, but trade liberalization was not brought about all at once. Rather, a process was set in motion that allowed liberalization to be implemented over a long period. It slowed up at times, especially when balance of payments problems arose, and at various later stages accelerated again. In the other seven countries, liberalization was more sudden.

Particularly noteworthy is the Chilean case. Before 1974, Chile had a highly differential and restrictive trade regime with more than five thousand tariff positions, 63 percent of which were subject to QRs. Some two hundred of these positions were completely banned while nearly two thousand positions were subject to a prohibitive ninety-day advance deposit requirement. Between 1974 and 1976, all QRs, except six minor items, were abolished. Tariff rates (which had been very high, up to 750 percent) were reduced in three stages to a uniform 10 percent by 1979, except for automobiles and other vehicles. Tariffs were increased in 1983, but the entire fourth period was one of openness.

As described in earlier chapters, an inflation and balance of payments crisis developed in Turkey in 1977 and culminated in a big devaluation and various other structural adjustment measures in 1980. Exports boomed after that. Turkish trade restrictions had been very tight, but from 1983 to 1985 there was significant import liberalization, so that by 1985 restrictions had been lifted on almost all imports of consumer goods, tariffs were reduced to an average 20 percent for the majority of goods, and the prohibited list was almost abolished.

The drastic changes in the Nigerian regime in 1986 have already been reported in chapter 8. Details for Indonesia, Korea, Mexico, Morocco, and Sri Lanka are given below. Four of the regime changes (in Morocco, Indonesia, Nigeria, Indonesia) were striking examples of "the new liberalization."

Why did countries liberalize? Two kinds of stories emerge, though they are not mutually exclusive.

The first story is simple. A country has a balance of payments problem in the years before 1974, created by external shocks or domestic expansionary policies, usually the latter. So it tightens import restrictions. Exports are handicapped by the difficulty of obtaining imported components and inputs, and sometimes by real appreciation. The restrictions have adverse effects on domestic output ("import starvation") and various other undesirable consequences, notably a preoccupation with rent-seeking. (Restrictions were particularly tight in Allende's Chile from 1970 to 1973 and in Sri Lanka from 1974 to 1976, after the first oil shock. The same was true in Turkey at various times, especially in 1977–80.) A gradual or sudden reaction against the situation develops. Policy changes are introduced following a rightward shift (to the extreme right in one case) of the political regime— as in Chile in 1973, Sri Lanka in 1977, and Turkey in 1980. Hence, the liberalization can be seen as part of an ideological shift, or alternatively as a reaction to the previous experience of the country itself. The worse the previous experience, the more drastic the change is likely to be. Liberalization in such cases must always be preceded by, or associated with, big devaluations (devaluation figures for our countries appear in table 8-2).

The second story can be called "the new liberalization," but it is not entirely different. Again, a country has an adverse experience. This time, the country already has tight restrictions, but it encounters a balance of payments problem, usually owing to an external shock. (The extreme cases here are the three oil exporters—Indonesia, Mexico, and Nigeria—which faced the adverse 1986 shock. Morocco in 1984 and possibly Turkey in 1980 could also be included.) Perhaps restrictions could be tightened even more—although this seems hardly to have been possible in the case of Nigeria. By now, the authorities can see that import restrictions are not a good policy, for all the familiar reasons. Hence, contrary to earlier practice, they institute a trade liberalization program or other measures associated with structural adjustment, such as devaluation, tight fiscal policies, and increases in public enterprise prices and privatization.

The balance of payments crisis creates the shock environment in which trade liberalization and other radical policy changes become possible. In the 1980s there was, in addition, an ideological shift toward outward and market-oriented policies. Furthermore, the recommendations and conditionality of the World Bank and the IMF played a decidedly major role. Countries with balance of payments problems needed the support of the two institutions, and that support was only forthcoming if some credible steps toward liberalization were taken. The fact that the two institutions, especially the World Bank, put so much emphasis on trade liberalization was itself a reflection of the worldwide ideological pro-market trend that was influenced by the successes of East Asia and the patent failures elsewhere.

The periods covered by this study end with 1990, but it may be noted that in 1991, two of the most protectionist countries—Argentina and India—embarked on liberalization programs. Argentina's measures have been quite drastic, while India had by 1992 greatly reduced the coverage of QRs on intermediate and capital goods imports. Argentina is clearly a case in which things had to get really bad before they would get better, and this point arrived in 1991. India provides a good example of our second story. Owing to excessive fiscal expansion, there emerged

Table 9.3   Trade Ratios, 1965–90

Country	1965–69	1970–74	1975–79	1980–85	1985–90
Argentina	0.18	0.20	0.20	0.20	0.23
Brazil	0.10	0.16	0.18	0.20	0.16
Cameroon	0.46	0.48	0.50	0.50	0.42
Chile	0.30	0.28	0.46	0.46	0.64
Colombia	0.26	0.30	0.30	0.26	0.30
Costa Rica	0.60	0.68	0.64	0.76	0.68
Côte d'Ivoire	0.68	0.66	0.74	0.76	0.68
India	0.10	0.10	0.12	0.16	0.16
Indonesia	0.22	0.36	0.44	0.50	0.45
Kenya	0.60	0.62	0.64	0.56	0.50
Korea	0.32	0.50	0.60	0.74	0.70
Mexico	0.20	0.16	0.18	0.26	0.30
Morocco	0.40	0.44	0.54	0.52	0.51
Nigeria	0.30	0.26	0.42	0.32	0.40
Pakistan	0.22	0.24	0.30	0.34	0.35
Sri Lanka	0.66	0.52	0.66	0.74	0.61
Thailand	0.36	0.38	0.44	0.50	0.64
Turkey	0.10	0.18	0.16	0.32	0.44

Note: Imports and exports of goods and nonfactor services in U.S. dollars as a ratio of GDP, at market prices in U.S. dollars.
Source: World Bank data.

for the first time in many years a serious balance of payments problem requiring support from the international institutions, and also highlighting the need for drastic stabilization and adjustment. It also appears that the worldwide change in thinking about these issues gradually made an impact in India (see the postscript to this chapter).

Table 9-3 provides an overview of the changes in openness over the study period. The table shows the ratios of trade (exports plus imports) to gross domestic product (GDP) in the four subperiods. Needless to say, the trade ratio depends on many factors, of which the degree of trade restrictiveness is only one. Normally, large economies are likely to have lower ratios than small economies, and this is borne out in the table. The two largest economies, Brazil and India, had by far the lowest ratios in all four periods; but these two were also very restrictionist countries that by 1990 had not yet embarked upon extensive liberalization. Argentina has a low ratio in comparison with that of Korea, even though the Korean economy is possibly twice the size of the Argentinian (on the basis of dollar figures). Obviously, this difference reflects the more outward-oriented policies of Korea— and no doubt explains in large part why the Korean economy was so much larger by 1990. If "openness" is defined as having a ratio of 0.40 or more, then the twelve open economies of 1985–90 include the six smallest economies (see table 1-1 for figures of aggregate GDP).

More relevant for the present discussion are the large changes that table 9-3 shows. In the first period, only six economies were "open" (had a ratio in excess of 0.40), these being five of the six small economies, the exception having been Chile. In that first period, Turkey was extremely closed. In the last period, twelve were open: the six additions to the group were Chile, Indonesia, Korea, Mexico, Nigeria, Thailand, and Turkey. The big changes in the case of Chile, Indonesia, Korea, Thailand, and especially Turkey, are very noticeable.

Trade and Exchange Rate Policy

As noted earlier in the volume, a country that seeks to maintain a fixed exchange rate and encounters a balance of payments problem is likely to impose or tighten import restrictions. The two policies are substitutes as instruments of balance of payments policy. This was actually a common response in the 1950s, a time when many developing countries encountered balance of payments problems as a result of the 1952 slump in commodity prices. Econometric evidence confirms the hypothesis that trade policy tightening and devaluations were substitutes up to 1983. Equation 9-5 in the appendix to this chapter illustrates a negative correlation between trade policy tightening and nominal devaluation.

Between 1965 and 1973, when balance of payments problems were rarer, they led to trade policy tightening in only three countries (see table 9-2): Kenya, Nigeria, and Pakistan. From 1974 to 1979, the period encompassing the effects of the first oil shock, there were nine such cases, with the severest tightening in Sri Lanka in 1973–75 and in Costa Rica sometime after its 1974 devaluation, which it had hoped not to repeat. The other fixed-rate countries that were adversely affected by the first oil shock were Thailand and Korea; they avoided both devaluation and tightening during that period, essentially by borrowing. In the later periods, trade policy tightening with a fixed exchange rate was undertaken in Côte d'Ivoire and Nigeria (see chapter 8). Restrictions in Nigeria were extremely severe.

It cannot be concluded that a country that has a flexible exchange rate regime, or that is willing to devalue when there is a balance of payments problem will necessarily avoid imposing or tightening trade restrictions. At most, the evidence from our case studies suggests that such a country is less likely to impose really tight restrictions, since the exchange rate instrument is available. This has certainly been true of Korea for the whole period since 1964, when its flexible exchange rate policy began. Except for the period after the 1974 devaluation until 1979, its exchange rate had been flexibly managed and trade policy tightenings have been avoided. In the years from 1965 to 1973, tightening episodes occurred in the other three countries that did not have longer-term fixed exchange rate commitments (Argentina, Colombia, and Chile), and in the next period, 1974–79, there was one such case (Brazil). Furthermore, when a really serious crisis came, as in the third period, many countries (seven in all) both devalued in real terms and tightened restrictions. The ones that confined themselves to using the exchange rate instrument were Chile, Korea, and Thailand (devaluation in 1984), all countries with a strong commitment to outward orientation in trade.

On the whole, the liberalization episodes indicate that liberalization was always preceded by or directly associated with devaluations, usually very large. Rates of devaluation are given in table 8-3, and table 9-2 shows that all but four out of thirty-three such episodes took place with devaluation or flexible rate regimes. In the case of flexible rate regimes, real devaluations were brought about, as described in chapter 8, by rates of nominal depreciation that exceeded inflation differentials.[2]

The eight regime changes tell an even more persuasive story. It is inconceivable that substantial liberalizations—and especially "the new liberalization"—would have been possible without some flexibility in exchange rates. Korea devalued in 1964, then began liberalization, and after that, until 1974, maintained a flexible rate regime. Chile (1974–79), Sri Lanka (1977), Morocco (1984), Indonesia (1986–89), and Nigeria (1986) all began liberalizing at roughly the same time that they devalued or, in the Nigerian case, allowed depreciation in the market, while Turkey (1983–85) liberalized three years after its devaluation.

The Mexican case is a little different because from 1988 on—when the liberalization process was incomplete and the full effects were yet to show—exchange rate flexibility was abandoned (see chapters 7 and 8), so that the real exchange rate actually appreciated. No doubt it was possible to sustain the exchange rate and liberalized trade regimes, thanks to capital inflow and to an export boom, the latter caused to some extent by the earlier devaluation and by the liberalization of imported inputs for export industries.

The Effects of Trade Policy Episodes

The various trade policy measures had important microeconomic and longer-term effects that have been studied in detail. The widely held view of economists—and, since the mid-1980s, of many policymakers in developing countries—is that detailed trade intervention, especially when it takes the form of quantitative import restrictions and when it fosters an inward-looking orientation, has, in general, adverse effects on real incomes and growth. The spreading of this belief helps to explain the liberalization trend of the 1980s and early 1990s. We will not recite the reasons for this belief, although we share it. The literature on the comparative growth effects of outward-oriented and inward-oriented trade policies is extensive.[3] Apart from some remarks on "import starvation," we have no new evidence to offer, since we confine ourselves to more narrow measurable macroeconomic effects.

Effects on Current Accounts

The short-term effects of trade policy episodes on outputs, exports, and imports are difficult to measure, at least in any comprehensive way, although we have something to say on outputs and imports below. We have tried to relate these episodes to subsequent current account developments (see table 9-4). An important point to remember here is that a trade policy episode never happens on its own. It may well be associated with expenditure changes and, as we have seen, with exchange rate changes. If the current account improves after a tightening episode that is associated with a devaluation, and when a fiscal contraction has also taken place, the subsequent current account development is presumably the result of the whole policy package. Furthermore, subsequent exogenous shocks, such as changes in export prices, will affect the result.

In the 1980s, the "new liberalization" was always associated with real devaluations, and often with crisis measures that involved fiscal and monetary contraction. Hence, the package would not necessarily worsen the current account. Nevertheless, liberalization was in many cases followed by such a deterioration. The problem was that even though the stabilization and structural adjustment packages recommended by the IMF and the World Bank involved both real devaluation and liberalization, they also brought with them extra financial support from these institutions, from governments, and eventually—as in the case of Mexico in 1991—from the private sector. Continued, and possibly greater, current account deficits were thus made possible. In the final analysis, a country can only sustain a current account that can be financed; it is the availability of finance (including financing obtained through rescheduling) that will determine the current account. If sufficient finance is not available, trade restrictions, exchange rate adjustment, and expenditure reductions together, in various combinations, will be needed to improve the current account.

To summarize, if the current account improves in the first or second year following tightening, the restrictionist policy is called a "success," and if not, a "failure." We find eleven "successes" and sixteen "failures," while emphasizing that "failures" were not necessarily policy failures, or attributable to the trade policy measures. With respect to liberalization episodes, in fifteen of the thirty-three cases the current account worsened after two years, and in eighteen cases it improved or stayed the same. On average, the current account worsened marginally following trade liberalizations and improved marginally following trade policy tightening. Econometric evidence reported in the appendix to this chapter suggests that current account improvements following tightenings do not last for more than three years. When the current account deficit is treated as the dependent variable in a reduced linear model of the current account, as in equation 9-6 of the appendix, trade policies affect the current account with a one-year lag. The six panels (I to VI for different time lags for equation 9-6) that describe the effects of the lagged trade policy variable show that the effect of a current account improvement following a trade tightening could be lost in three years.

Table 9.4 Changes in Trade Policies and the Response of the Current Account Balance CAB, 1971–88

(in current U.S. dollars)

	Tightening episodes					Liberalizing episodes			
Country	Period	CAB in year of policy	Cumulative CAB	Avg. of cumulative CAB	Country	Period	CAB in year of policy	Cumulative CAB	Avg. of cumulative CAB
Argentina	1971–73	-390	484	242	Argentina	1967	130	-283	-142
Argentina	1982	-2,353	-4,841	-2,421	Argentina	1976	651	2,982	1,491
Brazil	1973–74	-2,158	-14,570	-7,285	Argentina	1989	-1,305	1,641	1,641
Brazil	1981–84	-11,750	-23,147	-11,574	Brazil	1967	-276	-862	-431
Brazil	1988	4,159	-2,145	-1,073	Brazil	1979–80	-10,480	-24,560	-12,280
Cameroon	1973–74	-17	-170	-85	Chile	1968–70	-138	-2	-1
Cameroon	1976–77	-92	-278	-139	Chile	1974–79	-292	-342	-171
Chile	1971–73	-198	-750	-375	Colombia	1984–87	-1,401	-1,426	-713
Colombia	1967	0	-339	-170	Costa Rica	1986–88	-80	-435	-218
Colombia	1982	-3,054	-4,404	-2,202	Cote d'Ivoire	1986	-298	-2,049	-1,025
Costa Rica	1974	-266	-420	-210	India	1966–68	-930	-1,785	-893
Costa Rica	1982–84	-267	-431	-216	India	1980–85	-2,268	-5,638	-2,819
Côte d'Ivoire	1975–78	-379	-426	-213	Indonesia	1966–71	-108	-479	-240
Côte d'Ivoire	1982	-1,016	-1,002	-501	Indonesia	1986–89	-3,911	-3,495	-1,748

Country	Period			
India	1973–74	−430	−540	−270
Indonesia	1983–84	−6,338	−3,779	−1,890
Kenya	1971–75	−112	−194	−97
Kenya	1979–84	−498	−1,444	−722
Mexico	1980–82	−10,750	−22,367	−11,184
Morocco	1978	−1,338	−2,940	−1,470
Nigeria	1967–70	−201	−537	−269
Nigeria	1983–84	−4,354	2,681	1,341
Pakistan	1965–71	−459	−597	−299
Pakistan	1979–80	−820	−1,618	−809
Sri Lanka	1973–75	−25	−246	−123
Thailand	1983–84	−2,874	−3,646	−1,823
Turkey	1989	966	−2,611	−1,306
Average		−1,768	−3,372	−1,686

Country	Period			
Kenya	1976–78	−124	−633	−317
Kenya	1988–89	−454	−1,121	−561
Korea	1965–67	8	−296	−148
Korea	1978–79	−1,085	−9,472	−4,736
Korea	1981	−5,321	−7,296	−3,648
Mexico	1977–79	−1,854	−8,630	−4,315
Mexico	1985–90	1,130	2,295	1,148
Morocco	1984	−987	−1,100	−550
Nigeria	1973–74	−8	4,940	2,470
Nigeria	1986–88	366	−263	−132
Pakistan	1972–73	−241	−574	−287
Pakistan	1986–88	−774	−1,498	−749
Average		−974	−2,212	−1,081

Note: Annual average balances are for the two years following the year in which the trade regime changed.
Source: World Bank data.

Effects on Fiscal Balances

A common assumption is that a reduction in import tariffs and export subsidies would reduce fiscal revenues, while an increase would raise revenues. By extension, trade liberalization is expected to produce lower trade tax revenues and tightenings to cause increases, a further assumption being that tariffs and subsidies are the only or the more dominant trade instruments. The dynamic (growth) effects of trade policy episodes are also ignored.

The main method our countries used to tighten and liberalize trade policies was to vary QRs. Thus, a trade tightening based on an increase in QR coverage (at constant tariffs and subsidy rates) could lead to a decline in trade tax revenues. Conversely, a liberalization could raise revenues. These effects could be stronger or weaker, depending on growth effects, devaluations, the QR coverage, and of course, the initial conditions and the relevant elasticity of import and export demand.

In fact, trade policy liberalizations were followed by reduced trade tax revenues in some instances and by increases in others. Similarly, tightening trade policies raised trade tax revenues in some instances and reduced them in others (table 9-5). Data on trade tax revenue are available for thirty-four of the fifty-nine episodes. Of these, fourteen are trade-tightening cases, ten of which resulted in an increase in trade tax revenue, and four in a decrease. The remaining twenty are liberalization episodes. Here, trade tax revenues rose in fifteen cases and fell in five.

This modest sample suggests that both kinds of episodes may be followed by increases in trade tax revenues. Trade liberalization might be expected to increase trade tax revenues for several reasons. First, as QRs are reduced, more is imported, and even at lower tariffs and higher export subsidy rates, trade tax revenues could increase. Second, since devaluations usually accompany liberalizations, the valuation basis of exports and imports rises, which leads to higher trade tax revenues even at the same tax and subsidy rates. Also, since most trade liberalizations take place with some balance of payments support (so that the current account can deteriorate), the increase in imports specially designed to alleviate import starvation situations also leads to increased trade tax revenues.

Since our trade tax responses are lagged over an interval of only two years, the figures given here may in fact have a downward bias since export supply responds more slowly to trade liberalizations than do imports. Trade tax revenues are likely to go up because of export growth when sufficient time is allowed for this to take place.

The moral of the story is that it is impossible to predict the extent, and indeed the direction, of the change in trade tax revenues resulting from trade policy changes, and therefore the impact of these episodes on the fiscal balance. This is the main conclusion arising from our inquiry into the relationship between trade policy episodes and the fiscal effects. We turn now to a few country examples.[4]

Table 9.5   Changes in Trade Policies and the Response of Trade Tax Revenues, 1973–90

(annual average growth rate of trade tax revenues)

	Tightening episodes			Liberalizing episodes	
Country	*Period*	*Percent change*	*Country*	*Period*	*Percent change*
Argentina	1982	24	Brazil	1979–80	−50
Brazil	1981–84	64	Chile	1974–79	2
Cameroon	1976–77	19	Colombia	1984–87	39
Colombia	1982	−15	Costa Rica	1986–88	41
Costa Rica	1974	−8	India	1980–85	13
Costa Rica	1982–84	1	Indonesia	1986–89	2
Indonesia	1983–84	−7	Kenya	1976–78	27
Kenya	1971–75	10	Kenya	1988–89	−13
Kenya	1979–84	−6	Korea	1978–79	−7
Mexico	1980–82	15	Korea	1981	16
Morocco	1978	9	Mexico	1977–79	29
Pakistan	1979–80	10	Mexico	1985–90	14
Sri Lanka	1973–75	4	Morocco	1984	−9
Thailand	1983–84	7	Nigeria	1973–74	15
			Sri Lanka	1977	47
			Thailand	1986–88	27
			Turkey	1970	7
			Turkey	1979–80	−29
			Turkey	1983–85	1
			Turkey	1989	10
Average		9	Average		9

Note: Annual average growth rates for trade tax revenues are for the two years following the year in which the trade regime changed.
Source: World Bank data.

Two episodes from Argentina show that tax revenues can increase with a trade liberalization and decrease with a trade tightening. With the trade liberalization measures introduced in 1976, Argentina's tax ratio (tax collection to GDP) increased substantially, from 14 percent in 1976 to 23 percent in 1980. The import-duty ratio (the ratio of import duties to imports) increased from less than 10 percent in 1976 to 23 percent in 1980, principally because of the reductions in QRs. When Argentina tightened trade policies in 1982, however, both the tax ratio and the import-duty ratio declined, the former from 18.7 percent to 16 percent by 1984 and the latter from 5.9 percent to 4.6 percent in 1984. At the same time, total tax revenues increased by 1984.

In Mexico, tax revenues increased both when the government tightened its trade policies in 1980–82 and when it liberalized them during 1985–90. The increase following the tightening was due perhaps to the higher reference prices and hence the implicit tariffs. The increase during liberalization was due to the combination of reduced tariff rates, the withdrawal of reference prices (which valued imports at high prices), and the reduction in QRs. The effects of the first two measures offset the third, and trade revenues declined.

In Morocco, trade liberalization led to a small decline in trade tax revenue. With the liberalization in 1984, import duties and special import taxes were reduced. Subsequently, import tax revenues dropped slightly, from 15.5 percent of import value to 14.1 percent. The decrease from the reduction in the special import tax was offset by the increase in imports when QRs were reduced. It should also be noted that the effect of tariff reductions on budgetary revenue did not contribute to a macroeconomic disequilibrium.

"Import Starvation": Effects on Imports and Outputs

Import restrictions are widely thought to increase domestic output by protecting import-competing production and by diverting domestic spending away from imports toward home-produced goods and services of all kinds. This is the demand effect. Its disadvantage in relation to devaluation is that it only fosters import-competing production, and not exports. In addition, there is the supply-side "import starvation" effect, which is often neglected by advocates of import substitution but which can be very adverse.

First, as table 9-6 shows, in thirteen of the twenty-six trade tightenings, import growth was negative while in one case (Thailand) it remained unchanged, given its mild tightening. In the remaining twelve tightenings, import growth was positive but on average lower than when trade tightening was not present. Particularly strong declines were found in Brazil in 1981–84, Côte d'Ivoire in 1982–84, Mexico in 1980–84, and Nigeria in 1983–86. In these cases, the import level actually fell. In some cases, a few fortuitous circumstances helped imports rise, despite the tightening. Thus, although Côte d'Ivoire in 1975–77 tightened trade policies, imports increased as a result of the coffee boom. Similar situations arose in Colombia 1967–69 because of improved terms of trade and in Brazil in 1988 in response to a rather mild tightening episode.

The import-starvation phenomenon arises from stringent import restrictions that are associated with QR regimes. The QR regime robs the country of essential inputs and spare parts to run its factories or maintain crop yields. This obviously has an adverse effect on output. Thus, for example, in Nigeria (1983–86) and Mexico (1980–84) import growth was strongly negative as was output growth for these periods. Although direct evidence of import starvation is rare, there is adequate anecdotal material to suggest that the phenomenon is real.

Table 9.6   Changes in Trade Policies and Import Response
(average annual growth rate of imports)

	Tightening episodes			Liberalizing episodes	
Country	*Period*	*Percent-age*	*Country*	*Period*	*Percent-age*
Argentina	1971–73	−3	Argentina	1967	17
Argentina	1982	1	Argentina	1976	14
Brazil	1973–74	11	Argentina	1989	0
Brazil	1981–84	−12	Brazil	1967	17
Brazil	1988	12	Brazil	1979–80	−6
Cameroon	1973–74	3	Chile	1968–70	7
Cameroon	1976–77	10	Chile	1974–79	−20
Chile	1971–73	−1	Colombia	1984–87	−1
Colombia	1967	15	Costa Rica	1986–88	9
Colombia	1982	−7	Côte d'Ivoire	1986	−1
Costa Rica	1974	4	India	1966–68	−6
Costa Rica	1982–84	13	India	1980–85	1
Cote d'Ivoire	1975–78	26	Indonesia	1966–71	17
Cote d'Ivoire	1982	−10	Indonesia	1986–89	−9
India	1973–74	−10	Kenya	1976–78	23
Indonesia	1983–84	−1	Kenya	1988–89	1
Kenya	1971–75	−9	Korea	1965–67	42
Kenya	1979–84	−7	Korea	1978–79	3
Mexico	1980–82	−14	Korea	1981	4
Morocco	1978	−2	Mexico	1977–79	26
Nigeria	1967–70	6	Mexico	1985–90	−4
Nigeria	1983–84	−14	Morocco	1984	4
Pakistan	1965–71	3	Nigeria	1973–74	37
Pakistan	1979–80	−9	Nigeria	1986–88	−17
Sri Lanka	1973–75	−2	Pakistan	1972–73	1
Thailand	1983–84	0	Pakistan	1986–88	−1
			Sri Lanka	1968–70	0
			Sri Lanka	1977	28
			Thailand	1986–88	30
			Turkey	1970	21
			Turkey	1979–80	9
			Turkey	1983–85	17
			Turkey	1989	35
Average		0	Average		9

Note: Imports of goods and nonfactor services in 1987 U.S. dollars. Annual average growth rates of imports are for the two years following the year in which the trade regime changed.
Source: World Bank data.

Of course, domestic output and imports could also decline together because of a contraction of aggregate demand, and in crises situations this has clearly been a factor. It is our impression that in many cases output has declined because of tighter import restrictions rather than because of a decline in the demand for output.[5]

INDONESIA. Before the 1966–71 period, import starvation was acute in Indonesia. On the eve of the trade liberalization of 1966–71, the import volume index had fallen to 43.2 (1971 = 100), the lowest level since 1950. Per capita output in 1965 was 9 percent lower than its level in 1958, and capacity utilization in manufacturing was about 20 percent. By many accounts, the economy had shrunk in the period preceding the trade policy liberalization. Imports more than doubled between 1965 and 1972. Output growth rose from 1.1 percent in 1965 to 11 percent in 1968 and averaged more than 7 percent during 1969–71.

SRI LANKA. The increases in QRs following the first oil shock caused the volume of imports to fall 41 percent below the 1970–72 level, which in turn was only 60 percent of the average level of imports in the 1960s. The import cuts fell heaviest on investment goods imports, which fell by 52 percent in 1973–74, whereas intermediate goods fell by 47 percent and consumer goods by 37 percent over these two years. The ratio of imports to GDP dropped from 25.2 percent during 1960–69 to 12.40 percent by 1974.

Import starvation was most pronounced in manufacturing. The growth of manufacturing output turned negative in 1974 after moving up to 3 percent in 1973–74, while capacity utilization fell from 44 percent in 1972 to 40 percent in 1974. In agriculture, a part of the decline in output in plantation crops can be attributed to the declining investment in replanting and substantially reduced fertilizer use. Following the liberalizations in 1977, imports grew by 27 percent and between then and 1980 output rose from 3 percent to nearly 8 percent.

INDIA. Import starvation was evident in India in the mid-1960s, particularly among "maintenance" imports (that is, imports of inputs into further production, including fertilizers), which had been held down for several years by severe import controls (Bell and others 1965). Indeed, shortages of imported materials and components had become an important brake on production. The devaluation of July 1966 was intended to free India from this constraint. There may also have been some import starvation when import controls were tightened in 1974–75, with a consequential dip in the volume of imports of nonfoods other than fertilizers. Because there were also direct cuts in government investments (which were import-intensive), it is difficult to blame import controls directly for the loss of output.

NIGERIA. From 1983 to 1986 Nigeria's overall imports (at constant 1984 prices) declined by nearly 10 percent a year on average. All imports were subject to a highly stringent licensing system. It is estimated that Nigeria's GDP at factor cost fell by 8.5 percent in 1983, by 5.4 percent in 1984, and by another 3.2 percent in 1986, after a small recovery in 1985. Capacity utilization declined because essential imports were in short supply, particularly in manufacturing and construction activities.

Six Country Stories

The following six country stories discuss the motives for using trade policies to deal with macroeconomic imbalances, the types of policies used, and the results. Two of the countries are oil producers (Indonesia and Mexico), one is an enormously successful industrial exporter (Korea), one is an exporter of agricultural products (Sri Lanka), and one is a nonoil mineral exporter (Morocco). Korea liberalized its trade regime earlier than any other country in the sample (in 1965–67), while Mexico liberalized only at the end of the period (in 1985–90). Brazil is our familiar special case.[6]

Brazil

Constantly changing macroeconomic policies left Brazil with five trade policy episodes over the study period, and thus it shared with Argentina the largest number of episodes among our countries.

The first episode, a trade liberalization initiated in 1967, was preceded by a sharp devaluation in 1964 and a three-year stabilization program. The 1967 liberalization included a general reduction in import tariffs and the introduction of export promotion measures, such as the exemption of exports from the value added tax and a duty drawback system. The liberalization was weighted more toward exports rather than imports.

The second episode was a tightening of trade policies in 1973–74 that partly reversed the earlier liberalization. The export promotion measures, however, remained in place. This tightening, along with an increase in foreign borrowing, was Brazil's way of dealing with the first oil price shock. The main instruments used to tighten trade were an increase to 100 percent in the advance deposit requirement for imports, elimination of import financing for goods whose tariff exceeded 55 percent, and an increase in tariffs on consumer goods.

The third episode was a partial and weak liberalization in 1979–80. The measures taken at that time included the phasing out of advance deposit requirements, elimination of major subsidies to exporters, a large devaluation, and an increase in taxes on primary exports.

The fourth and fifth episodes were trade tightenings in 1981–84 and 1988. The 1981–84 episode saw the creation of a limit on import values to match export receipts through restricted allocation of import licenses and increases in the import financing tax. The negative list for QRs was also expanded following the 1982 debt crisis. Consequently, the volume of imports excluding oil fell to their 1970 level. The strongest decline was in capital goods imports. The last episode in 1988 included a reduction of export subsidies and the addition of various items to the QR list.

Brazil's episodes were closely related to macroeconomic shocks, only two of which were external events—the first oil price shock and the debt shock. Brazil tried to grow out of its macroeconomic problems following the first oil price shock, but the sharp reduction on external financing after 1982 put an end to that approach. The tightening of trade policies did not address the primary cause of disequilibrium, namely, the large fiscal deficits. The sharp cuts in imports in the early to the mid-1980s reduced investment, however, and no doubt contributed to the ensuing low growth rates. Although Brazil began to make a fundamental breach with the past in 1991 by adopting a liberal trade regime, its macroeconomic problems remained.

Indonesia

Indonesia benefited from the oil price increases of the 1970s and was hurt in the 1980s when oil prices declined sharply. The 1978 devaluation reversed the appreciation that had resulted from the oil boom and that had an unfavorable side effect on nonoil sectors (Dutch Disease effects). During much of the study period its trade regime was protectionist, and trade policies were used to deal with macroeconomic imbalances on at least three occasions. The first was the 1966–71 stabilization program described in chapter 7, which coincided with trade liberalization. The second occurred in 1983–84, when trade policies were tightened after oil prices fell. The third was a liberalization of the entire trade regime in 1986–89 as part of an overall program to increase the competitiveness of Indonesia's manufactured exports.

Under President Sukarno, Indonesia fell into the throes of disequilibrium in 1965, with the inflation rate running in excess of 600 percent. The rupiah was hopelessly overvalued and illegal transactions were pervasive. This period was one of severe import starvation in which output shrank sharply. President Sukarno was succeeded in 1966 by President Soeharto, who instituted far-reaching stabilization and trade liberalization programs. The liberalization began with the introduction of an export bonus scheme and abolition of the import licensing system. Tariffs were increased at the same time with the understanding that they would be gradually reduced over time. However, tariff reduction was stopped by 1968, and the average tariff actually rose. Trade liberalization, however, helped improve Indonesia's credibility with creditors in the West, and foreign aid helped to balance the budget. The end of import starvation helped increase production, which in turn raised the growth rate of the GNP.

The next trade policy episode was in 1983–84, when QRs were put into place in response to the sharp decline in oil prices and deterioration in Indonesia's nonoil terms of trade. The current account turned from a surplus in 1980 to a deficit of 8 percent of GDP in 1982. The government then devalued the rupiah by 38 percent (which restored the real exchange rate to the November 1978 level) and cut expenditures. It also introduced some export restrictions that reduced the domestic prices of exportables while raising their domestic value added.

The next episode was a trade liberalization in the 1986–89 period. The authorities no longer accepted the balance of payments rationale for trade controls and recognized that the restrictive measures of the early 1980s had not helped Indonesia develop a competitive manufacturing sector. The new trade policy reforms included a reduction of QR coverage from 41 percent of domestic production in 1986 to 29 percent in 1988, and tariff reform that reduced the average import tariff from 29 percent to 19 percent, and also reduced its variance. The number of items subject to QRs was further reduced and tariff bands were further narrowed in the 1988 and 1989 period. On the export side, a duty drawback and exemption scheme for inputs supplemented subsidized credit and preshipment insurance for exports, and most export license requirements were discontinued.

Korea

The relationship between Korea's trade policies and its macroeconomic situation was greatly influenced by the country's long-run goal of trade liberalization. Korea changed its trade regime from an inwardly oriented to an outwardly oriented one in the 1960s. It then responded to macroeconomic shocks by temporarily calling a halt to the trade liberalization process. When its balance of payments situation improved, reform resumed. Rapid growth in exports (except in 1979) helped sustain progress toward trade reform. Also, up to 1974, it had an active exchange rate policy—that is, it was willing to devalue in order to avoid real appreciation resulting from relatively high inflation—which made liberalization easier.

Korea experienced three distinct trade policy episodes (all involving liberalization): in 1965–67, 1978–79, and 1981.

The first episode (1965–67) was characterized chiefly by an increase in the number of items on the automatic approval (AA) list (that is, items not subject to QRs). The relaxation of trade controls began after the exchange rate reform of 1964–65 and was speeded up in the latter half of 1967. This process included a general reduction of tariffs on items on the AA list, a reduction in the number of items subject to a tariff rate exceeding 50 percent, and removal from the QR list of items whose domestic price exceeded the world price by more than 500 percent. Another significant change was the replacement of a negative list by a positive list.

After deteriorating in 1964 and 1965, Korea's balance of payments situation improved. The inflation rate (14.5 percent) was higher than the world rate, but the flexible exchange rate regime adopted in 1964 assured it of export competitiveness. Foreign debt was small, and there was a steady inflow of capital (mostly official funds). Various export incentives introduced during the 1961–65 period were continued. Progress in reducing trade controls slowed down between 1968 and 1977.

The second liberalization episode (1978–79) involved reductions in tariffs and QRs. As before, priority was given to goods whose domestic prices exceeded import prices substantially, while tariffs either replaced QRs or were reduced. The ratio of AA items to all tradeable items increased from 53.8 percent in early 1978 to 68.6 percent in early 1979. Domestic industries were given advance notice of impending import liberalization activities.

The third trade policy episode began in late 1981, when more items were transferred to the AA list. In the early 1980s, the current account deficit rose to high levels and there was concern about the short-term maturity of a large proportion of external debt. Nevertheless, the country did not go back to import restrictions; instead, it accelerated the process of liberalization in 1987 and 1988.

By 1990 the Korean trade regime was clearly a liberal one, even though there were a few pockets of resistance to greater openness, primarily among agricultural producers. Because the country had expanded its exports rapidly and remained creditworthy throughout the 1980s, it could repay debt obligations easily and did not use trade policies for macroeconomic purposes after the 1970s.

Mexico

Mexico's trade policy can be divided into four stages. During the first (1960–76), Mexico adopted a policy of import substitution. Bound by the prevailing ideology and committed to a fixed exchange rate, the country chose to tighten trade policies when its current account deficit started to climb, because of a spending boom that had begun in 1972 and that fueled inflation after 1973. By 1977, some 80 percent of all import categories were subject to licensing.

In the second stage, from 1977 to 1979, larger oil revenues encouraged the government to liberalize trade. By 1980, only 24 percent of import categories were subject to licensing. Tariffs were raised to give import-competing firms a chance to adjust to this change. Export licensing had been used to encourage domestic production and to keep domestic prices low. Now, the number of export categories under license was reduced from 800 to 580 (out of some 3,000). Trade policies during the period were highly influenced by an improvement in the current account and a declining inflation rate. Hence, import controls were reduced, primarily on intermediate and capital goods.

The third stage, running from 1980 to 1985, was marked by a tightening of trade policies in response to rising current account deficits and higher inflation. The discovery of new oil reserves had led to a spending boom in 1980 and 1981 that raised the public sector deficit to some 14 percent of GDP; QR coverage was raised to 100 percent in 1980, and tariffs were increased in 1981 and 1982 as the foreign exchange crisis became acute. The country failed to meet its debt-service obligations in 1982. By then, the current account deficit had risen to nearly 6 percent of GDP.

The fourth stage began in 1985. Strong trade liberalization measures were introduced, especially in 1987. This was part of the stabilization and reform program that followed the 1986–87 balance of payments crisis (see chapter 7). This time, a balance of payments problem was followed by liberalization instead of trade tightening. It was a notable example of the "new liberalization." The proportion of import categories subject to licensing was reduced from 47 percent in 1985 to 25 percent in 1987, and the average tariff to 12 percent. By 1988 the maximum tariff had been reduced to 20 percent, and by 1990 to 13 percent. Trade liberalization was made possible by the commitment of the de la Madrid and Salinas governments to reform, and was helped by the Brady debt-reduction scheme (see chapter 7). Under the Salinas administration, the Mexican trade regime became one of the most liberal regimes in Latin America.

Morocco

Two trade policy episodes can be distinguished in Morocco, the first a tightening of restrictions in 1978, the second a far-reaching liberalization in 1984 that compared favorably with those of Chile in 1974, Sri Lanka in 1977, and Turkey in 1980. Morocco's story is particularly interesting.

Morocco is a country that invariably depended on trade policies to deal with macroeconomic imbalances until giving them up completely after 1984—when it abandoned a fixed exchange rate and adopted strong fiscal and monetary policies. These changes improved the country's ability to deal with external shocks.

Morocco had a highly protected trade regime in the late 1960s and during most of the 1970s. A QR regime had been put into effect in 1967, tariffs were high, and the tariff structure was highly differentiated.

During the first trade policy episode (1978–80), trade policies were tightened through the introduction of advance import deposit requirements and an increase in the special import tax from 8 percent to 12 percent. These special import taxes had often been used before when balance of payments deficits appeared. This episode was the result of a steady two-year decline in the price of phosphates, Morocco's primary export. The tightening was combined with a sharp cut in absorption through a reduction in public investment from 20 percent of GNP in 1976–77 to 13 percent in 1978–80. Devaluation as a part of the solution was rejected, and two-thirds of the current account deficit was financed through foreign borrowing. The current account deficit declined in 1978 and 1979, while GDP growth in 1979 fell to 3.5 percent.

By 1982, private lenders had abandoned Morocco, and the current account deficit could not be financed by borrowing from abroad. In 1983, Morocco was hit by a full-fledged debt crisis.

The main elements of the 1984 liberalization of the entire trade regime were a reduction in the special import tax, elimination of the import deposit requirement, a reduction of the maximum tariff from 400 percent to 45 percent within two years, a broadening of the coverage of the free list to 75 percent of all imports, and a reduction of the average tariff from 66 percent to 39 percent. On the export side, licensing was removed from all but a few products, export procedures were simplified, and monopoly export marketing by the state was virtually abolished. Trade liberalization led to a small decline in trade tax revenues, resulting mainly from the reduction in the special import tax.

The 1984 liberalization did not place added pressure on the balance of payments, thanks to restrictive demand management in combination with favorable external conditions and an active exchange rate policy. Tariff reductions, however, had a negative impact on the budget, and alternative ways to raise revenues did not materialize. As a consequence, customs duties on all items had to be raised 2.5 percent. By 1990, many industrial items had been transferred to the free import list, and the remaining restrictions applied primarily to agricultural imports. The 1984 liberalization was successful in that the use of trade policy as a way of dealing with macroeconomic imbalances ended.

Sri Lanka

Adverse terms of trade, slow export growth, and substantial welfare expenditures forced the government of Sri Lanka to impose stringent import restrictions in 1960. A liberalizing episode in 1968–70 was reversed in 1973, but another such episode during the 1977–80 period was the equivalent of the trade regime liberalizations undertaken by Chile in 1974 and Turkey in 1980. Like those measures, the Sri Lankan overhaul was associated with a change in government leadership and an ideological shift. After this liberalization, Sri Lanka's governments avoided the use of trade policies to deal with macroeconomic imbalances, even though this approach was seriously challenged in the 1980s.

The 1968–70 liberalization was the contribution of a right-of-center government under Prime Minister Dudley Senanayake. About one thousand items on the import quota list were shifted to the free list, and revisions of the tariff schedule reduced the average tariff level and variance. Although the country did not have a formal devaluation, it adopted a dual exchange rate system that implied a depreciated rate for some transactions. Capacity utilization in the manufacturing sector increased rapidly, and GDP growth pulled up the following year, but adverse terms of trade led to an increase in the current account deficit and a sharp fall in reserves. A center-left government led by Mrs. Bandaranaike came to power in 1970. The free list was suspended, and Sri Lanka returned to a quota-based import regime.

The 1973–75 tightening of quotas began with a strong terms-of-trade shock arising from sharp increases in the prices of food imports and oil. The government cut imports—especially investment goods—sharply through QRs, and cut public expenditures as well, most notably Sri Lanka's traditional food subsidies. The fiscal deficit decreased in 1973–74 and was financed by foreign funds and loans from domestic social security funds. Devaluation was ruled out because of the potential political repercussions. The upshot was that capacity utilization fell, inflation rose, and both exports and imports declined. This was a period of strong import starvation when both manufacturing and plantation output fell because of import cuts.

The strongest cuts were in imports of investment goods that led to reduced growth prior to 1977.

The final episode was the liberalization of 1977, again the work of a right-of-center government, this one headed by President Jayawardana. The episode began with a sharp devaluation and a unification of exchange rates, accompanied by the removal of nearly all significant QRs. Some export promotion measures were also introduced, the main one being an import duty rebate scheme.

Exports grew rapidly following the 1977 liberalization. Domestic output expanded in response to increased imports of raw material and intermediate goods. Government revenues increased, thanks to the replacement of QRs with tariffs and devaluation. The positive response to the loosening of trade restrictions was counteracted, however, by large government expenditures on the Mahaweli River Development Program and on housing and urban renewal programs. The rupee appreciated, and a steady decline in the terms of trade, along with the second oil shock, impeded liberalization. Inflation rose to 40 percent and the current account deficit to 20 percent. As a result, macroeconomic policy during the 1982–89 period was dominated by a need to reduce imbalances.

The Sri Lanka story shows that import restrictions tend to be more costly in terms of output and employment than a cut in expenditure combined with a devaluation. The stringent import restrictions in place before 1977 had misallocated resources, but the benefits of the 1977 liberalization were offset to some degree by the huge public expenditure program mentioned above. Sri Lanka's policymakers then became preoccupied with reducing macroeconomic imbalances, and trade reform was relegated to the background.

Conclusion

Variations in trade policy—especially in quantitative import restrictions—appear to have played an important role in the macroeconomic histories of all the eighteen countries. For long periods, trade policy tightenings and occasional liberalizations were the main instruments of balance of payments policy. In the third (crises) period, tightening was associated with devaluations in seven cases. Most tightenings were preceded by a deterioration in the current account. In several, possibly many, cases, tight import restrictions had adverse effects on output, and hence on investment and growth. Variations in restrictions—what we called "episodes" —were usually part of a policy package, so it is difficult to isolate the effects of the episodes themselves. Sometimes they have been followed by current account improvements and sometimes by deterioration.

Our countries had various episodes of trade liberalization, particularly in the 1980s. There have been eight "regime changes," when generalized trade liberalization by a country brought about a break with the past use of QRs for balance of payments purposes and trade became much freer. The 1980s brought a "new liberalization," wherein balance of payments problems triggered liberalization rather than tightening.

There is no reason to expect the tightening of restrictions alone to improve the current account. An improvement requires an increase in national savings or a fall in investment, or both, and tightening would not necessarily bring this about. Where tighter import restrictions shift demand toward home-produced goods and output is initially demand-constrained, higher incomes would indeed result and then savings would normally increase, at least in the short run. At the same time, in an environment of "import starvation," as was present in some of our countries, incomes might fall as a result of tighter restrictions, and so savings might actually decline. A fall in imports would then be more than matched by a decline in exports.

The case for tighter import restrictions or devaluation when the current account has to be improved is that both measures divert demand away from imports toward home-produced goods and increase the profitability of import-competing industries. In addition, devaluation increases the profitability of exports. Thus, these policy instruments compensate for the reduction in demand for home-produced goods resulting from the decline in real expenditures that is usually necessary to bring about a current account improvement. They "switch" demand toward nontraded goods and output toward traded goods. This simple generalization is subject to qualifications: in particular, import restrictions may reduce the competitiveness of export industries when they use imported or import-competing inputs. Leaving this aside, there is a case for "switching policies" (as noted in chapter 1), even though a reduction in real expenditures (absorption) is, in the absence of initial excess capacity, the essential requirement for a current account improvement. Yet, the fundamental question is whether to use import restrictions or devaluation as the "switching" device.

This choice raises issues discussed at length in the literature, where the consensus is that import restrictions should be avoided, except perhaps temporary restrictions in extreme situations. In general, our material does not shed new light on these issues, and a discussion of various arguments for protection or intervention is beyond the scope of this book. Two important points do emerge here, however.

A country may have wide-ranging import restrictions because of earlier balance of payments problems or because of protectionist ideology, as was certainly true of many countries in the 1970s and early 1980s. Then it may be hit by a shock that compels a further reduction in imports. Even if the country devalues, an immediate increase in exports is unlikely, so that, one way or another, imports must fall. Yet imports have already been reduced to bedrock levels by earlier restrictions. The long-term solution is clearly to expand exports. Yet, in the crisis situation, "import starvation," with its adverse effect on domestic output, is then inevitable. The problem was caused by the import-substitution policies of earlier years. The failure to expand exports earlier has made the country excessively dependent on the imports that remain. There is no "slack" in imports. In other words, import starvation—which probably played a large part in the short-term output declines of many Latin American and African countries at times of their balance of payments crisis—could have been avoided if countries had been more outward-oriented to start with. It follows that outward-oriented policies are advantageous not only for the standard reasons, but also because, when they are followed in good times, they make it easier for a country to cope with the inevitable and often unpredictable bad times.

The second point, as is also indicated by simple theory, is that significant, general trade liberalization requires real devaluation either at the same time or beforehand. And, as shown in chapter 8, real devaluation is brought about by nominal devaluation. The evidence is clear that there has been such a connection between exchange rate policy and trade policy. A flexible exchange rate regime does not ensure that trade policy tightening will be avoided. This is apparent from the policies of the four South American countries in the first period of our story and those of many countries in the third period; but a fixed rate regime that rules out the possibility of devaluation makes significant liberalization improbable or even impossible. If a country has significant import restrictions over a wide area (or high tariffs), and it desires eventually to liberalize, then the government of the country must not make a fixed exchange rate commitment. Arguably, the "nominal anchor" argument can provide some justification for a fixed exchange rate policy, but—given that continued import restrictions are not desirable—such a policy should only be implemented (if at all), *after* a large devaluation and the required liberalization have taken place. Furthermore, once the fixed rate regime is in place, there is the danger that history will repeat itself: balance of payments problems develop, for whatever reason, and the only switching instruments available, namely, tariffs and quantitative import restrictions, will be used.

Postscript

Since 1990, our countries have experienced several trade policy episodes. These were trade liberalizations that were a continuation of the liberalization trends that began in the 1984–90 period. They appeared with force during 1990–92. Nowhere were these trends as strong as in the Latin American countries, particularly in Argentina, Brazil, and Colombia, with some adjustments to the already liberalized trade regimes in Chile and Mexico. Trade policies also underwent a significant change in India.

In Argentina by January 1992, import licensing was abolished for all but twenty-five products in the automobile sector and some items that were restricted on health and safety grounds. Tariffs were set at a three-band structure with zero tariffs for raw materials and noncompeting imports, 11 percent for intermediate goods, and 22 percent for finished goods and competing capital goods. All the export taxes were removed in late 1991.

In Brazil, the import licensing system was abandoned by 1990 and the import planning authority was closed down. A tariff reduction program was instituted with a target average tariff of 14.3 percent and a range of 35 percent by July 1993. Almost all the export taxes were abolished.

Colombia introduced a trade liberalization program in 1990 and decided to accelerate the program in late 1991. All import licensing requirements were abolished except for those justified by health and safety considerations. Under the tariff reduction program, the average tariff rate has been about 12 percent and has ranged from 0 to 40 percent. Colombia proposed to adopt a common external tariff with a four-tier structure of 0 to 20 percent by 1994, when the Andean Group would be formally established. Mexico and Chile had liberalized substantially by 1989 but subsequently announced further reductions in tariffs and in the variance in their structure.

For the Latin American countries as group, regional integration became an important consideration in the design of tariff reforms. The prospective North American Free Trade Agreement of Mexico with the United States and Canada influenced these tariff reforms. The new Andean Group, which is to be formed among Bolivia, Chile, Ecuador, Peru, and Venezuela, became a factor in the tariff revisions of Colombia. Argentina and Brazil were expected to adopt a common external tariff under the Mercosur arrangements by 1994.

India's trade liberalization measures were a significant departure from its past policies, even though they were not as extensive as in Latin America. In 1991 and 1992, the government made the QR regime less stringent and thus allowed the import of capital and intermediate goods virtually free. The previous import list, which had some twenty-six import categories, was made into a single negative list. Import tariffs were reduced from a maximum of 150 percent to 110 percent, while the tariff rates for the import of capital goods were reduced in the range of 80 to 55 percent. Meanwhile, export subsidies were eliminated and a scheme to grant freely tradable import entitlements to exporters was introduced. These reforms were made possible by the exchange rate reform, which introduced a floating rate that applies to 60 percent of all foreign exchange transactions.

Appendix 9A

This appendix examines cross-country relationships between the different trade policy episodes and the behavior of variables such as the current account deficit and the nominal exchange rate.[7] The analysis is based on a cross-sectional sample of fifty-nine trade episodes. The episodes are transformed into a qualitative variable that represents the episode characteristic (that is, 1 for tightening of trade policies, 0 for no change in the trade policies, and -1 for loosening of trade controls). Since trade policy changes are fairly isolated events that occur only sporadically, they are not easily subject to time-series regression methodology. This limitation forces the analysis to be somewhat descriptive. Therefore this appendix provides only a few simple correlations aimed at detecting some general regularities across countries.[8]

Hypothesis 1

First we examine the proposition that changes in trade controls are triggered by a current account deficit in the previous year. The regression that attempts to identify the correlation is

(9A-1) TI_t = $a + b \, CA_{t-1}$
   TI = 1 if there is a tightening of trade policies
   TI = 0 if there is a liberalizing of trade policies
   CA = Current account balance over GDP (that is, a negative figure means deficit in current account).

The results of the probit[9] analysis shows that we are more likely to encounter tightening in the trade policies when the countries experienced a deficit in the current account in the previous year, that is:[10]

(9A-2) TI_t = 0.489*** - 0.107 CA_{t-1}***
      (-3.50)   (-3.64)
   N = 153 LL = -97.71 AL = 0.53.

We have observed 153 events of trade policy tightening and liberalizing where the duration of each episode is enumerated.[11] When the data are restricted to the first year of each episode, the correlation between the trade episode and the current deficit increases, namely:

(9A-3) TI_t = -0.568** - 0.122** CA_{t-1}
      (-2.32)   (-2.51)
   N = 57 LL = -35.27 AL = 0.539.

The results indicate that there is a higher probability that tightening episodes are associated with current account deficits. Of course, not all current account deficits are followed by tightening.

The probit regressions for the two periods 1965–83 and 1984–89 are significantly different. While the coefficient for the lagged current account balance, (CA_{t-1}), is highly significant for the period 1965–83, it is not so for the period 1984–89. This points to significant differences in the response to current account balances between these two periods.

(9A-3a)   1965–83: $TI_t = -0.172 - 0.116CA_{t-1}$***
                    (-1.06) (-3.30)
           $N = 115$ $LL = -71.84$ $AL = 0.54$

(9A-3b)   1984–89: $TI_t = -0.854 - 0.053CA_{t-1}$***
                    (-2.60) (-0.68)
           $N = 37$ $LL = -20.29$ $AL = 0.58$.

Trade policy episodes from 1965 to 1983 responded much more clearly to the current account balances than did the episodes for 1984–89. For the latter period, the trade policy episodes show a weak relationship to the current account balances, which is further confirmed when we run an explicit regression for structural change using a dummy variable for the year effect.

(9A-3c) $TI_t = -0.317* -0.139CA_{t-1}$*** $+0.176D_t$***
                  (-2.22) (-4.07)   (2.98)
           $N = 153$ $LL = -94.36$ $Al = 0.54$

where D_t is zero for the period 1965–83 and 1 for the period 1984–89.

The structural change is indicated by the significant difference between intercepts for the two time periods 1965–83 and 1984–89.

Hypothesis 2

The second hypothesis relates the behavior of trade policies to the behavior of the nominal exchange rate. A qualitative variable *Dev* is constructed using the distinction made in chapter 8 between stepwise devaluations and devaluations that are followed by a crawling peg regime. This variable is defined as

> $Dev = 1$ if there is a stepwise nominal devaluation over 10 percent
> $Dev = 0$ otherwise.

The relation between devaluations and trade policies is specified as

(9A-4) $Dev_t = a + b\ TI_t$
          with: $TI = 1$ if there is a tightening on the trade policies
                 $TI = 0$ if there is no change on the trade policies
                 $TI = -1$ if there is a liberalizing of trade policies.

A coefficient of $b < 0$ will indicate a negative correlation between tightening and nominal stepwise devaluations. The result supports this proposition. Equation (9-5) supports the hypothesis that liberalizing—and not tightening—of trade policies has a greater probability of going together with devaluations of the nominal exchange rate.

(9A-5) $Dev_t = -0.765^{***} -0.254^{**} TI_t$
$$\qquad\qquad (-11.55) \qquad (-2.27)$$
$$N = 450 \; LL = -237.01 \; AL = 0.59.$$

Hypothesis 3

The third element to be investigated is the link between the behavior of the current account and trade policies. Specifically, we want to measure the impact of both liberalizing and tightening of the trade policies on the current account. To do so, we estimate a linear reduced model of the current account, namely:

(9A-6) $CA = f(RER, FD, ED, TT)$

where RER = the real exchange rate index defined as

$$RER_j \equiv \frac{\sum_{i=1}^{N} \alpha_i (WPI_i e_i us) \frac{e_j}{us}}{CPI_j} \qquad\qquad \alpha_i = \frac{GDP_i}{\sum_{i=1}^{N} GDP_i}$$

$$\sum_{i=1}^{N} = 1$$

where i = OECD countries, j = countries of the project, FD = fiscal deficit over GDP (a negative figure implies a deficit), and ED = change in the output of the OECD countries.

The output of the OECD countries was defined as:

$$GDP_{OECD} = \sum_{i=1}^{N} GDP_i$$

where $j = 1–18$, i = OECD 20 countries, and TT = terms of trade (Px/Pm).

Table 9A.1 The Relationship between the Current Account and Trade Policies (Panel Data Regressions Estimated by the AR(1) Method)

	Real exchange rate	Fiscal deficit/ GDP	GDP growth OECD	Terms of trade	Trade policy					RBAR**2	DB	DF
	t	t-1	t-1	t	t	t-1	t-2	t-3	t-4			
I	0.022^a (2.56)	0.166^c (1.73)	0.394^c (1.67)	0.020^b (2.16)						0.389	10.94^b	401
II	0.023^a (2.61)	0.169 (1.56)	0.402^c (1.69)	0.021^b (2.19)	0.143 (0.22)					0.385	9.53^b	400
III	0.023^a (2.62)	0.198^c (1.78)	0.445^c (1.89)	0.022^b (2.30)		1.223^b (1.91)				0.39	11.28^b	382
IV	0.023^b (2.29)	0.206^c (1.88)	0.457^c (1.74)	0.019^c (1.82)			1.180^c (1.67)			0.388	10.19^b	364
V	0.025^b (2.40)	0.184 (1.56)	0.402 (1.49)	0.021 (1.85)				0.380 (0.563)		0.383	8.41^b	346
VI	0.028^b (2.48)	0.174 (1.36)	0.380 (1.30)	0.024^c (1.91)					-0.485 (-0.63)	0.385	8.4^b	328

a. Indicates statistically significant at 1 percent level.
b. Indicates statistically significant at 5 percent level.
c. Indicates statistically significant at 10 percent level.
Note: GB is the Godfrey-Breusch test for autocorrelation. Figures in parentheses are *t* statistics. DF are the degrees of freedom.
Source: Authors' analyses.

The first two variables capture the internal conditions while the last two capture the external situation, and the expected sign for all of them is positive. The model will also include the qualitative variable for change in trade controls, that is:

TI = 1 if there is a tightening of trade policies
TI = 0 if there is no change on the trade policies
TI = -1 if there is a loosening on the trade policies

Given the simultaneous determination of the current account and the fiscal deficit, a one-period lag of the latter was used as the instrumental variable.

Table 9-7 presents the results of the panel data regressions estimated by AR(1) method. As the table shows, all the variables emerge statistically significant and with the expected sign. Also the Godfrey-Breusch test indicates the absence of serial correlation.[13] In terms of the units in which the variables are expressed, the results suggest that, say, a 1 percent drop in last year's output of the OECD countries will imply a deterioration of the current account by roughly half a point.

Regressions II to VI include the trade policy variable (TI). They show that trade policies affect the current account with a one-year lag. Thus, a tightening of the trade policies last year has a positive effect on this and next year's current account balance. The results also show that this is a short-term effect. In fact, when the trade policy variable is introduced with a lag larger than three years, it has no impact on the current account. This result supports the hypothesis that trade policy tightening improves the current account only in the short run.

Chapter 10

Fiscal and Monetary Policies

Governments play diverse and sometimes conflicting roles in society. Since the middle of the century, public expectations have risen to the point where governments are now asked to achieve growth, to eliminate unemployment, and to ensure social justice. These expectations were fed both by the socialist and by the Keynesian revolutions in thinking that occurred in the first half of the century. At its extreme, the former supplanted both decentralized and monopoly capitalism with central planning and state control of economic activity. The latter emphasized harnessing and guiding decentralized capitalism, partly through regulation, partly through the use of the government budget to compensate for the macroeconomic instabilities thought to be inherent in capitalism, and partly through the use of taxes and expenditures to ensure widespread distribution of the economic well-being made possible by capitalism.

In the 1950s and 1960s, government after government came to power promising and expecting to lead poor countries to the levels of prosperity known to be attainable from the experiences of Europe and North America. This prospect was in some respects the foundation of anticolonialism: if only the imperial shackles could be undone, newly independent countries could successfully pursue and achieve prosperity, led by the government. This was the psychological milieu of the 1960s and into the 1970s.

The government performs many functions. At a minimum, it sets the basic economic and social ground-rules for its citizens, it establishes a system for resolving their disputes, and it preserves domestic order and provides for defense against external enemies. The new expectations called for much more. The government was also to become the leading educator, the provider of social cohesion among diverse and sometimes historically antagonistic regions or factions, the founder of a social safety system for the poorest and least fortunate members of society, and also the entrepreneur and investor to ensure future growth. All these roles require resources, the amount increasing with the ambition under each heading. Although demands for resources under an expansive view of government are virtually unlimited, governments typically do not spend all the output of a country, even under Communist regimes. The reason is that the government must somehow finance its expenditures, and the available finance is limited, even in the extreme case when it simply prints money, since the public will find substitutes for a rapidly depreciating currency.

The government budget is supposed to bring the various elements of expenditure and financing together into a coherent whole, designed to ensure that expenditures are consistent both with its social objectives and with available financing, and to provide a disciplinary framework for its spending agents.

The purpose of this chapter is to examine fiscal and closely associated monetary policy in developing countries mainly with respect to just one of its many functions, namely, to mitigate or adjust to macroeconomic disturbances that have their origin elsewhere; in other words, to promote economic stabilization. Sometimes stabilization efforts may focus on increasing domestic output and employment (internal balance), at other times on improving the balance of payments (external balance). In either case, it is important to determine whether fiscal and monetary policy has been a possible source of macroeconomic disturbance, either because stabilization policy has gone awry, or because the government has not been conscious of the possible destabilizing role of its actions, or because it has been willing to ignore this effect for the sake of other objectives, such as stepping up the country's rate of investment. Here the aim is not to review specific episodes already covered in previous chapters, but rather to analyze the character of fiscal and monetary policies in their stabilizing or destabilizing roles in our eighteen countries, and through them to gain some insight into the policies of other developing countries.

Perhaps not surprisingly, in view of the discussion in earlier chapters, fiscal policy did not generally play a stabilizing role in most of our countries, and in several of them it was clearly destabilizing. During the 1980s, following the debt crisis, stabilization efforts necessarily focused predominantly on reestablishing external balance.

The Central Government Budget

First, however, it is helpful to examine the broad trends over the past two decades in government expenditure, revenues, and sources of financing. Some attention also needs to be given to state-owned enterprises and seigniorage as a source of finance.

Trends in Government Expenditure

Most of our countries experienced a marked increase in the ratio of central government expenditure (plus net lending) to GDP in the years from 1971 to 1982. This increase reflects the ambitious role for government discussed in chapter 2. In

Table 10.1   Types of Expenditure, Central Government
(percentage of GDP)

Expenditure	1972	1977	1982	1987
Industrial countries[a]				
Expenditures and net lending	24.9	28.1	31.8	31.0
Capital expenditures	1.8	1.9	1.8	1.3
Interest	1.2	1.7	3.1	3.8
Subsidies and other transfers	12.8	15.7	17.2	16.8
Net lending	1.0	1.0	1.0	0.2[b]
Current purchases of goods and services	8.3	7.8	8.8	8.9
Overall surplus	1.5	-3.3	-4.3	-3.5
Nonoil developing countries				
Expenditures and net lending	22.2	24.1	27.7	28.6
Capital expenditures	4.1	4.1	4.2	3.5
Interest	1.2	1.7	2.7	5.1
Transfers	6.8	7.2	9.3	7.9
Net lending	1.4[b]	2.5[b]	3.3	3.4[b]
Current purchases of goods and services	8.8	8.6	8.4	8.7
Overall surplus	-3.4	-5.2	-6.6	-6.5

a. Excludes Japan.
b. Estimated.
Source: IMF, *Supplement on Government Finance* (1986); *Government Finance Statistics Yearbook* (1989, pp. 71–79, 95–97); IMF, *International Financial Statistics* (1990).

nonoil developing countries as a group, the ratio rose from 22 percent in 1972 to 28 percent in 1982, or more than five percentage points.[1] The developing countries were not alone in this trend: developed countries showed an increase of over seven percentage points, from 25 percent of GDP in 1972 to 32 percent in 1982, a recession year (table 10-1). Our 18 countries all show an increase over this period except for Chile, where the ratio declined from the extraordinary 44 percent reached under the Allende regime in 1972 to 31 percent in 1982; and Costa Rica, where the ratio declined from 20 percent to 18 percent over the same period, having risen to a peak of 25 percent in 1980 (table 10-2). Colombia, Pakistan, and Thailand show only modest increases.

By 1982 the ratio of central government expenditure to GDP among our countries ranged from a low of 16 percent in Colombia to a high of 39 percent in Morocco, with all other countries (except Costa Rica, at 18 percent) lying between 20 and 35 percent (table 10-2).[2]

In the industrialized countries as a group, the ratio of government expenditure to GDP peaked in the early 1980s and fell by three percentage points between 1982

Table 10.2   Central Government Expenditures Plus Net Lending
(percentage of GDP)

Country	1967	1972	1977	1982	1987
Argentina	—	19.1	16.9	22.9	22.2
Brazil	11.2	19.5	23.5	27.6	45.4
Cameroon	—	17.9^d	17.2	20.5	22.0
Chile	19.9	43.9	32.9	31.2	28.5
Colombia	8.3	13.1	11.1	16.1	13.8
Costa Rica	14.2^a	19.7	19.8	18.4	27.6
Côte d'Ivoire	22.1^a	26.3	26.5	32.1	26.9^g
India	12.3	14.4^c	17.2	18.9	23.4
Indonesia	9.0^a	14.9	20.2	22.5	22.5
Kenya	—	24.0	23.3	32.4	29.8
Korea	18.2	17.9	18.3	22.0	16.8
Mexico	—	13.4	16.3	30.4	22.7
Morocco	23.4	23.0	40.2	38.9	30.2
Nigeria	—	14.8	27.0	14.6^g	24.5
Pakistan	13.3	19.9^b	22.5	21.2	24.8
Sri Lanka	28.3	25.4^b	23.2	33.8	32.5
Thailand	15.3	18.3	17.2	21.7	19.4
Turkey	—	21.7	25.9	23.1^f	21.9

— Not available.
a. 1968.
b. 1973.
c. 1974.
d. 1975.
f. 1981.
g. 1984.
Note: Figures may differ from published national figures because of the inclusion of separately budgeted state enterprises that serve governmental functions.
Source: IMF, *International Financial Statistics, 1972 Supplement; Supplement on Government Finance* (1986, pp. 78–79); *Government Finance Statistics Yearbook* (1990), pp. 94–95; Berthélemy and Bourguignon (forthcoming).

and 1987, because of a strong political reaction in many countries to what came to be considered excessive growth in government. In developing countries as a group, in contrast, the ratio continued to rise over the 1980s, although a rising interest burden accounted for all of this rise, and then some. The ratio continued to rise in nine of our countries, although at a more modest rate than it had during the preceding five years. In the other nine, the ratio peaked in the period 1980–83, and receded subsequently, as in the industrialized countries.

A number of our countries are federal in structure, and others have in addition devolved expenditure responsibility and taxing powers to the lower levels of government to varying degrees. Spending by provincial (= state) governments posed a serious problem in some countries—notably Argentina, Brazil, and

Nigeria—but in general central government expenditures will give an idea of the stabilizing or destabilizing role of fiscal policy, in part because in most countries the central government is the principal source of finance for state and local governments. State-owned enterprises (SOEs) and the central bank will be considered separately.

As a share of central government expenditure plus net lending, the large increases for all nonoil developing countries were concentrated in interest payments (from 1.2 percent of GDP in 1972 to 2.7 percent in 1982, and to 5.1 percent in 1987), and net lending to enterprises, public and private (from 1.6 percent in 1972 to 3.3 percent in 1982). Current purchases of goods and services declined by 0.4 percent of GDP over the same period, and recovered most of that by 1987. Subsidies and transfers rose during 1972–82, but declined sharply in the 1980s. Surprisingly, in view of the strong investment boom of the late 1970s, direct capital expenditures by central government remained unchanged in terms of GDP between 1972 and 1982, but declined 0.7 percentage points by 1987 (table 10-1).[3]

Defense spending among our countries in 1982 ranged from only 0.5 percent of GDP in Costa Rica and Mexico to 6.6 percent in Pakistan and 9.5 percent in Chile (table 10-3). Ten of the eighteen countries had defense expenditures of less than 4 percent of GDP. Argentina, Chile, Kenya, Morocco, and Thailand showed significant increases over the period 1972–82, that for Chile (+7.0) being especial-

Table 10.3   Defense Expenditures
(percent of GDP)

Country	1972	1982	1987	1989
Argentina	1.6	6.0	3.4	3.0
Brazil	1.6	1.6	1.1	1.2
Cameroon	1.7	1.7	2.1	2.1[a]
Chile	2.5	9.5	6.8	6.5
Colombia	1.2	1.8	2.0	2.6
Costa Rica	0.5	0.5	0.5	0.4
Cote d'Ivoire	1.2	1.1	1.2	1.2
India	3.3	3.1	3.9	3.3
Indonesia	3.6	4.2	2.5	2.0
Kenya	1.4	3.8	3.0	2.6[a]
Korea	4.8	5.8	4.5	4.4
Mexico	0.6	0.5	0.5	0.5[b]
Morocco	2.8	6.5	5.0	4.3
Nigeria	4.6	1.8	0.7	1.1
Pakistan	6.8	6.6	7.1	6.7
Sri Lanka	1.1	1.1	5.1	2.9
Thailand	3.5	4.9	4.3	3.2
Turkey	4.3	5.2	4.6	3.9

a. 1987.
b. 1988.
Source: SIPRI Yearbook, *World Armaments and Disarmament* (1990, 1991).

Table 10.4   Central Government Capital Expenditures
(percentage of GDP)

Country	1972	1977	1982	1987
Argentina	—	3.8	2.7	1.7
Brazil	2.4	1.5	1.8	1.3
Cameroon	5.0	5.9	8.7	9.1[a]
Chile	8.7	3.7	2.2	3.7
Colombia	5.8	4.1	3.9	2.7
Costa Rica	4.1	4.3	2.5	3.5
Côte d'Ivoire	6.0	9.3	8.3	5.5
India	1.6	1.5	1.9	2.5
Indonesia	6.0	8.0	10.4	6.6
Kenya	5.3	5.2	4.7	5.4
Korea	5.1	2.5	3.4	2.4
Mexico	3.6	3.4	6.8	3.7
Morocco	5.4	19.7	13.2	6.1
Nigeria	2.7	9.6	—	8.1
Pakistan	3.6	3.5	2.9	2.8[b]
Sri Lanka	5.7	5.5	15.5	11.6
Thailand	5.1	4.8	4.9	3.1
Turkey	6.9	7.1	6.7	3.9

— Not available.
a. 1985.
b. 1986.
Source: Author's calculations from IMF, *Supplement on Government Finance* (1986), country pages. For 1987, *Government Finance Statistics Yearbook* (1990, pp. 76–77, 94–95).

ly noteworthy, while five countries registered declines. Kenya was concerned with irredentist movements in Somalia, and Morocco had a serious insurgency over the Spanish Sahara. Korea's increase was a response to pressures by the United States, as Korea prospered, for greater burden-sharing in defense against the Democratic People's Republic of Korea, rather than to an actual change in the military threat. Argentina fought Britain over the Falkland Islands in 1982, and Argentina's military government and diplomacy were sufficiently threatening over territory claimed and occupied by Chile to induce a significant increase in Chilean defense spending. Defense spending declined in most of our countries during the 1980s, the notable exceptions being India, Pakistan, and Sri Lanka.[4]

Capital spending by the central government in our countries in 1982 ranged from lows of 1.8 percent of GDP in Brazil and 1.9 percent in India—figures that will surprise most observers, even after allowing for the fact that they must be roughly doubled to allow for state and local government capital expenditures—to 13.2 percent in Morocco and 15.5 percent in Sri Lanka, with a simple average of 5.9 percent (table 10-4). Seven of our countries showed significant increases over the period 1972–82, ranging from two to ten percentage points (the highest increase, in Sri Lanka, was associated with the ambitious Mahaweli power and irrigation project and other large public investments). A number of countries experienced declines, most notably Chile (-6.5 percentage points). The investment boom discussed in chapter 3, of course, included the countries mentioned above, but there was also a boom in investment by SOEs in a number of other countries, notably Brazil and Turkey, plus a sharp rise and fall in Costa Rica between 1977 and 1982.[5] Central government capital expenditure fell between 1982 and 1987 in thirteen of the countries, most sharply in Morocco and Sri Lanka.

Many countries had only modest (less than 1 percent of GDP) *net lending* programs in 1982, under which the central government acted as a financial intermediary, borrowing at home or abroad and relending to SOEs or private enterprises (table 10-5). Such activity was more than 2 percent of GDP in Kenya, Argentina, Korea, Côte d'Ivoire, and Pakistan, and was especially significant in Brazil (at 6.9 percent of GDP) and India (5.6). Brazil (+4.9 percent of GDP), India (+2.3), and Ko-

Table 10.5   Net Lending by Central Government

Country	1972	1977	1982	1987
Argentina	—	1.3	2.2	2.2
Brazil	2.0	4.8	6.9	21.2
Cameroon	0.1[a]	0.1	—	—
Chile	1.3	0.9	-2.9	-0.8
Colombia	0.3	-0.2	0.6[b]	0.0
Costa Rica	1.9	0.5	-0.1	0.3
Côte d'Ivoire	—	—	3.1[c]	0.4
India	3.3[d]	4.4	5.6	5.0
Indonesia	0.8	1.6	0.7	-0.2
Kenya	1.5	1.4	2.1	0.6
Korea	-0.1	2.6	2.9	1.1
Mexico	1.5	0.9	1.5	2.2
Morocco	-0.1	1.5	0.2	-0.0
Nigeria	2.7	5.5	—	0.9
Pakistan	3.2[e]	6.3	4.0	4.1
Sri Lanka	0.2[e]	0.2	0.6	0.8
Thailand	0.6	0.3	0.3	0.4
Turkey	0.1	1.1	0.5[b]	0.0

— Not available.
a. 1975.
b. 1981.
c. 1980.
d. 1974.
e. 1973.
Source: Author's calculations from IMF, *Supplement on Government Finance* (1986), country pages. For 1987, *Government Finance Statistics Yearbook* (1990, pp. 76–77, 94–95).

rea (+3.0) had substantial increases in net lending between 1972 and 1982, while Chile (-4.2) had a sharp reduction. This activity generally declined during the 1980s, although in Brazil it rose to an astounding 21 percent of GDP by 1987.[6]

Trends in Government Revenue

Central government revenues also increased over the period 1972–82, from 18.3 to 20.6 percent of GDP for all nonoil developing countries; that is, they rose by 2.3 percentage points, in comparison with expenditures that moved up 5.1 percentage points. Our countries reflected this general pattern, with half of them showing a rise of less than 2+ percentage points, and only Chile showing a decline (yet remaining in 1982 the most heavily taxed among our countries). Revenues generally increased further in the 1980s, but at a slower rate, and most show substantial increases over the entire 1967–87 period (table 10-6). However, the capacity to raise revenue varied greatly from country to country; by the late 1980s, central government revenues as a share of GDP ranged from 13 percent in Colombia to 29 percent in Chile, with half the countries clustered around 17–19 percent.[7]

The general rise in revenues over time reflected a gradual extension of tax coverage (and, in the case of oil exporters, a growth in oil revenues) rather than a high elasticity of revenue with respect to income growth. As shown in table 10-7, taxes on commodities, whether imports, exports, or domestic sales, accounted for more than half the revenue in ten of our eighteen countries in 1977, and for more than 40 percent of total revenues in fourteen of them. (The exceptions are Argentina, Brazil, Indonesia, and Nigeria, and the latter two drop below those thresholds because of oil revenue.) These taxes generally grow more slowly than income in developed countries, but in less developed countries they often grow proportionally with income, because of the commodity composition of the excise taxes.[8] Heavy reliance on foreign trade taxes exposes government revenues to fluctuations in demand for exports or to import squeezes necessitated by balance of payments difficulties; but the share of foreign trade taxes in total revenues has generally declined over time, and by 1989 was below 25 percent in all but three of our countries.

Financing

With expenditures rising more rapidly than revenues, deficits for all nonoil developing countries also grew, from 3.5 to 6.3 percent of GDP from 1972 to 1982. The same pattern obtained in industrial countries: revenues grew from 25.0 to 29.8 percent of GDP, that is, by 4.8 percentage points, compared with the 8.0 percentage point increase in expenditures (table 10-1). Over the subsequent five years, 1982–

Table 10.6   Central Government Revenue
(percentage of GDP)

Country	1967	1972	1977	1982	1987
Argentina	—	14.4	14.1	15.6	18.8
Brazil	9.5	19.0	22.4	24.9	33.3
Cameroon	—	—	16.2	18.0	18.6
Chile	19.2	30.9	30.6	29.5	29.0
Colombia	8.1	10.4	11.5	11.3	13.1
Costa Rica	12.6[a]	15.3	16.7	17.4	24.7
Côte d'Ivoire	24.2[a]	25.7	38.7	24.2	29.7[b]
India	7.8	10.8[c]	12.6	12.8	14.5
Indonesia	7.6[a]	12.4	18.2	19.3	19.3
Kenya	—	19.3	18.6	22.7	22.2
Korea	15.5	13.4	16.6	18.3	17.9
Mexico	8.6[d]	10.3	13.0	16.1	17.5
Morocco	18.2	18.8	24.8	26.2	23.5
Nigeria	—	13.7	21.3	10.5	15.7
Pakistan	7.0	12.4[e]	13.5	15.5	17.3
Sri Lanka	6.9	19.9[e]	17.2	16.3	21.4
Thailand	13.8	13.2	13.6	14.7	17.4
Turkey	—	19.6	20.2	20.0	17.5

—- Not available.
a. 1968.
b. 1985.
c. 1974.
d. 1964.
e. 1973.
Source: IMF, *International Financial Statistics, 1972 Supplement; Supplement on Government Finance,* 11 (1986, pp. 70–71); *Government Finance Statistics Yearbook,* (1990, pp. 86–87); Berthélemy and Bourguignon, forthcoming, annex I. Mexico for 1964 excludes net income of state owned enterprises and state agencies, amounting to 4.5 percent of GDP (Hansen 1971, p. 47).

87, deficits declined sharply in the industrialized countries but continued to rise slightly in the developing countries, as expenditures rose slightly and revenues declined slightly.

Deficits must be financed, either by borrowing or (temporarily) by drawing down cash balances. Borrowing can take place from foreigners (public or private), from domestic lenders (nonbanks or banks), and among banks, from commercial banks or from the central bank. Borrowing from banks involves monetizing the deficit, in the sense that on normal definitions (M1 or M2) the money supply increases, except insofar as bank lending to the government leads to a corresponding reduction in loans to the private sector. This proposition applies alike to deposit banks and to the central bank. Table 10-8 shows the sources of finance used by our

Table 10.7 **Sources of Central Government Revenue & Grants, 1977, 1989**
(percent of total revenue)

Country	On incomes & profits 1977	On incomes & profits 1989	On wages 1977	On wages 1989	On goods & services 1977	On goods & services 1989	Exports & imports 1977	Exports & imports 1989	Other taxes 1977	Other taxes 1989	Non-tax revenue 1977	Non-tax revenue 1989	Grants 1977	Grants 1989
Argentina	5.8	5.5	22.1	33.0	28.5	15.4	15.4	25.5	14.2	10.3	14.0	8.7	0.0	0.0
Brazil	17.0	4.8	33.6	5.8	29.9	3.8	5.6	0.5	7.0	0.8	6.0	84.1	0.9	0.2
Cameroon	13.6	45.2	7.1	6.4	17.1	20.2	43.4	14.0	10.0	9.1	5.3	5.1	3.5	0.0
Chile	11.4	21.8[a]	11.5	5.6[a]	35.9	34.7[a]	7.4	9.2[a]	7.0	5.3	22.9	23.5[a]	3.9	0.0
Colombia	28.5	27.4	14.0	12.4	21.3	27.3	21.8	17.5	5.1	6.6	7.1	7.4	2.1	1.4
Costa Rica	17.1	8.8	16.4	28.3	33.0	16.3	23.0	31.0	1.7	1.5	8.7	14.1	0.2	0.0
Côte d'Ivoire	12.3	14.5	5.5	6.7	23.9	24.1	40.9	35.0	5.8	10.6	11.4	9.0	0.2	0.0
India	20.0	14.3	0.0	0.0	39.7	33.8	16.1	26.1	0.8	0.4	20.6	24.0	2.8	1.3
Indonesia	67.4	57.5	0.0	0.0	13.2	25.1	10.1	6.0	1.9	3.0	7.3	8.3	0.0	0.0
Kenya	33.7	24.7	0.0	0.0	31.8	38.6	16.6	14.3	1.0	1.1	13.4	11.5	3.7	9.9
Korea	24.9	34.1	0.9	4.3	44.3	31.8	16.1	10.7	3.7	5.4	10.2	13.7	0.0	0.0
Mexico	34.1	25.3	15.9	9.8	34.0	45.7	9.7	4.4	1.9	0.6	4.3	14.2	0.1	0.0
Morocco	20.5	18.9[b]	4.5	4.9[b]	34.0	45.8[b]	19.8	12.6[b]	6.3	6.9	14.8	10.7[b]	0.0	0.0
Nigeria	60.6	34.9[b]	0.0	0.0	2.2	4.5[b]	13.0	5.8[b]	0.1	0.0	24.1	54.9[b]	0.0	0.0
Pakistan	12.3	9.0	0.0	0.0	33.7	32.6	30.5	28.0	0.2	0.2	18.3	25.0	5.1	5.2
Sri Lanka	13.8	8.5	0.0	0.0	32.0	38.4	35.4	27.3	1.5	4.5	9.8	10.7	7.4	10.6
Thailand	15.6	20.2	0.1	0.1	46.4	44.4	25.9	21.7	1.8	3.1	8.9	8.5	1.2	2.0
Turkey	46.9	42.9	0.0	0.0	24.8	29.3	15.9	6.3	6.5	3.1	5.8	18.1	0.0	0.4

a. 1988.
b. 1987.

Source: IMF, International Financial Statistics, Supplement on Government Finance, No. 11 (1986), pp. 18–29 IMF, Government Finance Statistics Yearbook (1991), pp. 52–57 (1992), pp.56–61.

Table 10.8 Financing Central Government Deficits, 1980, 1989

(as a percent of expenditures and net lending)

Country	Deficit/GDP		Deficit		Foreign Borrowing		Domestic Borrowing — Total		Domestic Borrowing — Deposit banks		Domestic Borrowing — Central bank	
	1980	1989	1980	1989	1980	1989	1980	1989	1980	1989	1980	1989
Argentina	3.6	2.7[a]	17.2	16.9[a]	0.4	8.1[a]	16.8	8.8[a]	—	-0.1	—	-1.6[b]
Brazil	2.3[c]	16.1	9.0[b]	14.9	-0.1[c]	0.2[d]	9.1[c]	36.9[d]	7.0[c]	0.4[d]	-1.8[c]	38.3[d]
Cameroon	-0.5	2.9[a]	-3.2	15.5	4.4	13.4	-7.7	2.0	-6.3	0.4	1.3	4.6
Chile	-5.4	0.2[a]	-8.5	0.8[a]	-2.6	7.6[a]	-16.2	-6.8[a]	-13.4	-20.6[a]	-5.2	13.8[a]
Colombia	1.8	1.9	13.3	12.8	—	5.7		7.2	-4.7	—	0.0	0.5
Costa Rica	7.4	2.1	29.3	8.0	4.4	2.7	24.9	5.3	15.3	5.8	-4.0	-0.4
Côte d'Ivoire	10.4	—	31.1	—	18.6	—	12.5	—	12.1	—	9.2	—
India	6.9	8.4	34.9	35.2	2.7	2.8	32.1	32.4	22.7	—	16.8	1.0
Indonesia	2.3	1.9	9.6	10.4	8.9	8.9	0.7	1.5	0.7	0.5	0.8	—
Kenya	4.9	6.9	16.5	21.2	8.6	7.5	7.8	13.7	5.7	0.7	1.5	-2.2
Korea	2.2	-0.2	11.0	-1.1	4.2	-2.3	6.8	1.2	18.0	—	18.0	2.3
Mexico	3.1	5.4	16.5	22.2	-0.4	2.3[b]	16.9	—	11.9	9.4[b]	8.3	-5.4[b]
Morocco	10.2	4.4[b]	29.1	15.9[b]	15.8	—	13.3	13.7[b]	29.4[e]	12.0[b]	15.3[e]	5.4
Nigeria	8.4[e]	8.9[b]	36.1[e]	35.8[b]	2.0[e]	9.0	31.7[e]	—	3.2	0.1[d]	-5.3	3.4
Pakistan	5.6	7.4	25.0	27.4	10.0	7.2	15.1	18.4	7.7	—	7.7	-4.0
Sri Lanka	18.3	8.7	43.1	26.5	10.6	0.5	32.5	19.3	18.2	0.5	9.7	-15.7
Thailand	4.9	-3.2	25.0	-20.4	5.9	—	19.2	-21.0	12.8	—	12.8	—
Turkey	3.4	4.5	14.4	19.3	2.1	—	13.0	—	—	—	—	11.6
All developing countries 1981		4.2		17.1		4.8		13.4		8.1		5.4
All developing countries 1984		4.3		16.7		3.3		14.5		—		5.9
All developing countries 1988		5.8		19.5		2.1		20.6		—		—

— Not available
a. 1988
b. 1987
c. 1981
d. 1986
e. Federal budgeted operations, 1982.

Source: IMF, *International Financial Statistics, Supplement on Government Finance* (1986), pp. 2–11; *International Financial Statistics Yearbook* (1989), *Government Finance Statistics Yearbook* (1991), pp. 44–49.

countries to cover their budget deficits in 1980, a year (in general) of rising budget deficits, although they peaked in 1982 and again in 1986. External funding was also generally available in 1980, and the external debt of developing countries grew sharply in that year. It is noteworthy, therefore, that only four of our countries (Côte d'Ivoire, Morocco, Indonesia, and Kenya, in order of relative size of external borrowing) financed more than half of their central government budget deficits externally. Even Sri Lanka, with its huge deficit, financed only a quarter of it abroad. Furthermore, there was very little direct external borrowing by the federal governments of Argentina, Brazil, and Mexico, countries that subsequently became the three largest debtors. The governments of those countries later became large debtors because they had given guarantees on borrowings by SOEs and because they assumed large amounts of private debt during the large devaluations and debt crises after 1982.

The remainder had to be borrowed from domestic sources. As can be seen in table 10-8, most domestic finance came from the banking system, although Costa Rica, Pakistan, and Sri Lanka relied heavily on nonbank sources of finance. True financial markets are in the main nonexistent in most developing countries, Brazil and Mexico being exceptions during much of our period, but that fact does not preclude borrowing from the nonbank public. There are many financial institutions, such as savings banks, insurance companies, pension funds, and specialized lending agencies, with sources of funds that can be placed, temporarily or indefinitely, in government securities. Thus a substantial fraction of government obligations are held by the nonbank public in some countries.

Table 10-9 shows average figures from 1977 to 1986 for developing countries of Asia and the Western Hemisphere (about fourteen countries in each group). Two striking features stand out: first, the overall central government deficits during this period as a whole were not much larger in Latin America than they were in Asia, and the share provided by foreign loans was very similar.[9] Second, nonbank domestic financing was more prevalent in Asia than in Latin America, whereas central bank financing was more common in the latter area. This second feature is at first glance the more surprising since domestic financial markets are rather more highly developed in Latin America than they are in Asia; but much of the nonbank financing in Asia is by postal or other specialized savings institutions, and by provident funds, which provide lump-sum payment to workers on retirement on the basis of employer and employee contributions, and which in the meantime are often invested in government bonds.

The median developing country in the late 1970s had 29 percent of its outstanding domestic debt held outside the banking system. The range for our countries is from 6.7 percent for Thailand to 53 percent for Sri Lanka and 57 percent in Kenya.[10] Argentina and Korea were above 33 percent.[11] When deficits are financed by long-term savings, they may crowd out private investments, but they are less likely to be inflationary than if they are financed by the banking system.

At the margin, however, almost all governments must turn to the banking system for incremental financing of budget deficits that cannot be financed overseas,

Table 10.9   Financing Budget Deficits
(percentage of central government expenditures plus net lending)

Region and year	Deficit	External	Nonbank domestic	Financing deposit money banks	Central bank
Asia					
1977	17.4	5.9	8.4	2.3	0.7
1978	18.0	6.9	8.5	1.5	1.0
1979	17.6	6.3	8.9	0.5	1.9
1980	19.9	5.3	10.3	3.6	1.2
1981	20.4	6.2	8.8	4.2	1.7
1982	21.6	6.3			
1983	19.8	5.2	11.8	3.1	0.8
1984	17.8	3.2	11.2	3.0	-1.2
1985	20.8	3.2	16.1	1.0	0.6
1986	23.5	4.0	15.8	3.6	0.4
1987	19.2	2.5			
Western Hemisphere					
1977	11.0	2.3			
1978	11.2	3.3			
1979	8.4	0.2			
1980	11.7	0.9			
1981	19.2	3.6	5.2	4.1	5.2
1982	25.0	2.8	-0.9	1.4	20.4
1983	22.9	5.2	3.5	0.5	12.3
1984	19.8	4.7	6.3	0.5	8.8
1985	22.5	2.4	9.0	1.8	10.8
1986	28.1	3.7	-0.7	0.6	24.1
1987	24.2	—			

— Not available.
Source: IMF, *Supplement on Government Finance* (1986, 11, pp. 2–11). IMF, *Government Finance Statistics Yearbook* (1990, pp. 44–47).

or that cannot be financed by drawing down liquid government assets. This financing is sometimes done almost exclusively by the central bank, as in Mexico, Turkey, and Indonesia; sometimes, as in Korea and Thailand, it is done mainly through deposit money banks (DMBs), which in turn have access to the central bank. Such financing is inflationary, of course, except insofar as the banks reduce their lending to private borrowers correspondingly. The question of seigniorage and the "inflation tax" are taken up further below, after a comment on the role of state-owned enterprises, which often act independently of the central government's budget, yet may have an important impact on macroeconomic stability.

State-Owned Enterprises

The public sector includes not only the central government and provincial and municipal governments, but also state enterprises. These are organizations that produce goods or services and sell them to customers, much as privately owned enterprises do. If state-owned enterprises behaved in all respects like private enterprises, there would be no need to address them in a chapter on fiscal and monetary policy, and indeed in a few countries state enterprises do approximate private enterprises in their behavior, while in others they are of relatively small quantitative importance. In most developing countries, however, SOEs are significant in number and magnitude, and they are sufficiently unlike private enterprises in some respects to warrant special mention. In particular, they often draw directly or indirectly on the government budget and thus can add substantially to public borrowing requirements. In a few cases—Brazil, Costa Rica, Turkey—they had direct access to the central bank, so their borrowing added directly to the money supply.[12]

Governments create or acquire state-owned enterprises for a variety of reasons: To begin with, their activities involve natural monopolies, and a simple way to regulate their prices and investment is to own them directly, as is done in many developed countries. Often they were acquired through the nationalization of a foreign-owned enterprise, such as a telephone service or a firm that generates and distributes electricity, when a political reaction developed to foreign ownership of such activities. Second, they are usually "strategic industries" for development, a concept that is so elusive as to be of doubtful validity, but that over the years has been taken to include steel production, petrochemicals, shipping, airlines, and in the 1980s integrated circuits. Third, governments at times absorb failing private firms, to avoid the social disruption that would arise with liquidation. This situation arises more frequently in developed countries, but it has also occurred in Brazil, Costa Rica, India, and (as a result of takeovers of banks) in Chile and Mexico.

Above all, public ownership has been driven by ideological considerations, either of a Marxist nature, calling for public ownership of the means of production, at least in manufacturing, or of a developmental bent, meaning the government is expected to play a leading role as capitalist and entrepreneur.

The relative number and economic importance of state-owned enterprises varies greatly among our countries. Nonfinancial national state-owned enterprises varied in number in 1980 from a low of 19 in Chile to a high of 287 in Mexico.[13] Although "privatization" became a byword in the 1980s, by 1988 only five of our eighteen countries had reduced the number of SOEs (in Mexico, drastically, to 177), while eleven showed increases (in Argentina and Brazil, sharp increases, partly through the formation of new subsidiaries by existing enterprises).[14] State-owned financial enterprises in 1980 ranged in number from 6 in Cameroon to 76 in Mexico, with declines in only three countries between 1980 and 1988.

Value added by SOEs for countries for which data are available ranged from 2 to 15 percent of GDP in the early 1970s, with an average of 8.6 percent for all developing countries in the mid-1970s. This figure rose slightly to 10.9 percent in the mid-1980s (see table 10-10). The relative importance in gross investment was much higher, ranging from 7 to 29 percent of total gross investment in the early 1970s, with an average of 27 percent in the mid-1970s for all developing countries, rising slightly to 28 percent in the mid-1980s. Our countries ranged from 13 percent in Costa Rica to more than 40 percent in Pakistan and India.[15] The time path also varied greatly from country to country. All our countries showed substantial increases from the late 1960s to the mid-1980s except Korea and Côte d'Ivoire, and the latter country had a dramatic increase in the late 1970s, followed by a dramatic decline in the mid-1980s. Thus, the relative importance of public

Table 10.10   Output and Investment Shares of Public Enterprises

Country	Percent of GDP		Percentage of gross investment	
	1970–73	*1985*	*1970–73*	*1985*
Argentina	4.8[a]	—	17.5	36.0
Brazil	—	3.5	14.0	17.5
Chile	15.2[b,c]	16.8	20.0[b,c]	27.5
Colombia	1.9[b,d]	—	10.3[b,d]	23.1
Costa Rica	—	4.3	7.3[e]	13.2
Côte d'Ivoire	10.5[a]	—	27.9	18.8
India	7.3	—	29.0	41.1
Kenya	8.7	8.0[f]	10.6	19.6[f]
Korea	7.0	3.3[g]	21.7	19.3[g]
Mexico	6.1[b,c]	11.3	27.0[b]	19.1[f]
Morocco	—	15.4	—	33.1
Pakistan	4.4	—	19.3	43.4
Sri Lanka	9.9[i]	—	19.4	35.9[j]
Thailand	3.6	—	8.5	17.1
Turkey	8.1	9.0	22.6	30.5
Developing countries	8.6[b]	10.9[f]	27.0[b]	28.2[f]

— Not available.
a. 1976–77.
b. 1974–77.
c. Large enterprises only.
d. Excluding local enterprises.
e. 1968.
f. 1984
g. 1982.
h. 1979.
j. 1974.
k. 1981.
Source: For the 1970s, Floyd, Gray, and Short (1984, pp. 118–22); for 1985, Nair and Filippides (1988, table 2.1).

enterprises in total investment increased over the period as a whole. Private investment in the mid-1980s was weak in a number of our countries, but that cannot account wholly for the relative increase in public enterprise investment.

This increase gives rise to a number of important questions: (1) Do earnings of state-owned enterprises cover their investments, or do they require additional savings from other sources? (2) Do they crowd out private investment? (3) Are they efficient; does their growth contribute to net national income? (4) Is their investment a source of macroeconomic disturbance, or is it countercyclical? Unfortunately, the data available for most countries do not readily permit complete answers to these questions.

Ideally, SOEs would produce their output efficiently, sell it at full cost, run operating profits, and produce revenues for the government. If the demand for the goods or services were growing, the SOEs would also invest their profits (and perhaps more) in ways that generated high rates of return when the investments were completed. Thus the SOEs would be net savers in the national accounts, although they might also be net borrowers from the government or the financial system to the extent that net new investment exceeded net earnings.

Too often in practice, SOEs are enlisted to serve public purposes other than producing goods or services, such as providing employment in excess of their labor requirements, as in Argentina in the mid-1970s,[16] or helping combat inflation through restraining increases in their output prices despite increases in their input prices, as in Brazil (and many other countries) in the late 1970s and 1980s. Serving either of these objectives reduces the net operating earnings of the SOEs and thus their contribution to national savings. Serving other objectives probably also reduces the efficiency of the SOEs, by complicating the problem of evaluating their performance both by managers and by ministers.

In our countries, only in Argentina and in Turkey (and in Costa Rica in the early 1980s) did these and other practices go so far as to produce deficits in the SOE sector, before allowing for capital expenditures.[17] The SOEs in most countries ran current surpluses (on operations plus debt service, before allowing for investments or amortization of debt), despite frequent restraints on their output prices; but they ran overall deficits because of their heavy investments. These overall deficits typically accounted for a substantial fraction of the overall public borrowing requirement, and in the cases of Brazil and Turkey in the early 1980s more than accounted for all of it. For Brazil, Côte d'Ivoire, Sri Lanka, and Turkey, and a few other countries for shorter periods of time (for example, Costa Rica in the early 1980s), the overall deficits of the SOEs were responsible for the principal movements in public sector deficits; for other countries, however, deficits were determined mainly by other factors, although the SOEs contributed to them.[18]

In general, borrowing by SOEs has not been heavy enough to displace private borrowing extensively, although in some countries and in some periods SOE borrowing represented a major claim on investable funds. For instance, in Brazil the SOE share of total new domestic credit rose from 11 percent in 1978 to 31 percent in 1985; the corresponding figures for Costa Rica are 13 and 36 percent, respectively;

in Turkey, in contrast, they fell from a peak of 35 percent in 1976–77 to 7 percent in 1985, and in Côte d'Ivoire from a peak of 28 percent in 1979 to 6.5 percent in 1984. Throughout the 1970s and early 1980s, this ratio was below 21 percent in Mexico, 16 percent in Pakistan, 7 percent in Kenya, and 3 percent in Thailand.[19] In combination with the possibility and (before 1983) actuality of borrowing abroad, it is unlikely that SOE borrowing "crowded out" private borrowing in the latter four countries, but it may have done so in Turkey and Côte d'Ivoire in the 1970s, and in Brazil and Costa Rica in the mid-1980s (when, however, demand for private investment was lower than normal). Among the eight countries listed, SOEs in Brazil, Costa Rica, and Turkey borrowed extensively directly from the central bank; the amounts reached 39 percent of total Brazilian SOE borrowing in 1985, 41 percent in Turkey in 1981, and 96 percent in Costa Rica in 1983–86. In Argentina, much domestic borrowing in the 1980s was undertaken by provincial and municipal enterprises, borrowing from province-owned banks, which in turn could and did discount readily at the central bank.[20]

Overall deficits of SOEs are desirable to the extent that they reflect investments that in future will yield high rates of return, enlarging future surpluses, and to the extent that they do not displace even higher-yielding private investments. Unfortunately, little work has been done to calculate true rates of return on SOEs, largely because of the lack of data on capital stock and on average lives of SOE investments, but some evidence suggests low efficiency. Joshi and Little (forthcoming) found that gross rates of return (that is, before depreciation) on public investments in manufacturing in India in the early 1970s averaged 6.7 percent, not enough to cover depreciation. Harberger calculated *negative* rates of return of 1 to 3 percent a year in Argentina over the period 1971–85.[21]

Publicly available figures on a number of large SOEs around the world make it possible to compare net earnings with assets. Of the seventy largest SOEs in the non-U.S. Fortune-500 list for 1984 (of which twenty-three are in developing countries), only five had earnings exceeding 10 percent of assets, four of which were in the petroleum industry (in India, Turkey, Venezuela, and Taiwan), and the fifth was CVRD, the large state-owned iron ore firm in Brazil. The weighted average ratio of earnings to assets for all SOEs was only 0.4 percent, and petroleum companies in many countries did not make money; Argentina's state-owned petroleum enterprise (YPF), in particular, ran large losses.

If a comparison is made with private companies listed in the same source, SOEs (excluding YPF with its large losses) earned less than half what private firms did, 1.7 percent of assets as against 4.0 percent. The pattern held for every separate industry as well, so the outcome was not a result of the different industry mix between public and private.[22]

Of course, comparisons of this type are somewhat treacherous, since (1) public enterprises are given some nonmarket objectives that most private firms do not have; and (2) interest payments on debt are treated as an expense, so that public enterprises that carry a larger share of their assets with debt will show lower net earnings without necessarily reflecting a less efficient use of capital. Against these points it may be argued that (1) governments frequently restrict the employment practices and output prices of private firms as well as public enterprises, although private firms generally have somewhat more freedom in these areas; (2) to equalize the return to capital at a 10 percent interest rate, this Fortune-500 sample of public enterprises would have to have a debt-to-asset ratio twenty-three percentage points higher than the corresponding private enterprises, which is possible but unlikely;[23] and (3) in any case, many public enterprises in developing countries in the mid-1980s enjoyed concessional interest rates on their borrowings, and even so sometimes did not pay their full interest obligations, thus artificially increasing net earnings.[24]

The extent of budgetary control over SOEs varies considerably from country to country, and from time to time. There is the notorious case of Indonesia's state oil firm Pertamina, which, on the strength of its enlarged earnings following the 1974 oil price increase, borrowed extensively in the Eurocurrency markets and diversified into a wide range of activities within Indonesia, often unwisely. It took a financial crisis and much political effort to establish effective finance ministry control over Pertamina's external borrowing and domestic investment activities, and over the popular and strong-willed general who headed Pertamina. Brazil's state-owned enterprises also enjoyed substantial autonomy and freedom from Finance Ministry control in the 1970s, although their investment splurge, it must be said, was consistent with government policy during the Delfim Neto period, 1979–80. It was not until 1982 that stronger central control was established, particularly over the external borrowing of Brazil's enterprises. Mexico distinguishes between the larger SOEs, whose budgets require congressional approval, and those that operate autonomously under general guidelines. Even the requirement for congressional approval did not prevent Pemex, Mexico's giant oil firm, from engaging in extensive commercial real estate development during the height of euphoria over the 1979–80 rise in oil prices. With steadily increasing Mexican oil output, a financial reversal for Pemex, or for Mexico, seemed inconceivable at the time.

Here is a real dilemma: effective management of any operating entity requires considerable autonomy for knowledgeable management to make operational decisions concerning the mix of outputs, inputs, and pricing. Tight government oversight inhibits SOE managers from managing effectively. At the same time, SOEs, being state owned, carry an implicit guarantee from the government that they will not be allowed to fail, in the sense that creditors are seriously at risk (but not in the sense that existing management can count on maintaining their positions until normal retirement age). Thus, SOEs are at an advantage with respect to private firms when it comes to long-term borrowing, apart from any special preferences the government may give them directly. This advantage may lead some SOE managers to undertake inappropriately risky investments. The implicit guarantee requires some degree of government oversight to avoid this problem. It is noteworthy, and ironic, that just as Brazil was moving in the early 1980s to assert more central control over its SOEs, Korea and India were moving in the opposite direction, to give them more autonomy. There is no ideal solution. The only way to avoid this particular dilemma is to sell the enterprises to private owners.

On the whole, the investment plans of SOEs were not keyed to macroeconomic stabilization, except in extreme cases in which total government spending had to be drastically cut. Rather, their investments were either autonomous (as in the case of Brazil in the 1970s) or conformed with the long-run development strategy of political leaders. A notable exception was Korea, where investments by SOEs were first restrained as part of the stabilization program of 1979, then accelerated to off-set in part the slowdown of 1980–81, then restrained again as part of the stabilization program of 1983–84. India also restrained SOE investments as part of its stabilization program in the late 1960s. But these exceptions stand out; for the most part, SOEs played some role, along with other government expenditure, in de-stabilizing economies rather than stabilizing them. During the 1980s, when governments found it necessary to reduce public expenditure, SOEs in many countries were gradually brought under tighter control and also reduced their investments.

Of course, SOEs were prevailed upon in other ways to advance the economic objectives of their governments. Argentina's SOEs were considered employers of last resort during the Peronist regime of the mid-1970s, and their employment jumped sharply. CODESA in Costa Rica, set up as an entrepreneurial holding company and financial intermediary for operating state-owned enterprises, with direct access to the central bank, found itself attempting to bolster, and eventually buying, a number of failing private firms. Many governments have limited the ability of SOEs to raise their prices autonomously—partly because they are often natural monopolies or protected sufficiently to be a monopoly, but partly also to avoid the public opprobrium of raising highly visible prices, for example, on gasoline or electricity or urban transit fares, especially in periods of threatened or actual inflation. Once started, these price controls are difficult to abandon: there never seems to be a time that is politically right for raising prices. The result is lower earnings to the SOEs, and ultimately lower revenues for the government—their products or services are indirectly subsidized, and if the restraints remain long enough in an inflationary environment, the government must subsidize the enterprises directly (or indirectly through nonrepayable loans from the central bank) in order to keep them in operation. Turkey offers a leading example, until its SOEs were moved toward financial autonomy with the reforms of 1980, but the practice was widespread. The extreme case among our countries is probably India, where price control is used as a mechanism to influence the distribution of income, and in 1986 about 30 percent of prices in the wholesale price index were subject to administrative control.[25]

State and Local Government

As noted above, our countries vary greatly in the unity of their fiscal systems. In many countries, the fundamental structure and the implementation of taxation is tightly controlled by the national government; in others, state and local authorities have substantial autonomy in some areas of taxation, typically within parameters laid down by the national government. Among our countries, Argentina and India are notable in this regard, with state and local authorities raising more than 30 percent of total government revenue; in Brazil and Pakistan, they raise more than 20 percent; and in Colombia, Korea, Mexico, and Turkey, more than 10 percent. In between are the countries in which state and local governments are in charge of a substantial amount of spending, but their main source of revenue is grants from the national government. In Brazil, Colombia, Indonesia, Nigeria, and Korea, grants and loans from the national government, along with own-source taxation, permit state and local governments to handle more than 30 percent of total government spending, and in India more than 50 percent.[26]

From the point of view of macroeconomic stabilization, however, it is generally possible to ignore state and local spending, since these authorities typically spend their revenue fairly quickly, and the grants they receive are included in the central government's budget, as well as any loans made. This stance creates difficulties only when the state and local governments have sources of finance independent of their own taxes and grants or loans from the central government, as was the case, among our countries, in Argentina and Brazil. In Nigeria, states had access to unbudgeted funds in the late 1970s and early 1980s. In India, states have temporary overdraft privileges at the Reserve Bank, which have been used especially in election years. In Argentina, the provinces own a number of state enterprises, including banks; these enterprises could borrow outside the budget, as commercial firms do, but with implicit government guarantees.[27] More significantly, as already noted, the provincial banks would often lend to the provincial governments, and the banks in turn could borrow from or rediscount at the central bank. In Nigeria during 1979–84 the national budgetary process simply broke down, and one of the substantial sources of leakage was federal grants to state and local governments, outside the formal budget process. Moreover, a large increase in legal grants to local governments, designed to strengthen their responsibilities, was partly siphoned off by intermediating state governments, who also more than doubled the number of local governments in order to increase federal transfers, which were based in part on the number of local government units.[28] In addition, state governments in Argentina and Brazil, like those in Australia, Canada, and the United States, were free to borrow abroad, and some did so. State governments in India, Nigeria, and Pakistan, in contrast, required federal government authorization to borrow abroad.

Financing: Debt and Seigniorage

To the extent that a government cannot finance its expenditures with its own tax and nontax revenues, or through grants from abroad, it must resort to borrowing, either from the banking system or from others. Over time, such financing cumulates in the form of outstanding debt, which can come to represent a substantial charge on the budget.[29] As already noted, for nonoil developing countries as a group, interest payments rose from 7 percent of total central government expenditure in 1977 to 10 percent in 1982, and moved to nearly 18 percent by 1987. Amortization of past debt, insofar as it could not be refinanced, increased the burden further. For a budget deficit to be sustainable, the available financing—domestically or abroad—must not be merely in the current period; there must be some prospect for financing it indefinitely if it is judged not to be strictly temporary. The long-run dynamics of budget deficits, which are often ignored in the budgeting process, are such that the growth of revenues must exceed the average interest rate paid on the outstanding debt as long as the government is running a primary deficit, that is, a deficit exclusive of interest payments. This requirement is mitigated to the extent that the government runs a primary surplus or, in other words, to the extent that interest payments exceed the overall deficit.[30]

The notion of primary deficit is useful, especially in a highly inflationary environment, where interest rates reflect the rate of inflation. In these circumstances some portion of interest payments in effect amortizes the debt, since a given nominal debt is declining in value in real terms.[31] This is true both for external debt and for internal debt, but in magnitude is especially important for internal debt willingly held by the public, such that holders will wish to preserve the value of their claims on the government in real terms and therefore will willingly reinvest the relevant portion of their interest earnings. In most of our high-inflation countries, however, domestic government debt was not acquired freely, but under compulsion, for example, by financial institutions or by pension funds. The notable exception was Brazil, where domestic debt was indexed, first (roughly) to the rate of inflation, then after 1982 to the exchange rate, and a substantial portion of the government deficit was financed by sales of securities to the nonbank public. In this case, the notion of operational (inflation-corrected) deficit made some sense, as the Brazilian government persuaded the officials of the IMF. In other cases, holders of debt will, if possible, allow the real value of their claims to erode with inflation, preferring investments in other assets. Under these circumstances, the "operational deficit" understates the financing problem of the government.

The notion of the primary deficit is useful in another respect as well. To the extent that government debt is held by foreigners, or by institutions (such as pension funds or life insurance companies) whose current disbursements are unrelated to their current earnings, interest payments by the government do not have the expansionary impact that other expenditures do. In developed countries where government bonds are widely held by the public, interest payments by the government increase the effective purchasing power of the public. In many developing countries, however, the primary deficit may give a better measure of the impact of government spending on the economy. This proposition depends, however, on exactly how the budget deficit affects monetary policy, a topic taken up below.

In any case, as table 10-11 shows, although overall budget deficits on average declined only slightly during the period 1982–87, primary budget deficits declined drastically, the difference being the sharp relative increase in interest payments, both to foreigners and to domestic holders of government debt. Indeed, by 1987 half of our countries ran primary surpluses. The primary deficits grew significantly only for Cameroon, Brazil, Costa Rica, and Pakistan, and the last three countries showed reductions by 1989. So the mid-1980s were a period of general budgetary retrenchment, the inevitable reaction to a crisis of excessive demand, as discussed in chapter 5.

External debt poses another problem. Not only must future revenue be increased to service the debt, but in effect the revenue must be raised in foreign currency, since the debt is overwhelmingly denominated in U.S. dollars or other foreign currency. A few governments enjoy direct ownership of exportable products

Table 10.11　Central Government Interest Payments and Primary Deficits
(percentage of GDP)

Country	Overall deficit		Interest payments		Primary deficit	
	1982	*1987*	*1982*	*1987*	*1982*	*1987*
Argentina	7.4	3.9	4.7	1.7	2.7	2.2
Brazil	2.5	11.7	3.1	9.4	−0.6	2.3
Cameroon	−1.3[a]	2.9[b]	.6[a]	1.1[b]	1.8[a]	1.8[b]
Chile	1.0	−0.5	0.5	2.3	0.5	−2.8
Colombia	4.7	0.7	0.8	1.4	3.9	−0.7
Costa Rica	0.9	2.9	1.6	2.3	−0.7	2.3
Côte d'Ivoire	3.1[c]	6.1	8.6[c]	6.2	−5.5[c]	−0.1
India	6.0	8.4	2.0	3.2	4.1	5.2
Indonesia	1.8	0.8	1.0	2.7	0.8	−1.9
Kenya	8.3	6.7	3.6	4.8	4.7	1.9
Korea	3.0	−0.4	1.2	1.0	1.8	−1.5
Mexico	15.4	13.6	4.2	18.4	11.2	−4.8
Morocco	11.4	4.5	3.5	4.6	7.9	−0.1
Nigeria		8.8		11.2		−2.4
Pakistan	4.7	9.1[d]	2.2	3.5[d]	2.5	5.6[d]
Sri Lanka	14.0	8.7	5.1	5.2	8.9	3.5
Thailand	6.7	2.3	2.0	3.0	4.7	−0.7
Turkey	4.2[a]	4.0	1.8[a]	3.3	2.6[a]	0.7
Non-oil-developing countries	5.9	5.9	2.7	5.2	3.2	0.7
United States	4.1	3.4	3.2	3.5	0.9	−0.1

a. 1983.
b. 1989.
c. 1984.
d. 1986.
Source: IMF, *Government Finance Statistics Yearbook* (various issues).

such as petroleum or other minerals; but most governments are unable to raise revenues directly in foreign currency. Instead, unless they can borrow further abroad, they must buy the foreign currency directly or indirectly from exporters, and the exchange rate at which they do so is important from a macroeconomic point of view. Large currency devaluations, in particular, can play havoc with the budget (for nonoil exporters), since the local-currency interest payments on foreign debt must rise abruptly by the amount of the devaluation.[32] Even gradual depreciations of the currency, as under a crawling peg regime, increase external debt-service requirements in terms of local currency; and when these depreciations go beyond merely compensating for domestic inflation, they raise the budgetary burden of external debt servicing in real terms.

Perhaps in part for this reason, most central governments did not borrow extensively abroad, the major exceptions being Côte d'Ivoire, Morocco, Pakistan, Sri Lanka, and Indonesia.[33] Rather, where external borrowing was extensive, it was done by SOEs, both nonfinancial and financial (such as national development banks, financial intermediaries that borrow abroad and relend to domestic enterprises), and by private firms. Debt problems in many countries arose because these borrowers' debts were often guaranteed by the government or by the central bank. If a currency devaluation led to a negative cash flow for the domestic institution, the government had to help resolve the problem. Typically, the external debts were directly or indirectly assumed by the central bank, which then ran the losses associated with application of the new exchange rate to debt servicing.

A characteristic transaction would permit external debt servicing by the SOE or private firm to be made at the predevaluation exchange rate, for instance, with the central bank absorbing the loss between what it paid exporters for their foreign exchange earnings and what it charged the debtor for foreign exchange to service its external debt. This arrangement was widely applied in Mexico following the 1982 devaluation, and by Costa Rica after the 1981 devaluation. In an alternative arrangement, the central bank could simply assume the external debt formally, in exchange for a domestic currency claim on the original debtor, whether it be private firm or SOE. This practice was followed by Brazil after 1982. In either case, the central bank ran large losses on these operations, which on balance were expansionary from a macroeconomic perspective. Korea, in contrast, engaged in no formal indemnification of external debtors caught by the devaluations of 1980 and 1985. Many debtors had offsetting increases in the local currency proceeds from exports, and others were expected to absorb the higher debt-service burden like any other unexpected increase in cost. Where firms ran into serious cash-flow difficulties, Korean banks under guidance extended low-interest credits, to help them through the period of adjustment.

Among our countries, ten experienced increases in the ratio of public or publicly guaranteed external debt to GDP in excess of ten percentage points between the end of 1978 and the end of 1983, an increase that was clearly not sustainable in the long run. The increases were due in part to extensive borrowing, in part to government absorption of private external debt, but also in part to currency depreciation, which raised the value of external debt in relation to GDP. Eight of these ran into repayment difficulties serious enough for one or more reschedulings to be required, as discussed in chapter 5. (Kenya and Thailand were the exceptions.)

An analogous problem attends domestic debt. A program to reduce a high rate of inflation will typically entail a sharp increase in real interest rates, sometimes for an extended period of time (see chapter 7), as it did in Mexico in 1988–89. This phenomenon arises in part because of the tight monetary policies that are introduced as part of the stabilization program, but even more because of continuing doubts about whether the stabilization program will survive even when inflation is falling rapidly, which lead to expectations of continuing currency devaluation. These high real interest rates, however, are a serious charge on the budget of any government (or other debtor) with large outstanding domestic debts that must be financed at prevailing interest rates. The high interest rates in some countries were more important than the growing debt in explaining the growth in interest payments as a share of public expenditure. Unless government revenue also rises sharply in response to the stabilization program, as the real value of revenue rises faster than its nominal value with a decline in the rate of inflation (the reverse Tanzi effect, discussed in chapter 6), the budget deficit may rise as a result of the stabilization and thereby threaten to undermine the credibility of the program. This is one of the legacies of large outstanding debt. It undermined Brazil's stabilization program in 1986, as interest payments (including monetary correction) rose to 44 percent of total government expenditures.

Seigniorage

Insofar as a budget deficit is not financed abroad or by the domestic public, it must be financed by the banking system—either by drawing down outstanding government deposits, which can only occur for a limited period of time, or by borrowing from the banks. Since on average about half of budget deficits in developing countries are financed in this way (table 10-8), fiscal and monetary policy are closely connected in most developing countries (chapter 6). Under a budget deficit, the money supply expands, either directly if the borrowing is from the central bank or indirectly if it is through the deposit money banks (DMBs).

That is expansionary and possibly inflationary. The typical developing country has a rapidly growing demand for money as the economy becomes more monetized and as households and firms increasingly hold assets in financial form, as currency, demand accounts, or savings accounts. The rise in demand for money—more rapid than the growth in GDP, unless discouraged by high inflation—permits governments, as issuers of money, to earn substantial seigniorage, the difference between the cost of issuing money and its face value. Needless to say, monetary expansion at a rate greater than this growing demand in an economy fully using its resources is inflationary and will lead to increased expenditures that will bid up prices. The rise in prices will in turn reduce the real value of outstanding money balances, which the public will want to replenish, at least in part. That development leads to more seigniorage, this additional portion being the "inflation tax," already discussed in chapter 6.

The government can command real resources by inflating and thereby inducing the public to spend less on goods and services, in order to replenish their cash balances in real terms, and this process acts like a tax on cash balances. The inflation tax is imposed on currency, on non-interest-bearing bank deposits, and on deposits or government securities that bear an interest rate that is not adjusted to the rate of inflation, either because that rate was underestimated by the public when they bought the bonds or because interest rates are held below a market-clearing rate and the purchase of the bonds is obligatory, for example, as secondary reserves by banks or insurance companies.

The amounts of seigniorage arising from growth and inflation together can be considerable, as shown in table 10-12, which calculates seigniorage only on base money (currency plus bank reserves) and therefore excludes the inflation tax, if any, on outstanding government debt. Seigniorage for half our countries amounted to more than 2 percent of GDP in the late 1970s, or about 10 percent of total government revenue. Seigniorage dropped in the early 1980s, both because of lower growth rates in many countries, and because of lower inflation rates in some; major exceptions are Costa Rica and Mexico, where inflation rose sharply. The inflation tax typically accounted for more than half of the seigniorage, even in such low-inflation countries as Thailand and Cameroon.[34] Brazil's seigniorage and inflation tax, while substantial, are remarkably small given Brazil's rate of inflation; that reflects the extensive indexing of the Brazilian economy and the development of noncash means of payment, resulting in by far the lowest ratio of currency to GDP (1 percent, compared with 4–12 percent in most of our countries; Mexico and Turkey, both countries with high inflation in the 1980s, had ratios below 3 percent; Argentina's ratio, remarkably, was about 7 percent).[35]

It has long been recognized that some inflation tax is an appropriate component of optimal tax policy, that is, policy that raises a given amount of revenue at the least social cost.[36] Tax revenue from other sources (for example, incomes or commodity sales) carries administrative and efficiency costs. Taxing cash balances through inflation is optimal as long as the social costs associated with reduced cash balances, along with any other costs of inflation, are lower per dollar of revenue raised than is true of alternative sources of revenue. The higher the costs of other sources of revenue, the higher should be the appropriate inflation tax. As a tax, inflation reaches all those who hold money, including those who evade other taxes or engage in nontaxed illegal activities. At the same time, higher inflation creates an incentive to hold lower cash balances, and that represents a social cost. In countries with poorly developed financial systems, the alternatives to holding cash or bank deposits are few, and the cost of the inflation tax is correspondingly less, since it comes closer to being the public finance specialist's desideratum, a lump-sum tax with no social cost. The costs of the inflation tax rise with the degree

Table 10.12   Seigniorage and Inflation Tax

Country	1965–69	1970–74	1975–79	1980–84	1985–88
Seigniorage[a]					
Argentina	—	9.53	13.42	14.70	6.38
Brazil	2.31	1.65	2.34	2.08	2.64[b]
Cameroon	1.02	0.68	0.96	0.79	0.23
Chile	2.28[b]	6.73[b]	2.43[b]	0.32[b]	—
Colombia	1.70	1.68	3.02	2.11	1.45
Costa Rica	1.19	1.40	2.82	4.45	4.31
Cote d'Ivoire	0.98	1.76	1.97	0.59	1.53
India	0.81	1.13	1.70	1.64	2.34
Indonesia	3.23	2.17	1.64	1.03	0.67
Kenya	2.45	0.77	1.27	0.54	1.27
Korea	2.79	2.34	2.83	0.20	1.22
Mexico	0.80	2.29	3.88	6.75	2.78
Morocco	1.17	1.78	2.22	1.32	1.58
Nigeria	0.35	1.64	1.73	1.30	1.43
Pakistan	1.26	1.96	2.44	1.99	2.14
Sri Lanka	0.54	1.07	1.57	1.67	1.51
Thailand	0.91	1.31	1.09	0.74	1.10
Turkey	1.67	3.30	4.22	3.62	2.95
Inflation Tax[c]					
Argentina	—	2.06	9.72	6.39	4.15
Brazil	1.87	1.16	1.68	1.68	1.60[b]
Cameroon	-0.02	0.61	0.58	0.60	0.19
Chile	1.38	1.63	2.11	1.01	—
Colombia	0.72	1.21	1.80	1.88	1.70
Costa Rica	0.25	0.92	0.77	3.50	2.25
Cote d'Ivoire	0.42	0.75	1.40	0.72	0.50[b]
India	0.62	1.17	0.31	1.03	1.10
Indonesia	0.40[b]	1.02	0.98	0.62	0.45
Kenya	-0.01[b]	0.63	0.90	0.88	0.52
Korea	—	1.06[b]	1.35	0.69	0.25
Mexico	0.18	0.90	1.90	5.24	4.17
Morocco	0.04	0.82	1.23	1.24	0.56
Nigeria	0.26	0.47	1.43	1.74	1.21
Pakistan	0.79	2.25	1.09	1.12	0.92
Sri Lanka	0.55	0.73	0.62	1.18	0.82
Thailand	0.31	0.78	0.62	0.49	0.24
Turkey	—	1.61	3.32	2.91	2.60

— Not available.

Note: Seigniorage is the change in base money divided by GDP for the year in question. Inflation tax is the geometric average base money in relation to GDP, $\{M(t)*M(t-1)\}^{1/2}$-$M(t-1)$/GDP, times $[i/(1+i)]$, where i is December-to-December change in the consumer price index.

a. Annual average in percentage of GDP.

b. Average over less than full period.

c. Annual geometric average in percent of GDP.

Source: World Bank data.

of financial intermediation. Even in a country whose financial system is as highly developed as Brazil's, inflation on one calculation must reach 700 percent annually before the public's demand for money declines so much that revenues from the inflation tax begin to decline.[37]

Moreover, countries with poorly developed administrative capabilities have difficulty finding alternative sources of revenue. Administrative problems and costs are the main reason that developing countries rely so heavily on import and export taxes for their revenue, which are typically concentrated on a few products entering or exiting the country through a few ports. So the relative advantages of the inflation tax are high in developing countries, and that may explain the prevalence of double-digit inflation in such countries.[38]

The key point for stabilization policy is that the inflation tax is an important source of real resources for governments in many developing countries, and to reduce inflation rates the government must cut its expenditures correspondingly, or find alternative sources of revenue. Thus, reducing average inflation may be costly in terms of public finance. This fiscal inhibition to reducing the average rate of inflation does not, of course, bear on the desirability of reducing fluctuations in inflation.

Fiscal Policy and Stabilization

A central question for this volume is what role fiscal policy played in stabilizing or destabilizing the economies of our eighteen developing countries during their two decades of turbulence, and more generally what role it played in helping them adjust to irrevocably altered circumstances. As noted earlier, the government budget was called upon to play many roles in developing countries—to provide for internal and external security, encourage growth, and redistribute income as well as help to manage the economy over a series of short runs of one to three years. Indeed, the other objectives typically took precedence over stabilization and adjustment, except when the latter were forced on the country.

One mechanical but nonetheless illuminating method for determining the extent to which fiscal policy had a stabilizing or destabilizing effect on national output is to correlate over time some measure of fiscal policy with deviations of annual economic growth rates from long-term (trend) growth. Some results of such an exercise for 1965–88 are shown in table 10-13, which reports the estimated relationship of fiscal policy, as measured by the overall deficit (in relation to GDP), to the deviations of annual growth in GDP from trend growth in each of our countries.

If fiscal policy is on balance stabilizing, this coefficient should be negative; that is, in a year of exceptional growth, the budget deficit should decline as output- and expenditure-sensitive revenues rise (automatically, at unchanged tax rates) and as government expenditures are reduced and tax rates perhaps increased in

Table 10.13 Fiscal Stabilization Coefficients

Country	Estimated coefficient	Standard error	R^2
Argentina	−.77	.42	.41
Brazil	−2.49[a]	1.07	.91
Cameroon	.80	.50	.99
Chile	.12	.56	.59
Colombia	−.17	.70	.98
Costa Rica	2.01[a]	.65	.90
Côte d'Ivoire	−.35	.51	.89
India	−.10	1.60	.98
Indonesia	−.27	.73	.99
Kenya	.47	.87	.97
Korea	−1.78	.97	.99
Mexico	.06	.61	.93
Morocco	.69[a]	.22	.98
Nigeria	.04	.50	.81
Pakistan	−.35	.27	.997
Sri Lanka	.11	.15	.99
Thailand	.13	.51	.99
Turkey	.33	.66	.94
United States	−2.04[a]	.53	.99

Note: Coefficient on central government deficit/GDP in a regression of (logarithm) real GDP against time and government deficit.
a. Coefficient exceeds two times standard error.
Source: World Bank data.

order to dampen the boom. Similarly, in a year of subnormal growth, revenues will fall (or rise less rapidly) and expenditures will be increased in order to raise aggregate demand.

If fiscal policy was destabilizing, in the sense that a burst of government expenditure or a cut in tax rates led to an exceptional contemporaneous growth in demand and output, the coefficient would be positive.

The results show eight countries with negative coefficients and ten with positive coefficients. The countries with negative coefficients (= stabilizing fiscal policy) include those we would expect on the basis of the discussion in earlier chapters: Colombia, India, Indonesia, Korea, and Pakistan. Perhaps surprisingly, they also include Argentina, Brazil, and Côte d'Ivoire, which suggests that as far as the central government's budget was concerned these countries responded in a stabilizing fashion. (Recall that it was provincial governments in Argentina and SOEs in Argentina, Brazil, and Côte d'Ivoire that generated much of the investment boom of the 1970s and the subsequent bust of the 1980s.)

Most of the coefficients are not statistically significant, in the sense that a hypothesis of "no impact, one way or the other" could be comfortably sustained. Of the countries with negative coefficients, only Argentina, Brazil, Korea, and Pakistan pass a significance test that can reject the "no impact" hypothesis, and only Brazil passes it strongly. (By comparison, the federal budget of the United States shows a strongly stabilizing role.) Of the ten countries with positive coefficients, only Cameroon, Costa Rica, and Morocco have coefficients that are sufficiently significant to warrant the conclusion that fiscal policy in those countries was clearly destabilizing on average over the period. The results are not radically altered if budget deficits are adjusted to exclude interest payments to foreigners, on the grounds that those expenditures are not expansionary for the domestic economy, except that Argentina and India then show destabilizing rather than stabilizing behavior, India significantly so.

Fiscal policy is used for "stabilization" in the above analysis on the assumption that the objective is to stabilize the growth of real output, such that income-disturbing changes in the terms of trade or elsewhere are discouraged from affecting the level (as distinguished from the composition) of output. This assumption is probably reasonable for most disturbances, since the path of employment will also be related to the path of output. For disturbances that affect the growth path of potential output, however, such as a decline in foreign capital directed at investment, fiscal policy should encourage "adjustment" rather than stabilization in the sense used above. In such cases, the underlying trend in output should be divided into segments on either side of the disturbance that altered the trend. For many countries, such a break might have occurred in the early 1980s. Unfortunately, not enough time has passed to permit confident analysis using annual data (that is, the period 1982–88 provides only seven observations, too few to fit three coefficients with any statistical confidence).

In summary, it seems that fiscal policy was not generally directed toward stabilization of output and employment in most of our countries throughout the 1970s and 1980s, with the exceptions of Brazil and Korea and, weakly, Colombia, Indonesia, and Pakistan. Moreover, according to Khan (1992), Pakistan was preoccupied with its balance of payments position and reserve levels, rather than with output; these variables, however, are correlated with movements in total demand. Thus, output stabilization for Pakistan was perhaps incidental to foreign exchange concerns.

Of course, an analysis such as this, covering roughly two decades, does not exclude individual episodes in which fiscal policy has been used for stabilizing purposes. India and Thailand both reacted strongly to inflation in 1973 and adjusted their fiscal stance accordingly. Korea tightened fiscal policy to dampen a boom in 1979, loosened it in 1980 to combat the recession of that year, and tightened it again to bring inflation under control in 1982–84. Colombia attempted to dampen the coffee boom of 1976–77 through fiscal action and then, as the boom receded, adopted a more stimulative fiscal stance in 1978–79.

Moreover, economic decisionmakers may be torn between conflicting objectives. Thus far, the analysis has focused on stabilizing output and employment (and, implicitly, on the effect of domestic demand on price levels). The authorities must also be concerned with supply-induced increases in prices, and with the country's balance of payments condition. To the extent that governments tightened their fiscal policies when confronted with external payments difficulties, and these difficulties were not due primarily to high domestic demand, the test described above would show, as it does, weak or nonexistent tendencies toward stabilization. Morocco applied fiscal stimulus on top of the phosphate boom of the mid-1970s, in the interests of long-term development; as phosphate earnings declined, Morocco continued to invest heavily by borrowing abroad. When foreign funds dried up, Morocco undertook fiscal retrenchment even though the economy was growing well below trend, thus destabilizing it by the standard applied above.

Fiscal policy can thus contribute toward "adjustment" to external shocks rather than toward internal stability. That is indeed what happened in many countries during the fiscal retrenchments of the 1980s, discussed in chapter 5. Over the period as a whole, however, fiscal policy (measured by the budget deficit relative to GDP) seems not to have been strongly influenced by contemporaneous payments difficulties (at least as measured by the current account deficit in relation to GDP). On the contrary, as in the case of output, fiscal policy made current account positions worse in about half the countries. Only in Brazil and Mexico were enlarged current account deficits associated significantly with a *decline* in budget deficits over the period 1970–88. In the remaining countries, there was no significant relationship between annual budget and current account deficits, and thus no significant causal link in either direction.[39]

Monetary Structure and Policy

Monetary policy relies on two main instruments, although they vary in detail: the interest rate at which the central bank lends to its various clients, mainly the government and the commercial banks, but including other financial and sometimes even nonfinancial institutions in a number of countries; and the rate at which the central bank issues liabilities against itself, that is, creates money (called base money, reserve money, or high-powered money). Control over the second instrument may be weakened to the extent that the monetary authorities (usually the government rather than the central bank) fix an exchange rate, thus obliging the central bank to issue money against the presentation of foreign exchange, if foreign exchange is in fact presented to the central bank in volumes that are significant in relation to whatever target increases in reserve money it may have. Of course, if it sets an attractive (low) interest rate for loans to its clients, it will also lose control over the growth of the money supply, or else (more typically) it will have to ration its allocation of credit at the attractive rate. To the extent that it is obliged to finance government deficits, as it often is, it yields control over money creation to the fiscal authorities.

The central bank can influence the composition of spending by determining which borrowers to favor with relatively low interest rates in capital-short economies. Central bank lending has been used to encourage particular forms of investment in all of our countries some of the time, and in some of our countries for the entire period under discussion. This has been an important dimension of development policy. Whether the central bank can influence aggregate demand and output by changing its lending rates is a more complicated and a more controversial question. Under some circumstances, when labor, entrepreneurial talent, and foreign exchange are all available, additional lending by the central bank to its clients, encouraged by low interest rates, may stimulate investment and aggregate output; under other circumstances, perhaps more typical in developing countries most of the time, such lending will simply reallocate spending away from other sources, without stimulating total output. And indeed, to the extent that it stimulates total spending (for example, through a multiple expansion of commercial bank credits), it may merely promote inflation.

The same may be said for the expansion of reserve money: under some circumstances, it may stimulate output (indeed, in a growing economy failure to allow reserve money to increase would almost certainly slow the rate of growth). Beyond some point, however, increasing the rate of expansion of reserve money will encourage excessive spending and lead to some combination of a worsening trade balance and increasing inflation.

The mediating factor in this case is the public's demand for money, and the capacity of the financial system to satisfy that demand on the basis of the reserve money that is made available by the central bank. Since governments everywhere these days have a monopoly on issuing bank notes, that particular form of money is supplied directly by the central bank. Demand and savings accounts are supplied by DMBs, sometimes called commercial banks, on the basis of their deposits at the central bank, which make up the other part of reserve money.

The Demand for Money

Economists typically construct their models of national economies on the assumption that the public's demand for money is fairly stable, or at least that it is a stable function of relatively few variables, notably money income plus some measure of the opportunity cost of holding money, such as interest rates on securities or savings deposits and the rate of inflation. Economic advisers often base their recommendations for even short-run macroeconomic management on the same assumption. It is therefore of interest to discover just how stable the public's demand for money is. To put it another way, just how reliable is the public's demand for money as an analytical tool for macroeconomic management?

The first point to note is that "money" is not a unique entity. By longstanding convention, it includes currency in the hands of the public (notes and coins in circulation) plus demand deposits at DMBs that can be transferred readily from one party to another. These are both means of payment, necessary for economic transactions in any monetary economy, and together they constitute M1. In most countries, DMBs also accept interest-bearing savings deposits, which in fact can be drawn on demand (although not typically transferred by check to another party), and the addition of such accounts to M1 results in a broader concept of money, M2. Financial institutions other than DMBs may also accept savings deposits, and the country may offer government securities for which there is an effective secondary market. So the concept of "money" can be broadened further. For most of our countries, however, financial institutions were not well-developed during most or all of our period, and M1 or M2 can be taken to represent a reasonable approximation to effective means of payment. As discussed in chapter 7, the notable exception is Brazil in the 1980s, with its short-term government paper that could in effect be used as money; and Argentina and Mexico during some periods in which foreign money (U.S. dollars) came to be used extensively for some domestic transactions (see table 10-14 for some comparative figures).

Over a period of twenty years the financial system of any growing economy can be expected to evolve ever more sophisticated institutions to respond to the growth in income and the changing structure of the economy. That has occurred in most of our countries. Concretely, the demand for money (M2) has typically grown more rapidly than GDP, as economies have become monetized and as savers have developed a willingness to hold their savings in financial institutions. Thus, there has been a secular rise in the ratio of M2 to GDP over the period 1965–88 in all our countries except Argentina, Brazil, Colombia, Mexico, and Turkey— which were more or less high-inflation countries, especially in the 1980s.[40] The rise was most striking in Indonesia, Korea, and Thailand, in each of which the ratio more than doubled over the period. Any assessment of the stability of the public's demand for money must be made against the long-run tendency in developing countries for the demand for money to grow more rapidly than GDP.

A second observation is that over a decade or two inflation rates across countries are highly correlated with increases in the money supply, whether measured by reserve money or M2.[41] Inflation cannot be sustained for long periods without an accompanying increase in the means of payment. So it is a truism to say that controlling inflation requires control over the growth of the money supply, and reducing the rate of inflation requires reducing the rate of growth of the money supply. That correct observation does not by itself establish that the public's demand for money is sufficiently stable to provide a reliable basis for framing short-run macroeconomic policy.

To assess that stability we performed two relatively simple calculations. First, we examined the relationship between year-to-year increases in velocity—the annual turnover of the money supply, the reciprocal of M2/GDP—and increases in domestic prices as measured by the GDP deflator. Second, for each of our countries

Table 10.14   Monetary Statistics, 1987

Country	Ratio of currency[a] to reserve money	Ratio of reserve money to money plus quasi money	Ratio of money plus quasi money to GDP[b]
Argentina	.69	.32	.18[c]
Brazil	.46[d]	.25[d]	.09[d]
Cameroon	.87	.26	.19
Chile	.73[e]	.10[e]	.28
Colombia	.49	.44	.21
Costa Rica	.52	.44	.35
Côte d'Ivoire	.74	.42	.29
India	.61	.34	.43
Indonesia	.64	.28	.25
Kenya	.64	.28	.29
Korea	.59	.14	.37
Mexico	.51	.30	.19
Morocco	.88	.30	.46
Nigeria	.64	.33	.24
Pakistan	.79	.39	.40
Sri Lanka	.65	.34	.29
Thailand	.74	.14	.61
Turkey	.44	.32	.26
United States	.76	.09	.63

a. Outside deposit money banks.
b. Average of end-1986 and end-1987.
c. 1986.
d. 1985.
e. 1984.
Source: IMF, *International Financial Statistics*, (various issues).

we estimated demand-for-money functions over the past two decades with a view to discovering how well such estimated functions fit the data. These exercises could be—and in some cases have been—greatly refined; but the underlying hypothesis, embodied in much theorizing and advice, is quite straightforward, and it is useful to test it in a similarly straightforward way, without attempting to mine the data for a superior fit.

Against the secular decline in velocity—the obverse of the trend increase in money in relation to output noted above—a rise in any particular year must be considered unusual. It could reflect a voluntary decline in the demand for money, caused, for example, by higher expected inflation. Or it could reflect an involuntary decline in real money holdings related to an exogenous rise in the price level, such as that brought about by a bad harvest or a sharp increase in oil prices. In the first case, the drop in demand for money, supply unchanged, will lead to an expansion of demand for goods and, under many circumstances, inflation. In this case, the rise in velocity will endure as long as the higher inflation expectations endure. In the second case, the increase in velocity is a response to a higher price level. Here, the increase clearly follows a rise in prices. Velocity should fall again (in relation to trend) following the involuntary rise, as the public restores its real money balances to its preferred level. Of course, a drop in demand for money *may* also follow a rise in prices, if that has created expectations about further inflation.

What can we say about actual increases in velocity? First, velocity rose in almost all of our countries in 1974, immediately following the first oil price shock (Cameroon, Côte d'Ivoire, and Argentina were the exceptions), and in seven countries the rise exceeded 10 percent in a single year, a large increase. Half our countries also experienced a rise in velocity in 1980, the most important year of the second oil shock. These increases are most obviously of the involuntary kind, associated with a temporary rise in the rate of inflation. Inflation rates in 1974 fell from the preceding year only in Argentina, India (where a good crop succeeded a poor one), and Thailand.

Apart from 1974 and 1980, velocity in our countries increased by more than 5 percent, a significant amount for purposes of macroeconomic management, on 55 occasions between 1965 and 1989, which, with 1974 and 1980, add up to 79 out of a total of 408 country-year observations. Data are not available for all our countries for the entire period, which would involve 18 x 24 = 434 country-year observations. Every country experienced at least one such increase. Most of these increases in velocity were associated with a contemporaneous increase in inflation, although in 18 instances the rate of inflation was lower than in the previous year, which suggests either an exogenous movement in velocity or an upward shift in inflationary expectations based on experience in previous years.

In most (thirteen) of our countries, velocity dropped back to trend following a sharp rise in 1973–74; this movement suggests the rise was involuntary, associated with the rise in oil and in other commodity prices in those years, and was restored as the public rebuilt money balances to correspond to the new, higher level of prices. Such an increase in velocity supports the "bubble inflation" discussed in Chapter 6. This pattern contrasts with what happened in the early 1980s, in association with some combination of the 1979–81 oil price increase and the debt crisis of 1982–83. In ten of our countries, the fact that velocity rose sharply and then stayed high or even continued to rise for several years suggests a rise in inflationary expectations that induced the public to reduce money holdings in relation to income. Only after several years and substantial economic retrenchment did velocity resume its downward trend.

The same issue can be approached in a slightly different way by comparing increases in prices with increases in the money supply, to see whether the result coincides with the observation that the demand for money grows more rapidly than GDP, so that prices ought generally to rise considerably less than the money supply in growing economies. Over the period 1965–87, prices (as measured by the GDP deflator, which excludes import prices) rose more rapidly than the money supply (M2) one-sixth of the time (52 out of 331 possible country-years, allowing for missing data), and rose more rapidly than M1 and reserve money nearly one-quarter of the time.

Invoking money growth in the preceding year does not generally provide an explanation for this otherwise puzzling result, and reductions in real GDP help explain only a few of the instances. Only 14 of the 52 cases of price increases exceeding contemporaneous money growth occurred in years of economic downturn, and 10 of those were in the world recession periods of 1975 and 1981–83. For instance, Brazil, Chile, and Mexico all fell into this category in 1983, and in no case could the decline in demand for money be adequately explained by the decline in real economic activity.

In summary, on these tests the velocity of money does not seem to be reliably stable for purposes of short-run macroeconomic analysis, since a 5 percent (or greater) unexplained movement in velocity introduces a significant amount of uncertainty into the public's response to any given event or action.

Formally estimated demand for money equations confirm the above results. Such equations were estimated for all our countries, in which both base money (M0) and M2 in real terms were regressed on real GDP, inflation in the same year, and inflation in the previous year, over the period 1965–88. The underlying idea is that demand for money will be positively related to growth in income, but negatively related to inflation, and possibly to last year's inflation since the public's expectations about inflation may be shaped by their recent experience.[42] Over this period, however, contemporaneous inflation was a statistically significant influence on demand for money in only two of the eighteen estimated equations for M0 and in only four of the estimated equations for M2, and one of those was negligible in magnitude. Inflation lagged by one year performed a little better, but not much: it was statistically significant in four of the equations for M0 and in six of the equations for M2, although of negligible magnitude in two of the latter. True, most of the equations gave a good overall statistical fit, but that was due almost solely to the fact that both real GDP and real money balances were rising in all our countries over this period; it does not provide a reliable basis for short-run analysis.[43]

Interest Rate Policy

Short-term interest rates are a principal indicator of monetary stance in industrialized countries, and changes in these rates are used operationally to restrain or to stimulate demand, or at least to signal to financial markets what the central bank thinks about the state of the economy. Interest rate policy in developing countries shows only a pale reflection of that role. At least until the mid-1980s, governments set almost all interest rates below market-clearing rates, with the result that credit had to be rationed to preferred customers. Nonpreferred customers were forced to seek credit outside the banking system when total demand for credit was high, which was usually the case. Indeed, interest rate policy has been used consciously as a component of *development* strategy, rather than as a component of stabilization strategy. Credit rationing has been deliberate, designed to steer credit toward preferred sectors of the economy, whether that be heavy industry, agriculture, or exports—each of which was favored in one or more countries. During considerable stretches of time, real interest rates were negative in most of our countries, at least when "real" interest rates are measured using controlled lending rates and the consumer price index.[44]

The short-run influence of interest rates in a developed economy is threefold: first, interest rates affect directly the costs of investment (and of consumer credit); changes in interest can therefore affect spending and savings, depending on their sensitivity to these rates. Second, interest rates can affect the exchange rate when it is free to move, thereby influencing the competitiveness of the country's products with respect to foreign goods and services; through that channel, they can affect demand for the country's output at home and abroad. Third, changes in interest rates affect the market value of long-term assets such as stocks, bonds, and houses; insofar as demand is influenced in the short-run by these changes in wealth, interest rates affect aggregate demand through that channel as well.

All three effects are muted or nonexistent in developing countries. Secondary markets for both long-term financial and nonfinancial assets in developing countries are by and large undeveloped, so there is little opportunity for changes in wealth induced by interest rates to be mobilized for spending in the short run. As discussed in chapter 8, exchange rates in developing countries were virtually all under direct control during most or all of our study period. Moreover, private international capital movements are also typically under formal control in most developing countries. Among our countries, Indonesia and Mexico marked a major exception to this last practice throughout the period, having no effective controls on capital movements, along with Chile and Argentina in the late 1970s and Thailand in the late 1980s. Moreover, Morocco, Pakistan, and Turkey all enjoyed large inflows of remittances from workers abroad, and those remittances could be accelerated or retarded according to prevailing monetary conditions, thus providing a considerable degree of private capital mobility even in the presence of formal controls on capital movements. In these countries, (deposit) interest rates and exchange rate policy could influence private international capital movements considerably; hence the liquidity of the domestic financial system.[45] Cameroon and Côte d'Ivoire had free capital movements with respect to France and other members of their respective monetary areas, although France itself maintained controls on resident capital outflows to non-franc zone destinations until the late 1980s.

Finally, excess demand for bank loans at the controlled interest rates prevailed virtually all the time, so spending was influenced only insofar as interest rates in the informal curb markets were raised or lowered, and that was more a question of overall monetary policy than of official interest rate policy.

However, the use of interest rate changes for stabilization purposes was not wholly absent. If we measure interest rate policy by changes in the discount rate of the central bank, to which other official interest rates were usually related, all countries had some changes in policy over the period 1965–89, with Morocco and Pakistan (four changes each) showing the least change, and with Argentina, Brazil, Chile, and Mexico changing their rates almost every year. Other countries ranged from five to thirteen changes over the twenty-three-year period.[46] The frequency of the changes was highly correlated with variability in inflation rates, being higher for high-inflation countries. Countries with low inflation tended to alter their discount rates infrequently.

The notable exception to this generalization was Thailand, which changed its discount rate fairly often over the 1977–89 period, in an attempt to modulate the economy and in particular to restrain increases in the rate of inflation. That was so despite the fact that Thailand's money market was not well developed and its secondary market in financial instruments was virtually nonexistent. Starting in 1979 the Bank of Thailand developed a limited form of open-market operations in the form of repurchase agreements for government bonds (typically of one- to three-year maturity), whereby the bank could alter commercial bank liquidity by buying or selling the bonds against a guaranteed reversal of the transaction within a specified period of time.[47] This instrument was used increasingly throughout the 1980s, especially in 1986–87 when the Bank of Thailand wanted to reduce bank liquidity arising from the balance of payments surplus; it also reduced the discount rate in 1986 to discourage capital inflow.

Most countries raised their discount rates with the general rise in world inflation in the late 1970s, and reduced them with the decline in world inflation in the mid-1980s, but the extent and pace of change varied greatly from country to country, and a few did not follow the pattern at all. Pakistan's discount rate remained unchanged at 10 percent from 1977 through 1990, for instance, and Morocco's official lending rate was unchanged at 7 percent from 1978 until 1985, when it was raised to 7.8 percent. India's official lending rate was raised to 16.5 percent in 1980, but then remained there throughout the 1980s.

Other countries, in contrast, used changes in interest rates to help control the economy. Colombia raised its discount rate in 1976 to restrain demand in the presence of the coffee boom, and lowered the discount rate to counter the recession of 1982. Korea raised its rate in 1978 to help counter inflationary pressures (a stabilization program was introduced in early 1979), and again in 1980, but lowered it in 1981 and 1982 to help stimulate demand.[48]

In the second half of the 1980s, at the end of our period, some of our countries moved cautiously toward liberalization of their domestic financial markets, including liberalization of interest rates from official control. Argentina and Chile led the way in the late 1970s, but temporarily reversed themselves in the early

1980s. Indonesia, Korea, Mexico, Thailand, and Turkey all liberalized substantially during the 1980s.

A key question for monetary policy was how well the central bank could control domestic credit creation, given the budget deficit. To what extent did an increase in the budget deficit increase total monetary expansion, and to what extent did it squeeze credit to the private sector? The answer seems to be that on the whole, short-run changes in the budgetary position, insofar as they were financed by the banking system, increased the rate of monetary expansion rather than crowding out credit to the private sector.[49]

Role of the Central Bank

The central bank of each country is a special kind of state-owned enterprise. It typically performs certain governmental functions, such as regulating and supervising the country's banks and perhaps also its other financial institutions. Typically, it is also the fiscal agent for the government, handling its cash balances, making disbursements, and covering deficits that have not been covered elsewhere. Most important, it issues the country's money, in the form of currency and deposits for government and financial institutions, which are its liabilities. Against these liabilities it holds various assets—claims on the government, in the form of loans or rediscounted paper; and—as holder and manager of the country's foreign exchange reserves—claims on foreign banks or governments, often U.S. Treasury bills denominated in foreign currency. It may also hold gold, although gold formed only a small fraction of the foreign exchange reserves of our countries, and in any case does not bear interest.[50]

The distinctive feature of a central bank as a financial institution is that its assets in principle bear interest, whereas at least most of its liabilities (currency and, normally, deposits by banks) do not bear interest. Central banks therefore should be very profitable, since the costs of operation and of printing new currency are small in relation to the difference between interest receipts on assets and interest payments on liabilities. After allowance for building reserves, these profits can be returned to the government as nontax earnings—that is the institutional embodiment of the seigniorage discussed earlier and in chapter 6.

As in table 10-12, seigniorage can be a significant source of revenue for governments in countries growing rapidly and experiencing moderate inflation. The transfers to government from central banks are typically less, and sometimes far less, than these calculations suggest. This shortfall can be explained at least in part by the fact that many governments do not pay interest on their obligations to the central bank, which reduces central bank earnings correspondingly. This practice represents a difference in form but not in substance, since the government still acquires the seigniorage. Central banks sometimes make loans at concessional interest rates to state-owned enterprises, however, or to specialized financial institutions established to promote agriculture, housing, exports, or the like, that will lower their earnings. The central bank can actually run losses through the sale of foreign exchange at domestic prices lower than the price at which the foreign exchange was purchased, or through the purchase from commercial banks of non-performing loans, which later have to be disposed of at a loss. One or both of these latter practices were common in our countries during the 1980s.

As discussed earlier, a major currency devaluation creates a serious problem for any institution that must service a debt denominated in foreign currency, but whose earnings are largely in domestic currency rather than in foreign exchange. Expenditures in local currency rise by the full amount of the devaluation, whereas there is no corresponding increase in receipts. The government budget will suffer if the government is a debtor to foreigners. Previously profitable firms can be thrown into the red, and previously solvent financial institutions can suddenly find not only that their operating statement has grown worse, but that they are actually insolvent if they have not built an adequate reserve against the contingency of a major devaluation.

To avoid wholesale bankruptcy, and even collapse of the financial system, central banks have sometimes made special provisions with respect to external debt—either by absorbing it directly, in exchange for claims in domestic currency on the domestic debtor, converted at an exchange rate favorable to the debtor relative to the new prevailing exchange rate; or by selling foreign exchange to the debtor at a rate more favorable than the new prevailing exchange rate for the purpose of servicing the external debt. The former practice occurred in Argentina, Brazil, and Chile in the early 1980s, and in Nigeria in 1986; the latter in Chile, Costa Rica, and Mexico.

Apart from devaluations (although sometimes related to them), half of our countries had financial crises in the first half of the 1980s. These crises arose in part from excessive domestic lending, and often uncritical lending, to domestic enterprises, including SOEs, in the late 1970s and early 1980s. Then the terms of trade shocks and rise in world interest rates exposed the fragility of the domestic debt structure. Although the details differ substantially from country to country, the common element was loans that deteriorated in the new situation, and banks or other financial institutions that were undercapitalized in relation to the risks that they were in fact running.[51]

Chile provides a dramatic example. Chile liberalized its economic system extensively in the late 1970s, reduced inflation, and ran substantial budget surpluses. In response, Chilean firms increased their investments and put strong upward pressure on local costs, especially on real estate values. These provided the basis for bank loans, which were supplied in part by an inflow of private capital from abroad.

A sharp drop in the price of copper, hence in Chilean income, from the temporary highs of 1979–80, exposed the underlying fragility of Chile's financial structure.[52] To compound the problem, several banks were owned by industrial combines, called *grupos*, which used the banks to channel loans to members of the combine, evidently without even the usual scrutiny of business loans. In November 1981, the Chilean government took over four insolvent banks whose assets together accounted for 35 percent of the entire banking system. Emergency loans to these banks expanded total credit by about 4.4 percent of GDP.

Fixing the exchange rate in the presence of wage indexation (see chapter 8) imposed serious macroeconomic strains that made it impossible to withstand the drop in copper prices, and Chile (contrary to stated policy) devalued the peso by more than 80 percent against the U.S. dollar from June to December 1982. By itself, this devaluation created a serious problem for banks and firms with dollar-denominated debt but without dollar-denominated assets or receipts. The central bank therefore created a preferential exchange rate for the repayment of external debt, which was to last four years at a rate 20 to 40 percent more favorable than the commercial exchange rate.

Despite these two relief measures, the Chilean economy and financial structure continued to deteriorate, and the government in January 1983 intervened in seven additional banks, accounting together for another 45 percent of the assets of the banking system. The central bank made further loans to the intervened banks and also purchased delinquent loans from other banks, to shore up their financial condition. Thus, a government bent on reestablishing a privately owned economy unwittingly found itself with extensive ownership and management responsibilities. By the end of 1983, emergency loans to the banking system amounted to more than 1.5 times the capital and reserves of the banking system.

Poor loans weakened the condition of the banks and reflected the weak condition of the borrowing firms. The government therefore sponsored a series of domestic debt reschedulings in 1983 and 1984, making many loans repayable over ten years at a real interest rate of 7 percent. For these rescheduled loans, the central bank lent to the commercial banks at 5 percent, thereby permitting a margin of 2 percent for the banks, at the expense of the central bank, whose opportunity cost was higher than 5 percent. Total transfers from the central bank to the financial system and to private borrowers during the period 1982–86 have been estimated at the equivalent of $6 billion, or 6 percent of GDP over the five years.[53]

Thus, an important part of the seigniorage generated by Chile's central bank was dissipated in bolstering the banking system and therefore was not turned over to the government as nontax revenue. The central bank was used as a nonbudgeted source of fiscal support. This practice is common, especially in the presence of financial crises, where the central bank is the natural source of support, and where for reasons of public confidence the government does not want to expose such support to a budgetary debate.

In 1981–82 the Argentine central bank, in order to encourage the rollover of private external debt to protect its foreign exchange reserves, offered exchange rate guarantees and swap arrangements to banks and private borrowers. When the peso was devalued sharply in 1981 and again in 1982, these guarantees had to be honored; and the swaps matured in late 1982. The central bank could not provide foreign exchange at the time, so it converted the obligations into dollar-denominated government bonds. In excess of $10 billion was involved. In this way, the Argentine government acquired much external debt without borrowing abroad directly. While the details differ, substantial private external debt was also acquired by the central government or central bank in Brazil, Chile, Mexico, Nigeria, and Turkey.

Often, seigniorage has also been used continuously for support for favored activities, usually in the form of low-interest loans or discount facilities, again representing a fiscal function that does not show up in the budget. In these circumstances it is inappropriate to count seigniorage (including the inflation tax) as contributing toward the financing of the normally recorded government expenditures.

Throughout the 1970s, Korea used most of its seigniorage to support favored industries through low-interest loans to banks making preferential loans. Korea's financial crisis in the early 1980s can be traced to some fraudulent activity in Korea's financial markets, but also to overextended loans, encouraged by earlier governments, to industries whose economic conditions turned out to be worse than originally hoped or expected, especially shipbuilding and overseas contract construction. Banks that had made these loans found themselves weakened financially, and threatened with insolvency if the bad loans had to be written off. Outstanding loans were rescheduled, and capital-strong firms were encouraged to buy the weak debtors, sometimes with new low-interest loans. The Bank of Korea in turn made concessional loans to the banks, whose outstanding claims were rescheduled and which made new loans to the acquiring firms.

The 55 percent depreciation of the won against the U.S. dollar between the end of 1979 and the end of 1982 also hit those with external debt in dollars. Fortunately, most of the debt was carried by firms with good export earnings, so no special arrangements were required. Those enterprises that ran into external debt-servicing difficulties because of the devaluation were treated no differently from other enterprises in financial difficulty: if their long-run prospects looked good, they were given loans at concessional interest rates to tide them over the transition. The cumulative result of these various rescue operations was that the Bank of Korea used up its substantial reserve and drove it to quite negative levels between 1981 and 1987. That is, the Bank of Korea not only used up its seigniorage, but also borrowed from the public (in the form of monetary stabilization bonds, issued against itself) in order to carry out what in effect were fiscal functions. Insofar as these activities involved operating subsidies, and not simply accounting recognition of bad loans that had been made earlier, for purposes of economic analysis they should be added to the government's budget deficit.[54]

Similar activities were undertaken by central banks in Argentina, Brazil, Colombia, Costa Rica, and Turkey. In some cases, the fiscal activities of the central banks were so great that they absorbed more resources than the seigniorage had yielded. Largely as a result of preferential exchange rates for selected customers and debtors, in connection either with providing exchange rate guarantees to ward off the consequences of expected devaluations (Argentina, Brazil) or with central bank absorption of external debt to avoid insolvency of the debtors after devaluation (Costa Rica, Mexico), some central banks ran truly enormous deficits. On one calculation, for instance, the Argentine central bank had deficits equal to 25 percent of GDP in 1982, 5 percent in 1983, 17 percent in 1984, and 7 percent in 1984.[55] Costa Rica's central bank was still running a deficit in excess of 3 percent of GDP into the second half of the 1980s. Some of these "deficits" arose from the accrual of interest on foreign loans, and thus did not involve immediate monetary expansion. Some of the large deficits represented accounting losses on low-value claims absorbed by central banks to avoid commercial bank insolvency, so they have a quite different macroeconomic impact from a purchase of goods or services. These operations were a far cry from providing seigniorage to government as an important nontax source of revenue.

It is perhaps worth noting that two recent studies suggest that the formalities of central bank independence do not seem to be sufficient to preserve central bank independence.[56] "Independence" in the first study was judged on the basis of eighteen criteria concerning the appointment and removal of central bank governors and their boards of directors, the presence of government representatives at central bank deliberations, and the control of central bank boards over the instruments of monetary policy. By this standard, the National Bank of Switzerland is the most independent central bank, followed closely by the Federal Reserve Board of the United States, the German Bundesbank, and the Netherlands central bank (all tied for second).[57] Central banks in developing countries are much less independent, with the most independent of the twenty countries studied (Tunisia) being the equivalent of ninth in the list of central banks of nineteen developed countries, and seven of them falling below the least independent central bank (Australia's Reserve Bank) among the developed countries.

More significant, the degree of independence as measured by these criteria of formal structure are *not* correlated with overall economic performance, or with inflation. Among our countries (eight of which are covered by the study), Argentina is the most independent (falling just below Tunisia), and Kenya, Korea, and Mexico are tied for least independent, with Brazil, Turkey, and Thailand all being only slightly more independent. By contrast, Thailand and Korea are among the best performers, and Argentina the worst, among our countries.

A second study examined the *laws* governing central banks in more than 100 countries, developed and developing, including ten of our countries; and in particular the legal limitations on central bank lending to the government. It concluded that there is little relationship between law and practice: some central banks remain well below their statutory limits, while others transgress their legal limits in various ways. Formal rules are no substitute for conviction when it comes to managing monetary policy.[58]

Côte d'Ivoire and Cameroon are unusual among our countries in that they do not have national central banks. Rather, each belongs to a regional monetary union involving five or six other countries, operating in cooperation with the Treasury of France. As a result, the national governments cannot turn automatically to a money-creating institution to finance budget deficits. In view of this limitation, it may be asked how Côte d'Ivoire ran into such financial difficulty, generated in part by large budgetary expenditures, in the late 1970s and early 1980s. The answer lies in a combination of external loans (during the time that was possible on a large scale) followed by involuntary external and domestic lending through the simple expedient of not paying bills, that is, building up arrears.

Côte d'Ivoire belongs to the West African Monetary Union (WAMU), along with six other west African countries, the most economically important of which is Senegal. These countries share a common central bank, BCEAO, located in Dakar, which issues the common currency (the Communauté financière africaine [CFA] franc) and governs monetary policy for the union as a whole. As discussed in chapter 8, the CFA franc has had an exchange rate fixed at 50:1 with the French franc since the beginning of the union in 1962. The BCEAO maintains an operations account with the French Treasury, which includes overdraft facilities, into which it must deposit at least 65 percent of its foreign exchange reserves.[59] The Council of Ministers provides guidance on overall monetary policy, but its decisions must be unanimous. Specific policy measures are decided by a board of administrators, made up of two representatives from each member country and two from France, on the basis of simple or two-thirds majority. A national credit committee from each member state makes recommendations annually on the growth in the money supply and in central bank credit, and until the late 1980s on the sectoral allocation of credit.

The BCEAO sets credit limits for all deposit banks that have rediscount privileges at the central bank and requires prior authorization for any loan to a single borrower in excess of CFA francs 100 million (about $400,000). Credit for crop financing can be entirely rediscounted at the BCEAO, but total financing through the BCEAO discount window is limited to 35 percent of each commercial bank's outstanding credit; BCEAO credit to governments, directly or indirectly through rediscounting government bills, is limited to 20 percent of tax receipts the previous year.

The BCEAO also operates a money market for reallocating excess funds within the region, or to the money market of Paris. The interest rates are determined by BCEAO, but with an eye on international rates to encourage remittance of foreign exchange to the WAMU, and to discourage outflows of private capital.

Under these arrangements, government borrowing from the central bank is far more limited in Côte d'Ivoire than in most other countries, but foreign exchange is freely convertible into CFA francs. Hence, in the study period, as long as external funds were available, the government could readily finance budget deficits; and during the early 1970s Côte d'Ivoire was considered the most promising of the non-oil-producing Sub-Saharan African countries, so external credit was readily available. That ceased to be the case in the early 1980s, when it became clear that Côte d'Ivoire had become overextended, and when the Latin American debt crisis induced international bankers to be much more cautious in their lending. Côte d'Ivoire had a serious slump in 1982–83 and cut way back on its high government expenditures, especially on investment projects. Revenues also suffered, so a deficit remained to be financed. Since the domestic capital market was nonexistent and access to the central bank strictly limited, the government financed its deficit by not paying some of its bills—its contractual external debt service (both principal and interest), and domestic bills to suppliers, farmers (under the price stabilization scheme), and even employees. Côte d'Ivoire arranged a debt rescheduling in 1984 to deal with the external arrears, and as the terms of trade and the general economy improved in 1984–86, it paid off the domestic arrears.

A similar phenomenon occurred in 1987–88. Internal support prices for cocoa and coffee, Côte d'Ivoire's two major export crops, had been raised by one-third between 1983 and 1986, and world prices increased sharply in 1985–86. These internal prices remained well below world prices, and the price stabilization fund (CSSPPA) normally was a substantial net earner of revenue for the public sector. Following a sharp decline in world cocoa and coffee prices in 1987, however, the CSSPPA retained its higher support prices for Ivoirean farmers (historically, the CSSPPA had never reduced prices), and began to run large losses. Thus not only did a normal source of public sector revenue dry up, but the CSSPPA could not pay its suppliers and even some of the exporters.

It might be thought that CSSPPA policy offers an important automatic stabilizer in the Ivoirean economy, at least with respect to movements in world cocoa and coffee prices, the most important components of Côte d'Ivoire's terms of trade. High world prices are skimmed, and low world prices are compensated to the farmer-exporters. If world prices and domestic production are not inversely correlated, this institutional arrangement should help to stabilize domestic income, hence aggregate demand within Côte d'Ivoire. Indeed, the calculation reported in table 10-13 shows tendencies toward stabilization, but they are small and not statistically significant.

The problem in practice is that in periods of high world prices, such as 1976–78, the government did not sequester the incremental revenues, but rather financed expanded government activities, both investment and current spending. The stabilizing feature was thus lost. (This expansionary activity was more restrained during the 1985–86 price boom.) Then when prices fell, the government could not pay all of its bills, including its obligations to the farmers. Farmers and wholesalers had (collectively) large seasonal loans that they were unable to pay, so total credit to the agricultural and commerce sectors rose substantially. Some of this could be discounted at the BCEAO, with the result that total credit increased, but banks had run up against their limits and consequently had to deny credit to other private borrowers, thereby contributing to the slump in economic activity. So CSSPPA's activities achieved less macroeconomic stabilization than might be expected at first sight.

Côte d'Ivoire's budget deficit grew from 1 percent of GDP in 1986 to 7 percent in 1987 and to more than 13 percent in 1988. By the end of 1988, total government arrears amounted to 5 percent of GDP, of which three percentage points were to domestic claimants. Additional financing of the budget deficit came from commercial banks and from running down cash balances. These expedients are all limited compared with an unlimited access to new central bank credit, so in the end they will force financial discipline on the government. In the short run of two or three years, the experience of Côte d'Ivoire suggests that the inability to monetize deficits at a central bank is not foolproof insurance against large budget deficits.

Summary

Although this chapter has provided much factual detail, it gives only a flavor of the role of fiscal and monetary policy in developing countries experiencing significant external or internal economic disturbances. That role, it seems, is exceedingly complex. Still, we will venture several generalizations.

First, fiscal policy has rarely helped to stabilize output and employment in our countries, and sometimes it has been a significant destabilizing factor. Fiscal policy in the 1980s often helped to reduce external imbalances, as governments could not continue to finance externally the large budget deficits they were running, and many of them found the inflationary consequences of central bank finance unacceptable. Even in these cases, however, fiscal policy had contributed to the large initial external imbalances.

Second, the central government did not always have effective control over fiscal policy for purposes of macroeconomic management, thanks to the relative independence of state-owned enterprises and in some cases provincial governments. In a few cases, largely associated with substantial unexpected increases in revenues, governments temporarily lost control over their own budgets.

Third, monetary policy is largely an adjunct of fiscal policy, and of the commitment to an exchange rate that is fixed in the short run. Many governments have turned extensively to their central banks for financing deficits, and even external borrowing typically results in monetary expansion under fixed exchange rates.

Fourth, seigniorage, especially when augmented by an "inflation tax," is a significant source of potential revenue to governments in developing countries, but it is often not, in fact, acquired by the government, being used instead to cushion the private sector in various ways, and is thus either dissipated or used consciously for the pursuit of policy objectives outside the budget.

Fifth, the demand for money varies greatly in most developing countries, in ways that are not easily predictable, and thus it does not provide a stable foundation on which to base short- to medium-run (one to three years) macroeconomic policy.

Sixth, endowing central banks with formal independence, or with legal restrictions on their capacity to lend to government, does not by itself seem to provide an adequate basis for separating fiscal from monetary policy, or for preventing inflationary finance. As discussed in chapter 12, effective monetary control seems to rest more on public or elite conviction, backed up by skilled technocrats who have the support of the country's leadership and of its public.

Finally, a large outstanding public debt, external or internal, whether acquired by borrowing or by capital losses through devaluation or by a takeover of private debt, can greatly reduce the room for maneuver of fiscal and other macroeconomic policy, since the fiscal implications of exchange rate changes or tighter monetary policy—or indeed even of a strong rhetorical stance that affects market interest rates—are roughly proportional to the relevant outstanding debt.

Chapter 11

Macroeconomic Management
and Long-Run Growth

This book has been primarily concerned with the way the governments of our eighteen countries have handled the instruments of macroeconomic policy, particularly when reacting to exogenous changes, and with the extent to which they have created problems for themselves. It does not go into those basic determinants of growth that are independent of macroeconomic policy, or only remotely connected to it. Nor does it consider the influence on growth of the long-run configuration of economic policy in relation to such matters as the extent of public ownership, redistribution, or of industrial and other policies likely to affect the pattern of domestic industrial and agricultural production and investment.

In this chapter we are thus concerned only with the probable repercussions on long-run growth of the government's handling of public expenditure and revenue in the short and medium term; its financing of deficits and control over money creation; its credit policies; and the manner in which it achieves or fails to achieve a viable balance of payments with the rest of the world.

Growth may be affected by many determinants that are wholly or largely independent of macroeconomic policy, such as climate, health, education and training, research, and so on. The determinant that is most directly affected by macroeconomic policy is investment, both public and private. Admittedly, when government expenditures are varied as part of macroeconomic policy, expenditure on health, education, and research may be affected. We did not study variations in such expenditures, and in any case, econometric studies have not been able to isolate the growth effects of such expenditures with much confidence.[1]

This chapter is therefore devoted mainly to the effects of macroeconomic policy on the level of gross investment in relation to GNP (the investment ratio), and the productivity of investment; and also in relation to the domestic savings ratio, since this largely determines the investment ratio. We also look at the relationship between growth and inflation.

Neoclassical growth theory made a distinction between changes that would affect the rate of growth of output, and those that would affect only the level of output. In particular, it was held that a rise in the investment ratio alone would eventually have no effect on the rate of growth of output. In long-run equilibrium, this latter rate was determined only by the rate of growth of population, and the rate of labor-augmenting (Harrod-neutral) technical progress, and these were independent of the investment ratio. We do not find value in this distinction, for we believe that investment causes technical progress (as well as being caused by it). Once this is admitted, it becomes possible for a higher investment ratio (or an increase in the productivity of investment) to cause a higher rate of economic growth indefinitely, indeed forever.[2] In any case, in the time frame that mortals usually consider, an increase in the rate of investment can influence the rate of growth by moving the economy from one (growing) level of output to a higher one.

Successful macroeconomic policy may, on the one hand, be identified with stabilization, that is, with minimizing the consequences of exogenous disturbances while avoiding the creation of unsustainable changes by the operation of the instruments of macroeconomic policy themselves. On the other hand, it is possible that living dangerously, with a consequential stop-go or boom-and-bust performance, will result in greater growth in the long run than a more orderly advance. We shall address this issue.

If stability seems to be advantageous for long-run growth, this must mainly be because either stable growth results in a higher level of investment in relation to GNP, or because investment within a framework of stable growth of both GNP and investment is more efficient than investment with a stop-go scenario. A priori, one would expect both of these hypotheses to be verified, especially the second. We shall pay particular attention to the stability of investment, and to its efficiency.

Investment must be matched by domestic or foreign savings. Although investment exceeded domestic savings in most years in all eighteen countries, the extent to which it was financed by foreign loans (or equity) or grants varied greatly. To the extent that foreign savings have to be paid for, a high level of self-financing should be more productive of GNP (but not GDP) than a low level.

Changes in the terms of trade may affect the growth of real GNP or GDP. The terms of trade do not affect real product growth directly, since this is measured at constant prices. Yet an improvement in the terms of trade should result in more profitable investment opportunities and thus be favorable to growth, raising both the level and the productivity of investment.

So far, we have not been precise about what we mean by growth. In what follows we define it by the exponential rate of growth of GNP per head. GNP is a better measure of success than gross domestic product, since net payments to foreigners are not part of national income and do not contribute to national welfare. We use GNP *per head* for two reasons. From a welfare point of view, it is obviously the relevant magnitude. From a production point of view, changes in population may be regarded as a crude measure of changes in the labor force, which are treated as exogenous in this study.

It is clear that growth in the labor force contributes exogenously to output, and therefore that growth in GNP per head is a better measure of success than growth in GNP. We have not attempted to estimate a multivariable comprehensive growth model. This would at least require as good a measure as possible of the quantity and quality of the labor input. In other words, the growth rate of the quality-adjusted labor force should be included as an independent variable, as well as the investment ratio, in any regression seeking to explain the growth of GNP (see Scott 1989).[3] Unfortunately our research did not extend to such an estimation of the labor input. This neglect may affect the relative "apparent productivity" of investment in our countries, as explained later in the chapter. At the same time, it does not invalidate what we have to say about the effects of macroeconomic policy on the level and efficiency of investment; and we do not think it could seriously undermine the significance of these determinants of the growth of GNP per head.

In the next section we turn to an overview of the growth of the eighteen countries from 1970 to 1989.

Growth, 1970–89

Table 11-1 records data on the growth of GNP per head, on the average ratio of investment to GNP and its variability, and on the ratio of domestic savings to GNP. It also relates growth to the investment ratio, and records the difference between investment and savings (that is, the reliance on foreign savings). The countries are arranged in order of growth (column 1). We divide them into three sets of six and refer to the sets as the first, second, and third divisions; and to their members as the good, the intermediate, and the bad performers.

Certain facts and implications from table 11-1 stand out:

- None of the good performers rescheduled debt from 1983 to 1988 (see chapter 5; as before, those that rescheduled are in italics). All the bad performers and two of the intermediates rescheduled. High growth may make high debt viable and this was clearly true of Korea. Nevertheless, the association of rescheduling and low growth suggests that unviable indebtedness in the 1980s was a cause of slow growth over the whole period.
- The average ratio of investment was highest for the good performers, and lowest for the bad: but the differences are not very great, much less than the differences in growth rates. From this it follows that the apparent productivity of investment (the growth rate divided by the ratio of investment to GNP; see column 3) was much higher for the good performers than the intermediate, and also much higher for the intermediate than the bad performers. Three of the bad performers experienced negative growth despite gross investment ranging from 17 to 22 percent of GNP. We shall see in the

Table 11.1   Growth Rates, Investment and Savings Ratios, 1970–89

Country	(1) Growth in GNP per head 1970–89	(2) Invest-ment GNP (%)	(3) (1)÷(2)	(4) Coeff. of variance. of (2)	(5) National Savings/ GNP (%)	(6) Invest-ment Savings/ GNP (%)	(7) GNP per head 1987–89/ 1976–78
Good performers							
Korea	6.5	29	21	.13	25	04	2.08
Indonesia	4.2	26	16	.20	26	00	1.58
Thailand	4.1	26	14	.09	22	04	1.67
Cameroon	4.0	22	20	.17	14	08	1.46
Sri Lanka	2.9	22	13	.26	12	10	1.37
Pakistan	2.5	18	15	.11	08	10	1.43
Means	4.0	24	17	.16	18	06	1.60
Intermediate performers							
Brazil	2.2	22	9	.12	19	03	1.12
Turkey	2.1	20	10	.13	16	04	1.19
India	2.0	22	9	.12	19	03	1.29
Morocco	1.8	25	8	.19	13	12	1.13
Colombia	1.7	20	8	.08	18	02	1.17
Kenya	1.3	25	6	.12	17	08	1.12
Means	1.9	22	8	.13	17	08	1.17
Bad performers							
Mexico	1.2	22	3	.12	19	03	1.06
Costa Rica	0.3	26	1	.10	14	12	0.98
Chile	0.3	16	2	.25	11	05	1.23
Côte d'Ivoire	-0.7	22	-3	.31	17	05	0.82
Argentina	-1.0	19	-5	.27	18	01	0.85
Nigeria	-1.5	17	-9	.36	16	01	0.70
Means	-2.3	20	-2	.24	16	05	0.94

Note: Countries in italics rescheduled their debt in 1983–88. The growth in column 1 is the fitted exponential rate expressed as a percentage per year. For some countries, the data must be regarded as especially unreliable in that there are large errors in the appendix tables of chapter 3, from which the
investment and savings figures are derived. These include Cameroon, Côte d'Ivoire, Indonesia, Mexico and Nigeria.
Source: World Bank data.

next section that the investment ratio is significant for growth, but by itself explains only a small part of the variance. Part of the variability in apparent productivity of investment could be that the contribution of labor to growth was greater where growth was greater.

- The variability of the investment ratio (column 4) was greatest for the bad performers, but somewhat higher for the best performers than for the intermediates. The correlation between the apparent productivity and the variability of investment was significantly negative ($r = -0.49$), however. This significance survives the exclusion of the five countries with the most suspect investment figures (but see the next section).
- The degree of reliance on foreign savings did not vary much between the groups. This may well be because this reliance is a poor measure of the costs of foreign savings. Thus a high reliance on foreign savings went together with a high level of aid, for example, in Cameroon, Sri Lanka, and Pakistan among the best performers.
- A few anomalies stand out. The most prominent is Costa Rica with very high and stable investment (but see below), and virtually no growth. This may be a statistical illusion, however (see note 13). Mexico is similar, but not quite as extreme an outlier. Its low growth is explicable in terms of ill-chosen investments and the drag of its high debt after 1982. Pakistan's achievement is remarkable, given the very low level of savings, and Sri Lanka is also remarkable, given the high volatility of its investment and the internal conflicts of recent years.

Some Growth Regressions

Consider now some regressions of long-run growth on its own variability, on the investment ratio and its variability, and on inflation.

We regressed the growth of GNP per head on the coefficient of variation of the annual growth rates of GNP (not shown in table 11-1). We did this for three periods: 1960–89, 1960–74, and 1974–89.[4] The coefficient of variation was significantly negative at the 5 percent level in each case. The correlation was remarkably high for the first two periods (r^2 equaling .49 and .47), but less so for 1974–89 ($r^2 = .22$).

We also regressed the growth of GNP per head (1970–89) on the average investment ratio (1970–88) and its coefficient of variation. The coefficient for the investment ratio was significantly positive at the 10 percent level, and that of the coefficient of variation significantly negative at the 10 percent level. Investment alone explains only 29 percent of the variance. The inclusion of the coefficient of variation raises r^2 to .42.

It is useful to examine the variability of investment in more detail, by considering the reasons for high variability in the case of the seven countries where the coefficient of variation was 19 or more. In four countries—Argentina, Chile, Côte d'Ivoire, and Nigeria—the main reason for the high variability was a collapse of the investment ratio beginning in the crisis year of 1982 (Chile's investment ratio was also very unstable in the 1970s). All of these were poor performers. In two cases—Morocco and Sri Lanka—the situation is best described as a tremendous boom followed by a downward trend. Thus in Morocco from 1972 to 1977 the investment ratio rose from .18 to .35, followed by a decline to about .25 in recent years. In Sri Lanka from 1977 to 1982, the investment ratio rose from .15 to .30, followed by a decline to about .22 in recent years. Indonesia is an exception, for it had no investment collapse. The high coefficient of variation results from a strong rising trend throughout the period, which took the investment ratio from .16 in 1970 to .37 in 1989.[5]

Note, however, that the importance of the variability of the investment ratio depends on a few countries with negative growth and very high variability of investment. Two of these, Nigeria and Côte d'Ivoire, are also countries for which the figures are especially unreliable. For this reason we reestimated the growth of GNP per head on the investment ratio and its variability for thirteen of the eighteen countries for which data are given in Serven and Solimano (1993) (excluded are Cameroon, Côte d'Ivoire, Indonesia, Morocco, and Nigeria), using their figures for investment.[6] The investment coefficient was significant at the 5 percent level, while the coefficient of variation was negative but insignificantly so. Since the excluded countries all had high coefficients of variation, this is, perhaps, not too surprising.[7]

There are, of course, good reasons to suppose that a stable investment ratio (or a stable trend of the investment ratio) will result in more efficient investment than an unstable one. As shown in chapter 3, there were some astonishing rises in the investment ratio within a year or two during the period 1974–81, largely as a result of expenditure on public sector projects. It is difficult to believe that such rapid rises could have been efficiently planned. In contrast, stable investment is associated with a stable growth of real demand, which makes investment easier to plan and less likely to disappoint as a result of excess capacity. Changes in relative prices are also likely to be less severe and easier to predict. The instability of GNP is also associated with cuts in public investment and increases in the cost of private investment, which often cause investment projects to be abandoned or delayed. Even if the cross-country evidence produced above is not totally compelling (econometric evidence never is!), we believe it clearly supports the common-sense a priori view that stability is good for growth.[8]

As for the relationship between inflation and long-run growth, the regression coefficient of growth in GNP per head in 1982–89 on the inflation rate of the consumer price index in 1982 was negative, but not remotely significant (chapter 5). The same was true of the change in the average rate of inflation in the period 1983–88 as compared with 1977–82.

Over the whole period 1965–89, we regressed growth in GNP per head on the inflation rate of the GDP deflator.[9] The coefficient was *negative*, but not significant at the 10 percent level. The same regression was repeated, excluding the three highest inflation countries: Argentina, Brazil, and Chile. The coefficient was *positive*, but again insignificant at the 10 percent level.

Cardoso and Fishlow (1990) found a significant negative correlation between growth in income per head (using Summers and Heston figures) and inflation for seventeen Latin American countries for the period 1950–80. The significance vanished altogether when four high-inflation countries—Argentina, Bolivia, Chile, and Uruguay—were excluded.

It is surely clear from country studies that very high inflation becomes a severe handicap. There is no evidence, however, that moderate inflation inhibits growth.

A Comparison of Shorter Periods

There is little to be learned about the determinants of long-term growth from growth in the shorter periods of the 1970s or 1980s, or from a comparison of them. These periods are too dominated by booms, recessions, and recoveries. As explained in chapters 3, 4, and 5, the investment booms of the late 1970s contributed to high short-term growth within the period, mainly through Keynesian effects rather than by contributing to the production potential of the economy. This experience was followed by actual recession in about half of our countries, with growth below trend in others. Although there was a recovery in the later 1980s, its strength and timing varied; also, the oil producers had a further setback in 1986.

Nevertheless, we have estimated the same regressions for shorter periods as for the period 1970–89. Little that was new emerged in all the trials made. In general, the investment ratio remained significant, but not always the coefficient of variation. For instance, for the period 1982–89, the coefficient of variation was negative but insignificant. We also regressed growth in GNP per head for 1982–89 on the investment ratio for 1982–88, and on the investment boom in the 1970s, defining the latter as the mean investment ratio for the years 1980 and 1981 divided by the mean investment ratio for the years 1974 and 1975. The coefficient of the investment ratio was, as always, positively significant, while that of the boom was negative, albeit insignificant. The correlation between the boom in the 1970s, and the investment ratio in the 1980s was quite low ($r = .22$). This weakly suggests that the boom of the 1970s added little to the investment ratio in the 1980s, and that it is better to achieve a high level of investment gradually.

A more promising approach is to compare GNP per head in the most recent years with that for years immediately preceding the shocks of 1979–82 and the beginning of the debt crisis. We compared average GNP per head for 1987–89 with that for 1976–78. The figures are given in column 7 of table 11-1.

This is a rather direct way of assessing the impact of the terms-of-trade shock and the debt crisis. A comparison of table 11-1, column 7, with table 4-2 shows at a glance that there was no relation between the rise or fall in income per head, and the severity of the 1979–81 shock. Of the six countries in the first division of table 11-1,[10] three (Korea, Sri Lanka, and Thailand) were among the five worst sufferers in 1979–81.[11] Similarly, the third division includes three countries for which the shock was positive (Nigeria and Mexico) or negligibly negative (Argentina). The story is very different for the eight severe debt-crisis countries (the italicized reschedulers). For them, the (unweighted) mean change in GNP per head over the eleven years (from 1976–78 to 1987–89) was –1.4 percent. For the ten nonreschedulers it was +43.6 percent.

The correlation between growth in this later period and the long-run trend (1970–89) is strong. This is to be expected, of course, since it includes eleven out of the nineteen years. Only Brazil and Chile show a large change of rank order. This change is explained by the fact that Brazil was the fastest grower in the 1970s, but has managed only modest growth since then; and the fact that the 1970s brought many troubles to Chile, although it has been experiencing a strong recovery since 1984.

Crises and Investment

From the foregoing discussion, it seems reasonably certain that instability—unsustainable high growth followed by recession or very low growth—is bad for long-run growth. The main transmission mechanism is via the effect of such instability on the average investment ratio over a long period of years, and on the productivity of such investment. The coefficient of variation of investment is negatively associated with the average investment ratio ($r = -.41$). It is also negatively associated with the apparent productivity of investment ($r = -.56$).

Severe falls in the investment ratio followed balance of payments and debt crises in most of the eight debt-crisis countries. In Argentina, Chile, Côte d'Ivoire, and Nigeria, the investment ratio collapsed in 1981 and 1982. Over the course of a few years or less, the ratio was cut in half or more. In Mexico, it fell from 28 percent in 1980 and 1981 to 21 percent in 1984, and in Brazil from 29 to 16 percent. In Morocco and Costa Rica, the fall was minor.[12] Turkey ran into a debt crisis in the 1970s, which pulled investment down from about 25 percent in 1976 and 1977 to about 19 percent in the next two years.

When investment fell, both public and private investment contributed to the fall in roughly equal proportions in most of these countries. The exceptions are Chile, where the collapse was mainly private, and Mexico, where it was almost wholly public. In Chile, the authorities did not cut public investment deeply because the public finances were in good shape.

In non-debt-crisis countries large falls in investment were rare. Kenya suffered a balance of payments crisis in the early 1980s, but did not reschedule. There was a sharp fall in investment from about 29 percent in 1980 and 1981, to about 22 percent in 1983 and 1984, to which both the public and private sectors contributed.

In Sri Lanka, as already mentioned, there was a long drawn-out retreat from the exceptional levels of around 30 percent in 1980 and 1981 to about 23 percent in the late 1980s.

The reasons investment suffers so much in a crisis are well known. The domestic absorption of resources has to be reduced. Governments find it politically easier to cut public investment than public consumption (see chapter 10). A fall in real public consumption will involve wage or employment cuts to a far greater extent than those caused by cuts in investment. They also find it politically and institutionally easier to use monetary policy rather than taxation as a means of quickly reducing private absorption. Thus, private investment is discouraged by either high interest rates or credit rationing, depending on the degree of control over the financial sector. Furthermore, import controls are usually tightened in a crisis: and it is politically easier to cut imports of machinery and equipment, than inputs into domestic production or "essential" items of consumption. Remember, too, that all the rescheduling countries were in recession in the period 1980–83 (see chapter 4). Lower incomes, reduced expectations of future growth, and the general uncertainty arising from the crisis would have greatly discouraged private investment.[13]

Given the disabsorption required to improve the current account of the balance of payments, however, it was necessary for private investment to fall unless consumption were more restrained than it was. To some extent, investment may create its own savings; this is likely to be true in the case of small businessmen and farmers who may restrain their own consumption in order to invest if there is a prospect of good returns. This qualifies the argument only to a limited extent. In fact, as a proportion of GNP, consumption was either maintained or rose in all the crisis countries, except Morocco. Morocco is an exception probably because the recession there was mainly agricultural. It was due to bad weather and did not last long (see chapter 4).

The degree of disabsorption required to improve the current account depends on the ease with which resources can be switched to the production of traded goods. As an unattainable best, the disabsorption required is equal to the amount by which the current account must be improved less any increase in the capacity to produce tradable goods. The adjustment may not require any recession, merely a temporary fall in the ratio of investment or consumption to GNP. At worst, the required fall in the absorption of tradable goods comes about entirely as a result of reduced imports consequent on reduced output.

As already noted in chapter 4, all the crisis countries suffered recessions in 1981 or 1982. It should be remembered that our account of the falls in investment referred to ratios of investment to GNP. To the extent that GNP fell, the absolute falls in investment were, of course, greater.

Also, we have used current prices to calculate the ratio of investment to GNP.[14] Since 1980 the real price of investment (relative to the GDP deflator) seems to have risen substantially in several countries (by about 25 percent), notably in Argentina, Brazil, Colombia, Costa Rica, Thailand, and Turkey (but not Chile, Kenya,

Korea, or Mexico).[15] The reasons for this have not been convincingly explained. It is obviously an important factor for growth that savings buy less real investment.

The lessons for long-term growth are clear. First, countries should avoid unsustainable booms that end in crisis and require subsequent large readjustments that almost inevitably bear hardest on investment. Second, countries should maintain such reserves or unused borrowing capacity as will enable them to ride out a temporary exogenous deterioration in the balance of payments without adjustment, or to adjust gradually to a permanent deterioration. Third, countries should avoid policies that reduce the flexibility with which resources can be shifted from one activity to another. Protective policies for labor that inhibit changes in relative wages or limit redundancies can be counterproductive for employment and labor's earnings by making recessions deeper and longer lasting than they otherwise would be. Fourth, when the need for adjustment becomes clear, governments should delay neither fiscal action when needed, nor prevent changes in the exchange rate that will encourage the production of tradable goods. As shown in chapter 5, inaction or delayed action in these respects is the best determinant of whether a country has suffered a damaging crisis. In all the above ways, the authorities can eliminate or reduce the need for any large and sudden disabsorption. Since disabsorption will probably be concentrated on investment, its avoidance can only enhance the prospects for long-run growth.

Investment Efficiency

Many early writers on development ignored the productivity of investment. Output growth followed investment automatically. Planning models required some marginal capital/output assumption. The optimistic figure of 3 was often used and was varied only a little country by country. In the event, there has been an enormous difference between countries in the apparent productivity of investment (see table 11-1). We cannot here explore all the many factors, apart from the effects of instability discussed above, that may help to account for these differences. One such factor is the differing contribution of labor, any investigation of which we have already disclaimed. Another is the varying degree to which investments are well chosen, and to this we now turn.

The cheap and easy credit of the 1970s tempted many countries into huge increases in public investment for which the decision and planning mechanisms were totally inadequate, and the framework consisted of distorted prices and entrenched nationalistic prejudice in favor of self-sufficiency and opposed to trade. The fact that many investments made in such conditions served to *reduce* GNP had become clear to a few researchers, but had not permeated the consciousness (or consciences) of civil servants, politicians, or presidents in developing countries.[16] The main difference in the 1970s to the long-standing emphasis on import substitution was new investment in "resource based" products for export, mainly on the part of oil exporters (but also Morocco). They seem to have implicitly accepted the false notion that it must always make good economic sense to process one's own materials. Most of these investments had low or negative returns for many different reasons.[17]

Distortions of relative prices affect the economic efficiency of investment. With such distortions, financial costs do not reflect opportunity costs, and revenues do not reflect economic benefits. The economic policies of developing countries have created many such distortions. The two distortion-creating policies that have been most researched are those of import substitution (trade repression) effected through import restrictions and tariffs, and the control of interest rates and credit allocation (financial repression).

The present study was not designed to elaborate or measure the inefficiencies that stem from the general style of a country's macroeconomic policies.[18] It has been primarily concerned with the stabilizing and destabilizing effects of a country's use of the instruments of macroeconomic policy. Trade and financial repression have been part of the background. Admittedly, variations in the degree of trade restrictions have been instruments of macroeconomic policy (see chapter 9), but we have not been able to relate such variations to the efficiency (apart from the level) of private investment. This section is therefore mainly concerned with the efficiency of public investment. As will become clear, the choice of public investments is seldom determined by relative prices: indeed causation often runs the other way.

Cost-benefit analysis was used in very few countries (Little and Mirrlees 1990), or had inadequate coverage and influence where it was used.[19] Feasibility studies by consultants that include a financial analysis are no adequate guard against ill-conceived investments. Sometimes unfavorable reports are ignored. Then, too, the consultant often profits from getting the project implemented, or is unwilling to risk the loss of goodwill involved in advising against a project that is known to be favored by very important persons (Auty 1990).

Cost-benefit analysis has been used by the World Bank and other lending or aid-giving agencies. The World Bank, however, seems to have been infected by the euphoria created in the second half of the 1970s by the success of the Organization of Petroleum Exporting Countries in raising oil prices and by the ease with which capital could be raised at low real interest rates (Little and Mirrlees 1990). In particular, the price projections made were extremely optimistic for the profitability of energy-saving projects and downstream petroleum-based activities including fertilizer production.[20] In addition, cost estimates for such projects were usually unrealistic, despite a mass of accumulated evidence that delays and overruns are endemic.

Macroeconomic evidence clearly indicates that investment in many developing countries has been of low productivity. There is also a mass of anecdotal evidence of bad public investment projects. At the same time, in-depth studies of the distribution of investments and their yields and ex post cost-benefit analyses are rare.[21] So the quality of investment is hard to document objectively. Our project, with its concentration on macroeconomics, was not planned to help fill this gap, but we proceed to record whatever can be learned from the country studies and a few other sources concerning the quality of investment, especially public investment. The related but somewhat different subject of rates of return on capital achieved in state-owned enterprises was considered in chapter 10.

In Brazil, incremental capital output ratios appear to have doubled (after allowing for estimated changes in capacity utilization) from about 2 to about 4 between the late 1960s and early 1970s to the mid-1980s. As partial causes, Coes (forthcoming) suggests a widening of the divergence of interest rates, and an increase in the variation of real exchange rates. There was a rise in the proportion of investment in construction: investment in housing had increased, encouraged by a reduced trust in the inflation indexing of financial assets. Coes further remarks that public investment since the late 1970s was not guided by costs and benefits, and that highly productive infrastructural investment was sacrificed in favor of programs with a demonstrably lower social rate of return. For instance, investment by Nuclebras trebled in the early 1980s, "despite the fact that nuclear power was probably the highest cost source of electricity available to Brazil."

In Cameroon, macroeconomic estimation suggests a high rate of return (see also table 11-1), but this was probably due entirely to oil. Public investment in all other sectors of activity seems to have produced financial losses (see Connolly unpublished).

In Costa Rica, the decision in 1972 to create CODESA, the Costa Rican development corporation which was given direct access to Central Bank credit, was a disaster. It invested in most spheres of economic activity, including such capital-intensive products as fertilizers and aluminum. All its twelve leading subsidiaries had losses in every year from 1976 to 1983, losses exceeding 25 percent of sales. In a report on CODESA, Arthur D. Little stated that "an examination of the feasibility studies for the projects showed serious deficiencies" (González-Vega forthcoming).

In Côte d'Ivoire, a single sugar cultivation and processing project, SODESU-CRE, constituted 37 percent of all public investment in agriculture. Berthelémy and Bourguignon (forthcoming) take this as indicative of the constituents of the enormous rise in public investment in the 1976–80 plan. It was decided on the sole authority of the president. They write: "This project would quickly prove—and probably appeared so to several observers at that time—economically unsound. This was the first time that such an enormous project had been launched. The lack of any serious evaluation before undertaking it has had severe negative effects upon the economy afterwards."

In the case of India, Joshi and Little (forthcoming) estimate a return on public investment of only about 6 percent for both the periods 1960/61 to 1975/76 and 1976/77 to 1986/87. Although the decisionmaking process for public investment seemed sound on paper, the process described, which includes cost-benefit analysis, covered only about a third of public investment. The authors dub the cost-benefit methods used as rudimentary and do not believe that the procedures were sufficiently objective and had enough political backing to adequately counter the chronic Indian preference for self-sufficiency over comparative advantage.

Indonesia gets relatively high marks for its choice of public investments from Woo and others (forthcoming) and other observers, at least for the period after the famous Pertamina crisis of 1975, if not before. As mentioned in chapter 3 and elsewhere, the crisis weakened the nationalist lobby that most favored highly capital-intensive import-substituting investments. As a result of this and the devaluation of 1978, Indonesia maintained rural and agricultural investment, in contrast to Nigeria, with which it is often compared. Nevertheless, Indonesia did promote many large industrial investments, especially in "resource-based" industries. These, however, appear to have been better planned than elsewhere (Auty 1990). Note, too, that when crisis threatened as oil prices fell after 1983, the Indonesian government acted quickly to shelve plans for further large-scale capital-intensive industrial projects.

Korea has the highest apparent productivity of investment among the eighteen countries. Debate goes on—as to whether this is because Korea's macroeconomic policies led to a framework of price incentives that guided investment (predominantly private investment, for Korea has a very low ratio of public investment to total investment, less than 20 percent on average since 1970) in the most socially profitable directions (largely labor-intensive exports) or whether Korea's industrial policies were an important factor. It is common ground that credit was steered at subsidized interest rates toward sectors that the government favored, especially after 1973 when President Park initiated a drive for heavy industry. Auty (1991) estimates low financial returns for steel, petrochemicals, and shipbuilding.[22] It is unlikely that these ventures had the high economic returns that have driven the Korean economy at such a remarkable pace since the early 1960s.[23] Note, however, that Korea's heavy industry projects are probably the most efficient in the developing world (with the possible exception of those in Taiwan). In most developing countries, the capital cost of a plant of the same capacity is 30–100 percent greater than in the United States or Japan. Korea has often achieved lower capital costs, despite the higher cost of imported equipment, because of exceptional speed and efficiency in site preparation, with low construction costs and short gestation periods. As in the case of Indonesia, the heavy industry program suffered rapid and substantial cutbacks when crisis threatened in the late 1970s.

The great Nigerian investment boom of the 1970s was accompanied by negative long-run growth. The boom was initially concentrated on transport, especially trunk roads, in addition to education. Feeder roads were apparently neglected. This was accompanied by administrative incompetence and corruption (so that some of the "investment" was probably consumption or capital flight). The new capital at Abuja was also planned, and work on it continues. In the late 1970s, the emphasis turned to industrial projects in fertilizers, refineries, petrochemicals, and above all steel. The $6 billion steel project runs counter to all advice. Despite continuing crisis, successive Nigerian governments have been obdurate in refusing to cancel or scale it down. The basic reasons for the failure of investment to procure growth would seem to have been the import substitution syndrome combined with overoptimistic assessment of domestic demand; an often grossly overvalued exchange rate, leading to manifold price distortions and uncertainty; and hasty planning and poor implementation.

As for Mexico, Gil Diaz (unpublished) writes of the Lopez Portillo administration from 1976 to 1982:

> The structural rigidities of the economy persisted and grew stronger as the State sector continued its expansion. The huge capital-intensive state enterprises which had been started in the former government, mostly in fertilizers and steel, continued now with incursions into petrochemicals. Mammoth investments into the development of new seaports were also initiated.
>
> It is very difficult to ascertain *a posteriori* if the huge waste involved in these projects was a result of the uncanny ability of the government to select fields in which international prices were going to decline, such as silver, steel, tuna fishing and petrochemicals, or a lack of an adequate study of alternatives when deciding to invest, in ports, for example. Or bad management. Or a bad selection of product lines, as was the case in steel. Perhaps it was a combination of all the factors enumerated above plus a few others which are the natural outcome of spending so much in such a short period.

Regarding the situation in Morocco, Claassen (unpublished) writes, "The fantastic investment boom of 1973–77, largely financed by foreign borrowing and allocated mainly to irrigation and capital-intensive production of import substitutes, constitutes the first reason of the later balance of payment crisis since it did not generate the expected foreign exchange earnings which were necessary in order to service the increasing indebtedness." He also points out that the average investment ratio was considerably higher from 1975 to 1985, while the growth of GDP was lower than in the late 1960s and early 1970s. Claassen criticizes the heavy investment in irrigation on three counts: it was capital-intensive, it favored the elite landowners, and the expected returns were based on an increasing real value of sales of fruit and vegetables to European markets that did not materialize.

Morocco is not the only country to have directed excessive investment into import-substituting capital-intensive industries. This criticism can be leveled at all eighteen countries except Korea for most of the period 1965–89. Morocco also embarked on resource-based export-oriented investment in phosphoric acid. We do not know whether this had good economic returns or not.

Sri Lanka provides an example of the ways in which the efficiency of investment may be diminished in a highly protected economy relying greatly on import controls (Athukorala and Jayasuriya forthcoming). Not only did Sri Lanka fail to exploit its comparative advantage, but the vulnerability of the economy was increased as all imports except capital goods became essential either for life or domestic production. The resulting uncertainty and discontinuities in the availability of imported capital goods bore heavily on investment efficiency. Some cuts in investment after the first oil shock may have been beneficial, however, since a number of negative value added industries, producing mainly intermediates, had been developed in the public sector.

After 1977, Sri Lanka became absorbed with the construction of the Mahaweli irrigation and power project. This, together with a large housing development project, accounted for much of the huge rise in public investment from 1977 to 1980. Initial cost-benefit analysis apparently suggested a yield of 11 percent, but subsequent analysis of the agricultural components of the project has suggested that this was a large overestimate. Athukorala and Jayasuriya (forthcoming) remark that "it is known that alternative less glamorous projects were assessed to have much higher rates of return." Whatever the projected returns, it would seem in any case to have been imprudent to put so many eggs into one basket, but Mahaweli was a pet project of the prime minister (later president), J. R. Jayawardana, whose electoral victory in 1977 and dramatic change of policies won the strong support of foreign capital suppliers.

Macroeconomic Policy and Savings

Given that the use of foreign savings is limited in the manner described in chapter 4, it follows that the ratio of savings to GNP is a constraint on the ratio of investment to GNP (notwithstanding the possibility that investment may to some extent create savings). A rise in private savings permits higher total investment unless such a rise merely compensates for a fall in public savings as the public sector relies more on borrowing and less on taxation.[24] Whether or not higher interest rates cause a rise in savings has been the subject of much debate and econometric investigation. The evidence on balance seems to support a positive effect (see Fry 1988, chap. 6). Further econometric evidence from our country studies, although limited, lends some support to this view.

Athukorala and Jayasuriya (forthcoming) found that the nominal interest rate on deposits (inflation was included as a separate regressor) was significant for private savings in Sri Lanka. They also found that the expansion of bank branches was significant. Onis and Riedel (1993) found that the real deposit rate was highly significant for private savings in Turkey, and that a one percentage point increase raised the savings/disposable income ratio by one percentage point. Joshi and Little (forthcoming) suggest that a rise in real deposit rates from negative to positive was a factor in the substantial rise in household savings/GDP during the 1970s in India. As in Sri Lanka, the fall in population per bank branch was also significant.[25]

Korea is one of the eighteen countries, but no country study was commissioned there. Collins (forthcoming), however, found that the real interest rate was significant in a regression similar to that of Onis and Riedel for Turkey (both include permanent and temporary income as regressors). The leverage was much less, requiring a doubling of real interest rates from about 5 percent to 10 percent to effect a rise in the savings ratio of one percentage point.

The other countries offer no useful evidence, mainly because they did not venture into financial liberalization to any extent until recently. Those that did try some earlier financial liberalization (for example, Argentina and Chile) ended up with very high inflation and financial chaos, which would have made any relationship between savings and its conjectural determinants fragile, to say the least.

Summary and Conclusions

The investment ratio is significantly related to the long-run (1970–89) rate of growth of GNP per head; but it explains only 29 percent of the variance of the intercountry growth rates.

Instability of the investment ratio (and of the annual growth rate of GNP) is negatively related to long-run growth, largely because the poor performers ran into acute balance of payments and debt crises in the early 1980s. This led to severe falls in investment, and to recession, followed only by weak recovery in most cases. It is notable that there is no relation between the severity of the shocks of 1979–82 and long-run growth. Policies matter more than adverse shocks, or windfalls.

The investment booms of the 1970s, financed by foreign borrowing, were part of the reason for the crises (though a few countries managed to have booms without crises). These booms did not compensate for the subsequent collapse.

While instability of investment goes some way toward explaining the huge variations in the apparent efficiency of investment (growth rate per head/investment ratio), much remains unclear. Among the many possible determinants of overall investment efficiency, we have drawn attention to the choice of projects in the public sector. We have found some reason to believe that decisionmaking processes and criteria were often idiosyncratic and imprudent, and seldom calculated to yield high economic or social returns. This, however, is an area in which more research, including *ex post* cost-benefit analysis, is surely desirable.

Our policy conclusions concerning long-run growth are simple indeed:

- The objective of stability should be given much weight in the design and implementation of macroeconomic policy.
- A sound system of cost-benefit analysis should underpin the selection of all large public sector investments.

Chapter 12

The Political Economy of
Stabilization and Adjustment

According to the conventional economic criteria of growth, inflation, and stability of growth, some of our eighteen countries performed well and some performed badly over the years from 1965 to 1990. As already emphasized, these differences cannot be explained by the frequency and the magnitude of external shocks to which they have been subjected. Their explanation lies in other directions.

First, key policymakers may not actually seek these economic objectives, despite the almost universal rhetorical commitment to them. Rather, their foremost concern may be the nation's political stability, security against external or internal aggression, substantial redistribution of income toward one or another favored group of the population, political longevity for themselves, or financial reward for themselves, their relatives, or their loyal supporters.

Second, although policymakers may wish to attain the national economic objectives mentioned above, they cannot do so because officials are unwilling or unable to implement the required policies, or the public will not endure the policies long enough for them to work.

Third, despite well-meaning decisions and implementation, the economies in question may be structured in such a way that the conventional and widely recommended actions to achieve growth and stability with low inflation will not work, as was argued for many years by the so-called structuralists; or, conversely, well-intentioned decisions and implementation following heterodox lines may fail to work because the economy in question is so structured that the conventional remedies would be more appropriate.

Fourth, we must allow for the logical possibility that everything was done more or less appropriately, but bad luck, for example, in domestic harvests or external terms of trade, prevented the country from achieving the desired results. (By the same token, it is possible that policymakers made a series of mistakes in framing or executing their plans, but the performance of the country did not suffer because of unrelated good luck.)

This chapter deals with the first two of these explanations: political factors that inhibit or prevent the attainment of generally acclaimed economic objectives. It also touches briefly on the fourth.

In their work, policy-oriented economists characteristically proceed by adopting the intellectual construct of a unitary governmental decisionmaking process, which involves defining national economic (and other) objectives and then pursuing them in a determined way. Their advice is designed to help clarify the objectives, and in particular to sharpen the need for choice among conflicting objectives; and then to help policymakers mobilize the instruments needed to attain the specified objectives with maximum efficiency. In short, their purpose is to introduce both consistency and efficiency into the pursuit of economic policy. This construct is always useful, sometimes even necessary, but it is totally inadequate for interpreting the economic performance of countries during a historical period, since, as noted above, the policymakers may have given predominant weight to noneconomic objectives; or there may have been no coherent policymaking process, but rather a collection of competing interests, all jockeying to manipulate the instruments in the hands of government for their diverse and typically conflicting aims.

This chapter therefore attempts in a sketchy way to place our countries' response to disturbances in a political setting, and to suggest which political settings are more or less conducive to framing and executing a national economic policy oriented to growth and stability.

By way of background, note that many developing countries have a relatively short history as nation-states, which dates from decolonization in the late 1940s for most of our Asian countries, and in the early 1960s for our African countries. The Latin American countries differ from the others in this respect, since they have been nation-states for well over a century, as has Thailand. Modern Turkey dates from 1920. Furthermore, almost all our countries have experienced periods of serious civil disorder within the past thirty years, since independence. There have been threatened coups (Cameroon, Kenya, Morocco), actual coups (Brazil, Korea, Thailand, Turkey), virtual civil war (Argentina, Chile, Colombia, India), or actual civil war (Indonesia, Nigeria, Pakistan, Sri Lanka). Moreover, some (Argentina, India, Morocco, Pakistan) were involved in international conflicts, and others (Kenya, Chile, Korea, Thailand) at times were deeply concerned about their external security. Among our countries, only Costa Rica, Côte d'Ivoire, and Mexico have avoided serious civil disorder throughout the past quarter century.[1] By comparison, the rich industrialized democracies have been politically calm, peaceful, and orderly during this period.

Despite these disadvantages, the period 1960–73 was an outstanding one for economic development, with unprecedented growth in a number of low and middle-income countries, as discussed in chapter 2. The world's communist countries were also growing rapidly. The climate of opinion was that the state should play a pivotal role in development, not merely or even mainly as a provider of a stable framework for private decisions, but as an entrepreneur, investor, and general manager of the pace and direction of economic development. A formal process of development planning came into vogue, encouraged by the apparent postwar success of the Soviet Union, with its five-year plans for determining investment and allocating key resources within the economy.

The vision of those who favored an activist state extended beyond the nation to the international economic order, which was alleged in the late 1960s to be biased against low-income countries in general and against the producers of primary products in particular. Foreign ministers and even heads of government from developing countries regularly attended international conferences of the Nonaligned Countries, the Group of Seventy-Seven, the Organization of African Unity, or the Association of South-East Asian Nations during which they framed, endorsed, or rallied around various proposals for a new international economic order, as described briefly in chapter 2. At various stages, India, Mexico, and Nigeria, among our countries, played an active and initiating role in these deliberations, which both reflected and reinforced the statist zeitgeist of the 1970s. The shock of the first oil price increase in 1974, although damaging to all oil-importing countries, was paradoxically *welcomed* by a number of leaders in developing countries outside the Organization for Petroleum Exporting Countries, who saw it as an economic weapon that could be used to force the rich countries to agree to the proposed changes in the international economic order. Thus, political considerations sometimes overrode economic interests, and it would not have been consistent with this expressed view to complain too much about, or to respond too vigorously to, the oil price shock.

Against this background, our countries launched their numerous public investment booms, made possible in part by an increased flow of development assistance from the rich countries, but even more by the rapid growth of the international money and capital market, to which developing countries had increasing access (see chapters 2 and 3). The possible reasons for their diverse performance can be found in each country's form of government, democratic or authoritarian; in the initial conditions inherited from the past (their traditions, convictions, and institutions); and in the role of nongovernmental actors—interest groups within the country, and external influences—in the formation of economic policy.

Form of Government

It has sometimes been suggested that authoritarian governments are better able to manage national economies in developing countries than are democratic governments since the former can quash opposition to occasional economic retrenchment, with its inevitable squeeze on some segments of society, often urban wage-earners. Moreover, over the longer term they are allegedly better able to establish and carry out a coherent program for economic development, to maintain fiscal discipline, and to direct resources—the limited surpluses that can be extracted from the public in poor countries, plus external borrowing—to the most productive ends. Democracies, in contrast, have difficulty maintaining a coherent policy over time and must constantly defer to special interests whose well-being is not always most conducive to longer-run growth.

A cursory examination of our eighteen countries does not support this frequently expressed view. Neither the form of government nor the degree of political freedom seems to have had a significant bearing on the adaptability of our countries to external shocks and their subsequent performance. Four of our countries—Costa Rica, Colombia, India, and Sri Lanka—were democracies (D) during the 1970s and 1980s; three (Brazil, Indonesia, and Korea) were military or quasi-military autocracies (MA), although both Brazil and Korea moved to elected governments in the period 1985–87; five (Cameroon, Côte d'Ivoire, Kenya, Mexico, and Morocco) were civilian autocracies (CA), although Mexico's was notably different in character from the others; and six experienced changes in type of government (CG). Since Chile and Pakistan were military autocracies during most of the period (both had democracies in the early 1970s and restored democracy in the late 1980s), that leaves Argentina, Nigeria, Thailand, and Turkey as the countries that underwent significant change for our purposes. Broadly speaking, these last four can be considered politically unstable during the 1970s and early 1980s, along with perhaps the borderline cases of India (because of Mrs. Indira Gandhi's national emergency in 1975) and Sri Lanka, with its radical change in government in 1977 and emerging civil war in the 1980s. The remaining countries were politically stable. Table 12-1 lists the countries' political leaders and changes in their form of government.

The political dimension can be approached in a somewhat different way. The organization Freedom House has ranked countries since 1973 according to their degree of political rights and civil liberties (Gastil 1987). The greater the freedom, it might be thought, the greater the influence of special interest groups on economic policy making. Averaging Freedom House scores over the period 1973–85 produces a list that runs from Costa Rica, the most liberal, to Cameroon, the least. They can be somewhat arbitrarily divided into two groups, the more free and the less free, ranked from the highest to the lowest degree of freedom:

More Free	*Less Free*
Costa Rica (D)	Nigeria (CG, 1979, 1983)
Colombia (D)	Morocco (CA)
India (D)	Kenya (CA)
Sri Lanka (D)	Indonesia (MA)
Mexico (CA)	Pakistan (CG/MA, 1973, 1977, 1988)
Turkey (CG, 1980, 1983)	Korea (South) (MA/CG, 1987)
Brazil (MA/CG, 1985)	Chile (CG/MA, 1973, 1989)
Argentina (CG, 1973, 1976, 1983)	Côte d'Ivoire (CA)
Thailand (CG, 1979, 1991)	Cameroon (CA)

Table 12.1 Political Leaders, 1965–90

Country	1965	1966	1967	1968	1969	1970	1971	1972	1973	1974	1975	1976	1977
Argentina	Illia	Organia				Levingston	Lanosse	Campora	Peron	I. Peron		Videla	
Brazil	Branco		da Costa e Silva		Medici						Geisel		
Cameroon	Ahidjo												
Chile	Frei					Allende			Pinochet[a]				
Colombia	Valencia	Restrepo				Pastrana				Lopez			
Costa Rica	Bolmarich	Trejos				Figueres				Oduber			
Côte d'Ivoire	Houphouet-Boigny												
India	Shastri	I. Gandhi											Desai
Indonesia	Sukarno	Suharto											
Kenya	Kenyatta												
Korea	Park												
Mexico	Ordaz					Echeverria						Lopez-Portillo	
Morocco	Hassan II												
Nigeria	Azikiwe	Ironsi/Gowon							Ramat	Obasanjo			
Pakistan	Arub Khan				Yahya Khan		Bhutto[b]						Isaq Khan[a]
Sri Lanka	Senanayake					Bandaranaike							Jayawardene
Thailand	Thanom								Sanya		Seni/ Kukrit	Seni/ Thanin	Kraingsak
Turkey	Demirel					Erim[a]	Melen		Ecevit[b]		Demirel		

364

Country												
Argentina				Viola	Galtieri	Alfonsín[b]						Menem	
Brazil		Figueiredo						Sarney[b]					Collor
Cameroon					Biya								
Chile													Alwin[b]
Colombia	Turbay				Betancur				Barco				Gaviria
Costa Rica	Carazo				Monge				Arias				Calderon
Côte d'Ivoire													
India		C. Singh	I. Gandhi				R. Gandhi					V.P. Singh	
Indonesia													
Kenya	Moi												
Korea	C. Park	Choi	Chun								Roh[b]		
Mexico					de la Madrid						Salinas		
Morocco													
Nigeria		Shagari[b]				Buhari[a]		Babangida					
Pakistan	Zia Ul-Haq										B. Bhutto[b]		
Sri Lanka												Premadasa	
Thailand			Prem[b]								Chatchai		
Turkey	Ecevit	Demirel	Evren[a]			Ozal[b]							

a. Indicates a coup.
b. Indicates a restoration of democracy.
Source: Compiled by authors.

The four most free countries are the democracies, and the least free are civilian autocracies, preceded by the military autocracies.

The question that needs to be asked is whether there is any discernible relationship between the various political attributes of these countries—their form of government, political stability, or degree of political freedom—and their economic performance. The issue can be formalized somewhat by dividing our countries into those that performed relatively well during the 1980s, following the shocks early in the decade, and those that performed relatively poorly. The main criterion will be economic growth, with some admixture of external debt problems and inflation. By these standards, the countries that performed badly during the 1980s are Argentina, Brazil, Cameroon (which performed well in the first half of the decade, but poorly thereafter), Chile, Colombia, Costa Rica, Côte d'Ivoire, Mexico, and Nigeria; those that performed relatively well were India, Indonesia, Korea, Morocco, Pakistan, Sri Lanka, Thailand, and Turkey. In terms of growth, Kenya and Sri Lanka are on the borderline, but because of Kenya's extraordinary growth in population it experienced little change in per capita income, so should be grouped with the poor performers, whereas Sri Lanka's growth in per capita income was 2.6 percent a year. Turkey, although a high-inflation country, saw its per capita income grow 2.4 percent a year during the 1980s, so we include it among the good performers. Chile's growth was impressive in the last few years of the decade, but not over the period as a whole. Moreover, its price level increased by a factor of five over the decade, in comparison with a doubling in Morocco, the country with the lowest per capita growth rate among the good performers. Colombia, a democracy, was the only one of our Latin American countries that did not reschedule its external debt.

These classifications can be summarized as shown in table 12-2. Here we have called those with dramatic changes in government "unstable" and all others "stable," although, as noted above, India and Sri Lanka might be considered borderline cases; Chile had a dramatic change to democracy in 1989, and Brazil and Korea introduced elected governments, both favored by the preceding military leaders, in 1985 and 1987, respectively.[2]

No clear pattern emerges in table 12-2. A roughly equal number of stable governments performed well and poorly, as was the case for unstable governments. Countries with a greater degree of freedom can be found in all four categories. Democracies and authoritarian governments alike can have poor—or good—economic performance. Simple generalizations about the effectiveness of various political systems in dealing with adverse—or favorable—external economic shocks do not seem to hold up.[3] It is true that if we move India and Sri Lanka into the northeast, politically unstable, corner, then all the countries in the northwest corner (that is, those that are politically stable with good economic performance) will be civilian or military autocracies, all of which fall in the lower half of the Freedom House list. Among these countries, however, Korea and Pakistan had free democratic elections in the late 1980s. And democratic Colombia's performance, classified as poor here, was not markedly inferior to authoritarian Morocco's.

Table 12.2   Political Regime and Economic Growth

Economic performance	*Stable*		*Unstable*	
Good	India[a]	3.0		
	Indonesia	3.3		
	Korea	7.2		
	Pakistan	2.9	Thailand[a]	5.3
	Sri Lanka[a]	2.6	Turkey[a]	2.9
Poor	Brazil[a]	0.2		
	Cameroon	-0.8		
	Costa Rica[a]	0.6		
	Côte d'Ivoire	-3.2		
	Kenya	0.4	Argentina[a]	-1.5
	Mexico[a]	-1.0	Nigeria	-1.3

a. Countries in upper half of Freedom House list.
Note: Trend annual growth rate in GDP per capita over the period 1980–90 follows each country.
Source: Authors' compilation.

Perhaps an authoritarian government has some edge when it comes to adopting difficult but desirable economic policies. Clearly, however, many authoritarian governments are not able or willing to do so, and the cases of India and Sri Lanka suggest that in some circumstances democratic governments in developing countries can also successfully implement policies of macroeconomic adjustment in response to adverse external shocks, which were admittedly modest in relation to GDP in the case of India, but were substantial for Sri Lanka.

The classifications used here no doubt could be refined. It has been suggested that a distinction needs to be made between "weak" authoritarian states and "strong" ones (Haggard and Kaufman, in Nelson 1989). Leaders of weak authoritarian states are insecure in tenure or not in complete command of the executive agencies of government, with the result that they may be unwilling to promulgate policies that are unpopular with the general public or with particular constituencies, or they may be unable to ensure that their policies are actually implemented. When applied to economic policy, this distinction runs the risk of being tautologous, with weak authoritarian states being defined as those that are unable to frame and carry out a coherent and effective macroeconomic policy. Nonetheless, some authoritarian governments clearly are weak in the respects mentioned above, and indeed should perhaps not be called "authoritarian" except for their low tolerance for civil and political liberty on the part of actual or feared opponents. Among our countries, Argentina, Brazil, Kenya, and Nigeria offer examples of weak authoritarian states during much of the 1970s or early 1980s, whereas Chile, Korea, and

Mexico were strong authoritarian states, with Côte d'Ivoire, Indonesia, and Pakistan being moderately strong.

Even "strong" authoritarian states must be concerned with their legitimacy at home and abroad and must pay attention to public opinion. Chile's Pinochet derived his security not only from the army's absolute control, but also from the fear of the alternative among many middle-class members of Chile's polarized society, who had already experienced it briefly under President Salvadore Allende in the early 1970s. In Brazil, Indonesia, Korea, and Turkey, military leaders attempted to legitimize their rule by founding political parties and converting to a civilian form of government. In doing so, they created forums (notably parliaments) where some opposition could be expressed, even if parliamentary power was limited. Even having a strong authoritarian government does not safeguard against policy errors. Chile, for example, fixed its exchange rate in 1979 without deindexing wage contracts and deregulated banking without providing for adequate regulation and supervision; and Côte d'Ivoire in the mid-1970s mistook a transitory increase in coffee and cocoa prices for a permanent one and budgeted accordingly.[4]

The examples of Colombia and India demonstrate that democratic countries can have a reasonably disciplined fiscal policy and a conservative fiscal tradition. Democratic countries can put together and implement a coherent macroeconomic policy. Incumbent governments in democratic countries are periodically concerned about the impact of their policies and performance on the polls, and upcoming elections may dictate the timing of macroeconomic policies. When President Jose Sarney of Brazil deferred the fiscal tightening necessary to make his Cruzado Plan work until after the constituent assembly elections of November 1986, that deferral spelled the collapse of his bold, if heterodox, effort to quash Brazil's inflation.[5] For this reason, democratic governments are likely to be less expansionist immediately after an election than they are immediately before, and thus an economic cycle sometimes develops in association with the timing of elections.

This problem is not peculiar to democratic countries. The most striking example of this phenomenon has been Mexico, a peculiar hybrid between authoritarianism and democracy. Mexico has been ruled by one party, the Party of Revolutionary Institutions (PRI), since 1929, and during most of this period its tolerance for serious political opposition has been low. At the same time, the party operates within a constitutional framework that restricts presidents to a six-year term and prohibits self-succession. For reasons best known to the PRI, it strives to win these elections by large majorities, perhaps to show that serious political opposition is really redundant, given its overwhelming popularity. Toward that end, it apparently increases government expenditures substantially in the last eighteen months before the end of each presidential term. During its first year in office, each incoming government, therefore, has to devote much of its political energy to reestablishing fiscal equilibrium.[6]

This pattern is the opposite of one sometimes associated with Latin America: the so-called populist electoral cycle, whereby relatively poor and uninformed electorates encourage candidates to promise all kinds of improvements. These politicians are elected and attempt to deliver on their promises by greatly increasing spending on public programs for health, education, foods subsidies, roads, and so on. It soon becomes clear that these programs cannot be conventionally financed on the scale on which they have been launched, so increased central bank financing is used, which helps speed up inflation. After a while, pressure from domestic groups dissatisfied or alarmed by the inflation or the deterioration in the country's international payments position leads authorities to recognize that macroeconomic policy needs to promote greater austerity. By this time, if an election is in prospect, the incumbent is likely to be removed in favor of a new politician who promises to deliver more (Dornbusch and Edwards 1989). Or a coup may occur before the cycle is complete.

This pattern, or at least part of it, is recognizable in Salvador Allende's election in Chile in 1970, and in Juan Peron's return to Argentina in 1973 (as well as in Alan Garcia's 1985 election in Peru, outside our sample of countries). Still, electorates are not always so undiscerning as the above model implies. Allende was elected by a minority, because the opposition was split. Peron was asked back to Argentina after an absence of nearly two decades in part because of a perception that only he could reduce the polarization in Argentina. That gamble did not work, but perhaps will be achieved by Peron's distant successor, Carlos Menem, elected in 1989.

Insofar as political incumbents shy away from taking constrictive fiscal or monetary action because they fear they will be chucked out of office, electoral results during the 1980s do not in general bear out this concern. Incumbents or their favored successors were returned to office in Sri Lanka (1982), Turkey (1983 and again in 1987), Costa Rica (1986), Korea (1987), and Thailand (1989), despite the fact that in each of these cases (except Sri Lanka) stringent fiscal policies had been in place earlier.[7] Incumbents or their preferred successors were removed by the electorate in Argentina (1983 and again in 1989), Colombia (1986), Pakistan (1988), and Chile (1989). Mexico (1989) might also be added to the list, for although the PRI presidential candidate Carlos Salinas, to no one's surprise, won in 1988, the regional elections of 1989 were considered a referendum and the PRI experienced its largest ever political losses. A number of these countries also had austerity programs.

The main difference between the two lists is that economic performance, on the standards we invoked earlier in this chapter, were generally good in those countries in which incumbents were returned (Costa Rica being the main exception), whereas they were generally poor in those countries in which the incumbent was dismissed (Pakistan being the main exception).[8] The lesson here, insofar as there is a lesson, is that electorates focus on end results, not on the means; if tight fiscal discipline is associated with good overall economic performance, the electorate is not likely to object.

New governments, whether democratic or authoritarian, are more likely to make drastic changes in economic policy—macroeconomic or structural—than are incumbent governments. Such changes were introduced among democratic governments following elections in Sri Lanka (1977), Costa Rica (1982), and Argentina (1989); and among authoritarian governments in Korea (1961–64), Indonesia (1966–69), Chile (1973–74), and Nigeria (1986). New governments can more easily break with the past and take the steps deemed to be necessary in order to correct the "chaos" left by the preceding regime. In all the authoritarian cases, gross mismanagement by the preceding government was a primary reason for the military coup, although in each case it took the new government some time to frame its new economic policy, as military leaders became apprised of the complexities of economic policy and engaged economic advisers or officials in whom they had confidence. Turkey (1980) provides an exceptional case, since the economic stabilization was actually begun under the democratically elected Demirel government, but had not yet been completed at the time of the military takeover. The military leadership not only continued but strengthened the economic reforms, and promoted the previous government's chief economic adviser Turgut Özal to the position of deputy prime minister in order to continue the macroeconomic and structural reforms.

In contrast, other countries (Colombia, India, Thailand and since 1964 Korea), and Cameroon (until 1988, among our eighteen) have demonstrated basic continuity in their policies, whereas still others (Côte d'Ivoire, Kenya, Mexico, and Morocco) managed to change policies gradually despite continuity in government, largely required by an adverse change in the external environment. "Basic continuity" does not exclude important changes in emphasis, as in Korea in 1982 and in Colombia in 1984.

It has been suggested that the governments experiencing the greatest difficulty in introducing or even maintaining tight macroeconomic policies are those in "democratic transition"—countries in which an authoritarian government has yielded to a democratic form, but the latter is not yet well established. There have been many examples of this transformation since 1975: among our countries, Thailand (1979), Nigeria (1979), Argentina (1983), Turkey (1983), Brazil (1985), Korea (1987), Pakistan (1988), and Chile (1989).[9] Political scientists Haggard and Kaufman (in Nelson 1989, pp. 59–60) suggest that democratic transitions are likely to lead to expansionist economic policies for three reasons:

- First, political transitions typically reflect an increased level of political mobilization and conflict. It is usually because such conflict cannot be overcome through repression that authoritarian regimes weaken and give way to constitutional ones. Because political mobilization generally increases in the last phases of authoritarian rule, it confronts new democratic leaders with previously repressed demands, heightened social and economic expectations, and strong pressures to reward supporters and incoming groups.
- Pressures from below are coupled with uncertainties at the top among new political elites. In the immediate post-transition period, the possibility ex-

ists that authoritarian forces will reenter politics. Short-run macroeconomic policies thus not only have coalitional consequences; they may also affect the survival of the new regime itself. These uncertainties shorten the time horizons over which politicians calculate the costs of policy choice. Difficult economic policy actions that create resistance or unrest—and that might provide an excuse for reversal of the democratization process—are likely to be avoided.

- Finally, democratization is likely to involve more substantial turnover in technical personnel and changes in decisionmaking institutions than is the case with changes of government in established democracies. With increased social demands, the uncertainties facing new political leaders, and the technocrats' own interest in supporting the democratic experiment, incoming economic teams are more likely to pursue expansionist programs that meet expectations and reduce social conflict in the short run.

By way of empirical support for their hypothesis, Haggard and Kaufman point out that during seven democratic transitions in the early 1980s increases in government expenditure were on average greater, budget deficits were higher, and central bank credit expansion was higher than in a control group of authoritarian countries and one of stable democratic countries. Furthermore, compliance with IMF programs was lower (Haggard and Kaufman, in Nelson 1989, tables 1 and 2). Countries undergoing a democratic transition do differ significantly, however, with some—Thailand, Turkey, Korea, among our countries—maintaining much continuity with the previous regime, especially among the technocrats. In all three cases, the new democratic leadership also reflected some continuity with the outgoing regime (although, ironically, Özal was not the military's favored candidate in Turkey's 1983 elections).

In other cases—Nigeria, Argentina, Brazil, among our countries, along with Peru—the transition to democracy reopened extensive populist or (in Nigeria's case) ethnic claims on government largess that had been suppressed by the previous regime (less so in Brazil than in the others), and rekindled debates on the basic thrust of economic policy. The new governments thus had to decide both on underlying principles of policy and on detailed implementation in ways that would build rather than erode support for democracy, in general, and for the incumbents, in particular. Moreover, in Argentina President Raul Alfonsin was preoccupied with establishing a system of justice and of administration that would endure future changes in government and that would discourage another military coup. Consequently, economic policy was at first given lower priority. In Nigeria, President Shehu Shagari was politically successful in his extended largess and patronage, in that he won a second term election in 1983; but the fiscal situation had deteriorated so extensively, and corruption was so widespread, that another military coup aborted his second term a few months after inauguration.

Even in Korea, where former general Roh Tae Woo as head of the party supported by the outgoing regime was elected president (but with less than half the popular vote, due to a split opposition) and where most technocrats continued in the administration, new freedoms (combined with an exceptionally strong export boom) permitted extensive labor unrest followed by exceptional wage increases in 1988 and 1989. Public expenditure became more expansionary in response to popular demand. In comparison with other countries, however, Korea maintained a high degree of fiscal control.

Governments in democratic transition are not the only ones to use public expenditures to strengthen national cohesion or to build political coalitions. In a sense, democratic governments are constantly engaged in these processes, especially the latter. Democratic leadership specializes, it might be said, in reconciling conflicting claims on public resources by various interest groups with the resources that are available, or that can be extracted from the public—or from abroad. Among our countries, the most dramatic single example is the pursuit by the new Jayawardana administration in Sri Lanka of the huge Mahaweli irrigation and water control project, designed in part to create employment and in part to bring prosperity to the countryside and to rural Sinhalese who, although a majority, felt disadvantaged next to the minority Tamils. This massive thirty-year project had been on the drawing boards for many years, but then was mobilized and accelerated to six years with the help of foreign donors who were eager to show support for the more liberal economic policies of the new administration in 1977, despite the fact that dispassionate economic analysis suggested the project did not offer an attractive rate of return. Indeed, as pointed out in chapter 11, the World Bank and other donors seem to have decided to support the project in principle even before the detailed economic analysis was undertaken. Unfortunately, even with extensive foreign assistance (amounting to the extraordinary figure of nearly 10 percent of GDP in 1982), substantial local resources were also required to undertake the project. Thus, expenditures on this project alone reached 22 percent of total government expenditures in 1982. Once embarked upon, it was difficult to abandon, although it was eventually scaled back somewhat.

Of course, authoritarian regimes also engage in fostering national cohesion and building coalitions of supporters. The public investment booms of the 1970s in both Morocco and Côte d'Ivoire, among others, were motivated by such considerations. Morocco's King Hassan II faced down two attempted military coups, in 1971 and 1972. To build more support among the elite, in early 1973 he dispossessed foreign landowners/farmers of the 600,000 hectares they still held (down from one million in 1960), allocated some of it to actual and potential supporters, and revived a 1930s plan for greatly extending the irrigation network, with a view to producing sugar for the domestic market and citrus and vegetables for export. Some thirty dams were built in the resulting investment boom (see Claassen unpublished). Ample financing seemed to be available at the time the projects were launched, thanks to strong world markets for phosphates in 1973–74.

President Felix Houphouët-Boigny of Côte d'Ivoire launched a major program of rural development, focused on cotton and sugar, during the five-year plan period 1975–79. This program was designed partly to quiet and occupy the restless "developmentalists" in his national party, partly to calm a serious feud within the politically important Coulibaly family in the north, and, most important, to tie central and northern ethnic groups more closely to the economically and politically dominant south (see Woods 1989). It fit nicely into the regime's continuing efforts to induce Ivoirians to stay on the land, or even to return to the land, and it seemed economically attractive on the basis of the high cotton prices of 1973–74 and the extraordinary sugar prices of 1974–75. The sharp price declines that subsequently occurred do not seem to have been contemplated. The fortuitous large increase in world coffee and cocoa prices in 1975–77 provided ample financing for a few years. When world prices for these leading export products declined, Côte d'Ivoire, like Morocco, continued with its projects, financing them largely with funds borrowed abroad and thereby laying the basis for its later debt problems.

In 1973 Korea launched its heavy and chemical industries (HCI) investment program, which was to move the Korean economy into a modern industrial structure. Although most of the investment was to be undertaken by private firms, these firms were "guided" by public policy and credit allocation. The financial requirements for the entire decade-long program were huge and alarmed financial officials at the time. Those concerned with economic development argued, however, that HCI was the right course, partly by analogy with the evolution of the Japanese economy. For his part, President Park Chung Hee was disturbed by what he (incorrectly) took to be the implications of the recently promulgated Nixon Doctrine, namely, that within the foreseeable future Korea would have to rely entirely on itself for its security, in particular against another attack by the Democratic People's Republic of Korea, materially supported by China or the U.S.S.R. He therefore wanted to build a strong foundation for a defense industry—steel, chemicals, and machinery—in Korea. As a result, Korea also participated in the general investment boom of the 1970s, although investments were temporarily postponed during the first oil shock, and many were postponed indefinitely after the second oil shock. The 1973 HCI program therefore turned out not to be an irrevocable one.

The general point of this discussion is that expenditures to strengthen national cohesion, or to build political coalitions, may in the minds of political leaders take precedence over the maintenance or restoration of macroeconomic equilibrium— as long as the expenditures can be financed somehow, or until inflation imposes risks to cohesion or coalition that appear to outweigh the gains from the expenditures. At times, these leaders appear to undertake large projects when adequate finance seems available without taking into account the possibility that the financial requirements may greatly exceed those initially postulated, or that the available financing may diminish because of world economic developments. Once launched, projects may be politically difficult or economically expensive to drop, although as Korea showed in the middle and late 1970s, ambitious investment programs can be curtailed or canceled if they threaten macroeconomic stability. Côte d'Ivoire, too, built only six of the twelve sugar mills it had originally planned, because the costs were much greater than anticipated, and the revenues less.

A less elevated focus on objectives other than growth and stability occurs in what has been called the predatory state, or more recently the "kleptocratic" state (by Whitehead 1990), in which individuals or groups of individuals more or less blatantly use the powers of the state to enrich themselves and their supporters. Every government has now and then tolerated this kind of behavior, although not always from its national leaders. Where national leaders have behaved this way, macroeconomic stability would be fostered only insofar as it enlarged the possible take, or was deemed to prolong the period over which government largess would be available.

External threats, real or perceived, are also likely to take priority over macroeconomic stability in the minds of most political leaders. Among our countries, Pakistan (1971), Argentina (1982), and Morocco (1977–90) were involved in actual conflicts, and Chile, Kenya, Korea, and Thailand all felt the pressure of external threats, the last two throughout our period. In addition, Nigeria, Kenya, and Sri Lanka had serious internal threats to security, requiring or thought to require substantial defense expenditures. Military expenditures have been discussed briefly in chapter 10 (see table 10-3). Curiously, several countries with actual or perceived external threats tended to maintain tighter budgetary discipline and less destabilizing fiscal policy than did countries with low military expenditures. Although in principle security considerations may dominate macroeconomic considerations in the minds of most political leaders, in fact the potential conflict between these two objectives seems to have been well managed in most of our countries.

Tradition, Convictions, and Institutions

Even if a political leader desires to establish a tightly managed fiscal policy, he needs to be able to implement it. For that, the institutional framework, the strength, competence, and authority of the public officials, and the general acceptability of the policy are all relevant.

Financial officials tend to be fiscally conservative in all countries. That attitude derives partly from their training, which in turn sometimes involves doctrine but even more, involves an acquaintance with balance sheets and the elementary proposition that every expenditure must somehow be financed. It derives also from the fact that their authority in government arises from the need for financial control. Countries—more precisely, the governing elite—have quite different histories and traditions, and these can strongly influence each country's approach to fiscal policy. Historical experience and tradition are reflected both in convictions about appropriate policies, and in institutions charged with implementing policy.

Some countries have deeply ingrained conservative fiscal convictions. Britain bequeathed to its former colonies both a Gladstonian tradition and an administrative setup conducive to "treasury control" (see Beer 1956). Both survive in India and Pakistan, although they seem to be weakening over time. They were gradually undermined in Sri Lanka under the populist administrations of Mrs. S. Bandaranaike during the early 1960s and early 1970s and could not easily be revived during the "foreign aid boom" of the late 1970s, despite the fact that aid donors typically favor good treasury control.

The British legacy could also be found in Kenya and Nigeria. Unlike the former Asian colonies, however, these countries had no widely accepted elite, and both were plagued by deep regional and tribal rivalries and mutual suspicions. In Nigeria, these differences led even to civil war within five years of independence (most Nigerian oil was in the breakaway region of Biafra).

A conservative fiscal tradition is eroded when governments are in constant search for supporters and potential supporters seek governmental favors. Intercession by financial officials in this kind of setting is likely to be interpreted narrowly, as one regional or tribal group attempting to assert its authority over others. The treasury control that survived these handicaps finally succumbed to the coffee boom in Kenya in 1975–77 and the oil boom in Nigeria during 1979–80, when funds were (temporarily, it turned out) so ample that treasury leverage disappeared and financial control seemed like an unnecessary nuisance.

A tradition similar to the British, but with different institutional details, was established in the former French colonies—Morocco, Cameroon, and Côte d'Ivoire. Indeed, as explained in chapters 8 and 10, the last two countries remain members of multinational monetary unions in which French Treasury officials continue to play an important role. While budgets are under national control, government debt to domestic banks by multinational agreement cannot exceed 20 percent of each nation's revenues in the preceding year. This puts a restraint on deficits that cannot be financed by borrowing abroad, which Côte d'Ivoire did extensively, and Cameroon more modestly. French Treasury officials must contend with the officials of other ministries in Paris—Commerce, Agriculture, Foreign Affairs—each of which for various reasons would sometimes urge that a more expansionist stance be permitted in the African countries.

Conservative financial traditions are not limited to former colonies. Thailand also has a "British" tradition of financial conservatism, said to stem from its desire in the nineteenth century to avoid giving Britain or France fiscal provocation to compromise its independence, as happened with a number of other countries (see Ingram 1954, pp. 170–74). More recently, Colombia, Korea, Indonesia, and Chile have all established a practice of fiscal conservatism, in reaction to a period of relative profligacy and the "chaos" that followed. Colombia had a vicious civil war in the early 1950s. The political truce that ended the war involved national power-sharing by the two leading parties for over fifteen years, 1958–74, combined with a resolve to put the economy on a sound basis and to avoid the turmoil of the past. Korea's Park Chung Hee was in part reacting to the fiscally undisciplined rule of Syngman Rhee before 1960; Indonesia's Suharto to the fiscal profligacy of Soekarno before 1965; and Chile's Pinochet to the unlimited spending (leading to inflation of 700 percent) of Salvador Allende in 1972–73. Each of these periods was traumatic for the informed public and created an environment that cried out for a high degree of fiscal discipline.

Convictions arise from such historical experiences, and they tend to be reflected also in the formal rules governing fiscal policy. Thailand, for instance, cannot run a budget deficit in excess of 20 percent of expenditures and did not do so during our period; foreign borrowing is considered a financing item rather than a receipt, but special provision is made for replacing maturing external debt. (State-owned enterprises are not covered by this rule, but their foreign borrowing has required central approval since 1977.)

In Korea, the national assembly can *reduce* budget expenditures submitted by the president for its approval, but it cannot increase them. Moreover, the Korean government cannot borrow from the central bank (with limited exceptions) without getting the explicit approval of the national assembly, a process likely to precipitate public debate and therefore to be avoided in the eyes of Korean officials.

The Indonesian government, at Suharto's insistence, has submitted only balanced budgets since 1967, although foreign loans count as receipts, and borrowing from the central bank is permitted under some circumstances. The government even alludes from time to time to the *constitutional* requirement for a balanced budget, although no such provision can be found in the constitution (Woo and others forthcoming). Thus are traditions established.

Chile cut government expenditures drastically in the mid-1970s and by 1975 was in budgetary surplus, despite the world recession and the sharp drop in copper prices. Moreover, Chile introduced a truly independent central bank in 1989, such that it is not obliged to lend to the government at any time. Colombia made a similar move in 1991, and Argentina in the same year prohibited its central bank from making domestic currency loans to the government.

The traditions get reflected in other ways as well. Presidents Park (1961–79) and Chun (1981–87) of Korea each took a strong *personal* interest in economic policy, even though they had no economic background; so did Prime Minister Prem (1980–88) of Thailand and, less so, President Suharto (1966–) of Indonesia. Korea and Indonesia created economic "superministers" who had responsibility for all facets of economic policy. Revenue forecasts have deliberately been conservative (that is, below outturn) in Korea, in order to restrain planned spending in the budget. As higher-than-projected revenues materialize, a supplementary budget is usually submitted, to ensure that spending occurs only as financing becomes available. Once a budget is approved, there is *no* history of overruns; that is, the administrative system maintains tight controls on outlays as well as on the budget. In Thailand, the discipline on actual spending is so tight that the outturn in our period was always below budgeted levels, sometimes by as much as 8 percent (Ramangkura and Nidhiprabha 1991, table 4).

Argentina and Brazil have quite different traditions. Juan Peron was a popular, charismatic leader during the 1940s, appealing especially to urban workers and denigrating the "stuffy" conservative European attitudes of other Argentinians. During his first period in office, the country enjoyed favorable exports and a buoyant income, after the bleakness of the Great Depression. He believed the state should play an active role and was known as a big spender, especially in the area of social programs and public employment. He was deposed in a military coup in 1955 and exiled (to Spain), but he remained a popular figure with significant segments of the population, thus making life difficult for any non-Peronista government that did not systematically suppress popular discontent. In 1973 he returned to Argentina as president and immediately launched a major program of public spending, encouraged by the high world grain prices of 1973. He died after less than a year in office, but had insisted that his wife be his vice-president, so Isabel Peron continued his policies until she was deposed by a military coup in March 1976. Partly as a consequence, Peronista statist expansionism retained its popularity with significant segments of the population, particularly urban blue-collar workers and many state employees.

Brazil as seen by Brazilians is a country with a large frontier and unlimited possibilities for development. Cheap, available credit was necessary for development. Historically, coffee growers were the dominant economic group, followed later by the business community in São Paulo, both of which liked easy credit. There has been no strong conservative financial tradition. Reflecting these views, Brazil did not create a central bank until 1964, and even that was achieved only by agreeing to open unlimited rediscount facilities, at a nominal 1 percent annual interest, for the Banco do Brasil, a leading commercial bank (partly government-owned) that had also been the government's banker and had strong ties to commercial borrowers. This facility was not eliminated until 1986. Within the government, the minister of finance not only did not control all government spending, he did not even know about all government spending. State-owned enterprises, specifically, were outside the control of the Ministry of Planning (the chief economic official), and sometimes had access to central bank financing, via Banco do Brasil.

Mexico started on a conservative financial tradition in the 1920s, in the aftermath of a long civil war. A quasi-independent central bank was established in 1926. The economic difficulties of the Great Depression of the 1930s compromised this independence, but established close working relations between the central bank and the (more expansionist) treasury. This team then succeeded in establishing and maintaining a relatively conservative financial tradition during the 1950s and 1960s. An implicit bargain seemed to exist within the ruling PRI: the president of the republic would defer to the secretary of the treasury on financial questions, and the secretary in turn would not become a *political* rival of the president or his chosen successor.

This "bargain" was in effect broken by President Luis Echeverria in the 1970s, when he exiled the traditional treasury man Hugo Margain to the Mexican embassy in the United States and appointed a more pliable successor, Jose Lopez Portillo. Late in his administration he established a new, rival Ministry of Planning and Budget to absorb the budgeting functions of the treasury and to challenge it institutionally. Expenditure rose by 3 percent of GDP between 1971 (Echeverria's first year of office) and 1975, precipitating a financial crisis and in 1976 the first devaluation of the peso since 1954. A modest retrenchment occurred, but expenditure increased further under President Lopez Portillo, Echeverria's chosen successor, rising by an astonishing 14 percent of GDP between 1977 and 1982. This great rise was made possible by the rapid increase in oil production that Mexico experienced in the latter half of the 1970s, by the sharp rise in oil prices in 1979–80, and by the external borrowing that such promising oil revenues permitted. The 1981–82 fall in oil demand, combined with oil pricing mistakes by Mexico, undermined Mexico's financial position, and the debt crisis of August 1982, discussed in chapter 2, was the consequence. In the meantime, the Ministry of Planning and Budget had been staffed by technically competent treasury or central bank officials, and the subsequent two presidents, Miguel de la Madrid (1982–88) and Carlos Salinas (1988–), were drawn from that group.[10]

Economic booms leading to large increases in government revenues typically weaken treasury control. An early example among our countries was Pertamina, Indonesia's state-owned oil company, following the first large oil price increase in 1974. It was led by an exuberant and entrepreneurial general, Ibnu Sutowo, who used the large inflow of funds not only to increase Pertamina's investments in oil exploration and development, but also to expand greatly Pertamina's range of activities, into manufacturing, transport, tourism, and even rice. To do so, Sutowo borrowed extensively in the Euro-currency market, against Pertamina's revenues.[11] Then, when oil demand slackened in 1975, Pertamina was found to be badly overextended.

A committee of financial officials was established to oversee Pertamina and other large state enterprises, to straighten out its financial situation, and to prevent a repetition. In the Javanese fashion, General Sutowo was eased out of his position and replaced by a less exuberant, more financially minded general. In the end, the Pertamina crisis, which attracted widespread adverse public attention, probably strengthened the position of the financial technocrats and helped avoid overextension during the next oil boom of the late 1970s.

Mexico's state-owned oil firm, Pemex, went through a similar phase in 1980–81, greatly expanding its activities, investing generously, paying large wage increases to its employees, and borrowing heavily abroad to accomplish it all, in an environment in which banks were eager to lend to an oil-rich firm. Oil demand and prices dropped sharply in 1982; Pemex's revenues suffered also from a Mexican reluctance, as in Nigeria, to lower posted oil prices, so market share was lost. Pemex was overextended, and its director general Jorge Diaz Serrano was finally dismissed.

Similarly, fiscal discipline was greatly weakened in Morocco, Côte d'Ivoire, and Costa Rica during their commodity export booms (in phosphates, cocoa, and coffee, respectively) of the mid-1970s. Once weakened, discipline was difficult to reestablish after commodity prices fell. Even more extreme was the loss of fiscal discipline, enhanced by ethnic, tribal, and regional rivalries and mutual suspicions, in Kenya during its coffee boom, and in Nigeria during the 1979–80 oil boom. Budgetary control virtually disappeared in these two countries for several

years, reinforced in the case of Nigeria by a newly established democratic government under President Shehu Shagari in need of building a supporting coalition
both for his party and for democratic government in general. As noted above, he
was deposed after his reelection in 1983, in large part because of the fiscal laxity
leading to cronyism and corruption.

The general point is that when funds are readily available, and known by all
to be available, it requires exceptionally strong traditions and strong-willed financial officials backed by their political leaders to maintain financial discipline in the
interests of avoiding difficulties in the future. Treasury control usually depends on
the leverage of a practical limit to revenues, which permits officials to impose con-
straints on spending.

Most governments, democratic and authoritarian alike, are preoccupied with
the short run and find it hard to resist spending a windfall in revenues. Among our
countries, Cameroon stands out as a notable exception, having used part of its unexpected increase in oil earnings in 1979–81 to prepay foreign debt, and part of it
to increase (secret) reserves abroad, not taking them into ordinary government
revenues. Even in that country, however, government spending rose by 7 percent
of GDP between 1979 and 1983. Colombia maintained its tight stabilization program through the small coffee boom of 1986, and Korea moved into budgetary
surplus and prepaid external debt extensively to help neutralize the expansionary
effects of a large export surplus in 1986–88, thus illustrating that a boom in revenues does not have to lead to an increase in expenditures.

This discussion of the dubious benefits of a boom in receipts illustrates a different point as well. The "government" is not a well-defined, cohesive unit in most
countries. At least three components must be viewed separately from those parts
of the government—including the economics or finance ministry and the central
bank—that are responsible for managing overall economic policy. First, there are
the "spending ministries," those responsible for carrying out the various functions
of government such as providing education or public infrastructure or health care.
Even leaving aside straightforward patronage, they almost always have unfulfilled
wishes or even plans that are constrained by the lack of finance. If finance is available, they will press forward.

Second, while economic policy is framed by the central government, many or
even most of the functions of government are carried out by its other units, provinces (called "states" in some countries), and local authorities. In many countries
these are simply units of the central government, subject to much the same kinds
of financial control as the spending ministries are. Some countries are organized
as federations, in which the provinces (or states) have a constitutionally independent existence, often with their own sources of revenue, and with a constitutional
division of responsibility between them and the central government. Among our
countries, Argentina, Brazil, Colombia, India, Indonesia, Korea, Mexico, Nigeria,
and Pakistan have federal structures, although the degree of provincial autonomy
varies substantially from country to country, being especially high in Argentina,
Brazil, India, and Nigeria.[12] In India, more than half of government expenditure

is undertaken by the states (and even more if the local government is included, but data are unavailable), and more than 30 percent by provinces and local government in Argentina, Brazil, Colombia, Indonesia, Korea, and probably Nigeria.[13] In most of our federal countries (Mexico has been an exception), a higher share of revenue has accrued to the national government than is true of spending responsibilities, so the national government shares revenues and makes grants (and sometimes loans) to lower levels of government. In India and Pakistan, for instance, an independent commission reviews and sets a revenue-sharing formula between center and states at five-year intervals.[14]

The existence of a federal system of government poses no special problem for macroeconomic management so long as the provinces and municipalities are fiscally constrained by their own revenue plus grants or loans from the national government. The problem arises either when national financial control has broken down, as in Nigeria in the late 1970s, such that subnational levels of government are authorized (by someone) to spend at levels collectively in excess of the revenues available; or when provinces can borrow abroad or have direct or indirect access to the central bank. The latter circumstances have prevailed especially in Argentina and Brazil. As already noted in chapter 10, a number of Argentine provinces own banks, from which they borrow, and these banks in turn have access to the central bank. In Brazil until 1986, the partly public Banco do Brasil had unlimited overdraft facilities at the central bank, and states in turn could borrow from the Banco do Brasil, as well as from state-owned banks that had direct access to the central bank. The internal politics of both countries, combined with the constitutional autonomy of provinces, made it difficult to curtail these practices. In particular, President Sarney depended for political support on several key state governors, and was disinclined to attempt to impose monetary discipline on them.

An analogous problem arises with respect to state-owned enterprises (SOEs). Although as the name suggests these are owned by the government and thus should in principle be under the control of the government, the degree of effective control varies greatly from country to country. Some SOEs have virtually become a state within a state, with a high degree of autonomy. We have already cited the cases of Indonesia's Pertamina and of Mexico's Pemex.

SOEs are subject to the same analytical observation as provincial governments: they cannot disrupt macroeconomic policy unless in practice they have unconstrained access to the government budget, or unless they can borrow abroad, or unless they can borrow directly or indirectly from the central bank. Unfortunately, examples can be found of all three of these "loopholes." Because governments are reluctant to allow SOEs to fail, and because managers of SOEs know that and are often politically powerful, they sometimes spend beyond what is formally allowed and then have the government pay the bill. Costa Rica's CODESA, a state-owned holding company whose function is to encourage development, had direct access to the central bank and spent some of its (borrowed) resources bailing out ailing firms, or buying them outright. The SOEs in Brazil could borrow from Banco do Brasil and thus until 1986 had indirect access to the central bank, and until about 1980 they could borrow directly abroad without restraint by the central authority, as could the SOEs in Turkey. Like any commercial firm, SOEs borrow routinely through suppliers' credits. In Côte d'Ivoire, Morocco, Nigeria, and Turkey, arrears on SOE borrowings in this form became a substantial part of the debt problem of the 1980s.

Some situations are highly complicated and do not necessarily involve loss of treasury control. A country's SOEs may run into financial trouble for a variety of reasons, some of which may have nothing to do with careless management. For example, a currency devaluation may have greatly and unexpectedly increased an SOE's debt-servicing costs; or as part of anti-inflation policy the government may impose controls on the SOE's product prices, even while its input prices continue to rise. When the firm runs into financial trouble, the government for a variety of reasons (for example, domestic or international prestige, to avoid contagion, and so on) may not want the firm to fail. It is allowed to borrow from a state-owned bank, even though its prospects are not good. The *bank* can certainly not be allowed to fail, it is thought. So it is allowed to borrow, or to rediscount its poor loan to the SOE, at the central bank. There are many examples of this pattern, especially following the widespread domestic financial crises of 1982–83 (see chapter 10), even in countries that run a relatively tight fiscal ship such as Korea and Thailand.

Government relations with SOEs are complicated by the fact that politically powerful interests are often associated with them, for example, through patronage rewards to important political figures, even potential political rivals of the incumbent leadership. Moreover, in some countries (Argentina, Brazil, and Indonesia, for instance) retired generals or even active military units are involved in managing SOEs, complicating the task of imposing financial discipline on them. Discipline is more easily maintained if the national leader is an economy-minded general or former general, such as Park and Chun in Korea, Suharto in Indonesia, Prem in Thailand, or Pinochet in Chile.

Interest Groups and External Actors

The function of politics, at least in democracies, is to reconcile the diverse and often conflicting interests of the citizens. This process in turn represents the core of the study of politics: who gets what, when, and how? The working assumption of political economists is that various elements of society will press the government for policies and actions favorable to their economic interests, and that they will strongly resist actions inimical to their economic interests. In short, prospective losers from a given line of policy action will try to block its adoption, or undermine its implementation. What can be said about interest group politics with respect to macroeconomic management in our countries?

Interest Groups

Surprisingly little, it turns out. This is partly because the various elements of society do not know, on balance, where their interests lie when it comes to an issue as complex as macroeconomic management. Most people in principle favor growth and oppose inflation; and they find it difficult to evaluate a policy that temporarily slows growth in order to reduce inflation, especially prospectively when the short-term trade-offs are not known. A policy to reduce inflation may be widely applauded at first, yet resisted later on, as people become aware of the lost output and higher unemployment. Currency devaluation raises the local currency prices of imports, unwelcome to those who purchase them; but in a regime in which imports have been suppressed through exchange controls, a devaluation with import liberalization may actually be welcome. Macroeconomic relationships are complex, and are not well understood even by the relatively well-informed elite. So governments can often garner support or at least acquiescence in policies by making claims for them that seem plausible in prospect even if they do not materialize in reality. No one, however, likes to pay higher taxes; and increases in urban bus fares come close to universal dislike.

In addition, with some notable exceptions, interest groups in most developing countries are not so well organized as they are in the wealthy democratic countries, so they are less able to translate their interests, even when they understand them, into political action. In what follows, we briefly examine the role of the principal (actual or potential) interest groups: urban labor, farmers, businessmen, military officers, employees of SOEs (labor and management), civil servants, and politicians themselves.

WORKERS. The "organized" or formal sectors of developing economies often have some form of labor organization, although its scope for political action is typically limited by custom or by law. Particularly when the capital city is also a large part of the formal nonagricultural economy, as it often is, workers could in principle have access to decisionmakers, and of course they can demonstrate publicly or go on strike. In practice, organized labor has often been co-opted by the leading political party, as in Mexico, or by the party attempting a stabilization program, as in Colombia and Costa Rica in the 1980s. In many other countries, labor is not permitted to demonstrate publicly or strike, and force may be used to suppress such actions. Even in Mexico, the government in 1986 cracked down sharply on labor that deviated from the accepted path of negotiating within the PRI, dismissing the dissident leaders. And a civilian government in Brazil used the military to suppress a strike in 1987. Argentina represents a partial exception to these generalizations, in that labor is well organized and at least since Peron of the 1940s has engaged in political action, contributing to the sectional standoff in Argentine politics. In reaction, the Videla military government (1976–80) was especially harsh with labor leaders, and even collective bargaining was banned from 1976 to 1986.

Only rarely does labor as an interest group greatly influence policy, and even then it usually has to appeal to a much wider constituency. An example is a strike by Chilean miners in 1983 over the regime's severe economic policies. This strike encouraged protests by others, and the Pinochet regime in response softened its macroeconomic actions temporarily (Nelson 1990). In Costa Rica of the late 1970s, however, organized workers in public enterprises successfully intimidated the (politically weak) Carazo government against cutting financial support to the SOEs, even though they were a substantial drain on the budget, and concern about labor unrest no doubt limits governmental action in many countries.

FARMERS. Farmers or agricultural workers in developing countries are even less well organized politically than are urban workers. They nonetheless represent important segments of the population, and for that reason governments often find it in their interest to appeal for rural support. We have seen the political impetus to rural development projects in the 1970s in the cases of Côte d'Ivoire, Morocco, and Sri Lanka. Similarly, both Suharto of Indonesia and Park of Korea felt that mass rural support for their governments was politically important, particularly in the former case because the communists were strong in the rural areas of Java. Hence, they devoted considerable resources to rural development and to price supports for some agricultural products. These examples involve political strategy by each country's leader rather than active political pressure by farmers.

Some farmers are well organized. The coffee growers have long been an important (although now diminishing) factor in Brazilian politics, one of the groups that has historically favored easy credit. Sugar growers in Costa Rica are well organized and have on the whole successfully resisted government efforts to reduce the protection they receive. And the large landowners of Argentina are well organized and politically active, like urban labor contributing to the political stalemate that existed for so long in that country.

BUSINESS. The business community is generally rather better organized to express its views on policy than either labor or farmers. This group, or various subsets of it, may also have a clearer idea of what its economic interests are. In any case, governments are more likely to pay attention to what the business community wants, but the relationships between business and the government vary. A number of governments, most notably Korea, have co-opted the business community, combining (until the relative liberalization of the late 1980s) guidance with incentives, largely in the form of foreign exchange allocations and low-interest credit. Great pains were taken to explain to the business community what government policy is, and why. The business community expressed its reactions to new policy directions and modified the content or timing, but it has not challenged new directions frontally.

In Chile and Thailand, too, the business community was generally favored by government policy, but often the government was pushed beyond what important elements of the business community would have preferred. Business muted its criticism of Chile's severe policy largely because it preferred the existing Pinochet government to the likely alternative of another divisive Allende-type government. It took considerable time and some anxiety before the business community in Chile began to criticize the extreme free-market ideology of Finance Minister Castro and his "Chicago boys," but eventually Castro was replaced with a more moderate minister (see Stallings, in Nelson 1990 and in Bates and Krueger 1993). In Thailand, policy was less extreme but still not to the liking of many in the business community, but they muted their criticisms because they preferred Prem to a less democratic, less business-oriented military government.

In Mexico, the geographically northern, more export-oriented parts of the business community became increasingly vocal in their criticisms of economic policy under President Lopez Portillo (1976–82), and support from this group was one of the factors that encouraged the change in structural orientation of Mexican economic policy in the 1980s. The business community in Brazil, mainly the São Paulo industrialists, is also well-organized and politically influential. This group has traditionally been growth-oriented and hostile to tight credit and high interest rates, so has generally opposed serious stabilization policies in Brazil; the financial community, in contrast, has been relatively weak.[15]

Wherever the business community is thought to be largely in the hands of a minority group, such as the Chinese in Indonesia or Asians in Kenya, the political influence of the business community is likely to be weak, and indeed businessmen are likely to shun any role that suggests political activism. The business community has little influence in India, perhaps because the commercially successful Parsees, Marwaris, and Gujeratis are regarded as being outside the mainstream of Indian society, both by themselves and by others. In other countries, such as Nigeria, business influence is exerted informally through relatives in the government and through traditional channels rather than through formal organizations and public statements.

MILITARY. Professional *military* men play a special role in many developing countries. They often see themselves as subordinate to the constitution and to the real "spirit" of the country, but not as subordinate to the existing government. Thus, half of our countries experienced military coups since 1965 *in the name of* true national purpose and proper governance (see table 12-1). Three others (Cameroon, Kenya, and Morocco) experienced attempted coups. The prospect of a military coup is thus something that many governments must constantly keep in mind. Costa Rica and Mexico dealt with this possible threat by eliminating, or virtually eliminating, the professional military. In other countries, the military, even when out of formal power, and sometimes merely by their presence, may influence policymaking. An obvious concern is the military budget; but preservation of personal prerogatives and military status and prestige can also be important;[16] and in some countries, as noted above, military figures or military units are involved directly in business activity, which governments must be cautious about threatening. Like other groups, professional military men do not always agree on what is best for the country, or even for them, and that gives astute leaders some room for maneuver. Furthermore, strong leaders that are former generals may find it easier to deal with the military than civilians do.

STATE-OWNED ENTERPRISES. The special role of SOEs in many developing countries has already been discussed. Their leaders are often individuals of considerable political influence, and their workers are often among the best organized of urban labor. Both management and labor may combine to oppose governmental actions that involve substantial cuts in output and employment in these often overstaffed enterprises, or to oppose actions that put them in a financial squeeze (such as having to service in full their external debt after a currency devaluation).

CIVIL SERVANTS. Civil servants can be divided into two groups, the higher-echelon professional administrators and technocrats, and the clerical and manual workers. The latter group makes up far the larger number, but they have little political power—not least because they risk losing their jobs if they become openly critical of policy, and their individual services are rarely crucial to the functioning of government because of widespread overstaffing.

Senior civil servants, in contrast, have substantial influence; it is their job to recommend policy, and often they are the most qualified people in the country to frame economic policy. In their advice and implementation, they are influenced by their formal training, by the traditions of the service in which they operate, and by the general intellectual currents of the time. U.S.-trained economists have played an especially important role as ministers and vice-ministers in Indonesia and Chile, where they were known as the "Berkeley mafia" and the "Chicago boys," respectively, and in Mexico during the late 1980s; but also as senior officials in Korea and in Thailand. Of course, most countries have some able economists; the key question is why they are or are not used.

Many officials will try to frame policy in what they consider the national interest, but they may also have more parochial interests, often involving their future scope of responsibility. Thus, "turf battles," common in any bureaucracy, are far from absent in developing countries. In the area of economic policy, these are often between the financial officials (generally in the finance ministry and central bank) and the economic planners or the officials of industry and agriculture ministries. Of course, there may also be serious substantive disagreements on policy; but the point here is that the disagreements often reflect differences in personal and financial interests, since the line between public and private is not typically drawn sharply and many officials are also engaged in private business. Indonesia, indeed, has made a public virtue of the dual role of official/entrepreneur or general/entrepreneur, but the practice is widespread (see Woo and Nasution 1989, p. 62).

POLITICAL LEADERS. Finally, in addressing interest groups we shall also include the political leaders themselves. To the extent that they or their relatives benefit financially from political power, and even if they do not, political leaders like to stay in power. To do so, as noted above, they typically must build public support for their tenure, and that often involves the inauguration of public works, the provision of public employment for loyal followers, and government purchases from favored suppliers. Too much budgetary discipline, and too much restraint on total government spending, may not be in either the personal or the political interests of the key policymakers.

External Actors

The world is organized into sovereign nations, enshrined in the Charter of the United Nations and fully free to make their own choices regarding domestic economic policy. The role of external actors—foreign governments, international organizations, foreign banks and businesses, human rights groups, and the like—is not to make domestic decisions for other countries. By holding out "carrots and sticks," they can influence the set of opportunities that domestic decisionmakers face, and in this respect they can influence national decisionmaking. The carrots and sticks normally have a financial dimension, but economic and political analysts sometimes underestimate the potency of simple international approval or disapproval of a country's course of action. Being a chief executive is lonely, and international approval and "understanding" from other leaders or prestigious international institutions can sometimes be important. The International Monetary Fund (IMF) and the World Bank are often cited as leading channels of foreign influence on economic policy. The role of external actors and the extent of their influence is beyond the scope of this study, but occasionally it has been important.

For instance, the U.S. Agency for International Development (USAID) played a critical role in leading Korea in the mid-1960s to adopt both stabilization policies and a policy of export orientation. The agency cajoled, but it also both offered and withheld aid at critical moments (see Haggard and others in Bates and Krueger 1993). U.S. assistance conditioned on changes in economic policy also seems to have played a crucial role in the Costa Rican stabilization of the mid-1980s. Obviously, such external influence cannot carry the policy alone; but sometimes it can be decisive in tilting the domestic decisionmakers, or in helping to overcome domestic resistance to directions that economic officials would like to take. For example, in 1984 the international community reinforced growing domestic dissatisfaction with the Betancur/Gutiérrez policy of fiscal expansion in Colombia, involving a larger budget deficit and a loss of foreign exchange reserves. Finance Minister Gutiérrez was subsequently dismissed and the policy reversed.

Some countries—most notably Brazil, Colombia, India, and Nigeria, among our countries—have shown extreme political sensitivity to international organizations, especially the IMF. "Going to the IMF" was politically unpopular, and came to be viewed as an act to be avoided if at all possible. Brazil in 1981 adopted a stabilization program arguably more severe than the IMF would have required at that time, without gaining access to IMF resources (see Bacha, in Williamson 1983). (Brazil did finally go to the IMF two years later.) Similarly, Colombia in

1985 and Nigeria in 1986 declined to go to the IMF. In Nigeria the military government of General Babangida opened the issue to public debate, and the response was a resounding negative. Nonetheless, each country needed IMF approval of its policies in order to qualify, in the case of Colombia, for a new jumbo commercial loan, and in the case of Nigeria for debt rescheduling under standard international practice, something they both wanted. The compromise was to allow the IMF to "monitor" domestically determined policies for the benefit of the international financial community (including creditor governments), while not drawing on IMF financial resources to which they would have been entitled under the agreement.

Other countries feel less constrained about going to the IMF, and indeed some have practiced it almost routinely in framing their economic policies. For instance, Kenya and Korea went to the IMF eight times during the period 1973–89, Pakistan seven times, and Costa Rica six times (see table 12-3). In truth, economic policy is *always* decided by the domestic government; no country is literally obliged to go to the IMF, although the costs of not doing so increased after the debt crisis of 1982, since alternative sources of funds were less readily available, and formal debt rescheduling typically required an IMF program. It is often convenient to blame some of the unpleasant consequences of stabilization policies on an external agency, a procedure that is sometimes politically useful, but in the long run it undermines confidence both in the national government and in the IMF.

One source of the difference between these two groups of countries has been disagreements between IMF officials and national policymakers regarding what is appropriate policy. In Brazil, where structuralist views held sway, this difference of opinion centered on macroeconomic management; in India, it was more over the principles that should govern the allocation of foreign exchange. Such countries went to the IMF reluctantly, for they resented its loan conditions (India's large extended fund facility in 1981 did not carry it into high conditionality).

In other cases, officials from the IMF and other international organizations have reinforced the convictions of national financial officials. The provision of international intellectual and financial support makes it easier for these officials to overcome opposition at home to their preferred policies. Such "side taking" of course sometimes creates resistance against the IMF in some segments of the population, precisely because of its support of financial officials in a domestic dispute over policy.

Mention should also be made of the general intellectual tendencies in world centers of opinion, which gradually diffuse throughout the world. During the late 1970s and especially the 1980s, academic opinion swung away from "planning" and an active role for the government. Many scholars had grown skeptical about the ability of governments to frame and especially to execute policies that were really in the interests of the average citizen, even in the long run. Correspondingly greater weight was given to the role of "market forces" in guiding economic decisions toward activities that were more likely to be efficient, hence more likely to raise average incomes over time. The market was also seen as a less personal force, diffusing power away from politicians and officials.

Table 12.3   International Monetary Fund Standby Arrangements for Eighteen Countries, 1973–89
(millions of SDRs)

Country	1973	1974	1975	1976	1977	1978
Argentina				Aug/260.0	Sep/159.5	
Brazil						
Cameroon						
Chile		Jan/79.0	Mar/79.0			
Colombia	Jun/20.0					
Costa Rica				Jul/11.6		
Côte d'Ivoire						
India						
Indonesia	May/50.0					
Kenya			Jul/67.2 (3 year EFF)			Nov/17.2
Korea, Rep. of	Apr/20.0 (8 mth)	May/20.0 (7 mth)	Oct/20.0 (8 mth)		May/20.0 (7 mth)	
Mexico					Jan/518.0 (3 year EFF)	
Morocco						
Nigeria						
Pakistan	Aug/75.0	Nov/75.0			Mar/80.0	Mar/80.0
Sri Lanka		Apr/24.5			Dec/93.0	
Thailand						Jul/42.2
Turkey						Apr/300.0 Apr/3,360.0 (9 mth)

Note: Blank cell = not applicable. EFF = Extended Fund Facility, canc. = cancelled.
Source: IMF Annual Reports, 1971–89.

1979	1980	1981	1982	1983	1984	Country
				Jan/1,500.0 (canc. 1/84)	Dec/1,182.0	Argentina
				Mar/4,239.0 (3 year EFF)		Brazil
						Cameroon
				Jan/500.0		Chile
						Colombia
	May/60.50 (2 year)	Mar/276.7 (3 year EFF) (canc. 12-81)	Dec/92.95			Costa Rica
		Feb/484.5 (3 year EFF)			Aug/82.7 (9 mth)	Côte d'Ivoire
		Nov/5,000.00 (3 year EFF) (canc. 5/84)				India
						Indonesia
Aug/122.4 (canc. 10/80)	Oct/241.5 (2 year) (canc. 1/82)		Jan/151.5	Mar/175.9 (18 mth)		Kenya
	Mar/640.0 (canc. 2/81)	Feb/576.0		July/575.8 (18 mth)		Korea, Rep. of
		Jan/3,611.0 (3 year EAR)		Jan/3,410.0 (3 year EFF)		Mexico
	Oct/810.0 (3 year EFF) (canc. 3/81)	Mar/817.0 (19 mth) (canc. 4/82)	Apr/281.2	Sep/300.0 (18 mth)		Morocco
						Nigeria
	Nov/1,268.0 (3 year EFF) (canc. 12/80)	Dec/919.0 (3 year EFF)				Pakistan
Jan/260.3 (3 year EFF)				Sep/100.0 (10 mth)		Sri Lanka
		Jun/814.5	Nov/271.5			Thailand
Jul/250.0 (canc. 6/80)	Jun/1,250.0 (3 year EFF)			Jul/225.0 (canc. 4/84)	Apr/225.0	Turkey

(The table continues on the following page)

Table 12.3 (continued)

Country	1985	1986	1987	1988	1989
Argentina			Jul/947.5 (14 mth)		Dec/1,104.0 (15 mth)
Brazil			·	Aug/109.0 (18 mth)	
Cameroon				Sep/69.0 (6 mth)	
Chile	Aug/825.0 (3 year EFF)				Dec/64.0
Colombia					
Costa Rica	Mar/54.0		Oct/40.0 (19 mth)		May/42.0
Côte d'Ivoire	Jun/66.2	Jun/100.0 (2 year) (canc. 2/88)		Feb/94.0 (14 mth)	Nov/75.8 (5 mth)
India					
Indonesia					
Kenya	Feb/85.2			Feb/85.0 (18 mth)	
Korea, Rep. of	Jul/280.0 (18 mth)				
Mexico		Nov/1,400.0 (18 mth)			
Morocco	Sep/200.0 (18 mth) (canc. 12/85)	Dec/230.0 (16 mth)		Aug/210.0 (16 mth)	
Nigeria			Jan/650.0		Feb/475.0 (14 mth)
Pakistan				Dec/273.0 (15 mth)	
Sri Lanka					
Thailand	Jun/400.0 (21 mth)				
Turkey					

Note: Blank cell = not applicable. EFF = Extended Fund Facility, canc. = cancelled.
Source: IMF Annual Reports, 1971–89.

These intellectual tendencies were seemingly supported empirically by some outstanding economic successes, especially in East Asia, where Hong Kong was a leading example of minimal governmental interference in commercial activity. These tendencies inevitably diffused to officials of international organizations and, partly through them, into intellectual and policy circles in many countries. They contributed to the dramatic policy changes that occurred in many developing countries during the 1980s, which greatly reduced the regulation of financial markets and of foreign trade, and even allowed some state-owned enterprises to be sold to the private sector.

Intellectual fashion in the area of macroeconomic management also changed, although no consensus developed on what mechanism other than an active government could be used to stabilize aggregate demand and combat inflation. Argentina and Chile, as we have seen, both experimented with an alternative approach emphasizing stabilizing expectations through exchange rate policy, and both experiments failed, although for different reasons. Changing attitudes toward the role of market forces very likely contributed to the greater flexibility of exchange rates in the 1980s than had prevailed in earlier periods.

The point here is that external actors and ideas are frequently influential in determining national economic policy in some developing nations, but that influence comes indirectly, by influencing the set of opportunities that national leaders face. The choice is theirs.

Summary

This chapter has briefly surveyed the political dimension of economic policymaking, which encompasses the form of government, the timing of transitional governments, the role of interest groups, and the role of history and tradition in shaping public expectations. It seems there is little correlation between the form of government and economic performance, as we have defined it—that is, on the basis of growth and inflation in the 1980s. Authoritarian governments have done both well and badly; democratic governments have also done both well and badly. Governments that suppress civil liberties do not, on average, perform better than governments that do not suppress civil liberties. There is a tendency, however, for *new* democratic governments, emerging from a period of authoritarian rule, to be somewhat more expansionist than other governments, regardless of whether underlying economic circumstances call for a more expansionist stance; when they do not, that can lead to later economic difficulties.

In general, interest groups are not as well organized in developing countries as they are in developed ones. In many countries, that may be because they are intimidated by the government, in others because the major political parties have channeled and co-opted them. The business community played an important role in resisting stabilization policies in Brazil, however, and labor in resisting stabilization policies in Argentina. Farmers are generally politically weak, but some leaders (in Indonesia, Korea, Sri Lanka, and Thailand, all Asian countries, and to some extent in Côte d'Ivoire) have nonetheless adopted policies favorable to rural populations, to acquire and keep their political loyalty.

History and tradition are extremely important in establishing what the public expects from the government and have considerable effect on the public's willingness to accept short-run hardship for the sake of desired longer-run aims that it believes the government is pursuing. How exactly these traditions are established is not well understood. Often a traumatic past event lingers in the collective memory and creates an environment conducive to certain policy actions. The German hyperinflation of 1923 is often mentioned in this regard, and the Colombian civil war of the early 1950s. India, Pakistan, and Sri Lanka inherited a tradition of firm treasury control from Britain. Such explanations are often no doubt correct, but they are incomplete, for they fail to indicate why equally traumatic events in other countries—hyperinflation in Brazil, a civil war in Nigeria, or a tradition of British Treasury control in Nigeria and Kenya—did not have a comparable impact. Full explanation is beyond the scope of this book; the important point is that the ability of the government to succeed in a course of macroeconomic stabilization depends not only on the economic circumstances confronting it, and on the policies formally adopted, but also on the convictions of the leaders and of the public with respect to desired outcomes.

It goes without saying that (apart from good luck, which sometimes comes) good policy depends on a cadre of technically competent officials who can recognize problems, analyze them skillfully, and propose courses of action to redirect the economy as desired. Although such skills were sometimes absent in the 1960s, officials with good technical training and experience were available in most countries by the 1980s, although not always in adequate numbers. They could often be augmented by foreign advisers, especially from the IMF and the World Bank.

Good policy advice is necessary, but far from sufficient. Such officials must carry enough weight to get their recommendations adopted, and then must be able to execute the policies effectively. To achieve this, they must have the support of the country's political leader(s), and preferably also of the public's convictions. The political leaders must insulate their officials from short-term or sectoral pressures that would undermine a coherent medium-run policy and must provide them with sufficient authority over the spending agencies to maintain budgetary control.[17]

Again, traditions are important. However, it requires exceptionally strong traditions, or an exceptionally strong political leadership, to protect a country's economy from a vigorous export boom. When incomes rise suddenly, and with them public revenues, treasury control and financial discipline can be too easily undermined. Once that happens, they are difficult to reestablish.

Finally, inflation is often the "impartial" reconciler of social conflict over resources. Politicians can avoid taking explicit decisions with respect to taxes and public spending priorities if they and the public are willing to tolerate some inflation to reconcile those differences through the hidden taxation of financial assets, especially currency. Fractious societies with weak or uncertain political leadership are more prone to inadvertent but sometimes continuing inflation than are countries with strong leadership and an anti-inflation consensus.

Thus, although all eighteen of our countries relied on the inflation tax to some extent over the study period, that reliance varied greatly from country to country, reflecting differences in public and official distaste for inflation as well as differences in politically irresistible pressures for expenditure running up against politically immovable resistance to explicit taxation. These differences have their origin more in the histories of countries than in their economic structure. As we have seen, governments responded in different ways to similar external shocks. The two major oil price increases of 1974 and 1979–80 necessarily resulted in a once-for-all immediate rise in the price level and in an inflation bubble, or adjustment inflation as we called it in chapter 6. In some countries, the bubble was burst; the rate of inflation subsequently dropped, as it should do after a once-for-all increase in the price level. In other countries, however, this adjustment inflation became spiral inflation, because the public could not agree on, or the government could not impose, the decline in real spending that a worsened terms of trade requires.

The possibility of borrowing abroad permits a country in this situation to temporize, in the hope perhaps that the adverse shock will be reversed and the difficult distributional decisions can be avoided. That sometimes works. If it does not, external borrowing only worsens the problem by creating yet another claimant, the foreign creditors, on a national output that is already too small to meet all the claims on it.

Societies with fragile social and political consensus are less likely to achieve appropriate macroeconomic management in the face of adverse external shocks than are others. Among our countries, Argentina and Nigeria, and Costa Rica and Turkey in the late 1970s, had such societies. Dissent was present but severely repressed in Chile until 1989, in Cameroon, and in Kenya in the late 1980s. Indeed, dissent was suppressed to some extent in many of our countries; it is a matter of degree. Sometimes, the economic or political situation gets so bad that a consensus can finally be formed around a corrective course of action, such as occurred in Colombia in 1958. That is the hope for Argentina and Nigeria in the 1990s.

Chapter 13

Conclusion: The Lessons of Experience

History does not repeat itself, but it does generate some lessons for the future. Compared with the previous two decades, the period from 1973 to 1989 was an exceptionally turbulent one for the world economy. That turbulence posed severe challenges to macroeconomic management in all countries, whether they had gained from the changes or had suffered. This volume contains accounts and analyses of many different policy reactions to similar circumstances and shocks. Despite this diversity, a number of common themes have emerged.

One is that it is not always possible to separate the effects of different policies from the effects of shocks of different magnitudes or kinds. The policies and general characteristics of an economy—especially its flexibility in responding to shocks—are more important than the size of shocks in determining their effects on growth rates. Indeed, the size of external shocks seems to have little bearing on subsequent economic difficulties: some countries adjusted well to large shocks, others adjusted poorly to small ones. Indeed, countries that experienced positive shocks, through mishandling, sometimes performed worse than countries that experienced negative shocks. Thus, although it is sometimes appropriate to point to disturbances emanating from the world economy as the source of a difficulty, countries cannot avoid responsibility for coping with those disturbances badly, since others coped well. There is need for policy control, policy flexibility, and flexibility in the economy, which in part reflects past policies.

Hence, we now reflect on the policies and in particular ask some counterfactual questions. Given the various changes in the world economy that the eighteen countries faced over the whole period, could policy reactions have been different and have avoided problems and painful adjustments? What was done wrong and what was done right?

Boom, Crisis, Adjustment

In the 1970s, borrowing on the international capital market became much easier for developing countries. Especially after the 1974 oil shock, it also became cheaper, as the earnings of oil-exporting countries were deposited in the world's large commercial banks. This enticed almost all our countries to engage in public investment booms financed by foreign borrowing. The timing differed, and some embarked on these investment spending booms quite late—after real interest rates had started rising—whereas others started early, usually motivated by some domestic political considerations. The debts incurred during this period led many of the countries into their debt crises. Should they not have borrowed?

This would not be a valid conclusion to draw, for when borrowing becomes easier and cheaper, it is rational to consider borrowing more. The problem is that the expected rate of return over the lifetime of an investment should exceed the expected rate of interest over the same period. The returns must also be convertible into foreign exchange for external debt service, which implies that extra investment should directly or indirectly earn or save foreign exchange. Furthermore, when the government borrows, or guarantees the debt, it should ensure that it can itself acquire the revenue and the foreign exchange needed to service the debt.

Since so much import replacement had already taken place as a result of restrictionist trade policies biased to inward-looking development, the new investment in most of our countries needed to go mainly into export industries or into infrastructure that would indirectly foster exports. Furthermore, whenever foreign borrowing became large enough for mistakes to have significant macroeconomic repercussions, the expected present value of investments should have been reduced in order to allow for this risk.

The first and main lesson is that thorough cost-benefit analyses must be made that take into account the need for export growth.[1] In general, sudden, big spending booms are unlikely to be sound. It takes time to plan and evaluate projects efficiently. Countries should beware of huge dramatic government-inspired investments, whether in the public or private sectors. This lesson emerges from many countries, particularly from Côte d'Ivoire, Sri Lanka, Mexico, Morocco, and even Korea.

The second lesson concerns the possibility that loans may not be refinanced. In other words, investments need to generate resources not just for interest payments but also for amortization payments. This implies that countries should beware of the risk of financing projects with short-term loans when the returns lie far in the future.

It is, of course, easy to be wise after the event. The sudden changes that took place in the world economy after 1979—the increase in oil prices in 1979–80 followed by the gradual decline, the rise in real interest rates at the end of 1979, and the drying up of private bank lending to developing countries from 1982 on—were not foreseen by commentators and advisers in the developed world, including the World Bank. It is fair to say that in many countries a good part of the extra borrowing for investment spending up to 1979 could be reasonably justified on the basis of generally accepted forecasts. The massive borrowing in the last stages, during 1980–82, cannot be justified in the same way. As noted in chapter 4, this was a period in which a potentially modest debt crisis turned into a very serious one for half our countries. In a few oil-importing countries the continued heavy borrowing went mainly to sustain consumption. This behavior was unwise since the deterioration in the terms of trade was not expected to be short-lived. In other countries, public investment financed by foreign borrowing continued apace. This, too, was unwise in the light of higher interest rates and the high debt already incurred. Only in Chile was the heavy foreign borrowing private. In the case of every country that became crippled by debt, the immediate cause was the failure of the government to take early action to correct unsustainably large current account deficits: the borrowing was not so much deliberate as the outcome of this failure.

A third lesson this borrowing period teaches is to beware of euphoria. Export price booms seem to be especially seductive. For many countries, especially up to 1980, growth rates were high, funds were easy to obtain, and the private and official international financial community was sympathetic. The country that, until a few years ago, was most subject to euphoria was Brazil—always the land of the future. The Mexican government and enterprises also seemed to be overcome by euphoria in their high borrowing period from 1979 and 1982 as a result of oil discoveries and the oil price rise. In Chile, and in Kenya during the coffee boom, the euphoria was in the private sector, but our remarks about government inaction still apply. The Chilean and Kenyan experiences show that a government cannot ignore the possibility of private sector excesses.

Euphoria was a problem not just for the governments of the borrowing countries, but also for the lenders—the international private and official financial community. The international commercial banks were certainly euphoric about Mexico after 1979. Furthermore, two countries—Chile and Sri Lanka—had made sharp shifts toward liberalization which the international community looked upon favorably. Hence, private funds flowed readily into the private sector in Chile and public concessional funds similarly went readily to the government of Sri Lanka. Earlier, Côte d'Ivoire had been considered a notable African success story, and this made it easier in the late 1970s for Côte d'Ivoire to borrow to finance its massive investment boom.

In retrospect, certain investment expenditures were clearly unsound on the basis of reasonable expectations at the time—they were projects that good cost-benefit analysis would have turned down. It is difficult, however, to generalize about the extent of the "excess" investment in various countries when using the criterion of "reasonable expectations." It could be argued that in many countries state-owned enterprises were so inefficient that the less they borrowed, the better. While one might agree that they would have been more efficient if privatized (a process that is now under way in several countries, notably Mexico and Argentina), it does not automatically follow from this that they were never justified in borrowing for investment.

For the most part, the crises arrived in 1982, sometimes earlier, and in a few cases later. Could these crises have been avoided or their impact moderated? We have noted that eleven countries had a recession in the 1980–82 period, and that eight had to reschedule their debt service in the 1983–88 period. Here a few lessons can again be drawn.

First, given the policy mistakes of the 1970s—and indeed both the size and suddenness of the public investment booms were mistakes, even if excusable—the unexpected external shocks of 1979–81 inevitably resulted in serious problems. The essential lesson here would seem to be that countries should constantly be aware that unexpected and unfavorable events will sometimes happen. Such awareness will help them recognize a damaging situation in its early stages.

Second, *policies* need to be flexible. Governments need to shift gears rapidly when circumstances change. Needless to say, this is easier said than done and does not necessarily imply that adjustment should be immediate and sudden. Sometimes, gradual adjustment is appropriate, but the decision to make the adjustment needs to be made quickly.

This recommendation may seem to conflict with the view that policies should be consistent and hence predictable so that governments should not shift gears too much. The most consistent approach is generally to follow cautious policies, which would include an appropriate adjustment when an adverse external shock occurs. Thailand, Korea, and Indonesia all provide good examples here, but we have also described many cases of obviously delayed adjustment. This is not to deny that there may sometimes be a genuine trade-off between commitment to a firmly proclaimed policy stance and adjustment to new circumstances. Chile faced this dilemma in 1982, and its delay in changing policies surely exacerbated the deep recession.

Third, *economies* need to be flexible. The more flexible they are, the less adverse the impact of the shock will be. Rigid real wages, sectorally immobile labor, and strong dependence on imported intermediate goods for domestic production make economies inflexible. The more inflexible the economy, the greater the recession when a compression of imports is required. Such flexibility cannot be created once a crisis comes, but needs to be achieved in advance.

Fourth, rapid export growth is crucial to successful recovery. When the balance of payments has to be improved, imports have to be cut or exports increased. Domestic production in most countries depends heavily on imported intermediate goods, and—because of earlier import-substituting policies—the scope for reducing imports of consumer goods is very limited. An ability to increase exports quickly is thus the best safeguard against a prolonged recession. The lesson here is twofold: countries should follow outward-oriented policies in good times and so develop a strong (and preferably somewhat diversified) export base; and devaluations may be helpful.

Finally, the ability to obtain foreign aid, concessional loans, or debt relief at a time of crisis—provided this is combined with strong adjustment policies—is helpful. This has certainly been true in a number of our countries, notably Indonesia

1966–70, and Turkey after 1980. In contrast, the severe decline in Mexico's growth rate after 1982 is at least partly explained by the lack of such relief and hence the need to generate a current account surplus and an average outward resource transfer from 1983 to 1988 of more than 7 percent of GNP.

Given the terms-of-trade shocks and the need to generate outward resource transfers, painful reductions in aggregate demand were inevitable. It was also inevitable that this shift would, above all, lead to declines in investment, especially public investment. It can be seen from table 5.1 that over the period 1983–88, only two countries—Mexico and Korea—actually ran current account surpluses on average; thus, all other countries were still borrowing. New borrowing often failed to cover the high interest payments, however, so outward resource transfers were in excess of 2 percent of GNP on average for Côte d'Ivoire, Chile, Brazil, Nigeria, and Argentina, as well as for Mexico and Korea. Thus, there was an inevitable adjustment problem.

Leaving aside Korea, where debt repayment was voluntary, these countries would have had decidedly less difficulty if they had obtained interest rate relief or more new funds.

In view of the need to cut aggregate demand, there were, of course, numerous choices to be made as to the pattern of the expenditure cuts. In general, the burden was borne by investment rather than public or private consumption, but some countries reduced real wages substantially, as well as various elements of public expenditure other than investment. The study of the distributional implications of expenditure cuts—such as the effects on the poor relative to the better-off, on the urban in relation to the rural sector, and so on—would deserve a separate book.

The Crucial Role of Fiscal Control

Yet another lesson to be learned—possibly the most important one to emerge from this study—is that fiscal control is essential, as discussed at length in chapter 10. Governments must not lose control of their fiscal situations.

It is particularly important to note that public sector deficits can arise in many quarters of the economy—not only the central government's budget, but also state economic enterprises that are financed directly by borrowing either from commercial banks or from the central bank, the budgets of provincial authorities, and the central bank itself (through past rescue operations of the private financial sector or through purchases of foreign exchange). It is striking that many of the public sector borrowing sprees originated not with the central government but with state economic enterprises, and it is also striking how large some Latin American central bank deficits were in the 1980s. The message is not that deficits should be zero, since borrowing for sound investment is often justified, but that the central government—and, above all, the Ministry of Finance—should maintain control: it should know how much the public sector as a whole is borrowing (which some governments in the 1979–82 period, for example, Brazil's or Mexico's, did not know), and what contingent obligations are being incurred through private sector borrowing. Provincial governments and state economic enterprises should certainly not have automatic access to central bank finance. Above all, the Finance Ministry should be able to cut back on spending quickly if a crisis develops. This is a tall order, and is a problem for all governments, whether developed or developing; but it focuses on the central macroeconomic policy issue for many or even all of those countries that faced crises in the 1980–83 period.

Deficits are not always the result of lack of control, if only because deficits can either be monetized or debt-financed. In some cases our countries had strong central control on borrowing, but conscious political decisions were made that led to the spending and borrowing booms. This was true, for example, of Korea, Sri Lanka, Thailand, and Colombia. Right through the 1980s, the fiscal control problem was overwhelming for Argentina and Brazil, and during the whole period from 1965 to 1990, Chile, Costa Rica, Indonesia, Kenya, Nigeria, and Turkey lost control on one or more occasions.

Inflation, Exchange Rates, and Trade Policies

Conclusions about inflation and stabilization have already been drawn in chapters 6 and 7. We have made no attempt to quantify the costs of inflation. These are very clear in high-inflation countries, notably Brazil and Argentina, but not so obvious when inflation rates are low or moderate and relatively steady. Here, there seems to be no statistical relationship between inflation rates and real economic growth. We pointed out that seigniorage, including that arising from inflation, has been a significant source of revenue for many of our countries. Perhaps the main argument in favor of keeping inflation low is that once it gets above a certain level, acceleration and hence the slide into high inflation are difficult to prevent. Unstable inflation creates uncertainties that inhibit investment and efficient economic decisionmaking and also causes social dissatisfaction. Once inflation hits a high level, stabilization will inevitably be called for, and this can impose large costs in lost output, depending on the considerations discussed in chapter 7.

As noted in chapter 6, the study of the low-inflation countries teaches two lessons. The first is that temporary increases in inflation, which we have called "bubbles," may be unavoidable at times of external or domestic shocks. Even so, it is important not to generate an expectation of high inflation. Rather, a firm commitment must be made to low inflation on average, and thus to the appropriate policies. The second lesson is an elementary one. As these countries show, it is possible to maintain relatively low inflation on average in spite of shocks, provided appropriate monetary-fiscal policies are pursued. The best examples come from the six Asian countries. At the same time, Colombia and Costa Rica show that policy mistakes can be made, or that there can be a brief loss of fiscal control, and yet matters need not get out of hand if there is a strong policy commitment to low inflation (or moderate, steady inflation, in the Colombian case).

Policy conclusions concerning stabilization from high inflation have been drawn in chapter 7 and need not be summarized here. Nevertheless, it is worth stressing the obvious: high inflation is difficult to reduce without cost—that is, without a recession—and certainly without considerable political cost. It is therefore best not to embark on the road of high inflation, and above all, not to monetize fiscal deficits. Of course, high inflation is not directly planned, but rather is the consequence of earlier and concurrent policy failures.

Conclusions about exchange rate policy have been drawn at the end of chapter 8 and, also, need not be repeated here. Nominal devaluations have clearly led to real depreciations that have been sustained for some time. Real depreciations can also lead to increases in exports, especially of manufactured goods. These generalizations do not apply at all times and to all countries, particularly when fiscal policy does not support the devaluation.

In a world of floating currencies, the case for fixing the nominal exchange rate to some leading currency or combination of them must be based on the idea that fixing an exchange rate to the currency of a low-inflation country "anchors" the country's rate of inflation. We have weighed this argument in chapter 8 and do not find that the evidence gives it strong support. A number of countries have remained low-inflation countries in spite of shifting from a (more or less) fixed to a flexible rate regime, while there have been several episodes in which fixing the exchange rate has not put a halt to inflation, but has rather intensified import restrictions. The costs of failure—that is, of fixing the rate while fiscal deficits or serious inflation, or both, continue—must be borne in mind.

As shown in chapter 9, variations in quantitative import restrictions have been very important in the macroeconomic histories of all the countries. For long periods, trade policy tightenings and occasional liberalizations have been the main instruments of balance of payments policy. The tightening of restrictions has had adverse effects on output through the "import starvation" effect. From a study of numerous crises, we have drawn the conclusion that countries with outward-oriented policies have been better able to cope with those crises because they did not have to cut imports to dangerously low levels.

An important conclusion concerning the relationship between exchange rate policy and import restrictions drawn in chapter 9 follows from simple theory and is clearly supported by the evidence. Trade liberalization, especially if it is substantial, requires simultaneous or preceding exchange rate adjustment. This has been true for all major liberalizations to which we have referred. We conclude that, if a country has significant import restrictions or high tariffs covering a wide range of actual and potential imports, it is unwise to make a long-term fixed exchange rate commitment on the basis of the "nominal anchor" argument. Such a commitment would make liberalization much more difficult and indeed might discourage such an initiative. Even if liberalization has taken place, the possibility of the reimposition of import restrictions in a future crisis cannot be ruled out if the exchange rate instrument ceases to be available. If one accepts (as we do) the undesirability of quantitative import restrictions, especially if—as is often the case—they stay on after the immediate need has passed, some degree of exchange rate flexibility is clearly necessary.

Macroeconomic Policy and Growth

The primary conclusion is that macroeconomic stability is good for long-run growth; and therefore that macroeconomic policies should be designed to stabilize real output in the face of exogenous disturbances, and to avoid the creation of unsustainable booms. Few of our countries—Brazil and Korea are the notable exceptions—systematically followed macroeconomic policies that tended to stabilize output growth around its trend. In many countries, fiscal policy was destabilizing.

All the many determinants of growth in real income per head act through the level of investment in relation to GNP (the investment ratio), or through changes in the amount of labor input (in relation to population), and through changes in the quality of investment and of the labor force. Our research did not include any work on the labor force. We therefore limit ourselves to the effects of macroeconomic policy on investment and its efficiency.

We found a negative relationship between the instability of GNP and investment, on the one side, and both the investment ratio and the apparent efficiency of investment, on the other side (by "apparent efficiency" we mean the growth rate of GNP per head divided by the investment ratio). When the authorities are forced to reduce demand in the face of a crisis, investment (both public and private) suffers most. The fact that often it was a previous boom in investment that partly caused the crisis does not usually compensate for the subsequent collapse.

Our countries differ greatly in their apparent efficiency of investment. Although instability explains something, many other factors come into play. One is the choice of investments in the public sector (remember that all the investment booms in the period 1974–82 were mainly public, or publicly inspired, except in the case of Chile). There is evidence from the country studies and elsewhere that much public investment was poorly conceived, although this is an area in which further detailed research is needed.

Aside from examining the investment ratio and the efficiency of investment, we did glance at the much discussed relationship between inflation and growth. Inflation may, of course, be both a symptom and a cause of instability. It is also liable to reduce the efficiency of investment by distorting prices and by increasing uncertainty. We found evidence of a negative relationship, but this vanishes when the very high inflation countries are removed from the sample. This finding, which implies that there is no econometric evidence that moderate inflation is harmful, echoes the work of others.

The large literature on the relationship between trade restrictions and economic growth indicates that outward-looking policies have favorable effects on long-term growth. Above all, the distortions that variable trade restrictions create—including the "rent-seeking" effects—reduce the productivity of investment. This is one channel through which macroeconomic policies can affect long-term growth. It is clearly desirable to avoid the use of trade restrictions and to take every opportunity to liberalize. As we have noted, this implies the need for some exchange rate flexibility. The first signs are that the "new liberalization" of the 1980s—where balance of payments crises led to liberalization rather than to trade policy tightenings—have had favorable growth effects, although in some cases it was, by 1992, too early to tell.

Political Economy: Any Lessons?

The form of government—democratic or authoritarian—does not determine the success or failure of macroeconomic policy. It is true that some of the most successful economies, notably Korea and Indonesia, have been authoritarian, but so have some of the least successful. Democratic transitions may create or intensify macroeconomic problems, as in Argentina and Brazil, but not, however, in Chile. Both authoritarian Pakistan and democratic India have followed conservative macroeconomic policies. There are no simple lessons here, other than that sound or cautious policies can be pursued under many forms of government.

Tradition and history—notably traumatic experiences of chaos or inflation—can influence current attitudes of elites and the general public. To simplify, things may have to get worse—possibly very bad indeed—before they get better. The stabilization success of Mexico since 1988 and the possible success of Argentina since 1991 seem to bear this out. There is no real policy lesson here, however, since one would not advocate creating chaos or a hyperinflation in order to teach the community the need for macroeconomic discipline or common sense. The conclusion we would derive is rather elementary. Those who determine government policy must be convinced of the correctness of responsible macroeconomic policies. In a democracy, the relevant group may be the larger community or a limited elite, and in an authoritarian state, it may be just one or a few individuals, or perhaps some influential members of the military. If high inflation is to be avoided, they must believe that inflation is undesirable and they must understand that financing budget deficits by monetization is likely to be inflationary; they must also understand that continuous debt financing, whether at home or abroad, will lead to trouble eventually if the debt grows too rapidly. They must appreciate the need for financial control.

In those countries where macroeconomic policy has on the whole been a success, there have usually been particular individuals in high government positions—above all the Ministry of Finance—who have been well qualified and who have been able to carry weight with the ultimate decisionmakers. They have been the actual makers and implementors of policy. In recent years these have often been professional economists. Such persons are increasingly available even in countries where they do not hold the high positions. Even when they do, their ability to persuade and to carry weight has been crucial; among other things, this ability has depended on all the considerations discussed in chapter 12—tradition, historical experiences, and the strength of pressure groups. In authoritarian states, the personal views of individuals—such as Presidents Park of Korea, Suharto of Indonesia, Pinochet of Chile, and Houphouët-Boigny of Côte d'Ivoire—have obviously been crucial.

Policy Advice

We can sum up our policy advice, derived from our findings in this study, in nine injunctions to policymakers:

- Assert firm overall budgetary control and budgetary accountability, including control over access to the central bank and to international capital markets.
- Be aware of the "unpleasant arithmetic," namely, the implications for the future of both external and domestic government debt; relate borrowing to returns on investment, to borrowing rates, and to the prospective growth of exports and of government revenues.
- Be sensitive to the maturity of debt, both external and internal. Maintain creditworthiness.
- The pursuit of sound long-run fiscal policy in the sense of the above points will normally permit the use of monetary and fiscal policy to stabilize nonagricultural output around its long-run trend.
- Resist euphoria when export prices rise exceptionally, new resources are discovered, or new borrowing opportunities open.
- Avoid jerky movements in the real exchange rate and thus periods of overvaluation, which can have adverse effects on tradable goods industries. It is generally better to have a flexible exchange rate regime, with frequent adjustments. Furthermore, do not make a fixed exchange rate commitment if there are still extensive trade restrictions.
- Avoid using import controls, except *in extremis*, and then remove them as soon as macroeconomic circumstances permit; if pursued credibly, this stance will enhance the effectiveness of import controls on the rare occasions they are used.
- Avoid building rigidities into the economy, such as persistent import controls or extensive wage indexation.
- Maintain flexibility in policy, and in particular correct mistakes quickly.

Caution

This study has revealed the diversity of macroeconomic experiences and policies of eighteen developing countries over a period of twenty years or so. Its primary aim has been to get the story straight and to try to answer various important policy-relevant questions. Caution must be exercised in drawing conclusions from our analyses, however, both because various aspects have not been fully researched and because so many generalizations are subject to important exceptions and qualifications. Furthermore, some important topics on which we have touched merit much more research. We have in mind particularly the need for ex post cost-benefit analysis of public investment spending, and the need to study further how much downward flexibility of nominal and real wages there is in various countries; our limited work in this area suggests substantial flexibility in real wages in most developing countries. We have not dealt with the pattern of government expenditures in any detail, with income distribution, and with numerous factors that affect growth and welfare apart from macroeconomic policies.

We would like to stress, finally, that a country's macroeconomic policies can explain only a part, often a small part, of its economic performance. A stable and sensible package of macroeconomic policies can be expected to provide only a solid framework both for other government policies and for private sector activities. However stable and sound this framework, if other policies are poor, or the private sector lacks dynamism or is inhibited by political uncertainties, a country can still have a low growth rate. Yet, when something goes wrong on the macroeconomic front, as it clearly did in the early 1980s in so many countries, concern with macroeconomic policy dominates everything else.

Annex I

Country Studies

Studies of the experiences of seventeen countries were commissioned in conjunction with the research project. No study was commissioned for Korea as there is an extensive literature available and a project on the Korean economy, in which Richard Cooper was involved, was under way. In particular, see Collins and Park (1989) and Haggard and others (forthcoming). We expect that nine of these studies will be published by the World Bank as part of the Comparative Macroeconomic Series. These nine are referenced in this study as "forthcoming" and are listed below with the provisional title of the finished work. The other studies will not be published by the World Bank and are referenced as "unpublished." Queries on these studies may be directed to the authors. A list of all the studies along with the authors and their affiliations is provided on the next page.

Country Studies

Argentina: Juan Carlos de Pablo, El Cronista Commercial, Buenos Aires

Brazil: *Macroeconomic Crises, Policies, and Growth: Brazil 1964-1990* Donald Coes, University of New Mexico, Albuquerque

Cameroon: Michael Connolly, University of Miami, Coral Gables

Chile: Hernan Cortes, International Monetary Fund

Colombia: *Macroeconomic Crises, Policies, and Long-Term Growth in Colombia, 1950–1986*
Jorge García García, The World Bank
Sisira Jayasuriya, Latrobe University, Australia

Costa Rica: *Macroeconomic Policies, Crises, and Long-Term Growth in Costa Rica*
Claudio Gonzalez-Vega, Ohio State University, Columbus

Côte d'Ivoire: *Growth and Crisis in Côte d'Ivoire*
Jean-Claude Berthelemy, Delta, Ecole Normale Supérieure, Paris
Francois Bourguignon, Delta, Ecole Normale Supérieure, Paris

India: *India: Macroeconomics and Political Economy, 1964-1991*
Vijay Joshi, Merton College, Oxford
Ian M.D. Little, Nuffield College, Oxford

Indonesia: *Macroeconomic Policies, Crises, and Long-Term Growth in Indonesia, 1965–1990*
Wing Thye Woo, University of California, Davis
Bruce Glassburner, University of California, Davis
Anwar Nasution, Bank Duta, Jakarta

Kenya: David Bevan, St. John's College, Oxford
Paul Collier, Institute of Economics and Statistics, Oxford
Jan Gunning, ESI-VU, Amsterdam

Mexico: Francisco Gil-Diaz, Ministry of the Treasury, Mexico

Morocco: Emil Claassen, Freie Universitat, Berlin

Nigeria: David Bevan, St. John's College, Oxford
Paul Collier, Institute of Economics and Statistics, Oxford
Jan Gunning , ESI-VU, Amsterdam

Pakistan: Nadeem Haque, International Monetary Fund
Mohsin Khan, International Monetary Fund

Sri Lanka: *Macroeconomic Policies, Crises, and Growth in Sri Lanka,*
1969-1990
Premachandra Athukorala, Latrobe University, Australia
Sisira Jayasuriya, Latrobe University, Australia

Thailand: *Macroeconomic Policies, Crises, and Long-Term Growth in*
Thailand
Peter Warr, Australian National University
Bhanupongse Nidhiprabha, Thammasat University, Bangkok

Turkey: *Macroeconomic Crises and Long-Term Growth in Turkey*
Ziya Onis, Bogazici University, Istanbul
James Riedel, School of Advanced International Studies,
The Johns Hopkins University, Washington, D.C.

Annex II

Tables

Table AII.1   GDP Growth Rates, 1966–91

Country	1966	1967	1968	1969	1970	1971	1972	1973	1974	1975	1976	1977
Argentina	0.7	3.2	3.8	9.0	4.6	4.4	2.1	3.8	5.5	-0.5	-0.2	6.5
Brazil	5.2	4.8	11.8	9.9	8.7	11.3	12.3	14.4	9.0	5.2	9.8	4.6
Cameroon	4.7	-12.0	6.5	4.9	2.9	3.8	2.3	5.5	10.7	-0.8	4.3	8.5
Colombia	5.7	4.1	6.5	6.3	7.1	6.0	7.6	6.7	5.7	2.1	4.8	4.1
Chile	11.0	3.3	3.6	4.1	2.0	9.1	-1.1	-5.5	0.8	-13.2	3.6	9.8
Costa Rica	7.8	5.6	8.4	5.4	7.6	6.8	8.2	7.8	5.4	2.0	5.4	8.9
Côte d'Ivoire	10.0	5.6	14.5	7.5	9.6	11.6	6.4	4.3	6.2	10.2	5.8	-0.2
India	0.0	7.9	3.3	6.5	5.2	1.6	-0.6	3.4	1.2	9.2	1.7	7.2
Indonesia	3.0	0.8	11.3	6.2	7.4	7.0	6.3	8.7	7.7	5.0	6.9	9.0
Kenya	13.9	3.7	8.3	7.8	-4.7	22.5	18.3	5.8	3.6	1.3	2.2	9.4
Korea, Rep.	11.7	6.4	11.6	13.9	8.9	10.0	5.8	15.2	8.9	7.7	13.5	11.0
Mexico	7.0	6.3	8.1	6.2	7.3	4.2	8.5	8.2	6.1	5.7	4.2	3.2
Morocco	—	—	8.5	9.9	4.9	5.6	2.4	3.5	5.4	6.7	11.0	4.9
Nigeria	-6.1	-14.6	4.6	17.5	19.3	11.5	1.0	7.6	11.2	-3.2	9.2	6.1
Pakistan	5.8	5.2	7.2	5.7	11.3	0.5	0.8	7.1	3.4	4.1	5.3	4.0
Sri Lanka	5.7	6.7	3.7	9.5	3.1	2.3	-2.4	9.5	3.8	6.5	3.5	5.1
Thailand	12.0	8.0	8.4	8.0	9.6	4.9	4.2	9.8	4.3	4.8	9.4	9.7
Turkey	11.6	4.8	6.4	5.5	4.6	9.0	6.6	4.2	8.6	8.9	8.8	4.8

— Not available.
Source: World Bank data.

Table AII.2   Inflation Rates, 1966–91

Country	1966	1967	1968	1969	1970	1971	1972	1973	1974	1975	1976	1977
Argentina	31.9	29.2	16.2	7.6	13.6	34.7	58.5	61.3	23.5	182.9	444.0	176.0
Brazil	41.3	30.5	22.0	22.7	22.4	20.1	16.6	12.7	27.6	29.0	42.0	43.7
Cameroon	—	—	—	-1.1	5.9	4.0	8.1	10.4	17.2	13.6	9.9	14.7
Chile	23.1	18.8	26.3	30.4	32.5	20.0	74.8	361.5	504.7	374.7	211.8	91.9
Colombia	19.9	8.2	5.8	10.1	6.9	9.1	13.5	20.8	24.3	22.9	20.2	33.1
Costa Rica	0.2	1.2	4.1	2.6	4.7	3.1	4.6	15.2	30.1	17.4	3.5	4.2
Côte d'Ivoire	5.6	2.3	5.3	4.5	9.4	-1.5	0.3	11.1	17.4	11.4	12.1	27.4
India	10.8	13.1	3.0	0.6	5.1	3.1	6.5	16.9	28.6	5.7	-7.6	8.3
Indonesia	636	112	85	10	6.5	4.4	6.5	31.0	40.6	19.1	19.9	11.0
Kenya	5.0	1.8	0.4	-0.2	2.2	3.8	5.8	9.3	17.8	19.1	11.5	14.8
Korea, Rep.	—	10.6	10.9	12.5	16.1	13.4	11.7	3.2	24.3	25.3	15.3	10.2
Mexico	4.2	3.0	2.3	3.4	5.2	5.3	5.0	12.0	23.8	15.2	15.8	29.0
Morocco	-1.0	-0.8	0.4	3.0	1.3	4.2	3.8	4.1	17.6	7.9	8.5	12.6
Nigeria	9.7	-3.7	-0.5	10.2	13.8	16.0	3.5	5.4	12.7	33.9	24.3	13.8
Pakistan	7.2	6.8	0.2	3.2	5.4	4.7	5.2	23.1	26.7	20.9	7.2	10.1
Sri Lanka	-0.2	2.2	5.9	7.5	5.9	2.7	6.4	9.6	12.3	6.6	1.3	1.2
Thailand	4.0	4.3	1.8	2.5	-0.1	0.5	4.8	15.5	24.3	5.3	4.2	7.6
Turkey	4.4	6.8	0.4	7.9	6.9	15.7	11.7	15.4	15.8	19.2	17.4	27.1

— Not available.
Note: Consumer Price Index inflation rates.
Source: World Bank data.

1978	*1979*	*1980*	*1981*	*1982*	*1983*	*1984*	*1985*	*1986*	*1987*	*1988*	*1989*	*1990*	*1991*
-3.4	7.2	1.9	-6.9	-5.5	2.9	2.3	-4.8	6.0	2.4	-3.0	-4.1	-0.5	5.0
3.2	6.8	9.1	-4.4	0.6	-3.4	5.4	7.9	8.0	3.3	-0.2	3.3	-4.2	1.2
14.7	13.3	15.6	12.9	2.7	7.8	5.8	7.7	8.0	-6.5	-7.7	-3.4	-2.5	0.5
8.5	5.4	4.1	2.1	1.0	1.6	3.6	3.3	6.1	5.4	4.1	3.4	3.9	2.0
8.4	8.3	7.8	5.6	-14.2	-0.7	6.3	2.5	5.7	5.7	7.3	10.1	2.1	6.0
6.2	5.0	0.8	-2.3	-7.0	2.8	7.9	0.9	5.5	4.8	3.5	5.6	3.7	1.3
13.9	2.9	-0.8	4.3	1.6	-1.2	-1.1	5.2	3.1	-1.2	-1.6	-1.0	-2.6	-2.1
-5.8	-5.3	6.7	6.5	3.8	7.4	3.8	5.3	4.5	4.9	9.8	6.2	5.5	2.2
7.7	6.2	7.9	7.4	-0.4	8.8	6.8	2.7	5.8	4.9	5.8	7.3	7.2	6.6
6.8	7.5	5.4	4.1	1.9	1.5	1.7	4.3	7.1	5.9	6.2	4.6	4.3	1.7
10.9	7.5	-3.3	6.9	7.4	12.1	9.2	6.9	12.3	11.8	11.5	6.1	9.0	8.4
8.2	9.3	8.4	8.8	-0.6	-4.2	3.7	2.8	-3.9	1.9	1.5	3.2	4.0	4.0
2.9	4.6	9.1	-2.8	9.6	-0.6	4.2	6.3	7.8	-2.3	10.2	2.3	4.0	4.8
-5.5	6.8	3.7	-9.3	-0.8	-6.5	-3.3	10.2	-0.6	-1.8	9.9	6.0	5.7	6.5
8.1	3.7	10.4	7.9	6.5	6.8	5.1	7.6	5.5	6.4	7.8	4.8	5.3	6.5
5.4	6.4	5.8	5.6	7.5	3.9	-0.3	9.8	4.4	0.7	2.7	2.1	6.3	4.7
10.6	5.0	4.7	6.3	4.0	7.2	7.2	3.4	5.1	9.6	13.4	12.2	10.3	8.0
-3.5	-1.2	-0.7	4.2	4.9	3.8	5.9	5.0	8.3	7.5	3.7	1.6	8.7	1.5

1978	*1979*	*1980*	*1981*	*1982*	*1983*	*1984*	*1985*	*1986*	*1987*	*1988*	*1989*	*1990*	*1991*
175.5	159.5	100.8	104.5	164.8	343.8	626.7	672.2	90.1	131.3	343.0	3079.8	2314.0	171.7
38.7	52.7	82.8	105.6	97.8	142.1	197.0	226.9	145.2	229.7	682.3	1287.0	2937.8	440.8
12.5	6.6	9.6	10.7	13.3	16.6	11.4	1.3	7.7	6.0	8.6	-0.03	—	—
40.1	33.4	35.1	19.7	9.9	27.3	19.9	30.7	19.5	19.9	14.7	17.0	26.0	21.8
17.8	24.7	26.5	27.5	24.6	19.8	16.1	24.0	18.9	23.3	28.1	25.8	29.1	30.4
6.0	9.2	18.1	37.1	90.1	32.6	12.0	15.1	11.8	16.9	20.8	16.5	19.0	28.7
13.0	16.6	14.7	8.8	7.3	5.9	4.3	1.9	7.3	0.4	7.0	—	—	—
2.5	6.3	11.4	13.1	7.9	11.9	8.3	5.6	8.7	8.8	9.4	6.2	9.0	13.9
8.1	16.3	18.0	12.2	9.5	11.8	10.5	4.7	5.9	9.2	8.0	6.4	7.5	9.2
16.9	8.0	13.9	11.8	20.4	11.5	10.2	13.1	3.9	5.2	8.3	9.8	11.7	14.8
14.5	18.3	28.7	21.3	7.2	3.4	2.3	2.5	2.8	3.1	7.2	5.7	8.6	9.7
17.5	18.2	26.4	27.9	58.9	101.8	65.5	57.8	86.2	131.8	114.2	20.0	26.7	22.7
9.7	8.3	9.4	12.5	10.5	6.2	12.5	7.7	8.7	2.7	2.4	3.1	6.9	8.0
21.7	11.7	10.0	20.8	7.7	23.2	39.6	7.4	5.7	11.3	54.5	50.5	7.4	13.0
6.1	8.3	11.9	11.9	5.9	2.5	10.1	5.6	3.5	4.7	8.8	7.8	9.1	6.6
12.1	10.7	26.2	18.0	10.8	14.0	16.6	1.5	8.0	7.7	14.0	11.6	21.5	12.2
7.9	9.9	19.7	12.7	5.3	3.7	0.9	2.4	1.8	2.5	3.9	5.4	5.9	5.7
45.3	58.7	110.2	36.6	30.8	31.4	48.4	45.0	34.6	38.9	75.4	63.3	60.3	66.0

Table AII.3   Current Accounts, 1965–91

(As a percentage of GNP)

Country	1965	1966	1967	1968	1969	1970	1971	1972	1973	1974	1975	1976	1977
Argentina	1.0	1.2	0.7	-0.3	-1.0	-0.7	-1.6	-0.9	1.8	0.2	-3.4	1.7	2.7
Brazil	1.3	-0.1	-0.9	-1.6	-0.9	-2.0	-3.4	-2.9	-2.7	-7.3	-5.7	-4.4	-3.0
Cameroon	—	—	—	—	—	-2.7	-3.9	-7.0	-1.0	-0.8	-6.0	-3.2	-3.0
Chile	-0.7	-1.4	-0.9	-2.0	1.2	-1.1	-2.0	-4.0	-2.7	-2.7	-7.1	1.6	-4.2
Colombia	-0.2	-5.3	-1.3	-2.8	-2.7	-4.2	-5.9	-2.3	-0.5	-2.9	-1.3	1.1	1.9
Costa Rica	-11.7	-7.0	-7.4	-5.7	-6.0	-7.6	-10.8	-8.3	-7.5	-16.4	-11.5	-8.6	-7.5
Côte d'Ivoire	-2.0	-2.9	-4.3	-0.0	-0.0	-2.7	-3.9	-7.0	-1.0	-0.8	-10.6	-5.9	-3.1
India	-2.5	-2.2	-2.4	-1.4	-0.4	-0.7	-0.6	-0.5	-0.5	-0.9	0.3	1.7	1.8
Indonesia	-1.3	-2.4	-4.2	-3.0	-3.8	-3.2	-3.8	-2.9	-2.8	2.3	-3.5	-2.3	-0.1
Kenya	0.1	-1.6	-5.0	-3.1	-0.6	-3.2	-6.5	-3.3	-5.3	-10.8	-7.0	-3.8	0.6
Korea, Rep.	0.3	-2.7	-4.1	-7.4	-7.3	-7.0	-8.7	-3.5	-2.3	-10.8	-9.1	-1.1	0.0
Mexico	0.7	-3.3	-2.7	-2.6	-1.9	-2.9	-2.1	-2.0	-2.5	-3.9	-4.4	-3.7	-2.2
Morocco	0.1	-1.8	-2.3	-1.8	-0.4	-3.2	-1.4	1.0	1.6	3.0	-5.8	-15.0	-16.9
Nigeria	-1.9	-1.5	-3.9	-4.4	-4.9	-3.0	-3.0	-2.2	0.0	16.3	0.1	-0.8	-2.0
Pakistan	-4.1	-3.9	-6.2	-3.1	-4.0	-6.7	-4.6	-2.6	-1.3	-5.7	-9.5	-6.3	-6.1
Sri Lanka	0.7	-3.3	-3.0	-3.2	-6.5	-2.6	-1.6	-1.3	-0.9	-3.8	-2.9	-0.2	3.5
Thailand	-0.3	0.5	-0.9	-2.3	-3.0	-3.5	-2.4	-0.6	-0.4	-0.6	-4.2	-2.6	-5.6
Turkey	0.0	-0.7	-0.5	-1.0	-0.8	-0.3	0.3	1.3	3.2	-1.9	-4.6	-4.9	-6.6

— Not available.

Source: World Bank data.

1978	1979	1980	1981	1982	1983	1984	1985	1986	1987	1988	1989	1990	1991
4.4	-1.0	-8.5	-8.4	-4.5	-4.1	-3.4	-1.6	-3.8	-5.5	-1.8	-2.4	1.9	-2.0
3.6	-4.8	-5.6	-4.7	-6.1	-3.6	0.0	-0.1	-2.1	-0.5	1.3	0.2	-0.6	—
4.5	-2.3	-5.8	-5.8	-4.8	-0.7	2.7	4.3	-6.0	-10.2	-7.5	-1.9	-2.6	—
7.2	-5.9	-7.4	-15.1	-10.2	-6.2	-12.2	-9.9	-8.0	-4.7	-0.8	-3.3	-3.2	0.3
1.1	1.6	-0.6	-5.5	-8.0	-8.0	-3.8	-5.4	1.1	1.0	-0.6	-0.5	1.8	6.2
10.6	-14.4	-14.4	-17.6	-12.3	-9.9	-4.5	-3.5	-1.9	-6.1	-4.2	-8.6	-9.5	-2.6
11.7	-16.9	-18.4	-17.8	-14.4	-14.8	-1.2	1.1	-3.4	-10.2	-12.0	-14.5	-14.6	-12.3
0.1	-0.3	-1.3	-1.7	-1.4	-1.3	-1.6	-2.7	-2.5	-2.4	-3.1	-2.8	-2.9	-1.0
2.7	1.9	4.0	-0.6	-5.9	-7.7	-2.2	-2.3	-5.1	-2.9	-1.7	-1.2	-2.9	-4.0
13.0	-8.3	-12.6	-8.4	-4.8	-0.8	-2.1	-1.9	-0.5	-6.5	-5.6	-7.3	-5.8	—
2.2	-6.5	-8.8	-6.9	-3.7	-2.0	-1.6	-1.0	4.5	7.7	8.4	2.4	-0.9	—
3.0	-4.0	-5.7	-6.7	-3.9	3.9	2.5	0.6	-1.4	3.0	-1.5	-2.0	-3.1	-4.9
10.2	-9.8	-7.8	-12.6	-12.7	-6.7	-8.1	-7.3	-1.3	1.0	2.2	-3.7	-0.8	—
6.8	2.4	5.7	-7.3	-9.4	-5.6	0.1	3.3	0.9	-0.3	-0.7	3.8	15.3	3.8
2.8	-4.2	-3.7	-2.7	-3.7	-0.6	-2.1	-3.9	-2.3	-1.0	-2.9	-3.3	-3.3	—
2.4	-6.8	-16.4	-10.3	-11.4	-9.1	0.0	-7.0	-6.5	-4.9	-5.7	-6.0	-3.7	-6.2
4.8	-7.7	-6.5	-7.5	-2.9	-7.3	-5.2	-4.2	0.6	-0.8	-2.8	-3.7	-9.0	-8.6
2.4	-2.1	-6.1	-3.4	-1.8	-3.9	-2.9	-2.0	-2.6	-1.2	2.3	1.2	-2.5	0.2

Notes

Chapter 1.   Introduction

1.   Multicountry studies of developing countries were pioneered in the field of trade policy by Little, Scitovsky, and Scott (1970); Bhagwati and Krueger (see Krueger, 1978); and Balassa (1982). More recent is the World Bank study of trade liberalization experiences, involving seventeen countries (Michaely, Papageorgiou, and Choksi, 1991). Apart from our own project, the principal multicountry project concerned with macroeconomic policies (focusing on the effects of international debt) is a National Bureau of Economic Research project (Sachs and Collins, 1989). It involves eight countries, including six of our group, and we have drawn extensively on the country studies produced by that project. The World Bank has sponsored several other multicountry research projects on various topics. A recent one of particular relevance here concerns the macroeconomics of the public sector deficit (Easterly, Rodriguez, and Schmidt-Hebbel, forthcoming).
2.   In this volume a billion is 1,000 million.
3.   The dependent economy model is expounded in Corden (1985, chapter 1). The model originated with Salter (1959) and Swan (1960), and the main elements go back to the writings of Meade (1951) and Johnson (1958). A fuller exposition of the basic theoretical framework for studying macroeconomic adjustment in developing countries is in Corden (1989).

Chapter 2.   A Brief Survey of the World Economy

1.   This gold convertibility applied only to the monetary authorities of other countries and to certain international institutions. Private citizens lost their right to convert dollars into gold freely in 1934.
2.   For convenience, we use the term "industrialized countries" to mean the twenty-four members of the Organization for Economic Cooperation and Development (OECD), which includes western Europe, Japan, Australia and New Zealand, Canada, and the United States—the rich, market-oriented economies. The OECD also includes several poor countries of Europe, however, among them Turkey, one of our eighteen countries.
3.   As already noted, the International Tin Agreement collapsed in 1986 when the International Tin Council (ITC) could no longer pay its debts collateralized on stocks of tin, the price of which was in decline. The Sugar Agreement collapsed on expiration in 1977, largely because the European

Community had become a large exporter of sugar and would not agree to restrain its exports. The Coffee Agreement collapsed in 1989 over leakages through nonagreement countries (mainly the German Democratic Republic) and because of Brazil's unwillingness to reduce its historically high export quota in favor of countries and coffees that consumers had come to prefer. The Cocoa Agreement was renewed in 1983, but without several major producers (Malaysia, Indonesia) and consumers (United States). Its purchases of cocoa ceased in 1988 when it reached its stockholding limit, producers went into arrears with the cocoa organization, and in any case it had too few resources to have a major impact on the market for cocoa.

4. National jurisdiction remains limited to a maximum of 12 miles from the coast, but for the control of fisheries, continental shelf minerals, and some aspects of pollution, about one-third of the ocean surface was appropriated.

5. These data are drawn from *International Financial Statistics*, and thus exclude several Communist countries. The United States developed an exceptionally large trade deficit during the mid-1980s as a consequence of its macroeconomic policies and a sharp appreciation of the dollar until early 1985; its share of world imports did not fall as much as its share of world exports. By the end of the decade, the U.S. trade deficit had declined substantially, but remained high by pre-1984 standards.

6. The IMF-sanctioned program did not always succeed, of course. See Gwin and Feinberg (1989).

7. See Cooper and Lawrence (1975).

8. Real gross domestic product in the industrialized countries declined 0.5 percent in 1975, in comparison with the 5.7 percent growth in 1973—a very sharp swing.

9. Figures are for net lending to developing countries from reporting banks in the industrialized countries; loans exclude those to offshore banking centers such as Singapore and the Cayman Islands. From the Bank for International Settlements, *Annual Report* (1990) and earlier issues.

10. See Cooper (1992) for a detailed discussion of the forecasts of late 1981 and early 1982.

11. The number is ten if the 1981 aid consortium to Pakistan is counted, since some official debt was rescheduled there, although that was not the main focus of the meeting. Cameroon rescheduled for the first time in 1989.

12. See Schultze and Lawrence (1987).

13. The exclusion of the U.S.S.R. and some other Communist countries accounts for only a small part of the discrepancy.

14. They failed to recognize that a strong principle of nondiscrimination in fact protects small countries against arbitrary actions by large ones, and later paid the price for this failure in the increasing use by the industrialized countries of "selective" safeguards against imports from developing countries.

15. One interesting characteristic of the 1970s is that the first oil shock, which hit a number of oil-importing developing countries severely, was officially welcomed by them, as at last giving the developing countries as a group a powerful enough "weapon" to get the serious attention of the industrialized countries. The OPEC decision to raise oil prices was motivated mainly by a desire for increased revenue to foster economic development, especially to advance the Shah of Iran's ambitious plans for his country (he hosted the December 1973 OPEC meeting). However, OPEC members, led by Algeria and Venezuela, were sensitive to the need to maintain "solidarity" with oil-importing developing countries and pressed the use of oil as a bargaining weapon into the discussions on a new economic order.

Chapter 3.   The Period of Cheap and Easy Credit

1. India was a net lender from 1975 through 1978. Nigeria and Indonesia were also lenders, but only very briefly in 1974.

2. The formula used for the terms of trade effect in year *t* is

$$\text{TOTEFF}_t = \text{EXP}_t \, \frac{p_I^{t-1}}{p_I^t} \div \frac{p_E^{t-1}}{p_E^t}$$

where EXP*t* *is the dollar value of exports, and* p_I and p_E are unit value indices for imports and exports respectively. TOTEFF*t* is expressed in the table as a percentage of GDP $_{t-1}$ and exports *t*-1. This formula is conventional and widely accepted by national income statisticians. (It is, however, arbitrary to use potential imports to express the gain or loss from a movement in the terms of trade.) For a critical discussion of this and other formulae see Scott (1979).

3. The issue of the choice between the exchange rate and import control measures is discussed in chapters 8 and 9. At this point it should be noted that many substantial real devaluations in the period 1984–88 did succeed in raising exports markedly and quite quickly.

4. In principle, the average price increase could be avoided by revaluing the currency. In view of the deterioration in the current account of the balance of payments, this was not contemplated by any of our countries (it was seriously considered in Taiwan [China], but finally rejected). The fear of further increasing prices was a deterrent against devaluation.

5. Indian fiscal years run from April 1 to March 31. References are always to fiscal years, unless a calendar year is specified.

6. Gelb (1988: table 5.2). The windfall is estimated in relation to a simple counterfactual.

7. In Indonesia, the investment boom continued through 1981 and reached 30.6 percent. In Nigeria, 1976 was the peak year.

8. There may even have been an absolute fall in Nigeria, but estimates are too unreliable to be sure.

9. The "coffee" boom was really a beverage boom. Cocoa and tea prices also rose. Cocoa was particularly important for Côte d'Ivoire.

10. Table 3.3 shows a larger rise for private investment in Cameroon and Indonesia. In these cases "private" includes public enterprises.

11. See, for example, Gelb (1988), Auty (1990), Bevan and others (unpublished).

12. See Gonzalez-Vega (forthcoming) for an extensive discussion.

13. See Bevan and others (unpublished).

14. Turkey had a minor investment boom in 1980 and 1981 that is not recorded in table 3.3.

15. See Little and Mirrlees (1974) and Squire and van der Tak (1975).

16. Net borrowing is equal to the change in foreign assets and liabilities, but it will fail to correspond to a change in recorded debt for several reasons. The latter excludes changes in reserves. It also necessarily excludes unrecorded and often illegal purchases and sales of foreign assets. The recorded debt measured in dollars will also change as the value of assets and liabilities in other currencies varies with the exchange rate of those currencies against the dollar. The value of the debt may in some cases in recent years also be affected by rescheduling, debt forgiveness, and debt/equity swaps. Table 3.4 is based on the appendix to this chapter, which lays out the algebra relating to the concepts used and for each country provides tables giving annual values for the relevant concepts, and the error implicit in the figures.

17. We speak of association rather than of the loans incurred being used for, or causing, investment. For instance, a rise in borrowing in relation to GNP may coincide with a rise in the ratio of investment to GNP. This latter rise might have taken place without the borrowing. The borrowing would thus be preventing a fall in consumption that would otherwise have taken place. It is, however, usually reasonable to suppose that in the absence of borrowing there would have been little change in the proportion of GNP saved, in which case it is legitimate to ascribe causation in one direction or the other to an association between borrowing and increased investment.

Chapter 4.   Heading for Crisis: 1979–1982

1.   For brevity, we frequently refer to deficits, debt, and so on, when we mean the ratio to GNP.
2.   The state of affairs described in this paragraph is known as the debt trap. The debt trap may arise also in the case of domestic borrowing. The simple mathematics behind the intuitive account of debt dynamics given in this section is laid out in chapter 10. Although the term "primary deficit" usually refers to a budget deficit, it is convenient to let it refer also to the current account of the balance of payments.
3.   Figures quoted for oil are average OECD spot import prices as given in the *OECD Economic Outlook* (1986).
4.   The formula used for the terms-of-trade effect is the same as in chapter 3.
5.   Interest Effect = $-(I_t - I_{t-1}[D_t/D_{t-1}])$, where I is interest payments on total debt (including short-term debt) and D is total outstanding debt, including public, publicly guaranteed, and private non-guaranteed debt.
6.   It was allowed for in Balassa and McCarthy (1984). Their calculations suggest that the effect of a fall below trend in the quantity of exports was, in most cases, small in relation to the terms-of-trade and interest effects.
7.   These volumes are calculated by taking the value of imports into all developed countries from each of our countries as given by the United Nations trade data system, and deflating by the World Bank export price indices for each of our countries.
8.   Three percent is about equal to the historical long-term rate of interest. This leads one to suspect that projectors were influenced by the Hotelling theorem (Hotelling 1931). If the price of oil is expected to rise by more than the rate of interest, then it pays to leave the oil underground, and the price rises until the expected price rise falls: and similarly, mutatis mutandis, if the price is expected to rise less than the rate of interest! Therefore, the expected price rise equals the rate of interest! As a corollary, it should have been predicted that the real rate of return obtainable by oil producers on their investments would fall to 3 percent. The Hotelling theorem has now been abandoned as a guide.
9.   An excellent comprehensive account is Edwards and Edwards (1991).
10.   As a percentage of GNP in current prices, this does not show up.
11.   The figures are from Claassen (unpublished). World Bank figures diverge considerably, and look wrong.
12.   Cardoso and Fishlow (1990) vividly describe his expansionary policies and their consequences.
13.   This is the so-called operational deficit, which is explained and discussed further in chapters 7 and 10. The figure comes from Coes (forthcoming).
14.   Figures for Cameroon are from Connolly (unpublished).
15.   Cameroon's relatively successful adjustment, despite a fixed exchange rate, is further analyzed in Devarajan and de Melo (1987).
16.   Gil-Diaz and Ramos Tercero (1988, table 8.1). The public sector borrowing requirement in such an inflationary situation is not, of course, a correct indicator of the destabilizing effects of the deficit (see chapters 6 and 10), although all deficit measures indicate a very large imbalance. For instance, the primary deficit was 8.4 percent and the "adjusted operational deficit" allowing for all inflation effects as calculated by the authors was 11 percent (Gil-Diaz and Ramos Tercero 1988, tables 8.1 and 8.5).
17.   A more comprehensive and longer-term comparison is made in Pinto (1987).

Chapter 5.   A Slow Recovery for Most: 1983–1989

1.   The figures given in appendix tables 5A.1 to 5A.18 are for interest paid, not due.

2. These surpluses do not arise only from a desire to reduce the debt. As in the case of Japan and Taiwan, it became politically difficult to reduce the trade surplus.

3. The simple correlation coefficients between the variables are given in the correlation matrix (table 5B-1) in appendix B to this chapter.

4. We do not have separate figures for public and private investment in all our countries. The following account derives from Serven and Solimano (1993). They give figures for Argentina, Brazil, Chile, Costa Rica, and Mexico among our eight reschedulers. When we compared the same periods as used in table 5-2, we found the larger part of the fall in Mexican investment was public. In Argentina the private fall was greater, but both fell heavily. In Chile public investment actually rose, but total investment fell. Of the nonreschedulers for which figures are available, total investment fell heavily in Kenya, mainly in the public sector. Serven and Solimano's figures differ from ours, but are not very different except for Costa Rica, where they found a drop in total investment of 4.2 percentage points of GNP, in comparison with our figure of 0.5.

5. The damaging effect of import starvation in Mexico is emphasized in Buffie (1990). Nigeria is another case in which import starvation was very damaging. See chapter 9 for a discussion of import starvation in Indonesia, Sri Lanka, India, and Côte d'Ivoire.

6. It may be argued that economic theory suggests that an increase in competitiveness would result in a higher *level* of exports in relation to GDP. However, the achievement of this new level would imply for some time a rate of growth of the value of exports greater than the rate of growth of GDP: and the greater the rise in competitiveness the higher this growth rate of exports is likely to be.

7. Celâsun and Rodrik (1989) make this point. They also cast doubt on whether the export drive can continue to rely so much on repeated real devaluations and subsidies. More export-oriented investment that requires less implicit and explicit subsidization will be needed.

8. This was also the case in Turkey in 1980.

9. See World Bank (1990), table 5.5.

10. The World Bank has made its own assessments. See World Bank (1989, 1990a).

11. We have used World Bank (1990c) here.

12. See Joshi and Little (forthcoming), especially chapters 5 and 9.

13. Nigeria's fiscal situation also deteriorated in 1989 when the economic reform plan introduced in 1986 broke down. External debt payments were in arrears and by 1992 the inflation rate was 45 percent.

Chapter 6. Inflation in the Eighteen Countries

1. The following figures come from *International Financial Statistics* and refer to average CPI inflation rates for 1980–89 for all developing economies. Only five countries averaged 300 percent inflation or more—Bolivia, Nicaragua, Argentina, Peru, and Brazil. Nine countries had average inflation rates of 50 to 200 percent; these included Mexico and Turkey from our group, and another sixteen had inflation rates ranging from 20 to 49 percent, including Costa Rica, Colombia, Chile, and Nigeria. All the rest (eighty-one) had rates less than 20 percent, and 51 less than 10 percent.

2. In several countries central banks also ran large deficits that are fiscal in character but not budgeted through the government. These also stimulate the growth of the money supply. This and other seigniorage issues are discussed further in chapter 10.

3. See Tanzi (1977). It is sometimes called the "Olivera-Tanzi effect" because the general idea can also be found in Olivera (1967).

4. These remarks do not refer to Morocco, which was an oil importer but benefited from a terms-of-trade improvement owing to the rise in the price of phosphates. They also do not refer to the five high-inflation countries discussed in chapter 7, three of which (Brazil, Chile, and Turkey) suffered significantly from the oil price rise.

5. The Sri Lankan inflation rate fluctuated a great deal. The 1983–89 average of 10.5 percent was well above the 1976–79 average of 6 percent. The fluctuations were caused by sharp changes in fiscal (public expenditure) and monetary policies, combined with a high flexibility of wages and nontradable (especially construction) prices.

6. Cameroon's debts were rescheduled in 1989.

7. See Woo and Nasution (1989), Woo, Glassburner, and Nasution (forthcoming) and Thorbecke (1991).

8. See Castillo (1988).

9. By 1993 Nigeria looked rather different. The fiscal situation had deteriorated since 1990, external debt was in arrears and in 1992 the inflation rate had leaped up again to 45 percent.

10. As noted in chapter 5, this is a particularly important but also relatively novel issue for India, which has a long tradition of low inflation but in 1990 was in an unstable public debt situation. There has been a steady rise in the ratio of public debt to GDP. This cannot go on indefinitely. The question is what combination of fiscal restraint and increased monetization will ultimately resolve the issue.

Chapter 7.   Stories of High Inflation and Stabilization

1. This discussion draws on Coes (forthcoming) and also on Baer (1987), Simonsen (1988), Cardoso and Dantas (1990), Cardoso and Fishlow (1990), Kiguel and Liviatan (1991), and World Bank and IMF sources.

2. Base money consists of currency issued to the public plus reserve deposits of the banking system with the Central Bank. M1, referred to below, also includes demand deposits (which are also non-interest-bearing).

3. At the beginning of 1991 the blocked cruzados were valued at 6 percent of GDP, and subsequently they were gradually deblocked. Other measures were taken to reduce liquidity (compelling banks to put more deposits into government long-term bonds).

4. This discussion draws on de Pablo (unpublished), Calvo (1986), Canavese and di Tella (1988), Corbo, de Melo, and Tybout (1986), Epstein (1987), Fernandez (1985), Machinea and Fanelli (1988), Rodriguez (1988, 1991), Dornbusch and de Pablo (1990), Kiguel and Liviatan (1988, 1991), Kiguel and Neumeyer (1989), Kiguel (1991), and on World Bank and IMF sources.

5. See especially Corbo, de Melo, and Tybout (1986), Calvo (1986), and Cumby and van Wijnbergen (1989).

6. Much of this discussion is based on Rodriguez (1991).

7. This discussion draws on Edwards and Edwards (1991), Corbo (1985), Corbo, de Melo, and Tybout (1986), Meller (1990), Corbo and Solimano (1991), and World Bank and IMF sources.

8. This discussion draws on Gil-Diaz (unpublished, 1984), Gil-Diaz and Ramos Tercero (1988), Buffie (1990), Beristain and Trigueros (1990), and various World Bank and IMF sources. See also Cardoso and Levy (1988), Dornbusch (1988), Ortiz (1991), and van Wijnbergen (1991).

9. The demand for money (the M1/GNP ratio) had been steadily falling from 1982, but this is not sufficient to explain the high inflation rates of 1987 and 1988.

10. See Khor and Rojas-Suarez (1991) for a detailed analysis of the determination of Mexican interest rates from 1987 to 1990. They find that the large expected exchange rate changes implicit in the interest rate differentials did not take place, but "that domestic interest rates of Mexican assets denominated in US dollars are closely linked to the behavior of the implicit yield derived from the secondary market for Mexican debt" (p. 852).

11. This discussion draws primarily on Onis and Riedel (1993), Celâsun and Rodrik (1989), Rodrik (1991), and World Bank and IMF sources. See also Kopits (1987), and Dervis and Petri (1987).

12. This continued to be the story in 1991 when the announcement that elections would be held led to various measures that increased the fiscal deficit. The inflation rate in 1991 was 66 percent, much the same as in 1989 and 1990.

13. Onis and Riedel (1993) have estimated the demand for money in 1965–86. They find that the elasticity of demand for aggregate real money balances with respect to inflation was -0.5 (but higher for real-time deposits alone).

14. There were substantial real wage increases (the result of strikes) in early 1991.

15. This discussion draws on Woo and others (forthcoming), Sundrum (1973), and Pitt (1991). See also Sutton (1984).

16. This observation is based on the revised figures calculated by Rosendale (1978) and reported in table 7-2. There is considerable doubt about the official figures over this period: the official figures (also reported in table 7-2) suggest that there was a deficit also in 1965–67, and that it increased in 1969.

17. For details, see Pitt (1991), who also gives real effective exchange rates for various categories of trade over the relevant period.

18. Views on inflation stabilization policies must, of course, be based also on experiences of other countries. Two countries that succeeded in stabilizing from very high inflation in the 1980s without declines in growth rates—and that are generally considered great successes in this respect—are Bolivia and Israel. On each of these there is a large literature. See Morales and Sachs (1990) on Bolivia, and Bruno and Piterman (1988) and Bruno and Meridor (1991) on Israel. The Bolivian program was purely "orthodox" and the Israeli program had the necessary orthodox elements but also contained important heterodox elements—that is, above all, a wage-restraining compact with the trade unions. The experiences of Germany and other European countries in the 1920s are also relevant. See Dornbusch and Fischer (1986). Overviews of stabilization issues can be found in Kiguel and Liviatan (1988) and Blejer and Cheasty (1988).

19. In Brazil various stabilization programs have also had other components, notably de-indexation or blocking of financial assets.

20. Wage indexation for the public sector was introduced in 1974 to avoid further declines in real wages that had resulted from the big inflation of 1972–74. From mid-1979 such 100 percent lagged indexation (i.e., nominal wages adjusted on the basis of price increases in the previous period) was extended compulsorily to all collective bargaining-determined wages in the private sector.

Chapter 8.   Exchange Rate Policy: Devaluations and Regime Changes

1. In table 8-1, a real depreciation is a *decrease* (nominal exchange rates being defined as units of foreign currency [dollars] per home currency [rupiahs]). Hence, to calculate from these indices a real devaluation between periods 1 and 2 using the definition adhered to in this book, the change must be expressed as a proportion of the period 2 figure.

2. Nigeria's real depreciation was about 400 percent. Korea and Mexico both appreciated in 1988, so their net real depreciations over the whole period were only 7 percent and 3 percent, respectively.

3. A thorough study of the erosion of the initial real effects of nominal devaluations in developing countries can be found in Edwards (1989a, chap. 7). Like the present study, it highlights the diversity of experiences; thirty-nine devaluation episodes over the period 1961 to 1982 are analyzed. When real exchange rates three years after devaluations are compared with the rates one year before, in general, some net effects remained, but there was significant erosion. In nine countries with a crawling peg regime, erosion was much less—though at the cost of increased inflation.

4. All figures of exports of manufactures cited come, unless otherwise stated, from the UN Trade Data System and refer only to exports to developed countries. They are based on figures of imports by the developed countries and are thought to be much more reliable in general than export data from the developing countries themselves. Only dollar value, not volume, indices are readily

obtainable. Some idea of volume growth can be obtained by relating the (more than) 20 percent dollar value growth per year in 1986–89, cited here, to the average annual rate of U.S. inflation, which was about 2 percent for producer prices and 3.6 percent for consumer prices.

5. These figures are based on national sources. The UN Trade Data System actually suggests that increases were substantially larger. The total increase 1986–88 was 121 percent according to these figures, and the annual rate of growth in 1986–89 was 44 percent.

6. The figure of 42 percent a year quoted in the text comes from Onis and Riedel (1993), who cite Turkish official sources. They also report that the value of exports to countries of the Organization for Economic Cooperation and Development grew at 20 percent a year over that period. The UN Trade Data System gives lower figures, but still shows large increases: an average rate of growth of exports to developed countries 1980–85 of 16 percent. For 1986–89, it gives a remarkable growth of 39 percent a year. Owing to export subsidies, there appears to have been a tendency for Turkish figures to overstate the true value of exports; hence data from partner countries (UN data) may be more accurate, although this may also have some problems. In any case, it can be agreed that since 1981 there has been a boom in Turkish manufactured exports!

7. An interesting result in Pritchett's paper is that the only discernible positive relationship is for the most recent short period, 1985–88, which suggests that the large real depreciations that have been discussed above did not just increase exports of manufactures but also played some role (to put it minimally) in improving the trade balance during that period.

8. The extensive theoretical literature on the contractionary effects of devaluation is surveyed in Lizondo and Montiel (1989)

9. This measure is also used by Edwards (1989a, p.103). He covers the period 1972–85 using quarterly data, and refers to 33 countries, including eleven in our group.

10. The figures come out as follows. The standard error of estimate of the equation for real exchange rates in 1978–88 (RER), where $RER = a + bt$ (where t is the year), is: Nigeria, 48.9; Argentina, 16.6; Colombia, 15.6; Chile, 15.2; Sri Lanka, 13.9; Indonesia, 13.4; and Mexico, 13.0. Turkey is only 7.3.

11. The following discussion is based on quarterly IMF figures, supported by figures in several country studies and World Bank sources. See also Edwards (1989a).

12. The second is the Martinez de Hoz episode discussed in chapter 7. The IMF real exchange rate index (where an increase is appreciation) shows a movement from 47.2 in 1978(1) to a peak of 116 in 1981(1) and down to 39.7 in 1983(1).

13. This explains the high standard deviation from the mean cited above, the highest of any country for the 1978–88 period.

14. It might be said that "flexible peg" is an oxymoron. How can a peg be flexible? There is clearly no firm line between an adjustable peg regime in which the rate is infrequently adjusted (as was usual under the Bretton Woods system) and one in which the adjustment is frequent; nor (as noted below) between the latter and a managed float. Some countries have had flexible peg regimes in the sense of the definition here, but have described them as managed floats.

15. The condition for absence of capital flows, that is, the equilibrium condition, is $r = r^* + d + q$, where r is the relevant domestic interest rate, r^* is the comparable foreign interest rate, d is the expected rate of depreciation of the domestic currency, and q is the risk factor. This is expounded in every international economics textbook. When the exchange rate is defined (as in this study) as pesos (domestic currency) per dollar (foreign currency), then the formula becomes $r = r^* + (E' - E)/E + q$, where E is the spot exchange rate and E' the expected exchange rate.

16. Figures of the parallel market premiums cited here have been calculated in the World Bank from figures of parallel market rates in various issues of the World Currency Yearbook.

17. An econometric attempt at measuring average capital mobility for the period 1969–87 in fifteen developing countries, including seven of our group, has been made by Haque and Montiel (1991). They needed to make rather heroic assumptions, including rational expectations that the expected rates of depreciation were equal to the later actual depreciations, and that the demand for money functions were constant. In addition, actual capital flight has been estimated by Cuddington (1986,1987). As noted earlier, however, there can be capital mobility without capital flight.

18. See Cuddington (1986, 1987) on which much of this discussion of capital flight is based. He showed econometrically that overvaluation of the real exchange rate was the main determinant. Problems of measurement are extensively discussed by him and in Lessard and Williamson (1987).

19. Venezuela is the only other country in which capital flight on this measure was large.

20. See Cuddington (1986, p. 29).

21. As noted in chapters 4 and 7, Chile had a large inflow of private capital 1980–81, the source of later problems. The capital market was liberalized in 1980.

22. Econometric work by García García and Jayasuriya (forthcoming) suggests that the domestic interest rate is very sensitive to external factors, though in the short run the monetary authority can influence it. See also Rennhack and Mondino (1988).

23. Berthélemy and Bourguignon (forthcoming). They estimate that such financial arbitrage flows were equal, on average, to 1 percent of GDP annually, that is, one-fifth of the total remittances.

24. Using the residual method, Joshi and Little (forthcoming) estimate that 40 percent of the (modest) increase in India's debt in 1980–84 was explained by private capital outflow.

25. See Devarajan and de Melo (1990) for a careful analysis comparing the growth rates of members of the zone with other sub-Saharan African countries, for the period 1973–81 (when the zone members did better) and 1982–89 (when they did worse). In the latter period zone members, notably, had larger declines in investment.

26. Berthélemy and Bourguignon (forthcoming) cite an index of the average real wage in the modern sector. Owing to quite high inflation, it fell sharply 1979–80, but has been quite steady after that. The minimum guaranteed nominal wage was constant 1982–86, so that it fell in real terms; but the authors point out that most workers are paid more, and that wage data in Côte d'Ivoire are not satisfactory (which is also true of many other countries in our study!).

27. There is an extensive literature on the concept of the real exchange rate. See especially Harberger (1986), Edwards (1988), Edwards (1989b), and Coes (1989). In preparing this note, Max Corden is indebted to Sisera Jayasuriya.

28. See Salter (1959) and Corden (1985, chap. 1), for full expositions of the "dependent economy" model.

29. The IMF real exchange rate indices are all derived from trade-weighted nominal rate indices (that is, "nominal effective exchange rates"). The weighting scheme takes into account both bilateral trade and third-country competition, and the trade flows used are averages of the three-year period 1980–82.

30. The most comprehensive study of real exchange rates in developing countries is by Edwards (1989a). He also defines the real exchange rate as p_t/p_n, that is, the Salter ratio. In his calculations, the foreign WPI is used to proxy the foreign price level. The domestic CPI is used to proxy the price of nontraded goods.

31. See Meller (1990), who reports the Chilean Central Bank's index, and Warr (1986), who calculated it for Indonesia in 1971–82.

32. One approach is to take into account all the differential effects of changes in trade regimes on different exports and imports. Thus, Athukorala and Jayasuriya (forthcoming) have calculated real effective exchange rate indices for Sri Lanka separately for traditional and for nontraditional exports, and have shown the following changes between 1976 and 1978 (that is, reflecting the effects of the 1977 devaluation and associated trade regime changes). For traditional exports, the index rose from 68 to 94; for nontraditional exports, it rose from 62 to 80. Hence, owing to reduction of export taxes, real devaluation was greater in the first case; that is, the bias in the system against this category was reduced.

33. Full explanations of the various real effective exchange rate indices calculated by the IMF for seventeen developed countries are given in each issue of *International Financial Statistics*.

Chapter 9.   Trade Policies: Tightening and Liberalization

1. These trade liberalizing episodes relate to the ten countries common to the present study and that of Michaely and others (1991) up to 1984, the last year of the period of the latter study.
2. The exceptions were the following. There were three episodes in period two of fixed rate liberalizations, all relatively minor and associated with balance-of-payments improvements (Kenya, Korea, and Nigeria). In period four, there was one, namely, Côte d'Ivoire (1985). The QRs were eliminated, while export subsidies and tariffs were raised. Subsequently, however, QRs were reintroduced following a strong deterioration in the terms of trade.
3. See Krueger (1978), World Bank (1987), Dollar (1990), Edwards (1991) and Michaely and others (1991).
4. The following information is based on Nogués and Gulati (1992) and other World Bank sources.
5. The following discussion is based on World Bank sources and on Pitt (1991), Athukorala and Jayasuriya (forthcoming), Joshi and Little (forthcoming).
6. Kwang Suk Kim (1991), Pitt (1991), Coes (forthcoming), Woo and others (forthcoming), Athukorala and Jayasuriya (forthcoming), Gil-Diaz (unpublished), Claassen (unpublished), and World Bank sources.
7. Help from Pedro Videla in preparing the statistical appendix to this chapter is gratefully acknowledged.
8. The source of the variables is the economic and social data base of the World Bank and the calculations are done with RATS 3.11 statistical package.
9. Given that the dependent variable takes values 0 and 1, the MLS model will give biased estimators for any sample size. The alternative is to use (binary choice) probit or logit models. These models take the form:

$$P[Y_i = 1/X_i] = F(X_iB).$$

The probit model uses a cumulative normal function while Logit uses a logistic function. Since the two functions are very similar and since the use of the standard normal cumulative density function is less contested in the literature, we use the probit model to test our hypotheses.
10. Here and in the subsequent equations, the t-statistic appears in parentheses. Superscript * indicates significance at the 0.1 level, superscript ** indicates significance at the 0.5 level, and superscript *** indicates significance at the 0.01 level. N indicates the number of observations, LL the log-likelihood, and AL the average likelihood.
11. The 153 events are the sum of all episodes times the duration of each episode counted as one for each year.
12. The Godfrey-Breusch test (GB) is used instead of DW because in the AR(1) method the dependent variable is regressed on itself and is lagged. The GB is an LM test for autocorrelated errors when the alternative hypothesis is either AR(q) or MA(q).

Chapter 10.   Fiscal and Monetary Policies

1. In developing countries as a group, the ratio rose from 21.9 percent in 1972 to 27.4 percent in 1982, or 5.5 percentage points. In general, for most years aggregate figures for all developing countries differ little from those for nonoil developing countries, so we cite only the latter. The source for all these figures is the IMF, *International Financial Statistics, Supplement on Government Finance*, Supplement 11 (1986), and its *Government Finance Statistics Yearbook* (1990). Statisticians convert national data into standardized categories, which means the IMF data are more likely to be comparable across countries. Because of these adjustments, however, the data

reported here may differ from those in national budgets, for example, in the treatment of state-owned enterprises that perform governmental functions, such as food price stabilization.

2. Most of our countries have a fiscal year that corresponds to the calendar year. In India, Indonesia, and Nigeria (until 1981), the fiscal year begins on April 1. In these cases, "1985" means fiscal 1985/86 in the tables. In Cameroon, Kenya, and Pakistan the fiscal year begins on July 1, and in Thailand it begins on October 1. In these cases "1985" means fiscal 1984/85.

3. The pattern in industrialized countries is somewhat different, with the 1972–82 rise being concentrated in transfer payments (up by 4.4 percentage points, to 17.2 percent of GDP) and interest payments (up 1.9 percentage points to 1982, and another 0.7 to 1987). Current consumption also rose by 0.5 percentage points, while capital expenditures and net lending remained unchanged in terms of GDP (table 10-1).

4. According to official data as reported to the International Monetary Fund, defense spending was substantially lower in Argentina in 1982 and in Chile in 1982 and 1987, and significantly lower in Indonesia (1973 and 1982), Sri Lanka (1987), and Turkey (1981 and 1987). We have relied on the Stockholm International Peace Research Institute (SIPRI) figures.

5. The distinction between capital expenditure by the central government and that by SOEs is usually clear; the former undertakes traditional infrastructure projects such as roadbuilding, major land irrigation, canal dredging, and so on; and the latter undertakes investments that can be expected to yield a commercial return. The distinction sometimes blurs, depending on whether or not large infrastructure projects are organized as a separate enterprise; in Côte d'Ivoire, for example, the sugar development program was switched at a certain stage from public expenditure to state-owned enterprise.

6. This figure reflects a substantial increase in lending from Brazil's social security funds in 1987, possibly associated with the elimination of the monetary correction as part of the 1986 Cruzado Plan.

7. Brazil shows 33 percent, but that includes interest and other income from the social security system that began to be loaned out in 1987. See note 6. Brazil's tax revenue fell from 19 percent of GDP in 1982, itself down from 25 percent in the mid-1970s, to 15 percent in 1987.

8. See Goode (1984), pp. 92–95. Where commodity taxes are specific rather than ad valorem, revenues will decline in relation to GDP when inflation occurs. By 1989 the number of countries relying on commodity taxes for more than half their revenue had fallen from ten to eight, and those relying on them for more than 40 percent dropped from fourteen to thirteen.

9. Asian deficits were somewhat larger than Western Hemisphere deficits in the period 1977–81 and were somewhat lower in every year after 1981.

10. In Sri Lanka, the leading investors in government securities are the National Savings Bank, the Employees' Provident Fund, and several insurance companies and savings banks. In Kenya, they included the government social security fund.

11. Goode (1984), pp. 200–1. The median ratio of the central government's debt to GDP in the late 1970s was 26.7 percent for all developing countries, and among our countries ranged from a low of 9.5 percent for Argentina to a high of 108 percent for Costa Rica, although figures for some countries, including these two, represent the budgetary central government only, excluding extrabudgetary accounts and state-owned enterprises.

12. This practice was stopped in all three countries in the second half of the 1980s.

13. Calculated from IMF, *Government Finance Statistics Yearbook* (1980). These figures exclude provincial enterprises and those owned by local governments. Such enterprises were numerous in Argentina, Brazil, Colombia, India, Korea, and Thailand. Shirley (1984, p. 5) shows a more than fourfold increase in number of SOEs between 1960 and 1980 in Argentina, Brazil, India, and Sri Lanka, and a trebling in Mexico, the only countries in our group reported there. Mexico began to privatize SOEs in a serious way in the mid-1980s; so did Argentina after the election of Carlos Menem as president in 1989.

14. Mexico greatly enlarged its number of SOEs in 1982 when it nationalized the banks and the government became owners of nonfinancial enterprises owned by the banks. So Mexico sold, consolidated, or liquidated more enterprises in the mid-1980s than the text figures suggest.

15. Short in Floyd, Gray, and Short (1984) for the 1970s; Nair and Filippides (1988) for the 1980s.

16. But not the 1980s, in Schenone's view. See Larrain and Selowsky (1991).

17. Short in Floyd and others (1984, table 5); and Nair and Filippides (1988, table 2-3). Schenone, however, reports current account surpluses for Argentine SOEs in each year during the period 1966–85. See Larrain and Selowsky (1991 p. 15).

18. Generalization from perusing table 2-2 and correlations on p. 8 of Nair and Filippides (1988).

19. The figures for these eight countries are from Nair and Filippides (1988, table 2-5).

20. See Schenone in Larrain and Selowsky (1991, p. 32).

21. Reported by Schenone in Larrain and Selowsky (1991, p. 37).

22. Ayub and Hegstad (1986, pp. 16, 75–76). This document arrays other circumstantial evidence, for example, from studies on Israel and India, that support this finding as well.

23. Onis and Riedel (1993) show that SOEs in Turkey had *lower* interest payments as a share of sales than did private enterprises in the 1980s.

24. To the extent that market prices are highly distorted in general, mainly through import controls but partly also through the direct governmental management of prices, financial rates of return such as those discussed above may provide a misleading guide to the true rates of return to the economy (although they are relevant to the financing problems of government). A study done of Egypt, admittedly an economy with greater-than-average price distortions, showed no meaningful correlation between financial rates of return and economic rates of return in 1980/81 over twenty-six branches of manufacturing. Shirley (1984, p. 33).

25. Joshi and Little (forthcoming).

26. World Bank (1988b, p. 155).

27. Argentine provincial and municipal deficits were exceptionally large in the mid-1970s, reaching 6.2 percent of GDP in 1975, and in the mid-1980s, when they exceeded 4 percent of GDP. See Schenone in Larrain and Selowsky (1991, p. 14).

28. World Bank (1988b, p. 165).

29. This formulation treats borrowing from the central bank as debt, on which interest should in principle be paid, even though under favorable circumstances most of that will be returned to the government in the form of earnings on seigniorage, discussed below. In fact, most governments do not pay interest on their debts to the central bank, in which case that portion of the debt should be excluded from this discussion.

30. The point in the text can be put more formally as follows:
$dD = G - R + iD$, where D is the outstanding government debt, R = government revenues, G = government expenditures exclusive of debt service, and i is the average interest rate on the government's debt. If the primary budget is balanced, $G = R$ and $dD = iD$. D/R will stabilize, the condition for long-run sustainability, when D and R are growing at the same rate. In the case of primary budget balance, this condition is met when $dR/R = dD/D = i$. When the primary budget is not in balance, the condition for long-run sustainability is more complicated:

$$dR/R = dD/D = i + (G - R)/D;$$

that is, the growth in revenue must exceed the interest rate by the size of the primary budget deficit in relation to outstanding debt.

Historical experience suggests that the revenues of developing countries can grow more rapidly than national production for many decades, but presumably this process has some limit, so ultimately $dR/R = dY/Y$, where Y is GDP, and a primary budget deficit will not be sustainable unless GDP growth exceeds the interest rate. For instance, with growth in GDP at 4.5 percent (the 1965–89 average for middle-income countries) and revenue growing at the same rate, a real interest rate of 4 percent permits a primary deficit of only 0.5 percent of GDP, far lower than what prevailed during the 1970s and early 1980s. Obviously, a country with a low initial D/R ratio can run a deficit in excess of that allowed by long-run sustainability for some time, by permitting D/R to rise, but at some point continued ability to service the debt will come into doubt, and the country will find itself having to pay a premium interest rate to continue to float debt with voluntary lenders. That in turn stiffens the requirements of sustainability.

This analysis does not allow for seigniorage, discussed further below. To the extent that seigniorage actually accrues to the government, it can be treated as revenue in the equation above, reducing the primary deficit and therefore, for a given interest rate, reducing the required rate of growth of revenue for D/R stability.

31. This phenomenon has given rise to the concept of "operational deficit," which is the nominal deficit reduced by the extent to which interest payments on outstanding debt simply preserve the real value of that debt. That is, the operational deficit is the nominal deficit less the inflation premium embodied in the interest payments. For a discussion of primary and operational deficits, see chapter 6.

32. Where oil or other export revenues accrue directly to the government, by the same token, currency devaluation results in a proportionate increase in domestic currency revenue, a point discussed in chapter 8.

33. See table 10.8, which shows that in 1980 the first four of these countries financed abroad 10 percent or more of their expenditures. A number of governments increased their external borrowing during the 1980s, when commercial credit to enterprises, public and private, became scarcer.

34. Direct comparisons between the lower and upper panels of table 10-12 are not always valid, because the lower panel was calculated on a fiscal-year basis and the upper panel on a calendar-year basis, and the two do not always coincide. See note 2.

35. In the United States, despite its highly sophisticated financial market and widespread use of credit cards, the ratio was more than 4 percent, although that figure is misleading to the extent that a substantial amount—perhaps more than one-quarter—of U.S. currency is held outside the United States.

36. See, for example, Bailey (1956) and Friedman (1971).

37. Coes (forthcoming), calculated over the period 1966–89, when extensive indexing prevailed. At this rate of inflation, seigniorage is estimated to be more than 3 percent of GDP. Of course, the optimal inflation tax will be lower than the maximum possible tax, the extent depending both on the social costs of inflation and of other forms of taxation. Onis and Riedel (1993) provide an estimate for Turkey that puts the maximum inflation tax revenue at 5 percent of GDP, at an inflation rate of 75 percent. Rodriguez (1991) calculates that the revenue-maximizing inflation tax in Argentina over the period 1960–88 was 22 percent a month (966 percent annually), yielding "revenue" equal to 7.3 percent of GDP. The first six percentage points are gained by an annual inflation of 213 percent; diminishing returns set in thereafter, as with other taxes.

38. It is often said that an inflation tax is highly regressive, falling disproportionately on the poorest members of society. This proposition is highly doubtful, since the poorest members of poor countries probably hold very little currency and have no bank accounts. On the contrary, in many societies they live largely on retail credit for their purchases. Rich persons can find ways to economize on their holdings of money, but they probably hold a higher ratio of money in relation to income than do the poorest members of society. If so, the inflation tax in poor countries would be progressive rather than regressive, on the usual definitions of those terms. This is an area in which some research on asset holdings by income class would be helpful. Such data for Mexico in 1980 suggest that the highest decile by income class is hit hardest by the inflation tax, and that fourth from the lowest decile the least. See Cooper (1992, chap. 2), drawing on Gil-Diaz, in Newbery and Stern (1987).

39. This paragraph is based on simple regressions for each country of the budget deficit on the current account deficit, both in relation to GDP, using annual data.

40. When a correction is made for inflation, as in the regressions described below, only Brazil shows a decline; that is probably due to the emergence of highly liquid government securities, not counted as part of M2, as a near-money.

41. Cross-section regressions of changes in the consumer price index on changes in reserve money (M0) over 1973–86 and on changes in money plus quasi-money (M2) for all our countries except Argentina and Brazil—the two countries with extreme inflations over the entire period—produced the following R^2:

	All	All except Chile	All except Chile, Mexico, and Turkey
CPI on M0	.95	.77	.72
CPI on M2	.99+	.92	.52

The correlations are high, but they are dominated by the high-inflation countries. Dropping the highest inflation country in the group, Chile, reduces the correlation substantially, and dropping the next two highest-inflation countries, Mexico and Turkey, reduces it further. Moreover, the regression coefficients are extremely sensitive to the sample of countries. For reasons noted in the text, inflation should be less than the growth in either reserve money or M_2, but this is not the case during the period in question for either Chile or Mexico with respect to reserve money. Thus, the regression coefficient of changes in the consumer price index on changes in reserve money is 3.36 for all sixteen countries, but drops to 1.0 if Chile is excluded, and drops further to .29 when Mexico and Turkey are excluded.

42. Concretely, the equation:

$$\ln(Mi/P) = a_0 + a_1(\ln[\text{GDP}/P]) + a_2(\text{Inf}) + a_3(\text{Inf})_{-1}$$

was fitted for each country with annual data over the period 1965–88 (or shorter periods when data availability required). Here $i = 0,2$ for base money and M2, respectively, P is the GDP deflator, and Inf (=inflation) is measured by the consumer price index. Interest rates are often included in such estimated equations, but in almost all of our countries interest rates were controlled and inflation rates represent a better indicator of the opportunity cost of holding money.

In the estimated equations for M2, only those for Argentina, Indonesia, Thailand, and Turkey showed a statistically significant (5 percent level) influence of contemporaneous inflation, and only those for Argentina, Chile, Indonesia, Pakistan, Thailand, and Turkey showed a statistically significant influence of inflation the previous year.

43. The adjusted R^2 exceeded .90 in all but five of the equations for M2, and in all but eight of the equations for M0, as can be expected from time series.

44. For business loans, a value added price index for business would be more appropriate for computing real interest rates, but such an index is not generally available in our countries.

45. To attract earnings of overseas workers, for instance, Turkey in the early 1970s created convertible lire accounts, whereby nonresidents could deposit foreign funds in Turkish banks at attractive interest rates. The banks sold the foreign exchange to the central bank for money-creating deposits; the central bank in turn sold the foreign exchange to the government, or government agencies, in exchange for (non-money-destroying) government securities, which in turn used the foreign exchange to finance the import content of government expenditures, including SOE investments. The result was a large expansion of the money supply owing to (desired) capital inflow. See Onis and Riedel (1993); also Celasun and Rodrik in Sachs and Collins (1989, pp. 640–54).

46. By comparison, the Federal Reserve Banks of the United States changed their discount rate on average more than once a year throughout this period.

47. See Emery (1991, chap. 8).

48. The motivation for these reductions may have lain elsewhere, however. Korea was trying to stimulate domestic demand in 1981, but its leading economic adviser, Kim Jae Ik, believed that interest rates were such an important part of business costs that they should be kept as low as consistent with monetary stability—a view maintained for years in the United States by Wright Patman, chairman of the House Banking Committee during the 1960s.

49. Concretely, regressions of year-to-year changes in (the logarithm of) bank credit to the private sector shows virtually no relationship to year-to-year changes in bank credit to the government, and therefore suggest that government financing did not crowd out private financing in the short run, although some countries show a gradual rise over time of the total share of bank financing that went to government, and some a gradual decline. Only the results for Pakistan and Thailand suggested some annual crowding out, and in those countries it was less than 50 percent of lending

to private borrowers. In contrast, the results for Brazil, Chile, and Mexico showed evidence for crowding *in*—that is, the greater the extension of credit to the government, the greater the extension of credit also to the private sector. In Brazil's case, this result may reflect accelerating inflation during the 1980s; in Chile's, the tight fiscal and monetary policy maintained both in the late 1970s and in the late 1980s.

50. Official gold holdings at national valuation in 1987 were typically less than one-quarter of foreign exchange reserves, and for some countries were negligible. The exceptions were Argentina and Thailand, which held about a third of their reserves in gold, and Turkey and Pakistan, where the ratio was one-half or more.

51. See Sundararajan and Balino (1991).

52. See Brock, Connolly, and Gonzalez-Vega (1989, p. 127), and Larrain and Selowsky (1991, pp. 124–33).

53. Larrain and Selowsky (1991, p. 131).

54. See Haggard and others (forthcoming, chapter 5). From an economic point of view, central bank purchase of a nonperforming loan from a commercial bank is not expansionary and may help avoid financial collapse. The expansionary impulse occurred when the loan was initially made.

55. Schenone in Larrain and Selowsky (1991, p. 22).

56. See Bodart (1990), and Leone (1991).

57. Much is made of the importance of central bank independence, and Germany's Bundesbank is often cited in illustration. It is true that the government cannot legally give instructions (as distinguished from suggestions) to the Bundesbank in its areas of competence. The Bundesbank is simply a creature of legislation, however, and this legislation can be changed by parliament. In a parliamentary system, a sitting government by definition controls enough votes to pass legislation. It is thus public opinion, not legal arrangements, that protects the "independence" of the Bundesbank. Similar statements can be made about the Swiss and Dutch central banks. The U.S. Federal Reserve System is also a creation of ordinary statute, but because of the separation of powers, legislation is more difficult to change in the United States than in a parliamentary system. Chile's new central bank, in contrast, has constitutional independence.

58. These results are augmented and confirmed in Cukierman and others (1992). For a sample of 117 developing countries, which includes 15 of our countries, they find that most of several measures of central bank independence have no significant influence on the rate of inflation over the period 1950–89, or on the growth of central bank credit to the public sector. The exception is turnover of central bank governors, which is significantly related to inflation rates, although it is unclear what is the direction of causation. Three of our countries—Argentina, Chile, and Brazil—show the highest turnover of central bank governors in their large sample. See also Cukierman (1992).

59. For a detailed discussion of the arrangements, see Bhatia (1985).

Chapter 11.   Macroeconomic Management and Long-Run Growth

1. A large number of cross-country studies relating many possible explanatory variables to long-run growth are surveyed and analyzed by Ross Levine and David Renelt (1991a, 1991b). They find very few variables robustly related to growth, in the sense that their statistical significance survives alterations in the list of independent variables included in the regressions. Indeed, they find the only policy-related variable that is robustly significant is the share of investment in GDP. This tends to excuse our neglect of many controlling variables in the simple correlations of this chapter. We ourselves are rather skeptical of the value of regressions for a hundred or more countries whose statistics are extremely unreliable.

2. As we understand them, this proposition should be acceptable to most proponents of non-neoclassical growth theories, characterized by the endogeneity of technical change and growth. For a recent example of such theorizing, see Romer (1990). The proposition is certainly accepted by

Scott (1989). It is also notable that most or all development economists have implicitly rejected the neoclassical growth model, which implies that policy with respect to savings is irrelevant for long-run growth.

3. None of the regressions we have seen include labor input, whether adjusted for quality or not. This is doubtless because employment figures are scarce in developing countries. It might be useful to select a set of countries on the basis of the existence and reliability of statistics for certain variables that theory and common sense suggest to be important for growth.

4. The GNP figures reach back to 1960, but our investment figures only to 1970. Thus, we could use a longer period for regressing growth on its own variability, than on investment and its variability.

5. This suggests that we should measure variability by the standard error of estimate (deviations from trend) divided by the mean, rather than the coefficient of variation (deviations from the mean) divided by the mean. Since Indonesia and, to lesser extent, Korea, were the only countries with a strong rising trend, this improvement would make little difference.

6. Their figures are given as percentages of GDP, not GNP. They appear to differ somewhat from ours, but not seriously.

7. For these thirteen countries, Serven and Solimano (1993) also give public and private investment separately. We regressed the growth of GNP per head on the total investment ratio and the ratio of public to private investment, since it is widely held that public investment is less efficient. The coefficient of the latter was insignificant. This, of course, provides no evidence for or against the hypothesis.

8. Scott (1989, chap. 16) explains the slowdown of productivity growth from 1973 to 1985 in OECD countries in terms of the rise in instability.

9. The growth rate of GNP per head was taken from *World Development Report* (1991), table 1. The growth rate of the GDP deflator was calculated from the same table.

10. The top set remains the same whether ordered by column 1 or column 7.

11. A fourth (Cameroon) also suffered greatly in 1979–81, according to table 4.2, but we distrust the figures.

12. Our figures for Costa Rica differ materially from those of Serven and Solimano (1993). Using constant prices, we found there *was* a severe fall in investment (see below).

13. The determinants of private investment are closely examined in several of the essays in Serven and Solimano (1993).

14. Constant price series were unavailable for some countries and were available for very few over the whole period 1970–89.

15. Costa Rica is an extreme example of the divergence of current and constant price series of investment. Starting from a peak in 1981, there was only a small fall in the investment ratio in 1982 and 1983 when measured at current prices; but in terms of constant prices, the falls were dramatic. Thus, according to Serven and Solimano (1993) and as seen in chapter 6, the price of investment rose by 82 percent from 1980 to 1982 in relation to the GDP deflator, before falling back by 1987 to a mere 6 percent above 1980. This is almost unbelievable, especially since no similarly large movement is recorded by them for any other country.

16. The work of Little, Scitovsky, and Scott (1970) is recognized as a landmark.

17. The probably low or negative returns on much of this investment are discussed in Gelb (1988) and in Auty (1990).

18. There have been numerous cross-country studies relating lower growth to trade repression. Chapter 4 presents some evidence suggesting that trade repression and low interest rates are negatively associated with investment efficiency. Another recent study (Gelb 1989) related real interest rates to the investment ratio, the "efficiency" of investment (the incremental output-capital ratio), and GDP growth, for thirty-four countries over the period 1965–85. Real interest rates and growth were positively and significantly associated. Most of this association stemmed from an association of interest rates and the efficiency of investment: the investment ratio related only weakly to interest rates. Gelb found that the relationship between interest rate and growth reflected mainly reverse causality. That is, growth and efficiency caused higher yields on all assets: but at least part of the relationship reflected a causal chain from interest rate levels to growth rates via the

degree of financialization of savings and investment efficiency. Similar results have been reported by Fry (1988, chap. 6).

19. The case of India, where this is true, is examined in Joshi and Little (forthcoming).

20. For an evaluation of fertilizer projects, see Kilby (1991). He suggests that many, perhaps most, fertilizer projects (including those supported by the World Bank) used more foreign exchange than they saved and were in the negative value added category.

21. There are more than two thousand reestimated rates of return (RERRs) on World Bank projects, but these do not rate as ex post cost-benefit analyses. See Little and Mirrlees (1991).

22. Auty (1991). Very high apparent returns to investment may partly be due to our neglect of labor's contribution, which may have been exceptionally high in the case of Korea. See Kim and Park (1985).

23. However, an ex ante economic return of 12 percent has been calculated for the heavy machinery project. See Sabin and Kato (1989).

24. That this might happen is implied by the dubious Ricardo equivalence theory.

25. Joshi and Little rely largely on Krishnaswami, Krishnamurti, and Sharma (1987).

Chapter 12. The Political Economy of Stabilization and Adjustment

1. A coup was attempted in Côte d'Ivoire in the early 1960s.

2. The characterization "unstable" for Thailand and Turkey applies largely to the 1970s; Thailand had five prime ministers and seven finance ministers during the period 1973–80; Turkey was run by a series of coalition governments, alternating between conservative and progressive until the military coup of September 1980. Both were more stable during the 1980s.

3. Helliwell (1993) has performed a more sophisticated analysis of ninety countries and found no significant relationship between democracy (measured quantitatively in several ways, including use of the Freedom House index on civil and political liberties) and economic growth over the period 1960–85. Democracy, however, is positively and significantly related to per capita income.

4. Here the *zeitgeist* discussed above may be especially relevant. Côte d'Ivoire President Felix Houphouet-Boigny may have reasoned that the international commodity agreement he strived to achieve for cocoa would prevent the high prices of cocoa prevailing in 1977–80 from declining to levels (in real terms) that they had experienced earlier, and that they subsequently experienced in the 1980s. As a condition for participating in a renewed international cocoa agreement, he insisted on a *floor* price of $1.10 per pound for cocoa, a price to which the United States and some other importing countries could not agree. The agreement limped forward without membership of either the major producer or the major consumer; prices in fact fell below $.70 per pound in 1982. Cote d'Ivoire joined the renewed agreement in 1983 (the United States did not), but the Cocoa Organization withdrew from the market in 1988 because it reached its stockholding limits.

5. See chapter 7. Sarney was in an especially weak political position, being an unpopular vice-presidential running mate of the popular Tancredo Neves, who died after being indirectly elected, but before he could take office. The length of Sarney's term was not even defined, and to bolster his weak position he tried to avoid alienating any segment of society, particularly those who would have some role in defining his constitutional position. See Kaufman in Nelson (1990).

6. Whitehead (1990, p. 1138) observes that these cycles go back to at least 1952.

7. Turkey is included here even though Turgut Özal in 1983 was not the preferred candidate of the outgoing military government, since he was the architect of the 1980 austerity program and was so identified in the public mind. Costa Rica's overall economic performance was not outstanding, but the government won the vote by doing an exceptionally good job (in Nelson's view) of appealing to urban dwellers by granting a large wage increase to government employees and launching an ambitious housing program. See Nelson in Haggard and Kaufman (1992).

8. The major issue in Pakistan, as also in Chile, was not economic policy, but a return to democracy and with that a restoration of civil liberties.

9. Of these, Nigeria (1983) and Thailand (1991) subsequently experienced military coups, although the military leadership in both cases proclaimed its intention to return to democracy as soon as possible; several other countries remained under close military watch.

10. Until Lopez Portillo took office, presidential candidates had generally been drawn from the Ministry of the Interior (Gobernaçion); thereafter, they came from the Ministry of Planning and Budget. When Luis Echeverria was selected, he was thought to be a center-right candidate, not well regarded by the liberal wing of the PRI. See Hansen (1971, p. 228).

11. A restraint on Pertamina's medium and long-term borrowing had already been imposed in 1972. Sutowo adopted the simple expedient of borrowing at short-term in the Euro-dollar market. For a discussion of the Pertamina episode, see Woo and Nasution (1989), Woo and others (forthcoming).

12. Cameroon was also a federation until 1972, when a unitary state was created under a new constitution.

13. Data from IMF, *Government Finance Statistics Yearbook*, various years; and from World Bank (1988b), pp. 155–58. Comprehensive data for Nigeria are not available, but the federal government passes over one-third of its tax collections to state and local governments; in addition, they have their own taxes.

14. In Pakistan, however, the commission did not meet between 1974 and 1991.

15. See Maxfield (1991), who notes especially the contrast with Mexico in the low influence of the financial community; and Kaufman in Nelson (1990). But with Brazil's extensive indexation of financial assets, the interests of the financial community are also less likely to be strongly opposed to inflation than in a less highly indexed economy.

16. The military coup in Thailand in 1991 is said to have been motivated mainly by "inadequate respect" paid to the military by Prime Minister Chatchai, although budget issues apparently were also involved.

17. As discussed in chapter 10, however, endowing the central bank with some degree of legal independence is not sufficient for ensuring effective monetary control.

Chapter 13. Conclusion: The Lessons of Experience

1. Proper cost-benefit analysis using shadow prices that take into account the distortions created by tariffs and import restrictions will do so. See Little and Mirrlees (1974). This work also deals with the need to allow for risk.

References

Aghevli, Bijan B., Mohsin S. Khan, and Peter J. Montiel. 1991. *Exchange Rate Policy in Developing Countries: Some Analytical Issues.* Occasional Paper 78. Washington, D.C.: International Monetary Fund.

Athukorala, Premachandra, and Sisira Jayasuriya. Forthcoming. *Macroeconomic Policies, Crises, and Growth in Sri Lanka, 1969–1990.* Washington D.C.: World Bank.

Auty, Richard M. 1990. *Resource-Based Industrialization.* Oxford: Clarendon Press.

——. 1991. "Creating Competitive Advantage: South Korean Steel and Petrochemicals." *Tijdschrift voor Econ. en Soc. Geografie* 82(1): 15–29.

Ayub, Mahmood Ali, and Sven Olaf Hegstad. 1986. *Public Industrial Enterprises.* Washington, D.C.: World Bank.

Baer, Werner. 1987. "The Resurgence of Inflation in Brazil, 1974–86." *World Development* 15(8):1007–34.

Bailey, Martin J. 1956. "The Welfare Cost of Inflationary Finance." *Journal of Political Economy* 64(April):93–110.

Balassa, Bela. 1982. *Development Strategies in Semi-Industrial Economies.* Baltimore, Md.: Johns Hopkins University Press.

——. 1989. "Outward Orientation." In H. Chenery and T. N. Srinivasan, eds., *Handbook of Development Economics* II:1646–89.

Balassa, Bela, and F. Desmond McCarthy. 1984. *Adjustment Policies in Developing Countries: An Update 1979–83.* World Bank Working Paper 675. Washington, D.C.

Bank for International Settlements. Various issues. *Annual Report.* Basel, Switzerland.

Bates, Robert, and Anne O. Krueger, eds. 1993. *The Political Economy of Policy Reform.* Oxford: Basil Blackwell.

Beer, Samuel H. 1956. *Treasury Control: The Coordination of Financial and Economic Policy in Great Britain.* Oxford: Clarendon Press.

Bell, Bernard R. 1965. *India's Economic Development Effort.* Washington, D.C.: World Bank.

Beristain, Javier, and Ignacio Trigueros. 1990. "The Three Major Debtors: Mexico." In John Williamson, ed., *Latin American Adjustment: How Much Has Happened?* Washington, D.C.: Institute for International Economics.

Berthelemy, J. C., and F. Bourguignon. Forthcoming. *Growth and Crisis in Cote D'Ivoire.* Washington D.C.: World Bank.

Bevan, David, Paul Collier, and Jan Willem Gunning. unpublished. "External Shocks and the Kenyan Economy." Research provided for the World Bank project "Macroeconomic Policies, Crisis, and Growth in the Long Run."

Bhagwat, Avinash, and Yusuke Onitsuka. 1974. "Export-Import Responses to Devaluation: Experience of the Non-Industrial Countries in the 1960s." *IMF Staff Papers* 21:414–62.

Bhatia, Rattan J. 1985. *The West African Monetary Union: An Analytical Review.* Occasional Paper 35. Washington, D.C.: International Monetary Fund.

Blejer, Mario, and Adrienne Cheasty. 1988. "High Inflation, Heterodox Stabilization and Fiscal Policy." *World Development* 16(8):867–81.

Bodart, Vincent. 1990. "Central Bank Independence and the Effectiveness of Monetary Policy: A Comparative Analysis." International Monetary Fund, Central Banking Department, Washington, D.C.

Brock, Philip L., Michael B. Connolly, and Claudio Gonzalez-Vega, eds. 1989. *Latin American Debt and Adjustment: External Shocks and Macroeconomic Policies.* New York: Praeger.

Bruno, Michael. 1991. *High Inflation and the Nominal Anchors of an Open Economy.* Essays in International Finance 183. Princeton, N.J.: Princeton University, International Finance Section.

Bruno, Michael, and Leora Meridor. 1991. "The Costly Transition from Stabilization to Sustainable Growth: Israel's Case." In Michael Bruno, Stanley Fischer, Elhanan Helpman, and Nissan Liviatan, eds., *Lessons of Economic Stabilization and its Aftermath.* Cambridge, MA: The MIT Press.

Bruno, Michael, and Sylvia Piterman. 1988. "Israel's Stabilization: A Two-Year Review." In Michael Bruno, Guido di Tella, Rudiger Dornbusch, and Stanley Fischer, eds., *Inflation Stabilization: The Experience of Israel, Argentina, Brazil, Bolivia and Mexico.* Cambridge MA: The MIT Press.

Bruno, Michael, Guido di Tella, Rudiger Dornbusch, and Stanley Fischer, eds. 1988. *Inflation Stabilization: The Experience of Israel, Argentina, Brazil, Bolivia and Mexico.* Cambridge, Mass.: MIT Press.

Bruno, Michael, Stanley Fischer, Elhanan Helpman, and Nissan Liviatan, eds. 1991. *Lessons of Economic Stabilization and Its Aftermath.* Cambridge, Mass.: MIT Press.

Buffie, Edward F. 1990. "Economic Policy and Foreign Debt in Mexico." In Jeffrey D. Sachs, ed., *Developing Country Debt and Economic Performance.* Chicago: University of Chicago Press.

Calvo, Guillermo A. 1986. "Fractured Liberalism: Argentina under Martinez de Hoz." *Economic Development and Cultural Change* 34(3):511–34.

Canavese, Alfredo J., and Guido di Tella. 1988. "Inflation Stabilization: The Experience of Israel, Argentina, Brazil, Bolivia and Mexico." In Michael Bruno, Guido di Tella, Rudiger Dornbusch, and Stanley Fischer, eds., *Inflation Stabilization: The Experience of Israel, Argentina, Brazil, Bolivia and Mexico.* Cambridge, Mass.: MIT Press.

Cardoso, Eliana A., and Daniel Dantas. 1990. "The Three Major Debtors: Brazil." In John Williamson, ed., *Latin American Adjustment: How Much Has Happened?* Washington, D.C.: Institute for International Economics.

Cardoso, Eliana A., and Albert Fishlow. 1990. "The Macroeconomics of the Brazilian External Debt." In Jeffrey D. Sachs and Susan M. Collins, eds., *Developing Country Debt and Economic Performance.* Chicago: University of Chicago Press.

Cardoso, Eliana A., and Santiago Levy. 1988. "Mexico." In Rudiger Dornbusch and F. L. Helmers, eds., *The Open Economy: Tools for Policymakers in Developing Countries.* London: Oxford University Press.

Castillo, Carlos Manuel. 1988. "The Costa Rican Experience with the International Debt Crisis." In Richard E. Feinberg and Ricardo French-Davis, eds., *Development and External Debt in Latin America.* Notre Dame, Ind.: University of Notre Dame Press.

Celásun, Merih, and Dani Rodrik. 1989. "Debt, Adjustment and Growth: Turkey." In Jeffrey D. Sachs and Susan M. Collins, eds., *Developing Country Debt and Economic Performance.* Chicago: University of Chicago Press.

Claassen, Emil-Maria. unpublished. "Macroeconomic Policies, Crises, and Growth in the Long Run: Morocco, 1967–1985." Research provided for the World Bank project "Macroeconomic Policies, Crisis, and Growth in the Long Run."

Coes, Donald V. 1989. "Real Exchange Rate: Definition, Measurement, and Trends in France, West Germany, Italy and the United Kingdom." In Donald R. Hodgman and Geoffrey E. Wood, eds., *Macroeconomic Policy and Economic Interdependence.* London: Macmillan Press.

———. forthcoming. *Macroeconomic Crises, Policy, and Growth: Brazil, 1964–1990.* Washington D.C.: World Bank.

Collins, Susan M. Forthcoming. "Savings, Investment and External Balance in South Korea." In Stephan Haggard, Richard N. Cooper, Susan M. Collins, Choongsoo Kim, and Sung-tae Ro, *Macroeconomic Policy and Adjustment in Korea, 1970–1990.* Cambridge, Mass.: Harvard Institute for International Development.

Collins, Susan M., and Won-Am Park. 1989. "External Debt and Macroeconomic Performance in South Korea." In Jeffrey D. Sachs and Susan M. Collins, eds., *Developing Country Debt and Economic Performance.* Chicago: University of Chicago Press.

Connolly, Michaely. Unpublished. "Macroeconomic Policies, Crises, and Long-Run Growth in Cameroon." Research provided for the World Bank project "Macroeconomic Policies, Crisis, and Growth in the Long Run."

Cooper, Richard N. 1971. *Currency Depreciation in Developing Countries.* Essays in International Finance 86. Princeton, N.J.: Princeton University, International Finance Section.

———. 1992. *Economic Stabilization and Debt in Developing Countries.* Cambridge, Mass.: MIT Press.

Cooper, Richard N., and Robert Z. Lawrence. 1975. *The Commodity Price Boom of 1972–1974.* Brookings Papers on Economic Activity 3. Washington, D.C.: Brookings Institution.

Corbo, Vittorio. 1985. "Reforms and Macroeconomic Adjustments in Chile during 1974–84." *World Development* 3(8):893–916.

Corbo, Vittorio, and Jaime de Melo. 1989. "External Shocks and Policy Reforms in the Southern Cone: A Reassessment." In G. Calvo and others, *Debt Stabilization and Development.* Oxford: Basil Blackwell.

Corbo, Vittorio, Jaime de Melo, and James Tybout. 1986. "What Went Wrong with the Recent Reforms in the Southern Cone." *Economic Development and Cultural Change* 34(3):607–40.

Corbo, Vittorio, and Andrés Solimano. 1991. "Chile's Experience with Stabilization Revisited." In Michael Bruno, Stanley Fischer, Elhanan Helpman, and Nissan Liviatan, eds., *Lessons of Economic Stabilization and Its Aftermath.* Cambridge, Mass.: MIT Press.

Corden, W. Max. 1984. "Booming Sector and Dutch Disease Economics: A Survey." *Oxford Economic Papers* 36(3):359–80.

———. 1985. *Inflation, Exchange Rates and the World Economy.* 3d. ed. Oxford: Clarendon Press.

———. 1989. "Macroeconomic Adjustment in Developing Countries." *World Bank Research Observer* 4(1):51–64. Also in Maurice Scott and Deepak Lal, eds., *Public Policy and Economic Development.* Oxford: Clarendon Press, 1990.

———. 1991a. "Exchange Rate Policy in Developing Countries." In Jaime de Melo and André Sapir, eds., *Trade Theory and Economic Reform—North, South and East: Essays in Honor of Bela Balassa.* Oxford: Basil Blackwell.

———. 1991b. "Macroeconomic Policy and Growth: Some Lessons of Experience." In *Proceedings of the World Bank Annual Conference on Development Economics, 1990, Supplement to the World Bank Economic Review*: 59–84.

Cuddington, John T. 1986. *Capital Flight: Estimates, Issues and Explanations.* Princeton Studies in International Finance 58. Princeton, N.J.: Princeton University, International Finance Section.

———. 1987. "Macroeconomic Determinants of Capital Flight: An Econometric Investigation." In Donald R. Lessard and John Williamson, eds., *Capital Flight: The Problem and Policy Responses.* Washington, D.C.: Institute for International Economics.

Cukierman, Alex. 1992. *Central Bank Strategy, Credibility, and Independence: Theory and Evidence.* Cambridge, Mass.: MIT Press.

Cukierman, Alex, Steven B. Webb, and Bilin Neyapti. 1992. "Measuring the Independence of Central Banks and Its Effect on Policy Outcomes." *World Bank Economic Review* 6(3):353–98.

Cumby, Robert E., and Sweder van Wijnbergen. 1989. "Financial Policy and Speculative Runs with a Crawling Peg: Argentina 1979–1981." *Journal of International Economics* 27(1):111–27.

de Pablo, Juan Carlos. Unpublished. "A Successful Case of Underdevelopment Process: Argentina." Research provided for the World Bank project "Macroeconomic Policies, Crisis, and Growth in the Long Run."

Dervis, Kemal, and Peter A. Petri. 1987. "The Macroeconomics of Successful Development: What Are the Lessons?" In Stanley Fischer, ed., *NBER Macroeconomics Annual.* Cambridge, Mass.: MIT Press.

Devarajan, S., and Jaime de Melo. 1990. "Membership in the CFA Zone: Odyssean Journey or Trojan Horse?" PRE Working Paper WPS 482. World Bank, Washington, D.C.

———. 1987. "Adjustment with a Fixed Exchange Rate: Cameroon, Côte d'Ivoire, and Senegal." *World Bank Economic Review* 1(3): 447–87.

Djajic, Slobadan. 1987. "Temporary Import Quotas and the Current Account." *Journal of International Economics* 22(3/4):349–62.

Dollar, David. 1990. *Outward Orientation and Growth.* Washington, D.C.: World Bank.

Dornbusch, Rudiger. 1988. "Mexico: Stabilization, Debt and Growth." *Economic Policy* 7:231–84.

Dornbusch, Rudiger, and Sebastian Edwards. 1989. *Macroeconomic Populism in Latin America.* Working Paper 2986. Cambridge, Mass.: National Bureau of Economic Research.

Dornbusch, Rudiger, and Stanley Fischer. 1986. "Stopping Hyperinflations Past and Present." *Weltwirtschaftliches Archiv* 122:1–46.

Dornbusch, Rudiger, and Juan Carlos de Pablo. 1990. "Debt and Macroeconomic Instability in Argentina." In Jeffrey D. Sachs and Susan M. Collins, eds., *Developing Country Debt and Economic Performance.* Chicago: University of Chicago Press.

Easterly, William, Carlos A. Rodriguez, and Klaus Schmidt-Hebbel, eds. Forthcoming. *Public Sector Deficits and Macroeconomic Performance.* New York: Oxford University Press.

Edwards, Sebastian. 1988. *Exchange Rate Misalignment in Developing Countries.* World Bank Occasional Paper 2, n.s. Baltimore, Md.: Johns Hopkins University Press.

———. 1989a. *Real Exchange Rates, Devaluation, and Adjustment: Exchange Rate Policy in Developing Countries.* Cambridge, Mass.: MIT Press.

——. 1989b. *Real Exchange Rates in Developing Countries: Concepts and Measurement.* Working Paper 2950. Cambridge, Mass.: National Bureau of Economic Research.

——. 1991. *Trade Orientation, Distortions and Growth.* Cambridge, Mass.: National Bureau of Economic Research.

Edwards, Sebastian, and Liaquat Ahamed, eds. 1986. *Economic Adjustment and Exchange Rates in Developing Countries.* Chicago: University of Chicago Press.

Edwards, Sebastian, and Alejandra Cox Edwards. 1991. *Monetarism and Liberalization: The Chilean Experiment.* 2d ed. Cambridge, Mass.: Ballinger.

Edwards, Sebastian, and Felipe Larrain, eds. 1989. *Debt, Adjustment, and Recovery.* Oxford: Basil Blackwell.

Edwards, Sebastian, and Guido Tabellini. 1990. *Explaining Fiscal Policies and Inflation in Developing Countries.* Working Paper 3493. Cambridge, Mass.: National Bureau of Economic Research.

Emery, Robert F. 1991. *The Money Markets of Developing East Asia.* New York: Praeger.

Epstein, Edward C. 1987. "Recent Stabilization Programs in Argentina, 1973–86." *World Development* 15(8):991–1006.

Feinberg, Richard E., and Ricardo French-Davis, eds. 1988. *Development and External Debt in Latin America.* Notre Dame, Ind.: University of Notre Dame Press.

Fernandez, Roque B. 1985. "The Expectations Management Approach to Stabilization in Argentina during 1976–82." *World Development* 13(8):861–92.

Floyd, Robert H., Clive S. Gray, and R. P. Short. 1984. *Public Enterprise in Mixed Economies.* Washington, D.C.: International Monetary Fund.

Friedman, Milton. 1971. "Government Revenue from Inflation." *Journal of Political Economy* 79(July/August):846–56.

Fry, Maxwell J. 1988. *Money, Interest, and Banking in Economic Development.* Baltimore, Md.: Johns Hopkins University Press.

García-García, Jorge, and Sisira Jayasuriya. Forthcoming. "Macroeconomic Crises, Policies, and Long-Run Growth in Colombia, 1950–1986." Washington D.C.: World Bank.

Gastil, Raymond D. 1987. *Freedom in the World.* New York: Greenwood Press.

Gelb, Alan H. 1988. *Oil Windfalls, Blessing or Curse.* Oxford: Oxford University Press.

——. 1989. "Financial Policies, Growth and Efficiency." Country Economics Department Working Paper WPS 202, World Bank, Washington, D.C.

Gil-Diaz, Francisco. 1984. "Mexico's Path from Stability to Growth." In Arnold C. Harberger, ed., *World Economic Growth.* San Francisco, Calif.: Institute for Contemporary Studies Press.

——. 1987. "Some Lessons from Mexico's Tax Reform." In David Newbery and Nicholas Stern, eds., *The Theory of Taxation for Developing Countries.* Oxford: Oxford University Press.

———. Unpublished. "Macroeconomic Policies, Crisis, and Growth in the Long Run: Mexico." Research provided for the World Bank project "Macroeconomic Policies, Crisis, and Growth in the Long Run."

Gil-Diaz, Francisco, and Raul Ramos Tercero. 1988. "Lessons from Mexico." In Michael Bruno, Guido di Tella, Rudiger Dornbusch, and Stanley Fischer, *Inflation Stabilization: The Experience of Israel, Argentina, Brazil, Bolivia and Mexico.* Cambridge, Mass.: MIT Press.

Gonzalez-Vega, Claudio. Forthcoming. *Macroeconomic Policies, Crises, and Long-Term Growth in Costa Rica.* Washington D.C.: World Bank.

Goode, Richard. 1984. *Government Finance in Developing Countries.* Washington, D.C.: Brookings Institution.

Guisinger, Stephen, and Gerald Scully. 1991. "Pakistan." In Demetris Papageorgiou, Michael Michaely, and Armeane Choksi, eds., *Liberalizing Foreign Trade 5: The Experience of Indonesia, Pakistan and Sri Lanka.* Oxford: Basil Blackwell.

Gwin, Catherine, and Richard Feinberg, eds. 1989. *The International Monetary Fund in a Multipolar World: Pulling Together.* Washington, D.C.: Overseas Development Council.

Haggard, Stephan. 1990. *Pathways from the Periphery.* Ithaca, N.Y.: Cornell University Press.

Haggard, Stephan, Richard N. Cooper, Susan M. Collins, Choongsoo Kim, and Sung-tae Ro. Forthcoming. *Macroeconomic Policy and Adjustment in Korea, 1970–1990.* Cambridge, Mass.: Harvard Institute for International Development.

Haggard, Stephan, and Robert Kaufman, eds. 1992. *The Politics of Economic Adjustment.* Princeton, N.J.: Princeton University Press.

Hansen, Roger D. 1971. *The Politics of Mexican Development.* Baltimore, Md.: Johns Hopkins University Press.

Haque, Nadeem Ul, and Peter Montiel. 1991. "Capital Mobility in Developing Countries: Some Empirical Tests." *World Development* 19(10):1391–98.

Harberger, Arnold. 1986. "Economic Adjustment and the Real Exchange Rate." In Sebastian Edwards and Liaquat Ahamed, eds., *Economic Adjustment and Exchange Rates in Developing Countries.* Chicago: University of Chicago Press.

Helliwell, John F. 1993. "Empirical Linkages between Democracy and Economic Growth." Harvard Center for International Affairs, Cambridge, Mass.

Hotelling, Harold. 1931. "The Economics of Exhaustible Resources." *Journal of Political Economy* 34(Feb-Dec):137–75.

Ingram, James C. 1954. *Economic Change in Thailand since 1850.* Stanford, Calif.: Stanford University Press.

International Monetary Fund (IMF). *International Financial Statistics.* (various issues). Washington, D.C.

———. *Government Finance Statistics Yearbook.* (Various issues). Washington, D.C.

Johnson, H. G. 1958. "Towards a General Theory of the Balance of Payments." In H.G. Johnson, ed., *International Trade and Economic Growth: Studies in Pure Theory*. London: Allen & Unwin.

Joshi, Vijay. 1990. "Exchange Rate Regimes in Developing Countries." In Maurice Scott and Deepak Lal, eds., *Public Policy and Economic Development*. Oxford: Clarendon Press.

Joshi, Vijay, and I. M. D. Little. Forthcoming. *India: Macroeconomics and Political Economy, 1964–1992*. Washington D.C.: World Bank.

Kamin, Steven B. 1988. *Devaluation, External Balance, and Macroeconomic Performance: A Look at the Numbers*. Princeton Studies in International Finance 62. Princeton, N.J.: Princeton University, International Finance Section.

Khan, Mohsin. 1992. "Macroeconomic Balances," In W.E. James and S. Roy, eds., *Foundations of Pakistan's Political Economy*. Delhi: Sage Publications.

Khor, Hoe E., and Liliana Rojas-Suarez. 1991. "Interest Rates in Mexico." *IMF Staff Papers* 38(4):850–71.

Kiguel, Miguel A. 1991. "Inflation in Argentina: Stop and Go since the Austral Plan." *World Development* 19(8):969–86.

Kiguel, Miguel A., and Nissan Liviatan. 1988. "Inflationary Rigidities and Orthodox Stabilization Policies: Lessons from Latin America." *World Bank Economic Review* 2(3):273–98.

———. 1991. "The Inflation-Stabilization Cycles in Argentina and Brazil." In Michael Bruno, Stanley Fischer, Elhanan Helpman, and Nissan Liviatan, eds., *Lessons of Economic Stabilization and Its Aftermath*. Cambridge, Mass.: MIT Press.

Kiguel, Miguel A., and Pablo Andres Neumeyer. 1989. "Inflation and Seigniorage in Argentina." PPR Working Paper WPS 289. World Bank, Washington, D.C.

Kilby, Peter. 1991. "Fertilizer Production: A Strategic Pitfall." Wesleyan University, Middletown, Conn.

Kim, K. S. 1991. "Korea" In Demetries Papageorgiou, Michael Michaely, and Armene Choksi, eds., *Liberalizing Foreign Trade 2: The Experience of Korea, The Phillipines and Singapore*. Oxford: Basil Blackwell.

Kim, K. S., and J. K. Park. 1985. *Sources of Economic Growth in Korea: 1963–92*. Seoul: Korea Development Institute.

Kopits, George. 1987. *Structural Reform, Stabilization, and Growth in Turkey*. Occasional Paper 52. Washington, D.C.: International Monetary Fund.

Krishnaswami, K. S., K. Krishnamurti, and P. D. Sharma. 1987. *Improving Domestic Resource Mobilization Through Financial Development*. India: Asia Development Bank.

Krueger, Anne. 1978. *Foreign Trade Regimes and Economic Development: Liberalization Attempts and Consequences*. Cambridge, Mass.: Ballinger.

Larrain, Felipe, and Marcelo Selowsky, eds. 1991. *The Public Sector and the Latin American Crisis*. San Francisco, Calif.: Institute for Contemporary Studies Press.

Leone, Alfredo. 1991. "Effectiveness and Implications of Limits on Central Bank Credit to the Government." In Patrick Dorones and Reza Vaez-Zadah, eds., *The Evolving Role of Central Banks*. Washington, D.C.: International Monetary Fund.

Lessard, Donald R., and John Williamson. 1987. *Capital Flight and Third World Debt*. Washington, D.C.: Institute for International Economics.

Levine, Ross, and David Renelt. 1991a. "Cross-Country Studies of Growth and Policy." Country Economics Department Working Paper <S>WPS<D> 608. World Bank, Washington, D.C.

———. 1991b. "A Sensitivity Analysis of Cross-Country Growth Regression." Country Economics Department Working Paper <S>WPS<D> 609, World Bank, Washington, D.C.

Little, I. M. D., and J. A. Mirrlees. 1974. *Project Appraisal and Planning*. London: Heinemann.

Little, I. M. D., Tibor Scitovsky, and Maurice Scott. 1970. *Industry and Trade in Some Developing Countries: A Comparative Study*. London: Oxford University Press.

Little, I. M. D., and J. A. Mirrlees. 1991. "Project Appraisal and Planning Twenty Year On." *Proceedings of the World Bank Annual Conference on Development Economics*. Washington, D.C.: World Bank.

Lizondo, J. Saul, and Peter Montiel. 1989. "Contractionary Devaluation in Developing Countries: An Analytical Overview." *IMF Staff Papers* 36(1):182–227.

Machinea, Jose Luis, and Jose Maria Fanelli. 1988. "Stopping Hyperinflation: The Case of the Austral Plan in Argentina, 1985–87." In Michael Bruno, Guido di Tella, Rudiger Dornbusch, and Stanley Fischer, eds., *Inflation Stabilization: The Experience of Israel, Argentina, Brazil, Bolivia and Mexico*. Cambridge, Mass.: MIT Press.

Maxfield, Sylvia. 1991. "Bankers' Alliances and Economic Policy Patterns: Evidence from Mexico and Brazil." *Comparative Political Studies* 23(January):419–58.

Meade, J. E. 1951. *The Balance of Payments*. London: Oxford University Press.

Meller, Patricio. 1990. "Three Policy Experiments: Chile." In John Williamson, ed., *Latin American Adjustment: How Much Has Happened?* Washington, D.C.: Institute for International Economics.

Michaely, Michael, Demetrios Papageorgiou, and Armeane Choksi, eds. 1991. *Liberalizing Foreign Trade, 7: Lessons of Experience in the Developing World*. Oxford: Basil Blackwell.

Modiano, Eduardo M. 1988. "The Cruzado First Attempt: The Brazilian Stabilization Program of February 1986." In Michael Bruno, Guido di Tella, Rudiger Dornbusch, and Stanley Fischer, eds., *Inflation Stabilization: The Experience of Israel, Argentina, Brazil, Bolivia and Mexico*. Cambridge, Mass.: MIT Press.

Morales, Juan Antonio, and Jeffrey D. Sachs. 1990. "Bolivia's Economic Crisis." In Jeffrey D. Sachs, ed., *Developing Country Debt and Economic Performance*. Chicago: University of Chicago Press.

Nair, G., and A. Filippides. 1988. *How Much Do State-owned Enterprises Contribute to Public Sector Deficits?* World Bank Working Paper WPS 45. Washington, D.C.

Nelson, Joan M., ed. 1989. *Fragile Coalitions: the Politics of Economic Adjustment.* Washington, D.C.: Overseas Development Council.

———, ed. 1990. *Economic Crisis and Policy Choice.* Princeton, N.J.: Princeton University Press.

Newbery, D., and N. Stern, eds. 1987. *The Theory of Taxation for Developing Countries.* Oxford: Oxford University Press.

Nogués, Julio, and Sunil Gulati. 1992. *Economic Policies and Performance under Alternative Trade Regimes: Latin America During the 1980s.* Washington, D.C.: World Bank, Latin America Technical Department.

Organization for Economic Cooperation and Development (OECD). 1986. *Economic Outlook.* Paris

———. 1991. *Development Cooperation: Efforts and Polices of Members of Development Assistance Committee.* Paris.

Olivera, Julio H. G. 1967. "Money, Prices and Fiscal Lags: A Note on the Dynamics of Inflation." *Banca Nazionale del Lavoro Quarterly Review* 20:258–67.

Onis, Ziya, and James Riedel. 1993. *Economic Crises and Long-Term Growth in Turkey.* Washington, D.C.: World Bank.

Ortiz, Guillermo. 1991. "Mexico beyond the Debt Crisis: Toward Sustainable Growth with Price Stability." In Michael Bruno, Stanley Fischer, Elhanan Helpman, and Nissan Liviatan, eds., *Lessons of Economic Stabilization and Its Aftermath.* Cambridge, Mass.: MIT Press.

Pazos, Felipe. 1972. *Chronic Inflation in Latin America.* New York: Praeger.

Pinto, Brian. 1987. "Nigeria during and after the Oil Boom." *World Bank Economic Review* 1(3): 419–45.

Pitt, Mark. 1991. "Indonesia." In Demetris Papageorgiou, Michael Michaely, and Armene Choksi, eds., *Liberalizing Foreign Trade 5: The Experience of Indonesia, Pakistan and Sri Lanka.* Oxford: Basil Blackwell.

Pritchett, Lant. 1991. "The Real Exchange Rate and the Trade Surplus: An Empirical Analysis for Non-Oil Exporting LDCs." World Bank, Washington, D.C.

Ramangkura, V., and B. Nidhiprabha. 1991. "The Macroeconomics of the Public Sector Deficit: The Case of Thailand." World Bank, Washington, D.C.

Rennhack, Robert, and Guillermo Mondino. 1988. *Capital Mobility and Monetary Policy in Colombia.* IMF Working Paper WP/88/77. Washington, D.C.

Rodriguez, Carlos Alfredo. 1988. "Comments." In Michael Bruno, Stanley Fischer, Elhanan Helpman, and Nissan Liviatan, eds., *Inflation Stabilization: The Experience of Israel, Argentina, Brazil, Bolivia and Mexico.* Cambridge, Mass.: MIT Press.

Rodriguez, Carlos Alfredo. 1991. *The Macroeconomics of the Public Sector Deficit: The Case of Argentina.* World Bank Working Paper WPS 632. Washington, D.C.

Rodrik, Dani. 1991. "Premature Liberalization, Incomplete Stabilization: The Özal Decade in Turkey." In Michael Bruno, Stanley Fischer, Elhanan Helpman, and Nissan Liviatan, eds., *Lessons of Economic Stabilization and Its Aftermath*. Cambridge, Mass.: MIT Press.

Romer, Paul M. 1990. "Endogenous Technological Change." *Journal of Political Economy* 98(5):S71–102.

Rosendale, Phyllis. 1978. "The Indonesian Balance of Payments 1950–1976: Some New Estimates." Ph.D. diss. Department of Economics, Canberra Australian National University.

Sabin, Lara L., and Hiroshi Kato. 1989. *Shadow Price Calculation and Application: A Case Study of Korea*. Discussion Paper 313. Cambridge, Mass.: Harvard Institute for International Development.

Sachs, Jeffrey D., and Susan M. Collins, eds. 1989. *Developing Country Debt and Economic Performance*. Chicago: University of Chicago Press.

Salter, W. E. G. 1959. "Internal and External Balance: The Role of Price and Expenditure Effects." *Economic Record* 35:226–38.

Sargent, Thomas J., and Neil Wallace. 1981. "Some Unpleasant Monetarist Arithmetic." *Federal Reserve Bank of Minneapolis Quarterly Review* 5:1–17. Reprinted in Thomas J. Sargent, ed., *Rational Expectations and Inflation*. New York: Harper and Row, 1986.

Scott, Maurice F. G. 1979. "What Price the National Income." In Michael J. Boskin, ed., *Economics and Human Welfare, Essays in Honor of Tibor Scitovsky*. New York: Academic Press.

———. 1989. *A New View of Economic Growth*. Oxford: Clarendon Press.

Schultze, Charles L., and Robert Z. Lawrence, eds. 1987. *Barriers to European Growth*. Washington, D.C.: Brookings Institution.

Serven, Luis, and Andrès Solimano, eds. 1993. *Striving for Growth after Adjustment: The Role of Capital Formation*. Washington, D.C.: The World Bank.

Shirley, Mary M. 1984. *Managing State-owned Enterprises*. World Bank Staff Working Paper 577. Washington, D.C.

Simonsen, Mario Henrique. 1988. "Price Stabilization and Incomes Policies: Theory and the Brazilian Case Study." In Michael Bruno, Guido di Tella, Rudiger Dornbusch, and Stanley Fischer, eds., *Inflation Stabilization: The Experience of Israel, Argentina, Brazil, Bolivia and Mexico*. Cambridge, Mass.: MIT Press.

Squire, Lyn, and Herman G. van der Tak. 1975. *Economic Analysis of Projects*. World Bank Staff Working Paper 194. Washington, D.C.

Srinivasan, T. N. 1990. "External Sector in Development: China and India 1950–89." In *American Economic Association Papers and Procedures* (May), 113–117.

Stockholm International Peace Research Institute (SIPRI). 1990. *World Armaments and Disarmament*. New York: Oxford University Press.

Sundararajan, V., and Tomas J. T. Balino, eds. 1991. *Banking Crises: Cases and Issues*. Washington, D.C.: International Monetary Fund.

Sundrum, R. M. 1973. "Money Supply and Prices: A Reinterpretation." *Bulletin of Indonesian Economic Studies*. 9(3): 73–86.

Sutton, Mary. 1984. "Indonesia, 1966–70." In Tony Killick, ed., *The IMF and Stabilization: Developing Country Experiences*. New York: St. Martin's Press.

Swan, T. W. 1960. "Economic Control in a Dependent Economy." *Economic Record* 36(73):51–66.

Tanzi, Vito. 1977. "Inflation, Lags in Collections, and the Real Value of Tax Revenue." IMF *Staff Papers* 24:154–67.

Thorbecke, Erik. 1991. "Adjustment, Growth and Income Distribution in Indonesia" . *World Development* 19(11):1595–1641.

van Wijnbergen, Sweder. 1991. "Debt Relief and Economic Growth in Mexico." *World Bank Economic Review* 5(3): 437–55.

Warr, Peter G. 1986. "Indonesia's Other Dutch Disease: Economic Effects of the Petroleum Boom." In J. P. Neary and S. van Wijnbergen, eds., *Natural Resources and the Macroeconomy: A Theoretical Framework*. Oxford: Basil Blackwell.

Warr, Peter G., and Bhanupongse Nidhiprabha. Forthcoming. "Macroeconomic Policies, Crises, and Long-Term Growth in Thailand." Washington D.C.: World Bank.

Whitehead, Lawrence. 1990. "Political Explanations of Macroeconomic Management: A Survey." *World Development* 18(8):1133–46.

Williamson, John, ed. 1983. *IMF Conditionality*. Washington, D.C.: Institute for International Economics.

——, ed. 1990. *Latin American Adjustment*. Washington: Institute for International Economics.

Woo, Wing Thye, and Anwar Nasution. 1989. "Indonesian Economic Policies and Their Relation to External Debt Management." In Jeffrey D. Sachs and Susan M. Collins, eds., *Developing Country Debt and Economic Performance*. Chicago: University of Chicago Press.

Woo, Wing Thye, H. Bruce Glassburner, and Anwar Nasution. Forthcoming. *Macroeconomic Policies, Crises, and Long-Term Growth in Indonesia, 1965–90*. Washington D.C.: World Bank

Woods, Dwayne. 1989. "Ethno-regional Demands Symbolic and Redistributive Politics: Sugar Complexes in the North of the Ivory Coast." *Ethnic and Racial Studies* 12(October):469–89.

World Bank. 1987. *World Development Report 1987: Industrialization and Foreign Trade*. New York: Oxford University Press.

——. 1988a. *Adjustment Lending, An Evaluation of Ten Years of Experience*. Washington, D.C.: Country Economics Department.

——. 1988b. *World Development Report 1988:* New York: Oxford University Press.

——. 1989. *World Development Report 1989: Public Finance in Development*. New York: Oxford University Press.

——. 1990a. *Adjustment Lending Policies for Sustainable Growth*. Washington, D.C.: Country Economics Department.

———. 1990b. *World Debt Tables 1990–91: External Debt of Developing Countries*. Washington, D.C.

———. 1990c. *Trends in Developing Economies 1990*. Washington, D.C.

———. 1991. *World Development Report 1991: The Challenge of Development*. New York: Oxford University Press.

———. 1992. *World Development Report 1992: Development and the Environment*. New York: Oxford University Press.

World Currency Yearbook. Various years. International Currency Analysis Inc. Brooklyn, N.Y.

Subject Index

Index of Names